THE GREAT WAR

MESSINES TO PASSCHENDAELE 1917

Menin Gate at Ypres

THE GREAT WAR

MESSINES TO PASSCHENDAELE 1917

RICHARD BROADHEAD

British 12 Inch gun at Brizlen August 1917

First published 2017

O&B Services
The Annexe
Poynder Place
Hilmarton, SN11 8SQ

British Library Cataloguing in Publication Data.
A catalogue record for this book is available from the British Library.

ISBN 978-0-9563825-5-9

CONTENTS

FOREWORD

As a Museum Director, you hear many stories of the sacrifices made on the battlefields of France and Belgium. But for me, the reality sank in when I laid a poppy at the grave of Captain E.C. Cunnington of the Royal Army Medical Corps, who died on 23 March 1918.

The first stop on a visit to the battlefields led by Richard Broadhead was the Cabaret-Rouge Cemetery at Souchez in the Pas-de-Calais. It was an early morning in November 2014, days after the commemorations of the Centenary of the outbreak of the War. The sun shone weakly through the chill mist, and we were tired after our long drive. Richard had not told us why this was our first stop.

Richard led us to the grave of Captain Edward Cunnington, the only son of Ben and Maud Cunnington. Ben was the first curator of the Devizes Museum and Maud, his wife, was the excavator of All Cannings Cross, the Sanctuary and Woodhenge in Wiltshire. She was awarded an MBE, the first woman to be recognised for her contribution to British Archaeology. Today, my colleagues and I follow in their footsteps and our Museum owes a deep debt of gratitude to their foresight and generosity.

Ben and Maud must have been so proud of their only son, as he qualified as a Doctor and volunteered to serve his country joining the Royal Army Medical Corps. He served in Egypt with the York and Lancaster Regiment before returning to the Western Front where he served with the Coldstream Guards. He lost his life while serving with the 95th Field Ambulance,. He had been serving with them for just four days.

As I stood by his grave, I saw nine other tombstones bearing the insignia of the Royal Medical Corps, all bearing the same date. I imagined them killed by a single bomb. Around me lay the graves of over 7,500 men from Great Britain and the Commonwealth countries. My mind went back to a time soon after I arrived in Devizes, when I had visited the house of one of our Trustees. He told me that his house had been the home of Ben and Maud Cunnington and had shown me the name 'Edward' carved on a bedroom door. I thought of my own sons and how Edward's was just one of the many lives cuts short by the horrors of Great War.

This book, Messines to Passchendaele 1917 contains the stories of hundreds of men who gave their lives in the service of their country in the Great War. Edward Cunnington had served as the medical officer with the 3rd Battalion Coldstream Guards and may have treated some of the men mentioned in this book. He survived the Battle of Passchendaele, though he must of seen many of those he served with lose their lives, only to lose his own life a few months later.

We remember them.

David Dawson
Diresctor
Wiltshire Museum

Introduction

When we think of the Flanders Battles of the Great War muddy trenches usually come to mind and no battle is more synonymous with mud than Passchendaele and the stories of men drowning in shell holes. Passchendaele, the name sometimes used for the Third Battle of Ypres in 1917 is a small village and the last to be captured by the allies during the battle. It is only a part of a battle that had its origins in the battle and capture of the Messines Ridge in June 1917, the success of this bite and hold operation acting as a precursor to the Third Battle of Ypres.

British commander in chief, Sir Douglas Haig, certainly gained confidence from General Herbert Plumers's Messine victory, which could be argued as the Allies quickest and most successful operation, if not the most successful operation in the Great war up to that date. After the failure of the Nivelle Offensive, named after the French commander Robert Nivelle in May 1917, was followed by widespread mutinies within the French army, Haig insisted that the British should push forward with a major offensive in the summer of 1917 in Flanders. The aggressive and meticulously planned offensive, ostensibly aimed at destroying German submarine bases located on the north coast of Belgium, whose submarines were causing havoc with the supply lines of Great Britain in the Atlantic and around the British coast. Haig believed that the German army was on the verge of collapse, and it would be broken completely by a major Allied victory.

On 18 July 1917, a heavy artillery barrage was launched on the German lines which lasted ten days. Three thousand artillery guns fired over four million shells, which could be heard in the southeast of England, and the German army expected a major Allied attack. However, no General can control the weather and though big advances were made, by General Hubert Goughs 5th Army when compared with previous battles, and large numbers of German prisoners were captured, the massive artillery barrage had succeeded in churning up the earth and breaking the banks of streams and large areas were turned into swamps. Halts in the fighting were needed before the guns were moved forward over broken muddy ground and the advances could only continue when the guns were in place. Haig, frustrated with the course of the battle, replaced Gough with the Messines victor Plumer at the end of August 1917 and the battle proceeded in a number of attacks ending on Passchendaele Ridge, 10km from Ypres in November 1917.

What is often overlooked about the battle was that not all areas were muddy.The lack of advance was also due to the German army defensive tactics that turned every farm into a concrete bunker bristling with machine guns and occupied by a platoon sized garrison with the determination to hold out against overwhelming odds. Plus the new tactics employed by the British with combined arms infantry, tanks, artillery and flying corps working together were significantly successful. Lessons learned in the Third Ypres went on to contribute to the 1918 battle and lead to the final victory.

No one can deny the loss of life and it has been estimated that 90,000 British and Commonwealth bodies were never identified and 42,000 never recovered from the battle. Bodies from the First World War are still being found and identified 100 years later.

Read the stories of these men visit their memorials or graves I am sure it will help you as it has helped me to have a better understanding of the Third Battle of Ypres and why those men carried on fighting when we, all too often today, judge these battles of the Great war to be such a futile waste of life.

But most of all remember them as they deserve to be remembered, as people and not names on grave stones and memorials.

1
June 1917

THE RESPONSIBILITY FOR ATTACK ON THE WESTERN FRONT IS PASSED TO THE BRITISH EXPEDITIONARY FORCE. FRENCH FORCES ARE TOO EXHAUSTED FOR CONSTANT ASSAULTS

WEATHER - FINE

Private Alec George Burbidge		*2nd Bn Wiltshire Regiment*	
Service No.	24192	Age:	20
Place of birth:	Bemerton, Wiltshire	Home Country:	England
Date of death:	02/06/1917	Cause of death:	Killed in action
Memorial:	Potterne		
War Cemetery:	Ramparts Cemetery Lille Gate - Grave J. 9.		
Next of Kin:	Frederick & Lucy Burbidge		
Address:	Ewart Croft, Potterne, Wiltshire		

Twenty year old Alec was the eldest son of Frederick and Lucy Burbidge and it is likely he was either conscripted into the army or joined under the Derby Scheme being sent to the front and joining D Company of the 2nd Battalion Wiltshire Regiment. On 30 May 1917 four officers and 151 other ranks were seconded to the 2nd Canadian Tunnelling Company as a permanent working party. He was killed on Saturday 2 June 1917, most likely near Mount Sorrell east of Ypres. A party of 30 Germans approached the British trenches and threw a number of hand grenades, the enemy raiders were repulsed. Alec was buried in Ramparts Cemetery, Lille Gate, Ypres, Belgium.

Lance Corporal William Caddy		*10th Bn Welsh Regiment*	
Service No.	30465	Age:	21
Place of birth:	East Knoyle, Wilts	Home Country:	Wales
Date of death:	02/06/1917	Cause of death:	Killed in action
Memorial:	Pontypridd, Glamorganshire		
War Cemetery:	Essex Farm Cemetery - Grave III. C. 2		
Next of Kin:	James & Rose Anna Caddy		
Address:	12 Richard Street, Cilfynydd, Pontypridd, Glamorganshire		

William, a coal miner, was the eldest son of James and Rose Caddy. He volunteered for service joining the 10th Service Battalion Welsh Regiment (the 1st Rhonda). He arrived in France on 2 December 1915 and in July 1916 took part in the attack at Mametz Wood during the Battle of the Somme. William was killed on Saturday 2 June 1917, most likely by German artillery fire, in the British front line at the Lancashire Farm Cemetery north of Ypres.

Tom Wheeler

Private Tom Wheeler *2nd Bn Wiltshire Regiment*

Service No.	32663	Age:	32
Place of birth:	Devizes, Wilts	Home Country:	England
Date of death:	03/06/1917	Cause of death:	Died of wounds
Memorial:	Trowbridge, Wilts		
War Cemetery:	Lijssenthoek Military Cemetery - Grave XII. C. 22A.		
Next of Kin:	Rose Wheeler (wife) – Thomas & Fannie Wheeler (parents)		
Address:	4 Ansties Court Mortimer Street, Trowbridge, Wiltshire		

Tom was employed as a stoker at the Wilts United Dairies and married Rose Turner in October 1916. He was called up for service early in 1917 and arrived in France during April 1917. On 30 May 1917 four officers and 151 other ranks were seconded to the 2nd Canadian Tunnelling Company as a permanent working party. Tom was wounded, on Saturday 2 June 1917, most likely near Mount Sorrell, east of Ypres when a party of 30 Germans approached the British trenches and threw a number of hand grenades, the enemy raiders were repulsed. He was taken to one of the base hospitals located at Lijssenthoek, Belgium where he died the following day leaving a widow and young child. Rose Wheelers' father had died a few weeks earlier and in June 1918 she inserted the following memoriam in a local paper:

In ever loving memory of my dear husband
Days of sadness still come o'er us
Secret tears do often flow,
Memory keeps are loved one near to us,
Though it's now one year ago

I often think and talk of him
And think how he died
To think I could not say goodbye
Before he closed his eyes
Could I but kneel beside his grave
And shed a silent tear
But now he sleeps somewhere in France
The one I love so dear

Private Alfred Conduit		*1st Bn Wiltshire Regiment*	
Service No.	3/8277	Age:	31
Place of birth:	Salisbury, Wiltshire	Home Country:	England
Date of death:	05/06/1917	Cause of death:	Killed in action
Memorial:	Salisbury, Wiltshire		
War Cemetery:	Wulverghem Lindenhoek Road Military Cemetery - Grave I. C. 5.		
Next of Kin:	Hilda Margaret Conduit (wife) - William G. & Harriet Conduit (parents)		
Address:	St. Edmunds, Salisbury, Wiltshire		

Alfred, a bricklayer, was the eldest son of William and Harriet Conduit and in the summer of 1911 married Hilda Margaret Emm. He was a member of the Wiltshire Regiment Special Reserve and was sent to France on 12 September 1914, being sent to the 1st Battalion Wiltshire Regiment on Tuesday 5 June 1917 Alfred was with the Wiltshires, who were preparing for a raid on the German trenches near Messines in the Wulverghem Sector, Belgium. They managed to penetrate into the German reserve line, the War Diary states for this day: 'Unfortunately, none of the enemy were encountered and the trenches were found to be quite unoccupied.' Alfred and two other men were killed on the raid, either from German snipers on the flanks or from British shells falling short. He was buried in Wulverghem Lindenhoek Road Military Cemetery.

Lance Corporal William Sutton		*6th Bn Wiltshire Regiment*	
Service No.	8215	Age:	28
Place of birth:	St Marks, Wiltshire	Home Country:	England
Date of death:	05/06/1917	Cause of death:	Killed in action
Memorial:	Salisbury, Wiltshire		
War Cemetery	Ypres Menin Gate - Grave Panel 53.		
Next of Kin:	Henry & Emma Sutton		
Address:	Salisbury, Wiltshire		

Regular soldier William was the third son of Henry & Emma Sutton and enlisted with the Wiltshire Regiment prior to the Great War. He was serving with the 2nd Battalion Wiltshire Regiment at Gibraltar at the outbreak of hostilities, landing a Zeebrugge, Belgium on 7 October 1914. He was wounded in 1916 and had won the Military Medal for bravery. At some point, most likely on his recovery, William was transferred and was sent to the 6th Battalion Wiltshire. He was killed in action on 5 June 1917, when two companies of the Wiltshire Regiment were relieving the 9th Welsh Regiment. It is likely he was killed by German shell fire, and is remembered on the Ypres Menin Gate Memorial, Belgium. He has no known grave. His Medals were never applied for by his family and a request was made by the Army Records office for their disposal in 1919.

Private Arthur Twine		6th Bn Wiltshire Regiment	
Service No.	26339	Age:	36
Place of birth:	Wootton Bassett, Wilts	Home Country:	England
Date of death:	05/06/1917	Cause of death:	Killed in action
Memorial:	Wootton Bassett, Wilts		
War Cemetery:	Ypres Menin Gate - Grave Panel 53.		
Next of Kin:	Thomas & Elizabeth Twine		
Address:	64 Church Street, Wootton Bassett, Wiltshire		

Regular Soldier Arthur was the fourth son of Thomas and Elizabeth Twine and had severed in India plus nine years on reserve. At the outbreak of hostilities he was recalled to the colours rejoining the 1st Battalion Wiltshire Regiment, arriving in France on 14 August 1914. He was wounded at the Battle of

Mons and was discharged. In September 1916 he re enlisted and was sent to France in October 1916 joining the 6th Battalion Wiltshire Regiment. He was killed in action on 5 June 1917 by a German shell, when two companies of the Wiltshire Regiment were relieving the 9th Welsh Regiment. On the 21 June 1917 Lieutenant T. Wing wrote the following to Arthur's parents;

"I am very sorry that I have not had an earlier opportunity of writing to you about your son, No. 26399 Pte. A. Twine. You will have already received the news about his death. Death was instantaneous, he being killed outright by a shell. He was an excellent soldier, smart, willing and conscientious and very popular everywhere. It is a great loss to his platoon and to the regiment. I hope that it may be some consolation to you in your bereavement to remember that he died doing his duty towards his King and Country as a gallant and honourable man. He was properly buried."

Arthur is remembered on the Ypres Menin Gate and has no known grave.

WEDNESDAY 6 JUNE 1917 - WEATHER - VERY HOT

Gunner Heber Theodore Smart — *Z - 41st Trench Mortar Bty Royal Field Artillery*

Service No.	102334	Age:	21
Place of birth:	Malmesbury, Wilts	Home Country:	England
Date of death:	06/06/1917	Cause of death:	Killed in action
Memorial:	Not known		
War Cemetery:	Dickebusch New Military Cemetery - Grave III. C. 13.		
Next of Kin:	Edmund Wilson & Thirza Smart		
Address:	Sawyers Hill, Minety, Wiltshire		

Twenty one year old farm Labourer Heber, was the youngest son of Edmund and Thirza Smart. It is likely he was conscripted into the army and was sent to the Royal Field Artillery. He was posted to the 41st Trench Mortar Battery who on Wednesday 6 June 1917 were engaged on a bombardment of German positions as a prelude to the assault on Messines Ridge. He was killed when one of the mortar bombs he was using prematurely exploded. One of Hebers comrades wrote to his parents stating:

"We are all sorry to lose Heber. He was dong so well. He had been put in charge of one of our guns and this was his fourth day at it, and we had almost finished firing when one of his own bombs burst prematurely in the gun pit, killing him instantly. This is one consolation because he never felt anything of it. This I know does not lessen the loss. All the boys in the battery wish me to convey their deepest sympathy to Mr & Mrs Smart, and I also myself, to you in your loss. The officer in charge had congratulated him on the way he carried out his duties on the previous day, and he could have been relieved, but preferred to stay with his gun. His devotion to duty caused his death. I was working in the next pit when it happened, and nearly got buried. I feel his loss keenly, as he was my best chum."

Private Frank Osborne — *2nd Bn Leinster Regiment*

Service No.	5370	Age:	31
Place of birth:	Singleton, Sussex	Home Country:	England
Date of death:	06/06/1917	Cause of death:	Killed in action
Memorial:	Westbury, Wilts – Singleton, Sussex		
War Cemetery:	Irish House Cememtery - Grave B. 15.		
Next of Kin:	Mille Louisa Osbourne (wife) - James & Kate Osborne (parents)		
Address:	1 Hayes Road, Westbury, Wiltshire – Singleton Sussex		

Left: Frank Osborne

Right: Richard Stanley Selwood

Frank was the eldest son of James & Kate Osborne and was employed as an ash loader for the Great Western Railway Company in the Loco and Carriage Department at Westbury. At the beginning of 1914 he married Mille Louisa Garlick at Westbury. It is likely Frank was conscripted into the army and was initially sent to the Dorset Regiment before being transferred to the 2nd Battalion Leinster Regiment. On Wednesday 6 June 1917, while in assembly trenches near St. Elooi, South of Ypres, while preparing for the assault on Messines Ridge, the 2nd Leinster Regiment were subjected a German artillery barrage consisting of tear gas and lethal gas. Frank was gassed and died soon after, he left a widow and a young daughter. In June 1918 Frank's wife inserted the following memoriam in a local paper:

Could we have been there at the hour of your death,
To have caught the last sigh of your parting breath,
Your last faint whisper, dear Frank, We might of heard,
And breathed in your ear just one loving word
Only those who have suffered are able to tell
The pain in the heart in not saying farewell

Messines Ridge

2
Battle of Messines

BRITISH LAUNCH ATTACK ON MESSINES - WYTSCHAETE RIDGE BY EXPLODING 19 LARGE MINES (Maps Page 416 - 417- 418)

THURSDAY 7 JUNE 1917 - WEATHER - FINE

A new British offensive on a large scale was launched on Thursday morning between Ypres and Armentieres. The main objective was the Messines Ridge. Sir Douglas Haig announced on Thursday night that this was carried out at the first blow. Later in the day the troops advanced and took the village of Oostaverne, and overran the enemy's rearward defences on a front of 6 miles. More than 5,000 prisoners have almost been counted. Many are still to come. The attack went with heavy air fighting. The enemy lost 18 machines; the British six. All hostile air squadrons were attacked and dispersed.

Private Richard Stanley Selwood		*52nd Bn Austrailian Infantry AIF*	
Service No.	1737	Age:	29
Place of birth:	Purton, Wiltshire	Home Country:	Australia
Date of death:	07/06/1917	Cause of death:	Killed in action
Memorial:	Purton, Wilts		
War Cemetery:	Ypres Menin Gate - Grave Panel 7 - 17 - 23 - 25 - 27 - 29 - 31.		
Next of Kin:	John & Annie Selwood		
Address:	The Common, Purton, Wiltshire		

Stock man Richard was the third son of John and Annie Selwood and emigrated to Australia prior to the Great War. He volunteered for service with the Australian Imperial Force on 13 January 1916 joining the 52nd Battalion. He arrived in England on 16 June 1916 and was sent to France on 17 September 1916. On 8 October 1916, the 52nd Battalion were in the front line at Spoil Bank, in the St Elloi Sector South of Ypres when the Germans strafed the Australians positions blowing in the parapet of the trench. Richard was wounded suffering from shell shock and sent to 17th Casualty Clearing Station at Hazebrouck. He rejoined his unit on 10 February 1917 and the following week he was detached for duty with the Anzac Light Railways. He again rejoined his unit on 14 May 1917 ready for the forthcoming attack at Messines Ridge. At 2.20am on 7 June 1917 the 52nd Battalion arrived at their assembly point, they were attacking the northern side of the village of Messines. The 6th Battalion Lincolnshire Regiment were on their left flank and the 49th Battalion was on the right flank. At about 3pm the 52nd Battalion reported they were not in touch with the Lincolnshire Regiment who should have been on their left flank. As the advance began D Company 52nd Battalion moved to the left coving the gap caused by the non-appearance of the Lincolns. After the capture of the first objective the 52nd Battalion advanced on east of Messines capturing Odour trench and the position was consolidated with a number of British units and the flanks were secure with the use of some tanks. The 52nd Battalion were hampered by the British artillery falling short throughout the action and at 11pm the Germans counterattacked along the front but failed to reach the captured trenches or get within bombing distance owing to the Australian machine gun and rifle fire. Richard was killed during the advance and is today remembered on the Ypres Menin Gate. In 1918 Richard's family inserted the following memoriam in a local paper:

He nobly answered duties call,
He gave his life for one and all;
And now to-day, so far away,
He sleeps in an unknown grave;
But the unknown grave is the bitterest blow,
None but an aching heart can know.
How little we thought as we said goodbye,
We parted forever and you were to die;
For the grief that we feel words cannot tell,
The only hope that is left us now
Is his brother's safe return.

Private Thomas Henry Mines		*49th Bn Australian Infantry AIF*	
Service No.	2948	Age:	33
Place of birth:	Rodden, Somerset	Home Country:	England
Date of death:	07/06/1917	Cause of death:	Killed in action
Memorial:	Frome, Somerset		
War Cemetery:	Ypres Menin Gate - Grave Panel 7 - 17 - 23 - 25 - 27 - 29 - 31.		
Next of Kin:	William & Mary Mines		
Address:	Chapmanslade Hill, Westbury, Wiltshire		

Thomas, a miner, was the second son of William and Mary Mines and emigrated to Australia in 1911 where he became a farmer. At the outbreak of hostilities, he volunteered for service with the Australian Imperial Force and embarked for Cairns, Queensland and was then sent to Thursday Island for garrison duties. He volunteered again for service outside Australia and left on the troopship Kanowa to take part in the capture of German New Guinea. The ship was forced to return to Townville following an incident with the ships firemen and did not take part in the action. Thomas was discharged on 18 September 1914. He then re-enlisted with the Australian Artillery on 8 December 1914 and was promoted to Lance Corporal on 22 September 1915, while serving with the Matupi Battery, in Rabaul. He was again discharged on 31st January 1916, when his service expired. Thomas then enlisted again on 26 March 1916 and embarked from Brisbane, Australia on 27 October 1916, arriving at Plymouth on 9 January 1917, and after training with the 13th Training Battalion at Codford, he was sent to France on 9 May 1917. At 2.20am on 7 June 1917 the 49th Battalion arrived at their assembly point for the attack on Messines Ridge, they were attacking the northern side of the village of Messines. The 52nd Battalion was on their left flank and the 45th Battalion was on the right flank. On the right flank the British Barrage was falling short and caused some casualties. At about 3pm the 52nd Battalion reported they were not in touch with the Lincolnshire Regiment who should have been on their left flank. This led to a 90-minute delay in the advance from 3.10am to 4.40am at which point the whole line moved forward. The British creeping barrage was 10 minutes behind schedule and the first objective could only be taken after the artillery had lifted. Only 2 Officers of the 12 who went forward made it to the first objective and all the Company Commanders were killed. Once the first objective was reached there was some confusion linking up the objective and at 5pm the the British barrage came back on the first objective causing some casualties. At 9pm the Germans massed for a counterattack but this was broken up by British artillery and Vickers guns. Thomas was killed during the advance and is today remembered on the Ypres Menin Gate.

Thomas Henry Mines

A machine gun officer who was standing on Messines Ridge, in order to give warning of German gas shells, which burst noiselessly, told of the history of the great mines which were exploded as the signal to begin the great attack stated:

"Nearly a year previously, a demand was made in the coalfields around Newcastle-on-Tyne and Cardiff for two hundred expert miners, skilled at digging and the art of explosions. They worked for about six months at digging, for a length of 2,000 yards under the slopes of the ridge, nineteen mine chambers under nineteen of the of the most formidable cemented and armed fortresses constructed by the enemy. A gallery for advancing had to be dug for 140 yards, and quadrangular pits similar to the cage of a lift, were constructed and crammed with high explosives, 25 tons of them. The electric wires, which were to cause the fatal spark in one second, were ready at the end of winter 1916. Since January 1917 the first line German troops have been living, without knowing it, a sleeping inferno. Such was the patient preparatory work to the outburst of the 7 June 1917. This convulsion of the old earth, vast as a supernatural cataclysm, wrecked the hill, filled up the marshes, and changed a wood into a lake of a misty green colour. It also changed in the twinkling of an eye, as well as the history of two years, the geography of two centuries. The marshes now sleep between two banks of soil and the road over which I passed had the elasticity of India rubber. The mines, in exploding did not make those deep craters which can be seen at Pozieres at the Somme. In this case great masses of earth were violently hurled into the air and fell back slowly in showers of dirt on the trenches, fortresses and their garrisons. It can be easily understood that the scene of each explosion became a cemetery, in which the frightened ran between the stones. Twelve hours after the attack repeated dull sounds from the remains of a dug-out were heard by some soldiers, who informed their officers. Digging was hastily begun and in the pit, were found four wounded officers dying of suffocation. They were saved and since then, along the whole vast ridge, soldiers are listening between the crash of shells for cries of frightened humanity, which seem too come from the other world."

Private Albert Edward Pearce MM		*1st Bn Wiltshire Regiment*	
Service No.	32312	Age:	35
Place of birth:	Imber, Wiltshire	Home Country:	England
Date of death:	07/06/1917	Cause of death:	Killed in action
Memorial:	Devizes, Wiltshire		
War cemetery:	Wulverghem Lindenhoek Road Military Cemetery Grave II. C. 6.		
Next of kin:	Albert & Mary G. Pearce		

Address:	New Copse Farm, West Lavington, Wiltshire

Regular soldier Albert was the eldest son of Albert and Mary Pearce and had originally enlisted with the Wiltshire Regiment on 20 January 1902 and served with the 1st Battalion in South Africa. He was discharged after completing his term of service on 19 January 1914. He was a member of the special reserve and rejoined his old unit the 1st Battalion Wiltshire Regiment and while serving with them was awarded the Military Medal. At 3.10am on the night of 6 -7 June the 1st Wiltshires attacked German positions near Wulverghem, Belgium as part of the operations at Messines. The attack was preceded by an intense barrage and several mines were exploded. The Wiltshires were the last battalion in the brigade to go forward and their first objective was to clear dugouts which they achieved and each German garrison was either killed or made prisoner. The second objective was an attack on 4 Huns Farm and October Support Trench but this was delayed when the British barrage failed to lift and some casualties occurred. The German positions were still captured and more prisoners taken. Albert was killed in action during the advance and later buried where he fell, east of Mortar Farm, near Nutmeg Reserve Trench. In October 1919, his remain s were moved to Wulverghem Lindenhoek Road Military Cemetery.

Lieutenant Charles Pomeroy Sainsbury MC		*1st Bn Wiltshire Regiment*	
Service No.	N/a	Age:	27
Place of birth:	Devizes, Wiltshire	Home Country:	England
Date of death:	07/06/1917	Cause of death:	Died of wounds
Memorial:	Devizes, Wiltshire		
War cemetery:	St Quentin Cabaret Military Cemetery – Grave II. N. 1.		
Next of kin:	Herbert and Margaret Fanny Sainsbury		
Address:	Greystone House, Devizes, Wiltshire		

Charles was the eldest son of Herbert, an ex-mayor of Devizes, and Margaret Sainsbury who was the daughter of Charles Pomeroy. He was educated at Devizes College before attending Taunton School and on leaving education he joined Capital and Counties Banks and served at Frome, Farnham, Marlborough and Lymington. At the outbreak of hostilities Charles could not get permission from the Bank quickly enough to join the army and so resigned his position and soon after secured a commission with the 1st Battalion Wiltshire Regiment in June 1915 arriving in France on 18 November 1915. In May 1916, he took part in the fighting at Vimy Ridge but was invalided home in June 1916. He was award the Military Cross for his part during the fighting at Vimy Ridge and the actions he took after a German mine had been exploded, the citation reads:

"For conspicuous gallantry and coolness. On two occasions, he succeeded by skilful leading, in occupying, under heavy fire, the near lip of the enemy craters immediately the hostile mine had been exploded."

After his recovery, he returned to the front in January 1916 and returned to the 1st Wiltshires. Charles was wounded in the early hours of Thursday 7 June 1917 during the attack on Messines, Belgium in the same action as Albert Pearce and died of his wounds later that day. Charles had been unable to attend Buckingham Palace to receive his Military Cross from the King because he was on active service in France and following his death Charles's father was awarded his sons Military Cross in August 1917 from General Sir Henry Slater, Commander in Chief of Southern Command.

Corporal Egbert Taylor		*1st Bn Wiltshire Regiment*	
Service No.	6754	Age:	31
Place of Birth:	Compton Bassett, Wiltshire	Home Country:	England
Date of Death:	07/06/1917	Cause of death:	Died of wounds
Memorial:	Trowbridge & Blacklands, Wiltshire		

Left: Egbert Taylor

Right: Charles Pomeroy Sainsbury MC

War cemetery: Bailleul Communal Cemetery Extension Nord - Grave III. C. 269.
Next of Kin: Ethel F Taylor (wife); Thomas & Emily Taylor (parents)
Address: Steeple Ashton, Wiltshire; Cherhill, Wiltshire

Egbert was employed as a farm labourer by Tom Tucker at Mill Farm, Steeple Ashton, where he took a keen intelligent interest in his work. In a ploughing competition organised by the Wiltshire Agricultural Education Committee at Keevil he won first prize and a special certificate. As a reservist, he was called to the colours on the outbreak of war and went over with the British Expeditionary Force. He was wounded in November 1915 by shrapnel in the chest and other parts of his body. He returned to France in the following June, but had only been with his regiment for a few weeks when he was again wounded and was treated at Chatham. On his recovery, he was transferred to Weymouth, where after doing duty at the reinforcement camp, he again left for the fighting line in September 1916. After repeatedly refusing promotion, upon his return to France he was prevailed upon to accept the non-commissioned officer's stripes, and became a corporal. During the following eight months, he saw much service with the Wiltshires and took part in every engagement, ultimately meeting his death on Thursday 7 June 1917, the date of his 31st birthday. The information of his death was conveyed in a letter from Sister McPherson, in charge of a base hospital, who writing to Ethel Taylor said:

"I am extremely grieved to tell you that your husband, Corporal Taylor, was admitted to this hospital with multiple wounds of his body and hands. He was collapsed on admission, and although everything was done for him he never recovered, but passed peacefully away at 2.30pm the same day. He did not lave any message, as he was quite unconscious."

Lieutenant Swayne, Egbert's commanding officer also wrote to Ethel expressing his regret and sympathy and said;

"Corporal Taylor was appointed brigade orderly and put there especially so as to be safer,as we realized his worth and the gallant services he had rendered, and we were hoping to get him a months leave due to him as a time-expired soldier."

It is likely that Egbert was wounded during the preparation for an attack on Messines Ridge and evacuated to the hospital at Baileul, France. Egbert had three brothers in the army. One, who had also served in the army before the war had been captured in 1914 and was held in a German prisoner of war camp. Ethel had lost two brothers during the Great War Albert, who is remembered on Keevil war memorial and John who is remembered on Bulkington war memorial.

Private William George Randall		*1st Bn Wiltshire Regiment*	
Service No.	26443	Age:	31
Place of birth:	Westbury, Wiltshire	Home Country:	England
Date of death:	07/06/1917	Cause of death:	Killed in action
Memorial:	Westbury, Wilts		
War Cemetery:	Ypres Menin Gate - Grave Panel 53.		
Next of Kin:	Emily Rosina Randall (wife) - John Alban & Mary Ann Randall (parents)		
Address:	Warminster Road, Westbury, Wiltshire		

Upholsterer William was the third son of John & Mary Randall and in the spring of 1909 married Emily Rosina Hart at Westbury. It is likely William was conscripted into the army and was sent to the 1st Battalion Wiltshire Regiment. He was killed in action in the early hours of Thursday 7 June 1917 during the attack on Messines, Belgium in the same action as Albert Pearce. William is remembered on the Ypres Menin Gate and has no known grave.

Private Sidney Frank Woolford		*1st Bn Wiltshire Regiment*	
Service No.	8794	Age:	28
Place of birth:	Swindon, Wiltshire	Home Country:	England
Date of death:	07/06/1917	Cause of death:	Killed in action
Memorial:	Not known		
War Cemetery:	Ypres Menin Gate - Grave Panel 53.		
Next of Kin:	George & Alice G Woolford		
Address:	25 Albion Street, Swindon, Wiltshire		

Sydney a general labourer was the fourth son of George & Alice Woolford It is likely Sydney was conscripted into the army and was sent to the 1st Battalion Wiltshire Regiment. He was reported missing in the early hours of Thursday 7 June 1917 during the attack on Messines, Belgium in the same action as Albert Pearce. Later he reported to have been killed in action on the day he was reported missing. Sydney is remembered on the Ypres Menin Gate and has no known grave. His brother Albert Edward Woolford was to be killed in action on 27 October 1917 during the battle that came to be known as Passchendaele. In June 1918 Sydney's family inserted the following memoriam in a local paper:

We miss our son, God alone can tell,
How we missed him when he fell;
Far away from those who loved him best
Comrades laid him down to rest;
A noble hero true and brave.
He peacefully sleeping in a soldiers grave.

Private Thomas Sherwood		*F Coy 1st Bn Wiltshire Regiment*	
Service No.	24197	Age:	20
Place of birth:	Sherston, Wiltshire	Home Country:	England
Date of death:	07/06/1917	Cause of death:	Killed in action
Memorial:	Sherston, Wiltshire		
War Cemetery:	Ypres Menin Gate - Grave Panel 53.		
Next of Kin:	Henry & Hilda Sherwood		
Address:	14 Silver Street, Sherston, Wiltshire		

Twenty year old Thomas was the sixth son of Henry & Hilda Sherwood. It is likely Thomas was conscripted into the army and was sent to the 1st Battalion Wiltshire Regiment. He was killed in action in the early hours of Thursday 7 June 1917 during the attack on Messines, Belgium in the same action as Albert Pearce. Thomas is remembered on the Ypres Menin Gate and has no known grave.

Lieutenant Noel Gilbert Bryan King		*1st Bn Wiltshire Regiment*	
Service No.	N/a	Age:	32
Place of birth:	Avebury, Wiltshire	Home Country:	England
Date of death:	07/06/1917	Cause of death:	Killed in action
Memorial:	Easterton & St. Edwards School Memorial Oxford		
War cemetery:	Ypres Menin Gate - Panel 53		
Next of kin:	Rev. Gilbert Alfred & Jane King		
Address:	Easterton, Wiltshire		

Teacher Noel was the only son of the Rev. Gilbert King, the Vicar of Easterton, and his wife Jane King and was educated at St. Edwards School, Oxford. He volunteered for service and was given a commission with the Wiltshire Regiment and sent to France on 9 September 1916. He was killed in action less than a year later during the early hours of the morning on Thursday 7 June 1917 during the attack on Messines, Belgium in the same action as Albert Pearce. He is remembered on the Ypres Menin Gate and has no known grave.

Corporal Edmund James Lawrence		*1st Bn Wiltshire Regiment*	
Service No.	19109	Age:	19
Place of birth:	Amesbury, Wiltshire	Home Country:	England
Date of death:	07/06/1917	Cause of death:	Killed in action
Memorial:	Amesbury, Wilts		
War Cemetery:	Ypres Menin Gate - Grave Panel 53.		
Next of Kin:	James & Edith Mary Lawrence		
Address:	Frog Lane, Amesbury, Wiltshire		

Edmund, known as James, was the eldest son of James & Edith Mary Lawrence. It is likely James was conscripted into the army and was sent to the 1st Battalion Wiltshire Regiment. He was killed in action in the early hours of Thursday 7 June 1917 during the attack on Messines, Belgium in the same action as Albert Pearce. James is remembered on the Ypres Menin Gate and has no known grave.

Private John Robinson		*1st Bn Wiltshire Regiment*	
Service No.	18099	Age:	42
Place of birth:	Ulverston, Lancashire	Home Country:	England
Date of death:	07/06/1917	Cause of death:	Killed in action
Memorial:	Highworth, Wiltshire		
War Cemetery:	Ypres Menin Gate - Grave Panel 53.		
Next of Kin:	Elizabeth Knight Robinson (wife) Thomas & Martha Robinson (parents)		
Address:	4 Whiteman Street, Gorse Hill, Swindon, Wilts - Ulverston, Lancashire		

Cabinet Maker John was the son of Thomas and Martha Robinson and in 1902 he married Elizabeth Knight Clark at Ulverston, Lancashire. He volunteered for service with the Wiltshire Regiment and arrived in France on 21 April 1915 and was sent to the 1st Battalion. He was killed in action in the early hours of Thursday 7 June 1917 during the attack on Messines, Belgium in the same action as Albert Pearce. John is remembered on the Ypres Menin Gate and has no known grave. He left a widow and young family.

Lance Corporal William James Stockham		*1st Bn Wiltshire Regiment*	
Service No.	8763	Age:	23
Place of birth:	Rowde, Wiltshire	Home Country:	England
Date of death:	07/06/1917	Cause of death:	Killed in action
Memorial:	Devizes, Wiltshire		
War cemetery:	Ypres Menin Gate Grave Panel 53		
Next of kin:	Samuel & Sarah Stockham		
Address:	3 Dunkirk, Devizes, Wiltshire		

Regular soldier William was the second son of Samuel and Sarah Stockham and landed with the 2nd Battalion Wiltshire Regiment at Zeebruuge, Belgium on 7 October 1914. William was wounded in June 1915 and after his recovery he returned to the front joining the 1st Battalion Wiltshire Regiment. He was killed in action during the early hours of the morning on Thursday 7 June 1917 during the attack on Messines, Belgium in the same action as Albert Pearce. He is remembered on Ypres Menin Gate and has no known grave.

Private Eric Raymond Leak		*1st Bn Wiltshire Regiment*	
Service No.	33005	Age:	21
Place of birth:	Marlborough, Wiltshire	Home Country:	England
Date of death:	07/06/1917	Cause of death:	Killed in action
Memorial:	Marlborough, Wiltshire		
War Cemetery:	Ypres Menin Gate - Grave Panel 53.		
Next of Kin:	Arthur Edward & Lizzie Annie Leak		
Address:	Luton House, Marlborough, Wiltshire		

Eric, an outfitters assistant was the second son of Arthur and Lizzie Leak and volunteered for service with Wiltshire Yeomanry. He transferred to the 1st Battalion Wiltshire Regiment and was sent to France. He was killed in action during the early hours of the morning on Thursday 7 June 1917 during the attack on Messines, Belgium in the same action as Albert Pearce. He is remembered on Ypres Menin Gate and has no known grave.

Private Alfred Henry James Allaway		*1st Bn Wiltshire Regiment*	
Service No.	8682	Age:	27
Place of birth:	Stratton St Margaret, Wilts	Home Country:	England
Date of death:	07/06/1917	Cause of death:	Died of wounds
Memorial:	Not known		
War Cemetery:	Bailleul Communal Cemetery Extension Nord - Grave III. C. 327.		
Next of Kin:	James & Lucy Ann Allaway		
Address:	Rodbourne Cheney, Swindon, Wiltshire		

Regular soldier Alfred had been a farm labourer before enlisting with the Wiltshire Regiment. He was the third son of James & Lucy Ann Allaway and was serving at Gibraltar with the 2nd Battalion Wiltshire Regiment at the outbreak of hostilities. He landed at Zeebrugge on 7 October 1914 with the 2nd Wiltshires. It is likely he was wounded at some stage during the first two years of the war and after his recovery was transferred to the 1st Battalion Wiltshire Regiment. He was wounded either during the preparation or on the first day of fighting in actions to capture Messine Ridge and evacuated to a casualty clearing station at Bailleul where he succumbed to his wounds on Thursday 7 June 1917.

Lance Coporal William James Harrell		7th Bn Royal Inniskilling Fusiliers	
Service No.	30183	Age:	25
Place of birth:	East Coulston, Wilts	Home Country:	England
Date of death:	07/06/1917	Cause of death:	Killed in action
Memorial:	Not known		
War Cemetery:	La Laiterie Military Cemetery - Grave XII. A. 17.		
Next of Kin:	Robert & Leah Harrell		
Address:	East Coulston, Westbury, Wiltshire		

William a farm labourer was the youngest son of Robert and Leah Harrell and it is likely he was conscripted into the army initially joining the Rifle Brigade. He was then transferred to the 7th Battalion Royal Inniskilling Fusiliers. In the early hours of Thursday 7 June 1917, the 7th Royal Inniskilling Fusiliers were forming up near Vierstraat to attack German positions at Wijtschate, Belgium. At Zero hour, 3.10am and immediately after the upheaval of the mines had subsided the A & B Company's of the 7th Royal Inniskilling Fusiliers advanced close to a creeping British artillery barrage. There was no opposition when the 7th Royal Inniskilling Fusiliers crossed the German front and support lines. When they reached their first objective the 7th Royal Inniskilling Fusiliers found that the German line ceased to exist following the effect of the mines and the ground had been turned into what resembled a swamp. The advance continued to the second objective with slight opposition from isolated small groups of Germans in shell holes who were soon dealt with. The Third objective, the Red line, was then captured and the A & B Companies 7th Royal Inniskilling Fusiliers began to consolidate the postion with the other Irish units on their flanks. C & D Company's 7th Royal Inniskilling Fusiliers then moved A and B Company's and advanced capturing the fourth objective the blue line consolidating the position. Over 100 German prisoners and two machine guns were captured during the advance. William was one of 14 men killed during the advance. In June 1918, his family inserted the following memoriam in a local paper:

In loving memory of our dear son
Gone is the Face we loved so dear
Silent the voice we loved to hear
Too far away from sight and speech
But not too far for our thoughts to reach

Private Harold Ernest Herring		*11th Bn Lancashire Fusiliers*	
Service No.	33487	Age:	19
Place of birth:	Ramsbury, Wiltshire	Home Country:	England
Date of death:	07/06/1917	Cause of death:	Killed in action
Memorial:	Aldbourne, Wiltshire – Shrivenham Oxfordshire		
War Cemetery:	Ypres Menin Gate - Grave Panel 33.		
Next of Kin:	William & Selina Ada Herring		
Address:	Newtown, Bishopstone, Wiltshire		

Farm worker, Harold, was the third son of William and Selina Herring and it is likely he was conscripted in to the army joining the Royal Field Artillery. He was transferred to the infantry and sent to France joining the 11th Battalion Lancashire Fusiliers. In the early hours of Thursday 7 June 1917, the 11th Lancashire Fusiliers were in the assembly trenches north west of Messines. While waiting in the trenches the British were shelled by the enemy with gas and lachrymatory (tear gas) shells. At 3.10am mines were exploded under the German front line; the mine in 74th Brigade sector was at Ontario Farm. The leading Company's of the 11th Lancashire Fusiliers left the British line and were subjected to a German artillery barrage in no mans land and the British front line trench system. A fairly strong easterly wind was blowing and this combined with the the dust of the barrage made it difficult to maintain the direction of the attack. The 11th Lancashire Fusiliers were keeping close to a creeping British barrage and as they reached the position of Steenbeck trench they found it did not exist and the River Steenbeck was non existent except for wet shell holes. Just after 4am Occu trench was captured, 2 machine guns and 61 prisoners were taken. At 4.27am the attackers reached Intermediate trench and found it too did not exist anymore. October trench was then captured capturing 2 machine guns. The 11th Lancashire Fusilers sustain some casualties caused by German snipers while waiting for the British barrage to lift from October Support trench. The snipers were dealt with by British rifle and rifle grenade fire. Sawayes Farm was captured followed by 4 Huns Farm and a concrete bunker captured in conjuctin with the 1st Wiltshires. By 11am the 11th Lancashire Fusiliers were consolidating their newly won position. Harold was one of the forty 11th Lancashire Fusiliers killed during the attack, and is remembered on the Ypres Menin Gate.

2nd Lieutenant James Chester Badgley		*6th Bn Wiltshire Regiment*	
Service No.	N/a	Age:	29
Place of birth:	Wootacumand, India	Home Country:	England
Date of death:	07/06/1917	Cause of death:	Killed in action
Memorial:	Devizes, Wiltshire		
War cemetery:	Klein-Vierstraat British Cemetery - Grave II. B.		
Next of kin:	Winifred E. Badgley – Col. William F. & Frances Badgley		
Address:	21 Hardwicke Road, Weymouth, Dorset - Vere Croft, Devizes		

James was the third son of Colonel William and Frances Badgley and emigrated to Canada with his brother and sister in 1903. He found employment with the Canadian Civil Service as a bookkeeper and was also a territorial soldier serving with the 90th Winnipeg Rifles. At the outbreak of the Great War James volunteered for service on 21 September with the 8th Battalion Canadian Infantry and on returning to England James obtained a commission with the Wiltshire Regiment. In the spring of 1916 he married Winifred E Kett at Christchurch, Hampshire and soon after he was sent to France joining the 1st Battalion Wiltshire Regiment. Early in July 1916 James had a lucky escape when two German shells landed each side of him at a distance of about 10 feet away, he was blown into the air and fell heavily, but was only bruised and able to carry on with his duties. He was more seriously wounded on 9 July 1916 during fighting at Trones Wood at the Somme. While going forward in attack James suffered shrapnel wounds and was evacuated to England being sent to the London General Hospital. After his recovery, he was sent to Weymouth where he served with the 3rd Battalion Wiltshire Regiment and on 7 February 1917 James returned to France joining the 6th Battalion Wiltshire Regiment. He was then attached to the 58th Trench Mortar Battery and while serving near Ypres, Belgium on Thursday 7 June 1917 James was killed in action. He is buried in Klein-Vierstraat British Cemetery.

6th Battalion Wiltshire - Thursday 7th June 1917 Belgium, In the Line

Battalion took part in the attack and capture by 2nd Army of the Messines - Wytschaete Ridge. The Battalion was the right front Battalion of the Right Brigade of left Divisions of IX Corps. At zero hour 3.10am 3 mines were exploded on the Hollande Salient on immediate front of Battalion. The objectives of the Battalion were the capture of the Hollande Salient in immediate front of the Battalion, the south east portion of Grande Bois and consolidation of Red Line. This was successfully carried out and 5 Machine guns, 3 Trench Mortars and 179 Prisoners were captured and 80 of the enemy being killed during the advance. On the capture of further objectives Battalion moved forward to Green Line in Support. Consolidation proceeded with and strong points established.

Hollande Salient is on the road from Vierstrat to Wytschaete. After you leave Vierstrat you will encounter the Wychaetebeek (stream) just after the first right turn. After crossing the Wytschaetebeek you will come to a second right turn. You are now crossing the British front line. As you continue you will come to a farm entrance on the left, this is the German front line and part of the Hollande Salient. Around this farm can be seen the craters, now pools, the effects of the three mines that were blown on 7 June 1917.

Private Orlando Edwards		*6th Bn Wiltshire Regiment*	
Service No.	18589	Age:	31
Place of Birth:	Chippenham	Home Country:	England
Date of Death:	07/06/1917	Cause of death:	Killed in action
Memorial:	Chippenham & St. Andrews Church Memorial		
War cemetery:	Ypres Menin Gate - Panel 53		
Theatre of war:	Belgium		
Next of Kin:	Joseph & Salina Edwards		
Address:	31 The Causeway, Chippenham		

Orlando had trained as a blacksmith and in May 1912 he took employment with the Post Office, first as a temporary postman and then as an auxiliary postman responsible for Tytherton. He was described as a quiet and well conducted lad. He volunteered for service with the 6th Battalion Wiltshire Regiment on 25 January 1915 and arrived in France on 19 July 1915. On 7 June 1917, the 6th Wiltshires took part in the attack on the German held Messines – Wytschaete Ridge in Belgium. At 3.10am three mines were exploded at the Hollandschschuur Farm forming the Hollande Salient near Vierstraat, Belgium. After capturing the Hollande Salient the Wiltshires went on to take the south east portion of the Grand Bois. At the end of June 1917 Joseph and Selina Edwards received the first intimation that their son had been killed in the following letter from Lieutenant Wing:

"He was as you doubtless know one of the special battalion bombers, so did not often parade with us, but we were always glad when he did so, for he was very smart, courageous, and painstaking and popular with everybody. I hope it maybe some consolation in your bereavement to reflect that he died the death of an honourable and gallant man for his King and country."

Orlando's parents received the following letter from Signaler Macdonald of the Royal Dublin Fusiliers:

"In the last advance, I found the body of your son, Orlando, with his pay book and letter lying beside him. On seeing this I thought it best to write to you and let you know he died a hero's death, and accept my deepest sympathy with you. I may also add that he had an instantaneous death. I saw that his body was removed and he had a soldier's funeral, being buried with hundreds of the bravest of the brave."

Orlando's grave was lost in subsequent fighting and he is today remembered on the Ypres Menin Gate.

Private Henry Charles Champion		*6th Bn Wiltshire Regiment*	
Service No.	23762	Age:	17
Place of Birth:	North Bradley, Wiltshire	Home Country:	England
Date of Death:	07/06/1917	Cause of death:	Killed in action
Memorial:	Trowbridge, Wiltshire		
War cemetery:	Klein-Vierstraat British Cemetery - Grave II. B. 14		
Next of Kin:	Charles & Mary Champion		
Address:	The Rank, North Bradley		

Left: Orlando Edwards

Right: Henry Charles Champion

Seventeen year old Henry, known as Charles, was an under age soldier. Before the war, he was employed by Salter and Co. but had been desperate to join the Navy but an affection to the throat debarred him. When the war broke out he repeatedly tried to join the army and was accepted on his seventh application in January 1916 and was sent to France in February 1917. He was killed in action on Thursday 7 June 1917 while serving with the 6th Battalion Wiltshire Regiment at the capture of Hollande Salient at Messines Ridge in the same action as Orlando Edwards. Charles Chapman senior received the following letter from his sons' platoon commander:

"He had not been with us very long, but he was certainly one of the most promising of the younger members of the platoon. He was always smart willing and courageous and was very popular with everybody. He would have certainly been promoted had he been spared longer. I hope that it may be some consolation to you in your bereavement to reflect that he died the death of an honourable and gallant man for his King and country"

In June 1918 Charles's family inserted the following memoriam in a local paper:

When last we saw his smiling face
He looked so strong and brave
We little thought how soon he would
Be in a Soldiers Grave
Sleep on dear one in and unknown grave
Your dear young life you nobly gave
No loved ones were with you to say Goodbye
But safe in God's keeping now you lie.

Private William John Simms — *6th Bn Wiltshire Regiment*

Service No. 9643 — Age: 25
Place of birth: Everleigh, Wilts — Home Country: England
Date of death: 07/06/1917 — Cause of death: Died of wounds
Memorial: Pewsey, Wilts
War Cemetery: Bailleul Communal Cemetery Extension Nord - Grave III. C. 273.
Next of Kin: William George & Mary Simms
Address: Fyfield, Wiltshire

Farm labourer William was the eldest son of William and Mary Simms and volunteered for service with the 5th Battalion Wiltshire Regiment. He arrived at Gallipoli on 20 June 1915 and it is likely William was either wounded or was suffering from illness or disease and evacuated to England. Following his recovery, he was transferred to the 6th Battalion Wiltshire Regiment and sent to France. He was wounded either during the preparation or on the first day of fighting in actions to capture Messines Ridge and evacuated to a casualty clearing station at Bailleul where he succumbed to his wounds on Thursday 7 June 1917.

Private William Frederick Godwin		*6th Bn Wiltshire Regiment*	
Service No.	21325	Age:	21
Place of Birth:	Alderton, Wiltshire	Home Country:	England
Date of Death:	07/06/1917	Cause of death:	Killed in action
Memorial:	Not known		
War cemetery:	Ypres Menin Gate – Panel 53		
Next of Kin:	Frederick & Mary Jane Godwin		
Address:	Rodwell, Hilmarton, Wiltshire		

Farm labourer William was the eldest son of Frederick and Mary Godwin and volunteered for Service with the Wiltshire Regiment. He was sent to the 1st Battalion and arrived in France on Christmas Day 1915. He was killed in action on Thursday 7 June 1917 while serving with the 6th Battalion Wiltshire Regiment at the capture of Hollande Salient at Messines Ridge in the same action as Orlando Edwards.

Private David James Berry		*6th Bn Wiltshire Regiment*	
Service No.	22714	Age:	21
Place of birth:	Sherston, Wiltshire	Home Country:	England
Date of death:	07/06/1917	Cause of death:	Killed in action
Memorial:	Sherston, Wiltshire		
War Cemetery:	Croonaert Chapel Cemetery - Grave B. 17.		
Next of Kin:	Thomas & Annie Berry		
Address:	6 Back Street, Sherston, Wiltshire		

Farm carter David, known as James, was the second son of Thomas & Annie Berry. It is likely James was conscripted into the army and was sent to the 6th Battalion Wiltshire Regiment. He was killed in action on Thursday 7 June 1917 while serving with the 6th Battalion Wiltshire Regiment at the capture of Hollande Salient at Messines Ridge in the same action as Orlando Edwards.

Lieutenant George Peak-Garland		*11th Bn Royal Inniskilling Fusiliers*	
Service No.	N/a	Age:	30
Place of Birth:	Lewannick, Cornwall	Home Country:	England
Date of Death:	07/06/1917	Cause of death:	Killed in action
Memorial:	Winterbourne Monkton & Heddington, Wiltshire		
War cemetery:	La Laiterie Military Cemetery - Grave II. AA. 2.		
Next of Kin:	James & Jane Peak-Garland		
Address:	Manor Farm, Avebury, Wiltshire		

George was the eldest son of James and Jane Peak-Garland and worked on his father's farm. He was a keen footballer and played for the village club and was well known in the local area. He was also assistant secretary of the Calne Christmas Fat Stock Show. Soon after the outbreak of hostilities he volunteered for service with the Wiltshire Yeomanry and arrived in France on 5 May 1916. In December 1916, he was given a commission and transferred to the 11th Battalion Royal Inniskilling Fusiliers. In the early hours of Thursday 7 June 1916, the 11th Royal Inniskilling Fusiliers were in British forming up trenches near the German front line at Spanbroekmolen, southwest of Wytschaete, Belgium. At 3.10am Peckham mine was blown under Spanbroekmolen resulting in a crater 80 yards in diameter and 80 feet deep. The British artillery which had been intermittent up to this point now began to pound the German front line. The 11th Royal Inniskilling Fusiliers deployed in to no mans land and reached the German front line as the British artillery barrage lifted. From this point the 11th Royal Inniskilling Fusiliers followed the British artillery barrage to their final objective the blue line meeting only slight enemy opposition, capturing nearly 200 prisoners, 2 machine guns and 1 field gun. George was one of three officers killed during the attack and is remembered on a private memorial at Heddington St. Andrews Church.

2nd Lieutenant William Herbert Dickson		*2/4th Bn Loyal North Lancashire Regiment*	
Service No.	N/a	Age:	40
Place of Birth:	Preston, Lancashire	Home Country:	England
Date of Death:	07/06/1917	Cause of death:	Killed in action
Memorial:	Chippenham & St. Andrew's Church Chippenham		
War cemetery:	Motor Car Corner Cemetery - Grave A 1		
Next of	Kin:George Herbert & Mary Eliza Ann Dickson		
Address:	Preston, Lancashire		

William, a solicitor, was the eldest son of George and Mary Dickson and was educated at Cheltenham. He was articled with Buck and Dickson Solicitors, a firm in which his father was a partner. Before the war William was practicing as a solicitor in Chippenham with Wood and Awdry and in 1916 he joined the London Scottish. He was attached to the Officer Training Corps and was given a commission with the 2/4th Territorial Battalion Loyal North Lancashire Regiment on 24 January 1917. He was sent to France in May 1917 and wounded after a few weeks' service and following his recovery, he rejoined his unit. In the early hours of Thursday 7 June 1917, the 2/4th Loyal North Lancashires were part of the flank defence in British trenches Southwest of Messines, Belgium, near the river Lys. The war diary states:

There was a lull for about 20 minutes and then to the minute there was a dull roar and the ground shook for miles around and simultaneously with this our real attack for the Ridge commenced with a magnificent barrage. The enemy was evidentally expecting trouble. Ploegstreet was heavily bombarded with 5.9's and shrapnel.

It is likely William was killed by hostile artillery fire on Thursday 7 June 1917. He was buried in Motor Car Cemetery.

Left: Memorial at Heddington St. Andrews Church. to George Peak-Garland

Right : William Herbert Dickson

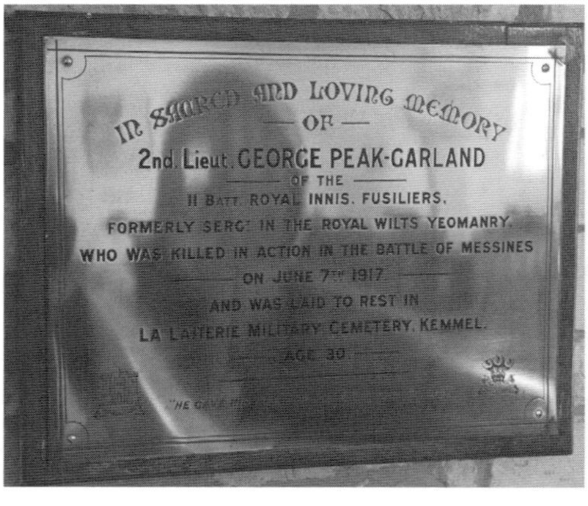

Monday afternoon's official German communiqué lays stress on the "most extreme violence" of artillery firing in the Wytschaete section (about five miles south of Ypres), and say it continued into the night. Aided no doubt by a favourable breeze, the sound of the guns was heard with remarkable plainness in many parts of the suburbs of London. On many previous occasions during the war have bombardments in Flanders been perceptible at great distances from the scene of operations, but rarely have reports of the artillery been so distinct as during the night of Sunday to Monday. A member of the editorial staff of the "Daily Telegraph" who resides in Beckenham states that he walked home from the station to his home at 2am, the gunfire was extraordinary audible. It resembled very much like the distant thudding of a steam launch's engine on the river upon a calm day, but punctuated at fairly frequent intervals by heavier sounds, no doubt the reports of the big howitzers. These latter even cause the slight rattling of ill-fitting villa windows. From various other points come similar statements, from Hounslow and Highgate, for example, where the gunfire was plainly heard.

FRIDAY 8 JUNE 1917 - WEATHER - FINE

General Sir Douglas Haig Stated:

"The position captured by our troops yesterday was one of the enemy's most important strong holds on the Western Front. Despite the difficulties and disadvantages which our troops had to overcome, further details of yesterday's fighting show that our first assault and subsequent attacks were carried out in almost exact accordance with the time-table previously arranged. By nightfall we had gained the whole of the day's objectives. The great number of German dead lying in the captured positions prove the severity of the enemy's losses. Our losses were light. The enemy made no attempt during the night to recapture his lost positions. The complete success gained may be ascribed chiefly to the distraction caused by our mines, to the violence of our bombardment, the very fine work of the Flying Corps, and the incomparable dash and courage of the Infantry."

Messines Ridge was one of the German's most important strong holds on the Western front. Dominating the Ypres Salient, and giving the Germans complete observation over it, they had neglected no precautions to render the position impregnable. These conditions enabled the enemy to overlook all the preparations for British attack, and the Germans had moved reinforcements up to meet the attack. The battle therefore became a gauge of the ability of the German troops to stop the British advance under conditions as favourable to them as any army could ever hope for, with every advantage of ground and preparation and with the knowledge that the attack was impending.

The German forward defences consisted of an elaborate and intricate system of well-wired trenches and strong-points, forming a defensive belt over a mile in depth. The numerous farms and woods were thoroughly prepared for defence, and included a large number of machine guns in their garrisons. Guns of all calibres had recently been increased in numbers, were placed to bear not only on the front, but on the flanks of the attack. Numerous communication trenches and switch lines, radiating in all directions, were amply provided with strongly constructed concrete dugouts and machine gun emplacements, designed to protect the enemy garrison and machine gunners from the effect of the British bombardment. In short, no precaution was omitted that could be provided by the incessant labour of years, guided by the experience gained by the enemy in previous defeats on the Somme, at Arras and on the Vimy Ridge. At 3.10am on Thursday 7 June 1917, 19 deep mines were exploded simultaneously beneath the enemy's defences, by which large portions both of his front and support trenches, including extensive dug-outs and mining systems, were completely wrecked.

Immediately upon the explosion of the mines the British Guns opened fire and the Infantry assault was launched. Within a few minutes the German first line trench system was taken on the whole front attacked. The British troops then pressed on, with scarcely a pause up the Western slopes of the Messines-Wytschaete Ridge, and three hours after the commencement of the attack they had stormed the entire crest line from north to south. Shortly afterwards the whole of Messines was captured, and before mid-day the capture of Wytschaete village had also been completed after hard fighting.

In the second stage of the attack the British troops pushed down the eastern slopes of the ridge, and advanced against a powerful line of German rear defences, which lay like a chord of an arc across the base of the salient formed by the ridge itself. Heavy fighting took place in a further series of fortified woods and strong points; but at 3.45pm the village of Oostaverne, lying just west of the centre of the line was captured. By nightfall, practically the whole of this trench system was also in our hands, and the British had gained the whole of the day's objectives. Great numbers of German dead lying in the captured positions prove the severity of the enemy's losses, a large proportion of which was borne by Bavarian troops. Unofficially it was stated that the British losses up to the night of Friday 8 June 1917, in the capture of Messines Ridge was about 10,000, and of these 60% were walking wounded. The Ridge was described as a vast mausoleum, and three wounded Germans declare that they were the only survivors of two whole companies. The British captured nearly 7,000 prisoners.

Private John Henry Odey		*13th Bn Durham Light Infantry*	
Service No.	54286	Age:	34
Place of birth:	Bath, Somerset	Home Country:	England
Date of death:	08/06/1917	Cause of death:	Killed in action
Memorial:	Swindon Christ Church, Wilts - Bath: St Mary the Virgin (Bathwick)		
War Cemetery:	Ypres Menin Gate - Panel 36 and 38.		
Next of Kin:	Rosie Mary Odey (wife) - James & Emily Odey		
Address:	3 Stanley Street, Swindon, Wilts - 7 Southville Terrace, Bath		

Upholsterer John was the second son of James and Emily Odey and was educated at St. Mark's school, Bath before attending Blue Coat School. While at the latter he became, and was employed as, an apprentice to Mr Holloway an antique dealer of Bath. At the start of 1906 he married Rosie Mary Parfitt at Bath and after 15 yeasrs employment with Mr Holloway, John moved to Swindon and was employed by Mr Batchelor as an upholsterer. John was a very enthusiastic bell ringer and was a member of the Diocesan Ringers' Association, holding the position of Tower Master at Swindon. It is likely he was conscripted into the army initially joining the Royal Field Artillery before being transferred to the 13th Battalion Durham Light Infantry. On Friday 8 June 1917, the 13th Durham Light Infantry were in captured German Trenches southwest of Hill 60 near Klein Zilbeke. It was described as a fairly quiet day; a British aeroplane flew over the British lines and droped a white light. The British artillery immediately opened a very heavy bombardment on German positions lasting until 10pm. The Germans heavily shelled the Durhams Battalion HQ. On of three men killed was John, he left a widow, an 8 year old son and eleven year old daughter , The Rev. E.G. Wells wrote the following letter to Rosie Odey:

"I want to offer on behalf of myself and and his comrades our sympathy in the death of your husband, Pte. Odey. He was killed by shell fire in the trying days that followed our recent successful operations. At least let us be thankful of that success which will assuredly bring the final victory nearer and for the fact that he and his comrades have not laid down their lives in vain. May God give you courage to bear your loss. I think we should continually pray to Him, that he will have mercy on the fallen and receive the service of their lives laid down for their country as service rendered to Himself, and let us pray too that he will give us faith to lookforward to a day of meeting again with those we love in a happier world. Let us prove ourselves worthy in this life of the great sacrifice that our loved ones have made for us. It is the best way to honour them."

Left: John Odey

Right: George Crook

Private George Crook		*37th Bn Austrailian Infantry AIF*	
Service No.	240	Age:	25
Place of birth:	Melksham, Wiltshire	Home Country:	Australia
Date of death:	08/06/1917	Cause of death:	Killed in action
Memorial:	Melksham, Wiltshire		
War Cemetery:	Ypres Menin Gate - Grave Panel 7 - 17 - 23 - 25 - 27 - 29 - 31.		
Next of Kin:	Joseph & Mary Crook		
Address:	New Broughton Road, Melksham, Wiltshire		

Gardener George was the fifth son of Joseph and Mary Crook and emigrated to Australia prior to the Great War. He volunteered for service with the 37th Battalion Australian Army on 16 February 1916 and after completing his training arrived in England on 25 July 1916. He arrived in France on 22 November 1916 and in the early hours of Thursday 7 June 1916 the 37th Battalion were preparing to take part in the attack on Messines Ridge. They faced a 3 mile march from their camp which led them through the wood under shelling from the enemy and a gas attack which slowed progress and claimed casualties. The battalion reached their jumping off points just in time for the start of the battle, signalled by the explosion of nineteen huge mines laid beneath a nine mile stretch of the enemy front line. The delay in the wood meant that many of the men went straight over the top, without pausing for the refreshments which had been planned. The 37th battalion attacked over ground northeast of Ploegsteert Wood, close to the Ultimo and Factory Farm mines. George a runner who delivered messages was initially reported to have been killed between 7 and 9 June. George's parents received the following letter from the regimental chaplain:

"Pte. Crook was killed on the 8 June, it was in the great battle of Messines a splendid victory but only one, as all such are, at the sacrifice of life, and is often the case the finest fellows are often those who go down, just because they are brave and dauntless. Your son was one of these, one of the fine fellows that make our victories possible. By the very giving of their lives they do it, and how finely they go to it! As their chaplain, I know how really and sincerely they were prepared for their ideal, such interest they showed in the religious side as well as the rest. You can be assured he was ready to face death, and they knew what to think about if such an opportunity came. He died a heros death in one of the greatest battles there have been. God gave him strength for his time of need, as He gives to all sorrowing relatives for their sorrow."

Two Soldiers came forward with information about George's death. Private D. Carter stated:

"He was killed by a bullet through the head and died instantaneously about mid day on the 8 June and was buried on the 9 June at Messines Ridge, I saw his grave."

Private A Campbell stated:

"He was a runner and was in the advance at Uncanny Support (trench), Messines Ridge. I did not see him killed but I saw him lying dead just near the objective. He was white and stiff when I got to him, I am not sure but I think he was buried at Hyde Park Corner Cemetery, Ploegsteert Wood."

The location of George's grave was later lost and he is today remembered on the Ypres Menin Gate.

Captured German pillbox on Messines Ridge

The message of congratulation which Field Marshall Sir Douglas Haig addressed to the General Officer Commanding the Second British Army the day after the victory at Messines Ridge has been published as a General Order of the Day. Stating:

"The complete success of the attack made yesterday by the Second Army, under the command of General Sir Herbert Plumer, is an earnest of the eventual final victory of the Allied cause.
The full effect of this victory cannot be estimated yet, but that it will be very great is certain. Following on the great success already gained, it affords final and conclusive proof that neither strength of position nor knowledge of any timely preparation to meet impending assault can save the enemy from complete defeat, and however brave and tenacious the German troops are it is only a question of how much longer they can endure the repetition of such blows.
Yesterday's victory was due to causes which always have given, and always will give success, viz., the utmost skill, valour and determination in the execution of the attack, following the greatest forethought and thoroughness in preparation for it.
I desire to place on record here my deep appreciation of the splendid work done, above and below ground, as well as in the air, by all arms, services, and departments and by commanders and staffs, by whom under sir Herbert Plumer's orders, all the means at our disposal were combined, both in preparation and in execution, with a skill, devotion and bravery beyond all praise. The great success gained has brought us along step nearer to the final victorious end to the war, and the Empire will be justly proud of the troops who have added such fresh lustre to its arms."

An idea of the gun-powder used preparatory to the attack on Messines Ridge can be gained from the fact that it is estimated that 6,000,000 shells were fired.

SATURDAY 9 JUNE 1917 - WEATHER - FINE

Private Albert Payne — *1st Bn Wiltshire Regiment*

Service No.	3/899	Age:	24
Place of birth:	Overton, Wiltshire	Home Country:	England
Date of death:	09/06/1917	Cause of death:	Died of wounds
Memorial:	West Overton, Wiltshire		
War Cemetery:	Bailleul Communal Cemetery Extension Nord - Grave III. C. 129.		
Next of Kin:	George & Elizabeth Frederica Payne		
Address:	Church Lane, Mildenhall, Wiltshire		

Shepherd Albert was the youngest son of George and Elizabeth Payne and volunteered for service joining the Wiltshire Regiment. He arrived in France on 18 May 1915 and was sent to the 1st Battalion Regiment. It is likely he was wounded on the first day of fighting in actions to capture Messines Ridge and evacuated to a casualty clearing station at Bailleul where he succumbed to his wounds on Saturday 9 June 1917.

Private Felix Edmund Sainsbury — *C Coy 51st Bn Australian Infantry A I F*

Service No.	2729	Age:	32
Place of birth:	West Lavington, Wiltshire	Home Country:	Australia
Date of death:	09/06/1917	Cause of death:	Died of wounds
Memorial:	Not known		
War Cemetery:	Pont D Achelles Military Cemetery Nieppe - Grave II. A. 6		
Next of Kin:	William & Susan Sainsbury		
Address:	Overton Hampshire		

Felix, a dairy hand was the fifth son of William & Susan Sainsbury and emigrated to Australia before the Great War. He volunteered for service with the Australian Army on 27 March 1916 and was sent to the 51st Battalion. He arrived in England on 2 December 1916 and proceeded to France in February 1917. In April 1917, he was sent to the 3rd Stationary Hospital, Rouen, and after his recovery he was returned to his unit in May 1917. On 7 June 1917 the 51st Battalion took part in the attack on German positions at Messines Ridge. Company's of the 51st Battalion were used to reinforce the 49th and 52nd Battalion attacking southeast of Wytshaete. C Company to which Felix belonged was sent to reinforce the 52nd Battalion and on the night of 8 June C Company were sent to reinforce the 49th Battalion. On the night of 9/10 June 1917, the 49th and 52nd Battalion were relieved and the 51st Battalion were sent to Nugent Support Trench. At about 8pm on the evening of 9 June Felix was wounded while in the front line. He was hit by a piece of shrapnel in the elbow. He was seen by some comrades walking back to the casualty clearing station. When he arrived at 9th Field Ambulance he was found not only to be injured in the right elbow but also in the right leg and scalp. His condition became worse and he died soon after.

Captain Gerard Montague Gordon — *12th Bn Royal Fusiliers*

Service No.	N/a	Age:	26
Place of birth:	Sherborne, Dorset	Home Country:	England
Date of death:	09/06/1917	Cause of death:	Killed in action
Memorial:	Durnford School, Sherborne, Dorset		
War Cemetery:	Reninghelst New Military Cemetery - Grave II. C. 23.		
Next of Kin:	George and Mary Gordon		

Left: Gerard Montague Gordon

Right: Cyril Ramsay Cook

Address: The Barn House, Sherborne, Dorset

Gerard was the youngest son of George and Mary Gordon and was educated at Durnford House, Wellington College and the South Eastern Agricultural College, Wye, Kent. Whilst at Wellington he played for two years in the cricket XI and also represented his school in the Public Schools' Racket competition at Queen's Club. He was a member of the MCC and of the Free Foresters and for several seasons played for the Dorset County XI. He was also a fine horseman and athlete. He volunteered on 15 August 1914 and was given a commission with the 3rd Battalion Royal Fusiliers and arrived in France on 9 Feb 1915 with the 12th (Service) Battalion and later became Adjutant. At the beginning of 1917, he was admitted to hospital suffering from appendicitis. After recovering from an operation to remove his appendix he returned to the front in May. On the evening of 9 June 1917, the battalion had just relieved the 1st Battalion Royal Fusiliers in trenches near Dammstrasse, adjacent to Hiele Farm south of St Elooi, Belgium. At 9.45pm, was one of four officers, including the Commanding Officer Lt. Col. Compton and the Medical Officer Capt. Whittingham, wounded by a shell which landed on Battalion headquarters. Gerard and Whittingham both died of wounds around midnight and were buried with full military honours at a funeral service in Reninghelst Military Cemetary, 10 km south west of Ypres, two days later. Lt Col Compton also later died of his wounds on 7 July at Etaples hospital. Two fellow officers paid tribute to Gerard:

"He was one of the bravest men I have ever met out here and his sense of duty in returning to the front soon after his recent operation filled us all with the deepest admiration. He was always so merry and bright and a great favorite with us all"

" His parting from us has caused a deep cloud over the battalion, because he was one of the best and one we could ill afford to lose"

2nd Lieutenant Cyril Ramsay Cook		*4th Bn. attd. 9th Bn Bn Sherwood Foresters*	
Service No.	N/a	Age:	19
Place of birth:	Warlingham, Surrey	Home Country:	England
Date of death:	09/06/1917	Cause of death:	Killed in action
Memorial:	Marlborough College, Wiltshire		
War Cemetery:	Ypres Menin Gate - Panel 39 and 41		
Next of Kin:	Frank & Sybil Cook		

Address: Endcliffe, Caterham Valley, Surrey

Nineteen year old Cyril was the eldest son of Frank and Sybil Cook and was educated at Marlborough College, before attending Nottingham University and Christ's College, Cambridge. While at university he became a member of the Officer Training Corps and was given a commission with the 4th Territorial Battalion Sherwood Foresters before being sent to Sunderland. He was sent to France on 6 April 1917 and attached to the 9th Battalion Sherwood Foresters, who in June 1917 took part in the attack on German positions at Messines Ridge. In the ealy hours of Saturday 9 June 1917 the 9th Battalion Sherwood Foresters were in Odour Trench South east of Oostaverne, east of Wytshaete. They were shelled with Geman 5.9's and during the Barrage Cyril was killed. His commanding officer wrote:

"I am told by his commanding officer that death was instantaneous. He had only been a short time with the battalion, but had made his mark, and was a splendid officer, who had the entire confidence and trust of his men. As his commanding officer, I had the highest opinion of him and he is a sad loss to us. He was buried close to where he was killed, and his grave has been marked and the exact locality sent to the Graves Registration Office. Your son struck me as being the exact type of what a young officer should be, and his company commander was full of his praises to me in recent operations."

Another officer wrote:

"I should like to tell you that in spite of the short time your son was with us, he was extremely popular, and when it came to actual work in action, I can assure you, his coolness and the thoroughness of his work was, in one of so little experience, utterly phenomenal. He only came to my company on the day he went up to the line, through one of my officers being suddenly sent for to join the Royal Flying Corps, but he lost no time in getting a thorough grip of his N.C.O.'s and men. There was one very extraordinary incident in connection with his death. He was in the front line talking to his platoon sergeant; as far as I remember, about 1 am, when he was hit by a piece of shell and instantaneously killed. His sergeant, who had already won the Military Medal for Gallantry early in the war, pounced on him immediately, took his revolver off him, and shouting something about "I'll avenge you sir, I'll kill some." Was away over the parapet before anyone could stop him. Of course, nobody expected to see him again, but he returned about an hour's time with an empty revolver and obviously quite mad."

His Chaplain wrote:

"The moment he joined he leapt straight into our hearts. We all knew we had a good boy, and he immediately took his place in all fun and gaiety. He was so full of life and enjoyment, and with it all so thoroughly good and clean and wholesome. He was extraordinarily popular, and we shall greatly miss his cheerfulness and good looks."

Cyril's grave was lost and he is today remembered on the Ypres Menin Gate.

SUNDAY 10 JUNE 1917 - WEATHER - FINE

Private Percy Evelyn King *6th Bn Wiltshire Regiment*

Service No.	19576	Age:	23
Place of birth:	Bromham, Wilts	Home Country:	England
Date of death:	10/06/1917	Cause of death:	Killed in action

Memorial: Bromham, Wiltshire
War cemetery: Oosttaverne Wood Cemetery- Grave I. A. 4.
Next of kin: Edward James & Emily King
Address: Church Hill, Bromham, Wiltshire

Percy, a labourer, was the eldest son of Edward and Emily King and volunteered soon after the start of the war arriving in France on 30 September 1915. He was severely wounded in action at Givenchy in November 1915 where he was struck in the chest by a bullet, but fortunately a cigarette case and matchbox diverted the bullets path saving Percy's life. He was evacuated to England and spent six months in Lincoln Hospital, after which he volunteered to return to France. He spent the next ten months on active service and was killed by a German shell on Sunday 10 June 1917 east of Oostaverne Wood, south of Ypres, Belgium. At 8.15pm the 6th Battalion Wiltshire Regiment had been on their way to the front line trenches to relieve the 8th Battalion East Kent Regiment when they were caught by a German barrage. Percy's parents received the following letter from 2nd Lieutenant J. A. Galley of the 6th Wiltshires:

"I was not his platoon officer at the time but as I had known him for a considerable time I asked if I might write to you. He was in the recent advance at Wytschaete, and had come safely through the attack on the 7th, but when returning to the trenches a piece of shell struck him in the head. If I can console you at all in your great bereavement it is that your boy died instantaneously, and doing his duty. He was liked by all, the men and all the officers of his company wish me to say that they have lost a man who can be ill spared at such a time, and one who could be relied on at all times, especially heavy shelling. He was always cheerful and smiling, and could always keep the men's spirits up during severe tests. I have tried to write to you before but we have passed through a very strenuous time, and we have now come out for a rest. It is my earnest wish that God will be near and comfort you in this sad trial. If you would like any further details I will consider it my duty to such a hero as your boy, and will willingly give them to you."

Percy's uncle Edwin Brown of Bromham wrote the following poem:

Toll the bell softly
Percy is dead
He like a soldier
Suffered and bled
Died for his country
Empire and King
We mourn our gallant son
We weep for him

Sing low the requiem
Percy is dead
Down through the ages
Let it be said
He was a hero
Valiant and brave
Fighting her battles
England to save

Bury the faithful dead
Our hearts his tomb
"Blessed" let it be said
Freed from the gloom
Living in memory now
Honoured and dear
England her loyal son's
Love and revere

Rifleman Frederick James Bolland — *21st Bn London Regiment*

Service No.	652258	Age:	22
Place of birth:	Devizes, Wilts	Home Country:	England
Date of death:	10/06/1917	Cause of death:	Killed in action
Memorial:	Devizes, Wiltshire		
War cemetery:	Ypres Menin Gate - Panel 54.		
Next of kin:	John and Sarah Bolland		
Address:	10 Linden Terrace, Devizes, Wiltshire		

Gardener Frederick was the fifth son of John and Sarah Bolland and it is likely he was either conscripted into the army or joined under the Derby Scheme. He was sent to the front joining the 21st London Regiment, known as the 1st Surrey Rifles. Frederick was killed in action on Sunday 10 June 1917 southeast of Hill 60 near Battle Wood, during the consolidating operations at Messines, Belgium. He is remembered on the Ypres Menin Gate and has no known grave. His brother Henry Bolland had been killed at Arras in April 1917.

Rifleman Frederick Barton — *2nd Bn Royal Irish Rifles*

Service No.	44103	Age:	34
Place of birth:	Hullavington, Wilts	Home Country:	England
Date of death:	10/06/1917	Cause of death:	Killed in action
Memorial:	Corston, Wilts.		
War Cemetery:	Messines Ridge British Cemetery - Grave I. A. 8.		
Next of Kin:	George & Elvira Barton		
Address:	Corston, Wiltshire		

Dock labourer Frederick was the third son of George and Elvira Barton and it is likely he was conscripted into the army initially joining the 9th London Rifles, before being sent to the 2nd Battalion Irish Rifles. On 7 June 1917, the 2nd Irish Rifles took part on the assault on Messines Ridge at Ontario Farm East of the village of Messines. Frederick was killed most likely by German artillery fire, on Sunday 10 June 1917 while in the front line. He was originally buried where he fell near Sloping Roof Farm, northwest of Messines and in December 1919 his remains were moved to Messines Ridge British Cemetery.

Monday 11 June 1917 - Weather - Dull Rain at Intervals

Private William James Williams — *13th Bn Middlesex Regiment*

Service No.	G/27450	Age:	25
Place of birth:	Ramsbury, Wilts	Home Country:	England
Date of death:	11/06/1917	Cause of death:	Killed in action
Memorial:	Liddington, Wiltshire		
War Cemetery:	Ypres Menin Gate - Panel 49 and 51.		
Next of Kin:	Maggie Williams (wife) - David & Elizabeth Williams (parents)		
Address:	Medbourne, Liddington, Wiltshire		

William a carter on a farm was the eldest son of David and Elizabeth Williams and in the spring of 1913 he married Margret M Sepour at Hambledon, Surrey. It is likely he was conscripted into the army joining the 13th Battalion Middlesex Regiment. He was killed in action on Monday 11 June 1917 most likely by German artillery, when the 13th Middlesex were in the British front line at Olive Trench, between Hollebeke and Ravine Wood. William's Mother and wife inserted the following memoriam in a local paper:

Left: William James Williams

Right: Harry Prosser

A bitter grief, a shock severe,
To part with one I loved so dear;
My loss is great, I'll not complain,
But hope in heaven to meet again.
Mother

I think of you in silence,
When no eye can see me weep;
But ever in my loving heart,
Your memory sweet I'll keep.
Maggie

Sergeant Harry Prosser		*1st Bn Wiltshire Regiment*	
Service No.	6972	Age:	33
Place of Birth:	Westbury, Wiltshire	Home Country:	England
Date of Death:	11/06/1917	Cause of death:	Killed in action
Memorial:	Trowbridge, Wiltshire		
War cemetery:	Messines Ridge British Cemetery		
Next of Kin:	Thomas & Mary Ann Prosser (parents)		
Address:	20 Prospect Place, Trowbridge		

Harry a bicycle tyre maker was the second son of Mary Ann Prosser and it is likely that he was a member of the national reserve volunteering on 7 August 1914. He arrived in France on 14 August 1914 and was promoted to Sergeant soon after. On 9 June 1917, the 1st Wiltshires took over the British front line from the 52nd Australian Infantry at Odious Trench southeast of Oostverne, Belgium. During daylight hours, the 1st Wiltshires were subjected to German snipers and at night to German machine gun and artillery fire. Harry was reported missing on Monday 11 June 1917 at a position near Odious trench. Official news was received by Harry's mother in May 1918, stating he had been killed on the day he was reported missing. In January 1920 Harry's remains were found east of Odious Trench, south west of Wambeke and were identified by means of a disc. His remains were moved to Messines Ridge British Cemetery.

Corporal William Charles Curtis		*1st Bn Wiltshire Regiment*	
Service No.	21129	Age:	30
Place of birth:	Bemerton, Wilts	Home Country:	England
Date of death:	11/06/1917	Cause of death:	Killed in action
Memorial:	Not known		
War Cemetery:	Wulverghem Lindenhoek Road Military Cemetery - Grave III. D. 8.		
Next of Kin:	Frederick Charles & Mary Ann Curtis		
Address:	7 Ema Terrace, Bemerton, Wiltshire		

Police constable, William was the eldest son of Frederick and Mary Ann Curtis and was serving with the Metropolitan Police in London. By 1917 around 2,300 members of the Metropolitan Police were serving in the armed forces. William joined the 1st Battalion Wiltshire Regiment. He was killed on Monday 11 June 1917 at a position near Odious trench southeast of Oostverne, Belgium in the same action as Harry Prosser. In October 1919 Williams grave was located near Gaapard east of Messines and his remains were moved to Wulverghem Lindenhoek Road Military Cemetery.

Private William Arthur Mullings		*1st Bn Wiltshire Regiment*	
Service No.	18413	Age:	36
Place of birth:	Darenth Kent, Wilts	Home Country:	England
Date of death:	11/06/1917	Cause of death:	Died of wounds
Memorial:	Edington, Wilts		
War Cemetery:	Bailleul Communal Cemetery Extension Nord - Grave III. C. 73.		
Next of Kin:	Mary Jane Mullings (wife) - William & Mary Mullings (parents)		
Address:	Salisbury Hollow, Tinhead, Wilts - Darenth, Kent		

Farm labourer William was eldest son of William and Mary Mullings and on Boxing Day 1904 he married Mary Jane Mathews at Edington, Wiltshire. He volunteered for service, joining the Wiltshire Regiment, and arrived in France on 6 July 1915, being sent to the 1st Battalion. While serving at the Somme in 1916 he was awarded a Distinguished Conduct Medal. The citation reads:

22 September 1916 - 18413 Pte. W. Mullings, Wilts. R.

For conspicuous gallantry during an attack and counter attack, when he volunteered to carry messages under very heavy shell and rifle fire. When an officer was hit, he carried him under heavy fire across the open to a place of safety.

It is likely William was wounded on 7 June 1917, when the 1st Wiltshires attacked German positions near Wulverghem, Belgium as part of the operations at Messines. The attack was proceeded by an intense barrage and several mines were exploded. The Wiltshires were the last battalion in the brigade to go forward and their first objective was to clear dugouts which they achieved and each German garrison was either killed or made prisoner. The second objective was an attack on 4 Huns Farm and October Support Trench but this was delayed when the British barrage failed to lift and some casualties occurred. The German positions were still captured and more prisoners taken. William was evacuated to a casualty clearing station at Bailleul, France where he succumbed to his wounds on Monday 11 June 1917. He Left a widow and two young sons.

TUESDAY 12 JUNE 1917 - WEATHER - FINE

Gunner Richard Charles Wood		*12th Bty Motor Branch Machine Gun Corps*	
Service No.	2438	Age:	18
Place of birth:	Marlborough, Wilts	Home Country:	England
Date of death:	12/06/1917	Cause of death:	Killed in action
Memorial:	Marlborough, Wilts		
War Cemetery:	Railway Dugouts Burial Ground - Grave Sp. Mem. E. 15.		
Next of Kin:	George & Eleanor Maud Wood		
Address:	78 High Street, Marlborough, Wiltshire		

Nineteen year old Richard, known as Charles, was the elder son of George and Eleanor Wood and was under age when he volunteered for service with the Wiltshire Regiment. He transferred to the Motor Machine Gun Service, Vickers machine guns mounted on motorcycles, arriving in France with the 12th Battery on 20 October 1915. He was killed in action on Tuesday 12 June 1916 southeast of Ypres during operations against German positions at Messines Ridge. He was buried in Railway Dugouts Burial Ground Railway but his grave was destroyed by later shelling of the cemetery and he is now commemorated on a special memorial as the location within the cemetery is not known.

Private Percy Henry Angell		*6th Bn Wiltshire Regiment*	
Service No.	13767	Age:	18
Place of Birth:	Calne, Wiltshire	Home Country:	England
Date of Death:	12/06/1917	Cause of death:	Killed in action
Memorial:	Calne, Wiltshire		
War cemetery:	Ypres Menin Gate - Panel 53		
Next of Kin:	Frederick & Sarah Angell		
Address:	23c New Road, Calne, Wiltshire		

Under age soldier Percy was the youngest son of Frederick and Sarah Angell and volunteered for service with the Wiltshire Regiment. He arrived in France on 6 March 1915 and was with either the 1st or 2nd Battalion He was wounded in December 1916 and following his recovery he was transferred to the 6th Battalion Wiltshire Regiment. On Tuesday 12 June 1917, the 6th Wiltshires were in trenches near Oostterveane Wood, northwest of Oosterverne, Belgium. During the afternoon, the Germans shelled the Wiltshires continuously and the casualties were 3 killed and 2 wounded. One of those killed was Percy, he has no known grave. His brother Arthur had died in Mesopotamia in April 1917.

Sergeant Arthur Weston		*6th Bn Wiltshire Regiment*	
Service No.	12051	Age:	31
Place of birth:	Chiseldon, Wiltshire	Home Country:	England
Date of death:	12/06/1917	Cause of death:	Killed in action
Memorial:	No 19 & 20 Shop Memorial Swindon Railway Museum		
War Cemetery:	Ypres Menin Gate - Panel 53.		
Next of Kin:	Francis M & Emma Weston		
Address:	42 Whitehead Street, Swindon, Wiltshire		

Arthur was the second son of Francis and Emma Weston amd was employed as a labourer in the Loco and Carriage Department in the Great Western Railway Works. He volunteered for service joining the 6th Battalion Wiltshire Regiment, arriving in France on 19 July 1915. On Tuesday 12 June 1917, the 6th Wiltshires were in trenches near Oostterveane Wood, northwest of Oosterverne, Belgium. During the afternoon, the Germans shelled the Wiltshires continuously and the casualties were 3 killed and 2 wounded. One of those killed was Arthur, he has no known grave.

Left: Arthur Weston

Above: Memorial to Edwin Alfred Keel on his step fathers grave in at Durrington Cemetery

Private Edwin Alfred Keel — *6th Bn Wiltshire Regiment*

Service No.	25872	Age:	34
Place of birth:	Netheravon, Wiltshire	Home Country:	England
Date of death:	12/06/1917	Cause of death:	Killed in action
Memorial:	Durrington, Wiltshire		
War Cemetery:	Ypres Menin Gate - Panel 53.		
Next of Kin:	Ethel May Keel (wife) – Charles & Emma Keel (parents)		
Address:	The Lane, Durrington, Wiltshire		

Labourer Edwin was the son of Charles and Emma Keel and following the death of Edwin's father his mother married George Macklin. In 1912 Edwin married Ethel May Hibberd at Wilton, Wiltshire. It is likely he was conscripted into the army joining the Wiltshire Regiment and being sent to the 6th Battalion. On Tuesday 12 June 1917, the 6th Wiltshires were in trenches near Oostterveane Wood, northwest of Oosterverne, Belgium. During the afternoon, the Germans shelled the Wiltshires continuously and the casualties were 3 killed and 2 wounded. One of those killed was Edwin, he has no known grave. Edwin is also commemorated on his step father George Macklin's grave marker in Durrington Cemetery.

Wednesday 13 June 1917 - Weather - Very Fine

Private Albert Robinson — *6th Bn Wiltshire Regiment*

Service No.	1771	Age:	39
Place of birth:	Rovenden, Kent	Home Country:	England
Date of death:	13/06/1917	Cause of death:	Killed in action
Memorial:	Salisbury, Wiltshire		
War Cemetery:	Ypres Menin Gate - Panel 53.		
Next of Kin:	Elizabeth Annie Robinson (wife) - George & Harriet Robinson (parents)		
Address:	Sandle Heath, Salisbury, Wiltshire		

Albert, a gardener, was the eldest son of George and Harriet Robinson and in the Summer of 1904 he married Elizabeth Annie Inkpen at Wimborne, Dorset. It is likely he was conscripted into the army joining the Wiltshire Regiment and being sent to the 6th Battalion. On Wednesday 13 June 1917, the

6th Wiltshires were in trenches near Oostterveane Wood, northwest of Oosterverne, Belgium. There had been heavy shelling by both sides during the day that Albert was killed. He is remembered on the Ypres Menin Gate and has no known grave. He left a widow and young family.

Private Arthur Stoodley		*6th Bn Wiltshire Regiment*	
Service No.	19218	Age:	30
Place of birth:	Corsham, Wiltshire	Home Country:	England
Date of death:	13/06/1917	Cause of death:	Killed in action
Memorial:	Corsham, Wiltshire		
War Cemetery:	Ypres Menin Gate - Panel 53.		
Next of Kin:	John Stoodley (father)		
Address:	Elley Green, Corsham, Wiltshire		

Arthur was the youngest son of John and Eliza Stoodley and was employed as a delver (worker) in a Bath stone quarry. He volunteered for service joining the Wiltshire Regiment and was sent to the 5th Battalion at Gallipoli. It is likely that Arthur was either wounded of suffered from illness or disease and was evacuated to England. Following his recovery, he was transferred to the 6th Battalion Wiltshire Regiment and sent to France. On Wednesday 13 June 1917, the 6th Wiltshires were in trenches near Oostterveane Wood, northwest of Oosterverne, Belgium. There had been heavy shelling by both sides during the day that Arthur was killed. He is remembered on the Ypres Menin Gate and has no known grave.

Private Richard Brookes		*6th Bn York & Lancaster Regiment*	
Service No.	32817	Age:	23
Place of birth:	Swindon, Wilts	Home Country:	England
Date of death:	13/06/1917	Cause of death:	Killed in action
Memorial:	Sheffield Council Official Roll of Honour		
War Cemetery:	Cabin Hill Cemetery - Grave A. 18.		
Next of Kin:	William & Eliza Brookes		
Address:	28 Barking Street Carbrook, Sheffield, Yorkshire		

Richard was the eldest son of William and Eliza Brookes and was employed as an underhand (assistant) furnace man at a steel works. He volunteered for service on 9 December 1915 under the Derby Scheme, where a man could enlist and would only be mobilised when he was needed. Richard was called up on 17 January 1917 joining the York & Lancaster Regiment and arrived in France on 4 May 1917, being sent to the 6th Battalion York & Lancaster Regiment. On Wednesday 13 June 1917, the 6th York & Lancasters were in the Oostterveane Line, northeast of Messines, Belgium. It is likely Richard was killed by German artillery while in the line.

Sergeant Walter James Banks		*5th Bn Dorsetshire Regiment*	
Service No.	202153	Age:	35
Place of birth:	Bradford on Avon, Wiltshire	Home Country:	England
Date of death:	13/06/1917	Cause of death:	Killed in action
Memorial:	Bradford on Avon Wesleyan, Wiltshire		
War Cemetery:	Ypres Menin Gate - Panel 37.		
Next of Kin:	Mabel A Banks (wife) - James & Elizabeth Banks (parents)		
Address:	5 Whitehead's Lane, Bradford on Avon, Wiltshire		

Walter was the eldest son of James and Elizabeth Banks and at the beginning of 1911 he married Mabel

Walter James Banks

A. Stafford at Bradford on Avon. He was employed as a rubber worker at Spencer Moulton & Co. Mills and was popular with his shop mates. He had been a member of the local Volunteer force for 17 years and a member of the shooting club. He was described as a first class shot and had won the monthly cup on many occasions. Out the outbreak of hostilities he volunteered for overseas service and was sent to India with the Wiltshire Territorial's. In May 1916, his time with the territorial's expired and he returned to England and was transferred to The Dorset Regiment and was sent to France in April 1917, joining the 5th Battalion. While in France he was employed on police duties and placed in charge of a number of patrols. On the night of 12/13 June 1917, the 5th Dorsets were given the task of digging two communication trenches east of Wytschaete, Belgium. They suffered 30 casualties, 6 dead and 24 wounded, caused by German shell fire. One of those killed was Walter. Mabel Banks received the following letter from her husband's commanding officer:

"It is with much regret that I have to inform you of the loss of your husband, Sergt. W.J. Banks, who was killed on the night of June 12-13. The Company was at the time employed in digging a communication trench to the front line, when a shell burst near your husband, killing him and wounding two others. Death was instantaneous. He suffered no pain at all. He was buried where he fell and a cross is being made and will be erected on the spot. As his commanding officer, I have always found Sergt. Banks a most capable non-commissioned officer, and his loss is greatly felt by the whole platoon. Please let me assure you of mine and the whole Company's sympathy in your great loss."

Walter's grave was lost in later fighting and he is today remembered on the Ypres Menin Gate.

THURSDAY 14 JUNE 1917 - WEATHER - VERY HOT

Private Charles William Andrews — *6th Bn Wiltshire Regiment*

Service No.	20774	Age:	23
Place of birth:	Deal, Kent	Home Country:	England
Date of death:	14/06/1917	Cause of death:	Killed in action
Memorial:	Salisbury, Wilts		
War Cemetery:	Oosttaverne Wood Cemetery - Grave III. A. 8.		
Next of Kin:	Caleb & Sarah Andrews		
Address:	St Martin, Salisbury, Wiltshire		

Charles a whip thong maker was the only child of Caleb and Sarah Andrews and it is likely he was conscripted into the army joining the Wiltshire Regiment. He was sent to France and to join the 6th Battalion. On Thursday 14 June 1916 at 7.30pm the Wiltshires made an attack on German positions near Oostterverne, southeast of Ypres, Belgium. The German artillery retaliated by shelling the Wiltshires in the front line trenches. Charles was one of two men killed during a German bombardment. Charles was originally buried in Oosttaverne Wood Cemetery No.2 which was in the northern part of Oosttaverne Wood. His remains were moved to their current position in July 1920.

Saturday 16 June 1917 - Weather - Extraordinarily Hot

Private Bertram Morris Macey		*6th Bn Wiltshire Regiment*	
Service No.	24527	Age:	19
Place of birth:	Chilmark Ridge, Wiltshire	Home Country:	England
Date of death:	16/06/1917	Cause of death:	Died of wounds
Memorial:	Newton Toney, Wilts		
War Cemetery:	Boulogne Eastern Cemetery - Grave IV. A. 6.		
Next of Kin:	Morris & Eliza Ann Macey		
Address:	Park Gate, Newton Toney, Wiltshire		

Nineteen year old Bertram, known as Bertie was the youngest son of Morris & Eliza Ann Macey and had been employed as a farm labourer. It is likely he was conscripted into the army joining the Wiltshire Regiment. He was sent to France joining the 6th Battalion. It is likely he was wounded during the opening stages of the battle for Messines Ridge, near St.Elooi, Belgium, and evacuated to a Military Hospital at Boulogne, where he succumbed to his wounds on Saturday 16 June 1916.

Private Edwin Hatter		*2nd Bn Leinster Regiment*	
Service No.	1052	Age:	28
Place of birth:	Corsham, Wilts	Home Country:	England
Date of death:	16/06/1917	Cause of death:	Killed in action
Memorial:	Corsham, Wiltshire		
War Cemetery:	Hooge Crater Cemetery - Grave XVIII. J. 13.		
Next of Kin:	William & Lucy Hatter		
Address:	Priory Street, Corsham, Wiltshire		

Under gardener Edwin was the youngest son of William and Lucy Hatter and volunteered for service with the Wiltshire Regiment on 7 September 1914. The Wiltshire Regiment was over subscribed and consequently Edwin was transferred with over 1,000 Wiltshire men to an Irish Regiment which were lacking recruits. In Edwins' case he was sent to the 6th Battalion Leinster Regiment and arrived at Gallipoli on 9 July 1915. It is likely Edwin was either wounded or was suffering from illness or disease and was evacuated to England. Following his recovery, he was transferred to the 2nd Battalion Leinster Regiment and sent to France. During the evening of 15 June 1917 the 2nd Leinsters moved into British trenches near Hill 60 southeast of Ypres, Belgium. On the morning of Saturday 16 June 1917 the left side of Battle Wood was shelled by German artillery. The afternoon was quiet, then during the evening the Germans shelled the British support lines. Between 9.30pm and 11.30pm the 2nd Leinsters trenches were heavily shelled by the Germans. The resultant casualties were described as light, one of those killed was Edwin Hatter. His brother Frank had been killed at the Somme in August 1916. In August 1919 Edwin's were remains found near Garde-Dieu, southeast of Wambeke and were identified by means of a disc, his remains were relocated to Hooge Crater Cemetery.

Left: Bertram Morris Macey

Right: John Hybart

Private John Hybart — *9th Bn East Surrey Regiment*

Service No.	25030	Age:	21
Place of birth:	Barry, Glamorgan	Home Country:	Wales
Date of death:	16/06/1917	Cause of death:	Killed in action
Memorial:	Not known		
War Cemetery:	Ypres Menin Gate - Panel 34		
Next of Kin:	Albert John Hybart		
Address:	26 Conway Road, Cardiff, Glamorganshire		

Twenty one year old John was the adopted son of Albert John Hybart and was educated at the Grammar School, Cowbridge. After leaving education he engaged in business at Cardiff Docks before joining Lloyds Bank Ltd. at Salisbury. He enlisted into the 31st Royal Fusiliers on 24 January 1916 and arrived in France on 6 Sptember 1916, being transferred to the 9th Battalion East Surrey Regiment. He acted as Company Runner for eight months and on Saturday 16 June 1917 the 9th East Surrey's were in British trenches at Mount Sorrel northeast of Hill 60. John was killed when the British trenches were subjected to a very intense German shelling through out the day. His commanding Officer wrote:

"He was selected for this duty because of his intelligence and the keen way he had been doing his work in the trenches, and for eight months he was my faithful follower and friend. I say "friend" because many talks we had as we went around on our rounds on current events of the day, and sometimes on politics, political economy, etc. As a runner he was always reliable, and showed a keen intelligence, and never once during the whole period he was with me had I occasion to find fault with him."

SUNDAY 17 JUNE 1917 - WEATHER - VERY HOT

Private Arthur John Bridgeman — *1st Bn Wiltshire Regiment*

Service No.	22889	Age:	23
Place of birth:	Shaw, Wiltshire	Home Country:	England
Date of death:	17/06/1917	Cause of death:	Died of wounds
Memorial:	Lydiard Millicent, Wilts		
War Cemetery:	Bailleul Communal Cemetery Extension Nord - Grave III. D. 35.		
Next of Kin:	Charles & Hannah Bridgeman		

Address: 9 Elms, Shaw, Wiltshire

Arthur was the only son of Charles and Hannah Bridgeman and was employed as a wagon painter in the Carriage and Wagon Department, at the Great Western Railway Works in Swindon. He enlisted with the Wiltshire Regiment in February 1916 and underwent training at Bovington Camp, He was sent to France in June 1916 joining the 1st Battalion and during his service was wounded twice and had home leave in December 1916. Arthur was wounded for a third time on 7 June 1917 when the 1st Wiltshires attacked German positions near Wulverghem, Belgium as part of the operations at Messines. He was evacuated to a medical facility at Bailleul, where he succumbed to his wounds on Sunday 17 June 1916.

Gunner Walter Palmer *168th Siege Bty Royal Garrison Artillery*

Service No.	78293	Age:	31
Place of birth:	Luckington, Wiltshire	Home Country:	England
Date of death:	17/06/1917	Cause of death:	Killed in action
Memorial:	Sherston, Luckington, Wiltshire		
War Cemetery:	Vlamertinghe New Military Cemetery - Grave I. B. 24.		
Next of Kin:	George & Fanny Palmer		
Address:	23 Brook Hill, Sherston, Wiltshire		

Walter, a hay trusser, was the third son of George and Fanny Palmer and enlisted in the army on 7 December 1915 under the Derby Scheme, where a man could enlist and would only be called up when the army needed him. He was mobilised on 4 May 1916 joining the Royal Garrison Artillery. He arrived in France on 22 September 1916 with the 168th Battery, equipped with four 6" Howitzers. Walter was wounded on 6 June 1917 and sent to hospital returning to his unit on 9 June 1917. He was killed most likely by German counter battery fire on Sunday 17 June 1916. His personal possessions consisting of 1 photo was returned to his mother.

Tuesday 19 June 1917 - Weather - Very Hot - Thunder Storms

Private Cecil Francis Deacon *1st Bn North Staffordshire Regiment*

Service No.	23307	Age:	20
Place of Birth:	Heath, Derbyshire	Home Country:	England
Date of Death:	19/06/1917	Cause of death:	Killed in action
War cemetery:	Ypres Menin Gate – Panel 55		
Next of Kin:	Frank Joseph & Elizabeth Deacon		
Address:	10 Warner Street, Hasland Road, Chesterfield, Derbyshire		

Cecil was the youngest son of Frank and Elizabeth Deacon and the grandson of Joseph Deacon of Eastbourne Road, Trowbridge. He was employed as a turner and enlisted in the army on 7 December 1915 under the Derby Scheme, where a man could enlist and would only be called up when the army needed him. He was mobilised on 27 April 1916 and after completing his training, he was sent to France on 2 January 1917. At just twenty years of age Cecil was killed in action in British trenches at Mount Sorrel, northeast of Hill 60, most likely due to German shell fire, on Tuesday 19 June 1917. He is remembered on the Ypres Menin Gate and has no known grave.

Private Lewis Henry Barnes Webb *4th Field Amb New Zealand Medical Corps*

Service No.	3/1800	Age:	28
Place of birth:	Christchurch, New Zealand	Home Country:	New Zealand

Arthur John Bridgeman

Date of death: 19/06/1917 Cause of death: Died of wounds
Memorial: Not known
War Cemetery: Wimereux Communal Cemetery - Grave II.M.12
Next of Kin: Ruth Webb (wife) - Arthur Henry & Helen Webb
Address: 28 Cheviot Street, Spreydon, Christchurch, New Zealand

Lewis, a carpenter joiner, was the second son of Arthur and Helen Webb and the nephew of George Barnes of Duke street, Trowbridge. He had already served with No.3 Field Ambulance and enlisted on 24 September 1915. He arrived in France in April 1916 with 4th New Zealand Field Ambulance and on 23 September 1916 he was wounded in action with gun shot wounds to the face, arms and legs. Following his recovery, he returned to his unit. He was wounded in operations at Messines on 10 June 1917 and evacuated to No. 8 Stationary Hospital. He was described as dangerously ill with gun shot wounds to the thigh and succumbed to his wounds on Tuesday 19 June 1917.

Private Arthur William Bull *1st Bn Wiltshire Regiment*
Service No. 3/63 Age: 28
Place of birth: Winterbourne Monkton, Wilts Home Country: England
Date of death: 19/06/1917 Cause of death: Killed in action
Memorial: Winterbourne Monkton, Wilts
War Cemetery: Poperinghe New Military Cemetery - Grave II. G. 11.
Next of Kin: Thomas & Anne Maria Bull
Address: Winterbourne Monkton, Wiltshire

Farm labourer Arthur was the second son of Thomas and Anne Maria Bull and was mobilised at the outbreak of hostilities arriving in France on 11 November 1914. He was sent to the 2nd Battalion Wiltshire Regiment. It is likely he was wounded and following his recovery returned to the front and was transferred to the 1st Battalion Wiltshire Regiment. Between 16th – 20th August the 1st Wiltshires we called on to supply working parties of 350 other ranks each evening from 8pm to 4am. They were employed digging a communication trench on Messines Ridge southeast of Messines to the front line. The 1st Wiltshires working parties were subject to considerable German shelling causing a number of casualties. One of those killed was Arthur, his brother James Bull had been killed at Givenchy in June 1915.

WEDNESDAY 20 JUNE 1917 - WEATHER - VERY HOT

Private James Gregory		*1st Bn Wiltshire Regiment*	
Service No.	7007	Age:	31
Place of birth:	Melksham, Wiltshire	Home Country:	England
Date of death:	20/06/1917	Cause of death:	Killed in action
Memorial:	Bromham, Wiltshire		
War Cemetery:	Ypres Menin Gate - Grave Panel 53.		
Next of Kin:	John & Martha Elizabeth Gregory		
Address:	Sandridge, Bromham, Wiltshire		

James known as Jim and a reservist, was the third son of John and Martha Gregory and at the outbreak of hostilities he was employed by the Avon Rubber Works at Melksham where he worked as a motor cycle tyre tread maker. He was called back to the 1st Battalion Wiltshire Regiment and sent to France on 14 August 1914. On the night of 19-20 June 1917, the 1st Wiltshires were called on to supply 350 men to dig a communications trench from Messines, Belgium to the front line in a south easterly direction. The operation was carried out under constant German shell fire. Jim was killed in the early hours of Wednesday 20 June 1918 while digging the communication trench. In July 1917 Jim's brother in law, Howard Pearce, received the following letters, the first from Captain G. D. Brown of the 1st Wiltshires:

"I am extremely sorry to have to write and tell you that your brother was killed instantly *by a shell, while working in the trenches on the night of 19th-20th June. He had been with the Battalion so long that his death is a great loss to us. Please accept my deepest sympathy."*

The second letter was from 2nd Lieutenant W. K. Holmes of the 1st Wiltshires:

"It is the deepest regret that I have to inform you of the loss of your brother, Pte. J. Gregory. He was killed in action on the evening of the 19th, whilst doing his duty gallantly as becomes a British soldier. I must take this opportunity of conveying to you the deep sympathy of the officers, N.C.O.'s and men of the company in your irreparable loss. Gregory was one of those men who I could always trust, even in the tightest of corners, and he showed an example which will be very hard to beat, to the younger men of the company. You will be glad to hear that he was not called upon to suffer any pain."

In June 1918 Jim's sisters Maud and Louise inserted the following memoriam in a local paper:

Days of sadness still come o'er us
Secret tears often flow
Memory keeps our loved one near to us
Though it's now one year ago
I often think and talk of him
And think how he died
To think he could not say good-bye
Before he closed his eyes
Could I kneel beside his grave
And shed a silent tear
But now he sleeps somewhere in France
The one I love so dear

Left: James Gregory

Right: William Rivers

Private William Rivers		*1st Bn Wiltshire Regiment*	
Service No.	19514	Age:	19
Place of birth:	Swindon, Wiltshire	Home Country:	England
Date of death:	20/06/1917	Cause of death:	Killed in action
Memorial:	Lyneham,Wiltshire		
War Cemetery:	Ypres Menin Gate - Panel 53.		
Next of Kin:	John and Fanny Rivers		
Address:	Freegrove Cottage, Goatacre, Wiltshire		

Nineteen year old William, known as Willie, was the third son of John and Fanny Rivers and volunteered for service at the age of seventeen in the summer of 1915, being sent to the front in September 1916. On the night of 19-20 June 1917, the 1st Wiltshires were called on to supply 350 men to dig a communications trench from Messines, Belgium to the front line in a south easterly direction. The operation was carried out under constant German shell fire. The first news of Willie's death was received by his parents from his uncle Shoeing E. Smith who was serving at the front. Official news followed soon after fron Captain G. D. Brown who wrote the following.

"I am extremely sorry to have to tell you that your son was killed instantaneously by shell fire while working in the trenches on the night of the 19th-20th. He and the others who fell were buried yesterday by the padre. Hiss loss is keenly felt by us all, and the battalion shares your grief. Please accept my deepest sympathy."

Willie's grave was lost in subsequent fighting and he is remembered today on the Ypres Menin Gate. His brother Walter Rivers was to die in October 1918.

Private James Ford		*1st Bn Wiltshire Regiment*	
Service No.	22301	Age:	30
Place of birth:	Steeple Langford, Wilts	Home Country:	England
Date of death:	20/06/1917	Cause of death:	Killed in action
Memorial:	Broadwey, Dorset – Amesbury, Wilts		
War Cemetery:	Ypres Menin Gate - Panel 53		
Next of Kin:	Edith Florence Ford (wife) - James & Elizabeth Ford (parents)		
Address:	Broadwey, Dorset -Durrington, Wiltshire		

Farm wagoner James was the youngest son of James & Elizabeth Ford and in the Summer of 1916 he married Edith Florence Hunt at Weymouth. It is likely he was conscripted into the army and was sent to the 1st Battalion Wiltshire Regiment. On the night of 19-20 June 1917, the 1st Wiltshires were called on to supply 350 men to dig a communications trench from Messines, Belgium to the front line in a south easterly direction. The operation was carried out under constant German shell fire. James was one of those killed, his grave was lost in subsequent fighting and he remembered today on the Ypres Menin Gate.

THURSDAY 21 JUNE 1917 - WEATHER - COLD AND RAINY

Private Arthur Edward Hancock — *1st Bn Dorsetshire Regiment*

Service No.	18412	Age:	31
Place of birth:	Edington, Wiltshire	Home Country:	England
Date of death:	21/06/1917	Cause of death:	Killed in action
Memorial:	Edington, Wiltshire		
War Cemetery:	Ramscapplle Road Military Cemetery - Grave II. A. 24.		
Next of Kin:	George & Eliza Hancock		
Address:	4 Church Street, Edington, Wiltshire		

Arthur, a carter, was the youngest son of George and Eliza Hancock and was a member of Ediington Church Choir. He was a prominent member of the Edington and Bratton Football Club and it is likely he was conscripted into the army in the spring of 1916, joining the Dorset Regiment. He was sent to France to serve with the 1st Battalion and in the winter of 1916 he was evacuated to England suffering from trench feet. Following his recovery, he returned to the front and was serving in trenches east of Nieuport, Belgium. He was one of 3 men killed, on Thursday 21 June 1917, when the Dorsets were bombarded by German heavy trench mortars. Arthur's mother received the following from his platoon officer:

"It is with the greatest sympathy that I write to inform you of the death of your son Pte. A Hancock. It is always such a great loss to the platoon to lose such a good man. He never failed to impress with his devotion to duty and bravery. He was respected by all and suffered no pain and his death being instantaneous."

Arthur was buried where he fell and in June 1919 his grave was located between Nose Trench and Nose Support Trench, south of Lombardsijde, with aid of an original burial report. His remains were then moved to Ramscapplle Road Military Cemetery

39-117

Private Christopher William Parfitt — *17th Bn Sherwood Foresters*

Service No.	4611	Age:	24
Place of birth:	Salisbury, Wiltshire	Home Country:	England
Date of death:	21/06/1917	Cause of death:	Killed in action
Memorial:	Loggerheads, Nottingham.		
War Cemetery:	Vlamertinghe Military Cemetery - Grave I. C. 13.		
Next of Kin:	John & Edith Parfitt		
Address:	Lammas Terrace, Meadow, Nottingham, Nottinghamshire		

Christopher, a printer, was the only son of John and Edith Parfitt and enlisted with the Special Reserve of the Notts and Derby Regiment (the Sherwood Foresters), on 14 August 1916. At the outbreak of hostilities, he was mobilised and then promoted to Lance Corporal 26 November 1914. He arrived in

France on 27 December 1914 and was sent to the 1st Battalion Sherwood Foresters. Christopher reported sick with myalgia at the end of January 1915, then again in February 1915, with a sprained ankle and was found to be suffering from frostbite and evacuated to England on 9 March 1915. Following his recovery, he returned to the front on 30 December 1915 and was posted to the 2nd Battalion Sherwood Foresters. In February 1916 he was admitted to 16th Field Ambulance suffering from scabies but returned to his unit soon after. Christopher was wounded with a gunshot wound to the back on 7 June 1916, while digging pits for dugouts at Frascati Farm, on the west bank of the canal north of Ypres. He was evacuated to England and after his recovery returned to France on 30 January 1917 and was transferred to the 17th Service Battalion Sherwood Foresters, (the Welbeck Rangers). He was killed by German shell fire, on Thursday 21 June 1917 while on the canal bank east of Vlamertinghe, Belgium. His personal property was returned to his family consisting of a disc, 3 coins, photographs, cards, pouch, pocket wallet and a note book.

FRIDAY 22 JUNE 1917 - WEATHER - HEAVY RAIN THUNDERSTORMS

Gunner William Henry Ponting		*203rd Siege Bty Royal Garrison Artillery*	
Service No.	87582	Age:	33
Place of birth:	Corston, Wiltshire	Home Country:	England
Date of death:	22/06/1917	Cause of death:	Died of wounds
Memorial:	Corston, Wiltshire		
War Cemetery:	Corston All Saints Chuchyard Malmesbury St Paul -		
Next of Kin:	Gertrude Alice Ponting (wife) - Henry & Thursa Ponting (parents)		
Address:	Corston, Wiltshire		

William was the only son of Henry and Thursa Ponting and had worked on the permanent way for the Great Western Railway Company, before being employed as a hay cutter for Mrs Denly of Corston. On Boxing Day 1911 he married Gertrude Alice Dunsby. He enlisted under the Derby Scheme, where a man could join the army but would only be called up when the army needed them, on 12 December 1915. While waiting to be called he worked for the Government on Salisbury Plain and was then mobilised 31 May 1916. He was sent to the Royal Garrison Artillery and after completing his training he was sent to France on 16 November 1916. On 18 March 1917, he was attached to the 203rd Siege Battery and while serving with them was badly wounded in the right arm, on 3 June 1917, most likely by German shell fire, during the bombardment of German position in preparations for the attack on Messines. He was evacuated to England on the Hospital Ship St Patrick and sent to Nottingham General Hospital where he succumbed to his wounds on Friday 22 June 1917. His body was sent to his family at Corston where he was buried with full military honours. He left a widow and three small children. In November 1917, his personal possessions were returned to his widow from his unit consisting of a safety razor with blades.

SATURDAY 23 JUNE 1917 - WEATHER - WET

Private William Samuel Orchard		*10th Bn Royal West Kent Regiment*	
Service No.	G/15484	Age:	30
Place of birth:	Salisbury, Wiltshire	Home Country:	England
Date of death:	23/06/1917	Cause of death:	Killed in action
Memorial:	Salisbury, Wiltshire – Folkestone, Kent		
War Cemetery:	Ypres Menin Gate - Panel 45 and 47.		
Next of Kin:	Susannah Rose Orchard (wife) - William & Rosa Orchard (parents)		
Address:	41 Queen Street, Folkestone - 100, Radnor Park Rd., Folkestone, Kent		

William a manager for a tobacco dealer was the eldest son of William and Rosa Orchard and in the summer of 1914 he married Susannah Rose Briscoe at Folkestone. It is likely he was conscripted into the army or joined under the Derby Scheme, arriving in France in September 1916. He was sent to the 10th Battalionn Royal West Kent Regiment, who on Saturday 23 June 1916 were in the British front line near Damme Strasse, south east of St.Eloi, Belgium. William was sent with a party of men to collect rations, one of his friends wrote to William's wife explaining what happened:

"We had been carrying up rations to the frontline, and were almost back to our own support trenches when Fritz opened out a very heavy shell fire, catching us in the open, which I will add is very frequent now. A piece of shrapnel caught Will in the back of the head, but he could not have felt anything. We laid him out nicely, and he was taken down the next morning, being buried in a properly dug grave, with his cross and number on."

In another letter, William's officers describe him as a thoroughly good and efficient soldier, and spoke of the regret felt by the whole company, officers and men alike, at this loss. William left a widow and two young children. His grave was lost in subsequent fighting and he is remembered on the Ypres Menin Gate. William's brother, Alfred was to be killed in September 1917 while serving with the Navy and his brother George was to be killed in April 1918 serving with the Royal West Surrey Regiment.

Private Stephen John Arthur Hughes		*H Coy.2nd Bn Wiltshire Regiment*	
Service No.	21244	Age:	20
Place of birth:	Swindon, Wiltshire	Home Country:	England
Date of death:	23/06/1917	Cause of death:	Died of wounds
Memorial:	Not Known		
War Cemetery:	Lijssenthoek Military Cemetery - Grave XIV. D. 2A.		
Next of Kin:	Abner & Rose Hughes		
Address:	30 Eastcott Road, Swindon, Wiltshire		

Stephen was the eldest son of Abner and Rose Hughes and it is likely he was conscripted into the army joining the 2nd Battalion Wiltshire Regiment. In June 1917, the 2nd Wiltshires were in the British front line near Zillebeke. On 20 June 1916 Stephen wrote home to his parents asking about the weather in Swindon as it had been raining in torrents for 2 days in Belgium. He said he would send his credits home only to be used for his brother, Harold, a carpenter to buy his tools. He also asked his mother to send him a bread pudding and a Khaki jacket, because the lice did not like those ones. He closed with fondest love from your loving son. While in the front line Stephen was wounded with shrapnel wounds to his left leg and elbow and evacuated to a military hospital at Lijssenthoek, east of Ypres. He succumbed to wounds on Saturday 23 June 1917 and was buried in the cemetery next to the hospital. In June 1918, his parents inserted the following memoriam in a local paper:

He sleeps beside his comrades,
In a grave we may never know;
But his name is written in words of love,
In the hearts he left at home.

It may be a soldier's honour
At his country's call to fall,
But we cannot think of the glory
With the sorrow it cause us all.

SUNDAY 24 JUNE 1917 - WEATHER - VERY CLEAR AND FINE

Private Henry James Mizen — *2nd Bn Wiltshire Regiment*

Service No.	3/753	Age:	44
Place of birth:	Bradford on Avon, Wiltshire	Home Country:	England
Date of death:	24/06/1917	Cause of death:	Killed in action
Memorial:	Westbury Leigh, Westbury, Wiltshire		
War Cemetery:	Perth Cemetery China Wall - Grave II. A. 32.		
Next of Kin:	Edith Virtue Mizen (wife) – Henry & Charlotte Mizen (parents)		
Address:	Westbury Leigh, Westbury, Wiltshire		

Old soldier Henry was the eldest son of Henry and Charlotte Mizen and enlisted with the Somerset Light Infantry on 29 December 1890 and served at Gibraltar and India and South Africa over a 12 year period. He was with the Indian expedition on the Punjab frontier in 1897-98 and went through the South African War, receiving the Queen's Medal with five bars, Transvaal, Relief of Ladysmith, Orange Free State, Tugela Heights, and Cape Colony. He also had the King's medal with two bars. He left the Army on 28 December 1902 and in 1903 married Edith Virtue Newman at Bradford on Avon. He found employment with Boulton Brothers Glove Factory and at the outbreak of hostilities was one of the first to re-enlist, giving his name at a big recruitment meeting in the Market Square at Westbury, on 6 September 1914. He joined the Wiltshire Regiment and arrived in France on 17 February 1915 and was sent to the 2nd Battalion. He was attached to the transport section and had only been granted one leave, in January 1916, but the last letter received by his wife stated he hoped to return home in July 1917. He was taking rations to the front line near Zillebeke on Sunday 24 June 1917 when it is believed he was struck by a German shell. His horse was wounded and returned without him. He left a widow, two sons and two daughters. Henry was originally buried northeast of Shrapnel Corner and in January 1919 his remains were moved to Perth Cemetery China Wall.

TUESDAY 26 JUNE 1917 - WEATHER - FINE

Sapper Christopher Whiteman — *104th Field Coy Bn Royal Engineers*

Service No.	520290	Age:	38
Place of birth:	Shilton, Berkshire	Home Country:	England

Left: Henry James Mizen

Right Christopher Whiteman

Date of death:	26/06/1917	Cause of death:	Killed in action
Memorial:	Not known		
War Cemetery:	Perth Cemetery China Wall - Grave I. G. 36		
Next of Kin:	Ellen Jane Whiteman (wife) - Edmund and Elizabeth Whiteman (parents)		
Address:	75 Omdurman Street, Swindon, Wilts - Quarry Farm, Poulton, Glos		

Bricklayer, Christopher, known as Chris, was the youngest son of Edmund and Elizabeth Whiteman and originally enlisted with the Royal Engineers on 9 November 1899. After spending one year in England Christopher was posted to St. Helena and on 5 December 1902, after spending 2 years on St. Helena, Christopher bought himself out of the army at a cost of £18. Returning to England he married Ellen Jane Walker in the summer of 1903. At some stage after this he began employment as a bricklayer with the Loco and Carriage Department at The Great Western Railway Works in Swindon. It is likely he was either conscripted into the army or joined under the Derby Scheme, rejoining The Royal Engineers and being sent to the front. Christopher was killed by German shell fire near Voormezeele, Belgium, on Tuesday 26 June 1916, while constructing new roads. He left a widow and a young family. Christopher was originally buried near Spoilbank Cemetery and in July 1919 was moved to Perth Cemetery China Wall.

WEDNESDAY 27 JUNE 1917 - WEATHER - VERY HEAVY RAIN

Private William George Gilbert — *15th Bn Hampshire Regiment*

Service No.	31607	Age:	25
Place of birth:	Field Barn, Wiltshire	Home Country:	England
Date of death:	27/06/1917	Cause of death:	Killed in action
Memorial:	Whiteparish, Wiltshire		
War Cemetery:	Dickebusch New Military Cemetery Extension - Grave II. A. 16.		
Next of Kin:	Florence Kate Gilbert (wife) - Thomas & Emily Gilbert (parents)		
Address:	Whistley Cottage, Potterne, Wiltshire – Titchbourne, Hampshire		

William, a carter on a farm was the only son of Thomas and Emily Gilbert and married Florence Kate Giles at Whiteparish on 31 July 1915. It is likely he was either conscripted or enlisted in the army under the Derby Scheme, joining the Hampshire Regiment and was sent to the front with the 15th Service Battalion. From 20 to 27 June 1917 the 15th Hampshires were sent out in working parties south of St. Eloi and William was killed, most likely by German shell fire, while on a working party on Wednesday 27 June 1916.

THURSDAY 28 JUNE 1917 - WEATHER - HEAVY RAIN WITH THUNDERSTORMS

Private Thomas Jenkins — *2nd Bn Wiltshire Regiment*

Service No.	21049	Age:	28
Place of birth:	Birmingham, Warwicks	Home Country:	England
Date of death:	28/06/1917	Cause of death:	Killed in action
Memorial:	Not Known		
War Cemetery:	Ypres Menin Gate - Panel 53.		
Next of Kin:	Ellen Jenkins (wife)		
Address:	Aldershot, Hampshire		

Thomas was a shepherd and resided in Salisbury prior to the Great War. It is likely he was either conscripted or enlisted into the army under the Derby Scheme, joining the Wiltshire Regiment and was sent to France to join the 2nd Battalion. He was wounded in November 1916 and after his recovery returned to his unit. On the night of 27/28 June 1917, the 2nd Wiltshires were in British trenches at Observatory Ridge north east of Hill 60. A raid took place on German trenches opposite consisting of 2 officers and 32 ranks. Although no prisoners were taken 3 Germans were killed (bayoneted) and the remainder wounded. A shoulder title and cap were secured and the Wiltshires withdrew. The following morning the Wiltshires were shelled in the front line. Thomas was presumed to have been killed on Thursday 28 June 1916 either during the raid or the German Bombardment that followed.

During the month of June 1917, the British captured the following during operations at Messines-Wytschaete Ridge and other parts of the front:

8,511 Rank and file

175 Officers

67 Guns (including two heavy guns)

102 Trench mortars

345 Machine guns

Besides great quantities of other war material.

Messines Village

3
Battle of Nieuport

GERMANS LAUNCH ATTACK ON NIEUPORT ON THE EAST SIDE OF THE YSER CANAL FORCING THE BRITISH TO WITHDRAW TO THE WEST BANK

TUESDAY 3 JULY 1917

German artillery intensely pounded British positions on the Nieuport front, and were attacked by a powerful enemy force and were unable to withstand the onslaught. The dunes area was isolated by the destruction of the Bridges and the enemy penetrated the British front on a width of 1400 yards to a depth of 600 yards and thus reached the banks of the Yser near the sea. German General von Ludendorff stated:

"The operation had been a great success and over 1,250 prisoners, including 27 officers, were brought in, and the English losses on the heavily shelled terrain between the sea and the river were very high."

Private Charles Henry Gillingham — *1st Bn Dorsetshire Regiment*

Service No.	16845
Age:	29
Place of birth:	Abbotsbury, Dorset
Home Country:	England
Date of death:	03/07/1917
Cause of death:	Killed in action
Memorial:	Not known
War Cemetery:	Nieuwpoort Communal Cemetery - Grave I. B. 3.
Next of Kin:	William George & Emily J. Gillingham
Address:	Stratford Sub Castle, Wiltshire

Charles, a butcher, was the third son of William and Emily Gillingham and it is likely he was either conscripted or enlisted into the army under the Derby Scheme, enlisting with the Dorset Regiment. He was sent to the front joining the 1st Battalion, who on Tuesday 3 July 1917 were in British trenches east of Nieuport, Belgium. The 1st Dorsets were subjected to German Shelling and Charles was one of two men killed on this day.

Private Percy Capel — *MT 37th Div. Sup. Col. Army Service Corps*

Service No.	M2/166793
Age:	37
Place of birth:	Cunmor, Berks
Home Country:	England
Date of death:	03/07/1917
Cause of death:	Died of wounds
Memorial:	Not Known
War Cemetery:	Dranoutre Military Cemetery - Grave II. J. 13.
Next of Kin:	George & Lucy Capel
Address:	Cunmor, Oxfordshire

Percy, a motor driver, was the third son of George and Lucy Capel and lived in Netheravon at the time of his enlistment. It is likely he was either conscripted or enlisted into the army under the Derby Scheme, and because of his trade, he joined the Army Service Corps and was sent to the 37th Division Supply Column. During the early hours of Tuesday 3 July 1917, they were based at Dranoutre and were bombed by a German aircraft. 10 men were killed and 12 wounded Percy was wounded and taken to 50th Field Ambulance Hospital where he succumbed to his wounds on the same day.

Gunner Alfred John Henry Pragnell — *17th Heavy Bty Bn Royal Garrison Artillery*

Service No.	283318	Age:	35
Place of birth:	Newport, Isle of Wight	Home Country:	England
Date of death:	03/07/1917	Cause of death:	Died of wounds
Memorial:	Porton, Wilts		
War Cemetery:	Wimereux Communal Cemetery - Grave II. N. 11.		
Next of Kin:	Florence Elizabeth Pragnell (wife) - Alfred & Eliza Pragnell (parent)		
Address:	Elm View, Gomeldon, Wiltshire		

Old soldier Alfred, know as Harry, was the eldest son of Alfred and Eliza Pragnell and had been a volunteer with the Hampshire and Isle of Wight Artillery. On 23 February 1901, he enlisted with the Hussars of the line and was posted to the 10th Hussars. On the 31 May 1902, he arrived in South Africa where he served until 22 September 1902 when he and the 10th Hussars were sent to India. While in India he extended his service to complete 12 years with the colours and returned to England in February 1911, transferring to the 18th Hussars. He was discharged in February 1913 on the completion of his service. In the summer of of 1915 he married Florence Elizabeth Sawyer at Amesbury and it is believed he re-enlisted into the army under the Derby Scheme joining the Royal Garrison Artillery being sent to France joining the 17th Heavy Battery. It is likely he was wounded during or soon after the bombardment of German positions at Messines and evacuated to the 32nd Stationary Hospital at Wimereux. Harry succumbed to his wounds at the hospital on Tuesday 3 July 1917.

Bugler John Henry Hatherell — *6th Bn Wiltshire Regiment*

Service No.	19452	Age:	19
Place of Birth:	Chippenham, Wiltshire	Home Country:	England
Date of Death:	04/07/1917	Cause of death:	Died of wounds

Left: Alfred John Henry Pragnell

Right: John Henry Hatherell

Memorial:	Chippenham, Wiltshire
War cemetery:	Boulogne Eastern Cemetery - Grave IV. A. 23
Next of Kin:	John William & Emily Hatherell
Address:	9 Lowden Hill, Chippenham, Wiltshire

Nineteen year old John was a twin and son of John and Emily Hatherell. He was employed as a signal worker with Saxby and Farmer Ltd prior to his enlistment with the 6th Battalion Wiltshire Regiment. He was sent to the continent where on Wednesday 4 June 1917 he was severely wounded during a German bombardment near Diependaalhoek, Belgium. He was evacuated to No 13 Base Hospital at Boulogne where he succumbed to his wounds. His parents received the following letter from Chaplain J. F. A. Branford:

"I am indeed most sorry to have to convey to you the sad news that your dear boy died this afternoon. Yesterday he seemed a little better, if anything, but he collapsed today. I saw him early this morning and we had a prayer together, but he quite suddenly, after dinner, got worse and expired in a few minutes. I know how much he longed to get back home and how much you longed to have him, so I can feel most sincere sympathy and I pray that our Heavenly Father may pour into your bleeding hearts His holy comfort and give you strength to bear bravely such a grievous blow."

In June 1918 John's parents inserted the following memoriam in a local paper:

In loving memory of our dear son
No one stood beside him to bid him a last farewell
Although his grave is far away he did his duty well
He's gone but not forgotten often we recall his name
But there is nothing left to answer but his photo in the frame
Sadly missed by his Mother, Father, Sisters and Brothers.

Sapper Albert Cook — *80th Field Coy Bn Royal Engineers*

Service No.	140182	Age:	29
Place of birth:	Swindon, Wilts	Home Country:	England
Date of death:	04/07/1917	Cause of death:	Died of wounds
Memorial:	St Mary's Swindon, Wilts		
War Cemetery:	Bailleul Communal Cemetery Extension Nord - Grave III. D. 184.		
Next of Kin:	John & Dinah Cook		
Address:	15 Taunton Street, Swindon, Wiltshire		

Carpenter Albert was the only son of John and Dinah Cook and it is likely he was either conscripted or enlisted into the army under the Derby Scheme, and because of his trade he joined the Royal Engineers. He was sent to France joining the 80th Field Company who in June 1916 were operating in the Zillebeke area. It is likely Albert was wounded by German shell fire and evacuated to the 11th Casualty Clearing Station at Boulogne where he succumbed to his wounds on Wednesday 4 July 1917.

Lieutenant Frank Remington Pretyman — *2nd Bn Scots Guards*

Service No.	N/a	Age:	26
Place of birth:	Edgewater, United States	Home Country:	England
Date of death:	04/07/1917	Cause of death:	Killed in action
Memorial:	Comton, Surrey – Marlborough College, Wiltshire		
War Cemetery:	Canada Farm Cemetery - Grave I. A. 4		
Next of Kin:	William & Jenny Pretyman		
Address:	Five Ways, Torquay, Devon		

Frank was the younger son of William and Jenny Pretyman and was educated at Stubbington and Marlborough College. He was an associate member of the Royal School of Mines and found employment

Frank Remington Pretyman

in Mexico, the United States and Canada. At the outbreak of hostilities he was attached to the Geological Survey of Wisconsin and decided to return home and enlist as a despatch rider with the Royal Engineers at the rank of Corporal. He was given a Commission with the Royal Engineers and sent to France arriving on 23 April 1915. He was sent to the 197th tunnelling company and on 14 September 1915 was gassed at La Boiselle, at the Somme. He was gassed again while trying to save the life of a Corporal underground. On 29 July 1916, he transferred to the Scots Guards and was serving with them on Wednesday 4 July 1917, when the Scots Guards were employed on fatigue work near Elverdinghe. Frank and his men had to march four miles at dusk and then took ammunition and stores to the front. Frank and fifteen other ranks were killed by German shell fire while undertaking this work which was preparation for the attack and subsequent capture of Pilckem Heights. His commanding officer wrote:

"I have never met a better, keener soldier, nor one who took a greater interest in the welfare of his men. All ranks mourn him. By his cheeriness, however hard the times were, and by his devotion to duty he made everyone proud of him, and by his death the regiment loses a fine officer and leader of men."

Another officer wrote:

He was an especial friend of all of us individually, all the more because he had during the nine months he was with us lived up to a reputation he quickly made for himself, of never having said an unkind thing about anybody and of being the straightest man out here."

Another wrote:

"I feel I have lost a very real friend. He always had the same cheerfulness, wherever he was, and there was no one with whom most of us would sooner have gone into action. We all loved him and as for the men, he was with them, one of, if not the, most popular officer."

Frank's brother Maurice had been killed in August 1914.

Gunner Albert Edward Higgins		*289th Siege Bty Royal Garrison Artillery*	
Service No.	110667	Age:	29
Place of birth:	Highworth, Wiltshire	Home Country:	England
Date of death:	05/07/1917	Cause of death:	Killed in action

Memorial:	Watchfield, Berks
War Cemetery:	Dickebusch New Military Cemetery - Grave II. B. 29.
Next of Kin:	Ada Helen Higgins (wife) – Albert & Mary Higgins (parents)
Address:	Hillside Cottage, Watchfield, Berkshire – Blunsdon, Wiltshire

Albert, a hay binder, was the eldest son of Albert and Mary Higgins and on 19 August 1911 he married Ada Helen Harris at Watchfield. He was conscripted into the army and called up on 10 August 1916 joining the Royal Garrison Artillery being posted to No. 3 Depot Royal Garrison Artillery. He was first sent to 45 Company and then to 224 Siege Battery before being sent to 289 Siege Battery in November 1916. He arrived in France on 28 March 1917 and was killed most likely by German shell fire east of Dickebusch on Thursday 5 July 1917. His personal possessions consisting of a 5 Franc Belgium note, a photo and two rosaries. He left a widow, a young son and two young daughters.

Bombardier George Bartlett *168th Siege Bty Royal Garrison Artillery*

Service No.	87580	Age:	30
Place of birth:	Ashton Keynes, Wilts	Home Country:	England
Date of death:	05/07/1917	Cause of death:	Died of wounds
Memorial:	Ashton Keynes, Wilts		
War Cemetery:	Lijssenthoek Military Cemetery - Grave XV. C. 12.		
Next of Kin:	Jennie Alberta Bartlett (wife) - Jessie & Eliza Bartlett (parents)		
Address:	Fore Street, Ashton Keynes, Wiltshire		

Groom, George, was the second son of Jessie and Eliza Bartlett and married Jennie Alberta Alletson at Swindon, on 6 April 1910. He enlisted under the Derby Scheme on 6 December 1915 and was mobilised on 31 May 1916, being posted to No. 3 Depot Royal Garrison Artillery. He was first sent to 45 Company and then to 168 Siege Battery on 27 June 1916. He arrived in France on 23 September 1916 and on 5 October 1916, was attached to the 2nd Army Signal School for a two week course. After returning to his unit he was promoted to Bombardier in March 1916. He was wounded, most likely by German shell fire, on 4 July 1916 and evacuated to No. 10 Casualty Clearing Station at Lijssenthoek, where he succumbed to his wounds on Thursday 5 July 1917. His personal possessions consisting of a coin, letters, photos, pipe, farmers calendar, cigarette case, tobacco pouch, penknife, spirit flask, lanyard, handkerchiefs, razor, cards and a disc were returned to his family. He left a widow, young son and two young daughters.

Friday 6 July 1917

Driver Alfred Harry Milner *15th Div Ammunition Col. Royal Field Artillery*

Service No.	18345	Age:	24
Place of birth:	Hastings, Sussex	Home Country:	England
Date of death:	06/07/1917	Cause of death:	Killed in action
Memorial:	Melksham, Wiltshire		
War Cemetery:	Brandhoek Military Cemetery - Grave I. L. 48.		
Next of Kin:	Sergent William & Elizabeth Georgina Milner		
Address:	5 Western Terrace, Melksham, Wiltshire		

Alfred, an engineer's fitter, was the second son of William and Elizabeth Milner and was employed at an aeroplane works in Bristol. He served his apprenticeship at Spencer & Co. Works and he was a member of the local Liberal Club. He joined the Royal Field Artillery soon after the outbreak of the war and arrived in France on 8 November 1915. He served in Salonika, Greece, where he contracted dysentery and was evacuated to England on sick leave. Following his recovery, he returned to France, joining the

15th Division Ammunition Column. He was killed most likely by German artillery east of Brandhoek, Belgium, on Friday 6 July 1917. Captain W. Read, Alfred's Commanding officer, wrote:

"I very much regret to have to inform you that your son, Driver A. H. Milner was killed in action on the night of 5/6 July. Death was instantaneous, and he suffered no pain I think you will be glad to know that we were able to bring him back, and he was buried yesterday afternoon by our chaplain, rev. Wilcock. I will see that a cross is erected over his grave and that his few belongings are forwarded. Will you please accept my deepest sympathy. We are very sorry to lose Driver Milner, but it is good to know he died gallantly doing his duty and that I think will prove to be your comfort in the years to come."

Saturday 7 July 1917

Captain Reginald Herbert Griffin		*attd 21st Siege Bty RGA Royal Field Artillery*	
Service No.	N/a	Age:	38
Place of birth:	Happenshire, Shropshire	Home Country:	England
Date of death:	07/07/1917	Cause of death:	Died of wounds
Memorial:	Marlborough College, Wiltshire		
War Cemetery:	Mendinghem Military Cemetery - Grave I. F. 12		
Next of Kin:	Marten Harcourt & Isabel Elizabeth Griffin		
Address:	Langfield, Bude, Cornwall		

Reginald was the fourth son of Marten and Isabel Griffin and was educated at Marlborough and Wye College before attending Corpus Christi College, Oxford. While at Oxford he took 1st class honours in Moderations and 2nd class in Literature and Humanities and was Captain of his college boat. In 1901 he joined the Home Civil Service and was employed in the War and Colonial Offices. In 1910 he was attached to the personal staff of the Governor General of the Union of South Africa and on his return to England became Private Secretary to the Secretary of State for the Colonies. In November 1915 Reginald was given a commission in the Royal Field Artillery and arrived in France in March 1916. Early in 1917 he was transferred to the Royal Garrison Artillery and given the command of the 21st Heavy Battery. He was wounded in action on Saturday 7 July 1917, most likely by German artillery, east of Mendinghem and succumbed to his wounds soon after.

Reginald Herbert Griffin

Left: Kenneth Mitchell Potter DSO

Right: Denham Charley Millard

SUNDAY 8 JULY 1917 - WEATHER - VERY WET

Major Kenneth Mitchell Potter DSO		*52nd Bde Royal Field Artillery*	
Service No.	N/a	Age:	35
Place of birth:	Ikley, Yorkshire	Home Country:	England
Date of death:	08/07/1917	Cause of death:	Killed in action
Memorial:	Marlborough College, Wiltshire		
War Cemetery:	Dickebusch New Military Cemetery Extension - Grave II. D. 29.		
Next of Kin:	William Furniss & Kate Potter		
Address:	Wharfemead, Bickley, Kent		

Kenneth was the third son of William Furniss & Kate Potter and was educated at Marlborough College. He was given a commission with the Royal Field Artillery in July 1901, and from then to 1912 he served in Ireland and Aldershot. In 1912 he was sent to India where he served until July 1916, he was promoted to Captain in 1914 and Major in November 1915. He returned to England following his service in India and was sent to France in November 1916, being involved in the fighting at Vimy Ridge and the Ypres Salient. In June 1917, he was awarded a Distinguished Service Order, for saving the lives of his men and horses at Dickebusch under heavy shell fire. He was killed most likely by German shell fire, near Dickebusch on Sunday 8 July 1917.

Lance Corporal Denham Charley Millard		*B Coy. 13th Bn Durham Light Infantry*	
Service No.	54241	Age:	30
Place of birth:	Westbury, Wiltshire	Home Country:	England
Date of death:	08/07/1917	Cause of death:	Killed in action
Memorial:	Westbury Leigh, Dilton Marsh, Wiltshire		
War Cemetery:	Ypres Menin Gate - Addenda Panel 57.		
Next of Kin:	Alice Elfreda Millard (wife) - Henry and Sinta Millard (parents)		
Address:	Clivey, Dilton Marsh, Wiltshire		

Denham, a wheelwright and painter, was the second son of Henry and Sinta Millard and was employed in the family's wheelwright business. On 18 October 1914 he married Alice Elfreda Noakes at Westbury. He enlisted in the army under the Derby Scheme on 11 December 1915 and was originally sent to the

Royal Field Artillery on 16 August 1916, but in November 1916 he was drafted into the Training Reserve. He arrived in France on 9 January 1917 and was initially attached to a South African Mining Company before being transferred to the 13th Battalion Durham Light Infantry. He was killed on Sunday 8 July 1917, by German shell fire, while in the British front line east of Hill 60, Belgium. Denhams wife received the following letters, the first from Pte P. Mundy states:

"No one misses him more than myself as we were always together in and out of the trenches. He was a man, every inch of him. Even in the trenches he knew no fear, and that is saying a lot. He got his promotion for knowing his duty and how to handle men in the time of need. His other sons are all sorry to hear the news."

The second was from 2nd Lt. L. F. Johnston of B Company and stated:

"I want to offer you my deepest sympathy at the sad death of your husband. It occurred on Monday night when our company were holding the front line and being heavily shelled by the enemy. It may be of some consolation for you to know that your husband suffered no pain, being killed instantaneously by a bursting shell. His body was brought down and buried in a British Cemetery near Ypres. Your husband was in my platoon and was very much respected by all the men in it. I cannot convey to you my deep sense of sympathy and sorrow, which I have with you in this irreparable loss. But I hope God will give you strength to bear the terrible blow; to look beyond the misery of the present, to the day when loved ones meet to part no more."

The last letter was from the Rev. E.G. Wells Chaplain, and stated:

"I want to offer my deepest sympathy at the sad death of your husband, Lance Corporal Millard. He was killed instantaneously by shell fire while guarding the trenches in the front line. His comrades succeeded in bringing out his body to a quiet spot behind the trenches, where we laid him to rest with three of his fellow soldiers. They were able to give him a Christian burial and his grave has been carefully marked so we hope it will be possible to identify it after the war. Let us pray to God to receive him in His mercy into that better life beyond the gate of death, and to give you faith and courage to look forward to the day when surely, we shall meet out loved ones again. And let us have patience and continue in God's service making ready for that time."

Denhams personal possessions were returned to his widow consisting of: photos, post card, pocket book, safety razor, letter case, cap badge and metal mirror. His grave was lost during subsequent fighting and he left a widow and two small children.

MONDAY 9 JULY 1917 - WEATHER - VERY HOT

Private Arthur Frank Bowron		*8th Bn Gloucestershire Regiment*	
Service No.	30003	Age:	31
Place of birth:	Croydon, Surrey	Home Country:	England
Date of death:	09/07/1917	Cause of death:	Killed in action
Memorial:	Not known		
War Cemetery:	Ypres Menin Gate - Panel 22 and 34.		
Next of Kin:	Constance Jessie Bowron (wife) – William & Mary Bowron (parents)		
Address :	28 Turner Street, Swindon, Wiltshire		

Arthur, known as Frank and a house painter, was the second son of William and Mary Bowron and at the beginning of 1912 married Constance Jessie Clark at Swindon. It is likely Frank was either conscripted into the army or enlisted under the Derby Scheme, joining the Gloucester Regiment. He was sent to France to join the 8th Service Battalion who on Monday 9 July 1917 were in the British trenches east of Oostaverne. The 8th Gloucester attacked German positions opposite, capturing 7 German prisoners and establishing a post. Frank was killed in action during the attack and Frank's wife received the following letter from 2nd Lt. R. H. Smythe:

"It is with the deepest regret that I write you with reference to the death of your husband. He was killed on the night of the 9th during an attack. His loss to the company is greatly felt, as he was an excellent soldier, and his platoon join me with expressions of the greatest sympathy in your bereavement. His body was brought back and buried, and a cross was erected over his grave. I'm not at liberty to tell you the exact spot, but you will be notified later."

Frank's grave was lost during subsequent fighting and he is today remembered on the Ypres Menin Gate.

TUESDAY 10 JULY 1917

GERMANS ATTACK NIEUPORT - BATTLE OF THE DUNES

For some days previous to Tuesday 10 July the Germans had subjected the British front line to intermittent bombardment, east of the River Yser. On the west of the river the Germans had shelled Nieuport Bains and hit or knocked out the majority of observation Posts. The trenches on the west side of the river were also shelled as were the three bridges at the mouth of the river causing some damage. There was considerable counter battery fire and the British rear areas behind the front line.

On the morning of Tuesday 10 July, the whole line and support lines were subjected to heavy German barrage's which became continuous. The three bridges were destroyed and the tunnels and covered trenches on the west side of the Yser were blown in. At around 7.50pm the German infantry began to attack, over running many of the British positions and working their way down the British trenches and support lines with flammemwerfer (flame throwers), smoke bombs and "stick handle" bombs. Dugouts were burning and British prisoners could be seen being taken away. By the early hours of 11 July the British positions on the east of the River Yser were in German hands. British casualties were estimated at between 70% and 80%. The two battalions in the front line, the 6th Battalion Kings Royal Rifle Corps and the 1st Battalion Northamptonshire Regiment, were practically annihilated. The majority of dugouts were blown in and their occupants either killed, wounded or imprisoned. Those who survived had to cross the River Yser under heavy fire.

2nd Lieutenant Arthur Clements Heberden		*6th Bn Kings Royal Rifle Corps*	
Service No.	N/a	Age:	30
Place of birth:	Stapleton, Gloucestershire	Home Country:	England
Date of death:	10/07/1917	Cause of death:	Killed in action
Memorial:	Marlborough – Marlborough College, Wiltshire		
War Cemetery:	Nieuport Memorial		
Next of Kin:	Rev Henry Buller & Mary Heberden		
Address:	The Grange, Charlton King's, Cheltenham, Gloucestershire		

Arthur was the youngest son of Rev. Henry and Mary Heberden and was educated at Rugby and Trinity College Oxford. He studied at the Royal College of Music, taking F.R.C.O. Degree, and Mus. Bac.

Left: Arthur Clements Heberden

Right: Sandford William Shippard

(Oxford). He was Director of Music at the Royal Naval College, Osborne, and Music Master and organist at Marlborough College. After a year's service with the Officer Training Corps, Arthur was given a commission with the Kings Royal Rifle Corps. He was wounded after a month's active service in January 1916. Following his recovery, he returned to France on 20 January 1917, joining the 2nd Battalion Kings Royal Rifle Corps. He was killed in action on Tuesday 10 July 1917 when Germans attacked British trenches east of the River Yser, near Nieuport. His body was not recovered and he is remembered on the Nieuport Memorial. In his will, he left Marlborough College his grand piano, all his books on music and his personal music.

Lieutenant Sandford William Shippard		*1st Bn Loyal North Lancashire Regiment*	
Service No.	N/a	Age:	21
Place of Birth:	Cape Colony	Home Country:	England
Date of Death:	10/07/1917	Cause of death:	Killed in action
Memorial:	Lacock – Lacock Church & Malthouse School Memorial		
War cemetery:	Nieuport Memorial		
Next of Kin:	Sir Sidney & Rosalind Shippard		
Address:	The Angel, Lacock, Wiltshire		

Sandford was the eldest son of Sir Sidney Shippard and his second wife Rosalind Shippard.He was educated the Old Malthouse School, Marlborough College and Sandhurst. On receiving his commission he was posted to the 1st Battalion Loyal North Lancashire Regiment arriving in France on 1 October 1915. On the morning of Tuesday 10 July 1917, four officers and 36 other ranks of the 1st Loyal North Lancashires, crossed the River Yser to the British trenches on the east bank and made their way to the left of the front line. Sandford was one of the officers and was present during the German attack. Only 2 other ranks returned. Sandford is remembered on the Nieuport Memorial and has no known grave.

Corporal Herbert Beezley Titchener		*1st Bn Northamptonshire Regiment*	
Service No.	31502	Age:	20
Place of birth:	Portsea, Hampshire	Home Country:	England
Date of death:	10/07/1917	Cause of death:	Killed in action
Memorial:	North Wilts Technical College, Swindon, Wiltshire		
War Cemetery:	Nieuport Memorial		
Next of Kin:	Ambrose Richard & Annie Titchener		

Address:	6 Euclid Street, Swindon, Wiltshire

Herbert a clerk, was the youngest son of Ambrose and Annie Titchener and was educated at Swindon Technical College. He enlisted with the Army Service Corps on 3 November 1913 at Swindon and after the outbreak of hostilities arrived in France on 6 October 1914. On 5 December 1916, he was compulsorily transferred to the 1st Battalion Northamptonshire Regiment and became an infantryman. He was killed in action on Tuesday 10 July 1917 when Germans attacked British trenches east of the River Yser, near Nieuport. His body was not recovered and he is remembered on the Nieuport Memorial.

Private Robert William Carter		*2/6th Bn Lancashire Fusiliers*	
Service No.	38981	Age:	37
Place of Birth:	Chippenham, Wiltshire	Home Country:	England
Date of Death:	10/07/1917	Cause of death:	Killed in action
Memorial:	Chippenahm – St. Andrews Church & Devizes Odd Fellows		
War cemetery:	Coxyde Military Cemetery - Grave I. E. 22		
Next of Kin:	Matilda M. Wheeler (wife) - George & Jane Carter (parents)		
Address:	Chippeham - 51 London Road, Chippenham		

Robert, a machinist, was the youngest son of George and Jane Carter and was a member of the Chippenham Odd Fellows Society. He married Matilda Wheeler in the summer of 1913 at Chippenham. It is likely he was conscripted into the army initially joining the Army Service Corps but because of a shortage of infantry recruits he was transferred to the 2/6th Battalion Lancashire Fusiliers, arriving in France in February 1917. Robert was killed, most likely by German shell fire, on Tuesday 10 July 1917 near Nieuport, on the Belgium coast. Robert left a widow and two small children.

Private Alfred Walter Goodfellow		*165th Coy Labour Corps*	
Service No.	98591	Age:	41
Place of birth:	Chilmark, Wiltshire	Home Country:	England
Date of death:	10/07/1917	Cause of death:	Killed in action
Memorial:	Chilmark, Wiltshire		
War Cemetery:	Coxyde Military Cemetery - Grave I. D. 59		
Next of Kin:	Annie Rhoda Goodfellow (wife) – George & Annie Goodfellow (parents)		
Address:	129 Old Street, Clevedon, Somerset		

Road worker Alfred was the third son of George & Annie Goodfellow and on 5 April 1915 he married Annie Rhoda Goodfellow at Chilmark. He was conscripted into the army and attested on 25 May 1916 and was placed on the Army Reserve. He was mobilised on 31 July 1916 joining the 13th Works Battalion Royal Bershire Regiment who were sent to France on 19 September 1916 to St Pol Camp near Dunkirk. On 9 May 1917, the 13th Works Battalion was incorporated into the Labour Corps and Alfred was transferred to the 165th Coy. Alfred was killed in action on Tuesday 10 July 1917 most likely by German shell fire near Nieuport, on the Belgium coast. He left a widow and a daughter.

Private William Hutchins		*165th Coy Bn Labour Corps*	
Service No.	98646	Age:	39
Place of birth:	Devizes, Wilts	Home Country:	England
Date of death:	10/07/1917	Cause of death:	Killed in action
Memorial:	Not known		
War Cemetery:	Coxyde Military Cemetery - Grave I. D. 56.		
Next of Kin:	Charles & Martha Hutchins		
Address:	3 Wharf Court, Devizes, Wiltshire		

Left: William Hutchins

Right: Philip Stanleigh Belcher

Masons labourer William was the youngest son of Charles and Martha Hutchins and prior to the Great War he was employed by the Great Western Railway Company repairing canals. It is likely he enlisted into the army under the Derby Scheme on 17 November 1915. He was mobilised on 10 August 1916 initially joining the 13th Works Battalion Royal Berkshire Regiment who were sent to France on 19 September 1916 to St Pol Camp near Dunkirk. On 9 May 1917, the 13th Works Battalion was incorporated into the Labour Corps and Alfred was transferred to the 165th Coy. Alfred was killed in action on Tuesday 10 July 1917 most likely by German shell fire near Nieuport, on the Belgium coast. He was buried in the nearby Coxyde Military Cemetery.

Sergeant Philip Stanleigh Belcher — *26th Field Company Royal Engineers*

Service No.	21026	Age:	26
Place of birth:	Trowbridge, Wiltsshire	Home Country:	England
Date of death:	10/07/1917	Cause of death:	Killed in action
Memorial:	Trowbridge, Wiltshire		
War Cemetery:	Nieuport Memorial		
Next of Kin:	George T & Mary A Belcher		
Address:	24 Gloucester Road, Trowbridge, Wiltshire		

Regular soldier Philip was the third son of George and Mary belcher and joined the Royal Engineers before the Great War, arriving in France on 17 August 1914. He was reported missing in action on Tuesday 10 July 1917, most likely from German shell fire, near Nieuport, Belgium. Philip was later assumed to have been killed on the day he was reported missing. He is remembered on the Nieuport Memorial and has no known grave.

Private Gilbert Charles Green — *2nd Bn Coldstream Guards*

Service No.	18314	Age:	18
Place of birth:	Salisbury, Wilts	Home Country:	England
Date of death:	10/07/1917	Cause of death:	Killed in action
Memorial:	Harnham, Wiltshire		
War Cemetery:	Artillery Wood Cemetery - Grave VII. E. 15.		
Next of Kin:	Jane Green (mother)		
Address:	Tower House, Coombe Road, Salisbury, Wiltshire		

Gilbert grew up with his brother in Salisbury Union Workhouse, where his mother was a laundress and on 8 July 1915 at the age of 15 he joined the Royal Navy as a boy. He firset served on H.M.S. Impregnable, before being transferred to H.M.S. Hampshire. While serving on the Hampshire he was given 60 days' imprisonment and discharged from the Navy for threatening to strike a superior officer. He left the Navy on 9 December 1915 and soon after joined the Coldstream Guards and was sent to the 2nd Battalion. He was killed on Tuesday 10 July 1917 most likely by German shell fire while in front line trenches on the canal bank at Boesinghe. It is likely that his remains were brought into the Artillery Wood Cemetery at the end of the war. Gilbert was originally buried on the west side of the canal bank, northeast of Boesinghe and in September 1919 his remains were moved to Artillery Wood Cemetery.

Private Stafford William Franklin		*9th Bn South Staffordshire Regiment*	
Service No.	14921	Age:	30
Place of birth:	Swindon, Wilts	Home Country:	England
Date of death:	10/07/1917	Cause of death:	Killed in action
Memorial:	Not known		
War Cemetery:	Dickebusch New Military Cemetery Extension - Grave II. B. 12.		
Next of Kin:	Henry & Harriett Franklin		
Address:	Trenance, Milton Avenue, Weston Super Mare, Somerset		

Stafford, a railway clerk, was the youngest son of Henry and Harriet Franklin and volunteered for service joining the 9th Battalion South Staffordshire Regimen, a pioneer battalion. He arrived in France on 24 August 1915 and served at the Somme and the Ypres Salient. On Tuesday 10 July 1917, the 9th Battalion were digging trenches near Dickebusch and constantly subjected to German bombardment by heavy calibre guns. It is likely Stafford was killed during this barrage.

Private Alfred Looker		*1st Bn Wiltshire Regiment*	
Service No.	26383	Age:	31
Place of birth:	Ramsbury, Wilts	Home Country:	England
Date of death:	10/07/1917	Cause of death:	Killed in action
Memorial:	Ramsbury, Wiltshire		
War Cemetery:	Vlamertinghe Military Cemetery - Grave I. F. 23.		
Next of Kin:	Elizabeth Jane Looker (wife) – Charles & Elizabeth Looker (parents)		
Address:	High Street, Ramsbury, Wiltshire		

Alfred, a carter on a farm, was the third son of Charles and Elizabeth Looker and in 1909 he married Elizabeth Jane Dowling. It is likely he was either conscripted into the army or enlisted under the Derby Scheme, joining the 1st Battalion Wiltshire Regiment. On Tuesday 10 July 1917, the 1st Wiltshires were called on to supply working parties in the forward area and parties for burying dead animals. The War diary states:

The casualties during this period were very largely due to a form of gas which was entirely new and was named 'Mustard Gas'. This gas destroyed the sense of smell and its presence was very difficult to detect but for its first symptom, continuous sneezing. In many cases several hours later vomiting and affectation of the eye ensued. Casualties other than those noted as "gas" were caused by hostile shelling and the casualties were as follows:-

10th killed, two other ranks wounded, Lieut and a/QM H Webber, and 3 other ranks, wounded, still at duty, 1 other rank.
11th killed, 1 other rank, wounded, 2 other ranks.
12th wounded, (gas) 20 other ranks, wounded, 2 other ranks, wounded still at duty, (gas) 4 other ranks.

13th wounded, (gas) 2 other ranks.
14th wounded, (gas) 1 other rank.

While on one of these working parties, German artillery fire killed Alfred. His wife, Elizabeth received the following letter from the chaplain who laid him to rest:

"I am writing to offer you my very deepest sympathy in the great sorrow that has come to you, and I pray God may comfort you in this great sacrifice which you have been called on to make. You may of heard by now that your husband was killed instantaneously, and I laid him to rest in a cemetery yesterday morning. A cross will be erected over his grave in the course of the next few days."

Alfred left a widow and a young family.

WEDNESDAY 11 JULY 1917

Private Albert Jesse Davis — *1st Bn Gloucestershire Regiment*

Service No.	23742	Age:	29
Place of birth:	Chelford, Gloucestershire	Home Country:	England
Date of death:	11/07/1917	Cause of death:	Killed in action
Memorial:	Not known		
War Cemetery:	Ramscapplle Road Military Cemetery - Grave VII. D. 7.		
Next of Kin:	Thomas Henry & Ellen Davis		
Address:	Level Crossing, Mintey, Wiltshire		

Albert was the eldest son of Thomas and Ellen Davis and joined the Royal Navy in July 1902 and was a stoker serving on many ships. He was discharged on 21 February 1913 after serving 42 days confinement for refusing to obey the orders of the Chief Stoker while serving on H.M.S. Impregnable. On 8 February 1915, he volunteered for service with the 2/1st Cyclist Company. He was initially promoted to Sergeant but after two offences for drunkenness was discharged as not likely to become an efficient soldier in July 1915. He volunteered for service with the Gloucestershire Regiment and arrived in France on 27 December 1915, joining the 1st Battalion. He was trained as a bomb (hand grenade) thrower and following the German attack on British positions on the east of the River Yser, at Nieuport, on 10 July, 2 Company's of the 1st Gloucesters were sent to Nieuport Bains. As the situation stabilizes one company returned to Jonia Camp leaving A Company in cellars in Nieuport Bains. A Company were given the task of repairing a tunnel and while this work was being undertaken Jesse was killed most likely by German shell fire. Albert was original buried in Nieuport Bains Military Cemetery and in March 1924 his remains were moved to Ramscapplle Road Military Cemetery.

Corporal Frank Jerman Parsons — *234th Siege Bty Royal Garrison Artillery*

Service No.	71900	Age:	33
Place of birth:	Walmer, Kent	Home Country:	England
Date of death:	11/07/1917	Cause of death:	Died of wounds
Memorial:	Morgans Vale, Wiltshire		
War Cemetery:	Etaples Military Cemetery - Grave XXII. M 13		
Next of Kin:	Eliza Amelia Parsons (wife) – Charles & Isabella Parsons		
Address:	Morgans Vale, Downton, Wiltshire		

Frank was the son of Charles & Isabella Parsons and enlisted with the Royal Marine Artillery on 2 July 1900. After completing his engagement with the marines, he married Eliza Amelia Hall at West Bromwich in 1909. prior to the Great War he was working as a plate layer for London and South Western

Railway. It is likely he was either conscripted into the army or joined under the Derby Scheme and given his previous artillery experience was sent to the 234th Siege Battery Royal Garrison Artillery. In July 1917 234th Siege Battery were on the left flank of Ypres and it is likely Frank was wounded by hostile German shell fire and evacuated to St. John's Hospital, Etaples where he succumbed to his wounds on Wednesday 11 July 1917. He left a widow and a young family.

Private Joseph Roper		*1st Bn Wiltshire Regiment*	
Service No.	33550	Age:	37
Place of birth:	Piddlehinton, Dorset	Home Country:	England
Date of death:	11/07/1917	Cause of death:	Killed in action
Memorial:	Not known		
War Cemetery:	Vlamertinghe New Military Cemetery - Grave I. F. 24		
Next of Kin:	Joseph Fowler & Sarah Mayo Roper		
Address:	Home Farm, Wilton, Wiltshire		

Joseph known as Joe was the third son of Joseph and Sarah Roper and following the death of his father managed Home Farm for the Earl of Pembroke. He was conscripted into the army being called up in January 1917 joining the Wiltshire Regiment. After completing his training, he arrived in France on 8 April 1917, being sent to the 1st Battalion. On Wednesday 11 July 1917, the 1st Wiltshires were called on to supply working parties in the forward area and parties for burying dead animals. Joe was killed by hostile shelling and the Wiltshire's Chaplain wrote to Joe's mother stating:

"I am writing to offer you my very deepest sympathy in the great sorrow that has come to you, and I pray God may comfort you in this great sacrifice which you have been called on to make. I was with your son when he was killed instantaneously. I laid him to rest in a cemetery yesterday morning and a small cross was erected over his grave."

THURSDAY 12 JULY 1917 - WEATHER - VERY HOT

Flight Sub Lieutenant Edward Hext Kendall		*Royal Naval Air Service*	
Service No.	N/a	Age:	22
Place of birth:	Chester, Cheshire	Home Country:	England
Date of death:	12/07/1917	Cause of death:	Killed in action
Memorial:	Marlborough College, Wiltshire		
War Cemetery:	Larch Wood Railway Cutting Cemetery - Grave I. B. 10		
Next of Kin:	Cptn. Edward Chambers & Nora Kendall		
Address:	Braeside, Ipplepen, Devon		

Edward was the youngest son of Edward and Nora Kendall and was educated at Marlborough College. At the outbreak of hostilities, he volunteered for service joining King Edward's Horse. He was given a commission with the Duke of Cornwall's Light Infantry and arrived in France on 6 May 1915 being sent to the 2nd Battalion. In November 1915, the 2nd Duke of Cornwall's were sent to Salonika arriving on 5 December 1915. While serving at Salonika Edward was wounded and evacuated to England and following his recovery in 1917 applied for a transfer to the Royal Naval Air Service. After completing his flying training, he was sent to No. 12 squadron RNAS on 27th June 1917 where he remained until 4th July 1917. He was then posted to No. 6 Squadron, at Frontier Aerodrome at Bray Dunes, who had just been equipped with Sopwith Camels, which Edward had not flown previously. On 11 July 1917, he was flying Sopwith Camel number N6331, and wrecked it while landing. At 10.20am Thursday 12 July 1917, the following morning he was sent on a patrol and took off from Bray Dunes, he was flying Camel N6350 and accompanied by Flight Sub Lieutennat R.R. Winter. Enemy spotter planes had been reported and the two British fighter planes were sent to intercept it.

Edward Hext Kendall

Flight Sub Lieutennat Winter reported that at 10:50 they were at 13,000 feet over Slype, (Slijpe) Belgium, Winter wrote:

"On looking around, I observed an enemy machine directly behind FSL Kendall. FSL Kendall dived, closely followed by the enemy aircraft, and I turned and dived also but was unable to fire at once as I was afraid of hitting our own machine. When I was able to I fired 200 rounds at the enemy aircraft, which left Kendall and continued to dive. I observed a trail of smoke and discovered Kendall's machine had been set on fire. The enemy was not seen again but I do not believe it was out of control."

Twenty two year old Edward was killed when his aircraft crashed in flames. He was originally buried Leffinghe German Military Cemetery and in 1925 his remains were moved to Larch Wood Railway Cutting Cemetery after the war.

Private Stephen William Emery		*8th Bn Somerset Light Infantry*	
Service No.	27839	Age:	19
Place of birth:	Malmesbury, Wiltshire	Home Country:	England
Date of death:	12/07/1917	Cause of death:	Killed in action
Memorial:	Malmesbury, Wiltshire		
War Cemetery:	Messines Ridge British Cemetery - Grave II. C. 12.		
Next of Kin:	Stephen Richard & Ellen Emery		
Address:	10 Gastons Road, Malmesbury, Wiltshire		

Stephen, known as William, was the second son of Stephen and Ellen Emery and originally enlisted with the Wiltshire Regiment in 1916. He was later transferred to the 8th Battalion Somerset Light Infantry arriving in January 1917. William was killed on Thursday 12 July 1917, most likely by German Shell fire when the 8th Somersets were in the British support line between Wytschaete and Messines near Limm Farm. In March 1918, a court case took place concerning William's will. His pocket book had been found on the battlefield and was sent to William's sweetheart Edith Reynolds as it contained her address. William had written a will while in the trenches stating he wished to leave his sweetheart a cow. The court decided that his sweetheart had no claim and the case was quashed. In July 1918 Williams' parents inserted the following memoriam in a local paper:

God called him home, it was his will,
But in our hearts he dwelteth still:
His memory is as dear today
As in the hour he passed away.

William was originally buried south Wambeke and in January 1920 his remains were moved to Messines Ridge British Cemetery.

FRIDAY 13 JULY 1917 - WEATHER - FINE COOL BREEZE

Acting Bombardier Edward Willett — *91st Bde Bn Royal Field Artillery*

Service No.	130096	Age:	31
Place of birth:	Banwell, Somerset	Home Country:	England
Date of death:	13/07/1917	Cause of death:	Killed in action
Memorial:	Not known		
War Cemetery:	Bard Cottage Cemetery - Grave III. A. 15.		
Next of Kin:	James & Helen Willett		
Address:	Towerhill Parcmain Street, Carmarthen, Carmarthenshire		

Edward was the second son of John and Helen Willett, he worked as a shop assistant in a fruiterer's in Chippenham prior to the declaration of war. It is likely he was conscripted into the army joining the Royal Field Artillery. He was sent to France joining the 91st Brigade and was killed in action north east of Vlamertinge, Belgium on Friday 13 July 1917, most likely by German artillery, when the 91st Brigade were moving into new positions to support the assault on Pilckem Ridge.

Sergeant Stanley William Price — *86th Coy Bn Machine Gun Corps*

Service No.	20941	Age:	29
Place of birth:	Easterton, Wiltshire	Home Country:	England
Date of death:	13/07/1917	Cause of death:	Died of wounds
Memorial:	Easterton, Wiltshire		
War Cemetery:	Lijssenthoek Military Cemetery - Grave XVI. B. 7A.		
Next of Kin:	William & Mary Jane Price		
Address:	Eastcott, Wiltshire		

William was the fourth son of William and Mary Price and volunteered for service. It is likely he intended to join the Wiltshire Regiment but they were over subscribed and over 1000 Wiltshire men were transferred to Irish Regiments who were suffering from a lack of recruits. He joined the 1st Battalion Royal Munster Fusiliers arriving in Gallipoli on 25 April 1915, it is likely he was either wounded or suffering from illness or disease and evacuated to England. Following his recovery, he transferred to the Machine Gun Corps and was sent to the 86th Company. He was wounded on 12 July 1917, when German artillery shelled Dragon Camp north east of Elverdinge. He was suffering from gun shot wounds to the lumbar region and evacuated to No. 3 Canadian Casualty Clearing Station at Lijssenthoek, Belgium where he succumbed to his wounds on Friday 13 July 1917.

Lance Corporal William Stanley Hobbs — *1st Bn Dorsetshire Regiment*

Service No.	18735	Age:	25
Place of birth:	Devizes, Wiltshire	Home Country:	England
Date of death:	13/07/1917	Cause of death:	Killed in action
Memorial:	Devizes, Wiltshire		

War Cemetery: Coxyde Military Cemetery - Grave I. H. 15.
Next of Kin: Sidney and Ellen Hobbs
Address: 8 Wharf Street, Devizes, Wiltshire

Baker William was the eldest son of Sidney and Ellen Hobbs. It is likely he was conscripted into the army and after completing his training he was sent to France joining the 1st Battalion Dorsetshire Regiment. William was killed in action on Friday 13 July 1917 when the Germans artillery attacked the British front line, with a heavy gas shell bombardment at Nieuport north of Ypres, Belgium. He was one of 25 men to be killed from the effects of the gas.

Gunner Enoch George Reeves *72nd Bde Royal Field Artillery*

Service No.	199145	Age:	30
Place of birth:	Corsham, Wiltshire	Home Country:	England
Date of death:	13/07/1917	Cause of death:	Killed in action
Memorial:	Corsham, Wiltshire		
War Cemetery:	Ramscapplle Road Military Cemetery - Grave II. A. 16.		
Next of Kin:	George & Sarah Reeves		
Address:	Green Lane, Neston, Wiltshire		

Enoch was the eldest son of George and Sarah Reeves and in the spring of 1915 he married Lucy Fido. Unfortunatley Lucy was to die in late 1916 and left Enoch a widower. It is likely he was conscripted into army in 1917 joining the Royal Field Artillery and was sent to France being sent to the 72nd Brigade. Enoch was killed by German atillery on Friday 13 July 1917 near Nieuport, on the Belgium coast. His parents received the following letter from his Captain:

"Three of his comrades had been badly wounded, and Private Reeves very gallantly helped to bandage them and to find splints for another man with a broken leg. The shelling became very heavy, and the men were ordered to get to a flank. Unfortunately, Private Reeves had forgotten his smoke helmet and rushed back to a trench for it, when a heavy shell fell close to him killing him instantly. I had the honour of reading the prayers over the body of a very gallant soldier."

Enoch was originally buried just south of Nieuport and in June 1919 his remains were moved to Ramscapplle Road Military Cemetery.

Enoch George Reeves

SATURDAY 14 JULY 1917 - WEATHER - VERY HOT

Private William Percy Fry		*1st Bn Wiltshire Regiment*	
Service No.	8419	Age:	32
Place of birth:	Westbury, Wiltshire	Home Country:	England
Date of death:	14/07/1917	Cause of death:	Killed in action
Memorial:	Not known		
War Cemetery:	Menin Road South Military Cemetery - Grave I. T. 21.		
Next of Kin:	Charles & Mary Fry		
Address:	Edward Street, Westbury, Wiltshire		

Regular soldier William known Percy was the third son of Charles and Mary Fry and had served 8 years with the Westbury Company of the Volunteers. He joined the Wiltshire Regiment and was serving with the 2nd Battalion at Gibraltar at the outbreak of hostilities and landed at Zeebrugge on 7 October 1914. Percy was wounded in both legs at Ypres and suffered from frost bite and rheumatism. He was evacuated to England and following his recovery he returned to France in December 1916 and was transferred to the 1st Battalion Wiltshire Regiment. On Wednesday 11 July 1917, the 1st Wiltshires were called on to supply working parties in the forward area and parties for burying dead animals. He was gassed on Saturday 14 July 1917 when the Wiltshires were exposed to mustard gas, the war diary states:

The casualties during this period were very largely due to a form of gas which was entirely new and was named ' Mustard Gas'. This gas destroyed the sense of smell and its presence was very difficult to detect but for its first symptom, continuous sneezing. In many cases, several hours later vomiting and affectation of the eye ensued. Casualties other than those noted as "gas" were caused by hostile shelling and the casualties were as follows:-

13th Wounded, (gas) 2 other ranks.
14th Wounded, (gas) 1 other rank.

Percy died on the way to a dressing station and was buried in Menin Road South Military Cemetery.

Lance Corporal Percy Walter Rowe		*1st Bn Wiltshire Regiment*	
Service No.	8860	Age:	23
Place of birth:	East Harnham, Wiltshire	Home Country:	England
Date of death:	14/07/1917	Cause of death:	Killed in action
Memorial:	Not known		
War Cemetery:	Ypres Menin Gate - Grave Panel 53.		
Next of Kin:	John & Eliza Rowe		
Address:	The Dell, Porchester Road, Fareham, Hampshire		

Reservist Percy was the second son of John and Eliza Rowe and was called up at the outbreak of hostilities and arrived in France on 20 October 1914 joining the 2nd Battalion Wiltshire Regiment. It is likely he was wounded and evacuated to England and following his recovery he returned to France, being transferred to the 1st Battalion Wiltshire Regiment. On Wednesday 11 July 1917, the 1st Wiltshires were called on to supply working parties in the forward area and parties for burying dead animals. Percy was gassed on Saturday 14 July 1917 when the Wiltshires were exposed to Mustard gas, and died soon after. He is today remembered on the Ypres Menin Gate and has no known grave.

William Percy Fry

Private Archibald Frank Pearce		*1st Bn Wiltshire Regiment*	
Service No.	10303	Age:	21
Place of birth:	Stanton St Bernard, Wilts	Home Country:	England
Date of death:	14/07/1917	Cause of death:	Killed in action
Memorial:	Stanton St Bernard, Wiltshire		
War Cemetery:	Ypres Menin Gate - Panel 53.		
Next of Kin:	David & Sarah Pearce		
Address:	Stanton St Bernard, Wiltshire		

Farm labourer Archibald was the fourth son of David and Sarah Pearce and volunteered soon after the outbreak of hostilities he joined the Wiltshire Regiment and was only 18 years old when he arrived in France on 26 January 1915, being sent to the 1st Battalion. He spent his 19th 20th and 21st Birthdays in France and was wounded three times. He was twice home on short leave, the last in June 1917. He wrote his last letter to his friends stating:

"Don't worry if you don't here from me for a short time."

On Wednesday 11 July 1917, the 1st Wiltshires were called on to supply working parties in the forward area and parties for burying dead animals. Archibald was gassed on Saturday 14 July 1917 when the Wiltshires were exposed to mustard gas, and died soon after. He is today remembered on the Ypres Menin Gate and has no known grave.

L/Cpl Reginald Herbert Percy Sheppard		*1st Bn Wiltshire Regiment*	
Service No.	8678	Age:	22
Place of birth:	Aldbourne, Wiltshire	Home Country:	England
Date of death:	14/07/1917	Cause of death:	Killed in action
Memorial:	Not known		
War Cemetery:	Ypres Menin Gate - Panel 53		
Next of Kin:	Ambrose & Lydia Sheppard		
Address:	Aldbourne, Wiltshire		

Regular soldier Reginald was the second son of Ambrose & Lydia Sheppard and joined the Wiltshire Regiment before the Great War. At the out break of hostilities, he was serving in Gibraltar with the 2nd Battalion and arrived at Zeebrugge, Belgium on 7 October 1914. It is likely he was wounded while serving with the 2nd Battalion and evacuated to England. Following his recovery, he was transferred to the 1st Battalion and returned to the front. On Wednesday 11 July 1917, the 1st Wiltshires were called on to supply working parties in the forward area and parties for burying dead animals. Reginald was gassed on Saturday 14 July 1917 when the Wiltshires were exposed to mustard gas and died soon after. He is today remembered on the Ypres Menin Gate and has no known grave.

Lance Corporal Frank Cecil Prosser		*8th Bn Somerset Light Infantry*	
Service No.	27798	Age:	20
Place of birth:	Melksham, Wiltshire	Home Country:	England
Date of death:	14/07/1917	Cause of death:	Killed in action
Memorial:	Melksham, Wiltshire		
War Cemetery:	Ypres Menin Gate - Panel 21.		
Next of Kin:	John & Fanny Prosser		
Address:	Redstocks, Melksham, Wiltshire		

Frank was the fourth son of John and Fanny Prosser and it is likely he was either conscripted into the army or enlisted unter the Derby Scheme initially joining the Wiltshire Regiment. He was transferred to the 8th Battalion Somerset Light Infantry and was killed on Saturday 14 July 1917, most likely by German shell fire when the 8th Somersets were in the British support line between Wytschaete and Messines near Limm Farm. He is remembered on the Ypres Menin Gate and has no known grave.

Gunner Walter Mumford		*199th Siege Bty Bn Royal Garrison Artillery*	
Service No.	91096	Age:	36
Place of birth:	Limpley Stoke, Wiltshire	Home Country:	England
Date of death:	14/07/1917	Cause of death:	Died of wounds
Memorial:	Westwood, Wiltshire		
War Cemetery:	Mendinghem Military Cemetery - Grave I. F. 28.		
Next of Kin:	Sarah Jane Mumford (wife) – Edward & Sarah Mumford (parents)		
Address:	Upper Westwood, Wiltshire		

Walter was the youngest son of Edward and Sarah Mumford and on 9 May 1907, he married Sarah Jane Poulson at Lower Westwood. He enlisted under the Derby Scheme on 9 December 1915 and was called up on 1 June 1916 and sent to the Royal Garrison Artillery. After completing his training he was sent to France on 27 November 1916 joining the 199th Siege Battery. He was wounded, with multiple gunshot wounds north west of Ypres on 27 June 1917 and was evacuated to No. 12 Casualty Clearing Station at Mendinghem. He succumbed to his wounds on Saturday 14 July 1917. He left a widow and two young children.

Private Francis William Hornblow		*6th Bn Wiltshire Regiment*	
Service No.	14288	Age:	24
Place of birth:	Calstone, Wiltshire	Home Country:	England
Date of death:	14/07/1917	Cause of death:	Killed in action
Memorial:	Seend, Wiltshire		
War Cemetery:	Oosttaverne Wood Cemetery - Grave III. A. 13.		
Next of Kin:	Samuel & Emily Hornblow		
Address:	12, Calstone, Wiltshire		

Francis, a farm labourer and carter, was the third son of Samuel and Emily Hornblow and volunteered for service in December 1914 with the 5th Service Battalion Wiltshire Regiment. He was sent to Gallipoli and arrived on 12 July 1915 and was invalided back to England after either being wounded or suffering from illness or disease. Following his recovery, he was transferred to the 6th Battalion Wiltshire Regiment and sent to France in September 1916. Francis was one of two men killed, most likely by German shell fire, on Saturday 14 July 1917, when the 6th Wiltshires were in trenches at Denys Wood, north of Oostaverne, Belgium. He was originally buried in Oosttaverne Wood No. 2 Cemetery and in August 1920 his remains were moved to Oosttaverne Wood Cemetery.

2nd Lieutenant Nelson Stuart Hibbard		*1st Bn Loyal North Lancashire Regiment*	
Service No.	N/a	Age:	32
Place of birth:	Bradford on Avon, Wilts	Home Country:	England
Date of death:	14/07/1917	Cause of death:	Killed in action
Memorial:	Bradford on Avon, Wesleyan		
War Cemetery:	Ramscapplle Road Military Cemetery - Grave II. D. 6.		
Next of Kin:	Lydia Hibbard (wife) - Albert & Ellen Hibbard (parents)		
Address:	Portsmouth, Hampshire – 118 Trowbridge Road, Bradford on Avon		

Nelson was the fourth son of Albert & Ellen Hibbard but lived with his uncle and aunt, Harry and Rose Edmunds, in Portsmouth. Prior to the war, he served 7 years with the 7th Hussars followed by 7 years on reserve. After leaving the army he spent some time working for Spencer – Mouloton & Co and was a mainstay of Bradford Football Club. Later, he moved to Portsmouth where he assisted the Football and Cricket Clubs. At the outbreak of hostilities, he was called up to his regiment and arrived in France on 15 August 1918. He took part in the early engagements of the war including the retreat from Mons, became detached from his squadron and was posted as missing for three months and eventually it was found he had become attached to the Lancers. On 30 January 1916 Nelson was given a commission and transferred to the Loyal North Lancashire Regiment and spent some time training new recruits. During this time, he married Lydia Bartlett of Glastonbury at Portsmouth and was given a silver sword and silver teapot by Portsmouth Football Club. He returned to the front in March 1917 and was sent to the 1st Battalion Loyal North Lancashire Regiment. He was looking forward to another period of leave when he was killed by German artillery fire on Saturday 14 July 1917. He was commanding a working party near Neiuport Bains repairing the damage that had been done during the German attack. The war diary of the 1st Battalion Loyal North Lancashires states:

Quiet day. 2nd Lieutenant Hibbard and 6 other ranks were killed - 8 other ranks wounded on working party during the night.

Left: Francis William Hornblow

Right: Nelson Stuart Hibbard

Nelson was originally buried in Nieuport Bains Military Cemetery and in March 1924 his remains were moved to Ramscapplle Road Military Cemetery.

SUNDAY 15 JULY 1917

Herbert Leslie Ridley — *1st Bn Royal Dublin Fusiliers*

Service No.	N/a	Age:	22
Place of birth:	Chelmsford, Essex	Home Country:	England
Date of death:	15/07/1917	Cause of death:	Killed in action
Memorial:	Chelmsford All Saints, Essex - Marlborough College, Wiltshire		
War Cemetery:	Canada Farm Cemetery - Grave I. D. 17		
Next of Kin:	Walter & Louise C. Ridley		
Address:	Springfield, Chelmsford, Essex		

Herbert was the fourth and youngest son of Walter and Louise Ridley and the grandson of the founder of the brewers and millers T. D. Ridley and sons. He was educated at Marlborough College and Trinity College, Cambridge. At the outbreak hostilities, he volunteered for service attending Sandhurst, and passed out in November 1914. He was given a commission with the 2nd Battalion Royal Dublin Fusiliers arriving in France on 18 January 1915. He was wounded in April 1915, at St. Julian, Belgium, and following his recovery he was sent to Gallipoli. Following the evacuation of the peninsular he was sent to Egypt before returning to France in March 1916, transferring to the 1st Battalion Royal Dublin Fusiliers. He was awarded the Military Cross in 1916 for general good service in the field. On Sunday 15 July 1917, the 1st Royal Dublin Fusiliers were in trenches on the canal bank near Boesinghe, Belgium. The British heavy artillery were bombarding German positions on the east side of the Yser Canal. Some of the shells fell short on the British positions and Herbert was killed during the evening by the blast of a British six inch shell falling short.

Private Job Holloway — *1st Bn Wiltshire Regiment*

Service No.	3/561	Age:	39
Place of birth:	Southwick, Wiltshire	Home Country:	England
Date of death:	15/07/1917	Cause of death:	Killed in action
Memorial:	Trowbridge, Wiltshire		
War Cemetery:	Menin Road South Military Cemetery - Grave I. T. 17.		

Next of Kin: John & Anne Holloway
Address: 22 Timbrell Street, Trowbridge, Wiltshire

Job was the sixth son of John and Annie Holloway and joined the army in 1898, spending 10 years in India. He received his discharge after 12 years service and at the outbreak of hostilities he rejoined the Wiltshires arriving in France on 23 October 1914. In July 1917 the Wiltshires were at Bellewarde to the east of Ypres, Belgium and while they were in the line they were subjected to considerable amount of German shell fire of both high explosives and gas. Job was one of two soldiers killed in action on Sunday 15 July 1917. In July 1918 his family inserted the following memoriam in a local paper:

"No one stood beside him to bid him a last farewell
Although his grave is far away he did his duty well
He is gone but not forgotten often his name we recall
But there is nothing left to answer but his photo on the wall

Private Jack Smith		*8th Bn Somerset Light Infantry*	
Service No.	27810	Age:	19
Place of birth:	Collingbourne Kingston	Home Country:	England
Date of death:	15/07/1917	Cause of death:	Killed in action
Memorial:	Not known		
War Cemetery:	Ypres Menin Gate - Grave Panel 21.		
Next of Kin:	Henry & Bessie Smith		
Address:	85 Sunton, Collingbourne Ducis, Wiltshire		

Jack was the fifth son of Henry & Bessie Smith and it is likely he was either conscripted into the army or enlisted under the Derby Scheme initially joining the Wiltshire Regiment. He was transferred to the 8th Battalion Somerset Light Infantry and was killed on Sunday 15 July 1917, most likely by German shell fire when the 8th Somersets were in the British support line between Wytschaete and Messines near Limm Farm. He is remembered on the Ypres Menin Gate and has no known grave.

MONDAY 16 JULY 1917

Private Charles Jones		*2nd Bn Wiltshire Regiment*	
Service No.	3/352	Age:	44
Place of birth:	Bradford on Avon, Wilts	Home Country:	England
Date of death:	16/07/1917	Cause of death:	Died of wounds
Memorial:	Bradford on Avon, Wiltshire		
War Cemetery:	Etaples Military Cemetery - Grave XXV. K. 10.		
Next of Kin:	Ellen Jones (wife) – Alfred & Fanny Jones		
Address:	21c Frome Road, Bradford on Avon, Wiltshire		

Charles was the eldest son of Alfred and Fanny Jones and in 1892 he married Ellen Hillier at Bradford on Avon. He had served with the Wiltshire Volunteers which became the Special Reserve and had volunteered for overseas serice soon after the outbreak of hostilities, arriving in France on 3 November 1914, being attached to the 2nd Battalion Wiltshire Regiment. On 24 June 1916, he was serving with the transport section taking rations to the men serving in the front line when he received severe wounds to the left leg, after coming under heavy German shell fire near Zillebeke, Belgium. He was evacuated to a Military hospital at Etaples, France. On 14 July 1917, Charles wrote home stating he was *"going on well,"* but his condition worsened and he succumbed to his wounds on Monday 16 July 1917. He left a widow and four children, his eldest son had been serving in the artillery in France since the start of the war and his son in law was also serving. In July 1919 Charles's widow inserted the following memoriam in a local paper:

This day brings back to our memory
Our dear one gone to rest
And we who think of him today
Are the ones who loved him best

Time may heal our broken hearts
And make the wound less sore
But it cannot stop us longing
For our loved one gone before

TUESDAY 17 JULY 1917 - WEATHER - VERY HOT

Gunner Francis Harold Hicks		*256th Bde Bn Royal Field Artillery*	
Service No.	636355	Age:	22
Place of birth:	Wanborough, Wiltshire	Home Country:	England
Date of death:	17/07/1917	Cause of death:	Killed in action
Memorial:	Swindon Christ Church, Wiltshire		
War Cemetery:	Poperinge New Military Cemetery - Grave II. D. 30.		
Next of Kin:	Thomas & Ellen Hicks		
Address:	5 Union Street, Swindon, Wiltshire		

Francis, a tin smith, was the eldest son of Thomas and Ellen Hicks and was educated at Lethbridge Road and National Schools. After completing his education, he served an apprenticeship with A.S. Payne in Victoria Road, Swindon and just before the outbreak of hostilities he was working near London. He initially joined the Wessex Brigade, Royal Field Artillery and attained the rank of Sergeant. When the Wessex Brigade left for India he was transferred to the Highland Division and sent to France. Francis was killed on Tuesday 17 July 1917 near Poperinge, Belgium. Gunner G. Ballantyne wrote the following to a close friend of Francis explaining how he met his death:

"It is with profound regret that I forward this note, enclosing a photograph which I found after a terrible explosion due to a German shell having struck one of our ammunition dumps. Evidently the ill fated sergeant, with two officers and a number of men, were sleeping in the vicinity of the disaster. I tried to identify him by the photograph, but it was well nigh impossible. No doubt you will be relieved to know he could have suffered no pain, death being instantaneous. The bodies were removed the same day and laid to rest in a small cemetery within sound of guns. My sympathy goes out to his people and friends in their sad bereavement. Should you care to write me I shall be pleased to forward any further particulars you may like to know."

Francis's father had been serving for two years with the Vetenary Corps. In 1918 his family inserted the following memoriam in a local paper:

Oh, look for those dear bright eyes,
And hear that voice that is still;
And, oh, the clasp of that vanished hand,
Yet must bend to God's holy will.

Private Thomas Foyle		*8th Bn Somerset Light Infantry*	
Service No.	16609	Age:	32
Place of birth:	Heytesbury, Wilts	Home Country:	England
Date of death:	17/07/1917	Cause of death:	Killed in action
Memorial:	Not known		
War Cemetery:	Cabin Hill Cemetery - Grave A. 5.		
Next of Kin:	Ethel Mary Foyle (wife) - John & Martha Foyle (parents)		
Address:	Compton Pauncefoot, Somerset		

Thomas, known as Tom and a shepherd, was the youngest son of John and Martha Folye and married Ethel Mary in 1910. He volunteered for service joining the Somerset Light Infantry and was initially sent to the 1st Battalion arriving in France on 29 June 1916. It is likely he was either wounded or suffered illness or disease and evacuated to England. Following his recovery, he was returned to the front and transferred to the 8th Battalion Somerset Light Infantry. He was killed, most likely by German artillery, on Tuesday 17 July 1917 while in British front line trenches northeast of Messines. He left a widow and a young son.

Lieutenant Roger Bolton Hay MC		*48th Sqdn Royal Flying Corps*	
Service No.	N/a	Age:	22
Place of birth:	Garsdon, Wilts	Home Country:	England
Date of death:	17/07/1917	Cause of death:	Died of wounds
Memorial:	Not known		
War Cemetery:	Oostende Communal Cemetery Extension - Grave A. 21.		
Next of Kin:	Reynell Wreford & Margaret Alice Hay		
Address:	Garsdon, Wiltshire		

Roger was the youngest son of Reynell and Margaret Hay and was educated at Dean Close School, Cheltenham and Blundell's, Tiverton, where he was head of his house and represented his school in the Public Schools Gym Competition at Aldershot in 1913. At the outbreak of hostilities he had planned to go to Oxford, but volunteered with his two brothers, joining the 16th Battalion Middlesex Regiment, the Public Schools Battalion. All three were given commissions in the Special Reserve in January 1915. Roger was sent to the 3rd Battalion West Yorkshire Regiment and arrived in France in February 1916. He returned to England in August 1916 and transferred to the Royal Flying Corps. After completing his training and gaining his pilots certificate he was sent to France and posted to 48th Squadron. In June 1917, he was awarded the Military Cross and the citation states:

For conspicuous gallantry and devotion to duty. On several occasions, he has shown the utmost courage and dash in attacking and dispersing hostile aircraft in superior numbers. His willingness to undertake the most hazardous duties has at all times set a fine example to other pilots and observers of his squadron.

Roger scored five victories between 23 April 1917 and 12 July 1917 but was reported missing in action on Tuesday 17 July while on patrol over the Belgium coast; his parents hoped he was safe and a prisoner of war. In early September 1917 news was received stating Roger had died of wounds while a prisoner of war. His commanding officer wrote the following letter to his parents:

"He was a top-hole pilot, a thorough sportsman, a brave and plucky fighter who downed more than one hostile machine. He was probably one of the best liked and most poplar officers in my squadron."

His observer on the day of 18 July 2017 wrote:

"We were attacked by six enemy scout aeroplanes. To start with, my gun jammed, and we were pretty

Left: Roger Bolton Hay MC

Right: Richard John Deane

well helpless, and it was impossible to remedy it. We were a good many miles over the line, and my pilot made a really wonderful flight from 14,000 feet down to the ground; he looped, he spun, and did everything he could to shake the enemy off. He was badly hit in the body before the end and had to land on the beach. We got out, and I helped him along, when I was shot in the leg as I was doing so. It was awful bad luck, for we were only three to four hundred yards from our line. I am sorry to say he died yesterday from his wound."

Roger was originally buried in Oostende German Cemetery and in October 1924 his remains were moved to Oostende Communal Cemetery Extension.

WEDNESDAY 18 JULY 1917

2nd Lieutenant Richard John Deane		*26th Bde Bn Royal Field Artillery*	
Service No.	N/a	Age:	19
Place of birth:	Fleetwood, Lancashire	Home Country:	England
Date of death:	18/07/1917	Cause of death:	Accident
Memorial:	Marlborough College, Wiltshire - Chailey, Sussex		
War Cemetery:	Dickebusch New Military Cemetery Extension - Grave II. D. 12		
Next of Kin:	Col Richard Woodforde & Harriet Deane		
Address:	Oldland, Hassocks, Sussex		

Richard was the youngest son of Richard and Harriet Deane and was educated at Marlborough College. After completing his education, he was placed on the Army Reserve and on 1 July 1916 he was passed as unfit by an Army Medical Board, noting that his chest was under-developed and that he had a scar from a tubercular glands' operation on the left side of his neck. On 7 July 1916 Richard's father sent him four guineas and directed him to attend a further board and on 18 July 1916 he was passed fit for service. On 5 November 1916, Richard Deane applied for a temporary commission with the army, the acting headmaster at Marlborough College, Mr J R Taylor, stated that he had known Richard for the last three years and Lt. Colonel Hall, commanding Marlborough College Officer Training Corps noted that he was a suitable candidate for a commission, stating he had been captain of his House and should make a good officer. On 28 December 1916, Richard was mobilised and sent to No 1 Royal Artillery Cadet School and on 5 May 1917, he was given a commission with the Royal Field Artillery. He was sent to France in July 1917, joining 117th Battery of the 26th Brigade, Royal Field Artillery on 9 July. On 18 July1917, Richard was discovered in his dug-out by Captain A E Rusher with a single bullet wound to his head. A court of enquiry was held and concluded the same day. Captain A E Rusher stated:

"Up to the time he went to bed last night 17 July, was quite normal and rational and seemed quite happy. The deceased officer appeared to have nothing on his mind either associated with his profession or personal affairs. He states further that at 8.50am this morning 18th July, he heard a shot fired. He himself was at the time in his own dug-out and as there is a good deal of rifle fire at aeroplanes in the vicinity he attached no significance to the report. Wondering why the deceased Officer had not appeared, he went to the deceased Officer's dug-out. He found 2/Lieut Deane lying in bed, with a revolver in his hand and bleeding from the nose. The pistol of the deceased Officer was used to shoot the wounded horse of an Australian driver about 2.30pm on the 15 July."

The enquiry found the deceased officer was handling his revolver in bed and accidentally shot himself. On 23 July 1917 Richard's father received an official War Office telegram which simply stated that his son had been killed in an accident. Shortly afterwards a few personal items were sent to his family consisting of a wrist watch, strap and guard, a fountain pen and an identity disc and chain.

However, on 29 July 1917, Surgeon General R Porter, Director of Medical Services for the Second Army, wrote that he was not convinced by the Court of Enquiry's findings into the officer's death, stating:

"I am of the opinion that 2/Lieut R J DEANE died from a Self-Inflicted Wound. The Medical evidence is not complete; the positions of the wounds of entrance and exit need to be stated, and whether there was any burning or discolouration of the skin; this might help to elucidate the fact as to whether the wound was accidental or not."

The Military however, took the official view that as there was nothing to show whether Richard's death was a case of suicide or accidental death it would give the benefit of the doubt. His death was recorded as accidental.

Gunner Percy Harold Leonard		*173rd Bde Royal Field Artillery*	
Service No.	183872	Age:	19
Place of birth:	Swindon, Wiltshire	Home Country:	England
Date of death:	18/07/1917	Cause of death:	Killed in action
Memorial:	Not known		
War Cemetery:	Vlamertinghe Military Cemetery - Grave I. G. 18.		
Next of Kin:	George & Elizabeth Louisa Leonard		
Address:	7 Warwick Road, Swindon, Wiltshire		

Nineteen year old Percy was the second son of George and Elizabeth Leonard and was employed as a boiler maker's labourer at the Great Western Railway Works at Swindon. He was conscripted into the Army in October 1916, being sent to the Royal Field Artillery. After completing his training in February 1917, he was sent to France joining the 173rd Brigade. He was killed on Tuesday 18 July 1917, east of Vlamertinghe, Belgium. Second Lieutenant McComb wrote the folling to Percy's parents:

"It is my sorrowing duty to inform you that your son, Gunner Leonard was killed in action on the morning of the 18 July. We were engaging the enemy at the time and your brave son was serving the gun. A shell burst in front of the gun-pit, and hit your son and another. Mr Mcorkindale, his section officer, with most gallent bravery rushed in under heavy fire and brought him out. Poor boy! He had

passed away even as he was brought out. Mr Mcorkindale, himself was hit. He suffered no pain and passes away quietly. I cannot express in words how sorrowful we all feel. He was a lovely boy, and every man in the battery liked him well. My Major has bidden me to write you and give you on behalf of the whole battery our heartfelt sympathy in your loss. Even as I write word comes that another of our number has been taken from us. Such is war, and such must we bear. I leave your consolation in higher and better hands than ours. Your boy has been buried in a military cemetery and lies peacefully with many other brave and heroic soldiers. He has done his duty and his reward will be given to him."

THURSDAY 19 JULY 1917 - WEATHER - VERY HOT

Sergeant Albert Victor Herrington		*16th Bn Middlesex Regiment*	
Service No.	PS/2026	Age:	31
Place of birth:	Stourton, Wiltshire	Home Country:	England
Date of death:	19/07/1917	Cause of death:	Killed in action
Memorial:	Mere, Wiltshire		
War Cemetery:	Ypres Menin Gate - Grave 49 and 51.		
Next of Kin:	Alfred & Hester Herrington		
Address:	Church Street, Mere, Wiltshire		

Albert, a shop assistant, was the third son of Alfred and Hester Herrington and volunteered for service with the 16th Battalion Middlesex Regiment, (the Public Schools Battalion), arriving in France on 17 November 1915. He took part in the battle of the Somme, France and on Thursday 19 July 1917 was near Yorkshire Trench east of Boesinghe, Belgium. He was killed, most likely by German artillery while in the British front line. Albert is remembered on the Ypres Menin Gate and has no known grave.

Private Sidney Harold Naile		*2nd Bn Coldstream Guards*	
Service No.	5574	Age:	31
Place of birth:	Bath, Somerset	Home Country:	England
Date of death:	19/07/1917	Cause of death:	Died of wounds
Memorial:	Warminster, Wiltshire		
War Cemetery:	Dozinghem Military Cemetery - Grave I. J. 4.		
Next of Kin:	Lucy Maud Naile (wife) – Robert & Mary Naile (parents)		
Address:	2 Vicarage Street, Warminster, Wiltshire		

Reservist Sidney was the fifth son of Robert and Mary Naile and was working as a mail cart driver, between Warminster and Bath, when he married Lucy Maud Burgess at Warminster on 1 June 1911. At the outbreak of hostilities, he was recalled to the colours rejoining the 2nd Battalion Coldstream Guards. He arrived in France on 12 August 1914 and was wounded during the retreat from Mons. While serving in Belgium in July 1917 he was attached to the Assistant Military Provost and was severely wounded in the abdomen, most likely by German artillery, east of Dozinghem, Belgium. He was evacuated to No. 4 Casualty Clearing Station where he succumbed to his wounds on Thursday 19 July 1917. He was buried the following day with full military honours, leaving a widow and two young daughters. When Warminster War Memorial was dedicated in 1921, a wreath was laid, with the following inscription:

In ever loving memory of our dear daddy Pte S H Naile, from Sylvia and Joan.

Above: Memorial at Hilmarton Church to the memory of Frederick Doble Smale

Right: Sidney Harold Naile

FRIDAY 20 JULY 1917

Private Frederick Doble Smale		*253rd Siege Bde Royal Army Service Corps*	
Service No.	M/304534	Age:	23
Place of birth:	Kentisbeare, Devon	Home Country:	England
Date of death:	20/07/1917	Cause of death:	Killed in action
Memorial:	Hilmarton, Wiltshire		
War Cemetery:	Lijssenthoek Military Cemetery - Grave XVI. C. 2.		
Next of Kin:	Frederick & Mary A Smale		
Address:	Cowage, Hilmarton, Wiltshire		

In July 1916 Frederick, known as Fred, was passed fit for General Service. He was his parents only son and his father appealed to the local Tribunal for the exemption of his son from Military Service. His father stated that twenty two year old Fred was a shepherd and stockman at the farm at Cowage with 500 sheep and 145 grazing young cattle. All the staff consisted of two men in their 50's, another man medically unfit and Fred. He found it impossible to get a shepherd to take his son's place, and three of his men had joined the Colours. Fred's father was given until 1 October 1916 to find an ineligible man to replace his son. At the end of September 1916 Frederick's father made a further appeal to the County Tribunal for the exemption of his son, he stated;

"I will have to dispose of his flock if my son goes, he is my only son, and I bought the farm two years ago with the sole object of leaving it to my son."

Lord Bath chair of the County Tribunal stated;

"We will give further exemption till 14th November 1916 on the condition that there is no further appeal."

Fred was conscripted into the army joining the Royal Army Service Corps. After completing his training, he was sent to the front and attached to 253rd Siege Battery Royal Field Artillery. On the morning of Friday 20 July 1917, he was killed by a German Artillery shell while serving near Poperinge, West of Ypres Salient.

Gunner William Clifford		*324th Garrison Artillery RGA*	
Service No.	46479	Age:	42
Place of Birth:	Chippenham, Wiltshire	Home Country:	England
Date of Death:	20/07/1917	Cause of death:	Died of wounds
Memorial:	Not known		
War cemetery:	Dozinghem Military Cemetery		
Next of Kin:	Ada Phylis Clifford (wife) - William & Sophia Clifford (parents)		
Address:	Euston Court Road, Epsom, Surrey		

William, an asylum assistant, was the son of William & Sophia Clifford and married Ada Phylis Beeching on 12 May 1907 at Epsom. He volunteered for service joining the Royal Garrison Artillery on 7 September 1914 arriving in France on 22 May 1915. In November 1915 William became ill and having spent a few days in hospital was granted extended leave, due to his medical condition, in order to return to England in December 1915. He rejoined his unit on 28 December 1915 but was admitted to hospital on 23 February 1916 and then evacuated to England on 3 March 1916. He then rejoined his unit on 1 May 1917. He was subsequently wounded with gunshot wounds on 20 July 1917 and evacuated to No. 4 Casualty Clearing Station where he succumbed to his wounds, later that day. William's personal items were returned to his wife and included correspondence, two pipes, three pocket books, religious book, tobacco pouch, knife, whistle and strap, metal wrist watch (no glass). William left a widow and two children and in January 1918 Ada Clifford was granted a pension of 22 shillings and eleven pence a week.

SATURDAY 21 JULY 1917 - WEATHER - VERY HOT

Lieutenant Valentine Leslie Douglas Uzielli		*Royal Field Artillery*	
Service No.	N/a	Age:	29
Place of birth:	Staines, Middlesex	Home Country:	England
Date of death:	21/07/1917	Cause of death:	Killed in action
Memorial:	Marlborough, Wiltshire		
War Cemetery:	Coxyde Military Cemetery - Grave I. A. 6		
Next of Kin:	Catherine Uzielli (wife) – Douglas & Emily Uzielli (parents)		
Address:	34 Warwick Gardens, West Kensington, London		

Valentine was the youngest son of Douglas and Emily Uzielli and was educated at Park Hill New Forest and Marlborough College. After completing his education, he went to South Africa in 1909 to become a mining engineer, joining the Transvaal Horse Artillery in 1910. At the outbreak of hostilities, he returned to England and volunteered for service and was given a commission with the Royal Filed Artillery on 22 October 1914. He arrived in France in March 1915 and returned to England to marry Catherine Hopkins on 18 August 1915. He was severely wounded at Loos in October 1915, losing the sight in one eye and evacuated to England. Following his recovery, he returned to France in March 1917. He was killed on Saturday 21 July 1917, most likely by German artillery fire, near Nieuport, Belgium, while laying out a telephone wire. A fellow officer stated:

"His death was a sad blow to us, as he was absolutely without fear, and inspired everyone with his coolness and courage."

He left a widow and a young daughter.

SUNDAY 22 JULY 1917

Left: Valentine Leslie Douglas Uzielli

Right: Eric George Lander King

Lieutenant Eric George Lander King		*1st Bn Grenadier Guards*	
Service No.	N/A	Age:	22
Place of birth:	Sutton, Surrey	Home Country:	England
Date of death:	22/07/1917	Cause of death:	Killed in action
Memorial:	Marlborough College, Wiltshire		
War Cemetery:	Canada Farm Cemetery - Grave I. F. 35.		
Next of Kin:	George Lander & Bertha King		
Address:	Gloucester House, Overton Road, Sutton, Surrey		

Eric was the third son of George and Bertha King and was educated at Marlborough College. In November 1915, he enlisted with the 28th London Regiment, the Artist's Rifles, and was given a commission with the Grenadier Guards in January 1916. He was sent to France joining the 1st Battalion and wounded in September 1916 at the Somme, being evacuated to England. Following his recovery, he returned to the front in April 1917. He was killed on the night of 22 July 1917, most likely by German artillery when the 1st Grenadier Guards were employed on fatigues near Boesinghe, Belgium, in preparation for the forthcoming attack.

Sapper John William Lewis		*12th Light Railway Operating Coy Royal Engineers*	
Service No.	269356	Age:	44
Place of birth:	South Marston, Wiltshire	Home Country:	England
Date of death:	22/07/1917	Cause of death:	Died of wounds
Memorial:	Not known		
War Cemetery:	Trois Arbres Cemetery Steenwerck - Grave I. V. 6.		
Next of Kin:	Emma Annie Lewis (wife) – William & Charlotte Lewis		
Address:	47 Winifred Street, Swindon, Wiltshire		

John, known as Jack, was the eldest son of William and Charlotte Lewis and as a youth was employed by the Great Western Railway Works at Swindon. At the age of 17 years he enlisted with the Oxfordshire Light Infantry and served seven years before leaving and joining the reserve. He was called to the colours when the Boer War broke out and served for some time in South Africa. He was wounded in 1900 and evacuated to England and following his recovery he was discharged with a pension. Jack married Emily Annie Woolford at the end of 1904 in Swindon. He again worked for the Great Western Railway works for a period of time before moving to Barrow in Furness and working for Vickers. At the outbreak of hostilities, he returned to Swindon and volunteered for service and initially joined the Wiltshire Regiment, before being transferred to the Dorset Regiment, then the Cameronians, being given home service duty in England and Scotland. While serving at Dundee he was transferred to the Royal Engineers and was sent to France in May 1917. In July 1917 Jack became ill and he wrote to his wife explaining he was going into hospital that was the last letter she was to receive from him. On Sunday 22 July 1917 Jack was killed, by a bomb dropped from a German aircraft, while being a patient of the 2nd Australian Casualty Clearing Station at Steenwerck, France. Jack's widow received the following letter from E.M. Collick a Chaplain at the hospital:

"It is with deepest sorrow I have to inform you of the sad death of your husband, Sapper J.W. Lewis, of the Royal Engineers. Will you accept my very sincere sympathy in your great bereavement. He was brought into this hospital sick on 19 July, and was killed by a bomb dropped by a German airman on the 22 July. Your husband was killed instantly, and suffered no pain. I laid him to rest in the little cemetery nearby, and a cross will be erected over the grave. I know how keenly you will feel the loss, but you will be cheered by the thought that your husband did his duty, and did it well. He was given his life, it is true, but only to gain a higher one, which will last for ever. His sacrifice has been great, but you may feel sure his reward will be greater."

Jack left a widow and three young children. His brother Charles would be killed in October 1918 while serving with the Canadians.

Private Herbert Culverhouse		*13th Bn Welsh Regiment*	
Service No.	55031	Age:	32
Place of birth:	North Bradley, Wiltshire	Home Country:	England
Date of death:	22/07/1917	Cause of death:	Died of wounds
Memorial:	North Bradley, Southwick		
War Cemetery:	Bard Cottage Cemetery - Grave III. B. 4.		
Next of Kin:	Evelyn Culverhouse (wife) – Enoch & Mary Jane Culverhouse		
Address:	2 Frome Road, Southwick, Wiltshire		

Herbert, a bricklayer, was the eldest son of Enoch & Mary Jane Culverhouse and married Evelyn Gerrish after the outbreak of war in 1914. It is likely he was conscripted into the army or joined under the Derby Scheme initially enlisting with the Wiltshire Regiment but was then transferred to the Welsh Regiment. He was wounded most likely by German artillery, on 21 July 1917 when the 13th Welsh were on working parties east of Elerverdinghe, Belgium. He was evacuated to 131st Field Ambulance, where he succumbed to his wounds on Sunday 22 July 1917. In July 1918 Herbert's wife Evelyn inserted the following memoriam in a local paper:

Twelve months gone how I miss him
Some may think the wound is healed
But little do they know the sorrow
that lies within my heart concealed

Private William Highman		*1st Bn Wiltshire Regiment*	
Service No.	10792	Age:	32
Place of birth:	Brinkworth, Wiltshire	Home Country:	England
Date of death:	22/07/1917	Cause of death:	Died of wounds
Memorial:	Lyneham, Wiltshire		
War Cemetery:	Hazebrouck Communal Cemetery - Grave III. D. 34.		

Next of Kin:	Richard & Mary Ann Highman
Address:	Bradenstoke, Wiltshire

William, known as Willie, a draper's assistant, was the youngest son of Richard & Mary Ann Highman and volunteered for service in August 1914, enlisting with the 5th Service Battalion Wiltshire Regiment. He arrived at Gallipoli on 12 July 1915 and while serving on the peninsular contracted enteric fever and was evacuated to England. Following his recovery, he was transferred to the 1st Battalion Wiltshire Regiment and sent to France. He was dangerously wounded with gunshot wound to the head, most likely around 20 June 1917, while on a working party near Messines, Belgium, and evacated to No.1 New Zealand Stationary Hospital at Hazebrouck, France, where he succumbed to his wounds on Sunday 22 July 1917. Willie's mother received a letter from the chaplain stating:

"Your gallent son was buried by me at Hazebrouck, where his name is marked with a cross, with his name and regiment upon it."

Lance Corporal Ernest Edwin Booy		*1st Bn Coldstream Guards*	
Service No.	9283	Age:	27
Place of birth:	Stanton St Quintin, Wilts	Home Country:	England
Date of death:	22/07/1917	Cause of death:	Killed in action
Memorial:	West Kington - Stanton St Quintin, Wiltshire		
War Cemetery:	Canada Farm Cemetery - Grave I E 31		
Next of Kin:	Henry & Emma Booy		
Address:	Didmarton, Gloucestershire		

Regular soldier Ernest was a farm labourer prior to his enlistment with the Coldstream Guards and was the second son of Henry and Emma Booy, arriving in France on 13 August 1914. He was killed in action on Sunday 22 July 1917 most likely by German artillery, near Bosinghe, Belgium, while carrying out fatigues during preparations for the Third Battle of Ypres.

Ernest Edwin Booy

Monday 23 July 1917 - Weather - Very Hot

Bombardier Jehu Simon Wakefield Chester *119th Brigade Bn Royal Field Artillery*

Service No.	W/809	Age:	24
Place of birth:	Ludgershall, Wiltshire	Home Country:	England
Date of death:	23/07/1917	Cause of death:	Killed in action
Memorial:	Not known		
War Cemetery:	Voormezeele Enclosure No 3 - Grave XIII. A. 1.		
Next of Kin:	Jehu & Alice Mary Chester		
Address:	4 Cribbwr Square, Pyle, Bridgend, Glamorganshire		

Jehu, a collier filler, was the second son of Jehu and Alice Mary Chester and volunteered for service joining the Royal Field Artillery. He arrived in France on Christmas Eve 1915 joining D Battery of the 119th Brigade. He was killed on Monday 23 July 1917, most likely by German artillery near Voormezeele, Belgium. His memoriam card states he was killed on 24 July 1917 and bears the words.

Just my boy
Into the great Forever,
Of that far land of rest,
Where Summer passes never,
My soldier lad's "Gone West"

Could I have raised his dying head,
Or said a last farewell,
The pain would not have been so hard
For those who loved him well.

Jehu was originally buried near where he fell just north of Snipers Barn, east of St. Elooi and in September 1919 his remains were moved to Voormezeele Enclosure No. 3.

Private Gerald Harvey Barnfield *1st Bn Wiltshire Regiment*

Service No.	32282	Age:	19
Place of birth:	Rangeworthy, Gloucester	Home Country:	England
Date of death:	23/07/1917	Cause of death:	Killed in action
Memorial:	Chippenham - St.Andrews Church Chippenham		
War Cemetery:	Ypres Menin Gate - Panel 53.		
Next of Kin:	William & Sarah Barnfield		
Address:	46 Lowden, Chippenham, Wiltshire		

Nineteen year old Gerald was the eldest son of William and Sarah Barnfield and it is likely he was conscripted into the army or enlisted under the Derby Scheme, joining the 1st Battalion Wiltshire Regiment. On Monday 23 July 1917 the 1st Wiltshires were southeast of Ypres, Belgium, and were called on to provide working parties in the forward area for burying dead animals. Throughout the night the Wiltshires were subjected to German shelling causing a number of casualties. One of these casualties was Gerald. He is remembered on the Ypres Menin Gate and has no known grave. In August 1917 Gerald's parents inserted the following memoriam in a local paper:

Christ shall clasp the broken chain
Closer when we meet again

Left: Jehu Simon Wakefield Chester

Right: Gerald Harvey Barnfield

Private Robert John Kibble		*8th Bn Somerset Light Infantry*	
Service No.	27840	Age:	40
Place of birth:	Harnhill, Gloucestershire	Home Country:	England
Date of death:	24/07/1917	Cause of death:	Died of wounds
Memorial:	Brinkworth, Wiltshire		
War Cemetery:	Etaples Military Cemetery - Grave XXV. L. 17.		
Next of Kin:	Theresa Ellen Kibble (wife) – Robert & Ann Kibble (parents)		
Address:	Sunday's Hill, Brinkworth, Wiltshire		

Robert, a farm labourer, was the eldest son of Robert and Ann Kibble and on 26 October 1905 married Theresa Ellen Webb at Brinkworth. It is likely he enlisted with the army under the Derby Scheme, initially joining the Wiltshire Regiment, before being transferred to the 8th Battalion Somerset Light Infantry. Robert was wounded while serving in the British front line east of Messines, most likely by German artillery, on 8 July 1917. He was evacuated to a hospital at Etaples, France, where he succumbed to his wounds on Tuesday 24 July 1917. Before enlisting in the army, Robert spoke to his father in law, stating:

"Dad, if I should be killed always remember to tell my children when they are big enough to understand, that their father died as a good British soldier to save them and their mother from the Germans, that he would not have the name of a shirker or a coward."

Robert left a widow, two children and a 75 year old mother to mourn his loss. In August 1917, his widow inserted the following memoriam in a local paper:

For honour and country, he bravely fought and died
We glory in his deed yet we miss him from our side

Corporal Albert Thomas Hamblin		*218th Siege Bty Royal Garrison Artillery*	
Service No.	87620	Age:	36
Place of birth:	Holcombe, Somerset	Home Country:	England
Date of death:	24/07/1917	Cause of death:	Killed in action
Memorial:	Frome, Frome Christchurch Church, Somerset		
War Cemetery:	Bus House Cemetery - Grave G. 6.		

Left: Albert Thomas Hamblin

Right: Wilfred Frederick Fisher

Next of Kin:	Alice Selina Hamblin (wife) - Edward J. & Louisa Eliza Hamblin (parents)
Address:	2 Bythesea Road, Trowbridge - Keyford Dairy, Frome, Somerset

Albert, a malsters foreman, was the eldest son of Edward J. & Louisa Eliza Hamblin and in the spring of 1906 he married Alice Selina Hayward at Frome in Somerset. He enlisted with the army under the Derby Scheme on 11 December 1915, was called up on 1 June 1916 and after completing his training, he was given one weeks leave before arriving in France on 17 January 1917. He was killed during German shelling in the early hours of the morning of Tuesday 24 July 1917 while engaged in the construction of a gun pit near St. Elooi, Belgium, in preparation for the Third Battle of Ypres. He left a widow and a young son. Albert's battery officer wrote to his widow stating:

"He was a conscientious and willing NCO, always carrying out his orders to the best of his ability."

2nd Lieutenant	*Wilfred Frederick Fisher*	*12th Bn Royal Sussex Regiment*	
Service No.	N/a	Age:	19
Place of birth:	Withyham, Sussex	Home Country:	England
Date of death:	24/07/1917	Cause of death:	Killed in action
Memorial:	Cuckfield, Sussex – Marlborough College		
War Cemetery:	Ypres Menin Gate - Panel 20		
Next of Kin:	Rev. Robert & Mary F Fisher		
Address:	Friars Gate, Chichester, Sussex		

Nineteen year old Wilfred was the youngest son of Rev. Robert and Mary Fisher and was educated at Marlborough College. On leaving education he served with the Inns Court, Officer Training Corps and was subsequently given a commission on 9 July 1915 with the Royal Sussex Regiment. He arrived in France on 21 June 1916 and was attached to the 9th Battalion Devonshire Regiment and was wounded at Ginchy at the Somme in July 1916. Following his recovery, he was returned to the front transferring to the 12th Battalion Royal Sussex Regiment. On the night of 23/24 July 1917 Wilfred was sent on a patrol to inspect the German wire near the Canal Bank opposite Bosinghe, Belgium. His patrol was ambushed and he was wounded and thought to have been taken prisoner. He was never seen again and is today remembered on the Ypres Menin Gate.

Gunner Wilfred Wiggins *161st Siege Bty Royal Garrison Artillery*

Service No.	126022	Age:	28
Place of birth:	Sevenhampton, Berkshire	Home Country:	England
Date of death:	24/07/1917	Cause of death:	Killed in action
Memorial:	Marlborough, Wiltshire		
War Cemetery:	Hospital Farm Cemetery - Grave B. 22.		
Next of Kin:	Margaret K Wiggins (wife) – Charles & Emily Wiggins (parents)		
Address:	94 High Street, Marlborourgh, Wiltshire		

Wilfred, a labourer, was the second son of Charles and Emily Wiggins and in the spring of 1915 he married Margaret K. Landfear at Marlborough. It is likely he was either conscripted into the army or enlisted under the Derby Scheme, joining the Royal Garrison Artillery. He was sent to France joining the 161st Siege Battery, who, in July 1917 were in action near Elverdinge, Belgium. Wilfred was killed, most likely by German artillery counter battery fire, on Tuesday 24 July 1917.

WEDNESDAY 25 JULY 1917 - WEATHER - MORNING WET AFTERNOON FINE

Private William James Leaver *15th Bn Royal Welsh Fusiliers*

Service No.	291958	Age:	21
Place of birth:	Bradford on Avon, Wiltshire	Home Country:	England
Date of death:	25/07/1917	Cause of death:	Killed in action
Memorial:	Bradford on Avon, Wiltshire		
War Cemetery:	Ypres Menin Gate - Grave Panel 22.		
Next of Kin:	James & Caroline Leaver		
Address:	37 Wine Street, Bradford on Avon, Wiltshire		

William, a cowman, was the only son of James and Caroline Weaver. He was conscripted into the army, attesting on 28 January 1916 and was called up on 18 August 1916 and sent to the Royal Welsh Fusiliers. He was long sighted and had difficulty seeing things close to him and his condition was not improved with glasses. He arrived in France on 16 June 1917 joining the 15th Battalion on 9 July 1917. On 23 July 1917, the 15th Royal Welsh Fusiliers were ordered to dig assembly trenches for the forthcoming attack on the west bank of the Ypres Canal neat Tugela Farm almost opposite Yorkshire Trench. On 24 July 1917 they were called on to undertake fatigues in the same area and were subject to German artillery shelling with gas shells. Many of the offers and men were suffering from the effects. The following day the 15th Royal Welsh Fusiliers conducted a large scale raid against German positions on the east side of the Ypres Canal. At 9am the British barrage opened on German positions and at 9.10am the British raiders advanced toward the German trenches. Little enemy opposition was found in the first German line but the second line was heavily occupied by German troops. After the British raiders returned it was believed that Second Lieutenant Lloyd and 150 other ranks were in the hands of the enemy. William was reported missing while on the raid. In late April 1918 William's mother received official information stating he was presumed to have been killed on the day he was reported missing.

2nd Lieutenant Basil Alderson Carr *Special Reserve Royal Garrison Artillery*

Service No.	N/a	Age:	37
Place of birth:	Broadstairs, Kent	Home Country:	England
Date of death:	25/07/1917	Cause of death:	Killed in action
Memorial:	Marlborough College, Wiltshire		
War Cemetery:	Coxyde Military Cemetery - Grave I. L. 54		
Next of Kin:	Rev. Canon James Haslewood & Elizabeth A Carr		
Address:	Aldisham, Kent		

Left: Basil Alderson Carr

Centre: Daniel Johnson

Right : James William Birt

Basil was the youngest son of Rev. James and Elizabeth Carr and was educated at Marlborough College which he entered with a Foundation Scholarship in 1893. After completing his education he became an Assistant Master at Sunningdale School. He joined up in February 1917 and after 5 months training he was sent to the front. He joined his battery near Nieuport, Belgium on 20 July 1917 and was killed most likely by German artillery 5 days later.

THURSDAY 26 JULY 1917

Sergeant Daniel Johnson		*10th Bn South Wales Borderers*	
Service No.	20216	Age:	41
Place of birth:	Malmesbury, Wiltshire	Home Country:	Wales
Date of death:	26/07/1917	Cause of death:	Killed in action
Memorial:	Ebbw Vale Christchurch, Monmouthshire		
War Cemetery:	Bard Cottage Cemetery - Grave III. F. 4.		
Next of Kin:	Emily Johnson (wife) – George & Ruth Johnson (parents)		
Address:	5 Letchworth Road Willow Town, Ebbw Vale, Monmouthshire		

Old soldier Daniel was the second son of George and Ruth Johnson and originally enlisted with the South Wales Borderers on 23 April 1894. He served in Gibraltar and India and left the army on 12 November 1906. Soon after he married Emily Harding at Chipping Sodbury. The couple moved to Ebbw Vale, Monmouthshire, where Daniel took employment in a steel factory, where he worked as a spring maker. He volunteered for service soon after the outbreak of the Great War joining the 10th Battalion South Wales Borderers arriving in France on 3 December 1915. During 1917 he was attached to 151st Field Company Royal Engineers, who, in July 1915 were building an advanced dressing station and pontoon bridges on the bank of the Ypres Canal south of Boesighe, Belgium. On Thursday 26 July 1917 Daniel and Major Jack McMurtrie were visiting men working on a communication trench when a German shell exploded close by. Daniel and the Major were both killed and buried side by side in Bard Cottage Cemetery. He left a widow and four children.

2nd Lieutenant James Mortimer Strong		*23rd Bn Machine Gun Corps*	
Service No.	N/a	Age:	24
Place of birth:	Everleigh, Wiltshire	Home Country:	England

Date of death:	26/07/1917	Cause of death:	Died of wounds
Memorial:	Dauntsey's School Memorial, Everleigh, Wiltshire		
War Cemetery:	Brandhoek Military Cemetery - Grave I. C. 6.		
Next of Kin:	James & Charlotte Strong		
Address:	Park Dale House, Devizes, Wiltshire		

James was the eldest son of James and Charlotte Strong and was educated at Dauntseys School prior to being employed on his father's farm. He volunteered for service joining the Royal Fusiliers and arrived in France on 14 November 1915. He transferred to the Machine Gun Corps and was given a commission on 25 September 1916. James was killed by German artillery fire while serving near Ypres, Belgium and was evacuated to a casualty clearing station at Brandhoek where he succumbed to his wounds on Thursday 26 July 1917.

Gunner James William Birt		*244th Siege Bty Royal Garrison Artillery*	
Service No.	91035	Age:	26
Place of birth:	Painswick, Gloucestershire	Home Country:	England
Date of death:	26/07/1917	Cause of death:	Killed in action
Memorial:	Marlborough, Wiltshire		
War Cemetery:	Ypres Menin Gate - Grave Panel 9.		
Next of Kin:	Florence Mabel Birt (wife) - Martin John & Ada Sophia Birt (parents)		
Address:	St Johns Close, Marlborourgh, Wiltshire		

Butcher, James, was the third son of Martin and Ada Birt and on 24 March 1913 he married Florence Mabel Mutton at Stroud, Gloucestershire. He enlisted with the army under the Derby Scheme on 2 December 1915 and was called up on 1 June 1916, being sent to the Royal Garrison Artillery Depot. After completing his training as a signaler - telephonist he arrived in France on 29 January 1917 and was sent to the 244th Siege Battery. He was killed on Thursday 26 July 1917, most likely by German artillery, near Ypres, during the preparations for the third battle of Ypres. He left a wife and two small children. His personal possessions were sent home to his widow and consisted of correspondence and a metal watch (broken).

Private Albert George Osborne		*139th Field Amb. Royal Army Medical Corps*	
Service No.	74086	Age:	20
Place of birth:	Chippenham, Wiltshire	Home Country:	England
Date of death:	26/07/1917	Cause of death:	Killed in action
Memorial:	Moulton, Bradford on Avon, Wiltshire		
War Cemetery:	Bus House Cemetery - Grave G. 20.		
Next of Kin:	Alfred & Emily Osborne		
Address:	252, Monument Road, Birmingham, Warwickshire		

Albert was the only son of Alfred and Emily Osborne and was employed by the Spencer Moulton Works at Bradford on Avon. It is likely he was either conscripted into the army or enlisted under the Derby Scheme. He joined the Royal Army Medical Corps and was sent to the 139th Field Ambulance. He was killed instantly on Thursday 26 July 1917 North west of Hill 60, when a shell hit the side of No. 3 Regimental Aid Post.

FRIDAY 27 JULY 1917

Private Walter Inkpen		*200th Coy Army Service Corps*	
Service No.	S4/064782	Age:	30
Place of birth:	Salisbury, Wiltshire	Home Country:	England
Date of death:	27/07/1917	Cause of death:	Died of wounds
Memorial:	Not known		
War Cemetery:	Menin Road South Military Cemetery - Grave II. B. 2.		
Next of Kin:	Walter & Ann Inkpen		
Address:	Skew Bridge Wilton Road, Salisbury, Wiltshire		

Walter, a grocer's clerk, was the second son of Walter and Ann Inkpen and volunteered for service on 1 March 1915, joining 200th Company Army Service Corps. He arrived in France on 25 September 1915, and in 1917 was attached to 25 Division Train. He was wounded on Friday 27 July 1917 near Ypres, most likely by German shell fire. He was taken to 96th Field Ambulance where he succumbed to his wounds soon after.

Private Walter Aubrey Buckingham		*227th Coy Machine Gun Corps*	
Service No.	57527	Age:	26
Place of birth:	Taynton, Gloucestershire	Home Country:	England
Date of death:	27/07/1917	Cause of death:	Killed in action
Memorial:	Audit Department Memorial Great Western Railway Works Swindon		
War Cemetery:	Canada Farm Cemetery - Grave II. A. 5.		
Next of Kin:	John & Harriet Buckingham		
Address:	Stanton, Harcourt Road, Newland, Witney, Oxfordshire		

Walter was the youngest son of John and Harriet Buckingham and it is likely he was conscripted into the army or enlisted under the Derby Scheme. He initially joined Oxford & Bucks Light Infantry but soon after transferred to the Machine Gun Corps. He was sent to the front to the 227th Company and was killed in action on Friday 27 July 1917, north east of Ypres.

Corporal Charles White		*13th Bn Royal Welsh Fusiliers*	
Service No.	235509	Age:	23
Place of birth:	Tilshead, Wiltshire	Home Country:	England
Date of death:	27/07/1917	Cause of death:	Died of wounds
Memorial:	West Lavington, Wiltshire		
War Cemetery:	Dozinghem Military Cemetery - Grave I. H. 9.		
Next of Kin:	John R. & Elizabeth A. White		
Address:	Lower Farm West Lavington, Wiltshire		

Twenty three year old Charles known as Charlie and a farm labourer, was the fourth son of John and Elizabeth White. Charlie volunteered for service joining the 8th Battalion Wiltshire Regiment before being transferred to the 4th Battalion Royal Welsh Fusiliers on 21 October 1916 arriving in France on 5 June 1917. He was then transferred to the 13th Battalion Royal Welsh Fusiliers joining them on 24 June 1917. He was wounded, most likely by German artillery, during preparations for the attack on Pilckem Ridge Belgium, which was to be the start of the third battle of Ypres. He was evacuated to No. 4 Casualty Clearing Station near Westvleteren, Belgium, where he died on Friday 27 July 1917. Charlie's mother received the following letter from the chaplain of the casualty clearing station:

"It is with profound regret that I the C of E Chaplain, write to tell you of the death of your gallant son, Corp. C. White, 235509 Royal W. Fusiliers. No man can die a soldier or a more heroic deed than fighting in the cause of all that Christianity stands for and his King and Country. May God in his Divine Love

Left: Charles White

Right: Thomas Sheppard

help strengthen and comfort you. He was buried by me this morning. The place of burial and particulars of graves may be obtained from the War Graves Commission."

SATURDAY 28 JULY 1917 - WEATHER - VERY HOT

Gunner Thomas Sheppard — *58th Bde Royal Field Artillery*

Service No.	135349
Age:	27
Place of birth:	Box, Wiltshire
Home Country:	England
Date of death:	28/07/1917
Cause of death:	Killed in action
Memorial:	Corsham, Wiltshire
War Cemetery:	Ypres Menin Gate - Panel 5 and 9.
Next of Kin:	Gladys Annetta Sheppard (wife) - Frederick G. & Annie E. Sheppard (parents)
Address:	Bay Cottage Elley Green, Corsham, Wiltshire

Thomas, known as Tom and a mason, was the eldest son of Frederick and Annie Sheppard and at the beginning of 1915 he married Gladys Annetta Lilly in Corsham. He was described as having a gentle and kindly disposition and it is likely he was either conscripted into the army or enlisted under the Derby Scheme joining the Royal Field Artillery. Tom was killed on Saturday 28 July 1917, most likely by German artillery, north of Ypres, Belgium. His battery commander wrote to Gladys Sheppard stating:

"I sincerely regret the loss of a capable, and willing man, who always did his duty even in the most trying circumstances. A military chaplain presided at his burial service and the exact position of his grave will be forwarded to you later."

Tom's grave was lost and he is today remembered on the Ypres Menin Gate. He left a widow and young child.

Sapper George James Skippence — *475th Field Coy Bn Royal Engineers*

Service No.	496811
Age:	24
Place of birth:	Great Bedwyn, Wiltshire
Home Country:	England
Date of death:	28/07/1917
Cause of death:	Died of wounds
Memorial:	Great Bedwyn, Wiltshire

War Cemetery: Abbeville Communal Cemetery Extension - Grave III. B. 21.
Next of Kin: James & Eliza Ann Skippence
Address: Frogmore Farm, Great Bedwyn, Wiltshire

George, a farmhand, was the eldest son of James and Eliza Skippence and it is likely he was either conscripted into the army or enlisted under the Derby Scheme. He joined the Royal Engineers and was sent to the 475th Field Company. He was most likely wounded while working on shelters and bridges on the canal bank north of Ypres. The 475th Field Company were subjected to German shelling with mustard gas shells, which affected their eyes and breathing. The gas also soaked into the soil and it was found it would cause large blisters, even through clothing. George was evacuated to the 1st South African General Hospital at Abbeville, France, where he succumbed to his wounds on Saturday 28 July 1917.

Private Edward James Andrews *15th Bn Welsh Regiment*
Service No. 54810 Age: 20
Place of birth: Aldershot, Hampshire Home Country: England
Date of death: 28/07/1917 Cause of death: Killed in action
Memorial: Westbury, Wiltshire
War Cemetery: Bard Cottage Cemetery - Grave III. G. 26.
Next of Kin: George & Annie W E Andrews
Address: Fair View, Bratton Road, Westbury, Wiltshire

Edward was the second son of George and Annie Andrews and was the son of a soldier. He was educated at the Duke of York's School, Guston, near Dover, which was a school for the children of serving soldiers. It is likely he was either conscripted into the army or enlisted under the Derby Scheme initially joining the Queens Regiment. He was transferred to the 15th Battalion Welsh Regiment and sent to the front. Edward was killed on Saturday 28 July 1917, most likely by German artillery when a patrol was sent out to the German front line trenches at Kiel Cottage, not far from Yorkshire Trench. The German positions were found to be unoccupied.

Private John Bertie Blackford *8th Bn Gloucestershire Regiment*
Service No. 29193 Age: 41
Place of birth: Purton, Wiltshire Home Country: England
Date of death: 28/07/1917 Cause of death: Killed in action
Memorial: Not known
War Cemetery: Ypres Menin Gate - Panel 22 and 34.
Next of Kin: Sarah Annie Blackford (wife) – Joseph & Rosanna Blackford (parents)
Address: 140 Beatrice Street, Swindon, Wiltshire

John, a butcher, was the youngest son of Joseph and Rosanna Blackford and in the spring of 1903 he married Sarah Ann Fletcher. It is likely he was either conscripted into the army or enlisted under the Derby Scheme joining the 8th Service Battalion Gloucestershire Regiment. On Saturday 28 July 1917, the 8th Gloucesters were in the British front line at Oosttaverne, Belgium. At 1.25am the Germans raided the British trenches with what the Gloucesters war diary described as *"Sturmtrupp,"* storm troops. John was killed during the attack but the enemy were repulsed with considerable loss. Second Lieutenat Kimber who joined the Gloucesters in the trenches on the same day as John was killed wrote the following letter to Sarah Ann Blackford:

"It is with very great regret that I have to offer you my sympathy and that of all the officers and men of this company upon the death of of your late husband, Private Blackford. He was killed by a bomb,

(hand grenade), during a German raid in the early morning of the 28th July, a raid which, however, was successfully repulsed. Private Blackford was an excellent soldier, and trusted and liked by his comrades, so that we, too, share in the great loss which you have sustained."

John is remembered on the Ypres Menin Gate, he left a widow and young family.

SUNDAY 29 JULY 1917 - WEATHER - VERY HOT

Private Gerald King		*3rd Bn Coldstream Guards*	
Service No.	15458	Age:	26
Place of birth:	Athlone, West Meath	Home Country:	Ireland
Date of death:	29/07/1917	Cause of death:	Killed in action
Memorial:	Chippenham, Police HQ Devizes		
War Cemetery:	Ypres Menin Gate - Panel 11.		
Next of Kin:	George & Mary King		
Address:	10 Myrtle Avenue, Warminster, Wiltshire		

Gerald, a Wiltshire policeman, lived at Lowden, Chippenham, and was the only child of George and Mary King. He volunteered for service with the Coldstream Guards arriving in France on 12 October 1915. On the evening of Sunday 29 July 1917, the 3rd Coldstream Guards were near Bosinghe, north of Ypres, Belgium, preparing for the third battle of Ypres. In mid August 1917 George and Mary received the following letter from Company Sergeant Major J. Gornall stating:

"Private King was my servant, or batman, as we say. We were digging quite close together when a shell burst very close to us. Your son was struck with a piece. I saw it myself. Death was instantaneous, there was no suffering, which is a mercy. He was very much liked by his officers and comrades, which shows that he always did his work well and pleasantly. He went to the sacrament on the Sunday before going to the trenches. That too says a lot, I think."

Captin Dorrian of the Coldstream Guards also wrote expressing his regrets and stating:

"Private King, poor fellow, was killed in action during the last battle of Ypres. All the men and myself will miss him. He was one of the finest soldiers we had and a great personal friend of mine. My sympathies are with you. The food parcel received from you has been given to his pals."

It is likely Gerald was buried and his grave lost during subsequent fighting. He is today remembered on the Ypres Menin Gate.

Private William Parsons		*13th Bn Welsh Regiment*	
Service No.	55042	Age:	19
Place of birth:	Trowbridge, Wiltshire	Home Country:	England
Date of death:	29/07/1917	Cause of death:	Killed in action
Memorial:	Trowbridge, Wiltshire		
War Cemetery:	Ypres Menin Gate - Grave Panel 37.		
Next of Kin:	Frank & Laura Parsons		
Address:	4 West Ashton Road, Trowbridge, Wiltshire		

Nineteen year old William was the eldest son of Frank and Laura Parsons and employed at Yates & Company wire mattress manufacturers. He volunteered for service with the Wiltshire Regiment in February 1916 and after completing his training was sent to the continent in February 1917. He was

Left: William Parsons

Right: Reginald Loader

then transferred from the Wiltshire Regiment to the 13th Battalion Welsh Regiment. William was killed in action on Sunday 29 July 1917 most likely by German artillery, on the canal bank east of Elverdighe, Belgium, while the 13th Welsh were preparing for the third battle of Ypres. Frank and Laura Parsons received the following letter from Captain Richards of the 13th Welsh:

"Your son served under me and I thought quite a lot of him. He was always so very cheerful and will be greatly missed by all the boys in the Regiment."

In August 1918 William's parents inserted the following memoriam in a local paper:

"We were not there to see him die
The one we loved so dear
But we know he died a hero
And died without a fear
He fought for King and Country
He died a hero's death
He's now with our Heavenly Father
God Grant him peace and rest.

Guardsman Reginald Loader		*1st Bn Grenadier Guards*	
Service No.	27323	Age:	20
Place of birth:	Ludgershall, Wiltshire	Home Country:	England
Date of death:	29/07/1917	Cause of death:	Killed in action
Memorial:	Ludgershall, Wiltshire		
War Cemetery:	Duhallow ADS Cemetery - Grave VII. G. 13.		
Next of Kin:	William & Annie H Loader		
Address:	2 Newton Villas, Ludgershall, Wiltshire		

Reginald was the youngest son of William and Annie Loader and was employed by Richard Dickeson & Co. Ltd, a wholesale grocers who supplied the army. He was conscripted into the army joining the Grenadier Guards and arrived in France on 3 April 1917, being sent to the 1st Battalion. On Sunday 29 July 1917, the 1st Grenadier Guards were in trenches on the Ypres canal bank near Boesinghe, Belgium and were continually shelled by German artillery. Reginald's mother received a letter from a chaplain stating that Reginald was properly buried in a soldier's cemetery near the spot where he was killed by shell fire. Later, a cross made by the Battalion was made to mark the place. He was originally buried just south of Boesinghe Chateau and in August 1919 his remains were moved to Duhallow ADS Cemetery.

Private William E. Bristow		*10th Bn Worcestershire Regiment*	
Service No.	31204	Age:	37
Place of birth:	Vauxhall, Middlesex	Home Country:	England
Date of death:	29/07/1917	Cause of death:	Died of wounds
Memorial:	Not known		
War Cemetery:	Voormezeele Enclosure No 3 - Grave Pheasant Wood Cem. Mem. 3.		
Next of Kin:	Fanny Louisa Bristow (wife) - John & Martha Dellaway (grandparents)		
Address:	2 Frederick Place, Sidbury, Worcestershire		

William, a tailor, had grown up in Devizes with his grandparents John and Martha Dellaway and in the summer of 1906 he married Fanny Louisa Pittaway. It is likely he was either conscripted into the army or enlisted under the Derby Scheme and after completing his training he was sent to France joining the 10th Battalion Worcestershire Regiment. William was wounded near Rose Wood northeast of Oostaverne, Belgium by German shell fire and probably died soon after. He was originally buried at Pheasant Wood Cemetery and after the war when the graves from there were relocated to Voormezeele Enclosure No. 3, William and four other men's graves could not be found and he is now commemorated on a special memorial.

Lieutenant Horace Michael H. Allenby MC		*T Bty 14th Bde Royal Horse Artillery*	
Service No.	N/a	Age:	19
Place of birth:	Donhead St Andrew, Wiltshire	Home Country:	England
Date of death:	29/07/1917	Cause of death:	Died of wounds
Memorial:	Houses of Parliament		
War Cemetery:	Coxyde Military Cemetery - Grave II. D. 1.		
Next of Kin:	Edmund Henry Hynman & Adelaide M Allenby		
Address:	The Residency, Cairo, Egypt		

Horace was the only child of General Edmund, later Viscount, and Adelaide Allenby and was educated at Wellington House, Kent. He volunteered for service and was given a commission with the Royal Horse Artillery, arriving in France on 18 January 1916, being sent to the T Battery, 14th Brigade. He was awarded the Military Cross for devotion to duty in the field. The citation reads:

"For conspicuous gallantry in action. He ran out communications to the two forward companies and sent back very useful reports on the situation. Later, he rescued a wounded man under heavy fire. He displayed marked courage and determination throughout the operations."

While serving near Nieuport, Belgium, on Sunday 29 July 1917. Horace was hit by a splinter of shell which went through his steel helmet while he was walking from a detached gun to the remainder of the battery. He was evacuated to the 24th Casualty Clearing Station and lived five hours, but never recovered consciousness. His battery commander wrote:

"He had absolutely no notion of fear, and in every operation wished to go forward as Forward Observing Officer, but, of course, was only allowed to do it in his turn. He was the finest practical gunner of his rank that I have ever seen in France. The men all loved him and would do anything for him. In the mess he amused us greatly with his socialistic views and his defence of conscientious objectors. He was a good rider and a thorough sportsman.'

Left: Horace Michael H. Allenby MC

Right: The special memorial to Leonard White in Hedge Row Trench Cemetery

Horace's mother was presented with her sons Military Cross at an investiture on 18 September 1917. He was originally buried at Oosthoek Military Cemetery, Adinkerke, 4 Kms South-West of Coxyde and relocated after the war.

MONDAY 30 JULY 1917

Gunner Leonard White — *86th Army Bde Bn Royal Field Artillery*

Service No. 59080
Place of birth: Lea, Wiltshire
Date of death: 30/07/1917
Age: 22
Home Country: England
Cause of death: Died of wounds
Memorial: Seagry, Wiltshire
War Cemetery: Hedge Row Trench Cemetery - Grave Sp. Mem. G. 13.
Next of Kin: John Humphrey & Mary White
Address: West End, Minchinhampton, Gloucestershire

Leonard, a baker's assistant, was the second son of John and Mary White who had lived at Upper Seagry. He volunteered for service joining the Royal Field Artillery and arrived in France on 18 July 1915 being sent to D Battery 86th Brigade. He died of wounds, most likely due to German artillery, on Monday 30 July 1917 on the eve of the third battle of Ypres, southeast of the Hill 60, Belgium. Leonard is today buried in Hedge Row Trench Cemetery, which suffered very severely from shell fire, and after the Armistice the positions of the individual graves could not be found or reconstructed. The headstones are therefore arranged symmetrically round the Cross of Sacrifice. John & Mary White lost two more sons: Cecil had been killed in France in April 1917 and Arthur was to be killed in France in April 1918.

Gunner Frederick George Clifford — *168th Siege Bty Bn Royal Garrison Artillery*

Service No. 87052
Place of birth: Calstone, Wiltshire
Date of death: 30/07/1917
Age: 30
Home Country: England
Cause of death: Killed in action
Memorial: Poulshot, Keevil
War Cemetery: Belgian Battery Corner Cemetery - Grave I. F. 3.
Next of Kin: Amy Lilian Clifford (wife) - George H & Fanny J Clifford (parents)
Address: Mill Lane, Poulshot, Wiltshire

Sawmill worker Frederick was the eldest son of George and Fanny Clifford and on 27 November 1911 he married Amy Lilian Weston at Calstone. He attested to join the army on 12 December 1915 at Devizes, under the Derby Scheme. Named after Lord Derby the Scheme allowed men to register for the army and to be called up when they were needed. Frederick was called up six months later and joined the Royal Garrison artillery on 29 May 1916. After his short training, he embarked from Southampton on 22 September 1916 arriving at Le Harve the following day. During November 1916, he was attached to 2nd Army Signal School, for training as a signaler and then he returned to his unit. Frederick was killed in action on Monday 30 July 1917, most likely by shelling from German artillery, and buried at Belgian Battery Corner Cemetery. The cemetery is at a road junction where three Belgium artillery batteries were situated in 1915 and nearly all the 566 graves are from artillery units. Frederick's personal possessions were returned to his wife Amy and consisted of letters, photos, religious book, penknife, 2 Cigarette holders, cards, Australian cap badge, medallions, safety razor, 9 blades and a tin cigarette case. He left a widow and young son.

Private Martin Chubb — *13th Bn Royal Welsh Fusiliers*

Service No.	253319	Age:	38
Place of birth:	Silton, Dorset	Home Country:	England
Date of death:	30/07/1917	Cause of death:	Died of wounds
Memorial:	Zeals, Wiltshire		
War Cemetery:	Bard Cottage Cemetery - Grave I. M. 5.		
Next of Kin:	Thomas & Anne Chubb		
Address:	Knowle Green, Bowerchalke, Wiltshire		

Martin, a general labour, was the youngest son of Thomas and Anne Chubb and was an old soldier. He had originally joined the militia before enlisting with the Wiltshire Regiment on 7 December 1897. He served in England and two tours of South Africa before being discharged on 9 April 1901, having been found medically unfit for further service. Martin was then conscripted into the army on 12 January 1917 rejoining the Wiltshire Regiment. He arrived in France on 5 June 1917 and on 21 June he was transferred to 13th Battalion Royal Welsh Fusiliers. On Monday 30 July 1917, the 13th Royal Welsh Fusiliers were positioned in and around Yorkshire Trench and were subjected to German artillery bombardments. Martin was wounded during the bombardment and evacuated to 131st Field Ambulance where he succumbed to his wounds soon after. His personal property was returned to his brother, Hubert and consisted of identity disc, watch and chain (damaged), key, purse, belt and testament.

Private Reginald George Dimmer — *2nd Bn Wiltshire Regiment*

Service No.	33230	Age:	20
Place of birth:	Bowerchalke, Wiltshire	Home Country:	England
Date of death:	30/07/1917	Cause of death:	Killed in action
Memorial:	Not known		
War Cemetery:	Ypres Menin Gate - Panel 53.		
Next of Kin:	George Edward & Kate Elizabeth Dimmer		
Address:	Ebbesbourne Wake, Wiltshire		

Reginald a farm worker was the eldest son of George and Kate Dimmer and it is likely he was either conscripted into the army or enlisted under the Derby Scheme joining the Wiltshire Regiment. He was sent to the 2nd Battalion, who on Monday 30 July 1917 were in assembly trenches at the southern end of Sanctuary Wood, Belgium. Reginald was killed most likely by German artillery while in these trenches. He is remembered on the Ypres Menin Gate and has no known grave.

4
The Battle of Pilckem Ridge

START OF THE THIRD BATTLE OF YPRES (Maps Page 419 - 420 - 421)

TUESDAY 31 JULY 1917 - TEMPERATURE 20°c OVERCAST WITH 21.7mm OF RAIN

After artillery preparation extending over many days, the long expected British offensive was begun at dawn on Tuesday 31 July 1917, in Belgium. On a broad front, extending north and south of Ypres, the British forces broke the German line and made an advance to a depth of between four and five thousand yards. The British attacked extended from Boesinghe, at the northern end of the Ypres salient, to a point on the south near Warneton, on the River Lys. French forces joined in the assault on the British left. There was no element of surprise in the undertaking, except the exact moment chosen by Sir Douglas Haig. The Germans were well aware that they were to be attacked, and the German newspapers have contained many references to the expected onslaught. The Kaiser himself sent a telegraphic message a day or two before, to his troops in the battle-line, in which he referred to the coming British offensive. The Germans had strengthened their means of resistance, had brought up many additional guns, and had massed supports at all critical points.

This was the fourth major offensive of the British Army in 1917, the three previous being Vimy Ridge, Arras and Messines. It was no secret and at least three or four weeks before the attack, British officers were told the attack would take place on either the 31 July or the 1 August 1917, and for a long time the artillery preparation had continued with ever increasing intensity. At no time since the war began had the firing been heard over such a large area of England, and millions of people living in London and the Southeast heard this tremendous firing going on day and night at distances from 100 to 200 miles from the guns. During all this firing, the British Army was preparing and had been helped by the staff work and the Flying Corps who have taken many photographs that when the British began the advance they knew exactly the location of every German trench and barbed wire entanglement.

During the darkness on the morning of the advance the assaulting troops were able to form up for the attack very close to the German lines. Lines of shell craters, in the fields where our storms of fire had swept away all trenches, all buildings and all trees. The Germans held these forward positions lightly, by small groups of men who knew themselves to be doomed, and waited for that doom in their pits, like animals in death traps. The German second line defences, were less damaged but awful enough in the wreckage of earthworks, the Germans were in greater strength, and from these positions flares were sent up all through the night, giving blurred white light along the barriers of mist, and rising high into the cloudy sky. Scores of thousands of British soldiers, lying in the wet earth in puddles and mud holes, watched those flares, and hoped they would not be revealed before that second when they would have to rise and go forward to meet their luck. They lay silently, never stirring nor coughing nor making any rattle of arms, while the German shells passed over them or smashed among them, killing and wounding some of those who lay close. German aircraft came out in the night, bolder than by day, since they had been chased and attacked and destroyed in great numbers by British pilots who had been determined to get the mastery of the air and to blind the Germans eyes before the battle, and were beyond any doubt successful. The German aircraft swooped over the places where they thought the British batteries were hidden, and dropped bombs; but as they could see nothing in the darkness their aim was bad, and not much damage was done.

Shortly after 3.30am the artillery noise quickened and intensified to a monstrous over whelming tumult. It was so great that 12 miles behind the lines big houses moved and were shaken with great trembling. People farther away were awakened with fear, and went to their windows and stared out into the darkness and saw fireballs in the sky, and knew that men were fighting and dying in Flanders. The drum fire of the guns never slackened for hours. At 9am it beat over the countryside with the same great terror as it started before 4am. Strangely above this hammering and thundering of two thousand or more British guns, answered by the Germans barrage, railway whistles screamed from trains taking up more and more shells to the very edge of the fighting lines and in between the massed batteries, using them as fast as they could be unloaded. Over at Warneton and Oostaverne, in the valley below Messines Ridge, the Germans were pouring fire along the British line, with shells of the heaviest calibre, which burst monstrously and raised great pillars of white smoke. It was a valley of death and the British were fighting for the slopes beyond.

The first official report of the battle recorded that both the British and French, who were attacking to the north of the British, had captured on the whole front, more than 15 miles, their first objectives, and were reported to be making satisfactory progress at all points. Considerable numbers of prisoners had been captured before noon. Later Sir Douglas Haig sent news that the main advance had been made north of Ypres and that 3,500 prisoners had been taken. To resist the British attack were 13 German divisions and the prisoners came from every German regiment in the line. The main depth of the British advance was between 4,000 and 5,000 yards and it broke out on all sides of the bounds of the famous Ypres salient. The great majority of the troops that took part in the attack were English, though both Scots, Welsh and Australians bore a part of it. A correspondent accompanying the attack spoke in glowing terms of the Welsh who had a place of honour in the line, the Guards, and Highland Regiments but adds that none of them could have done better than the Englishmen.

A German report on the battle alleged that the British attacks were repulsed and added:

"After changeable, bitter fights on a large scale the enemy who attacked with superior forces many ranks deep, had to content himself with the possession of a crater position in our defence zone."

Sapper Arthur Henry Carr		*422nd Field Coy Royal Engineers*	
Service No.	183127	Age:	40
Place of birth:	Edington, Wiltshire	Home Country:	England
Date of death:	31/07/1917	Cause of death:	Killed in action
Memorial:	Trowbridge, Wiltshire		
War Cemetery:	Ypres Menin Gate - Grave Panel 9.		
Next of Kin:	Emily F Carr (wife) – Elizabeth Carr (parent)		
Address:	11 Gladstone Road, Trowbridge, Wiltshire		

Arthur, a carpenter, was the only son of Elizabeth Carr, later Elizabeth Penny, and married Emily

Left: Arthur Henry Carr

Right: Percival Lorenzo Oram

Florence Gifford on Boxing Day 1899. He was well known as a skilled tradesman and worked on many local buildings including Winsley Sanatorium and County Offices in Trowbridge where he was appointed foreman in charge of the carpenters. In June 1916 he was conscripted into the army but was placed on reserve and sent home. He was recalled on 26 October 1916 and sent to North Wales. In April 1917, he was sent to France and was transferred to the West Lancashire Engineers. Emily Carr received a letter from Arthur on Tuesday 31 July 1917 stating he was going up the line for the second time after a few days' rest. Unfortunately, Arthur was killed in action on the same day that his wife received the letter, having been killed near Wieltje, Belgium, on the first day of the third battle of Ypres. He is remembered on the Ypres Menin Gate and has no known grave. He left a widow and five young children.

Private Percival Lorenzo Oram		*166th Bn Machine Gun Corps*	
Service No.	102811	Age:	20
Place of birth:	Market Lavington, Wilts	Home Country:	England
Date of death:	31/07/1917	Cause of death:	Killed in action
Memorial:	Market Lavington, Wiltshire		
War Cemetery:	Ypres Menin Gate - Panel 56.		
Next of Kin:	William & Louisa Oram		
Address:	New Inn, Market Lavington, Wiltshire		

Percy was the only son of William and Louisa Oram and was employed by the Great Western Railway Company as a clerk in the traffic department at Trowbridge. It is likely he was either conscripted into the army or joined under the Derby Scheme, initially joining the Wiltshire Regiment and then transferring to the Machine Gun Corps. Percy was killed in action on Tuesday 31 July 1917 near Wieltje, north east of Ypres, Belgium when the 166th Machine Gun Coy were called to lay down barrage fire on German positions during the advance. He is remembered on the Ypres Menin Gate and has no known grave. In August 1918 Percy's parents inserted the following memoriam in a local paper:

When the roll is called up yonder
And our Saviour counts the brave
Our son shall be amongst them
For his precious life he gave
No loved one stood beside him
When he gave his last farewell

Not a word of comfort could he have
From those who loved him so well
No one knows the silent heartache
Only those can tell
Who have lost their loved and dearest
Without saying Farewell

Private Frank Smart		*116th Coy Bn Machine Gun Corps*	
Service No.	9891	Age:	30
Place of birth:	Maiden Bradley, Wiltshire	Home Country:	England
Date of death:	31/07/1917	Cause of death:	Killed in action
Memorial:	Chilcompton, Somerset		
War Cemetery:	Ypres Menin Gate - Panel 56.		
Next of Kin:	Lucy May Smart (wife) – Alfred James & Rosina Smart		
Address:	Norton Down, Stratton on the Fosse, Somerset		

Coal miner Frank was the eldest son of Alfred and Rosina Smart and at the end of 1914 he married Lucy May Willis. It is likely he was either conscripted into the army or joined under the Derby Scheme, initially joining the Somerset Light Infantry and then transferring to the 116th Coy Machine Gun Corps. It is likely Frank was killed around 3.50am, by German artillery, when he was in the assembly trenches preparing for the attack on St. Julien, Belgium, on Tuesday 31 July 1917. He left a widow and young daughter.

Rifleman Frederick John Brown		*2nd Bn Rifle Brigade*	
Service No.	S/28484	Age:	20
Place of birth:	Down Ampney, Wiltshire	Home Country:	England
Date of death:	31/07/1917	Cause of death:	Died of wounds
Memorial:	Not known		
War Cemetery:	Menin Road South Military Cemetery - Grave II. E. 12.		
Next of Kin:	Frederick & Sarah A Brown		
Address:	Down Ampney, Gloucestershire		

Frederick, a farm labourer, was the eldest son of Frederick and Sarah Brown and it is likely he was either conscripted into the army or enlisted under the Derby Scheme joining the Gloucester Regiment. He was sent to the front and transferred to the 2nd Battalion Rifle Brigade who, on Tuesday 31 July 1917, were near Halfway House north east of Zillebeke, Belgium. It is likely Frederick was wounded by German shell fire and died soon after. It is interesting to note, the Register of soldier's effects states he died of wounds on 3 August 1917.

Private Ernest Fisher		*10th Bn Royal West Kent Regiment*	
Service No.	205663	Age:	18
Place of birth:	Lincoln, Lincolnshire	Home Country:	England
Date of death:	31/07/1917	Cause of death:	Killed in action
Memorial:	North Wilts Technical College, Swindon.		
War Cemetery:	Ypres Menin Gate - Panel 45 and 47.		
Next of Kin:	Jesse & Clara Fisher		
Address:	105 William Street, Swindon, Wiltshire		

Eighteen year old Ernest was the eldest son of Jesse and Clara Fisher and was educated at North Wilts Technical College, Swindon. He enlisted with the Royal West Kent Regiment and was sent to France joining the 10th Battalion. He was killed on Tuesday 31 July 1917 as the 10th Royal West Kent's advanced towards Zandvoorde taking two of their objectives. Ernest is remembered on the Ypres Menin Gate and has no known grave.

Lance Coporal Gilbert Charles Whatley		*10th Bn Liverpool Regiment*	
Service No.	357989	Age:	24
Place of birth:	Winsley, Wiltshire	Home Country:	England
Date of death:	31/07/1917	Cause of death:	Killed in action
Memorial:	Not known		
War Cemetery:	Ypres Menin Gate - Panel 4 and 6.		
Next of Kin:	Ada Whatley (wife) – Thomas & Sarah Whatley (arents)		
Address:	No 2 Westwood Road Northgate, Leyland, Lancashire		

Gilbert, a tyre repairer, was the youngest son of Thomas and Sarah Whatley and on 10 May 1913 he married Ada Weir at Leyland, Lancashire. He was a Wiltshire Regiment Territorial but at some stage he transferred to the 10th Liverpool Regiment. He was killed on Tuesday 31 July 1917 when the 10th Liverpool Regiment, advanced East of Wieltje, Belgium. The first objective on the east side of the Steen Beek, were taken with the aid of tanks that knocked out German machine guns. Gilbert is remembered on the Ypres Menin Gate and has no known grave. He left a widow and a young son.

Private Bertram Robert Dent		*1st Bn Cambridgeshire Regiment*	
Service No.	326027	Age:	23
Place of birth:	Cambridge, Cambridgeshire	Home Country:	England
Date of death:	31/07/1917	Cause of death:	Killed in action
Memorial:	Not known		
War Cemetery:	Ypres Menin Gate - 50 and 52.		
Next of Kin:	Ethel B Dent (wife) - Alfred & Harriet Dent (parents)		
Address:	12 Gloucester Terrace, Swindon, Wiltshire		

Bertram, a grocer's assistant, was the youngest son of Alfred and Harriet Dent and in the spring of 1915 he married Ethel B. Saunders at Cambridge. He volunteered for service joining the 1st Battalion Cambridgeshire Regiment and arrived in France on 14 February 1915. He was killed on Tuesday 31 July 1917 while advancing toward St. Julien, Belgium. The British attacks were subjected to repeated counterattacks when they reached the west side of St. Julien and were forced to retire. Bertram is remembered on the Ypres Menin Gate and has no known grave.

Private Albert Edward Miflin		*12th Bn Royal Fusiliers*	
Service No.	5047	Age:	24
Place of birth:	Lyneham, Wiltshire	Home Country:	England
Date of death:	31/07/1917	Cause of death:	Killed in action
Memorial:	Lyneham, Wiltshire		
War Cemetery:	Ypres Menin Gate - Panel 6 and 8.		
Next of Kin:	William and Elizabeth Miflin		
Address:	Church Farm, Lyneham, Wiltshire		

Albert, known as Bert and a solicitor's clerk, was the second son of William and Elizabeth Miflin and volunteered for service joining the 12th Battalion Royal Fusiliers. He was trained as a signaler and arrived in France on 1 September 1915. He took part in the attacks at Loos in 1915 and Guillemont at the Somme in 1916. Bert was reported missing on Tuesday 31 July 1917 when the 12th Royal Fusiliers attacked German positions to the east of Sanctuary Wood. Later Bert's parents received official information stating that their son was presumed to have been killed on the day he was reported missing. He is remembered on the Ypres Menin Gate and has no known grave.

Private Henry Joseph Brindle		*6th Bn Royal Berkshire Regiment*	
Service No.	16296	Age:	31
Place of birth:	Marston Maisey, Glos	Home Country:	England
Date of death:	31/07/1917	Cause of death:	Died of wounds
Memorial:	Avebury, East Kennett, Wiltshire		
War Cemetery:	Lijssenthoek Military Cemetery - Grave XVI. G. 8A.		
Next of Kin:	Edith Brindle (wife) – Joseph & Mary Brindle (parents)		
Address:	East Kennet, Wiltshire		

Henry, a brewery hand, was the second son of Joseph and Mary Brindle and in the spring of 1913 he married Edith Hawkins. He volunteered for service enlisting with the 6th Battalion Royal Berkshire Regiment. His father, Joseph, was an old soldier and had served in the Zulu wars and six of his seven sons volunteered for service but the seventh was rejected as medically unfit. Henry arrived in France on 11 June 1915 and on Tuesday 31 July 1917 the 6th Royal Berkshires attacked German positions east of Sanctuary Wood. Henry was wounded during the attack with gunshot wounds to the forearm, left thigh and face and evacuated to No 3 Casualty Clearing Station. He succumbed to his wounds soon after and left a widow and young son.

2nd Lt Henry Geoffrey Nelson Tarrant MC		*6th Bn Royal Berkshire Regiment*	
Service No.	N/a	Age:	22
Place of birth:	Bromley, Kent	Home Country:	England
Date of death:	31/07/1917	Cause of death:	Killed in action
Memorial:	Not known		
War Cemetery:	Hooge Crater Cemetery - Grave II. H. 7.		
Next of Kin:	Walter AgnesTarrant		
Address:	73 Croyden Road, Anerley, Kent		

Henry, known as Geoffrey, was the grandson of Mr Hayden of Trowbridge. At the outbreak of the war he volunteered for service with the Artists Rifles, the 28th London Regiment, and was sent to France on 27 March 1915. On 22 November 1916, he was given a commission with the Royal Berkshire Regiment and while serving with them he won a Military Cross for valour. He was killed in action on Tuesday 31 July 1917, when the 6th Royal Berkshires attacked German positions north of the Menin Road near Sanctuary Wood. Henry was originally buried near Surbiton Villas and after the war his remains were moved to Hooge Crater Cemetery.

Private Joseph Topp		*6th Bn Wiltshire Regiment*	
Service No.	8735	Age:	23
Place of birth:	Hilmarton, Wiltshire	Home Country:	England
Date of death:	31/07/1917	Cause of death:	Killed in action
Memorial:	Calne, Wiltshire		
War Cemetery:	Somer Farm Cemetery - Grave C. 18.		
Next of Kin:	Henry & Jane Topp		
Address:	Cowitch Cottages, Hilmarton, Wiltshire		

Reservist Joseph was the second son of Henry and Jane Topp and had joined the Wiltshire Regiment before the Great War. He arrived in France on 20 October 1914 and was sent to the 2nd Battalion

Wiltshire Regiment. It is likely he was either wounded or was suffering from illness or disease and was evacuated to England. Following his recovery, he was transferred to the 6th Battalion Wiltshire Regiment and returned to the front. At 3.50am on Tuesday 31 July 1917, the first day of the third battle of Ypres, the 6th Wiltshires were supporting the 56 Brigade in an attack on German positions east of Oostaverne, Belgium, near Green Wood and Junction Buildings. It is likely Joseph was killed by German artillery fire during the advance.

2nd Lt Frederick Charles Westmacott		*11th Bn Royal West Kent Regiment*	
Service No.	N/a	Age:	19
Place of birth:	St Germans, Cornwall	Home Country:	England
Date of death:	31/07/1917	Cause of death:	Killed in action
Memorial:	Marlborough College, Wiltshire		
War Cemetery:	Ypres Menin Gate - Panel 45 and 47		
Next of Kin:	Canon Walter & Helen Maria Maud Westmacott		
Address:	The Sanctuary, Probus, Cornwall		

Frederick was the eighth son of Canon Walter and Helen Westmacott and was educated at Marlborough Collage and had planned to go on to Trinity College, Cambridge. However, he was given a commission with the 3rd Battalion Royal West Kent Regiment. He arrived in France on 4 December 1916 and was attached to the 11th Battalion, who at 3.50am on Tuesday 31 July 1917 left their assembly trenches northwest of Hollebeke, Belgium. They attacked on the south side of the Ypres Canal capturing all their objectives and securing Hollebeke. Frederick was wounded during the attack but refused to leave his post and succumbed to his wounds soon after. He is remembered on the Ypres Menin Gate and has no known grave. His brother, Spencer Ruscombe Westmacott's name appears on panel 44 of the Menin Gate. He had been killed in action in May 1915 while serving with the Leinster Regiment.

2nd Battalion Wiltshire Regiment

At 3.40am on Tuesday 31 July 1917 the 2nd Battalion Wiltshire Regiment left the assembly trenches on the east side of Sanctuary Wood. As they made their way through the wood a German barrage came down on the old British front line and there was considerable machine gun fire from the right that hampered the 2nd Battalion Yorkshire Regiment, who were attacking on the 2nd Wiltshires right flank. There was some confusion as the attackers made their way through Sanctuary Wood and different battalions became mixed up. However, by 6.15am the first objective was taken and the trenches cleared, along with 40 German prisoners of war. The captured positions were consolidated and C Company 2nd Battalion Wiltshire Regiment attempted to bomb (hand grenade) their way down Jam Row and Jam Lane trenches killing a number of Germans. There was considerable hostile machine gun fire from the German held Stirling Castle and the woods west of Dumbarton Lakes and Inverness Copse. An attempt to capture Stirling Castle failed. At about 2pm A Company 2nd Wiltshires reported enemy massing around Dumbarton Lakes but no development took place. Heavy shelling continued around the British reserve positions and "No Man's Land" throughout the whole day.

Private Herbert Leonard Fisher		*2nd Bn Wiltshire Regiment*	
Service No.	32197	Age:	19
Place of birth:	Collingbourne Kingston	Home Country:	England
Date of death:	31/07/1917	Cause of death:	Killed in action
Memorial:	Collingbourne Ducis, Wiltshire		
War Cemetery:	Ypres Menin Gate - Panel 53		
Next of Kin:	Frederick & Elizabeth Fisher		
Address:	Southton Cottages, Collingbourne Ducis, Wiltshire		

Left: Frederick Charles Westmacott

Right: Arthur William Maill

Nineteen year old farm worker, Herbert, was the youngest son of Frederick and Elizabeth Fisher. It is likely he was either conscripted into the army or enlisted under the Derby Scheme, joining the Wiltshire Regiment. He was sent to the 2nd Battalion and was killed during the attack from Sanctuary Wood on Tuesday 31 July 1917, the first day of the third battle of Ypres. He is remembered on the Ypres Menin Gate and has no known grave. His brother Frank had been killed in France in March 1915 while serving with the Wiltshire Regiment.

Private Arthur William Maill *2nd Bn Wiltshire Regiment*

Service No.	3/9949	Age:	26
Place of birth:	Clyffe Pypard, Wiltshire	Home Country:	England
Date of death:	31/07/1917	Cause of death:	Killed in action
Memorial:	Trowbridge, Wiltshire		
War Cemetery:	Ypres Menin Gate - Panel 53.		
Next of Kin:	Albert Herbert & Alice Maill		
Address:	5 Kemp's Building's Mortimer Street, Trowbridge, Wiltshire		

Regular soldier Arthur was the only son of Albert and Alice Maill and had worked in a foundry prior to enlisting in the Wiltshire Regiment some months before the outbreak of war. He was a special reservist and arrived in France on 23 October 1914 seeing a good deal of action. William was wounded four times and on one occasion he was so seriously injured his father journeyed to France to see him in hospital. He was killed in action by a German shell on Tuesday 31 July 1917 during the attack from Sanctuary Wood, on the first day of the third battle of Ypres. He is remembered on the Ypres Menin Gate and has no known grave.

Private Edwin John Wilson *2nd Bn Wiltshire Regiment*

Service No.	203054	Age:	19
Place of birth:	Swindon, Wilts	Home Country:	England
Date of death:	31/07/1917	Cause of death:	Killed in action
Memorial:	Not knoiwn		
War Cemetery:	Ypres Menin Gate - Panel 53.		

Next of Kin:	Alfred & Bessie Mary Wilson
Address:	41 Bright Street, Swindon, Wiltshire

Nineteen year old Edwin, known as Jack was the youngest son of Alfred and Bessie Wilson. It is likely he was either conscripted into the army or enlisted under the Derby Scheme, initially joining the Somerset Light Infantry before being transferred to the Wiltshire Regiment. He was sent to the 2nd Battalion and was killed during the attack from Sanctuary Wood on Tuesday 31 July 1917, the first day of the third battle of Ypres. He is remembered on the Ypres Menin Gate and has no known grave. His brother William was to be killed in Palestine in May 1918 while serving with the Wiltshire Regiment.

Private Francis George Harper — *2nd Bn Wiltshire Regiment*

Service No.	203065	Age:	37
Place of birth:	Amesbury, Wiltshire	Home Country:	England
Date of death:	31/07/1917	Cause of death:	Killed in action
Memorial:	Alderbury, Wiltshire		
War Cemetery:	Hooge Crater Cemetery - XIII. F. 13		
Next of Kin:	Mary Harper (wife) – William & Sarah Ann Harper (parents)		
Address:	Lower Lane, Alderbury, Wiltshire		

Frances, known as Frank and a domestic gardener, was the youngest son of William and Sarah Ann Harper and toward the end of 1905 he married Mary Ann Gilbert. It is likely he was either conscripted into the army or enlisted under the Derby Scheme, initially joining the Somerset Light Infantry before being transferred to the Wiltshire Regiment. He was sent to the 2nd Battalion and was killed during the attack from Sanctuary Wood on Tuesday 31 July 1917, the first day of the third battle of Ypres. He left a widow and two young sons. In June 1919 Francis's remains were located between Clonmel Copse and Bodmin Copse and moved to Hooge Crater Cemetery.

Private George Raymond Burton — *2nd Bn Wiltshire Regiment*

Service No.	203052	Age:	23
Place of birth:	Tisbury, Wilts	Home Country:	England
Date of death:	31/07/1917	Cause of death:	Killed in action
Memorial:	Tisbury, Wiltshire		
War Cemetery:	Ypres Menin Gate - Panel 53.		
Next of Kin:	Helena Margaret Burton (wife) - George & Adelaide Burton (parents)		
Address:	High Street, Tisbury, Wiltshire		

George, a photographer, was the only child of George and Adelaide Burton and married Helena Margaret Armstrong on 1 November 1915 at St Andrews Church, Willesden. It is likely he was either conscripted into the army or enlisted under the Derby Scheme, initially joining the Somerset Light Infantry before being transferred to the Wiltshire Regiment. He was sent to the 2nd Battalion and was killed during the attack from Sanctuary Wood on Tuesday 31 July 1917, the first day of the third battle of Ypres. He is remembered on the Ypres Menin Gate and has no known grave.

Sergeant Frederick William Morriss — *2nd Bn Wiltshire Regiment*

Service No.	12245	Age:	36
Place of birth:	Wandsworth, London	Home Country:	England
Date of death:	31/07/1917	Cause of death:	Died
Memorial:	Not known		
War Cemetery:	Ypres Menin Gate - Panel 53		

Next of Kin: Blanche Ruth Morriss (wife) – Richard & Sarah Morriss (parents)
Address: Bodenham, Wiltshire

Frederick, a domestic gardener, was the second son of Richard and Sarah Morriss and on 15 October 1905 he married Blanche Ruth Fulford. He volunteered with the Wiltshire Regiment in September 1914 and arrived in France on 11 November 1914, being set to the 2nd Battalion. He was killed during the attack from Sanctuary Wood on Tuesday 31 July 1917, the first day of the third battle of Ypres. He is remembered on the Ypres Menin Gate and has no known grave. Frederick left a widow and a young family.

Private Francis Thick *2nd Bn Wiltshire Regiment*
Service No. 23652
Age: 27
Place of birth: Bishopstone, Wilts
Home Country: England
Date of death: 31/07/1917
Cause of death: Killed in action
Memorial: Bishopstone, Wiltshire
War Cemetery: Ypres Menin Gate - Panel 53.
Next of Kin: John & Martha Thick
Address: Faulston Field Barn, Bishopstone, Wiltshire

Francis, known as Frank and a carter on a farm, was the seventh son of John and Martha Thick. It is likely he was either conscripted into the army or enlisted under the Derby Scheme joining the Wiltshire Regiment. He was sent to the 2nd Battalion and was killed during the attack from Sanctuary Wood on Tuesday 31 July 1917, the first day of the third battle of Ypres. Frank is remembered on the Ypres Menin Gate and has no known grave.

Private James Perry *2nd Bn Wiltshire Regiment*
Service No. 22728
Age: 21
Place of birth: Enford, Wiltshire
Home Country: England
Date of death: 31/07/1917
Cause of death: Killed in action
Memorial: Not Known
War Cemetery: Ypres Menin Gate - Panel 53.
Next of Kin: Frederick & Emily Perry
Address: Wichester Street, Ludgershall, Wiltshire

James, a builder's labourer, was the youngest son son of Frederick and Emily Perry. It is likely he was either conscripted into the army or enlisted under the Derby Scheme joining the Wiltshire Regiment. He was sent to the 2nd Battalion and was killed during the attack from Sanctuary Wood on Tuesday 31 July 1917, the first day of the third battle of Ypres. James is remembered on the Ypres Menin Gate and has no known grave.

Private William John Burness *2nd Bn Wiltshire Regiment*
Service No. 33501
Age: 37
Place of birth: Canning Town, Middlesex
Home Country: England
Date of death: 31/07/1917
Cause of death: Killed in action
Memorial: Not known
War Cemetery: Ypres Menin Gate - Panel 53.
Next of Kin: Katie C. Burness (wife) – Joseph & Elizabeth Burness (parents)
Address: 46 Goddard Avenue, Swindon, Wiltshire

William, a tailor, was the second son of Joseph and Elizabeth Burness and in the summer of 1910 married Katie C. Clissold at Swindon. It is likely he was either conscripted into the army or enlisted under the Derby Scheme joining the Wiltshire Regiment. He was sent to the 2nd Battalion and was killed during the attack from Sanctuary Wood on Tuesday 31 July 1917, the first day of the third battle of Ypres. William is remembered on the Ypres Menin Gate and has no known grave. He left a widow and two young sons.

Private William Frederick Nicholson		*2nd Bn Wiltshire Regiment*	
Service No.	33250	Age:	30
Place of birth:	Barton St David, Somerset	Home Country:	England
Date of death:	31/07/1917	Cause of death:	Killed in action
Memorial:	Not known		
War Cemetery:	Ypres Menin Gate - Panel 53.		
Next of Kin:	Annie Nicholson (wife) - George & Elizabeth Nicholson (parents)		
Address:,	Atworth, Wiltshire - Freshford, Somerset		

William, a horseman on a farm, was the eldest son of George and Elizabeth Nicholson and at the begining of 1910 married Annie Carter at Bradford on Avon. It is likely he was either conscripted into the army or enlisted under the Derby Scheme joining the Wiltshire Regiment. He was sent to the 2nd Battalion and was killed during the attack from Sanctuary Wood on Tuesday 31 July 1917, the first day of the third battle of Ypres. William is remembered on the Ypres Menin Gate and has no known grave. He left a widow and three young sons.

Private Ernest Weeks		*2nd Bn Wiltshire Regiment*	
Service No.	23744	Age:	31
Place of birth:	Colerne, Wiltshire	Home Country:	England
Date of death:	31/07/1917	Cause of death:	Killed in action
Memorial:	Colerne, Wiltshire		
War Cemetery:	Ypres Menin Gate - Panel 53.		
Next of Kin:	Henry & Sarah Weeks		
Address:	Colerne, Wiltshire		

General labourer Ernest was the youngest son of Henry and Sarah Weeks and it is likely he was either conscripted into the army or enlisted under the Derby Scheme joining the Wiltshire Regiment. He was sent to the 2nd Battalion and was killed during the attack from Sanctuary Wood on Tuesday 31 July 1917, the first day of the third battle of Ypres. In late August 1917, the following letter from Captain W. B. Wood was received by Ernest's sister:

"It is with great regret that I am writing to inform you of the death of your brother, No. 23744 Private E. Weeks. He was killed in action by a German sniper on the 31st July and his death must have been quite painless. I hope that it will be a great comfort to you to know that he died doing his duty for King and Country, and I am sure that no one could wish for a better death than that. Again, wishing to express my most sincere sympathy for you in your great trouble."

The following memoriam appeared in a local paper in 1917:

Could we have raised his dying head
Or heard his last farewell
The grief would not have seemed so hard
To those who loved him well
No one knows the silent heartache

only those can tell
Who have lost their loved and dearest
Without saying Farewell

Ernest is remembered on the Ypres Menin Gate and has no known grave.

Private George William Mackinnon		*2nd Bn Wiltshire Regiment*	
Service No.	25782	Age:	29
Place of birth:	Urchfont, Wiltshire	Home Country:	England
Date of death:	31/07/1917	Cause of death:	Killed in action
Memorial:	Easterton, Wiltshire		
War Cemetery:	Ypres Menin Gate - Panel 53		
Next of Kin:	Ethel Mackinnon (Wife) – William & Ellen Mackinnon (parents)		
Address:	Easterton, Wiltshire		

Cowman George was the fourth son of William and Ellen Mackinnon and married Ethel Sainsbury on Christmas Eve 1910. It is likely he was either conscripted into the army or joined under the Derby Scheme, being sent to the front joining the 2nd Wiltshire Regiment. George was killed during the attack from Sanctuary Wood on Tuesday 31 July 1917, the first day of the third battle of Ypres. He is remembered on the Ypres Menin gate and has no known grave. George left a widow who was pregnant with his daughter and two young sons.

Private Reginald William Butler		*2nd Bn Wiltshire Regiment*	
Service No.	10640	Age:	19
Place of birth:	Semington, Wiltshire	Home Country:	England
Date of death:	31/07/1917	Cause of death:	Killed in action
Memorial:	Seend, Semington, Wiltshire		
War Cemetery:	Ypres Menin Gate - Panel 53.		
Next of Kin:	William & Matilda Butler		
Address:	Seend Park Farm, Semington, Wiltshire		

Reginald, known as Reggie, was the eldest son of William and Matilda Butler and volunteered for service soon after the outbreak of hostilities. He enlisted with the Wiltshire Regiment and arrived in France on 11 December 1914, being sent to the 2nd Battalion. Reggie was reported missing during the attack from Sanctuary Wood on Tuesday 31 July 1917, the first day of the third battle of Ypres. In 1920 Reggie's parents received official information stating that their son was presumed to have died on or since the day he was reported missing. He is remembered on the Ypres Menin gate and has no known grave.

Private Reginald John Matthews		*2nd Bn Wiltshire Regiment*	
Service No.	18286	Age:	25
Place of birth:	Wootton Bassett, Wiltshire	Home Country:	England
Date of death:	31/07/1917	Cause of death:	Killed in action
Memorial:	Clyffe Pypard, Wiltshire		
War Cemetery:	Ypres Menin Gate - Panel 53.		
Next of Kin:	Robert & Eliza Matthews		
Address:	The Street, Clyffe Pypard, Wiltshire		

Reginald, a gardener domestic, was the eldest son of Robert and Eliza Matthews and volunteered for service with the Wiltshire Regiment. He arrived in France on 25 June 1916 and was sent to the 2nd Battalion. Reginald was killed during the attack from Sanctuary Wood on Tuesday 31 July 1917, the first day of the third battle of Ypres. He is remembered on the Ypres Menin gate and has no known first day of the third battle of Ypres. He is remembered on the Ypres Menin gate and has no known grave. In 1918 Reginald's parents placed the following memoriam in a local paper:

Stars shine upon a silent grave,
Of one who died our land to save:
We loved him dearly, God thought best
To take him to eternal rest.

Private Leslie Edward J Lawrence		*2nd Bn Wiltshire Regiment*	
Service No.	13956	Age:	19
Place of birth:	Calne, Wiltshire	Home Country:	England
Date of death:	31/07/1917	Cause of death:	Killed in action
Memorial:	Calne, Wiltshire		
War Cemetery:	Ypres Menin Gate - Panel 53.		
Next of Kin:	Edward John & Florence Beatrice Lawrence		
Address:	36 Pippin Road, Calne, Wiltshire		

Leslie was the eldest son of Edward John and Florence Beatrice Lawrence and volunteered for service when he was seventeen years of age. He enlisted with the Wiltshire Regiment and arrived in France on 18 May 1915, being sent to the 2nd Battalion. Leslie was killed during the attack from Sanctuary Wood on Tuesday 31 July 1917, the first day of the third battle of Ypres. He is remembered on the Ypres Menin gate and has no known grave.

Private Wilfred Manley Greenman		*2nd Bn Wiltshire Regiment*	
Service No.	33245	Age:	22
Place of birth:	Swindon, Wiltshire	Home Country:	England
Date of death:	31/07/1917	Cause of death:	Killed in action
Memorial:	Swindon Christ Church, Wiltshire		
War Cemetery:	Ypres Menin Gate - Panel 53.		
Next of Kin:	Thomas & Ada Greenman		
Address:	128 Victoria Road, Swindon, Wiltshire		

Wilfred was the youngest son of Thomas and Ada Greenman and was employed at Nightingale Farm working with his father. He was described as a gentle lad and in his spare time had gained something of a reputation as a billiard player, at the Christ Church Young Men's Club. He was conscripted into the army in April 1916 and was attached to the Wiltshire Yeomanry before being transferred to the Wiltshire Regiment. At Christmas 1916 he was sent to France joining the 2nd Battalion and was killed during the attack from Sanctuary Wood, during the third battle of Ypres. The Commonwealth War Grave Commission state he was killed on Tuesday 31 July 1917. However, the following letter from Lieutenant S. Collier states:

"It is with the very deepest pain that I have to write to you and confirm the death in action of your son, W. Greenman on the evening of August 1st. He was the gunner of my Lewis gun team, and I had always thought a great deal of him, as he was a good upright boy. I believe he had been with the Royal Wiltshire Yeomanry, which is my own regiment. He followed me closely in the attack the day before and he and I were the first in the enemy's trenches. It is characteristic of him that although a first-class soldier he was very kind-hearted and I shall never forget the way he stopped me from killing the German I had captured. All through the battle he behaved with great gallantry. He was severely wounded by a shell on the evening of August 1st and died before we could get him to the dressing station. He is buried in the German position which he helped to capture. If I can give you any further particulars, I will do so if you write."

Above: A roadside dressing station near Bosinghe

Right: Percy White

Wilfred's burial site was lost and he is today remembered on the Ypres Menin Gate.

Private Percy White		*2nd Bn Wiltshire Regiment*	
Service No.	31786	Age:	19
Place of birth:	Bradford on Avon, Wilts	Home Country:	England
Date of death:	31/07/1917	Cause of death:	Killed in action
Memorial:	Moulton, Bradford on Avon, Wiltshire		
War Cemetery:	Ypres Menin Gate - Panel 53.		
Next of Kin:	Mark & Emma White		
Address:	44 Newtown, Bradford on Avon, Wiltshire		

Nineteen year old Percy was the youngest of Mark and Emma White and was employed as a rubber worker by Spencer Moulton and Co. He originally volunteered for service with the Wiltshire Regiment on 16 February 1915 with the intent of joining the band of the 8th Battalion Wiltshire Regiment. However, he was discharged on 17 May 1915, being an under-age soldier. He was called up and conscripted into the army in July 1916 and after completing his training was sent to France on his 19th birthday, joining the 2nd Battalion Wiltshire Regiment. Percy was killed during the attack from Sanctuary Wood on Tuesday 31 July 1917, the first day of the third battle of Ypres. Lieutenant W.C. Shaw of the Wiltshire Regiment wrote the following to Percy's parents:

"I deeply regret to inform you that your son Pte. Percy White, was killed instantaneously by a shell. His death is a great loss to me, for he was such a brave little fellow and such a good soldier, always cheerful and popular with everyone. I am so very sorry for you in your great trouble."

He is remembered on the Ypres Menin gate and has no known grave. In1918 Percy's parents inserted the following memoriam in a local paper:

For many years, our family chain
was fondly linked together
But oh, that chain has broken now
One link has gone for ever

Left: Albert Edward Newton

Right: Kenneth Mountney James Fergusson

Corporal Albert Edward Newton		*2nd Bn Wiltshire Regiment*	
Service No.	22560	Age:	40
Place of birth:	Regents Park, London	Home Country:	England
Date of death:	31/07/1917	Cause of death:	Killed in action
Memorial:	Great Western Railway, Paddington		
War Cemetery:	Ypres Menin Gate - Panel 53.		
Next of Kin:	Elizabeth Hasterley Newton (wife) – Albert & Mary Newton (parents)		
Address:	82 Cricklade Road, Gorse Hill, Swindon, Wiltshire		

Albert was the eldest son of Albert and Mary Newton and was employed as a labourer in the Carriage and Wagon department of the Great Western Railway Works in Swindon. At the beginning of 1906 he married Elizabeth Hasterley Williams at Swindon and it is likely he was either conscripted into the army or enlisted under the Derby Scheme, joining the Wiltshire Regiment. He was sent to the 2nd Battalion and was killed during the attack from Sanctuary Wood on Tuesday 31 July 1917, the first day of the third battle of Ypres. He is remembered on the Ypres Menin Gate and has no known grave. Albert left a wife and a young family.

Lt. Kenneth Mountney James Fergusson		*2nd Bn Lincolnshire Regiment*	
Service No.	N/a	Age:	24
Place of birth:	London, London	Home Country:	England
Date of death:	31/07/1917	Cause of death:	Killed in action
Memorial:	Littlehampton, Sussex – Marlborough College, Wiltshire		
War Cemetery:	Ypres Menin Gate - Panel 21		
Next of Kin:	James & Constance Fergusson		
Address:	4 Wynnstay Gardens, London, London		

Kenneth was the only son of James and Constance Fergusson and was educated at Marlborough College. At the outbreak of hostilities he joined the University and Public Schools battalion and in October 1914 he went to Sandhurst. In March 1915, he was given a commission with the 2nd Battalion Lincolnshire Regiment and was sent to France in February 1916. He was promoted to Lieutenant in April 1916 and later attached to a trench mortar battery, who he was serving with when he was killed in action on Tuesday 31 July 1917. He is remembered on the Ypres Menin Gate and has no known grave.

Rifleman Howard Cook *3rd Bn Rifle Brigade*

Service No.	S/28492	Age:	21
Place of birth:	Alderton, Wiltshire	Home Country:	England
Date of death:	31/07/1917	Cause of death:	Killed in action
Memorial:	Alderton, Wiltshire		
War Cemetery:	Ypres Menin Gate - Panel 46 - 48 and 50		
Next of Kin:	Thomas John & Florence Cook		
Address:Little	Stoke, Patchway, Bristol, Gloucestershire		

Howard, a farm labourer was the second son of Thomas John and Florence Cook and enlisted with the army under the Derby Scheme on 13 November 1915. He was called up on 23 June 1916 joining the 11th Battalion Gloucester Regiment and in September 1916 transferred to the Training Reserve. He arrived in France on 2 December 1916 and was attached to the 178th Tunnelling Company Royal Engineers. In January 1916 he was evacuated to No 2 Canadian Casualty Clearing Station suffering from trench feet and then sent to the 10th General Hospital at Rouen where his condition was found to be severe which then led to his evacuation to England. Following his recovery, he returned to France on 16 June 1917 and was sent to the 3rd Battalion Rifle Brigade on 12 July 1917. At 3.50am on Tuesday 31 July 1917 the 17th Brigade, left their assembly trenches near Mount Sorrel and attacked through Shrewsbury Forest in the direction of Gheluvelt. The 3rd Rifle Brigade were used to consolidate positions and were subjected to German machine gun fire from a strong point at Tower Hamlets and German pill boxes at Lower Star Post. Howard was initially reported wounded during the attack, and later reported wounded and missing. In February 1918 Howard's parents were officially informed he was presumed to have been killed in action on the day he was reported missing. Howard is remembered on the Ypres Menin Gate and has no known grave.

Private Charles William Lawrence *2nd Bn Devonshire Regiment*

Service No.	204880	Age:	38
Place of birth:	Lambeth, Surrey	Home Country:	England
Date of death:	31/07/1917	Cause of death:	Killed in action
Memorial:	Amesbury, Wiltshire		
War Cemetery:	Ypres Menin Gate - Panel 21.		
Next of Kin:	Frances Maria Lawrence (wife) – Alfred & Rosina Lawrence (parents)		
Address:	Yew Tree Laundry, Salisbury Street, Amesbury, Wiltshire		

Charles was the youngest son of Alfred and Rosina Lawrence and was a whitesmith (tinsmith) in a government balloon factory. Toward the end of 1909 he married Frances Maria Pike at Amesbury and it is likely he was either conscripted into the army or joined under the Derby Scheme, being sent to the front joining the 2nd Battalion Devonshire Regiment. Charles was killed on Tuesday 31 July 1917, the first day of the third battle of Ypres. At 3.50am the 2nd Devons left their assembly trenches near Railway Wood and advanced north east on the south side of the Ypres – Roulers railway, toward Zonnebeke. The attackers were subjected to German artillery and machine gun fire throughout the advance, but achieved all their objectives. At the end of the day the 2nd Devons were positioned near South Station Buildings and Sexton House. Charles is remembered on the Ypres Menin Gate and has no known grave. He left a widow and three young daughters.

Private William John Franklin *2nd Bn Devonshire Regiment*

Service No.	27079	Age:	41
Place of birth:	Warminster, Wiltshire	Home Country:	England
Date of death:	31/07/1917	Cause of death:	Killed in action
Memorial:	Warminster, Wiltshire		
War Cemetery:	Ypres Menin Gate - Panel 21.		

Left: Alfred Joseph Elton Sunderland

Right: Eric Arthur Frank Coleman

Next of Kin:	Minnie Florence Franklin (wife) – William & Elizabeth Franklin (parents)
Address:	26 Worcester Buildings, Larkhall, Bath, Somerset

William, a brick layer, was the eldest son of William and Elizabeth Franklin and in 1903 he married Minnie Florence Read at Warminster. It is likely he was either conscripted into the army or joined under the Derby Scheme being sent to the front joining the 2nd Battalion Devonshire Regiment. William was killed on Tuesday 31 July 1917, the first day of the third battle of Ypres. At 3.50am 2nd Devons left their assembly trenches near Railway Wood and advanced north east on the south side of the Ypres – Roulers railway, toward Zonnebeke. The attackers were subjected to German artillery and machine gun fire throughout the advance, but achieved all their objectives. At the end of the day the 2nd Devons were positioned near South Station Buildings and Sexton House. William is remembered on the Ypres Menin Gate and has no known grave. William left a widow and a young son. His brother Richard James Franklin had been killed at Gallipoli in August 1915.

Lieutenant Col. Alfred Joseph Elton Sunderland 2nd Bn Devonshire Regiment

Service No.	N/a	Age:	42
Place of birth:	Bedford, Bedfordshire	Home Country:	England
Date of death:	31/07/1917	Cause of death:	Killed in action
Memorial:	Eggington, Bedfordshire - Marlborough College, Wiltshire		
War Cemetery:	Belgian Battery Corner Cemetery - Grave I. F. 2.		
Next of Kin:	James & Florence Margaret Sunderland		
Address:	Egginton Vicarage, Leighton Buzzard, Bedfordshire		

Alfred was the eldest son of Rev. James and Florence Sunderland and was educated at Marlborough College. After leaving Marlborough he went to the Royal Military College at Sandhurst and in 1895 he was given a commission with the Devonshire Regiment. He served in the Boer War from 1899 to 1902 and in 1902 was promoted to Captain, being given home duties. He arrived in France on 3 November 1914 with the 2nd Battalion Devonshire Regiment, but was invalided to England in 1915. He returned to France in 1916, where he was promoted to Lieutenant Colonel and given command of the 2nd Battalion Devonshire Regiment, being mentioned twice in despatches. Alfred was killed at 10.50am, by German rifle fire, while leading the battalion along the line south of the Roulers railway, toward Zonnebeke. His body was recovered from the battlefield and taken to Belgian Battery Corner Cemetery south west of Ypres.

2nd Lt. Eric Arthur Frank Coleman		*3rd Bn. Norfolk Regiment attd Machine Gun Corps*	
Service No.	N/a	Age:	31
Place of birth:	Coleshill, Buckinghamshire	Home Country:	England
Date of death:	31/07/1917	Cause of death:	Killed in action
Memorial:	Marlborough College, Wiltshire		
War Cemetery:	Ypres Menin Gate - Panel 4		
Next of Kin:	Lilian Coleman (wife) – Capt. George Drury & Edith Isabel Coleman (parents)		
Address:	5 St. John's Terrace, Wakefield, Yorkshire		

Eric was the third son of Capt. George and Edith Coleman and was educated at Brighton and Marlborough College. At the outbreak of hostilities he was in Vancouver, Canada, and volunteered for service with the Canadian Royal Engineers. He came to England with the Canadian 1 Division and was given a commission in January 1915 transferring to the Norfolk Regiment. In August 1915 he married Lillian Harris at Wakefield, Yorkshire. She was the daughter of the Chief Constable of Wakefield. After serving with the 3rd and 10th Battalions Norfolk Regiment, he transferred to the Heavy Branch Machine Gun Corps (Tanks), and went with a tank unit to France in June 1916. Eric was killed Tuesday 31 July 1917 near Wieltje, Belgium, his Colonel wrote:

"He was very keen and inspired every member of his crew with the same feelings. They would have done anything for him. Major Hawkins, his Company Commander, is writing to you and will give you all such particulars as we have; for myself I can only say that we have lost a friend, and the battalion an officer whom I cannot replace."

One of his men wrote:

"I offer you my deepest sympathy in your sad loss and bereavement, and so do all the crew who had the pleasure of serving under such a gentleman and hero as Lieutenant Coleman was. When I sit, and think of this awful tragedy that has befallen us, it makes me ill, as I lost an officer who was a chum to all, always merry and bright, ready for any danger when duty called. He respected all and sundry, and helped many in distress; worked hard for our comfort and benefit, and I can assure you every brother officer and man in the battalion respected him and would have followed him anywhere, as we did, for we had implicit trust and every confidence in such a brave gentleman, who fought game to the last.

A British knocked out Tank near St. Julien

Although an officer and I his driver, we shared the confidence in each other, and had various views in common. I feel now I have lost a friend who was dear to me, a hero and a man. We crawled up on the 30th, at night, waiting for morning to go over the top to strafe a cunning, and cruel foe. Lieutenant Coleman and seven of us, his crew, slept near each other, waiting for the light of day to bid for victory or death. At the given time, we went over as merry as sandboys, our Governor, as we called him, leading the way. He never seemed to care what was falling around us. He just led us like a hero would. We did good work too, but it was a hot time and difficult."

Another officer wrote:

"I was not actually present when Eric met his death, which you will be glad to know must have been instantaneous, and that he cannot have suffered at all. He died in the execution of his duty, and that he performed always to the satisfaction of his superior officers. In this, his first Tank action, he was working on the left of the company; was first over, and, while advancing to push through the first waves of infantry, had led his Tank on foot all the way. Consequently, he had reached his objective early on, and was rendering good assistance to the infantry, who were held up by machine gun fire at the time, near the strong point at Spree Farm, east of Wieltje. Up till then he had been outside his Tank, leading it over very difficult ground, sodden with rain and aerated by shell fire. When summoned to the assistance of the infantry on his right, he got inside and went to their help, which he seems to have rendered satisfactorily. Then a shell hit the the left track, breaking six track plates and stopping the Tank. He said: "What's that?" got outside to examine, and another shell came, hitting the Tank and killing him, and wounding one of the crew. I may say that if all the junior officers in this action had shown the same devotion to duty and led their Tanks forward, the company would have done better than it did. He always worked hard, and could be relied on to execute any duty to the best of his ability."

Eric was buried in the track of his Tank near Spree Farm south of St Julien, Belgium. His grave site was lost and he is today remembered on the Ypres Menin Gate.

2nd Lieutenant Edwin Horler		*122nd Coy Machine Gun Corps*	
Service No.	N/a	Age:	29
Place of birth:	Bath, Somerset	Home Country:	England
Date of death:	31/07/1917	Cause of death:	Killed in action
Memorial:	North Wilts Technical College, Swindon, Wiltshire		
War Cemetery:	Voormezeele Enclosure No1 and No2 - Grave I. E. 21.		
Next of Kin:	John & Emma Horler		
Address:	Stoney Littleton, Shoscombe, Bath, Somerset		

Edwin, a school master, was the only son of John and Emma Horler and was educated at North Wilts Technical College. He enlisted under the Derby Scheme on 27 November 1915 joining the Somerset Light Infantry. He was called up on 29 February 1916 and transferred to the Machine Gun Corps on 13 May 1916. He was given a commission with the Machine Gun Corps on 25 January 1916 and sent to France on 6 June 1917 joining 122nd Coy Machine Gun Corps. On Tuesday 31 July 1917 Eric was given command of 2 and 3 Sections who were supporting the 11th Battalion Royal West Kents and the 18th Kings Royal Rifle Corps, attacking German positions near Hollebeke, Belgium. They left the British assembly trenches at 3.50.am between the Ypres Canal and St. Eloi. Edwin was shot by a sniper during the early part of the advance.

Private William George Baker		*11th Bn South Wales Borderers*	
Service No.	40481	Age:	29
Place of birth:	Devizes, Wilts	Home Country:	England
Date of death:	31/07/1917	Cause of death:	Killed in action

Memorial: Devizes, Wiltshire
War Cemetery: Poelcapelle British Cemetery - Grave XLIX. C. 10
Next of Kin: Susan E. Baker (wife) - Frank & Annie Baker (parents)
Address: 1 St James Place, Devizes, Wiltshire

William, a boot maker, was the eldest son of Frank and Annie Baker and married prior to the start of the Great War. It is likely he was conscripted into the army or enlisted under the derby scheme. He joined the Wiltshire Regiment but was transferred to the 11th Service Battalion South Wales Borderers. He arrived in France in January 1917 and had been wounded twice. On Tuesday 31 July 1917 the 11th South Wales Borderers had assembled at Hulls farm on the west bank of the Ypres Canal, south of Boesinghe, Belgium. At 5.30am they crossed the canal and advanced northeast in the direction of Langemarke. As the 11th South Wales Borderers approached the Steenbeke they got into attack formation and met considerable resistance and German machine gun fire. All the opposition was mopped up and the Germans were cleared from the Steenbeke, and the 11th South Wales Borderers crossed at the Au Bon Gite bridgehead. They were then subjected to considerable German artillery fire and machine gun fire coming from the area around Langemarke. William was killed by a German sniper on Tuesday 31 July 1917. He left a widow and two small children and in August 1918 William's widow inserted the following memoriam in a local paper:

He little thought when leaving home
That he would never return
And now he lies in a soldier's grave
Somewhere in France
His cheery ways his smiling face, are a pleasure to recall
There is nothing left to answer but his photo on the wall

In October 1920 William's remains were located near Chien Farm on the west side of the Steenbeke Stream. He was identified by the means of a disc and his remains relocated to Poelcappelle British Cemetery.

8th Battalion Somerset Infantry Oostaverne
On Tuesday 31 July 1917, the 8th Battalion Somerset Infantry were in the second phase of the attack east of Oostaverne, Belgium. At 7.50am the British were shelled by German artillery causing some casualties and just afterwards the 8th Somersets advanced to clear Beek Wood, establishing a new line from the Wambeek just south of Wam Farm. By 9am the attack had succeeded and the 8th Somersets were digging in near Beek Farm. They then went forward and began clearing Beek Enlosures. Toward the end of the day the 8th Somersets began to consolidate their positions. Throughout the advance the 8th Somersets faced hostile snipers, machine guns and artillery.

Lance Corporal Harry Benjamin J Ferris *8th Bn Somerset Light Infantry*
Service No. 27820 Age: 35
Place of birth: Rowde, Wiltshire Home Country: England
Date of death: 31/07/1917 Cause of death: Killed in action
Memorial: Weston Super Mare, Somerset
War Cemetery: Ypres Menin Gate - Panel 21.
Next of Kin: Mary E. Ferris (wife) – Harry & Harriet Ferris (parents)
Address: Weston Super Mare, Somerset – No 5 Short Street, Devizes

Harry was the eldest son of Harry and Harriet Pearce and after the death of Harry's father his mother Harriet, remarried Staff Drummer Pearce of the Wiltshire Regiment. Young Harry influenced by his step father enlisted with the Wiltshire Regiment as a boy drummer at fourteen years of age and was sent to serve with the 3rd Battalion Wiltshire Regiment at St Helena, guarding Boer prisoners of war. After seven years service with the Wiltshire Regiment he left the army and with his step father's health failing he came back to Devizes to help his mother. He found employment with Eastman's Butchers Ltd and worked with the firm for fifteen years, nine of which were as manager of the Weston-Super-Mare branch. Harry was a keen member of the Buffaloes being secretary for 3 years in the town and in the summer of 1911 he married Mary Offer at Weston-Super-Mare. Because of his position in the company Harry did not enlist at the outbreak of hostilities ut was called up in February 1917 initially rejoining the Wiltshire Regiment and after a short period of training he was sent to France being transferred to the 8th Battalion Somerset Light Infantry. Harry was described as having the kindest of hearts, the pleasantest of manners, the most gentlemanly instincts and wrote to his wife and little son every 6th day but no letter was received after 6 August 1917. In his last letter dated 30 July 1917 Harry had simply stated:

"Moving in a day or two."

One of those killed during the advance was Harry. He is remembered on the Ypres Menin Gate and has no known grave. He left a widow and young son.

Private Thomas Butterworth		*8th Bn Somerset Light Infantry*	
Service No.	27819	Age:	37
Place of birth:	Bradford on Avon, Wilts	Home Country:	England
Date of death:	31/07/1917	Cause of death:	Killed in action
Memorial:	Bradford on Avon, Bradford on Avon Christ Church		
War Cemetery:	Ypres Menin Gate - Panel 21.		
Next of Kin:	James & Rebbecca Butterwoth		
Address:	Bradford on Avon, Wiltshire		

Thomas, a house painter, was the youngest son of James and Rebbecca Butterwoth and it is likely he was either conscripted into the army or joined under the Derby Scheme initially joining the Wiltshire Regiment. He was sent to the front and transferred to the 8th Battalion Somerset Infantry. He was killed in action on Tuesday 31 July 1917 when the 8th Somersets attacked German positions east of Oostaverne, Belgium. He is remembered on the Ypres Menin Gate and has no known grave.

Lance Sergeant Edgar Fiander		*8th Bn Somerset Light Infantry*	
Service No.	19206	Age:	22
Place of birth:	Milton Abbas, Dorset	Home Country:	England
Date of death:	31/07/1917	Cause of death:	Killed in action
Memorial:	Laverstock, Wiltshire		
War Cemetery:	Ypres Menin Gate - Panel 21.		
Next of Kin:	Robert & Catherine Fiander		
Address:	Lower Village, Offwell, Honiton, Devon		

Edgar, a hotel worker, was the second son of Robert and Catherine Fiander and volunteered for service joining the 8th Battalion Somerset Infantry. He arrived in France on 11 October 1915 and was promoted to the rank of Lance Sergeant. Edgar was killed in action on Tuesday 31 July 1917 when the 8th Somersets attacked German positions east of Oostaverne, Belgium. He is remembered on the Ypres Menin Gate and has no known grave.

Private Walter Chunn		*8th Bn Somerset Light Infantry*	
Service No.	27803	Age:	19
Place of birth:	Mildenhall, Wiltshire	Home Country:	England

Date of death: 31/07/1917 Cause of death: Killed in action
Memorial: Not known
War Cemetery: Ypres Menin Gate - Panel 21.
Next of Kin: Edward & Eliza Chunn
Address: Mildenhall, Wiltshire

Walter, a thatchers labourer was the second son of Edward and Eliza Chunn and it is likely he was either conscripted into the army or joined under the Derby Scheme joining the 8th Battalion Somerset Infantry. He was killed in action on Tuesday 31 July 1917 when the 8th Somersets attacked German positions east of Oostaverne, Belgium. He is remembered on the Ypres Menin Gate and has no known grave. His brother Frank Chunn had been killed at Loos in 1915.

Private Samuel Tyler Gillard *8th Bn Somerset Light Infantry*
Service No. 27762 Age: 29
Place of birth: Swindon, Wiltshire Home Country: England
Date of death: 31/07/1917 Cause of death: Died of wounds
Memorial: No. 3 Shop Memorial, Great Western Railway Works
War Cemetery: Ypres Menin Gate - Panel 21
Next of Kin: Frederick & Maria Gillard
Address: 23 Cromwell Street, Swindon, Wiltshire

Samuel was the youngest son of Frederick and Maria Gillard and was employed as a labourer at No. 3 shop, Great Western Railway Works at Swindon. It is likely he was either conscripted into the army or enlisted under the Derby Scheme joining the 8th Battalion Somerset Infantry. He was killed in action on Tuesday 31 July 1917 when the 8th Somersets attacked German positions east of Oostaverne, Belgium. He is remembered on the Ypres Menin Gate and has no known grave.

Private Herbert Pullin *8th Bn Somerset Light Infantry*
Service No. 27861 Age: 19
Place of birth: Nettleton, Wiltshire Home Country: England
Date of death: 31/07/1917 Cause of death: Killed in action
Memorial: Leigh Delemere, Wiltshire
War Cemetery: Ypres Menin Gate - Grave Panel 21.
Next of Kin: George & Ellen Pullin
Address: Green Barrow Farm, Summer Lane, Castle Combe, Wiltshire

Herbert, was the youngest son of George and Ellen Pullin and volunteered for service with the Somerset Light Infantry in July 1915 at the age of seventeen, his character was described as bright and cheerful. He was killed in action on Tuesday 31 July 1917 when the 8th Somersets attacked German positions east of Oostaverne, Belgium. He is remembered on the Ypres Menin Gate and has no known grave.

CSM Herbert Moody *8th Bn Somerset Light Infantry*
Service No. 27850 Age: 27
Place of birth: Sherfield, Hampshire Home Country: England
Date of death: 31/07/1917 Cause of death: Killed in action
Memorial: Dorchester, Dorset
War Cemetery: Ypres Menin Gate - Grave Panel 21.
Next of Kin: Ethel Ellen Moody (wife) - Walter & Annie Moody (parents)
Address: Whiteparish, Wiltshire

Herbert, a groom and gardener, was the eldest son of Walter and Annie Moody. It is likely he enlisted within the Wiltshire Regiment before the Great War, but was transferred to to the Somerset Light Infantry. On Boxing Day 1916 when he was serving at Littlemoor Camp Weymouth, he married Ethel Ellen Perkins at St Mary's Fordington, Dorchester. He was killed in action on Tuesday 31 July 1917 when the 8th Somersets attacked German positions east of Oostaverne, Belgium. Herbert had been serving as Company Sergeant Major and had been recommended for a commission and was about to be promoted to an officer at the time of his death. He is remembered on the Ypres Menin Gate and has no known grave.

Private Thomas Kimber		*8th Bn Somerset Light Infantry*	
Service No.	27855	Age:	30
Place of birth:	Hodson, Wiltshire	Home Country:	England
Date of death:	31/07/1917	Cause of death:	Killed in action
Memorial:	Not known		
War Cemetery:	Ypres Menin Gate - Grave Panel 21.		
Next of Kin:	Ethel M Kimber (wife) – Charles & Mary Ann Kimber (parents)		
Address:	3 Swindon Road, Swindon, Wiltshire		

Thomas, a tailor, was the youngest son of Charles and Mary Ann Kimber and toward the end of 1912 he married Ethel Fry at Swindon. It is likely he was either conscripted into the army or enlisted under the Derby Scheme joining the 8th Battalion Somerset Infantry. He was killed in action on Tuesday 31 July 1917 when the 8th Somersets attacked German positions east of Oostaverne, Belgium. He is remembered on the Ypres Menin Gate and has no known grave. He left a widow and a young daughter.

2nd Lieutenant Osmond Pickard Brown		*11th Bn Bn Royal West Kent Regiment*	
Service No.	N/a	Age:	19
Place of birth:	Aylestone, Leicestershire	Home Country:	England
Date of death:	31/07/1917	Cause of death:	Died of wounds
Memorial:	Marlborough College, Wiltshire		
War Cemetery:	Oak Dump Cemetery - Grave C. 21		
Next of Kin:	Albert Edward & Florence Mary Brown		
Address:	The Firs, Aylestone, Leicestershire		

Osmond was the only child of Albert and Florence Brown and was educated at Marlborough College. At Easter 1916, he went to Cambridge joining the Officer Training Corps and was given a commission with the 3rd Battalion Royal West Kent Regiment. He was sent to France in April 1917 and attached to the 11th Battalion. At 3.50am on Tuesday 31 July 1917 the 11th Royal West Kent's left assembly trenches east of St. Elooi and advanced through White Chateau Woods toward Hollebeke and dug in just west of Hollebeke. Osmond was mortally wounded while leading his men and succumbed to his wounds soon after.

Captain Arthur Lea Harris		*4th Bn Loyal North Lancashire Regiment*	
Service No.	N/a	Age:	31
Place of birth:	Blackburn, Lancashire	Home Country:	England
Date of death:	31/07/1917	Cause of death:	Killed in action
Memorial:	Walton-le-Dale - St. Leonards Church,		
War Cemetery:	Ypres Menin Gate - Panel 41 and 43		
Next of Kin:	Winifred Margaret Harris (wife) - Seymour Frederick & Mary E. Harris (parents)		
Address:	Pear Tree Bank, Ashton on the Ribble, Lancashire		

Left: Osmond Pickard Brown

Right: Arthur Lea Harris

Arthur was the only son of Seymour and Mary Harris and was educated at Marlborough College. On leaving he studied law and qualified to be a solicitor in 1909. He became a partner of Houghton Myres and Reveley, Preston in 1911. In April 1912, he married Winifred Margaret Arminson at Preston. He was well known in Preston and was secretary to the Grasshoppers Rugby Football Club, an active member of the tennis club and an amateur actor. He volunteered for service with the Loyal North Lancashire Regiment, the day following the declaration of war. He arrived in France in April 1915 with the 4th Battalion, as transport officer, and was there until November 1915 when he came back to England for an operation on his knee. Following his recovery, he returned to his unit in February 1917. He was killed on Tuesday 31 July 1917 while leading A Company northeast of Wieltje Belgium. Arthur is remembered on the Ypres Menin Gate and has no known grave. He left a widow and young daughter.

Rifleman Reginald Robert Henstridge		*18th Bn Kings Royal Rifle Corps*	
Service No.	A/201845	Age:	20
Place of birth:	Battersea, Surrey	Home Country:	England
Date of death:	31/07/1917	Cause of death:	Killed in action
Memorial:	St Augustines, Swindon, Wiltshire		
War Cemetery:	Ypres Menin Gate - Panel 51 and 53.		
Next of Kin:	Henry George & Fanny Henstridge		
Address:	89 Bruce Street, Rodbourne, Swindon, Wiltshire		

Reginald, known as Reggie was the third son of Henry and Fanny Henstridge and it is likely he was either conscripted into the army or enlisted under the Derby Scheme joining the 18th Battalion Kings Royal Rifle Corps. He was killed on Tuesday 31 July 1917 during the advance toward German positions at Hollebeke. The 18th Kings Royal Rifle Corps attacked on the south side of the Yser- Comines Canal and it is likely Reggie met his death when they were held up by German machine gun fire coming from Hollebeke church. He is remembered on the Ypres Menin Gate and has no known grave. In 1918 Reggie's parents inserted the following memoriam in a local paper:

When alone in our sorrow and bitter tears flow,
There stealeth a dream of a sweet long ago;
And unknown to the world He stands by our side
And whispers these words, "Death cannot divide."

Left: Percy Stanley Abel Edwards

Right: George E. Randall

Just when his hopes were brightest,
Just when his thoughts were best,
He was called from this world of sorrow
To that home of eternal rest.

"Called to a higher service."

Private Percy Stanley Abel Edwards		*13th Bn Royal Welsh Fusiliers*	
Service No.	235313	Age:	20
Place of birth:	Bristol, Gloucestershire	Home Country:	England
Date of death:	31/07/1917	Cause of death:	Killed in action
Memorial:	Not known		
War Cemetery:	Dragoon Camp Cemetery - Grave B. 26.		
Next of Kin:	Joshua Abel & Mary Ann Edwards		
Address:	46 Senaca Street St George, Bristol, Gloucestershire		

Percy was the only son of Joshua and Mary Ann Edwards and was employed as a porter in the Traffic Department of the Great Western Railway at Devizes. He enlisted under the Derby Scheme on 10 December 1915, joining the Wiltshire Regiment and was called up on 27 February 1917. He was sent to France with a draft for the Wiltshire Regiment on 5 June 1917 and transferred to the 13th Battalion Royal Welsh Fusiliers on 24 June 1917. Percy sent his last letter home on 28 July 1917 stating only he and a Corporal had been transferred to the 13th Royal Welsh Fusiliers, who at 3.50am on 31 July 1917 advanced behind a British barrage toward Pilckem Ridge. The attackers were met with opposition from Marsoin and Stray Farms on the right and Pilckem on the left. Percy was killed in the attack and later buried in Villa Gretchen Cemetery which later had its name changed to Dragoon Camp Cemetery. Percy's death greatly troubled his parents and Joshua Edwards wrote to the army asking for details of other men who had been transferred from the Wiltshires to the 13th Welsh Fusiliers to find out the circumstances of his son's death. It is not known whether he received any further information.

Private George E. Randall		*1st Bn Coldstream Guards*	
Service No.	19204	Age:	28
Place of birth:	Farrington Gurney, Somerset	Home Country:	England
Date of death:	31/07/1917	Cause of death:	Killed in action

Memorial:	Not known
War Cemetery:	Ypres Menin Gate - Panel 11
Next of Kin:	Joseph & Ann Randall
Address:	Rush Hill, Farrington Gurney, Somerset

George was the youngest son of Joseph and Ann Randall and had been employed by the Great Western Railway, in the Traffic Department at Dauntsey. It is likely he was either conscripted into the army or enlisted under the Derby Scheme joining the 1st Battalion Coldstream Guards who at 3.50am on Tuesday 31 July 1917 left their assembly trenches near Boesinghe, crossing the Yser Canal. After the first objective had been taken the 1st Coldstream Guards formed up and advanced taking the second objective on Pilckem Ridge. They then dug in and consolidated the position. George was one of 22 men killed during the attack and is remembered on the Ypres Menin Gate memorial.

Lance Coporal Arthur George Reed *3rd Bn Grenadier Guards*

Service No.	14577	Age:	22
Place of birth:	Nettleton, Wiltshire	Home Country:	England
Date of death:	31/07/1917	Cause of death:	Killed in action
Memorial:	Nettleton, Burton, Wiltshire		
War Cemetery:	Artillery Wood Cemetery - Grave IV. F. 3.		
Next of Kin:	Doris Amelia Reed (wife) - George & Sarah Reed (parents)		
Address:	Nettleton, Wiltshire		

Arthur joined the Grenadier Guards in 1910 using the name George Reed and stated his age was nineteen years when in fact he was fifteen years of age. He left the army prior to the Great War and joined the police force in Abergavenny and at the outbreak of hostilities he was an attendant at the Brecon and Radnor Asylum. Being a member of the reserve he was called back to the colours rejoining the 3rd Battalion Grenadier Guards and arriving in France on 12 September 1914. He fought at the retreat from Mons, the Marne, the Aisne and the first battle of Ypres. He was wounded in the head at Le Bassee by an explosive bullet and was sent to England to recover for six weeks. While convalescing he married nurse Doris Amelia Pewtner in early 1915. He returned to France taking part in the fighting at Loos, the Somme and the capture of Vimy Ridge. At 3.50am on Tuesday 31 July 1917 the 3rd Battalion Grenadier Guards left their assembly trenches and advanced, crossing the Ypres Canal, south of the railway and moving northeast on the line of the railway from Boesinghe. The canal in the area had become a boggy mass because of recent shelling. The 3rd Battalion Grenadier Guards succeeded in capturing all their objectives moving through Artillery Wood. Arthur was killed instantly by a shell at about 10:30am on Tuesday 31 July 1917 while working in a trench near Grande Barriere House, north of Pilckem, Belgium, where the Pilckem - Bixschoote Road crossed the railway line. Sergeant W. Robertson, who was in the same company as Arthur, wrote:

"He was one of the bravest men I have ever seen, and was the most respected and best-liked non-commissioned officer in his company."

At the time of his death Arthur had spent almost 3 years on the continent with the exception of six weeks in England. He left a widow and young son. Arthur was originally buried near the railway line north of Pilckem and in September 1919, he was identified by means of a disc and his remains moved to Artillery Wood Cemetery.

Guardsman Mark Day *2nd Bn Grenadier Guards*

Service No.	25285	Age:	23
Place of birth:	Broadtown, Wiltshire	Home Country:	England
Date of death:	31/07/1917	Cause of death:	Killed in action

Memorial: Castle Eaton, Wiltshire
War Cemetery: Ypres Menin Gate - Grave Panel 9 and 11.
Next of Kin: Antony & Alice Day
Address: Droveway Cottage, Castle Eaton, Wiltshire

Mark was the youngest son of Antony and Alice Day and was employed as a labourer in the Loco Department of the Great Western Railway Works at Swindon. It is likely he was either conscripted into the army or enlisted under the Derby Scheme, joining the Grenadier Guards. He was sent to the front to the 2nd Battalion, who on Tuesday 31 July 1917 were given the task of the capture of the furthest objectives two and a half miles from the British front line. When the 2nd Grenadiers reached the Ypres Canal they were subjected to heavy German shelling and had several casualties. The canal was crossed at 6am by means of small bridges and advanced a further 2,000 yards from the British front line and were subject to heavy German machine gun fire. By 8am they were 3,000 yards from the British front line and paused to prepare for the attack. The 2nd Grenadiers reached the Green Line which was consolidated and one company pushed on capturing Signal Farm and Ruisseau Farm, west of Langemarck and taking 20 to 30 German prisoners. The 2nd Grenadiers then dug in some on the east bank of the Steenbeck and some on the west bank where they were subjected to heavy German artillery and machine gun fire. Mark was killed during the advance and is remembered on the Ypres Menin Gate. In August 1918 Mark's family inserted the following memoriam in a local paper:

One year has passed, our hearts still sore,
As time flies on we miss him more;
His welcome smile, his loving face,
No one can fill the vacant place.
We loved him then, we love him still,
Forget him, no, we never will;
God's will be done we'll meet again,
And then we'll part no more.

WEDNESDAY 1 AUGUST 1917 - TEMPERATURE 15°c WITH 5.3mm OF RAIN

The official British despatch on the evening of Wednesday 1 August 1917, stated:

"Rain has continued to fall throughout the day. By a successful local operation carried out today on our new battle front our line has been advanced slightly in the neighbourhood of the Zillebeke to Zonnebeke road. On the left flank of our attack our Allies have gained further ground along the east bank of the Yser Canal. During the night our new positions east and northeast of Ypres, between Westhoek and St. Julian, were heavily counter attacked by strong forces of the enemy. Our troops successfully resisted the enemy's repeated attempts to drive us from important positions on the high ground captured yesterday in this neighbourhood, but under the weight of his assaults, and after stubborn fighting, we were compelled to withdraw our advanced troops from the village of St. Julien. Fighting was particularly fierce for the possession of the village of Westhoek, of which our troops now hold the western outskirts. This afternoon the enemy again attacked in the neighbourhood of the Ypres- Roulers railway, and at the second attempt succeeded in entering our advanced positions on a narrow front. Fighting is still in progress.

The number of prisoner captured by British troops in the course of Yesterday's operations is now known to exceed 5,000, including 95 officers. A few guns and a number of machine guns and trench mortars have also been taken, but the exact figures cannot be ascertained.

Yesterday, in spite of weather which made flying almost impossible, our aeroplanes kept contact with our advancing infantry throughout the day. The enemy's aerodromes, transport, and infantry were successfully attacked with bombs and machine gun fire. The few enemy machines that attempted to fly were attacked and six of them were brought down. Three of our machines are missing.

The number of German prisoners captured by us in the month of July is 4,039, of whom 85 are officers. These figures include such of the prisoners captured in Yesterday's operations as had reached collecting stations by 6pm. Captured materials includes 8 field guns, 53 machine guns, and 32 trench mortars.

The French official reports of Wednesday 1 August 1917, relating to the Flanders front announced simply that:

"With persistent rain, the day was spent organising the positions won."

Gunner Ephriam John Baker		*A Bty 38th Bde Royal Field Artillery*	
Service No.	189167	Age:	33
Place of birth:	Hilmarton, Wiltshire	Home Country:	England
Date of death:	01/08/1917	Cause of death:	Killed in action
Memorial:	Not known		
War Cemetery:	Railway Dugouts Burial Ground - Grave VII. A. 2.		
Next of Kin:	William Lewis & Sarah Baker		
Address:	7 Swindon Road, Swindon, Wiltshire		

Ephriam was the second son of William and Sarah Baker and was employed as a carman for John Toomer & Sons. It is likely he was either conscripted into the army or enlisted under the Derby Scheme joining the Royal Field Artillery. He was sent to the 38th Brigade, who on Wednesday 1 August 1917 were near Zillebeke, Belgium. It is likely Ephriam was killed by German counter battery artillery fire.

Private Frederick Angel Greenman		*1st Bn Wiltshire Regiment*	
Service No.	24120	Age:	34
Place of birth:	Hullavington, Wiltshire	Home Country:	England
Date of death:	01/08/1917	Cause of death:	Killed in action
Memorial:	Hullavington, Wiltshire		
War Cemetery:	Divisional Collecting Post Cemetery and Extension - Grave I. K. 14.		
Next of Kin:	Thomas & Mirriam Greenman		
Address:	Jesamine Cottage, Hullavington, Wiltshire		

Frederick, a farm labourer, was the fourth son of Thomas and Mirriam Greenman It is likely he conscripted into the army or enlisted under the Derby Scheme, joining the 1st Battalion Wiltshire Regiment. On Wednesday 1 August 1917, the 1st Wiltshires were at Half Way House Dugout east of Ypres, Belgium, and at noon were ordered to relieve the 1st Battalion Sherwood Foresters on the Westhoek Ridge. When they reached Bellewaerde Lake the Wiltshires were subjected to such heavy German shelling that no further movement could take place and they were forced to find what ever cover they could. At about 5pm the bombardment was less intense and the Wiltshires proceeded in small groups and relieved the Sherwood Foresters. Frederick was one of five men killed during the German bombardment at Bellewaerde Lake. In January 1925 Frederick's remains were located east of Bellewaerde Lake and identified by means of his shoulder titles. His remains were moved to the Divisional Collecting Post Cemetery and Extension.

Lance Corporal Ernest William Gard		*1st Bn Wiltshire Regiment*	
Service No.	25803	Age:	33
Place of birth:	Melbury Osmond, Dorset	Home Country:	England
Date of death:	01/08/1917	Cause of death:	Died of wounds
Memorial:	Bradford on Avon, Bradford on Avon Christ Church		
War Cemetery:	Menin Road South Military Cemetery - Grave II E. 13.		
Next of Kin:	Stella Ann Gard (wife) – William & Jane Gard (parents)		
Address:	Stone Easton, Bath, Somerset		

Ernest, a gardener, was the second son of William and Jane Gard and on 27 May 1912 he married Stella Ann Robins at Stone Easton, Somerset. It is likely he conscripted into the army or enlisted under the Derby Scheme, joining the 1st Battalion Wiltshire Regiment. He was wounded on Wednesday 1 August 1917 by German shell fire near Bellewarrde Lake east of Ypres, Belgium, as the Wiltshires relieved the 1st Battalion Sherwood Foresters on the Westhoek Ridge. Ernest was evacuated to Ypres where he succumbed to his wounds soon after.

Lance Corporal Reginald George Moseley		*1st Bn Wiltshire Regiment*	
Service No.	18926	Age:	20
Place of birth:	Stanford Headley, Hampshire	Home Country:	England
Date of death:	01/08/1917	Cause of death:	Killed in action
Memorial:	West Ashton, Wiltshire		
War Cemetery:	Railway Dugouts Burial Ground - Grave VI. S. 27.		
Next of Kin:	Lewis & Jane Moseley		
Address:	Edgerley Cottage, Glastonbury, Somerset		

Reginald, a servant, was the youngest son of Lewis and Jane Moseley and volunteered for service with the Wiltshire Regiment arriving in France on 9 August 1915. He was one of five men killed in action on Wednesday 1 August 1917 by German shell fire near Bellewarrde Lake east of Ypres, Belgium, as the Wiltshires relieved the 1st Battalion Sherwood Foresters on the Westhoek Ridge. In December 1924 Reginald's remains were located northeast of Bellewaerde Lake, near Idiot Drive Trench and identified by means of his shoulder titles, boots, and badges of rank. His remains were moved to Railway Dugouts Burial Ground.

Private Henry Joseph Harfitt		*2nd Bn Irish Guards*	
Service No.	11302	Age:	35
Place of birth:	Salford, Wiltshire	Home Country:	England
Date of death:	01/08/1917	Cause of death:	Accident
Memorial:	Salisbury, Wiltshire - Rode, Somerset		
War Cemetery:	Canada Farm Cemetery - Grave II. E. 8.		
Next of Kin:	Edith M Harfitt Felix Herbert & Lucy Louisa Harfitt		
Address:	Exceter Street, Salisbury, Wiltshire		

Henry, a cabinet maker, was the third son of Herbert and Louisa Harfitt and in the summer of 1915 married Edith M. Whapshare at Winchester, Hampshire. It is likely he conscripted into the army or enlisted under the Derby Scheme, joining the Irish Guards. He was sent to the front joining the 2nd Battalion and was wounded as the result of an accident on Wednesday 1 August 1917. He was taken to Canada Farm, a farmhouse used as a dressing station, north- of the town of Ypres, where he succumbed to his wounds on the same day. He left a widow and a baby daughter.

Left: Henry Joseph Harfitt

Right: Sidney Howard Motion

Lieutenant Sidney Howard Motion *7th Bn Northamptonshire Regiment*

Service No.	N/a	Age:	22
Place of birth:	Sutton, Surrey	Home Country:	England
Date of death:	01/08/1917	Cause of death:	Died of wounds
Memorial:	Amersham, Buckinghamshire - Marlborough College, Wiltshire		
War Cemetery:	Brandhoek New Military Cemetery - Grave I. B. 11.		
Next of Kin:	Sidney H. & Clara Louise Motion		
Address:	Leigh, Surrey		

Sidney was the elder son of Sidney and Clara Motion and was educated at Marlborough College where he was a member of the Officer Training Corps. In 1913 he went to Caius College, Cambridge, to study medicine and at the outbreak of hostilities he volunteered for service. He was given a commission with the 7th Battalion Northamptonshire Regiment and was sent to France on 1st September 1915. He took part in the Battle of Loos on 25 Septemer 1915 and he was wounded on 14 August 1916, while acting as Company Commander, at Guillemont, Somme. Following his recovery, he, at his own request, returned to his regiment in France in May 1917. He took part in the battle of Messines, when he again acted as Company Commander. Sidney was wounded on 31 July 1917 while leading his men in an attack on German positions at Shrewsbury Forest south east of Zillebeke, Belgium. He succumbed to his wounds at an advanced dressing station the following day. His company commander wrote:

"There is one thing I may tell you, that he had charge of my company in the Messines show, whilst I was on leave, and when I returned my Company Sergeant Major came to me on behalf of my Non commissioned officers and men of the company, to ask if, "Mr Motion could be put in for something, as his conduct in cheering up the men during a terrifically intense bombardment was the best thing they had ever seen, and they again expressed the wish that he should be recommended. I discussed it with the commanding officer, and accordingly I recommended him for the Military Cross; unfortunately, the regiment was not giving any."

Private Henry Shurmer *9th Bn Welsh Regiment*

Service No.	46456	Age:	37
Place of birth:	Swindon, Wiltshire	Home Country:	England
Date of death:	01/08/1917	Cause of death:	Killed in action
Memorial:	Chepstow, Monmouthshire.		
War Cemetery:	Oosttaverne Wood Cemetery - Grave II. C. 10.		

Next of Kin:	Alice Elizabeth Shurmer (wife) – George & Jane Shurmer (parents)
Address:	3 Lights Court, Church Street, Chepstow, Monmouthshire

Henry, known as Harry, a carter for a coal company, was the eldest son of George and Jane Shurmer and in the spring of 1906 he married Alice Elizabeth Batchford at Chepstow. It is likely he conscripted into the army or enlisted under the Derby Scheme, joining the 9th Battalion Welsh Regiment. He was killed most likely by German artillery fire on Wednesday 1 August 1917 in captured trenches west of Oostaverne, Belgium, while relieving the 9th Royal Welsh Fusiliers. The 9th Battalion Welsh Regiment war diary states the weather was very bad and many of the trenches waterlogged. Henry left a widow and a young daughter.

Gunner Wilfred Harry Merefield — *82nd Bde Bn Royal Field Artillery*

Service No.	57938	Age:	35
Place of birth:	Compton Abbas, Dorset	Home Country:	England
Date of death:	01/08/1917	Cause of death:	Killed in action
Memorial:	Semley, Wiltshire		
War Cemetery:	Dickebusch New Military Cemetery Extension - Grave 11.F.14		
Next of Kin:	Louisa Gertrude Merefield (wife) – James & Amelia Merefield (parents)		
Address:	229 Gutch Common, Semley, Wiltshire – Compton Abbas, Dorset.		

Wilfred, a cowman on a farm, was the youngest son of James and Amelia Merefield and married Louisa Gertrude Woodrow on the 18 January 1904 at St. James Church, Shaftesbury. It is likely he conscripted into the army or enlisted under the Derby Scheme, joining the Royal Field Artillery. He was sent to the front joining the 82nd Brigade and was killed most likely by German artillery fire on Wednesday 1 August 1917 near Dickebusch. He left a widow and two young children.

Private Christopher Francis Pound — *89th Coy Machine Gun Corps*

Service No.	7241	Age:	20
Place of birth:	Portsmouth, Hampshire	Home Country:	England
Date of death:	01/08/1917	Cause of death:	Died of wounds
Memorial:	Not known		
War Cemetery:	Longuenesse St. Omer Souvenir Cemetery - Grave IV. D. 2.		
Next of Kin:	William & Emma Elizabeth Pound		
Address:	Ball Road, Home Lodge, Pewsey		

Christopher was the youngest son of William and Emma Pound and volunteered for service joining the Royal Berkshire Regiment. In 1915, he transferred to the Machine Gun Corps and was sent to France joining the 89th Company. He was wounded in fighting south of Hooge, Belgium and evacuated to 10th Stationary Hospital at St. Omer, France, where he succumbed to his wounds on Wednesday 1 August 1917.

THURSDAY 2 AUGUST 1917 - TEMPERATURE 15°c SHOWERS WITH 5.3mm OF RAIN

Lance Corporal Richard Henry Smith — *2nd Bn Wiltshire Regiment*

Service No.	8758	Age:	27
Place of birth:	Preshute, Wiltshire	Home Country:	England
Date of death:	02/08/1917	Cause of death:	Killed in action

Memorial: Marlborough, Wiltshire
War Cemetery: Ypres Menin Gate - Grave Panel 53.
Next of Kin: Henry Richard & Mary Jane Smith
Address: 86 The George, Overton, Wiltshire

Regular soldier, Richard, was the second son of Henry and Mary Smith and enlisted with the Wiltshire Regiment before the outbreak of hostilities. He was serving in Gibraltar with the 2nd Battalion when war was declared and landed at Zeebrugge on 7 October 1914. He was killed near Observatory Ridge east of Zillebeke, Belgium, on Thursday 2 August 1917, when the Wiltshires experienced a good deal of German machine gun fire from the northeast corner of Bodmin Copse. He is remembered on the Ypres Menin Gate and has no known grave.

Private George William John Woodward *15th Bn Royal Welsh Fusiliers*
Service No. 56509
Age: 19
Place of birth: Swindon, Wiltshire
Home Country: England
Date of death: 02/08/1917
Cause of death: Died of wounds
Memorial: Not known
War Cemetery: Dozinghem Military Cemetery - Grave II. J. 3.
Next of Kin: Frederick William & Clara Ann Woodward
Address: 101 Eastcott Hill, Swindon, Wiltshire

George was the only son of Frederick and Clara Woodward and it is likely he conscripted into the army or enlisted under the Derby Scheme, initially joining the Wiltshire Regiment. He was transferred to the 15th Battalion Royal Welsh Fusiliers and was sent to the front. He was wounded near Pilckem Ridge and taken to a medical facility near Dozinghem where he succumbed to his wounds on Thursday 2 August 1917.

Lance Corporal Arthur John Thomas *2nd Bn Coldstream Guards*
Service No. 14109
Age: 28
Place of birth: Forston, Dorset
Home Country: England
Date of death: 02/08/1917
Cause of death: Died of wounds
Memorial: Porton, Wiltshire
War Cemetery: Mendinghem Military Cemetery - Grave III. E. 25
Next of Kin: Edward George & Harriet Thomas
Address: The Dairy House, Idminston, Wiltshire

Arthur, a dairyman, was the third son of Edward and Harriet Thomas and it is likely he was conscripted into the army or enlisted under the Derby Scheme, joining the 2nd Battalion Coldstream Guards. He was wounded near Pilckem Ridge and taken to No. 46 Casualty Clearing Station at Mendinghem where he succumbed to his wounds on Thursday 2 August 1917. His brother Oliver Robert Thomas had been killed while serving with the Wiltshire Regiment in October 1914.

Private Charles Hill *6th Bn Wiltshire Regiment*
Service No. 26057
Age: 38
Place of birth: Highworth, Wiltshire
Home Country: England
Date of death: 02/08/1917
Cause of death: Killed in action
Memorial: Highworth, Wiltshire
War Cemetery: Oosttaverne Wood Cemetery - Grave II. B. 2
Next of Kin: Maud Mabel Hill (wife) – Alfred & Annie Hill (parents)
Address: Swindon Street, Highworth, Wiltshire

Charles was the eldest son of Alfred and Annie Hill and at the start of 1901 he married Maud Mabel Greenway at Swindon. He was employed at the The Oriental Fibre and Matting Company, known as the Vorda Works, Highworth, where he worked as a fibre mat maker, and had worked for many years. It is likely he conscripted into the army or enlisted under the Derby Scheme, joining the Wiltshire Regiment, and was sent to the front joining the 6th Battalion. He was killed on Thursday 2 August 1917, near Oosttaverne, when the Wiltshires were in rain soaked trenches which were in a very bad state and led to a postponement of a further attack. Charles left a widow and two children.

FRIDAY 3 AUGUST 1917 - TEMPERATURE 15°c WITH 9.9mm OF RAIN

Corporal William John Bailey — *2nd Bn Wiltshire Regiment*

Service No.	32993	Age:	27
Place of birth:	Malmesbury, Wiltshire	Home Country:	England
Date of death:	03/08/1917	Cause of death:	Killed in action
Memorial:	Little Somerford, Wiltshire		
War Cemetery:	Ypres Menin Gate - Panel 53.		
Next of Kin:	Mildred Jane Bailey (wife) - Edward & Georgina Bailey (parents)		
Address:	East end Lane, Little Somerford, Wiltshire		

William was the eldest son of Edward and Georgina Bailey and in the summer of 1911 he married Mildred Jane Minty. He was employed as second horseman at Westonbirt and at the outbreak of hostilities he joined the Wiltshire Yeomanry. In November 1916, he was transferred to the 2nd Battalion Wiltshire Regiment, and just before Christmas sent to France. On Friday 3 August 1917, the Wiltshires were near Klien Zillebeke southeast of Ypres, Belgium and while in the trenches they were subjected to German shelling. In late August 1917 Mildred Bailey received the following letter from William's platoon officer Second Lieutenant F.R. Lewis:

"It is with deep regret that I have to inform you of the death of your husband, Corporal W. Bailey. He was killed by a shell on the battlefield south east of Ypres, during the attack of July 31st. He was a corporal in my platoon and both a capable and popular non-commissioned officer, and his loss is keenly felt by all his comrades. He was killed after fighting bravely and doing invaluable service during an action, and he was buried where he fell. I trust you will find some consolation in the fact that he died the most noble death fighting for his country. Once again, I express my deepest sympathy."

William's grave was lost during further fighting and he is today remembered on the Ypres Menin Gate, he left a widow and three young children.

Private Frederick Holloway Isaacs — *2nd Bn Wiltshire Regiment*

Service No.	203069	Age:	27
Place of birth:	Burbage, Wiltshire	Home Country:	England
Date of death:	03/08/1917	Cause of death:	Died of wounds
Memorial:	W Shop Great Werstern Railway Works, Swindon		
War Cemetery:	Mendinghem Military Cemetery - Grave III. E. 16.		
Next of Kin:	Elsie May Isaacs (wife) - Edward & Mary Annie Isaacs (parents)		
Address:	31 Kingshill Road, Swindon, Wiltshire		

Frederick was the second son of Edward and Mary Isaacs and was employed as a labourer in W Shop, Great Western Railway Works in Swindon. It is likely he was conscripted into the army in October 1916, initially joining the Somerset Light Infantry and was sent to Whiststable for training. In February 1917, he married Elsie May Bathe at Swindon and he was sent to France on 25 June 1917, when he was transferred to the 2nd Battalion Wiltshire Regiment. He was wounded on the morning of Friday 3 August

Left: Frederick Holloway Isaacs

Right: James Pillans

1917, near Klien Zillebeke southeast of Ypres, Belgium when, while in the trenches, the Wiltshires were subjected to German shelling. He was evacuated to a medical facility at Mendinghem where he succumbed to his wounds later the same evening. Frederick's widow received the following letter from Rev. F.G. Walmsley (chaplain):

"It is with great regret that I write to tell you that your dear husband passed away last night. He only came into us that day, so badley wounded above the legs that all we could do was to make his end peaceful as possible. He spoke of you and sent his love. It is very sad, but you may indeed feel he has given his life for his country and for that peace for which we are all praying so earnestly. We have told you all we can of the short time he was with us, but we do assure you of our deep sympathy in your great loss. May God help you to be brave as he was. 'Greater love hath no man than this, that a man lay down his life for his friends.'"

Lance Corporal James Pillans		*2nd Bn Wiltshire Regiment*	
Service No.	9873	Age:	32
Place of birth:	Biggar, Lanarkshire	Home Country:	England
Date of death:	03/08/1917	Cause of death:	Died of wounds
Memorial:	Ludgershall, Wiltshire		
War Cemetery:	Mendinghem Military Cemetery - Grave III. B. 14.		
Next of Kin:	Hilda S Pillans (wife) - John and Helen Pillans (parents)		
Address:	2 Lansdowne Villas, Ludgershall, Wiltshire		

James was the son of John and Helen Pillans and enlisted with the Cameron Highlanders on 5 February 1907. In the summer of 1909 he married Hilda Susanah Edwards at Ludgershall. However, the following year on 19 May 1910 James went absent and stole a bicycle. He was given two months' imprisonment with hard labour. He also forfeited 9 days pay for the absence and was discharged from the army on 15 June 1910. At the outbreak of hostilities James volunteered for service joining the 6th Service Battalion Wiltshire Regiment and after undergoing his final battle training at Perham Down in March 1915 he arrived in France on 19 July 1915. At Christmas 1915 he was given a week's home leave after which he returned to his Regiment in France. James had been a Sergeant Major with the 6th Wiltshires, but trouble found him again and he was court martialled and reduced to the rank of Private. In January 1917, he spent 3 weeks in hospital in France, before being evacuated to England suffering from dysentery. After his recovery, he was given 10 days' home leave before being sent back to France in January 1917 and transferred to the 2nd Battalion Wiltshire Regiment. James was wounded with gunshot wounds to the head, most likely on Friday 3 August 1917, near Klien Zillebeke southeast of Ypres, Belgium when, while in the trenches, the Wiltshires were subjected to German shelling. He was evacuated to a casualty clearing station at Mendinghem where he succumbed to his wounds. He left a widow and a young daughter.

SATURDAY 4 AUGUST 1917 - TEMPERATURE 19°c WITH 4.9mm OF RAIN

Private John Stephen Johnson		*1st Bn Wiltshire Regiment*	
Service No.	26407	Age:	27
Place of birth:	Warminster, Wiltshire	Home Country:	England
Date of death:	04/08/1917	Cause of death:	Killed in action
Memorial:	Bradford on Avon		
War Cemetery:	Ypres Menin Gate - Panel 53.		
Next of Kin:	Esther Ellen Johnson (wife) – Stephen & Anna Johnson (parents)		
Address:	9 Church Street, Bradford on Avon, Wiltshire		

John was the only son of Stephen and Anna Johnson and was employed as a rubber worker in the Avon Rubber Mills in Baradford on Avon. In the summer of 1915 he married Esther Ellen Butt at Bradford on Avon. He was called up in April 1916 but because he was engaged in Government work he was sent home for three months. He was called up again in July 1916 joining the Wiltshire Regiment and after completing his training he arrived in France in October 1916, being sent to the 1st Battalion. John was killed on Saturday 4 August 1917 when the Wiltshires were subjected to a German artillery barrage while in the area of Bellewaarde Ridge, east of Hooge, Belgium. They also had to contend with the British artillery firing a number of *"shorts"* on the British positions. John's widow first heard the news of his death in a letter from her brother in mid August 1917 and in September 1917 she inserted the following memoriam in a local paper:

I could not raise his dying head,
Or kiss him a last good-bye,
But as I look around our home,
I feel that he is nigh.

Loved one, so true in life,
Snatched from my side in death;
Somewhere in France, they have laid thee,
Beloved take thy peace and rest.

He is remembered on the Ypres Menin Gate and has no known grave.

Gunner Edward Howard Pickard MM + Bar		*4th Field Amb. Australian Army Medical Corps*	
Service No.	10083	Age:	44
Place of birth:	Southwick, Wiltshire	Home Country:	England
Date of death:	04/08/1917	Cause of death:	Died of wounds
Memorial:	Rode, Somerset		
War Cemetery:	Godewaersvelde British Cemetery - Grave I. C. 14.		
Next of Kin:	Thomas & Martha Pickard		
Address:	Dilly Brook Farm, North Bradley, Wiltshire		

Edward was the second son of Thomas and Martha Pickard and at the outbreak of the Great War, Edward was a poultry farmer in Australia. He had been a seaman and settled in Australia and enlisted with the

Left: *John Stephen Johnson*

Right: *Edward Howard Pickard*

Australian artillery on 15 September 1915. He left Sydney on 17 December 1915 and was initially sent to Egypt and in June 1916 arrived in Marseilles, France. In December 1916, he transferred to the 4th Australian Field Ambulance and attached to duty with the 10th Australian Artillery. He was awarded the Military Medal for bravery on 20 June 1917 and later was awarded a Bar for another act of bravery. He was wounded in action on 28 July 1917 with multiple gun shot wounds and was taken to the 4th Australian Field Ambulance. He was then transferred to No. 41 Casualty Clearing Station where he died on Saturday 4 August 1917. His personal property was returned to his next of kin consisting of letters, pipe cleaner, 2 numerals and 2 badges.

Private Harry Gibbs		*15th Bn Welsh Regiment*	
Service No.	53961	Age:	20
Place of birth:	Swindon, Wiltshire	Home Country:	England
Date of death:	04/08/1917	Cause of death:	Killed in action
Memorial:	Not known		
War Cemetery:	Ypres Menin Gate - Panel 37.		
Next of Kin:	George & Elizabeth Gibbs		
Address:	22 Dover Street, Swindon, Wiltshire		

Harry was the youngest son of George and Elizabeth Gibbs and was employed as a labourer in the Loco Department at the Great Western Railway works in Swindon. It is likely he conscripted into the army or enlisted under the Derby Scheme, joining the Welsh Regiment, and was sent to the front joining the 15th Battalion. He was killed on Saturday 4 August, most likely by German artillery, when the 15th Welsh, relieved the 16 Royal Welsh Fusiliers near Pilckem Ridge, east of Boesinge, Belgium. Harry is remembered on the Ypres Menin Gate and has no known grave.

Driver Arthur Alexander Attwood		*C Bty 52nd Bde Royal Field Artillery*	
Service No.	94701	Age:	22
Place of birth:	Swindon, Wiltshire	Home Country:	England
Date of death:	04/08/1917	Cause of death:	Died of wounds
Memorial:	Not known		
War Cemetery:	Lijssenthoek Military Cemetery - Grave XVII. G. 16.		
Next of Kin:	William & Eliza Attwood		
Address:	St Mark, Swindon, Wiltshire		

Arthur was the second son of William and Eliza Attwood and volunteered for service joining the Royal Field Artillery. He arrived in France on 13 May 1915 and was sent to C Battery of the 52nd Brigade. He was wounded most likely by German artillery in the opening stages in the third battle of Ypres and taken to a casualty clearing station at Lijssenthoek, where he succumbed to his wounds on Saturday 4 August 1917.

Private Arthur Leonard Green		*10th Bn Royal West Kent Regiment*	
Service No.	G/23722	Age:	23
Place of birth:	Blunsdon, Wiltshire	Home Country:	England
Date of death:	04/08/1917	Cause of death:	Died of wounds
Memorial:	Blunsdon, Wiltshire		
War Cemetery:	Etaples Military Cemetery - Grave XXII. O. 22A.		
Next of Kin:	John & Martha Green		
Address:	44 St Mary's Grove, Swindon, Wiltshire		

Arthur was the fifth son of John and Martha Green and was employed as a market gardener for Mr D.E. Hall. He was described as being tender hearted and having a loveable disposition. From a young age had been a member of the parish church choir and was an active bell ringer. It is likely he conscripted into the army or enlisted under the Derby Scheme, joining the 10th Battalion Royal West Kent Regiment. He was wounded in action in early August 1917 near Klein Zillebeke and evacuated to a medical facility near Etaples, France, where he succumbed to his wounds on Saturday 4 August 1917. The first news of Arthur's death came in a letter from a comrade and then soon after official news was received. In 1918 Arthur's parents inserted the following memoriam in a local paper:

We'll know why clouds instead of sun,
Were over many a cherished plan;
Why songs were hushed, when scarce begun,
Yes, there, sometime, we'll understand.

Corporal Eli Job Rose		*10th Bn Royal West Surrey Regiment*	
Service No.	T/23069	Age:	33
Place of birth:	Trowbridge, Wiltshire	Home Country:	England
Date of death:	04/08/1917	Cause of death:	Killed in action
Memorial:	Trowbridge, Wiltshire		
War Cemetery:	Ypres Menin Gate - Panel 11 - 13 and 14.		
Next of Kin:	Minnie Adelaide Rose (wife) - William & Ellen Rose (parents)		
Address:	10 Allen Road, Trowbridge, Wiltshire		

Eli was the fourth son of William & Ellen Rose and worked with his parents in their grocers shop in Bond Street, Trowbridge. He had married Minnie Adelaide Sumption in 1908 and was a keen member of the Upper Studley Baptist Church and Sunday School. Eli voluntarily enlisted in the Army Service Corps and after passing a trade test at Aldershot was promoted to the rank of Corporal. In spring 1917 orders were received by Northern Command that all men in the Army Service Corp, irrespective of rank, who were passed fit for general service, were to be transferred to the infantry and Eli was reduced to the rank of a private soldier and sent to the training reserve. He was given leave in June 1917 and visited Trowbridge before being sent to France at the end of the same month. He was transferred to the Border Regiment and sent to the front. On reaching the front line he was again transferred, to the West Surrey Regiment, who were preparing to attack the following morning. He was killed in action during his first time under fire near Hollebeke, Belgium. Minnie Rose received the following letter from 2nd Lieutenant K. R. Weame of the West Surreys:

Left: Eli Job Rose

Right: George William Barnes DCM

"It is with extreme sorrow that I have to inform you that your husband was killed in action whilst doing his duty on the 4th August. His death was instantaneous. Although he had not been with the company long, it was long enough to prove him a good and willing soldier, and his loss is felt by all in the company. I trust that your grief will be lighted by the knowledge of the noble manner of his death."

Eli left a widow and two children and is remembered on the Ypres Menin Gate and has no known grave.

SUNDAY 5 AUGUST 1917 - TEMPERATURE 23°c RAINFALL NIL

Private George William Barnes DCM		*1st Bn Wiltshire Regiment*	
Service No.	18266	Age:	33
Place of birth:	Longbridge Deverill, Wiltshire	Home Country:	England
Date of death:	05/08/1917	Cause of death:	Killed in action
Memorial:	Longbridge Deverill, Wiltshire		
War Cemetery:	Ypres Menin Gate - Panel 53.		
Next of Kin:	George & Hannah Barnes		
Address:	52 Sand Street, Longbridge Deverill, Wiltshire		

George, known as William and a horseman on a farm, was the eldest son of George and Hannah Barnes and volunteered for service on 29 December 1914 joining the Wiltshire Regiment. He arrived in France in May 1915 and was sent to the 1st Battalion. In June 1917 during the attack on Messines he was awarded the Distinguished Conduct Medal. He went forward in front of his company and British tanks, armed only with a revolver and captured, single handedly a German machine gun team of eight. He took them prisoner and brought back the German machine gun. The official citation reads:

'For conspicuous gallantry and devotion to duty. He captured an enemy machine gun and single handed, at the point of the bayonet, displaying throughout the action admirable qualities of initiative and leadership.'

On the evening of the 4/5 August the 1st Wiltshires were in forward positions on Bellewarde Ridge and were relieved by other British units. During the relief, one company was near Chateau Wood when the Germans commenced to shell very heavily using a large number of mustard gas shells and some phosphorous shells. William was killed by a shell, his parents received the following letter from Captain R.F.J. Hayward of A Company:

"I beg to inform you that your son, No. 18266 Pte. Barnes G.W. of my company, was killed instantaneously by a shell on the night of 5 August 1917. I may state that he was one of the best stretcher bearers we have ever had, and always most willing to carry out any duties allotted to him. He did so well with me at Messines that I got him awarded the D.C.M. for great bravery. The Officers, N.C.O.'s and men of his company join with me in sympathising with you in your great bereavement for so great a loss."

Lance Corporal A. Dean wrote the following.

"I am writing just these few lines hoping it will console you in the great loss of your son. As I knew him personally and was in the same company for the past two years and more, I thought I would just write on behalf of the Boys to tell you how esteemed he was by all who knew him and how he was liked in the Company. By the time you get this letter I expect you will have heard from other sources how he died, but from what I know he died instantaneously from a shell splinter; he did not suffer any pain. He was such a brave fellow, so cool, and we always knew that if anyone got wounded 'Barney' and his mate were on the spot to take him away with the stretcher. It seems so hard just after winning the medal. I got one, too, at the same time, so you can guess how I feel now. We all feel the loss of such a gallant soldier. Hoping again that these few lines will help to console you in your terrible bereavement."

In August 1918 William's parents inserted the following memorium in a local paper:

A soldier's grave - a touching thing,
Where loving hands no flowers can bring;
But God, in his great and loving care,
Will guard his loved one sleeping there.

His King and country called him,
The call was not in vain;
On Britains Roll of Honour
You will find my dear son's name.

Gone but not forgotten

William is remembered on the Ypres Menin Gate and has no known grave.

Private Charles Ernest Ball		*8th Bn Royal Inniskilling Fusiliers*	
Service No.	41698	Age:	19
Place of birth:	Winterbourne Monkton, Wilts	Home Country:	England
Date of death:	05/08/1917	Cause of death:	Killed in action
Memorial:	Winterbourne Monkton, Wiltshire		
War Cemetery:	Ypres Menin Gate - Panel 22.		
Next of Kin:	Ernest & Elizabeth A Ball		
Address:	191, Winterbourne Monkton, Wiltshire		

Charles was the eldest son of Ernest and Elizabeth Ball and it is likely he conscripted into the army or enlisted under the Derby Scheme, joining the 8th Battalion Royal Inniskilling Fusiliers. He was killed on Sunday 5 August 1917, most likely by German shell fire, west of Zonnebeke, Belgium, when they were subjected to a heavy German artillery barrage, with 4.2's and 5.9's. He is remembered on the Ypres Menin Gate and has no known grave.

Guardsman James Chappell — *1st Bn Grenadier Guards*

Service No.	17965
Age:	26
Place of birth:	Sherston, Wiltshire
Home Country:	England
Date of death:	05/08/1917
Cause of death:	Killed in action
Memorial:	Sherston, Wiltshire
War Cemetery:	Ypres Menin Gate - Panel 9 and 11.
Next of Kin:	Worthy & Cetha Chappell
Address:	Sherston, Wiltshire

Farm labourer James was the second son of Worthy & Cetha Chappell and volunteered for service joining the Grenadier Guards. He arrived in France on 16 March 1915 and was sent to the 1st Battalion. He was killed on Sunday 5 August 1917, most likely by German shell fire near Pilckem Ridge, Belgium. James is remembered on the Ypres Menin Gate and has no known grave.

Private Arthur Charles Bowers — *15th Bn Hampshire Regiment*

Service No.	23164
Age:	36
Place of birth:	Andover, Hampshire
Home Country:	England
Date of death:	05/08/1917
Cause of death:	Killed in action
Memorial:	Lyndhurst, Hampshire
War Cemetery:	Ypres Menin Gate - Panel 35.
Next of Kin:	John James & Harriet Bowers
Address:	Grovely Wood, Barford St Martin, Wiltshire

Arthur, a gardener, was the third son of John and Harriet Bowers and it is likely he conscripted into the army or enlisted under the Derby Scheme, joining the 15th Battalion Hampshire Regiment. On Sunday 5 August 1917, the 15th Hampshires were holding the British front line at Hollebeke Belgium. At 4am they were subjected to a German attack and Arthur was killed during this action. His parents received the following from his officer:

Left: Grenadier Guards at Pilckem Ridge 5 August 1917-
Above: Wounded near Elverdinge 31 July 1917

"He was a good soldier and greatly missed by his officers and comrades. He was shot through the head while repulsing a German counterattack at daybreak and was buried behind the lines."

In November 1917, an alter-cloth and oak re-table were dedicated to the memory of Arthur at the Earl of Pembroke's Mission Church, Grovely Wood. The location of Arthur's grave was subsequently lost and he is today remembered on the Ypres Menin Gate.

MONDAY 6 AUGUST 1917 - TEMPERATURE 21.5°c WITH 0.1mm OF RAIN

Sergeant Ernest Frederick Goddard — *P Special Coy Bn Royal Engineers*

Service No.	147024	Age:	29
Place of birth:	Shrewton, Wiltshire	Home Country:	England
Date of death:	06/08/1917	Cause of death:	Killed in action
Memorial:	Not known		
War Cemetery:	Vlamertinghe New Military Cemetery - Grave VI. C. 2.		
Next of Kin:	Frederick & Ellen Goddard		
Address:	Shrewton, Wiltshire		

Regular soldier Ernest was the eldest son of Frederick and Ellen Goddard and landed in France with the 1st Battalion Wiltshire Regiment on 14 August 1914. At some stage he transferred to the Royal Engineers and was attached to P Special Company, who were poison gas cylinder operators. He was killed, most likely by German artillery, on Monday 6 August 1917.

Private William George Lock — *6th Bn Wiltshire Regiment*

Service No.	9209	Age:	27
Place of birth:	Fermoy, Cork	Home Country:	England
Date of death:	06/08/1917	Cause of death:	Killed in action
Memorial:	Bradford on Avon - Moulton Spencer Memorial		
War Cemetery:	Oosttaverne Wood Cemetery - Grave II. B. 11.		
Next of Kin:	James & Annie Lock		
Address:	6 Tory Place, Bradford on Avon, Wiltshire		

William, a labourer, was the second son of James and Annie Lock and was employed at Spencer Moulton Mills, Bradford on Avon. He volunteered for service in August 1914, on the same day his brother, a reservist was called to the colours. He was sent to France in June 1915 and within a short time he was wounded with shrapnel in the legs. He was evacuated to England and following his recovery he was sent back to France joining the 6th Battalion Wiltshire Regiment. William was given home leave at the beginning of July 1917 and returned to France soon after. On Monday 6 August 1917, the 6th Wiltshires were at Polka Estaminet south east of Oostaverne. William was on duty as a gas sentry and was killed by a stray shell. The following week his parents received unofficial information concerning William's death. The following week the news of his death was confirmed in the following letter from his comrade, Private H. Rumbold:

"It is with feelings of the deepest regret that I am forwarding these few treasures which we removed from your son's pockets after the great misfortune which took place on Sunday evening the 5 August. I am writing these few lines on behalf of our small section of which your son was a most fearless, cheerful, and at all times a pleasant member, to express our very deepest sympathy with you in your sorrowful bereavement. Its sadness is felt by us all very much, and the loss of such a companion will not be forgotten for many a long day. He was at the time on duty as a gas sentry at battalion headquarters, and after a

terrific 'strafe' by the enemy, a stray shell exploded very near him, causing almost instantaneous death. I am pleased to say an Army Chaplain was able to hold a service in the cemetery near by, and a memorial cross has been erected as best weather conditions would allow, and although it is poor comfort, you can rest assured it will be well cared for and be tended often."

The letter states he was killed on the 5 August 1917, while the Commonwealth War Graves Commission states his name as Locke and that he died on 6 August 1917.

Private Walter Harold Cox		*1st Bn Wiltshire Regiment*	
Service No.	33562	Age:	27
Place of birth:	Holywell, Somerset	Home Country:	England
Date of death:	06/08/1917	Cause of death:	Died of wounds
Memorial:	Police HQ Devizes, Wiltshire		
War Cemetery:	Lijssenthoek Military Cemetery - Grave XVII. B. 3A		
Next of Kin:	Walter & Rebecca Cox		
Address:	Cloford, Somerset		

Walter known as Harold was the eldest son of Walter and Rebecca Cox and was a Wiltshire Police Constable. It is likely he was either conscripted into the army or joined under the Derby Scheme being sent to the front joining the 1st Battalion Wiltshire Regiment. It is likely he was wounded near Hooge, Belgium, by shrapnel wounds penetrating his chest, face and legs, and then evacuated No. 3 Canadian Casualty Clearing station at Lijssenthoek where he succumbed to his wounds on Monday 6 August 1917.

TUESDAY 7 AUGUST 1917 - TEMPERATURE 20.5°c RAINFALL NIL

Gunner George William Hayles		*B Bty 153rd Bde Royal Field Artillery*	
Service No.	30262	Age:	21
Place of birth:	Carisbrooke, Isle of Wight	Home Country:	England
Date of death:	07/08/1917	Cause of death:	Killed in action
Memorial:	Not known		
War Cemetery:	White House Cemetery, St Jean Les Ypres - Grave III. B. 20.		
Next of Kin:	George & Bertha Hayles		
Address:	97 Kingsdown Road, Upper Stratton, Wiltshire		

George, a van man, was the eldest son of George and Bertha Hayles and volunteered for service joining the Royal Field Artillery. He was sent to France on 26 November 1915, joining B Battery 153rd Brigade. He was killed, most likely by German counter battery fire, near St. Jean on Tuesday 7 August 1917. In 1918 George's family inserted the following memoriam in a local paper:

One year has passed since that sad day,
When our dear boy was called away;
A loving son, true and brave,
He peacefully sleeps in a soldier's grave.

Geore was originally buried west of St. Jean and in July 1919 his remains were moved to White House Cemetery.

Left: Alfred George Millard

Right: Charles Humphrey Bayley

2nd Lieutenant Alfred George Millard *9th Bn East Surrey Regiment*

Service No.	N/a	Age:	27
Place of birth:	Windsor, Berkshire	Home Country:	England
Date of death:	07/08/1917	Cause of death:	Died of wounds
Memorial:	Felsted, Essex – Marlborough College, Wiltshire		
War Cemetery:	Aeroplane Cemetery - Grave IV. B. 15		
Next of Kin:	Alfred William & Beatrice Millard		
Address:	153 Langdale Road, Thornton Heath, Surrey		

Alfred was the only son of Alfred and Beatrice Millard and was educated at Eton Choir School and the Royal College of Music. After leaving education he became the Assistant Music Master at Marlborough from 1911 to 1915, and then he went to Felstead School. In 1916, he joined the 28th London Regiment, the Artists Rifles and soon after was given a commission with the 9th Battalion East Surrey Regiment. He was wounded on Tuesday 7 August 1917 most likely by German shelling in the British front line at Shrewsbury Forest near Klien Zillebeke, Belgiun. He succumbed to his wounds soon after. Alfred was originally buried near where he fell north of Klien Zillebeke. In September 1919, his remains were moved to Aeroplane Cemetery.

Captain Charles Humphrey Bayley *7th Bn South Lancashire Regiment*

Service No.	N/a	Age:	37
Place of birth:	Stockport, Lancashire	Home Country:	England
Date of death:	07/08/1917	Cause of death:	Died of wounds
Memorial:	Ambleside, Cumbria – Marlborough College, Wiltshire		
War Cemetery:	Outtersteene Communal Cemetery Extention - Grave I. A. 8		
Next of Kin:	Zoe Charlotte Marshall Bayley (wife) – Rev. Charles James & Mary Bayley		
Address:	2 Clarence Parade, Southsea, Hampshire		

Charles was the only son of Rev Charles James & Mary Bayley and was educated at Marlborough College before attending Kings College Cambridge. He served for two years in the South African War as a trooper for six months and afterwards in the militia. He married Zoe Charlotte Marshall Hannagan at Jubblepore, Bengal in 1903. He served in India with the 1st Battalion South Lancashire Regiment, was given a commission and in October 1910 he was appointed as a Lieutennant. He was serving with the 7th Bn South Lancashire Regiment on 31 July 1917 when he was wounded on the Oostverne Road, most likely by German artillery. He was evacuated to Outtersteene, France, where he succumbed to his wounds on Tuesday 7 August 1917. He left a widow and a son and daughter.

Sergeant Frederick Ashbee *126th Siege Bty Royal Garrison Artillery*

Service No.	26040	Age:	30
Place of birth:	Billericay, Essex	Home Country:	England
Date of death:	07/08/1917	Cause of death:	Died of wounds
Memorial:	Not known		
War Cemetery:	Mendinghem Military Cemetery - Grave IV. A. 38		
Next of Kin:	Alice Eliza Ashbee (wife)		
Address:	Seend Cleve, Seend, Wiltshire		

Regular soldier Frederick had joined the Royal Garrison Artillery before the Great War. He arrived in France with the 126th Siege Battery, Royal Garrison Artillery on 17 September 1914. Toward the end of 1915 he married Alice Eliza Helloco at Alverstoke, Hampshire. He was wounded, most likely by German counter battery fire to the northwest of Ypres and taken to No 12 Casualty Clearing Station at Mendinghem, where he succumbed to his wounds on Tuesday 7 August 1917. He left a widow and a young daughter.

WEDNESDAY 8 AUGUST 1917 - TEMPERATURE 21.5°c - 25% CLOUD COVER WITH THUNDERSTORMS - RAINFALL 10.2mm

Sergeant Sidney Cannons *1st Bn Wiltshire Regiment*

Service No.	5828	Age:	33
Place of birth:	Idstone Ashbury, Berkshire	Home Country:	England
Date of death:	08/08/1917	Cause of death:	Died of wounds
Memorial:	Carriage & Loco Department, Great Western Railway Works, Swindon.		
War Cemetery:	Mendinghem Military Cemetery - Grave IV. B. 12.		
Next of Kin:	Elizabeth Cannons (wife) – John & Elizabeth Cannons (parents)		
Address:	Swindon, Wiltshire		

Old Soldier, Sidney, was the eldest son of John and Elizabeth Cannons and had served with the Wiltshire Regiment before the Great War. At the outbreak of hostilities he was working as a labourer in the Carriage and Loco Department of the Great Western Railway Works, Swindon. He re-enlisted and at the beginning of 1915 he married Elizabeth Greenwood at Devizes. He was wounded most likely by German artillery near Hooge, Belgium and was evacuated to No 46 Casualty Clearing Station at Mendinghem, where he succumbed to his wounds on Wednesday 7 August 1917. He left a widow, a son and a daughter.

Sidney Cannons

Official British Despatch

There was a great activity in the air again on Tuesday, and severe fighting took place, in the course of which nine German aeroplanes were brought down and five others driven down out of control. Seven British aeroplanes are missing, two of which were overtaken by a violent storm when working over the enemy's lines.

Hostile raiding parties attacked new British positions east of Klien Zillebeke, were completely repulsed, leaving 14 prisoners in British hands. Stormy weather continues, and heavy rain has fallen.

On the Ypres battle front, a hostile attack against British positions in the neighbourhood of the Pilkem-Langemarck road was completely repulsed.

A correspondent described the German defences in the region of the fighting as a waste of ruined buildings, of industrial suburbs, and railway cuttings, *"reticulated in all directions with lines of trenches thickly wired and defended by strong points with machine guns everywhere."*

Artillery Wood Military Cemetery looking toward Boesinghe

5

The Capture of Westhoek

Map page 422

FRIDAY 10 AUGUST 1917 - TEMPERATURE 20.5°c CLEAR - RAINFALL 1.5mm

Gunner Thomas William Lawrence Flangham — *1st Siege Bty Bn Royal Garrison Artillery*

Service No.	87577	Age:	33
Place of birth:	Ramsgate, Kent	Home Country:	England
Date of death:	10/08/1917	Cause of death:	Died of wounds
Memorial:	Calstock, Cornwall		
War Cemetery:	Brandhoek New Military Cemetery - Grave VI. B. 16.		
Next of Kin:	Isabel Flangham (wife) - Harry Lawrence & Sarah Flangham (parents)		
Address:	Chapel See, Albaston, Tavistock, Devon		

Thomas was a gardner and had married Isabel Jolliffe on 31 October 1908 at Cheshunt, Hertfordshire and they lived for some time in Curzon Street, Calne. He attested under the Derby Scheme on 10 December 1915 and was called up on 9 June 1916. After Training he was sent to France and the 1st Siege Battery in December 1916 and in February 1917 he spent 3 days' sick in hospital and then returned to his unit. On 5 May 1917 Thomas was charged and awarded 3 days' field punishment No2 for: *"hesitating to obey an order."* He was wounded on 9 August 1917, most likely by German artillery fire while supporting the advance during third battle of Ypres and died the following day at 32nd Casualty Clearing Station. Isabel and her son Edward received a pension of 18 Shillings and nine pence per week and his personal possessions, which were sent home, consisted of disc, letters, photos, 2 religious books, purse, 2 copper coins, photo case and stylus pen.

Private Harry Brown — *9th Bn Royal Inniskilling Fusiliers*

Service No.	43667	Age:	19
Place of birth:	Salisbury, Wiltshire	Home Country:	England
Date of death:	10/08/1917	Cause of death:	Killed in action
Memorial:	Salisbury, Salisbury Post Office, Wiltshire		
War Cemetery:	New Irish Farm Cemetery - Grave XII. D. 13.		
Next of Kin:	George & Lucy A Brown		
Address:	45 Clarendon Road Elm Grove, Salisbury, Wiltshire		

Harry was the second son of George and Lucy Brown and it is likely he was conscripted into the army or enlisted under the Derby Scheme. He initially joined the Royal Fusiliers, but was transferred to the 9th Battalion Royal Inniskilling Fusiliers. He was killed in action on Friday 10 August 1917, most likely by German artillery fire, near St. Julien, along with ten other members of the battalion. In January 1919 Harry's remains were located near Fotuin, South of St. Julien and moved to New Irish Farm Cemetery.

Saturday 11 August 1917 - Temperature 18°c Cloud Cover - Rainfall 4.8mm

Private Frederick Yeates		*1st Bn Wiltshire Regiment*	
Service No.	32227	Age:	31
Place of birth:	Highworth, Wiltshire	Home Country:	England
Date of death:	11/08/1917	Cause of death:	Killed in action
Memorial:	Not known		
War Cemetery:	Ypres Menin Gate - Panel 53.		
Next of Kin:	James & EmmaYeates		
Address:	59, Collingbourne Kingston, Wiltshire		

Frederick, a farm labourer, was the second son of James and EmmaYeates and it is likely he was conscripted into the army or enlisted under the Derby Scheme, joining the Wiltshire Regiment. He was sent to the 1st Battalion who, on Saturday 11 August 1917, were at Westhoek and Bellewaarde Ridge near Hooge, Belgium. They were subject to shelling by German artillery and Frederick was killed as a result of an enemy shell. He is remembered on the Ypres Menin Gate and has no known grave.

CSM Bertram Charles Arter		*1st Bn Wiltshire Regiment*	
Service No.	5510	Age:	35
Place of birth:	Devizes, Wiltshire	Home Country:	England
Date of death:	11/08/1917	Cause of death:	Killed in action
Memorial:	Devizes, Wiltshire - Weymouth, Dorset		
War Cemetery:	Ypres Menin Gate - Panel 53.		
Next of Kin:	Margaret Mary Arter (wife) - George and Mary Marian Arter (parents)		
Address:	Rocky Knapps, Dorchester Road, Weymouth, Dorset - Devizes		

Regular soldier Bertram was the youngest son of George and Mary Arter and had served about 18 years with the Wiltshire Regiment. He had just finished his training when he was sent to South Africa serving throughout the campaign and toward the end of 1912 Bertram married Margaret Mary Kavanagh at Devizes. Bertram was a well-known footballer in Devizes and the surrounding area playing as a back in the Depot team in the Wiltshire league. At the outbreak of hostilities Bertram was serving on the permanent staff at the Wiltshires barracks and was posted to Weymouth where he acted as an instructor. In June 1917 Bertram was sent to France joining the 1st Battalion Wiltshire Regiment and was promoted to Sergeant Major. In the early hours of the morning on Saturday 11 August 1917 the Wiltshires were in positions at Westhoek and Bellewaarde Ridge near Hooge, Belgium. They were subject to shelling by German artillery and Bertram was killed as a result of an enemy shell. He is remembered on the Ypres Menin Gate and has no known grave. He left a widow and two infant children.

Private Reginald Frank Archer		*1st Bn Wiltshire Regiment*	
Service No.	3/3547	Age:	19
Place of birth:	Highworth, Wiltshire	Home Country:	England
Date of death:	11/08/1917	Cause of death:	Killed in action
Memorial:	Highworth, Wiltshire		
War Cemetery:	Ypres Menin Gate - Panel 53.		
Next of Kin:	Phineas & Kate Archer		
Address:	Church Street, Highworth, Wiltshire		

Reginald was the elest son of Phineas and Kate Archer and was employed as an apprentice at the Gas Works. It is likely he enlisted as a special reserve, joining the Wiltshire Regiment. He was sent to the

1st Battalion who, on Saturday 11 August 1917, were at Westhoek and Bellewaarde Ridge near Hooge, Belgium. They were subject to shelling by German artillery and Reginald was killed as a result of an enemy shell. His parents received the following letter from Second Lieutenant H. Clarke:

"I am deeply sorry to have to inform you that your son, Pte. R Archer, was killed on August 11th, 1917. He was one of our best, and was invariably most cheerful under every and all trying circumstances. The officers, N.C.O.'s and men of my company wish to join me in expressing to you their deepest sympathy in your sad bereavement. It may be of some comfort to you to know that his death was instantaneous, being struck by a shell."

He is remembered on the Ypres Menin Gate and has no known grave.

Private John Thomas Cook		*1st Bn Wiltshire Regiment*	
Service No.	26401	Age:	39
Place of birth:	Salisbury, Wiltshire	Home Country:	England
Date of death:	11/08/1917	Cause of death:	Killed in action
Memorial:	Salisbury, Wiltshire		
War Cemetery:	Ypres Menin Gate - Panel 53.		
Next of Kin:	Edith Mary Cook (wife) - Eva Cook (parent)		
Address:	The Close, Salisbury, Wiltshire		

Brewers drayman, John, was the eldest son of Eva Cook and in the summer of 1904 he married Edith Mary Dennis at Lambeth. It is likely he was conscripted into the army or enlisted under the Derby Scheme, joining the Wiltshire Regiment. He was sent to the 1st Battalion who, on Saturday 11 August 1917, were at Westhoek and Bellewaarde Ridge near Hooge, Belgium. They were subject to shelling by German artillery and John was killed as a result of an enemy shell. He is remembered on the Ypres Menin Gate and has no known grave. He left a widow and a young family.

Private Isaac Cox		*1st Bn Wiltshire Regiment*	
Service No.	18049	Age:	31
Place of birth:	Shipston, Oxfordshire	Home Country:	England
Date of death:	11/08/1917	Cause of death:	Killed in action
Memorial:	Highworth, Wiltshire – Great Western Railway		
War Cemetery:	Ypres Menin Gate - Panel 53.		
Next of Kin:	Edith Emily Cox (wife) – John & Jane Cox (parents)		
Address:	11 Kings Hill Road, Swindon, Wiltshire – Highworth		

Isaac was the youngest son of John and Jane Cox and was employed as a labourer in BB Shop at the Great Western Railway Works in Swindon. At the beginning of 1912 he married Edith Emily Sutton at Swindon and volunteered for service with the 5th Service Battalion Wiltshire Regiment on 5 December 1914. He arrived at Gallipoli on 12 July 1915 and after serving on the peninsular for four months he was evacuated to England suffering with dysentery and enteric fever in November 1915. He returned to the front in February 1916 and was sent to France and transferred to the 1st Battalion Wiltshire Regiment, serving at the Battle of the Somme. In November 1916, he was invalided to England suffering fron dysenrtry and poisoned feet (trench foot). Following his convalescence, he was given a week's home leave in May 1917 before returning to the 1st Wiltshires. He was killed on Saturday 11 August 1917 when the Wiltshires were at Westhoek and Bellewaarde Ridge near Hooge, Belgium. They were subject to shelling by German artillery and Isaac was killed as a result of an enemy shell, while he was acting as a stretcher bearer taking a wounded man to a dressing station. Issac's widow received the following letter from Captain J. T. Wood, Isaac's company commander:

Left: Isaac Cox

Right: Geoffrey Maynard Evans

"I am very sorry to have to tell you that No. 18049 Pte. Cox was killed in action on August 11th. He was one of our stretcher bearers, and was taking a wounded man across the dressing station when a shell burst near them, killing Pte. Cox instantaneously. It is a great mercy that he can have suffered no pain. About your husband I cannot speak too highly. He and Pte. Way (the other stretcher bearer with whom he used to work) were both men of the same sort, always ready to help the wounded, and not caring the least for any danger they might meet while doing their duty. His loss is deeply felt by us all."

He is remembered on the Ypres Menin Gate and has no known grave.

Chaplain 4th Class Geoffrey Maynard Evans MC		*Royal Army Chaplains Department*	
Service No.	N/a	Age:	35
Place of birth:	Harwich, Essex	Home Country:	England
Date of death:	11/08/1917	Cause of death:	Killed in action
Memorial:	Marlborough College, Wiltshire		
War Cemetery:	Divisional Collecting Post Cemetery and Extension - Grave II. E. 12.		
Next of Kin:	Samuel & Eleanor Sophia Evans		
Address:	Cartref, Dovercourt, Essex		

Geoffrey was the only son of Samuel and Eleanor Sophia Evans and was educated at Marlborough College, where he won 13 prizes. He served in the South African war with the Leicestershire Militia and was later given a commission with the 1st Battalion Welsh Regiment, serving in South Africa, Egypt and England. He retired in 1911 and took Holy Orders at Bishop College, Cheshunt, and was ordained Deacon in October 1913 by the Bishop of London, when he was Gospeller in St. Paul's Cathedral. He was ordained as a Priest in October 1914 and was a curate at the Marlborough College Mission at St. Mary's Tottenham. He was given a commission as a Chaplain on 19 May 1915 and arrived in France on 27 May 1915, being attached to the 3rd Battalion Worcestershire Regiment. Geoffrey was awarded the Military Cross for Gallant and distinguished service in the field in June 1917. He was killed by a German shell at Westhoek Ridge and originally buried at Bellewarde Cemetery. His Colonel wrote:

"He was an ideal Chaplain to the troops, and was simply worshiped by the men. He knew just how to deal with them, and there wasn't a man in either Battalion to which he ministered, who could help being affected by his courage and energy, cheerfulness and total absence of side."

In September 1925 Geoffrey's remains were located and he was identified by his clothing, epaulet, buttons and a pocket book, and his remains were moved to Divisional Collecting Post Cemetery and Extension. In the two days of fighting the 3rd Battalion Worcestershire Regiment lost one third of its strength.

SUNDAY 12 AUGUST 1917 - TEMPERATURE 22°c - 75% CLOUD COVER

RAINFALL 1.7mm

Lance Corporal William Holder *1st Bn Wiltshire Regiment*

Service No.	22827	Age:	20
Place of birth:	Colerne, Wiltshire	Home Country:	England
Date of death:	12/08/1917	Cause of death:	Killed in action
Memorial:	Colerne, Wiltshire		
War Cemetery:	Ypres Menin Gate - Panel 53		
Next of Kin:	George & Sarah Holder		
Address:	Martins Croft, Colerne, Wiltshire		

William was the fourth son of George and Sarah Holder and was employed as a paper mill worker. It is likely he was conscripted into the army or enlisted under the Derby Scheme, joining the Wiltshire Regiment. He was sent to the 1st Battalion who on Sunday 12 August 1917 were at Westhoek and Bellewaarde Ridge near Hooge, Belgium. They were subject to shelling by German artillery and William was killed as a result of an enemy shell. He is remembered on the Ypres Menin Gate and has no known grave.

Lance Coporal Francis Sidney Williams *1st Bn Wiltshire Regiment*

Service No.	32648	Age:	26
Place of birth:	Swindon, Wiltshire	Home Country:	England
Date of death:	12/08/1917	Cause of death:	Died of wounds
Memorial:	Calne, Wiltshire		
War Cemetery:	Brandhoek New Military Cemetery - Grave VI. C. 11.		
Next of Kin:	William Sperring & Sarah Ann Williams		
Address:	No. 2 Church Street, Calne, Wiltshire		

Frank was the youngest son of William and Sarah Williams and was employed as a fishmonger in the family business. He was conscripted into the army and called up in early 1917 joining the Wiltshire Regiment. He was sent to the front in July 1917 and attached to the 1st Battalion who in mid August 1917 were were at Westhoek and Bellewaarde Ridge near Hooge, Belgium. On 11 August 1917, he was struck by a shell splinter and died the following day at a casualty clearing station at Brandhoek. A comrade of Frank's, Lance Corporal Warwick, who was in the Red Cross Hospital at Exeter, wrote the following letter about the action:

"On Friday night, August 10th, we were ordered to take rations up to the front line, after which we were to go back for a good rest. We started from a dump in the Menin Road under shell fire. When we got near the front line our guide lost us, and we had to return with our burden to the place we had started, but that did not down hearten us. We received orders that the rations must be got up at all costs, and we succeeded in getting there and back without losing a man. No sooner had we returned when, 'pon my word, we had orders to go straight back again to the front line and hold it, but for how long we did

not know. You can picture our thoughts and feelings to receive orders 3 times in succession to go to the front-line trenches, but though foot sore and weary it was no good to grumble; we just had to do it.

We reached the line again much to our sorrow, as we were in a proper death trap. We arrived at 8am on August 11th, and I am deeply sorry to say that poor old Frank was hit by a piece of shell, commonly known as a "whiz-bang." The shell burst on top of the trench where he and several others of his comrades were digging in. Our sergeant-major and two men were killed by it, and Frank and another wounded. I saw him immediately after he was hit, and I understood him to say he was hit in the back and the right leg. We got him onto a stretcher and in less than half an hour he was on his way to the hospital. He told me to let his people know but I got wounded the next morning with a similar shell, and it is a miraculous how I escaped death. The strange thing about it is I must have been lying in the hospital bed where he died, but being badly wounded I did not realise where I was until I arrived at Hospital."

The Rev. Leonard T Pearson, C.F., writing from a casualty clearing station to Frank's mother, states;

"I am sorry to have to report the death of your dear son in this hospital, after being wounded in action. Everything possible was done for him, but without avail. I ministered to him before he died, and have buried him in the military cemetery."

In a subsequent letter the chaplain stated that Frank was wounded in the back by shell splinters which also penetrated his abdomen, he wrote;

"There is One in your home who can help you bear your sorrow, the Friend that sticketh closer than a brother, the Man of Sorrows acquainted with grief."

The following memoriam was inserted in a local paper by Frank's parents in August 1918;

In loving Memory of Frank youngest son
Far from his home he is laid to rest
And strangers tend his grave
But in the hearts that loved him best
Is dear the life he gave"

Private William Henry Jefferies		*1st Bn Wiltshire Regiment*	
Service No.	33531	Age:	19
Place of birth:	Swindon, Wiltshire	Home Country:	England
Date of death:	12/08/1917	Cause of death:	Killed in action
Memorial:	Not known		
War Cemetery:	Ypres Menin Gate - Panel 53.		
Next of Kin:	Henry & Ellen Madors Jefferies		
Address:	53 Lansdown Road, Swindon, Wiltshire		

William was the eldest son of Henry and Ellen Jefferies and it is likely he was conscripted into the army or enlisted under the Derby Scheme, joining the Wiltshire Regiment. He was sent to the 1st Battalion who on Sunday 12 August 1917 were at Westhoek and Bellewaarde Ridge near Hooge, Belgium. They were subject to shelling by German artillery and William was killed as a result of an enemy shell. He is remembered on the Ypres Menin Gate and has no known grave.

Private Edgar Rupert Patrick Noyes		*6th Bn Royal Irish Regiment*	
Service No.	4014	Age:	22
Place of birth:	Poulshot, Wiltshire	Home Country:	England

Date of death: 12/08/1917 Cause of death: Killed in action
Memorial: Poulshot, Wiltshire
War Cemetery: Ypres Menin Gate - Panel 33.
Next of Kin: Henry & Eliza Noyes
Address: Poulshot Lodge Cottage, Poulshot, Wiltshire

Farm worker Edgar was the fifth son of Henry and Eliza Noyes and volunteered for service initially joining the Wiltshire Regiment and then being transferred to the Royal Munster Fusiliers. He arrived at Gallipoli in September 1915 and it is likely he was either wounded or suffering from sickness and evacuated from the peninsular. Following his recovery, he was transferred to the 6th Service Battalion Royal Irish Regiment and returned to France. In June 1917, he was commended by the General of his Division for his:

"Gallant conduct and devotion to duty in the field."

On Sunday 12 August 1917, the 6th Royal Irish Regiment were at Square Farm between Wieltje and Zonnebeke, where they were subjected to a heavy German artillery barrage. Official sources state Edgar was killed in action on Sunday 12 August 1917, east of Ypres, however private John Salmon of Hinton, Chippenham and a friend of Edgar, stated that he was wounded at the same time and they had to lie in a shell hole for some time. Edgar passed peacefully away and his last thoughts were for his mother, whose name was the last words he uttered. Edgar is remembered on the Ypres Menin Gate and has no known grave.

Private Richard Dobson *6th Bn Royal Irish Regiment*
Service No. 5370 Age: 22
Place of birth: Chilton Foliat, Wiltshire Home Country: England
Date of death: 12/08/1917 Cause of death: Killed in action
Memorial: Chilton Foliat, Wiltshire
War Cemetery: Ypres Menin Gate - Panel 33
Next of Kin: Thomas & Lucy Dobson
Address: Chilton Foliat, Wiltshire

Farm labourer Richard was the eldest son of Thomas and Lucy Dobson and it is likely he was conscripted into the army or enlisted under the Derby Scheme, initially joining the Royal West Kent Regiment. He was sent to the front and transferred to the 6th Service Battalion Royal Irish Regiment. Richard was killed on Sunday 12 August 1917, when the 6th Royal Irish Regiment were at Square Farm between Wieltje and Zonnebeke, where they were subjected to a heavy German artillery barrage. He is remembered on the Ypres Menin Gate and has no known grave.

THURSDAY 14 AUGUST 1917 - TEMPERATURE 26°c RAINFALL 18.1mm

Private Joe Saunders *2nd Bn Devonshire Regiment*
Service No. 30784 Age: 24
Place of birth: Winterslow, Wiltshire Home Country: England
Date of death: 14/08/1917 Cause of death: Killed in action
Memorial: Horsell, Surrey – South Wonston, Hampshire
War Cemetery: Ypres Menin Gate - Panel 21
Next of Kin: Sarah Ann Jane Saunders (wife) - Sydney & Emma Saunders (parents)
Address: 17 South Road, Horsell, Surrey - South Wonston, Hampshire

Joe, a farm labourer, was the third son of Sydney and Emma Sanders and in the spring of 1913 he married Sarah Ann Jane Johnson at Fareham, Hampshire. It is likely he was conscripted into the army or enlisted under the Derby Scheme, initially joining the Dorset Regiment. He was sent to the front and transferred to the 2nd Battalion Devonshire Regiment. Joe was killed on Tuesday 14 August 1917, most likely by German artillery fire near Bellewarde Ridge on the left side of the Ypres – Roulers Railway. Joe is remembered on the Ypres Menin Gate and has no known grave. The Commonwealth War Graves Commission states his name as Joseph Sanders

Private John Henry Fishlock		*2nd Bn Devonshire Regiment*	
Service No.	25578	Age:	25
Place of birth:	Pewsey, Wiltshire	Home Country:	England
Date of death:	14/08/1917	Cause of death:	Killed in action
Memorial:	Wanborough, Wiltshire		
War Cemetery:	Bedford House Cemetery - Enclosure No.4 IV. F. 1		
Next of Kin:	Mary Ann Fishlock (wife) - William & Sarah Fishlock (parents)		
Address:	Highworth, Wiltshire - Pewsey, Wiltshire		

John, a carter on a farm, was the second son of William and Sarah Fishlock and in the spring of 1914 he married Mary Ann Read at Swindon. It is likely he was conscripted into the army or enlisted under the Derby Scheme, initially joining the Dorset Regiment. He was sent to the front and transferred to the 2nd Battalion Devonshire Regiment. John was killed on Tuesday 14 August 1917, most likely by German artillery fire near Bellewarde Ridge on the right side of the Ypres – Roulers Railway. After the war John's remains were located, South of the Ypres – Roulers Railway, east of Lake Farm. He was identified by means of a disc and moved to Bedford House Cemetery.

Private Frank Reginald Candy		*7th Bn Somerset Light Infantry*	
Service No.	265878	Age:	25
Place of birth:	Seend, Wiltshire	Home Country:	England
Date of death:	14/08/1917	Cause of death:	Killed in action
Memorial:	Seend, Wiltshire		
War Cemetery:	Duhallow ADS Cemetery - Grave VII. C. 2.		
Next of Kin:	Maud E. Candy (wife) – Frank Sidney & Hebe Jane Candy (parents)		
Address:	21 Scotland Road, Melksham, Wiltshire		

Frank was the eldest son of Frank and Hebe Candy and employed as a labourer on the Kennet and Avon Canal. At the start of 1913 he married Maude E. Turtle at Melksham and it is likely he was conscripted into the army or enlisted under the Derby Scheme, initially joining the Wiltshire Regiment Somerset Light Infantry. He was sent to the front and transferred to the 7th Battalion Somerset Light Infantry, who on Tuesday 14 August 1917 were at Solferino Farm, southwest of Boesinge, Belgium. Just as the men were putting on their equipment and getting ready to move out on their way to the front line, German artiulley opened fire on a British 8inch howitzer battery near the farm. An enemy shell exploded right in the middle of platoon B Company, killing seven men and wounding twenty, the platoon was almost wiped out. One of those killed was Frank. In 1918 his widow inserted the following memoriam in a local paper:

One year passed but still we miss him
Some may think the wound is healed
But they little know the sorrow
That lies within our hearts concealed

Jesus has called him far away
From this sinful land today
He will guide him ever more
On that sweet eternal shore

The Commonwealth War Graves commission state his regimental number as 265678, all other sources state 265878. In August 1919, Frank's grave was located near Magenta Farm and moved to Duhallow ADS Cemetery.

Private Edward Fisher		*7th Bn Somerset Light Infantry*	
Service No.	265014	Age:	36
Place of birth:	Box, Wiltshire	Home Country:	England
Date of death:	14/08/1917	Cause of death:	Killed in action
Memorial:	Box, Wiltshire		
War Cemetery:	Duhallow ADS Cemetery - Grave VII. C. 6.		
Next of Kin:	Florence Fisher (wife) – Joseph Edward & Mary Ann Fisher (parents)		
Address:	22 Brook Road, Twerton, Somerset – Box, Wiltshire		

Edward, an upholstery porter, was the third son of Joseph and Mary Ann Fisher and married in 1908. It is likely he was conscripted into the army or enlisted under the Derby Scheme, initially joining the Worcestershire Regiment in June 1916. He was sent to the front in June 1917 and transferred to the 7th Battalion Somerset Light Infantry. He was killed on Tuesday 14 August 1917 at Solferino Farm, southwest of Boesinghe, Belgium, by a German shell in the same incident as Frank Candy. In August 1919, Edward's grave was located near Magenta Farm and moved to Duhallow ADS Cemetery.

Private Lewis Gray		*7th Bn Somerset Light Infantry*	
Service No.	25576	Age:	35
Place of birth:	Mere, Wiltshire	Home Country:	England
Date of death:	14/08/1917	Cause of death:	Killed in action
Memorial:	Marston, Frome Trinity Church Frome, Somerset		
War Cemetery:	Duhallow ADS Cemetery - Grave VII. C. 4.		
Next of Kin:	Sarah Ellen Gray (wife) – Moses & Elizabeth Gray (parents)		
Address:	55 Selwood Road, Frome, Somerset		

Lewis, a farm labourer was the fourth son of Moses and Elizabeth Gray and toward the end of 1904 he married Sarah Ellen Stainer. He had been employed by Mrs Tucker of Mere and it is likely he was conscripted into the army or enlisted under the Derby Scheme, joining the Somerset Light Infantry on 29 May 1916. He was sent to the front in October 1916 and joined the 7th Battalion Somerset Light Infantry. He was killed on Tuesday 14 August 1917 at Solferino Farm, southwest of Boesinghe, Belgium, by a German shell in the same incident as Frank Candy. He left a widow and four children. In August 1919, Lewis's grave was located near Magenta Farm and moved to Duhallow ADS Cemetery.

Driver William Joseph Lock		*240th Bde Bn Royal Field Artillery*	
Service No.	825413	Age:	21
Place of birth:	Holt, Wiltshire	Home Country:	England
Date of death:	14/08/1917	Cause of death:	Killed in action
Memorial:	Not known		
War Cemetery:	Vlamertinghe New Military Cemetery - Grave V. C. 10.		
Next of Kin:	William & Catherine Alice Lock		
Address:	Broughton Giffard, Wiltshire		

Left: William Leonard Moss

Right: John Lionel Knight

William was the second son of William and Catherine Alice Lock and volunteered for service joining the Royal Field Artillery. He arrived in France on 20 March 1915 and was sent to the B Battery, 240th Brigade who on Tuesday 14 August 1917 were north west of Ypres. He was wounded most likely by German counter battery artillery fire and taken to a medical facility at Vlamertinghe, where he succumbed to his wounds soon after.

WEDNESDAY 15 AUGUST 1917 - TEMPERATURE 20°c - OVERCAST RAINFALL NIL

Private William Leonard Moss		*1st Bn Wiltshire Regiment*	
Service No.	24543	Age:	20
Place of birth:	Collingbourne Kingston, Wilts	Home Country:	England
Date of death:	15/08/1917	Cause of death:	Died of wounds
Memorial:	Collingbourne Ducis, Wiltshire		
War Cemetery:	St Sever Cemetery Extension Rouen - Grave P. II. D. 8B.		
Next of Kin:	William George & Elizabeth Moss		
Address:	Victoria House, Collingbourne Ducis, Wiltshire		

William was the eldest son of William and Elizabeth Moss and was employed in his father's drapery business. It is likely he was conscripted into the army or enlisted under the Derby Scheme, joining the Wiltshire Regiment. He was sent to the front to serve with the 1st Battalion and was wounded most likely by German artillery near Bellewarde Ridge, Belgium. He was evacuated to a base hospital at Rouen, France, where he succumbed to his wounds on Wednesday 15 August 1917.

6
The Battle of Langemarck

THURSDAY 16 AUGUST 1917 - TEMPERATURE 20°c OVERCAST - RAINFALL NIL

Private John Lionel Knight		*7th Bn Somerset Light Infantry*	
Service No.	12149	Age:	24
Place of birth:	Wells, Somerset	Home Country:	England
Date of death:	16/08/1917	Cause of death:	Killed in action
Memorial:	Great Western Railway Memorial		
War Cemetery:	Tyne Cot Memorial - Panel 41 to 42 and 163A		
Next of Kin:	Richard & Jane Knight		
Address:	Wells, Somerset		

John, known as Jack, was the second son of Richard and Jane Knight and was employed as a porter in the Traffic Department of the Great Western Railway at Westbury, Wiltshire. He volunteered for service joining the 7th Service Battalion Somerset Light Infantry, arriving in France on 24 July 1915. On Thursday 16 August 1917, the British attacked German positions south west of Langemarke the 7th Somersets attacking on the south side of the railway from Ypres. They crossed the Steenbeck with some difficulty as the banks of the stream were flooded, slippery and boggy. Soon after midnight the Germans bombarded the area with 5.9cm shells. They were also observed by German infantry and a 7.7cm gun that fired on the British attackers causing some casualties. The 7th Somersets dug in and were subjected to sporadic enemy fire while the Germans frequently sent up lights from Au Bon Gite south west of Langemarck. At 4.45pm the British creeping barrage commenced and the 7th Somersets advanced but they were fired on from a German machine gun in Au Bon Gite. The German position was captured by B Company, 7th Somersets. After this position fell there was little enemy opposition until the German front line was reached to the west of Langemarck. The condition of the ground became much worse and the attackers were frequently getting stuck in the mud and having to be pulled out by their comrades. All this while under withering Geramn machine gun fire from a line of pill boxes near Reitres Farm, west of Langemarke, where the advance was stopped. After a hold up of about fifteen minutes the 7th Somersets followed the creeping barrage through Langemarck and were fired on from German machine guns northwest of Langemarck. By 7am B Company, 7th Somersets, were at Alouette farm south east of Langemarck and by 7.15am the 7th Somersets had secured all their objectives although they had been subjected to heavy German machine gun and artillery fire throughout the attack. Jack was killed during the attack. He is remembered on the Tyne Cot Memorial and has no known grave.

Private Archie Arthur Portingale		*7th Bn Somerset Light Infantry*	
Service No.	265988	Age:	22
Place of birth:	Monkton Deverill, Wiltshire	Home Country:	England
Date of death:	16/08/1917	Cause of death:	Killed in action

Memorial: Codford St Mary, Wiltshire
War Cemetery: Tyne Cot Memorial - Panel 41 to 42 and 163A
Next of Kin: Edmund & Elizabeth Portingale
Address: 33 Cheapside, Codford St Mary, Wiltshire

Archie, a shepherd, was the youngest son of Edmund & Elizabeth Portingale and it is likely he was conscripted into the army or enlisted under the Derby Scheme, initially joining the Wiltshire Regiment. He was sent to the front and transferred to the 7th Service Battalion Somerset Light Infantry. Archie was killed during the battle of Langemarck on Thursday 16 August 1917, in the same action as Jack Knight. He is remembered on the Tyne Cot Memorial and has no known grave. Archie's brother Walter was to be killed in Palestine in 1918.

Private Frederick White — *7th Bn Somerset Light Infantry*

Service No.	204239	Age:	32
Place of birth:	Great Tew, Yorkshire	Home Country:	England
Date of death:	16/08/1917	Cause of death:	Killed in action

Memorial: Lechlade, Gloucestershire
War Cemetery: Tyne Cot Memorial - Panel 41 to 42 and 163A.
Next of Kin: Caroline White (wife) – George & Elizabeth White (parents)
Address: Redland, Highworth, Wiltshire – Station Road, Lechlade, Gloucestershire

Frederick, known as Fred and a stone mason, was the son of George and Elizabeth White and was employed by King & Bowley of Lechlade. At the beginning of 1915 Fred married Caroline Eagles at Swindon, and it is likely he was conscripted into the army or enlisted under the Derby Scheme, initially joining the Worcestershire Regiment in June 1916 at Bristol. He was sent to Herne Bay for training and transferred to the Devonshire Regiment and then sent to the front in June 1917 and transferred to the 7th Service Battalion Somerset Light Infantry. Fred was killed during the battle of Langemarck on Thursday 16 August 1917, in the same action as Jack Knight. Fred's officer wrote to his parents stating Fred had been buried with other comrades on the spot on which they fell. The location of the sight was lost in later fighting and Fred is today remembered on the Tyne Cot Memorial and has no known grave. In 1918 Fred's widow inserted the following memoriam in a local paper:

All souls are Thine; we must not say
That those who are dead pass away,
From this our world of flesh set free,
We know them living unto Thee.

He left a widow and a young family.

Private Charles William Gingell — *7th Bn Somerset Light Infantry*

Service No.	20134	Age:	35
Place of birth:	Box, Wiltshire	Home Country:	England
Date of death:	16/08/1917	Cause of death:	Killed in action

Memorial: Corsham, Wiltshire
War Cemetery: Tyne Cot Memorial - Panel 41 to 42 and 163A.
Next of Kin: Alfred & Hannah Jane Gingell
Address: Elly Green, Corsham, Wiltshire

Charles was a coal carter and the only son of Alfred and Hannah Gingell and it is likely he was enlisted under the Derby Scheme, joining the Somerset Light Infantry. He was sent to the front to the 7th Service

Battalion Somerset Light Infantry. Charles was killed during the Battle of Langemarck on Thursday 16 August 1917, in the same action as Jack Knight. He is remembered on the Tyne Cot Memorial and has no known grave.

Private Herbert Henry Taylor (Amor)		*144th Coy Bn Machine Gun Corps*	
Service No.	70622	Age:	20
Place of birth:	Devizes, Wiltshire	Home Country:	England
Date of death:	16/08/1917	Cause of death:	Killed in action
Memorial:	Melksham, Wiltshire		
War Cemetery:	Tyne Cot Memorial - Panel 154 to 159 and 163A.		
Next of Kin:	Frank William & Sarah Taylor		
Address:	Redstacks, Melksham, Wiltshire		

Twenty year old Herbert, a labourer, was the eldest son of Sarah Taylor and his real name was Amor. He initially volunteered at the age of seventeen joining the Wiltshire Regiment. Sarah Taylor complained to the army that her son had enlisted under age sending Herbert's birth certificate (stating his name was Amor) and leaving home had placed her family in financial hardship. The Army wrote to the Wiltshire Constabulary asking for clarification concerning the name, age and circumstances of the young soldier's enlistment and received the following reply.

"I beg to inform you that the enclosed certificate does refer to N.10439 Pte. Taylor of your Battalion who is an illegitimate child, but I believe has always gone in the name of Taylor since his mother married her present husband.

Taylor's parents are in poor circumstances the father some what deformed in the feet, his earnings as a Farm Labourer only 14 shillings per week with a wife and five children dependant on him, ages 10, 7, 4, 2 years and one 10 months, with a cottage rent of 4 Shillings and 6 pence per week. The sixth child aged 14 years has just been put out into a situation.

Pte. Taylor previous to enlisting was in a situation earning 4 shillings per week with board of which 2 shillings per week he gave to his mother. Since enlisting I am informed he has not seen fit to send his mother any money if it was only a little it would be very acceptable to her under the present circumstances."

Herbert was discharged from the army for being under age on 12 February 1915. Later he again enlisted with the Wiltshire Regiment, then transferring to the Machine Gun Corps. He was killed in action on Thursday 16 August 1917 west of Langemarck, Belgium. He is remembered on the Tyne Cot Memorial and has no known grave.

Gunner Edwin Victor Pitcher		*Z 36th Trench Mortar Bty Bn Royal Field Artillery*	
Service No.	163954	Age:	19
Place of birth:	Dorchester, Dorset	Home Country:	England
Date of death:	16/08/1917	Cause of death:	Killed in action
Memorial:	Not known		
War Cemetery:	Tyne Cot Memorial - Panel 4 to 6 and 162.		
Next of Kin:	Edwin Charles & Maria Pitcher		
Address:	Stockclose Farm, Aldbourne, Wiltshire		

Edwin was the third son of Edwin and Maria Pitcher and it it is likely he was conscripted into the army or enlisted under the Derby Scheme, initially joining the Royal Field Artillery. He was sent to the front and attached to Z Trench Mortar Battery of the 36th Brigade. He was killed in action most likely by German artillery on the first day of the battle of Langemarck. He is remembered on the Tyne Cot Memorial and has no known grave.

Rifleman Walter Shrapnell		*1/5th Bn London Regiment*	
Service No.	315056	Age:	32
Place of birth:	Trowbridge, Wiltshire	Home Country:	England
Date of death:	16/08/1917	Cause of death:	Killed in action
Memorial:	Trowbridge, Wiltshire		
War Cemetery:	Ypres Menin Gate - Panel 52 and 54.		
Next of Kin:	Mabel G M Shrapnell (wife) - Charles & Agnes Kate Shrapnell (parents)		
Address:	43 Mountfield Road, Ealing, London - 6 Eastbourne Terrace, Trowbridge		

Walter, a domestic gardener, was the third son of Charles and Agnes Shrapnell and married Mabel G. M. Jones in 1912 in Kent. It is likely he was conscripted into the army or enlisted under the Derby Scheme, initially joining the 9th then 12th London Regiment. He was sent to the front and transferred to the 5th Battalion London Regiment, who on Thursday 16 August 1917 attacked German positions at Glencourse Wood, south of Westhoek. No opposition was found until they reached the east side of the wood when one party of A Company reached the final objective, the race course in Polygon Wood, but were not heard of again. It is likely Walter was with this group because he was reported missing during the attack. In 1919 Walter's widow and family received official information stating that he was presumed to have been killed in action on Thursday 16 August 1917. His family inserted the following memoriam in a local paper

They are not dead who die in battle,
Giving there lives for honour, smiling at death's dart;
They are not dead whose memory still is living
within their loved ones hearts.

Walter left a widow and young family. He is remembered on the Ypres Menin Gate and has no known grave.

Rifleman Luther William Dancey		*1/5th Bn London Regiment*	
Service No.	301709	Age:	36
Place of birth:	Beanacre, Wiltshire	Home Country:	England
Date of death:	16/08/1917	Cause of death:	Killed in action
Memorial:	Melksham, Dauntseys School Memorial, Wiltshire		
War Cemetery:	Ypres Menin Gate - Panel 52 and 54		
Next of Kin:	Thomas and Lydia Dancey		
Address:	Beanacre, Melksham, Wiltshire		

Luther was the only son of Thomas and Lydia Dancey and was educated at Dauntseys School. He had held the position of Assessor of Income Tax and Rate Collector at Melksham and was well known in the town. He was a Freemason being a member of the "Chaloner Lodge" and was secretary of the local miniature shooting club. He volunteered for service in August 1915 and was sent to France in December 1916 joining the 1/5th Bn London Regiment. Luther's sisters received a letter from him dated 13 August 1917 in which he wrote in his usual cheerful manner. The next day the sister received a letter from a lieutenant from his regiment dated 14 August 1917 stating Luther had been killed in action and said:

"It is with deep regret that I have to inform you of the death of your brother, Rifleman Luther Dancey,

Left: Walter Shrapnell

Right: Luther William Dancey

who was killed in action on August 14th. He was struck by a fragment of shell and died instantaneously. He was greatly respected and his coolness at all times was a fine example to his comrades. His loss will be keenly felt by the whole company."

The letter states Luther was killed on the 14 August 1917. However, official records state Luther was killed in action in the same action as Walter Shrapnell on Thursday 16 August 1917. He is remembered on the Ypres Menin Gate and has no known grave.

Rifleman Reginald Albert Butler		*1/5th Bn London Regiment*	
Service No.	315215	Age:	25
Place of birth:	Chippenham, Wiltshire	Home Country:	England
Date of death:	16/08/1917	Cause of death:	Killed in action
Memorial:	Chippenham, Devizes Odd Fellows		
War Cemetery:	Ypres Menin Gate - Panel 52 and 54.		
Next of Kin:	George & Maria Butler		
Address:	27 Foghamshire, Chippenham, Wiltshire		

Reginald was a footman in service at Mayfair and the second son of George & Maria Butler. It is likely that he was either conscripted into the army or enlisted under the Derby Scheme, joining the 1/5th Battalion London Regiment. He was killed in action on Thursday 16 August on the first day of the battle of Langemarck, in the same action as Walter Shrapnell. He is remembered on the Ypres Menin Gate and has no known grave.

Lance Corporal William George Duckles		*2nd Bn Royal Berkshire Regiment*	
Service No.	19017	Age:	25
Place of birth:	Greenwich, Kent	Home Country:	England
Date of death:	16/08/1917	Cause of death:	Killed in action
Memorial:	Devizes, Wiltshire		
War Cemetery:	Hooge Crater Cemetery - Grave IV. H. 12.		
Next of Kin:	Wiliam & Elizabeth Duckles		
Address:	11 Prior Park Cottages, Bath, Somerset		

Bookstall clerk William was the only son of William and Elizabeth Duckles and it is likely he was either conscripted into the army or joined under the Derby Scheme being sent to the front joining the 2nd Battalion Royal Berkshire Regiment. At 4.45am on Thursday 16 August 1917, the 2nd Royal Berkshires attacked German positions east of Bellewarde Ridge, Belgium. The first objective fell without great opposition. The Hamebeke was crossed, however the British attacking unit on the right of the 2nd Royal Berkshires had been held up and the Germans in Nonne Boshen and Polygon Wood were shooting into the side of the 2nd Royal Berks as they advanced. The British creeping barrage continued and the 2nd Royal Berkshires captured the Iron Cross Redoubt, along with 50 German Prisoners. The British attackers continued to attack but as they reached their objective the Germans counter attacked the British battalions on the right who fell back and the 2nd Royal Berkshires sustained a large number of casualties. By 3pm the 2nd Royal Berkshires consisted of 4 officers, one wounded and 100 men. The German attacks continued and the British units on either side of the 2nd Royal Berkshires fell back forcing the 2nd Royal Berkshires to retire. William was reported missing on Thursday 16 August 1917, during the attack and later his parents were officially informed he was presumed to have been killed on the day he was reported missing. Some time after, In March 1919 William's remains were located, north east of Westhoek and he was identified by means of a disc. His remains were moved to Hooge Crater Cemetery.

2nd Lieutenant Albert Edward Mills		*2nd Bn Royal Berkshire Regiment*	
Service No.	N/a	Age:	21
Place of birth:	Westbury, Wiltshire	Home Country:	England
Date of death:	16/08/1917	Cause of death:	Killed in action
Memorial:	Dilton Marsh, Westbury Wesleyan Church, Wiltshire		
War Cemetery:	Tyne Cot Memorial - Panel 105 to 106 and 162		
Next of Kin:	Albert & Sarah Jane Mills		
Address:	Eastcot Newtown, Westbury, Wiltshire		

Albert was the eldest son of Albert and Sarah Jane Mills and volunteered for service with the Wiltshire Regiment in March 1915. After being promoted to Sergeant he applied for a commission which was granted in March 1917 and he was sent to Keble College, Oxford, for training for four months. He was sent to the front in July 1917 joining the 2nd Battalion Royal Berkshire Regiment. A letter from Albert was received by his parents on 10 August 1917 in which he stated that he would probably be going to the firing line again and that if he came out safely he would be coming home on leave in three weeks' time. Albert was reported missing on Thursday 16 August 1917, in the same action as William Duckles. His parents received the following letter from Lt. Colonel A.A. Danbury-Sparrow:

"It it is with the deepest regret that I am writing to tell you that your son Second Lieutenant A.E. Mills, is missing, and I am afraid there can be little doubt but that he is killed. The Battalion took part in the battle of August 16th and was subsequently driven back from the ground it had gained. It was during this retirement that your son was seen to fall and it was impossible to recover his body. I had not known him very long, but I had learned to like him very much, and his loss is felt very much by us all."

Later Albert's parents received official information that their son had presumed to have died on the day he was reported missing. He is remembered on Tyne Cot Memorial and has no known grave.

Sergeant Frederick George Woodhams		*13th Bn London Regiment*	
Service No.	490109	Age:	22
Place of birth:	Kensal Green,	Home Country:	England
Date of death:	16/08/1917	Cause of death:	Killed in action
Memorial:	Great Western Railway Audit Department Swindon Railway Museum		
War Cemetery:	Hooge Crater Cemetery - Grave XVI. C. 16.		
Next of Kin:	Frederick W. & Sophia G. Woodhams		

Address: 71 Ilbert Street, Queen's Park, Paddington, London

Frederick was the eldest son of Frederick and Sophia Woodhams and in 1910 took employment as a clerk in the Audit Department of the Great Western Railway Company. He volunteered for service joining the 13th Battalion London Regiment and arrived in France on 3 November 1914. He was killed in action on Thursday 16 August 1917, most likely by German artillery fire, when the 13th Londons were southwest of Zonnebeke. In July 1919 Frederick's remains were located near Anzac Farm southwest of Zonnebeke and were identified by means of a disc, before being moved to Hooge Crater Cemetery.

Private Arthur Minchin		*1/1st Bn Ox & Bucks Light Infantry*	
Service No.	204102	Age:	30
Place of birth:	Wargrave, Berkshire	Home Country:	England
Date of death:	16/08/1917	Cause of death:	Killed in action
Memorial:	Police HQ Devizes, Wiltshire		
War Cemetery:	Tyne Cot Memorial - Panel 96 to 98.		
Next of Kin:	Maud Minchin (wife) - Jacob & Jane Minchin (parents)		
Address:	Emscote House, 62 Market Place, Henley on Thames, Oxfordshire		

Wiltshire policeman Arthur was the eldest son of Jacob and Jane Minchin and had been stationed at Trowbridge and later Melksham. It is likely he was either conscripted into the army or joined under the Derby Scheme in January 1917 and just before he was sent to France he married Maud May at Henley in the spring of 1917. On his arrival on the continent he joined the 1/1st Battalion Ox & Bucks Light Infantry who on Thursday 16 August 1917 at 4.45am formed up on the west side of the Steenbeek west of St. Julien. After crossing the stream, the 1/1st Ox & Bucks made their way up the ridge on the east side of the Steenbeek and were met by heavy German machine gun fire. The leading company was entirely annihilated and it took the second and third waves to rush the German positions and hand to hand fighting ensued, before the enemy put up their hands and surrendered. After advancing another 150 yards to the east the 1/1st Ox & Bucks came under a cross fire by German machine guns. About 25 men were seen to reach Springfield northeast of St. Julien and some were seen to fall and at 9.30am others were seen to be led away as prisoners of the Germans. Arthur was killed on Thursday 16 August 1917 during the attack. He is remembered on the Tyne Cot Memorial and has no known grave. He left a young widow.

Corporal Herbert Arthur Rendell		*5th Bn Dorsetshire Regiment*	
Service No.	7878	Age:	31
Place of birth:	West Coker, Somerset	Home Country:	England
Date of death:	16/08/1917	Cause of death:	Died of wounds
Memorial:	Salisbury, Wiltshire		
War Cemetery:	Bard Cottage Cemetery - Grave IV. C. 33.		
Next of Kin:	James & Emma Rendell		
Address:	15 York Road, Fisherton, Salisbury, Wiltshire		

Herbert, known as Arthur, was the only son of James and Emma Rendell and enlisted with the Dorset Regiment on 10 March 1906, serving in England and India. He left the army in 1913 and as a reservist was called up at the out break of hostilities, arriving in France 27 August 1914, being sent to the 1st Battalion. He was gassed in February 1915 and evacuated to a base hospital at Rouen, then to England. Following his recovery, he was transferred to the 5th Service Battalion and was sent to Gallipoli in December 1915, then on to Egypt in January 1916 and then back to France arriving on 9 July 1916. He was attached to the 34th Trench Mortar Battery in August 1916 and rejoined the 5th Service Battalion in January 1917. Arthur was wounded during the attack southwest of Langemarke, near Haanixbeck Farm on Thursday 16 August 1917, and evacuated to Bard Crossing on the Yser Canal where he succumbed to his wounds soon after. It is likely he was originally buried at Marengo Farm Cemetery just south of Bard Cottage and relocated after the war. His personal property was returned to his father and consisted of metal ring, ribbon DCM, correspondence, 2 Identity discs, 3 coins, cigarette case, tobacco pouch, pipe, purse, religious book, wallet, locket, 2 cloth badges, pair of shoulder titles, cap badge, 5 photographs, wrist watch, match box cover, handkerchief.

Sergeant George Robert Batson *5th Bn Dorsetshire Regiment*

Service No.	14561	Age:	34
Place of birth:	Trent, Dorset	Home Country:	England
Date of death:	16/08/1917	Cause of death:	Killed in action
Memorial:	Sedgehill, Wiltshire		
War Cemetery:	Tyne Cot Memorial - Panel 92		
Next of Kin:	Flora Ellen Batson (wife) - Charles & Jane Batson (parents)		
Address:	Sedgehill, Wiltshire – Trent, Dorset		

George was the eldest son of Charles and Jane Batson and enlisted in the army on 22 August 1901, joining the 2nd Battalion Dorsetshire Regiment. On 15 January 1903, he was transferred to the 1st Battalion and sent to India. In July 1904, he was tried by District Court Martial, for offering violence to his superior officer and striking his superior officer in the execution of his duties. He was sentenced to 112 days Imprisonment with hard labour. He returned to duty and on 22 October 1906 he was transferred to the 2nd Battalion. One year later he was again tried by District Court Martial, for receiving stolen goods, taken from a Regimental Institution and sentenced to 90 days' imprisonment with hard labour. After his return to duty in January 1908 he was discharged from the army for misconduct. On leaving the army he took employment as a carter and on 30 May 1909 he married Flora Ellen Smith at Sherborne. At the outbreak of hostilities, he volunteered for service joining the 5th Service Battalion and was sent to Gallipoli in December 1915, then on to Egypt in January 1916 and then back to France arriving on 9 July 1916. George was killed during the attack southwest of Langemarck, near Haanixbeck Farm on Thursday 16 August 1917 and is remembered on the Tyne Cot Memorial. He left a widow and a young family.

Private John Abner Oliver *2nd Bn Devonshire Regiment*

Service No.	26019	Age:	32
Place of birth:	Newbury, Berkshire	Home Country:	England
Date of death:	16/08/1917	Cause of death:	Killed in action
Memorial:	Trowbridge, Wiltshire		
War Cemetery:	Tyne Cot Memorial - Panel 38 to 40.		
Next of Kin:	Elizabeth Oliver (wife) - Frederick & Mary Oliver (parents)		
Address:	107 Elm Park Road, Reading, Berkshire		

John was the second son of Frederick and Mary Oliver and was a painter in the employ of Mr W. Hussey. He was a prominent member of the Salvation Army which he had been associated with for 17 years and he had been a member of the Reading Corps prior to moving to Trowbridge. He was an enthusiastic musician and a band sergeant and band master of the young people's section. John married Elizabeth Gordon Mclean at Reading in the spring of 1908 and he joined the army in June 1916. After completing his training, he was sent to France in July 1917. He was killed in action on Thursday 16 August 1917 when the 2nd Devons were in reserve and two companies were sent to support the attacking units. It is likely he was killed near Hannebeke , North east of Hooge, Belgium. He is remembered on Tyne Cot Memorial and has no known grave.

Left: John Abner Oliver

Right: William Alexander Dixon

2nd Lieutenant William Alexander Dixon — *3rd Bn attd 8th Bn Royal Irish Fusiliers*

Service No.	N/a	Age:	18
Place of birth:	Bogota, Columbia	Home Country:	Columbia
Date of death:	16/08/1917	Cause of death:	Killed in action
Memorial:	Marlborough College, Wiltshire		
War Cemetery:	Tyne Cot Memorial - Panel 140 to 141		
Next of Kin:	Christopher E. & Esther Dixon		
Address:	Bogota, Columbia		

Eighteen year old William, was the eldest son of Christopher and Esther Dixon and volunteered for service enlisting with the Inns of Court, Officer Training Corps. He was given a commission with the Royal Irish Fusiliers in October 1915 and was sent to the front in July 1916, serving with the 8th Battalion. He took part in the attack on Messines Ridge in early June 1917 and was reported missing on Thursday 16 August 1917 during a British attack near Boory Farm north west of the Zonnebeke, Belgium. His parents later received official information stating their son was presumed to have been killed on the day he was reported missing. He is remembered on the Tyne Cot Memorial and has no known grave.

Private Heywood Francis Cluett — *7th Bn Royal Inniskilling Fusiliers*

Service No.	41724	Age:	19
Place of birth:	Heytesbury, Wiltshire	Home Country:	England
Date of death:	16/08/1917	Cause of death:	Killed in action
Memorial:	Sturminster Newton, Dorset		
War Cemetery:	Dochy Farm New British Cemetery - Grave VI. B. 21.		
Next of Kin:	Francis Jabez & Charlotte Cluett		
Address:	Bridge Street, Sturminster Newton, Dorset		

Nineteen year old Heywood was the only child of Francis Jabez and Charlotte Cluett and it is likely he was either conscripted into the army or joined under the Derby Scheme joining the Royal Inniskilling Fusiliers. He was sent to the front to the 7th Battalion and reported missing in fighting near Delva Farm, north west of the Zonnebeke on Thursday 16 August 1917. His parents were initially officially informed that he was presumed to have been killed on the day he was reported missing. His remains were later located and he is today buried in Dochy Farm New British Cemetery not far from where he fell.

Private Allan Jesse Wort		*7th Bn Royal Inniskilling Fusiliers*	
Service No.	41648	Age:	23
Place of birth:	Nomansland, Wiltshire	Home Country:	England
Date of death:	16/08/1917	Cause of death:	Killed in action
Memorial:	Nomansland, Wiltshire – Bramshaw, Hampshire		
War Cemetery:	Potijze Burial Ground Cemetery - Grave D. 16		
Next of Kin:	Frank & Maria Wort		
Address:	Nomansland, Wiltshire		

Allan, a builder's labourer, was the only son of Frank and Maria Wort and it is likely he was either conscripted into the army or joined under the Derby Scheme initially joining the Devonshire Regiment. He was sent to the front and transferred to the 7th Battalion Royal Inniskilling Fusiliers and was killed most likely by German artillery barrage while preparing for the attack west of Zonnebeke, Belgium.

Private Charles Alfred Tilley		*7/8th Bn Royal Inniskilling Fusiliers*	
Service No.	41754	Age:	19
Place of birth:	Fisherton, Wiltshire	Home Country:	England
Date of death:	16/08/1917	Cause of death:	Killed in action
Memorial:	Salisbury, Wiltshire		
War Cemetery:	Tyne Cot Memorial - Panel 70 to 72.		
Next of Kin:	John & Julia Tilley		
Address:	9 Farley Cottages Friary, Salisbury, Wiltshire		

Nineteen-year-old Charles was the youngest son of John and Julia Tilley and it is likely he was either conscripted into the army or joined under the Derby Scheme joining the 7th Battalion Royal Inniskilling Fusiliers. He was reported missing in fighting near Delva Farm, north west of the Zonnebeke on Thursday 16 August 1917. His parents were officially informed that he was presumed to have been killed on the day he was reported missing. He is remembered on Tyne Cot Memorial and has no known grave.

Rifleman Henry Albert Sumner		*14th Bn Royal Irish Rifles*	
Service No.	41115	Age:	34
Place of birth:	Finsbury, London	Home Country:	England
Date of death:	16/08/1917	Cause of death:	Killed in action
Memorial:	Not known		
W-ar Cemetery:	Tyne Cot Memorial - Panel 138 to 140 and 162 to 162A and 163A		
Next of Kin:	Sarah Beake (mother)		
Address:	Stert, Wiltshire		

Henry was the eldest son of Sarah Beake and was employed in the stables of Cater, Stoffell and Fortt of Bath, Somerset before working as a shoeing smith for a veterinary surgeon. He tried to enlist before the war but was rejected on account of deafness. He volunteered at the outbreak of hostilities and was accepted by the 4th Hussars and was sent to Curraugh, Ireland, where he was employed as a shoeing smith. In October 1916, he was sent to France being transferred to the 14th Battalion Royal Irish Rifles. He was killed during an attack near Somme Farm, a German strong point, north west of the Zonnebeke on Thursday 16 August 1917. Henry's mother received a letter from his company commander stating:

"He was a good soldier who bore himself well under the circumstances. He was killed while going 'over the top' and was killed instantaneously."

He is remembered on the Tyne Cot Memorial and has no known grave. His step brother was serving with the Royal Dublin Fusiliers at the time of Henry's death.

Private John Frederick Ernest Hutchinson *1/5th Bn Gloucestershire Regiment*

Service No.	240707	Age:	25
Place of birth:	Swindon, Wiltshire	Home Country:	England
Date of death:	16/08/1917	Cause of death:	Killed in action
Memorial:	Not known		
War Cemetery:	Tyne Cot Memorial - Panel 72 to 75.		
Next of Kin:	Robert & Eleanor Hutchinson		
Address:	7 Stroud's Hill, Chiseldon, Wiltshire		

John was the youngest son of Robert and Eleanor Hutchinson and had served an apprenticeship as a coach builder in the Great Western Railway Works in Swindon. He volunteered for service joining the 1/5th Territorial Battalion Gloucestershire Regiment and was sent to France on 29 March 1915. He was killed in action on Thursday 16 August 1917 when the 1/5th Gloucesters attacked German positions at St Julien. They were held up by German machine guns in Janet Farm to the east of St. Julien and sustained heavy casualties and were forced to dig in. John is remembered on the Tyne Cot Memorial and has no known grave.

Private Archibald Harry Merchant *1/5th Bn Gloucestershire Regiment*

Service No.	240605	Age:	21
Place of birth:	Sherston, Wiltshire	Home Country:	England
Date of death:	16/08/1917	Cause of death:	Killed in action
Memorial:	Sherston, Wiltshire		
War Cemetery:	Tyne Cot Memorial - Panel 72 to 75.		
Next of Kin:	Harry & Rosa Merchant		
Address:	Church View, Sherston, Wiltshire		

Archibald, known as Bert, was the youngest son of Harry and Rosa Merchant and was an agent for the Western Gazette. He volunteered for service on 17 August 1914 with the 1/5th Territorial Battalion Gloucestershire Regiment and was sent to France on 23 March 1915. He was killed instantaneously by a German shell on Thursday 16 August 1917 when the 1/5th Gloucesters attacked German positions at St. Julien. They were held up by German machine guns in Janet Farm to the east of St. Julien and sustained heavy casualties and were forced to dig in. His death was almost 3 years from the day he enlisted and signed on for 3 years or the duration of the war. At the time of his death he had been recommended for a commission. Bert's parents received the following letter from the Sergeant in charge of the signal section:

"I do not know how to express the sorrow of poor Bert's' fellow comrades in the signal section and myself in your sad loss. He was held in such high respect by all of us, he had an utter contempt for any danger. He was killed by a shell which wounded his Company Officer at the same time, while doing his duty in the manner worthy of a good and brave soldier during an attack in which the battalion was engaged. No woprds are too high in his praise, and I sincerely trust you will find consolation in the fact he suffered no pain, his death being instantaneous. Allow me on behalf of the Signal Section to express our very deepest sympathy in your sad loss and bereavement."

Bert's Company Commander wrote:

"I am awfully sorry to have to inform you of the death of your son, 24605 Lance Corporal A.H. Merchant. He was killed by a shell on the 16th August in the attack of that day. I need not say how sorry I am for you. He was a very good soldier, and worked well and cheerfully all the time he was out here. He was

in the Signal Section, and most reliable. He had been recommended for a commission. It may be some consolation to you that his death was instantaneous and he can have felt no pain."

A further letter was also received from a private in Bert's platoon who wrote:

"On behalf of the platoon, I beg to convey our united sympathy to you. This is due, as your dear son was killed in going into action on the 16th. He suffered no pain whatever, having been killed instantaneously. As a chum of your son, I can, with all sincerity and truth, say he was won of the best fellows one could meet, and one whom everybody respected and admired. Prior to going into the line, the platoon had a few most beautiful hymns, the favourite being 'Nearer my God to Thee' and your beloved son joined in the singing of all of the same. The platoon prays that God will comfort you in the sad hour of trial and sorrow, and let us try and remember at all times 'His Will be done.' Again expressing our united sympathy."

Bert is remembered on the Tyne Cot Memorial and has no known grave.

Private Archibald James Perry		*1/7th Bn Worcestershire Regiment*	
Service No.	41352	Age:	19
Place of birth:	Malmesbury, Wiltshire	Home Country:	England
Date of death:	16/08/1917	Cause of death:	Died of wounds
Memorial:	Malmesbury, Wiltshire		
War Cemetery:	Brandhoek New Military Cemetery No 3 - Grave II. B. 2.		
Next of Kin:	George & Emily Perry		
Address:	Kingswall, Malmesbury, Wiltshire		

Archibald known as Archie was the second son of George and Emily Perry and was educated at Westport Boys' School. He was a member of the Scouts and a patrol leader and a Kings Scout in the King Athelstan Troop, which his father had founded. When he was 13 he received from Chief Scout General Baden Powell the Merit Medal of the Scouts for saving the life of a boy in the river Avon at Malmesbury. On leaving education he went into service with Mr G.P. Fuller at Neston Park, before taking a position in the service of Henry Farquhar, at Mauchhne, Scotland, as a second footman. While at Mauchhne he was Assistant Scoutmaster of the 1st Mauchhne (Ayrshire) Troop of Boy Scouts. In 1915 he enlisted with the Army Ordanance Corps and when he became 19 years of age he was transferred to the Norfolk Regiment. He was sent to France and transferred again to the 1/7th Battalion Worcestershire Regiment. On 14 August 1917 Archie's parents received a letter stating he was going into battle and after it was all over he hoped to have a long rest. Archie was wounded most likely by German artillery while moving up for the attack at Langemarke, Belgium. He was evacuated to an Australian Casualty Clearing Station at Brandhoek where he succumbed to his wounds on Thursday 16 August 1917. Sister Ida O'Dwyer wrote to Archie's parents stating:

"I am writing to tell you about your son, Pte. A. J. Perry, 41352. He was brought into this hospital yesterday morning early about 2am, quite collapsed and very badly wounded in the abdomen and right leg. Everything possible was done to revive him, but he did not improve at all, and he died at 7am. I told him I would write home and say that he was wounded and he sent his love and said he would write as soon as he was well enough, as he had no idea he was dying. I am afraid it is so very little to tell you, but I thought it might be of some consolation to you to know that he was in hospital where he received every possible care and attention, and that he was relieved of his pain."

Gunner Frank Oram		*186th Bde Royal Field Artillery*	
Service No.	3813	Age:	22
Place of birth:	Uffington, Berkshire	Home Country:	England

Left: Frank Oram

Right: Graham Strange Whiting

Date of death:	16/08/1917	Cause of death:	Killed in action
Memorial:	No 15 Shop Memorial Swindon Railway Museum		
War Cemetery:	Vlamertinghe New Military Cemetery - Grave V. C. 38.		
Next of Kin:	Charles & Fanny Oram		
Address:	Uffington, Berkshire		

Frank was the youngest son of Charles and Fanny Oram and was employed as a labourer in No. 15 Shop, Carriage and Waggon Department, at the Great Western Railway Works at Swindon. He volunteered for service joining the Royal Field Artillery, arriving in France on 30 May 1915, being sent to the 186th Brigade. Frank was killed on Thursday 16 August 1917, most likely by German counter battery artillery fire. He left his money to his sweetheart Mary Hinder.

FRIDAY 17 AUGUST 1917 - TEMPERATURE 22°c - CLEAR - RAINFALL NIL

Lance Corporal Graham Strange Whiting		*1/8th TF Bn Royal Warwickshire Regiment*	
Service No.	306642	Age:	31
Place of birth:	Trowbridge, Wiltshire	Home Country:	England
Date of death:	17/08/1917	Cause of death:	Killed in action
Memorial:	Trowbridge, Wiltshire		
War Cemetery:	Tyne Cot Memorial - Panel 23 to 28 and 163A.		
Next of Kin:	Abraham & Ruth Whiting		
Address:	25 Gloucester Road, Trowbridge, Wiltshire		

Graham, a livery stable coachman, was the eldest son of Abraham and Ruth Whiting and joined the army under the Derby Scheme on 10 December 1915. He was called up on 15 March 1916 and sent to the 3/8th Royal Warwickshire Regiment and sent to France on 29 June 1916 joining the 1/8th Territorial Battalion Royal Warwickshire Regiment. In Late July1916 he was evacuated to No. 44 Casualty Clearing Station and then on to 36th Australian General Hospital at Bologne. He returned to his unit in late September 1916 and was treated again for diarrhoea in October 1916 and sent to 16th General Hospital. Following his recovery, in May 1917, he was sent to No. 2 Railway Construction and Maintenance Company, before returning to the 1/8th Warwickshires in late July 1917. Graham was reported missing on Friday 17 August 1917 near St. Julien when the 1/8th Warwickshires were subjected to heavy and prolonged German artillery shelling. In March 1918 Graham's mother received the following letter from the British Red Cross Enquiry Department:

"Since writing to you on the 5th December we have received another report as follows from Pte. Sowter who was in the same company now in 3rd London General Hospital states:

'L/Cpl. Whiting was wounded in the leg about the 16th August 1917. My pal Neath carried him out the next morning. We were in a shell hole near St. Julien, Ypres front. He was taken back to a dressing station and I think he died there. (Neath is probably with my battalion now, 10th Platoon. He is a smart fellow.) L/Cpl whiting was hit by shell fire and was wounded also in the body. He was dark, medium height, nice looking, had a moustache."

Having regard to the long time which has now gone by we fear that what Pte. Sowter thinks occurred most probably did actually happen."

Later official information was received by Grahams' parents stating he was presumed to have been killed on the day he was reported missing. He is today remembered on the Tyne Cot Memorial and has no known grave.

Tanks at the Third Battles of Ypres

Tanks cooperated, and it was a cooperation which made our success so absurdly easy and it is not as if it were a mere non-descript bit of open country which we advanced over, for the ground taken included a number of strong points, where the foundations and cellars of old farms and other clusters of buildings had been converted by the lavish use of ferro-concrete into really strong fortresses. The concrete is sometimes 8 feet and upwards thick, and in the best form is strengthened with layers of iron rods of hairpin shape embedded in the material. When a supply of rods of the proper shape was not available the Germans made use of all sorts of strange makeshifts, like the frames from bedsteads, stoves, fenders and similar articles of furniture, gathered among the local ruins, all welded in the solid mass of one huge thickness of concrete. I have already explained that though the results are formidable defence works, they are also traps for the garrisons when our men come along.

The operation was practically a trial of strength between our movable landships and the stationary forts, and the latter were hopelessly outmatched. The attack was largely a surprise, and before the Germans new anything was happening each fort had one or two tanks sitting on its doorstep. In several cases the mere sight of the monsters looking in at the windows was enough, and the garrisons surrendered out of hand. In some cases, they tried to get out the back doors and run for it, and our machine gunners had their chance, but invariably this was when the Tank was called at the front door only. The presence of another Tank behind was always enough to command discretion and prompt surrender. One tank got into trouble 200 yards before reaching its objective, so it made itself into a stationary fort also, and opened fire with all its guns when the Germans came pouring out and tried to run. Our infantry coming close behind dealt with them, and then the crew of the Tank got out, and, taking their machine guns with them, went on to new conquests, just as marines from a real ship might do or dismounted cavalry.

Another Tank got behind its particular for and opened fire on the back door, but two shots were enough; the garrison came streaming out to surrender. Two other Tanks wet to indicated strong points and found them already deserted, and came back grunting their disapproval, and so great was the terror spread among the enemy by this novel invasion that our men saw the Germans running far off in the distance from positions which it was not part of our programme to attack. The infantry engaged in the attack had, as the casualties show, an easy job, and their chief business was to take over batches of prisoners surrendering to the Tanks. In several of the forts the Tank crews found the Germans just about to begin breakfast, and our men sat down and ate the meals gratefully.

This was by no means the first service rendered by the Tanks on the Ypres front, though the ground here, from its nature, and more especially from the wetness, is singularly ill adapted to Tankmanship. In the attack on the 31 July 1917, Tanks accounted for something over 30 machine guns in various

British Tanks abandoned at Zillebeke in September 1917

positions, and one Tank alone took 80 prisoners. The affair yesterday, however, was the first in which Tanks undeniably played the chief part in the victory, the infantry part being altogether secondary. They won for us, at a purely trifling expense, ground and positions which might have been very costly to take by direct infantry assault.

Sergeant Edward Albert Frederick W. Hornblow 84th Bde Royal Field Artillery

Service No.	44410	Age:	28
Place of birth:	Blunsdon, Wiltshire	Home Country:	England
Date of death:	17/08/1917	Cause of death:	Killed in action
Memorial:	Not known		
War Cemetery:	Artillery Wood Cemetery - Grave I. A. 24.		
Next of Kin:	Edward & Fanny Hornblow		
Address:	6 Church Street Caversham, Reading, Berkshire		

Regular soldier Edward was the youngest son of Edward and Fanny Hornblow and joined the Royal Filed Artillery and arrived in France on 16 August 1914. He was killed on Friday 17 August 1917 most likely by German Counter battery artillery fire east of Boesinge Belgium.

Captain Felix George Buckley MC *8th Bn Northumberland Fusiliers*

Service No.	N/a	Age:	22
Place of birth:	West Oystesmouth, Glam.	Home Country:	England
Date of death:	17/08/1917	Cause of death:	Died of wounds
Memorial:	Not known		
War Cemetery:	New Irish Farm Cemetery - Grave X. B. 7.		
Next of Kin:	Maj. Edmond D. H. & Ellen C. Buckley		
Address:	New Hall, Salisbury, Wiltshire		

Felix was the younger son of Maj. Edmond and Ellen Buckley and was educated at Wellington College before attending Brasenose College, Oxford. He was given a commission with the 8th Service Battalion Northumberland Fusiliers and arrived at Gallipoli in September 1915. Following the evacuation of the peninsular the 8th Northumberland Fusiliers were sent to Egypt where they remained until they were transferred to France in July 1916. Felix was awarded the Military Cross in June 1917 for good service and bravery in the field. On the night of 14/15 August 1917, the 8th Northumberland Fusiliers relieved

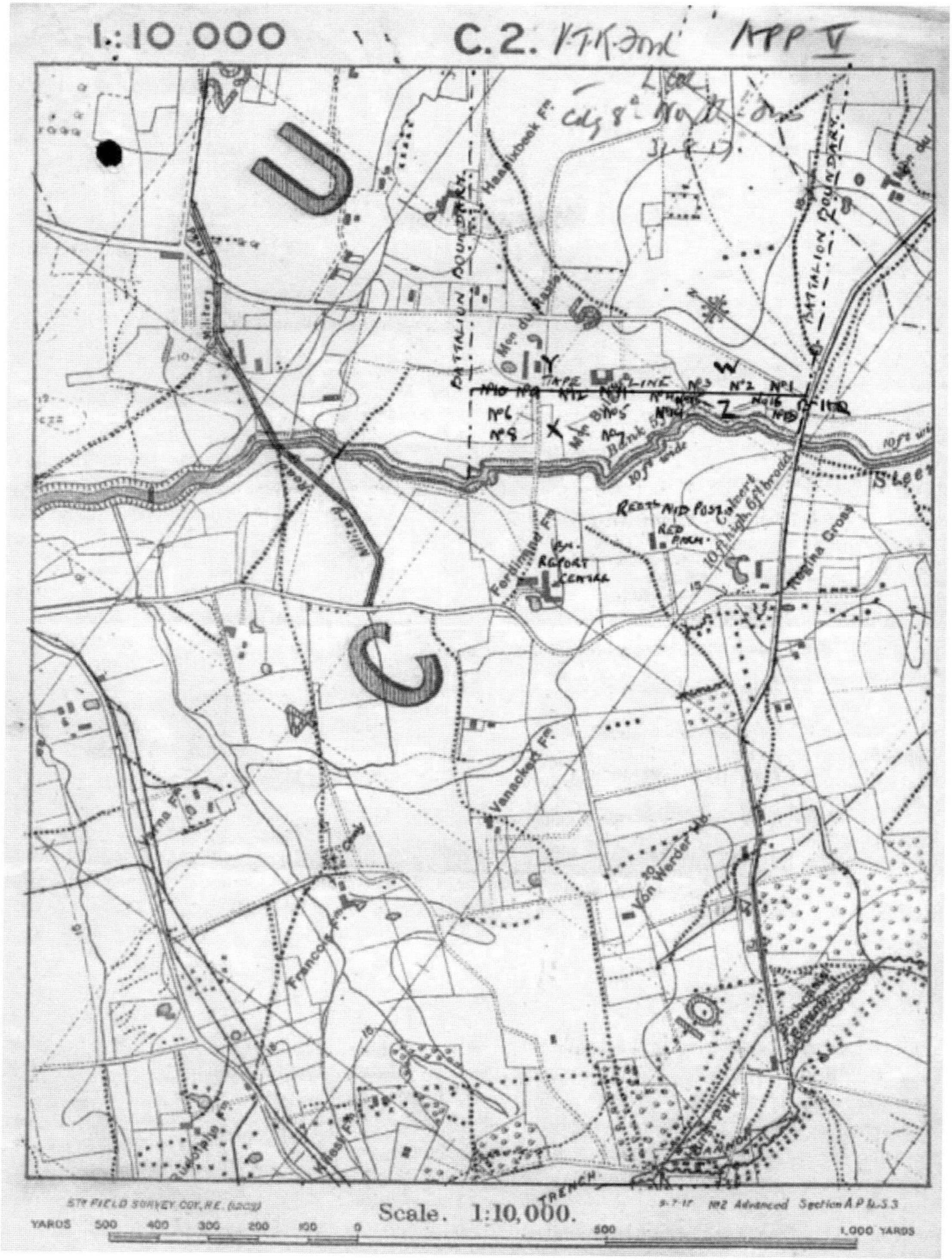

Map showing where the 8th Battalion Northumberland Fusiliers attacked near Langemarck on 17 August 1917, when Felix Buckley was killed

the 6th York and Lancashire Regiment in the British front-line, south of Langemarke. This was not completed until 4am because of the very muddy ground and scattered dispositions of the front-line posts. Felix was W Company Commander and slightly wounded in the head but insisted on remaining with his company. The following night of 15/16 August 1917 the 8th Northumberland Fusiliers moved into battle positions near Ferdinand Farm south of Langemark, and crossed the Steenbeck which at this point was 10 feet wide and the banks were 5 feet high. At 4.45am the 8th Northumberland Fusiliers, who were in the first wave, advanced. W Company were met by withering German rifle and machine gun fire and the war diary states Felix was killed. However another report states he was very severely wounded and died a few hours after and before reaching a dressing station. He was originally buried in Ferdinand Farm Cemetery, near where he fell, and his remains were relocated to New Irish Farm Cemetery In December 1919. The Commonweath War Graves Commission states he was killed on Friday 17 August 1917, while the War Diary states he was killed on the night of 15/16 August 1917.

Lance Corporal Alfred Henry Marsh *2nd Bn Royal Berkshire Regiment*

Service No.	12852	Age:	24
Place of birth:	Pewsey, Wiltshire	Home Country:	England
Date of death:	17/08/1917	Cause of death:	Died of wounds
Memorial:	Lambourn, Berkshire		
War Cemetery:	Brandhoek New Military Cemetery No 3 - Grave II. J. 1.		
Next of Kin:	Frances Ann Wooldridge		
Address:	Lambourn, Berkshire		

Farm labourer Alfred was the oldest son of Frances Ann Wooldridge and was the first man to volunteer at a recruiting meeting at Lambourn, soon after the outbreak of hostilities. He enlisted with the Royal Berkshire Regiment and arrived in France on 25 July 1915, being sent to the 2nd Battalion. He was wounded in the chest and both legs, when the 2nd Royal Berkshires attacked German positions east of Bellewarde Ridge and was evacuated to a casualty clearing station at Brandhoek. Alfred's mother received the following letter from Sister Luard:

"He was wounded in the chest and both legs on August 17th, and died the same day. We made him comfortable and did all we could for him, but he soon became unconscious, and at 6pm passed peacefully away."

The Chaplain of the casualty clearing station wrote;

"The bodies of our gallant soldiers are laid by our chapel altar until buried in the military cemetery. Their graves will be cared for and crosses put up. We hope you will get his name put on your church roll for remembrance before God. I grieve to say he did not survive the wounds with which he was brought in. I hope you will meet this trial of your faith with Christian bravery. God made him brave to dare and will give you power to carry on and through."

Lance Corporal Horace Albert Millard *1/5th Bn London Regiment*

Service No.	301571	Age:	24
Place of birth:	Islington, London	Home Country:	England
Date of death:	17/08/1917	Cause of death:	Died of wounds
Memorial:	Not known		
War Cemetery:	Mendinghem Military Cemetery - Grave III. F. 9.		
Next of Kin:	Henry Curtis & Catherine Sinta Millard		
Address:	The Laurels, Elmsleigh Drive, Leigh on Sea, Essex		

Horace, a civil service clerk, was the fourth son of Henry and Catherine Millard and the Grandson of

Mrs Millard of Westbury. He volunteered joining the 1/5th Battalion London Regiment and was for the early part of the war employed as a musketry instructor at Fovant, Wiltshire. He was sent to the front in December 1916. He was shot through the head and leg on Thursday 16 August 1917 when the 1/5th London Regiment attacked German positions at Glencourse Wood, south of Westhoek. He was taken to No. 12 Casualty Clearing Station at Mendinghem, where he succumbed to his wounds on Friday 17 August 1917. His uncle Denham Charley Millard had been killed on 8 July 1917 near Hill 60.

SATURDAY 18 AUGUST 1917 - TEMPERATURE 23°c -CLEAR RAINFALL NIL

Private Ernest Arthur Bassett		*184th Bn Machine Gun Corps*	
Service No.	30461	Age:	24
Place of birth:	Warminster, Wiltshire	Home Country:	England
Date of death:	18/08/1917	Cause of death:	Died of wounds
Memorial:	Warminster, Wiltshire		
War Cemetery:	Brandhoek New Military Cemetery No 3 - Grave II. E. 10.		
Next of Kin:	Richard & Ellen Bassett		
Address:	51 Brook Street, Warminster, Wiltshire		

Ernest, a carter, was the youngest son of Richard and Ellen Bassett and it is likely he was either conscripted into the army or enlisted under the Derby Scheme, joining the Machine Gun Corps. He was sent to the front and served with the 184th Company. He was wounded east of Ypres and evacuated to a casualty clearing station at Brandhoek, where he succumbed to his wounds on Saturday 18 August 1917. Ernest's parents received the following letter from Lieutenant H. G. Allen:

It is with the greatest regret that I have to inform you of the death of your son Ernest, which occurred as the result of wounds received on the 18th August. He was at work at the time building a gun emplacement, when a shell burst practically at his feet, and severely wounded him in the head. We did what we could for him and got him away on a stretcher, but heard later he passed away on arrival at the dressing station. I do not think he regained consciousness after his wound and would suffer no pain. Your son has been in my section ever since I joined the Company some nine months ago. He was No. 1 of his gun team, and one of the best lads I have ever had or ever wished to have under me. I have on several occasions been in quite hot places with him, and he has always been cool and fearless and ready to do his job, no matter how heavy the shelling. He was always most willing, and I shall miss him more than I can express. He was loved by me and all his comrades. He was their leader in sports, particularly football, and the whole section feel the loss tremendously. On behalf of his comrades and myself I wish to express to you and all his relatives our very sincere sympathy with you in your bereavement."

Rifleman Arthur Robert William Hall		*12th Bn Rifle Brigade*	
Service No.	S/16036	Age:	20
Place of birth:	Melksham, Wiltshire	Home Country:	England
Date of death:	18/08/1917	Cause of death:	Killed in action
Memorial:	Not known		
War Cemetery:	Tyne Cot Memorial - Panel 145 to 147.		
Next of Kin:	Arthur James & Rosina Hall		
Address:	127 Queen's Road, Peckam, London		

Arthur, a clerk, was the eldest son of Arthur and Rosina Hall and volunteered for service joining the Rifle Brigade. He was trained as a Lewis gunner and arrived in France on 21 June 1916, being sent to the 12th Battalion on 30 June 1916. At the end of August 1916, Arthur was seen by the Regimental Medical Officer, at the No. Camp Reception Station (a medical inspection room when out of the fighting),

Albert John Sansom

and was diagnosed with ICT feet, inflammation of the connecting tissue in his feet, better known as trench foot. He was evacuated to No 3 Stationary Hospital at Rouen, and after a two-week recovery period he returned to his unit in mid September 1916. On Saturday 18 August 1917, the 12th Rifle Brigade were south of Langemarck in the area of Alouette Farm and were subjected to continuous hostile German artillery shelling and sniping from Germans in Rat House to the southeast. Arthur was killed during this action. In 1918, Arthur's personal property was returned to his parents and consisted of a pipe, wallet, purse, photo's, cases and a registration card. He is remembered on the Tyne Cot Memorial and has no known grave.

Private Albert John Sansom		*1/6th Bn Royal Warwickshire Regiment*	
Service No.	306733	Age:	38
Place of birth:	Smethwick, Staffordshire	Home Country:	England
Date of death:	18/08/1917	Cause of death:	Killed in action
Memorial:	Carriage & Wagon Paint Shop Memorial Great Western Works, Swindon		
War Cemetery:	Tyne Cot Memorial - Panel 23 to 28 and 163A.		
Next of Kin:	John & Elizabeth Jane Sansom		
Address:	136 William Street, Swindon, Wiltshire		

Albert, known as Bert, was the eldest son of John and Elizabeth Sansom and was employed as a painter in the carriage and wagon paint shop at the Great Western Railway Works at Swindon. He enlisted under the Derby Scheme on 26 November 1915 and was called up on 20 March 1916, being sent to the 3/8th Royal Warwickshire Regiment. He arrived in France on 22 July 1916 and in December 1916 he was evacuated to No. 9 Casualty Clearing Station suffering from diarrhoea. He was then sent to No. 11 Stationary Hospital at Rouen, where he was diagnosed with debility, better known to us as "shell shock," or chronic fatigue syndrome. Bert was evacuated to England on Christmas Day 1916 and following his recovery was returned to the France on 11 June 1917. He was transferred to the 1/6th Battalion Royal Warwickshire Regiment in Belgium on 27 July 1917 who on Saturday 18 August 1917 were near the Steenbeck North of St. Julien. Bert was killed most likely by German artillery fire. His personal property was returned to his family consisting of a mirror, a belt and a pocket knife. He is remembered on the Tyne Cot Memorial and has no known grave. In 1918 his family inserted the following memoriam in a local paper:

A wooden cross is the only sign,
Neath the rays of the setting sun,
To denote the place of one who did his duty,
Facing the dangers as each day dawned
And like a hero fell.

Airmen at the Third Battle of Ypres

Before the battle began, that is by the 31 July 1917, British Airmen had, in spite of inferior observation during the last few days, established absolute control of the air over the whole battle area, just as they did on the Somme and at Messines. Then came that long spell of unprecedented weather, when four days it rained continuously, and for nearly a week afterwards thick white mists hung over all the Flanders plains, so that work in the air was almost impossible. These were ten days of blessed rest for the German flyers. They could reorganise their shattered squadrons, bring up reinforcements, both of new machines to replace those lost and of those special auxiliary forces known as "circuses," which move from one point to another at the front, wherever they are most needed. More important than all, the individual pilots had ten days' rest for their nerves, ten long days in which they had every excuse for not going up, and in which the British pilots could not get at them. So that when the air cleared again and fighting was once more possible, our British work had been largely undone, and there was a rejuvenated flying corps.

Driving down the German machines was only a minor and accidental item of the Flying Corps' work. The real essential function of aeroplanes was observation, to assist the artillery and by photographing and bringing back intelligence, to help the High Command in their battle plans. Secondary to this was the work of actual co-operation in the battle, flying low and firing on the German infantry. Fighting enemy machines was only necessary to prevent the enemy's interference with the more important work and to make it impossible for the German flyers to do similar with their ground forces.

In the course of a single day the British artillery guns, guided by the Royal Flying Corps, silenced 73 hostile batteries. Observation showed 21 gun pits entirely destroyed and 35 others badly damaged. Eighteen explosions of ammunition stores were caused and 15 other fires. The British aircraft raided the German lines, on a daily basis, dropping between a dozen to 20 tons of explosives. From early dawn till dark the British pilots fired with their machine guns into the enemy trenches and at German troops in shell holes or marching on roads. The British aircraft attack and silence batteries and dive down and wipe out machine guns on the ground and anti-aircraft guns which constantly fired at them. They chased trains along the railways, firing into the engine cabs and through the roofs and windows of the carriages.

One British pilot who went to attack a German aerodrome found a machine just about to rise from the ground, so he dived and fired into and wrecked it, then circled round and continued to shatter the wreckage. He made a tour of the aerodrome, firing into the sheds from below the level of the roof, but as no more life appeared he went away and found a German battery in action. He fired along the line of enemy guns silencing the lot. Then he "sat on" the battery for five minutes in case it recommenced firing, but as it did not he returned home using the remainder of his ammunition on enemy trenches he was flying over.

Another British airman had a similar morning. He took on first an enemy aerodrome, then a German battery, then a train and finally the enemy infantry trenches at Polygon Wood. Another had the luck to find a large body of German troops on a road, so he went down and flew above them, firing as he went, and when they scattered and hid in ditches and a wood the road was dotted with dead.

Another spent his time at altitudes of between 50 to 100 feet. He found three enemy machines getting ready to take off from an aerodrome, so he wrecked them all. Then he found a wagon and horses on the road and shoot both horses. Next, he visited a railway station and as no train was there, shot the guard on duty and finished up by attacking and stampeding a column of horses on the road.

Still another tackled a German aerodrome, circling round at a height of 20 feet, firing into every shed and setting one on fire. A nice two-seater machine was being got out when he arrived, so he wrecked that and used all the rest of the ammunition he could spare flying up and down a railway train full of troops in a siding, firing into it through the roofs and windows. Another flew up and down the main street of Zonnebeke at a height of 500 feet, firing on German troops which were crowded in the street

An Australian R. E. 8 after a forced landing in Flanders mud on the battlefield near Westhoek, following engine trouble

till they had all taken cover. Then visited a train on a railway siding; then finding an enemy battery firing, he silenced that and dived on and raided enemy trenches on the way home.

Another youthful pilot who had been gaining notoriety, started by visiting an enemy aerodrome where he bombed a group of machines on the ground and fired into the sheds. He went off and found a railway siding full of German troops waiting for a train, so he scattered them and returned to the aerodrome. One machine was just rising, so he attacked it and it crashed. A second rose from the ground, but he attacked that also, and when it was only 20 feet or so up it side-slipped and likewise crashed. As he left a machine gun opened fire on him so he went for that and silenced it before returning home.

SUNDAY 19 AUGUST 1917 - TEMPERATURE 20.5°c -CLOUD COVER - RAINFALL NIL

Private Harold Smith Locke		*2/8th Bn Worcestershire Regiment*	
Service No.	263059	Age:	37
Place of birth:	Swindon, Wiltshire	Home Country:	England
Date of death:	19/08/1917	Cause of death:	Killed in action
Memorial:	Halesowen, Worcester		
War Cemetery:	Tyne Cot Memorial - Panel 75 to 77		
Next of Kin:	Maud Locke (wife) - James Joseph & Mary J. Locke		
Address:	Halesowen, Worcester		

Grocer's manager, Harold, was the second son of James and Mary Locke and in the spring of 1915 married Maud Wilcox. It is likely he was either conscripted into the army or enlisted under the Derby Scheme joining the Worcestershire Regiment. Harold was sent to the front, serving with the 2/8th Battalion and was killed on Sunday 19 August 1917 when the 2/8th Worcesters were subjected to heavy hostile German artillery shelling east of Wieltje, in the area of Uhlan Farm. He is remembered on the Tyne Cot Memorial and has no known grave. He left a sorrowing widow.

Private Edwin Charles Soper		*2/6th Bn Gloucestershire Regiment*	
Service No.	38431	Age:	32
Place of birth:	Salisbury, Wiltshire	Home Country:	England
Date of death:	19/08/1917	Cause of death:	Killed in action
Memorial:	Not known		
War Cemetery:	Oxford Road Cemetery - Grave I. A. 6.		
Next of Kin:	Elsie Annie Soper (wife) - Alfred E. & Elizabeth Soper (parents)		
Address:	7 Midland Terrace, Keighley, Yorks - 92 Addington Road., Reading.		

Edwin, a carpenter, was the eldest son of Alfred and Elizabeth Soper and in the spring of 1911 married Elsie Annie Luxton at Christchurch, Hampshire. It is likely he was either conscripted into the army or enlisted under the Derby Scheme initially joining the Devonshire Regiment before being transferred to the Somerset Light Infantry. He was then sent to the front and transferred to the 2/6th Territorial Battalion Gloucestershire Regiment. Edwin was killed on Sunday 19 August 1917, while in the British front line east of Wieltje, by hostile German artillery shelling. His brother John Elford Soper was to be killed three days later while serving with the Oxford and Bucks Light Infantry.

Private Joseph Harper Thorne		*2nd Bn Hampshire Regiment*	
Service No.	27805	Age:	28
Place of birth:	Great Durnford, Wiltshire	Home Country:	England
Date of death:	19/08/1917	Cause of death:	Died of wounds
Memorial:	Amesbury, Wiltshire		
War Cemetery:	Etaples Military Cemetery - Grave XXII. P. 2.		
Next of Kin:	Henry & Emma Thorne		
Address:	66 Salisbury Street, Amesbury, Wiltshire		

Joseph, a carrier, was the only son of Henry and Emma Thorne and it is likely he was either conscripted into the army or enlisted under the Derby Scheme initially joining the 6th Duke of Cornwalls Light Infantry. He was sent to the front and transferred to the 2nd Battalion Hampshire Regiment, who in August 1917 were in action west of Langemarck. Joseph was wounded and evacuated to St. Johns Hospital at Etaples where he succumbed to his wounds on Sunday 19 August 1917.

MONDAY 20 AUGUST 1917 - TEMPERATURE 21.5°c -50% CLOUD COVER - RAINFALL NIL

Private Herbert Frank Love		*2nd Bn Royal Fusiliers*	
Service No.	G/65762	Age:	27
Place of birth:	Tisbury, Wiltshire	Home Country:	England
Date of death:	20/08/1917	Cause of death:	Died of wounds
Memorial:	Tisbury, Wiltshire		
War Cemetery:	Dozinghem Military Cemetery - Grave IV. I. 19.		
Next of Kin:	Frank & Mary Love		
Address:	Style Cottages, Tisbury, Wiltshire		

Frank, a grocer's assistant, was the eldest son of Frank and Mary Love and it is likely he was either conscripted into the army or enlisted under the Derby Scheme joining the Royal Fusiliers. He was sent to the front serving with the 2nd Battalion who attacked German positions near Langemarck. Herbert was wounded at this time and taken to a casualty clearing station at Dozinghem, where he succumbed to his wounds on Monday 20 August 1917.

Sapper Harry George Hiscock		*153rd Field Coy Bn Royal Engineers*	
Service No.	95996	Age:	23
Place of birth:	Devizes, Wiltshire	Home Country:	England
Date of death:	20/08/1917	Cause of death:	Died of wounds
Memorial:	Devizes, Wiltshire		
War Cemetery:	Locre Hospice Cemetery - Grave I. B. 26.		
Next of Kin:	Charles and Mary Elizabeth Hiscock		
Address:	Station Road, Gillingham, Dorset		

Metal worker and fitter Harry was the youngest son of Charles and Mary Hiscock and volunteered for service on 24 April 1915 joining the Royal Engineers. After completing his training, he arrived in France on 19 November 1915 being sent to 153rd Field Company. Harry was wounded on the night of 19 August 1917 while in forward positions in near Vierstraat, Belgium. He was with his officer, a non-commissioned officer, and comrades working in the trenches when a shell burst amongst the party. The shell caused three deaths with Harry dying of his wounds on Monday 20 August 1917. Mary Hiscock received the following letter from a Lieutenant in Harry's company:

"Your son was nobly doing his duty in our advanced organized shell holes, well in front of our front line, at the time of the accident. Your dear boy was acting as orderly to his section officer, who was killed outright by the same shell, which struck your son. He will be greatly missed amongst his chums and the accident has cast a terrible gloom over the whole company, as he was a general favourite and was marked out for promotion. He was a good honest worker, clean, alert, attentive and obedient and the jolliest of lads between the hours of duty. The proudest tribute I can pay to his memory is that he died for his country and was loved and respected by all"

In the above letter, the lieutenant states that the shell was an accident which indicates that Harry was killed by friendly fire. Harry's personal possessions were returned to his mother and consisted of 2 discs, letter, notebook, cigarette case, electric torch and purse. Harry was buried in Locre Hospice Cemetery, Belgium.

TUESDAY 21 AUGUST 1917 - TEMPERATURE 21.5°c -CLEAR - RAINFALL NIL

Private Tom Walter Candy — *2/1st Bn Ox & Bucks Light Infantry*

Service No.	204214	Age:	38
Place of birth:	Salisbury, Wiltshire	Home Country:	England
Date of death:	21/08/1917	Cause of death:	Killed in action
Memorial:	Not known		
War Cemetery:	Tyne Cot Memorial - Panel 96 to 98		
Next of Kin:	Florrie Candy (wife) – Joseph Candy (parent)		
Address:	27 Roslyn Road, Redland, Bristol, Gloucestershire		

Tom, a carter, was the son of Joseph Candy and on 1 May 1899 he married Florrie Beatrice Smith at Westbury on Trym. It is likely he was either conscripted into the army or enlisted under the Derby Scheme joining the 2/1st Battalion Oxfordshire and Buckinghamshire Light Infantry. He was killed on Tuesday 21 August 1917, most likely by German artillery fire, at Pommern Castle, northwest of Zonnebeke. He is remembered on the Tyne Cot Memorial and has no known grave. He left a widow and a young son.

Private William Underwood — *2/4th Bn Royal Berkshire Regiment*

Service No.	220209	Age:	23
Place of birth:	Milton, Wiltshire	Home Country:	England
Date of death:	21/08/1917	Cause of death:	Killed in action
Memorial:	Not known		
War Cemetery:	White House Cemetery St Jean Les Ypres - Grave III. B. 2.		
Next of Kin:	Thomas & Mary A. Underwood		
Address:	Pewsey, Wiltshire		

William was the only son of Thomas and Mary Underwood and was employed as a farm worker for Mr Maidment of West Wick. It is likely he was either conscripted into the army or enlisted under the Derby

Scheme initially joining the Wiltshire Regiment, in February 1916. In mid 1917 he was transferred to the Berkshire Regiment and arrived in France in July 1917, being sent to 2/4th Battalion Royal Berkshire Regiment. He was killed by a German shell on Tuesday 21 August 1917, near Weiltje. William's parents received the following letter from his company commander:

"I have the sad duty of writing to tell you that your son, Private W. Underwood, was killed in action by a shell on August 21st. The service was read over his grave by the regimental chaplain. I may not tell you where he is buried, but we have put a cross over the spot. Although he had been so short a time with us, he was liked by all, and his comrades join with me in sympathising with you in your time of great loss."

Rifleman Reginald Llewellyn Maple		*9th Bn Kings Royal Rifle Corps*	
Service No.	R/18558	Age:	23
Place of birth:	Salisbury, Wiltshire	Home Country:	Wales
Date of death:	21/08/1917	Cause of death:	Died of wounds
Memorial:	Tumble Carmarthenshire		
War Cemetery:	Birr Cross Roads Cemetery - Grave III. E. 20.		
Next of Kin:	Ada Florence Kate Maple (wife) - Thomas & Elizabeth Maple		
Address:	10 Railway Terrace, Llanelly, Carmarthenshire		

Reginald, a labourer, was the second son of Thomas and Elizabeth Maple and married Ada Florence Kate Mager at Llanelli on 6 May 1914. He volunteered for service with East Lancashire Regiment on 20 August 1914, his daughter Gladys, was born on 9 September 1914. He was discharged from the army on 16 October 1914, the reason given was not being likely to become an efficient soldier on medical grounds. Reginald was suffering from heart disease. Later, it is likely he was either conscripted into the army or enlisted under the Derby Scheme initially joining the Kings Royal Rifle Corps and was sent to the front, to the 9th Battalion. From 18 August 1917 the 9th Battalion were between Hooge and Westhoek Ridge an area they shared with a number of British artillery battery's while there the 9th Battalion suffered a number of casualties from German counter battery fire. It is likely Reginald was wounded by the German shelling and succumbed to his wounds on Tuesday 21 August 1917. Reginald left a widow and a young daughter. His Brother Cecil Owen Maple had been killed at the Somme in July 1916. In January 1919, Reginald's grave was located just near Leinster Farm, south of the Menin Road and his remains were moved to Birr Cross Roads Cemetery.

Private Walter Hazell		*2/8th Bn Worcestershire Regiment*	
Service No.	260336	Age:	26
Place of birth:	Westwood, Wiltshire	Home Country:	England
Date of death:	21/08/1917	Cause of death:	Killed in action
Memorial:	Westwood, Wiltshire		
War Cemetery:	Vlamertinghe Military Cemetery - Grave VII. E. 10.		
Next of Kin:	Alfred & Sarah Hazell		
Address:	Upper Farm, Westwood, Wiltshire		

Walter was the youngest son of Alfred and Sarah Hazell and was employed on his father's farm. It is likely he was either conscripted into the army or enlisted under the Derby Scheme initially joining the Hampshire Regiment. He was transferred to the 2/8th Battalion Worcestershire Regiment and sent with them to the front. On the night of the 20/21 August 1917, they were relieved at the front line and returned to Ypres North Camp, near Vlamertinghe. The 2/8th Worcestershires camp was shelled during the afternoon causing a few casualties. Walter was killed by the German shell fire.

Private Arthur Douglas Pile		*1st King Edwards Horse*	
Service No.	1084	Age:	21
Place of birth:	Salisbury, Wiltshire	Home Country:	England
Date of death:	21/08/1917	Cause of death:	Killed in action
Memorial:	Durnford - Dauntsey's School Memorial, Wiltshire		
War Cemetery:	Divisional Collecting Post Cemetery and Extension - Grave I. C. 19.		
Next of Kin:	Richard & Beatrice Pile		
Address:	Netton, Wiltshire		

Twenty one year old Arthur was the second son of Richard and Beatrice Pile and was educated at Dauntsey's School. He volunteered for service and arrived in France on 15 September 1915 joining the 1st King Edwards Horse. He was killed in action near Ypres, Belgium, as a result of German artillery fire on Tuesday 21 August 1917. Arthur was buried in Divisional Collecting Post Cemetery and Extension and is commemorated on a private memorial at Durnford Church.

WEDNESDAY 22 AUGUST 1917 - TEMPERATURE 22°c -CLEAR - RAINFALL NIL

Private Frederick Ernest Duck		*2/4th Bn Royal Berkshire Regiment*	
Service No.	13587	Age:	23
Place of birth:	Swindon, Wiltshire	Home Country:	England
Date of death:	22/08/1917	Cause of death:	Killed in action
Memorial:	Boilermaker Loco and Carriage Works, Great Western Railway Works, Swindon		
War Cemetery:	Tyne Cot Memorial - Panel 105 to 106 and 162.		
Next of Kin:	Frederick John & Mary Anne Duck		
Address:	25 Shelley Street, Swindon, Wiltshire		

Frederick, known as Ernest was the eldest son of Frederick and Mary Duck and was employed as a boiler maker at the Great Western Railway Works at Swindon. He volunteered for service joining the Royal Berkshire Regiment and arrived in France on 19 September 1915, being sent to the 2/4th Battalion. At 5.45 on Wednesday 22 August 1917 61 Division attacked German positions near Frezenberg, West of Zonnebeke. The 2/4th Royal Berkshires were divided into 13 platoons and given the task of attacking the following German strong points; Somme, Cross Cott, Aisne House, Schuler, Pond Farm, Hindu, Martha House, Green House. The 13 platoons followed close behind the leading infantry and on nearing their objectives dashed through the leading waves and assaulted the strong points. The 2/4th Royal Berkshires war diary states;

The first strong point encountered was Pond Farm. This was attacked from both flanks, 2nd Lieut F.A. N. Wilmot working in from the right, and 2nd Lieut. G.A.F. Gilmour from the left. Both these Officers were wounded before reaching the farm. Owing to heavy machine gun fire Sgt. Shackleford, then in charge of No 13 platoon found he was unable to take the farm, revelries of these platoons kept the garrison of the strong point strongly engaged, thus enabling the assaulting waves and the platoons for the further objectives to push forward without any serious trouble. Sgt. Shackleford then reorganised his platoon and made a fresh attack on the farm but on getting within 20 yards of his objective he was again held up by very heavy machine gun fire. However, he succeeded in surrounding the Farm, keeping the garrison fully occupied till late in the afternoon he joined two platoon of the 2/5th Glosters and helped to successfully assault and enter the farm. There were 35 prisoners taken by us at this strong point.

The next Strong Point encountered on the left was Hindu, 2/Lt F. Exler was wounded as soon as the infantry advanced, but the platoon carried on and owing to the marshy state of the ground were unable to enter the farm. However, they succeeded in advancing beyond and surrounding the strong point, thus enabling the assaulting waves to push forward. Pte. Pike of A Company having lost his own platoon succeeded in entering this strong point, and found it garrisoned by 19 Germans, 13 of whom were unwounded. He took all these prisoners, and himself remained there alone for two days guarding them until he was relieved by an Officer of the 2/6th Glosters.

The remaining strong point on the left was Schuler. Despite the fact that the left Division was held up and that his flank was exposed 2nd Lieut H.W. JEWELL pushed forward and stormed the Schuler Galleries, taking 2 Officers and 74 OR prisoners. These he dispatched to the rear. He then consolidated and held his post breaking up three local counter attacks. This post was almost isolated owing to the right flank falling back, but by great determination they held on for two days, till they were relieved by the 2/6th Glostors.

The first strong point encountered on the right was Somme. On nearing this 2nd Lieut. G.W. de St Legier pushed forward ahead of the leading waves and together with two men rushed through our own barrage and entered this post from the rear, killing the whole of the garrison. He afterwards consolidated the position and broke up several local counter attacks and held his post until he was relieved two days later.

Owing to the 15th Division being held up, and very heavy flanking machine gun fire being directed on our troops from Hill 35 and Gallipoli, the attacks on Green House, Cross Cott and Martha House were unsuccessful but these platoons helped the 2/1st Bucks to form a line running roughly from Somme in rear of Aisne House close to the gun pits at D13 Central, on to Schuler Galleries. Three enemy Counter attacks were repulsed.

Tanks were employed, but were unsuccessful owing to the marshy state of the ground. The line was taken over on the night of the 23/24th by the 183rd Infantry Brigade and the battalion marched back to a camp at Goldfish Chateau, the last platoon arriving about 6am. Casualties for the 22nd/23rd were as follows: -

7 Officers - 2nd Lieuts F.A.N. Wilmot, G.A.F. Gilmor, F. Exler, C.L.B. Kirkland, A.K. Glover, A.H. Robinson and A.E. Saw - wounded.
2 Officers - 2nd Lieuts H.S. Griffin and D. Mackinon, wounded and missing.
32 other ranks killed.
111 other ranks wounded.
25 other ranks wounded and missing.
54 other ranks missing.

Ernest was reported missing during the attack on one of the strong points. Later his parents received official information that he was presumed to have been killed on the day he was reported missing. He is remembered on the Tyne Cot Memorial and has no known grave.

Private Albert Ernest Watts		*2/4th Bn Royal Berkshire Regiment*	
Service No.	202702	Age:	22
Place of birth:	Clyffe Pypard, Wiltshire	Home Country:	England
Date of death:	22/08/1917	Cause of death:	Died of wounds
Memorial:	Not known		
War Cemetery:	Tyne Cot Memorial - Panel 105 to 106 and 162.		
Next of Kin:	Joseph & Tryphina Watts		
Address:,	Manton, Wiltshire		

Albert was the youngest son of Joseph and Tryphina Watts and it is likely he was either conscripted into the army or enlisted under the Derby Scheme initially joining the Wiltshire Regiment. He was transferred

Left: Frederick Ernest Duck

Right: John Park Oak

to the 2/4th Battalion Royal Berkshires Regiment and sent to the front. Albert was reported missing on Wednesday 22 August 1917 in the same attack as Ernest Duck on the German strong points at Frezenberg. Later his parents received official information that he was presumed to have been killed on the day he was reported missing. He is remembered on the Tyne Cot Memorial and has no known grave.

Private Edwin Reginald Amos — *2/4th Bn Royal Berkshire Regiment*

Service No.	202945	Age:	25
Place of birth:	Swindon, Wiltshire	Home Country:	England
Date of death:	22/08/1917	Cause of death:	Killed in action
Memorial:	Not known		
War Cemetery:	Tyne Cot Memorial - Panel 105 to 106 and 162.		
Next of Kin:	Edwin & Florence Harriett Amos		
Address:	69 Goodhind Stapleton Road, Bristol, Gloucestershire		

Edwin, a black and white artist, was the only son of Edwin and Florence Amos and it is likely he was either conscripted into the army or enlisted under the Derby Scheme joining the Royal Berkshire Regiment. He was sent to the 2/4th Battalion and was reported missing on Wednesday 22 August 1917 in the same attack as Ernest Duck on the German strong points at Frezenberg. Later Edwin's parents received official information that he was presumed to have been killed on the day he was reported missing. He is remembered on the Tyne Cot Memorial and has no known grave.

Private John Park Oak — *2/1st Bn Ox & BuckS Light Infantry*

Service No.	285162	Age:	41
Place of birth:	Weston Colville, Cam.	Home Country:	England
Date of death:	22/08/1917	Cause of death:	Killed in action
Memorial:	Weston Colville, Cambridgeshire		
War Cemetery:	Tyne Cot Memorial - Panel 96 to 98.		
Next of Kin:	Elizabeth Ann Oak (wife) Charles & Augusta Oak (parents)		
Address:	80 Ponting Street, Swindon, Wiltshire		

John, a print compositor, was the youngest son of Charles and Augusta Oak and married Elizabeth Ann Davies in the summer of 1903. It is likely he was either conscripted into the army or enlisted under the Derby Scheme initially joining the Hampshire Regiment. He was sent to the front and transferred to the

2/1st Battalion Oxfordshire and Buckinghamshire Light Infantry, who on Wednesday 22 August 1917 were one of the attacking battalions in the action at Frezenberg, see Ernest Duck, 2/4th Battalion Royal Berkshires Regiment. The 2/1st Ox & Bucks were attacking the German strong points, Somme and Aisne, which were captured, but other strong points remained in the Germans hands. Four company's 2/1st Ox & Bucks advanced and it is thought they reached their objectives but no news was heard from them throughout the day. The fighting was from shell hole to shell hole and the situation became very confused. At the end of the day the 2/1st Ox & Bucks were relieved and went back to the rear areas. The war diary states:

"The majority of the survivors arrived in camp near Goldfish Chateau by 5am, dog tired, but so excited and full of their experiences that the camp resounded with laughter well into the morning. Should I attempt to relate half of these exciting experiences and acts of gallantry, we shall have to indent for a General Service Wagon to carry the library, so let it suffice to relate a few of the most conspicuous acts during this period of real 'WAR.' It is hard to feel cheerful when so many of our best and dearest companions are lost to us, but we must always and will always be thankful that, in the generals own words, the battalion has been tried and has not been found wanting, remembering especially the share of those who have gone, never again to answer their names in the role of the battalion. The casualties to the battalion were heavy, the total taken into the line was 13 officers and 637 other ranks, of theses 11 officers and 338 other ranks are reported as casualties."

John was reported missing during the attack on Wednesday 22 August 1917 and later his widow received official information that John was presumed to have been killed in action on the day he was reported missing. He is remembered on the Tyne Cot Memorial and has no known grave.

Private Theodore Thorne		*2nd Bn Hampshire Regiment*	
Service No.	27817	Age:	39
Place of birth:	Milborne Port, Somerset	Home Country:	England
Date of death:	22/08/1917	Cause of death:	Killed in action
Memorial:	Westbury, Westbury Congregational Church		
War Cemetery:	Tyne Cot Memorial - Panel 88 to 90 and 162.		
Next of Kin:	Katie Thorne (wife) - Joseph & Catherine Thorne (parents)		
Address:	Chalford, Westbury, Wiltshire		

Theodore, a glove cutter, was the third son of Joseph and Catherine Thorne and in the summer of 1903 he married Katie Cowburn at Yeovil. It is likely he was either conscripted into the army or enlisted under the Derby Scheme initially joining the Duke of Cornwalls' Light Infantry. He was sent to the front and transferred to the 2nd Battalion Hampshire Regiment. Theodore was killed on Wednesday 22 August 1917 most likely by German artillery near Broenbeek north west of Langemarck. He left a widow and young family and is remembered on the Tyne Cot Memorial, he has no known grave.

Private John Turner		*45th Coy Machine Gun Corps*	
Service No.	89484	Age:	23
Place of birth:	Wardour, Wiltshire	Home Country:	England
Date of death:	22/08/1917	Cause of death:	Killed in action
Memorial:	Tisbury, Wiltshire		
War Cemetery:	Tyne Cot Cemetery - Grave LIV. D. 10.		
Next of Kin:	Nellie Turner (wife) – William & Sarah Turner (parent)		
Address:	Lower Hillmorton, Rugby, Warwickshire - Wardour, Wiltshire		

John Beacham

John, a butcher, was the youngest son William and Sarah Turner and married Nellie Davies at Rugby in the spring of 1916. It is likely he was either conscripted into the army or enlisted under the Derby Scheme initially joining the Army Service Corps. He was sent to the front and transferred to the 45th Company Machine Gun Corps, who on Wednesday 22 August 1917 were supporting a British attack west of Zonnebeke. The 45th Company Machine Gun Corps were in the area of Square Farm and subject to a heavy German artillery barrage which was a mix of gas and explosive shells, forcing the British to wear gas masks. At one stage, a Corporal came back to the 45th Company MGC, Headquarters with a machine gun that had been hit with a piece of shell, putting a hole in the cooling jacket. John was reported missing during this action and later his widow received official information that John was presumed to have been killed on the day he was reported missing. In November 1920 John's remains were located east of Iberberian Farm, which lies west of Zonnebeke. He was identified by his disc and his remains moved to Tyne Cot Cemetery.

Private John Beacham — *6th Bn Somerset Light Infantry*

Service No.	235024	Age:	28
Place of birth:	Fonthill Bishop, Wiltshire	Home Country:	England
Date of death:	22/08/1917	Cause of death:	Killed in action
Memorial:	Not known		
War Cemetery:	Tyne Cot Memorial - Panel 41 to 42 and 163A		
Next of Kin:	James & Elizabeth Beacham		
Address:	Fonthill Bishop, Wiltshire		

John, known as Jack, was the youngest so of James and Elizabeth Beacham and was employed as a valet and footman for Francis Baring, of Barings Bank, at Timsbury Manor House, near Romsey. It is likely he was either conscripted into the army or enlisted under the Derby Scheme initially joining the Hampshire Regiment. He was sent to the front and transferred to the 6th Battalion Somerset Light Infantry who on Wednesday 22 August 1917 were in action at Inverness Copse, just north of the Menin Road and south of Westhoek. After carrying out an attack on German positions the 6th Somerset Light Infantry were part of a force that successfully repulsed three German counter attacks. Jack was reported missing during the action. Later his family received official information that he was presumed to have been killed on the day he was reported missing. He is remembered on the Tyne Cot Memorial and has no known grave. No request was made for his medals and they were never issued. His brother Henry was to die from wounds in France on Boxing Day 1917.

Sir Douglas Haig reported on the evening of Wednesday 22 August 1917, more heavy fighting on the Ypres front. Near the Ypres-Menin road the British line has been carried forward about 500 yards on a front of about a mile. A position giving important observation eastward has been taken, and the British troops have established themselves in the western part of Inverness Copse.

Farther north, the advanced reached a depth of more than half a mile at its farthest on a front of 2½ miles. The enemy resistance was most stubborn, and consequently the prisoners taken "bear a more than usually small proportion to the total losses inflicted on the enemy."

Thursday 23 August 1917 - Temperature 23°c 50% Cloud Cover

Rainfall 1.4mm

Lance Corporal John Pearce — *6th Bn Somerset Light Infantry*

Service No.	26932	Age:	20
Place of birth:	Rowde, Wiltshire	Home Country:	England
Date of death:	23/08/1917	Cause of death:	Killed in action
Memorial:	Rowde, Wiltshire		
War Cemetery:	Tyne Cot Memorial - Panel 41 to 42 and 163A.		
Next of Kin:	James & Sarah J Pearce		
Address:	Rowde Common, Rowde, Wiltshire		

John was the eldest son of James and Sarah Pearce and it is likely he was either conscripted into the army or joined under the Derby Scheme initially joining the Wiltshire Regiment before being transferred to the 6th Battalion Wiltshire Regiment. He was killed in action on Thursday 23 August 1917 when the 6th Somersets were attacked and were counter attacked by German forces near Inverness Copse south of Westhoek, Belgium. The 6th Somersets war diary states that that the German shelling was the heaviest ever encountered and during one German counter attack 10 boxes of small arms ammunition were fired at the attackers. John is remembered on the Tyne Cot Memorial and has no known grave.

Lance Corporal Albert King — *6th Bn Duke of Cornwalls Light Infantry*

Service No.	31609	Age:	37
Place of birth:	All Cannings, Wiltshire	Home Country:	England
Date of death:	23/08/1917	Cause of death:	Killed in action
Memorial:	All Cannings, Wiltshire		
War Cemetery:	Poelcapelle British Cemetery - Grave VIIA. C. 8.		
Next of Kin:	Eliza King (wife) - William & Ruth King (parents)		
Address:	2 Greenhouse Road, All Cannings, Wiltshire		

Farm labourer, Albert, was the third son of William and Ruth King and married Eliza Sims toward the end of 1902. He volunteered for service initially joining the Wiltshire Regiment and arrived in France on 17 February 1915. It is likely he was wounded in action while with the Wiltshires and after his recovery he returned to the front joining the 6th Service Battalion Duke of Cornwall's Light Infantry. Historical information indicates Albert was posted missing in action on Thursday 23 August 1917 when the 6th Duke of Cornwall's Light Infantry attacked and were counter attacked by German forces near Inverness Copse south of Westhoek, Belgium and later presumed to have been killed in action. However, Albert is buried in Poelcapelle British Cemetery, and his wife was informed he had died of wounds. This could mean that he died when the 6th Duke of Cornwall's Light Infantry were near St. Julien a few days earlier. Albert left a widow and young family. In August 1918 Eliza King inserted the following memoriam in a local paper:

We little thought when last we met
He'd never more return
And now he lies somewhere in France
And we are left to mourn
No loved one near to see him die
To hear his last farewell
No word of comfort could he have
From those who loved him best

Albert's remains were located in October 1923, north of Inverness Copse and identified by means of his shoulder titles and a piece of strap marked R.J. King. His remains were relocated to Poelcapelle British Cemetery.

Instructor Staff Sgt. Leslie Vivian Hurle Bath		*83rd Bde Bn Royal Field Artillery*	
Service No.	90189	Age:	25
Place of birth:	Salisbury, Wiltshire	Home Country:	England
Date of death:	23/08/1917	Cause of death:	Killed in action
Memorial:	Salisbury, Wiltshire		
War Cemetery:	The Huts Cemetery - Grave III. B. 8.		
Next of Kin:	Fred & Hannah H. Bath		
Address:	Fisherton Anger, Salisbury, Wiltshire		

Leslie was the youngest son of Fred and Hannah Bath and was educated at Salisbury School. After leaving education he was apprenticed to Peter & Sons, engineers, of Yeovil, serving with them for four years until 1 May 1914. He remained in the experimental department until the outbreak of hostilities when he and five other employees offered their services to either the Royal Flying Corps or the Royal Engineers. He was accepted by the latter and served on the east coast until March 1915 when he, with another, were selected to go to Woolwich for gun training, afterwards passing with the full 100 marks and was at once made Instructor Staff Sergeant. He subsequently went to France, arriving on 26 July 1915 having charge of two batteries of howitzers, remaining all through the fighting with only one short leave of absence. Leslie was killed on Thursday 23 August 1917, most likely by German artillery counter battery fire near Dickebusch, Belgium.

Private George John Newell		*2/6th TF Bn Gloucestershire Regiment*	
Service No.	242553	Age:	20
Place of birth:	Frome, Wiltshire	Home Country:	England
Date of death:	23/08/1917	Cause of death:	Killed in action
Memorial:	Warminster, Wiltshire		
War Cemetery:	New Irish Farm Cemetery - Grave Spree Farm Mem. 14.		
Next of Kin:	George Charles Hearsy & Bessie Maria Newell		
Address:	Warminster, Wiltshire		

George, known as John, was the youngest son of George and Bessie Newell and was employed as a labourer at a saw mill. It is likely he was either conscripted into the army or joined under the Derby Scheme joining Gloucestershire Regiment. He was sent to the front with the 2/6th Territorial Battalion, who on Thursday 23 August 1917 were in support for an attack on German positions west of Zonnebeke. Two company's were called on to go forward to Pond Farm South east of St. Julien and it is likely john was killed during this action. He was originally buried in Spree Farm Cemetery, Langemarck, 800 metres South-East of St. Julien, which contained the graves of 14 soldiers from the United Kingdom and three from New Zealand who fell in August and October 1917. These graves were lost in subsequent fighting and he is today remembered on a special memorial in New Irish Farm Cemetery.

Sergeant Ernest James Shergold		*5th Bn Shropshire Light Infantry*	
Service No.	8573	Age:	27
Place of birth:	Steeple Langford, Wilts	Home Country:	Wales
Date of death:	23/08/1917	Cause of death:	Died of wounds
Memorial:	Newport, Monmouthshire		
War Cemetery:	Lijssenthoek Military Cemetery - Grave XVIII. B. 14A.		
Next of Kin:	Sidney & Annie Shergold		
Address:	5 Henry Street, Newport, Monmouthshire		

Regular soldier Ernest, was the second son of Sidney and Annie Shergold and was serving in India with the 2nd Battalion Shropshire Light Infantry at the outbreak of hostilities. He arrived in France on 21 December 1914 and it is likely at some stage of his service he was wounded and following his recovery transferred to the 5th Battalion. It is also likely he was again wounded during an attack on German trenches near Glencourse Wood, east of Hooge on 22 August 1917. He was evacuated to a casualty clearing station at Lijssenthoek, where he succumbed to his wounds on Thursday 23 August 1917.

Gunner Albert Henry Hooper		*286th Siege Bty Royal Garrison Artillery*	
Service No.	116264	Age:	29
Place of birth:	Gillingham, Dorset	Home Country:	England
Date of death:	23/08/1917	Cause of death:	Died of wounds
Memorial:	Gillingham, Dorset		
War Cemetery:	Mendinghem Military Cemetery - Grave V. B. 14		
Next of Kin:	Alice Louisa Hooper (wife) – Albert & Emma Hooper (parents)		
Address:	Merton Cottage, Merton Park, London – Gillingham, Dorset		

Albert, a railway worker, was the only son of Albert and Emma Hooper and married Alice Louisa Price at Warminster on 20 October 1914. He enlisted under the Derby Scheme on 11 December 1915 and was called up for service on 17 August 1916, being sent to the Royal Garrison Artillery. After completing his training, he was sent to France on 22 May 1917 and posted to the 286th Siege Battery on 2 June 1917, who on the 24 June 1917 came into action west of Ypres between Asylum and Kruistraat. Albert was wounded on Thursday 23 August 1917 with a gunshot wound to the head, which fractured his skull. He was evacuated to 64 Casualty Clearing station at Mendinghem, where he later succumbed to his wounds. He left a widow and a young daughter. His personal property was returned to his widow and consisted of correspondence, photos, 2 wallets, belt, cigarette case, a card, metal ring, key, purse and a pencil case.

FRIDAY 24 AUGUST 1917 - TEMPERATURE 20°c - 50% CLOUD COVER

RAINFALL 0.1mm

Captain Harold Cecil Round DSO MC		*6th Bn attd 9th Bn Rifle Brigade*	
Service No.	N/a	Age:	21
Place of birth:	Godstone, Surrey	Home Country:	England

Left: Albert Henry Hooper

Right: Harold Cecil Round DSO MC

Date of death:	24/08/1917	Cause of death:	Killed in action
Memorial:	Marlborough College		
War Cemetery:	Tyne Cot Memorial - Panel 145 to 147		
Next of Kin:	Francis Richard & Frances Emily Round		
Address:	Avenue House, Witham, Essex		

Harold was the youngest son of Francis and Frances Round and was educated at Marlborough College, where he was a cadet lieutenant in the Officer Training Corps. After leaving Marlborough he was rejected several times for military service on medical grounds and spent a short time in a munitions works. He finally was given a commission with the 6th Battalion Rifle Brigade and was attached to the 9th Battalion. He went to France and was awarded the Military Cross and in May 1917 was awarded the Distinguished Service Order, near Arras. The citation reads:

"For conspicuous gallantry and devotion to duty. When our troops were forced to withdraw, he collected a few men and made a strong point within 70 yards of the enemy trench. This position he held for two days without supplies of any kind. He was finally able to get a valuable report through, before being ordered to withdraw."

On Friday 24 August 1917, the 9th Battalion Rifle Brigade relieved the Kings Royal Rifle Corps astride of the Menin Road East of Hooge. While commanding a company Harold was killed when the Germans attacked the British front line positions with a strong force using flame throwers. The line near Stirling Castle was later consolidated. Harold's brothers were also killed in the Great War. Auriol, in September 1915 and James at the Somme in November 1916.

Sergeant John Orchard DCM		*8th Bn Kings Royal Rifle Corps*	
Service No.	A/3186	Age:	23
Place of birth:	Aldbourne, Wiltshire	Home Country:	England
Date of death:	24/08/1917	Cause of death:	Killed in action
Memorial:	Aldbourne, Wiltshire		
War Cemetery:	Hooge Crater Cemetery - Grave VIII. A. 1.		
Next of Kin:	John & Sarah R Orchard		
Address:	Post Office, Aldbourne, Wiltshire		

John, known as Jack, was the second son of John and Sarah Orchard and volunteered for service joining the 8th Battalion Kings Royal Rifle Corps. He arrived in France on 18 May 1915 and was awarded the Distinguished Conduct Medal at the Somme in 1916. The citation reads;

"For conspicuous gallantry in an attack when he led the first wave of his company. Although himself wounded, he controlled the few survivors, and established a post in the enemy trench, holding it for two hours, when he brought back two prisoners.

Jack was killed on Friday 24 August 1917, east of Hooge on the Menin Road, when the Germans attacked the British front line positions with a strong force using flame throwers. The line near Stirling Castle was later consolidated. In April 1919, Jack's remains were located near Clapham Junction on the Menin Road. He was identified by his sergeants stripes and his remains were moved to Hooge Crater Cemetery.

Major Tom Louis Bourdillon MC		*8th Bn Kings Royal Rifle Corps*	
Service No.	N/a	Age:	29
Place of birth:	Chupra Bengal, India	Home Country:	England
Date of death:	24/08/1917	Cause of death:	Killed in action
Memorial:	Durnford School – Marlborough College, Wiltshire		
War Cemetery:	Tyne Cot Cemetery - Grave LVIII. E. 44		
Next of Kin:	Sir James & Mary Wake Bourdillon		
Address:	Westlands, Liphook, Hampshire		

Tom was the only son of Sir James and Mary Bourdillon and was educated at Durnford School and Marlborough College, before attending Corpus Christie College Oxford. He passed the exam for the Colonial Civil Service in 1911 and in November of the same year left England for the Malay Straights. He spent three years in the Immigration Department and at the outbreak of hostilities he returned to England and was given a commission with the Kings Royal Rifle Corps. He arrived in France in May 1915 and was severely wounded at Hooge on 30 July 1915 and evacuated to England. After being passed fit for light duty in February 1916 he was attached to the Reserve Battalion, as Company Commander and Assistant Adjutant. He returned to France in July 1916 and on 15 September 1916, he was slightly wounded near Flers at the Somme and awarded the Military Cross. On Friday 24 August 1917, east of Hooge on the Menin Road, Tom was slightly wounded and being carried into a dug out was killed by a German shell. He was one of six officers of the 8th Kings Royal Rifle Corps to be killed when the Germans attacked the British front line positions with a strong force using flame throwers. The line near Stirling Castle was later consolidated. In January 1921 Tom's remains were located south of Stirling Castle and he was identified by correspondence he had in his possession. His remains were moved to Tyne Cot Cemetery.

Sergeant William Emmett		*8th Bn Rifle Brigade*	
Service No.	6581	Age:	37
Place of birth:	Exeter, Devon	Home Country:	England
Date of death:	24/08/1917	Cause of death:	Killed in action
Memorial:	Not known		
War Cemetery:	Tyne Cot Memorial - Panel 145 to 147		
Next of Kin:	Edith Emily Emmett (wife) - William & Mary Ann Emmett (parents)		
Address:	Lower Salisbury, Salisbury, Wiltshire – Romsey, Hampshire		

William was the second son of William and Mary Ann Emmett and in the spring of 1914 he married Edith Emily Biddlecombe. He volunteered for service and joined the 8th Battalion Rifle Brigade arriving in France on 15 March 1915. On Friday 24 August 1917, the 8th Rifle Brigade were east of Hooge on the Menin Road. An account at the time states:

Left: *Tom Louis Bourdillon MC*

Right: *Harold Edward Street CMG MID*

"During the afternoon, reinforcements of the 8th Bn. Rifle Brigade arrived, and after a conference, it was decided to post them south of the Menin Road, strengthen the line (and) offensive flank, and push forward posts into Inverness Copse while one platoon, being overcrowded, spread up north of the Menin Road. Later the 7th Bn. 60th and 7th Bn. Rifle Brigade came up to relieve all troops in this sector. I made myself responsible for the relief of all troops north of the Menin Road while O.C., 10th Bn. D.L.I. and O.C. 8th Bn. Rifle Brigade handed over all south of the Menin Road.

William was killed when the Germans attacked the British front line positions with a strong force using flame throwers. The line near Stirling Castle was later consolidated.

SATURDAY 25 AUGUST 1917 - TEMPERATURE 20°c - 50% CLOUD COVER RAINFALL NIL

Colonel Harold Edward Street CMG MID		*106th Bde Bn Royal Field Artillery*	
Service No.	N/a	Age:	41
Place of birth:	Marylebone, Middlesex	Home Country:	England
Date of death:	25/08/1917	Cause of death:	Killed in action
Memorial:	Caterham St Mary The Virgin, Surrey – Marlborough College		
War Cemetery:	Reninghelst New Military Cemetery - Grave III. A. 19.		
Next of Kin:	Gladys Mary Street (wife) - Joseph Edward & Edith Jane Street (parents)		
Address:	Summer Tree, Herstmonceux, Hailsham, Sussex		

Harold was the second son of Joseph and Edith Street and was educated at Marlborough College, before attending The Royal Military Academy at Woolwich. He was given a commission with the Royal Field Artillery and served in Gibraltar and at the commencement of the Boer War was sent to South Africa where he was mentioned in dispatches three times. At the end of hostilities, he served in India and after passing for Staff College, was appointed Brigade Major to the 1st Division at Aldershot. He arrived in France on 18 August 1914 and the following year accompanied the 29th Division to Gallipoli, where he was awarded the Companion of the Order of St. Michael and St. George and the Legion of Honour. In the summer of 1916 he married Gladys Mary Douglas at St Pancras, and later served in Egypt and France and was mentioned nine times in dispatches. On Saturday 25 August 1917, he was commanding two brigades of Royal Field Artillery, south east of Ypres, when he was killed most likely by German counter battery fire.

SUNDAY 26 AUGUST 1917 - TEMPERATURE 21°c OVERCAST - RAINFALL 19.6mm

Major Thomas Weeding — *1st Bn Royal West Surrey Regiment*

Service No.	N/a	Age:	38
Place of birth:	Addlestone, Surrey	Home Country:	England
Date of death:	26/08/1917	Cause of death:	Killed in action
Memorial:	Addlestone, Surrey – Marlborough College, Wiltshire		
War Cemetery:	Coxyde Military Cemetery - Grave III. C. 1		
Next of Kin:	Thomas & Alice Weeding		
Address:	Kingthorpe, Addlestone, Surrey		

Thomas was the eldest son of Thomas and Alice Weeding and was educated at Marlborough College, before attending the Royal Military Academy at Sandhurst. He was given a commission with the Royal West Surrey Regiment and served eight years in India, where he became a very keen polo player and was described as a very good shot. He was one of the first British officers to learn to fly and after obtaining his pilots certificate at Brooklands in 1912, he returned to duty at his regiment who were serving in Bermuda. At the outbreak of hostilities, he was serving with the 2nd Battalion Royal West Surrey Regiment in South Africa and landed with the Division at Zeebrugge on 7 October 1914. He was severely wounded at Gheluvelt on 31 October 1914 and after returning to the front was wounded during fighting near the Hohenzollern Redoubt, near Loos, France on 30 September 1915. He returned to France in December 1916 transferring to the 1st Battalion Royal West Surrey Regiment. On Sunday 26 August 1917 Thomas and three other officers left on horseback to reconnoitre the sector of the line near Nieuport, prior to the battalion going into the line. The party proceeded down the Wupen – Nieuport Road and reached the road to Ramscapelle when a shell burst close by killing Thomas and his horse instantaneously. His brother John Richard Baggallay Weeding had been killed serving with the Welsh Regiment in December 1915.

MONDAY 27 AUGUST 1917 - TEMPERATURE 14°c - 50% CLOUD COVER - RAINFALL 19.6mm

Private John Yockney Burchell — *2/8th Bn Worcestershire Regiment*

Service No.	260310	Age:	20
Place of birth:	Winchester, Hampshire	Home Country:	England
Date of death:	27/08/1917	Cause of death:	Killed in action
Memorial:	Great Western Raiway Memorial		
War Cemetery:	Tyne Cot Memorial - Panel 75 to 77.		
Next of Kin:	John & Annie E. I. Burchell		
Address:	14 Quarters, HM Prison, Wandsworth, London		

John was the eldest son of John and Annie Burchell and lived with his grandparents in Marlborough. He was employed as a telephone attendant, in the Locomotive and Carriage Department in the Great Western Railway Works at Swindon. It is likely he was either conscripted into the army or enlisted under the Derby Scheme initially joining the Hampshire Regiment. He was sent to the front and transferred to the 2/8th Battalion Worcestershire Regiment, who in late August 1917 were taking part in attacks on German positions north west of Zonnebeke. John was killed on Monday 27 August 1917 during an attack on Somme and Gallipoli, German strong points. He is remembered on the Tyne Cot Memorial and has no known grave.

Left: Thomas Weeding

Right: John Yockney Burchell

Private Frederick James Batchelor — *1/8th TF Bn Royal Warwickshire Regiment*

Service No.	306529	Age:	28
Place of birth:	Buckinham, Buckinghamshire	Home Country:	England
Date of death:	27/08/1917	Cause of death:	Killed in action
Memorial:	Fringford, Oxfordshire		
War Cemetery:	Tyne Cot Memorial - Panel 23 to 28 and 163A		
Next of Kin:	Mabel Annie Batchelor (wife) - Robert & Anne Batchelor (parents)		
Address:	4 Wharf Road, Wroughton, Wiltshire		

Frederick, a gardener and labourer, was the youngest son of Robert and Anne Batchelor and enlisted under the Derby Scheme on 7 December 1915 joining the Royal Warwickshire Regiment. He was called up on 29 February 1917 and four months later on 7 June 1916 he married Mabel Annie Miller at the parish church in Wroughton. He was sent to the front four days later on 11 June 1916 and attached to the 1/8th Warwicks. Frederick was killed on Monday 27 August 1917, when the 1/8th Warwicks attacked German positions of Springfield and Winnipeg, north east of St. Julien. A comrade wrote:

"His death was instantaneous, as he was shot through the head by a machine gun bullet."

His officer wrote:

"He was always ready to do his duty under all conditions."

Frederick's personal possessions were returned to his wife consisting of letters, photos and a leather pocket wallet. He is remembered on the Tyne Cot Memorial and has no known grave.

Private Alfred Sidney Harding — *1/8th TF Bn Royal Warwickshire Regiment*

Service No.	306722	Age:	34
Place of birth:	Sedgehill, Wiltshire	Home Country:	England
Date of death:	27/08/1917	Cause of death:	Killed in action
Memorial:	Semley Baptist Chapel Memorial		
War Cemetery:	Poelcapelle British Cemetery - Grave XLII. C. 19.		
Next of Kin:	Thomas Baker & Mary Ann Harding		
Address:	Hugglers Hole Cottages, Semley, Wiltshire		

Alfred, a gardener, was the second son of Thomas and Mary Harding and enlisted under the Derby

Scheme on 8 December 1915. He was called up on 23 March 1916 and sent to the Royal Warwickshire Regiment. He arrived in France on 30 July 1916 and was attached to the 1/8th Warwicks who on Monday 27 August 1917 attacked German positions of Springfield and Winnipeg, north east of St. Julien. Alfred was reported missing and later his parents received official information that their son was killed in action on the day he was reported missing. His personal possessions were returned to his mother consisting of letters, two mirrors and religious books. In May 1920 Alfred's remains were located south of Vancouver Corner and identified by a disc, before being moved to Poelcapelle British Cemetery.

Private Frank Reynolds		*1/8th TF Bn Royal Warwickshire Regiment*	
Service No.	306687	Age:	39
Place of birth:	Trowbridge, Wiltshire	Home Country:	England
Date of death:	27/08/1917	Cause of death:	Killed in action
Memorial:	Trowbridge, Wiltshire		
War Cemetery:	Tyne Cot Memorial - Panel 23 to 28 and 163A.		
Next of Kin:	Eli & Hannah Reynolds		
Address:	30 Bradford Road, Trowbridge, Wiltshire		

Frank was the youngest son of Eli and Hannah Reynolds and was employed by Sirdar Rubber Mills in Bradford on Avon. He joined the army in March 1916 most likely under the Derby Scheme and after completing his training he was sent to France in June 1916 serving with the Warwickshire Regiment. On 26 August 1917 Hannah Reynolds received a letter from Frank explaining that he expected to come home on leave very soon. Frank was killed on Monday 27 August 1917, when the 1/8th Warwicks attacked German positions of Springfield and Winnipeg, north east of St. Julien. In early September Hannah Reynolds received official notification from the record office in Warwick that her son had been killed in action on Monday 27 August 1917. He is remembered on the Tyne Cot Memorial and has no known grave.

Lance Corporal William Thomas Dunlop		*1/8th TF Bn Royal Warwickshire Regiment*	
Service No.	306604	Age:	26
Place of birth:	Trowbridge, Wiltshire	Home Country:	England
Date of death:	27/08/1917	Cause of death:	Killed in action
Memorial:	Trowbridge, Wiltshire		
War Cemetery:	Poelcapelle British Cemetery - Grave VIIA. D. 9.		
Next of Kin:	Annie Dunlop (wife) - Thomas & Agnes Dunlop		
Address:	18 St Margaret Street, Bradford on Avon - 87 Park Street, Trowbridge		

William, known as Billy, was a travelling draper and he married Annie Mason in October 1915 joining the army two months later. He was called up on 16 March 1916 and after completing his training he was sent to France on 7 September 1916. He was killed on Monday 27 August 1917, when the 1/8th Warwicks attacked German positions of Springfield and Winnipeg, north east of St. Julien. In August 1918 Annie Dunlop inserted the following memoriam in a local paper:

Sleep on, dear Billy, in a far-off land
In a grave, we will never see
But as long as life and memory last
I will remember thee

In October 1923, Billy's remains located just outside St. Julien and his widow received a letter from the infantry records office stating that they had in their possession an identity disc and a badly damaged wrist watch had been found on her late husband's body. Annie Dunlop asked that the items be forwarded to her. His remains were moved to Poelcapelle British Cemetery.

Left; Frank Reynolds

Right: William Thomas Dunlop

Private Claud Humphrey Smith — *1/8th TF Bn Royal Warwickshire Regiment*

Service No.	306822
Age:	36
Place of birth:	Islington, London
Home Country:	England
Date of death:	27/08/1917
Cause of death:	Killed in action
Memorial:	Not known
War Cemetery:	Tyne Cot Memorial - Panel 23 to 28 and 163A
Next of Kin:	Myra Alice Smith (wife) - William Henry & Sophia Ann Smith (parents)
Address:	46 York Road, Chichester, Sussex – Islington, Middlesex

Carpenter Claud was the youngest son of William and Sophia Smith and was working in Durrington most likely building military camps, when he enlisted under the Derby Scheme on 8 December 1915. He was called up on 23 March 1916 and sent to the 3/8th Battalion Royal Warwickshire Regiment. After completing his training, he arrived in France on 9 July 1916 being sent to the 1/8th Territorial Battalion Royal Warwickshire Regiment. He was awarded 14 days' field punishment No. 1, for disobedience, fouling the grounds in the camp. On 20 January 1917, he was evacuated to England suffering from dysentery and while he was convalescing he married Myra Alice Newman, in the spring of 1917 at Islington, Middlesex. Following his recovery, he returned to the front arriving in France on 11 June 1917. Claud was reported wounded and missing on Monday 27 August 1917, when the 1/8th Warwicks attacked German positions of Springfield and Winnipeg, north east of St. Julien. In July 1918 Claud's widow received official information that he was presumed to have died of wounds on or since the day he was reported missing. He is remembered on the Tyne Cot Memorial and has no known grave.

Sergeant Charles Grant — *1/8th Bn Royal Warwickshire Regiment*

Service No.	306775
Age:	32
Place of birth:	Chapmanslade, Wiltshire
Home Country:	England
Date of death:	27/08/1917
Cause of death:	Killed in action
Memorial:	Chapmanslade, Wiltshire
War Cemetery:	Tyne Cot Memorial - Panel 23 to 28 and 163A.
Next of Kin:	Eli & Elizabeth Grant
Address:	Chapmanslade, Westbury, Wiltshire

Charles, a market gardener, was the second son of Eli and Elizabeth Grant and enlisted under the Derby Scheme on 10 December 1915. He was called up on 24 March 1916 and sent to the 3/8th Battalion Royal Warwickshire Regiment. After completing his training, he arrived in France on 22 July 1916 being sent to the 1/8th Territorial Battalion Royal Warwickshire Regiment. Charles was killed on Monday 27 August 1917, when the 1/8th Warwicks attacked German positions of Springfield and Winnipeg, north east of St. Julien. On 10 August 1918 Elizabeth Grant was sent Charles's personal property which consisted of an identity disc. She wrote to the army records office asking:

"I should be pleased to learn from you to know if any more articles have been returned to you belonging to my son, Sgt. C. Grant. Is it not known he had many things by him?"

Charles is remembered on the Tyne Cot Memorial and has no known grave.

Private John Henry Bothwell		*2/4th TF Bn Gloucestershire Regiment*	
Service No.	202626	Age:	33
Place of birth:	Horningsham, Wiltshire	Home Country:	England
Date of death:	27/08/1917	Cause of death:	Died
Memorial:	Horningsham,		
War Cemetery:	Tyne Cot Memorial - Panel 72 to 75.		
Next of Kin:	James & Annie Bothwell		
Address:	Horningsham, Wiltshire		

John, a grocer's traveller, was the third son of James & Annie Bothwell and he volunteered for service joining the Gloucestershire Regiment, arriving in France on 6 January 1915. He was initially sent to the 1st or 2nd Battalions and it is likely he was wounded or suffered from illness or disease and evacuated to England. Following his recovery he returned to the front and transferred to the 2/4th Territorial Battalion, who in late August 1917 were taking part in attacks on German positions north west of Zonnebeke. John was reported missing on Monday 27 August 1917 during an attack on Winnepeg and Schulen Farm, German strong points. Later his parents received official information that John was presumed to have been killed on the day he was reported missing. He is remembered on the Tyne Cot Memorial and has no known grave.

Gunner Stanley Arthur Perry		*16th Heavy Bty Royal Garrison Artillery*	
Service No.	116733	Age:	20
Place of birth:	Figheldean, Wiltshire	Home Country:	England
Date of death:	27/08/1917	Cause of death:	Killed in action
Memorial:	Figeldean, Wiltshire		
War Cemetery:	Bard Cottage Cemetery - Grave IV. E. 18.		
Next of Kin:	Edward & Jane Perry		
Address:	Figheldean, Wiltshire		

Stanley, a carter, was the second son of Edward and Jane Perry and enlisted with the army under the Derby Scheme on 27 November 1915. He was called up on 1 September 1916 and was soon after sent to Heavy Section, No. 7 Brigade Royal Artillery. He was posted to France arriving on 23 May 1917 and on 15 July sent to 16th Heavy Battery Royal Garrison Artillery. Stanley was killed on Monday 27 August 1917, most likely by German counter battery fire north of Ypres. His personal possessions were returned to his parents and consisted of leather waist belt, wrist watch with strap and guard, pocket knife, pair of folding scissors, watch key, note book, damaged photo case, letters, photos,cards, purse and wrist watch with no glass.

TUESDAY 28 AUGUST 1917 - TEMPERATURE 16.5°c - 50% CLOUD COVER - RAINFALL 0.9mm

Private Sidney Herbert Compton — *6th Bn South Wales Borderers*

Service No.	17459	Age:	23
Place of birth:	Warminster, Wiltshire	Home Country:	England
Date of death:	28/08/1917	Cause of death:	Died of wounds
Memorial:	Warminster, Wiltshire		
War Cemetery:	Lijssenthoek Military Cemetery - Grave XVIII. G. 19		
Next of Kin:	Edmund John & Thirza Ann Compton		
Address:	Warminster, Wiltshire		

Sidney was the second son of Edmund and Thirza Compton and was employed as a smith at Monmouth Steel Works near Newport, South Wales. He volunteered for service with the 6th Battalion South Wales Borderers (Pioneers) at the outbreak of hostilities in August 1914. After completing training as a signaler, he arrived in France with his battalion on 24 September 1915. He had been through many engagements while at the front without a wound, but his luck ran out in late August 1917. The 6th Battalion South Wales Borderers were working between Bellewarde and Railway Wood and were subject to a heavy German barrage, during which Sidney was wounded by a shell. He was evacuated to a casualty clearing station at Lijssenthoek, where he succumbed to his wounds on Tuesday 28 August 1917. He left a sorrowing sweetheart, Daisey Thornbury. His younger brother, Roy, had been reported missing in Mesopotamia in February 1917.

Private Frederick H Powell — *2nd Bn Wiltshire Regiment*

Service No.	25688	Age:	20
Place of birth:	Ebbesbourne Wake, Wiltshire	Home Country:	England
Date of death:	28/08/1917	Cause of death:	Died of wounds
Memorial:	Not Known		
War Cemetery:	Bailleul Communal Cemetery Extension Nord - Grave III. E. 217.		
Next of Kin:	Anne Powell (grandparent)		
Address:	Ebbesbourne Wake, Wiltshire		

Twenty year old Frederick, a farm labourer, was the grandson of Anne Powell. It is likely he was conscripted into the army or enlisted under the Derby Scheme. He joined the Wiltshire Regiment and was sent to the front being sent to the 2nd Battalion. Frederick was wounded most likely when the 2nd Wiltshires were at the front in the Messines sector. The front line was a series of shell holes and while on duty at the front the 2nd Wiltshires worked to connect the shell holes into a continuous trench. It is probable Frederick was wounded by German shell fire and evacuated to a hospital facility at Bailleul, where he succumbed to his wounds on Tuesday 28 August 1917.

Captain John Lindsay Kelsall — *B Battery 86th Bde Royal Field Artillery*

Service No.	N/a	Age:	26
Place of birth:	Crieff, Perthshire	Home Country:	England
Date of death:	28/08/1917	Cause of death:	Killed in action
Memorial:	Marlborough College, Wil		
War Cemetery:	The Huts Cemetery - Grave IV. B. 7		
Next of Kin:	Henry & Mary Eudoxia Kelsall		

Left: John Lindsay Kelsall

Right: William Henry Gay

Address: Moss Side Estate, Rochdale, Lancashire

John was the second son of Henry and Mary Kelsall and was educated at Marlborough College. He volunteered for service on 28 August 1914, and was given a commission with the Army Service Corp but soon after transferred to the Royal Field Artillery. He was mentioned in dispatches in May 1917 and was killed in action on Tuesday 28 August 1917 while serving with the 86th Brigade at Zillebeke Lake. His original grave marker is now displayed at Marlborough College Chapel. He is buried in the Huts Cemetery, Belgium and the epitaph on his gravestone reads:

"Died at the guns heartening his men at Zillebeke Lake"

Wednesday 29 August 1917 - Temperature 16°c - 50% Cloud Cover - Rainfall 2.6mm

Private William Henry Gay — *2nd/3rd (Home Counties) Field Amb RAMC*

Service No.	497418
Place of birth:	Staverton, Wiltshire
Date of death:	29/08/1917
Memorial:	Staverton, Wiltshire
War Cemetery:	Divisional Collecting Post Cemetery and Extension - Grave I. C. 9.
Next of Kin:	Hubert John & Alice Gay
Address:	Factory Lodge, Staverton, Wiltshire
Age:	21
Home Country:	England
Cause of death:	Killed in action

William was the third son of Hubert and Alice Gay and was employed as a butter maker at the Nestle Anglo Swiss Milk Company factory at Staverton. He volunteered for service with the Royal Army Medical Corps on 21 April 1915 and arrived in France on 25 January 1917. He was killed in action north east of Ypres on Wednesday 29 August 1917. His personal possessions that were returned to his parents consisted of a 9 carat gold signet ring (bent), small silver watch (damaged) in metal case, silver cigarette case (damaged), purse – wallet one and three quarters francs – 25 centimes, photos and cards.

Algernon Alfred Nicholas Bull

Wednesday 29 August 1917

Stormy weather continued on the Flanders front and at Langemarck a German strong point of trouble had been cleared immediately in front of the new British line. By a counter-thrust the Germans claimed to have driven the British out of the indent they previously admitted in the line at Frezenburg.

THURSDAY 30 AUGUST 1917 - TEMPERATURE 17°c - 50% CLOUD COVER - RAINFALL 0.7mm

Private Algernon Alfred Nicholas Bull *2nd Bn Wiltshire Regiment*

Service No.	33248	Age:	22
Place of birth:	Fyfield, Wiltshire	Home Country:	England
Date of death:	30/08/1917	Cause of death:	Killed in action
Memorial:	West Overton		
War Cemetery:	Torreken Farm Cemetery No 1 - Grave D. 10.		
Next of Kin:	Edgar Theodore & Gertrude Mary Bull		
Address:	Bayardo Farm, Clench Common, Marlborough, Wiltshire		

Algernon was the fourth son of Edgar and Gertrude Bull and was employed on his father's farm. He enlisted with the Royal Wiltshire Yeomanry but was sent to the front and transferred to the 2nd Battalion Wiltshire Regiment. On Thursday 30 August 1917, the 2nd Wiltshires were in the British front line south of Oostaverne. At about 10.30pm after an intense barrage on the British front line the Germans raided the 2nd Wiltshires right front, D Company. After a stout resistance with Lewis guns, under heavy shelling and machine gun fire, the German raiders penetrated some of the 2nd Wiltshires posts and took nine prisoners, one of whom escaped into no man's land and made his way back to the 2nd Wiltshires lines. Heavy losses are thought to have been inflicted on the German raiders, who were identified as being the 22nd Pioneer Battalion by the dead bodies found near the British wire. The 2nd Wiltshires losses were 1 killed, 14 wounded and 9 missing. Algernon was the man killed during the German Raid.

Private William Arthur Sinclair		*2/6th TF Bn Gloucestershire Regiment*	
Service No.	16647	Age:	27
Place of birth:	Reading, Berkshire	Home Country:	England
Date of death:	30/08/1917	Cause of death:	Died of wounds
Memorial:	Not known		
War Cemetery:	Mendinghem Military Cemetery - Grave V. A. 1.		
Next of Kin:	Peter & Elizabeth Sinclair		
Address:	16 Devizes Road, Swindon, Wiltshire		

William was the eldest son of Peter and Elizabeth Sinclair and after completing his education he served a hair dressing apprenticeship with his brother in law, W.F. Dodgson of Swindon. He was working at Weston-Super-Mare at the outbreak of hostilities and volunteered for service joining the 2/6th Territorial Battalion Gloucestershire Regiment. He arrived in France on Christmas Eve 1915 and took part in the advance at Vimy Ridge. He was given home leave and returned to the front in mid July 1917 and had been with his battalion for six weeks, when he was wounded by German artillery fire while in the British front line trenches near Wieltje. He was evacuated to a casualty clearing station at Mendinghem and succumbed to his wounds on Thursday 30 August 1917. The Rev. G.H. Peskett, an Army chaplain wrote the following letter to William's parents:

"It is with regret that I follow up the field card I sent you on the 28 August, by writing to tell you of the death of your son. He was admitted to this hospital in an unconscious condition at 5.45pm on the 28 August, suffering from severe shell wounds in the head, left arm and right thigh. I can assure you that he received most careful attention from very skilled surgeons and nurses, who did their utmost for him. I saw him at frequent intervals, hoping that he would at least recover sufficiently to give me a message for you, but unfortunately, he never rallied at all. He passed away peacefully at 2.40pm yesterday. I laid him to rest this afternoon in the military cemetery here; and a cross, suitably inscribed, will mark his grave. I cannot express my sorrow for you in your bereavement. You have my deepest sympathy."

The village of Hooge

7
September

SATURDAY 1 SEPTEMBER 1917 - TEMPERATURE 15°c - 50% CLOUD COVER - RAINFALL 0.2mm

Private Tom Berrett — *1st Bn Wiltshire Regiment*

Service No.	18349	Age:	30
Place of birth:	Wilcot, Wiltshire	Home Country:	England
Date of death:	01/09/1917	Cause of death:	Died of wounds
Memorial:	Wilcot, Wiltshire		
War Cemetery:	Tyne Cot Memorial - Panel 119 to 120.		
Next of Kin:	Frances E. Berrett (wife) - Arthur & Lucy Berrett (parents)		
Address:	Wilcot, Wiltshire		

Tom, a farm labourer, was the second son of Arthur and Lucy Berrett and toward the end of 1910 he married Frances Smith at Wilcot. He volunteered for service joining the Wiltshire Regiment and was sent to the Gallipoli peninsular, arriving on 17 November 1915, being sent to the 5th Service Battalion. He arrived during a period of severe cold weather on the peninsular, just a few weeks before the evacuation, and it is likely he was either wounded or suffered from illness or disease and was evacuated to England. Following his recovery he was transferred to the 1st Battalion and sent to the western front. Tom was wounded, most likely by German artillery fire, when the 1st Wiltshires were making their way along the British front line on the western edge of Inverness Copse, east of Hooge. Tom succumbed to his wounds soon after on Saturday 1 September 1917, his company officer wrote the following to his wife Frances Berrett:

"He was a most efficient soldier, being always willing and keen. The officers and N.C.O.'s and men wish me to convey to you their deep sorrow in your great loss."

Tom's grave was lost and he is today remembered on the Tyne Cot Memorial. He left a widow and young family.

Captain Harold Frank Barclay Turner — *1st Bn Wiltshire Regiment*

Service No.	N/a	Age:	22
Place of birth:	Uxbridge, Middlesex	Home Country:	England
Date of death:	01/09/1917	Cause of death:	Died of wounds
Memorial:	Holt, Wiltshire		
War Cemetery:	Menin Road South Military Cemetery - Grave II. A. 12.		
Next of Kin:	Frank Melville & Harriet Fanny Turner		
Address:	Holt Court, Holt Wiltshire, England		

Harold was the only son of Frank Melville and Harriet Fanny Turner, both his parents died when he was young and he went to live with his aunt and uncle at Holt Court. He was educated at Chigwell, where he was a keen sportsman and member of the officer training corps. Soon after the outbreak of hostilities, in September 1914, he volunteered for service with the university and public school battalion. He was in training at Epsom a few weeks before he was given a commission with the 6th Battalion Wiltshire Regiment, being promoted to Lieutenant and arriving in France in October 1915. He was wounded at the Somme in June 1916 and evacuated to England and following his recovery he returned to duty in July 1916 with the 3rd Battalion at Weymouth, before returning to France on 20 September 1916, being transferred to the 1st Battalion. He was promoted to Captain on 1 June 1917 and was recommended for the Military Cross. His Colonel wrote:

"He did splendid work on the Messines Ridge, leading his men splendidly and very greatly assisting his whole battalion in the fight for Wyschaete Ridge."

He was given a brief leave to England and returned to the 1st Wiltshires on 25 June 1917. He was mortally wounded by a German sniper while reconnoitring the ground in front of his section of trenches, when the 1st Wiltshires were in the British front line on the western edge of Inverness Copse, east of Hooge, on the evening of 31 August 1917. He died of his wounds on Saturday 1 September 1917. He was buried on 2 September in Menin Road South Military Cemetery, his Colonel wrote:

"He was absolutely fearless always keen and considerate to his men, and one of the most popular Company Commanders the battalion has ever had. He will be very difficult to replace, and his loss will be felt for a very long time."

Another officer wrote:

"He was a deservedly popular officer in the battalion, and much liked by his company, which he commanded with great tact and skill and constant thought for his men and their comfort, most successfully keeping up the traditions of C Company, which always relied on the suaviter in modo (doing what is to be done) system. He was brave at times to recklessness, and cool in danger, and it is wholly lamentable that so promising a company commander has been taken from us."

Private Thomas Mildenhall		*1st Bn Wiltshire Regiment*	
Service No.	24545	Age:	19
Place of birth:	Ramsbury, Wiltshire	Home Country:	England
Date of death:	01/09/1917	Cause of death:	Killed in action
Memorial:	Ramsbury, Wiltshire		
War Cemetery:	Tyne Cot Memorial - Panel 119 to 120.		
Next of Kin:	William & Kitty Mildenhall (parent)		
Address:	Mill Lane, Ramsbury, Wiltshire		

Thomas known as Tom was the youngest son of William & Kitty Mildenhall it is likely he was either conscripted into the army or enlisted under the Derby Scheme. He joined the Wiltshire Regiment and was sent to the front to the 1st Battalion. Tom was killed on Saturday 1 September 1917, most likely by German artillery fire, when the 1st Wiltshires were making their way along the British front line on the western edge of Inverness Copse, east of Hooge. He is today remembered on the Tyne Cot Memorial and has no known grave.

SUNDAY 2 SEPTEMBER 1917 - TEMPERATURE 17°c OVERCAST - RAINFALL 1.1mm

Sergeant William Henry Bowles		*1st Bn Wiltshire Regiment*	
Service No.	3/811	Age:	46
Place of birth:	Stratton St Margaret, Wiltshire	Home Country:	England
Date of death:	02/09/1917	Cause of death:	Killed in action
Memorial:	Not known		
War Cemetery:	Tyne Cot Memorial - Panel 119 to 120.		
Next of Kin:	Annie Amelia Bowles (wife)		
Address:	Fernham, Berks		

Special reservist William, a cowman on a farm, married Annie Amelia Westal toward the end of 1910. He volunteered for overseas service arriving in France on 4 January 1915 and was sent to the 1st Battalion Wiltshire Regiment. He was killed on Sunday 2 September 1917 most likely by German artillery fire, when the 1st Wiltshires were in the British front line on the western edge of Inverness Copse, east of Hooge. The location of his grave was lost and he is remembered on the Tyne Cot Memorial. He left a widow and young family. In October 1917 Annie Bowles inserted the following memoriam in a local paper:

And now he is sleeping his last long sleep,
And his grave I may never see;
But some gentle hand in that distant land
May scatter some flowers for me.

He little thought when he left home,
That he would never return;
His heart was good, his spirit brave,
His resting place a soldier's grave

Private Arthur Charles Smith		*1st Bn Dorsetshire Regiment*	
Service No.	18721	Age:	38
Place of birth:	Calne, Wiltshire	Home Country:	England
Date of death:	02/09/1917	Cause of death:	Killed in action
Memorial:	Calne, Calne Methodist Memorial, Wiltshire		
War Cemetery:	Coxyde Military Cemetery - Grave III. E. 18.		
Next of Kin:	Martha Smith (wife); George & Emma Smith (parents)		
Address:	39 Pippin Road, Calne, Wiltshire		

Arthur was the youngest son of George and Emma Smith and had been employed as a mason at the Bowood Estate. In 1904, he married Martha Drewett at Calne and they had one child. It is likely that he joined the army under the Derby Scheme or was conscripted. For some years prior to his enlistment he was a teacher in the Primitive Methodist Sunday School, and was a founding member of the Male Voice Choir. In September 1917, Martha Smith received the following letter from the chaplain of the Regiment;

"It is with very great regret that I have to write to you about your husband, Private A. Smith. He was killed here in the line alas on the 1st; he met his end on duty doing his bit in the war, where a man should be. We all share in your loss and would send our sympathy to you. The awful toll of this war! It is hard to write to you, his wife; you must try to bear the dreadful blow with a courage and a brave heart worthy of those who bear so much every day. If we really believe our Lords words about faithful service, "Enter thou into the joy of thy lord," and if we really took Him at His word, how much our grief and feeling of loss would be lessened. Do not think of him as we say as "dead" but alive still, caring still, loving still, and only just passed on and before you into life. He will be so much missed; he has been so well spoken

Left: Arthur Charles Smith

Right: Herbert John Holloway

of. I have been in the line with the Regiment so another Chaplain officiated at the graveside some way back. I do not like leaving the Regiment to go away in times like those."

It is interesting to note that official records state he was killed on 2 September 1917 and the Chaplain states he died on 1 September. It is likely he was killed during the night. A comrade, W. Cox, wrote to Martha on 3 September and stated that he had just heard of her poor husband's death. The writer did not know what had happened as he was wounded at the time, but said he and all the rest of his mates were upset to hear of his death. It is likely that Arthur was killed in the Lombartzyde sector of the front line near Neiuport, Belgium. He is buried in Coxyde Military Cemetery, Belgium with over 1500 soldiers who died in the Great War.

Corporal Herbert John Holloway — *1st Bn Dorsetshire Regiment*

Service No.	25457	Age:	27
Place of birth:	Chapmanslade, Wiltshire	Home Country:	England
Date of death:	02/09/1917	Cause of death:	Killed in action
Memorial:	Chapmanslade, Wiltshire		
War Cemetery:	Coxyde Military Cemetery - Grave III. E. 3.		
Next of Kin:	John & Martha Holloway		
Address:	9 Thomas Street, Walcot, Bath, Somerset		

Herbert was the fifth son of John and Martha Holloway and on leaving education he was employed at the Leigh Leather Works. He was a prominent member of Chapmanslade Football Club and at the outbreak of hostilities was working for the Great Western Railway at Cardiff. He volunteered for service with the 6th Battalion Wiltshire Regiment and arrived in France on 19 July 1915, his first engagement being the Battle of Loos, where he was the only survivor of his platoon. He was badly wounded, with a shattered leg, at the Somme in July 1916. He was evacuated to England and following his recovery he was returned to the front on 6 June 1917, being transferred to the 1st Battalion Dorsetshire Regiment. Herbert was killed on Sunday 2 September 1917 while in the British front line in the Lombartzyde sector of the front line near Neiuport, Belgium. A Sergeant in his platoon wrote the following letter to his parents:

"He had been with us but a short time, but his willingness and cheerful disposition under all circumstances had won him many friends, and we all feel it as a very personal loss in the Lombartzyde

sector of the front line near Neiuport, Belgium. I may add that he suffered nothing, being hit by a machine gun bullet from the German line. He passed away very peacefully as a soldier would wish to die, doing his duty."

Lieutenant Christopher John Masterson		*10th Bn Worcestershire Regiment*	
Service No.	N/a	Age:	22
Place of birth:	Collingbourne Ducis, Wilts	Home Country:	England
Date of death:	02/09/1917	Cause of death:	Killed in action
Memorial:	Collingbourne Ducis, Wiltshire		
War Cemetery:	Underhill Farm Cemetery - Grave A. 37.		
Next of Kin:	James Robert & Elizabeth Masterson		
Address:	Collingbourne Ducis, Wiltshire		

Regular soldier Christopher was the second son of James and Elizabeth Masterson and was serving with the 12th Lancers at the outbreak of hostilities. He arrived in France on 15 August 1914 and took part in the retreat from Mons and the Battle of the Marne. When he had home leave he often talked of how he enjoyed riding across the countryside and how they had to leave their horses and go into the trenches. He was given a commission with the 10th Battalion Worcestershire Regiment on Christmas Day 1916 and soon after was sent to the front and attached to the 1st Battalion Worcestershire Regiment. Christopher was killed instantaneously, with his servant, on Sunday 2 September 1917, most likely by German artillery, while in the British front line north west of Warneton, Belgium.

Private Frederick Cyril Lawrence		*2/1st Bn Ox & Bucks Light Infantry*	
Service No.	285148	Age:	21
Place of birth:	Bethnal Green, Middlesex	Home Country:	England
Date of death:	02/09/1917	Cause of death:	Killed in action
Memorial:	Not known		
War Cemetery:	Tyne Cot Memorial - Panel 96 to 98.		
Next of Kin:	Harry & Minnie Lawrence		
Address:	13 Lethbridge Road, Swindon, Wiltshire		

Frederick was the eldest son of Harry and Minnie Lawrence and after completing his education was employed by the Halford Cycle Company at Regents Street, Swindon. He was then sent to work in the Bath branch and at the outbreak of hostilities he was managing the Southampton depot. In November 1915, he joined the Cycle Corps of the Hampshire Regiment on the Isle of Wight, where he was employed as an auxiliary artificer. In June 1916, he was sent to the Royal Ordinance College at Woolwich, where he passed out at the top of a list of 120 soldiers and was promoted to Lance Corporal and artificer. In May 1917, he was sent to Lyndhurst, where he undertook a bombing course and qualified as an instructor. He was sent to France in July 1917 and transferred to the 2/1st Battalion Ox & Bucks Light Infantry. On 22 August 1917, he wrote the following letter to his parents stating his experiences in action, north west of Zonnebeke:

"During the past, few weeks I have been up the line and over the top. I am safe, but nerves are a little shaky. Don't worry. I will tell you a few of my experiences. We went into the front line on Monday night, walked up there in the open. The trench was just a lot of shell holes connected up, affording little cover. On Tuesday morning Fritz got his wind up and thought we were going to attack. He dropped a barrage fire on our trench. I got partly buried. It lasted about an hour. On Wednesday morning, we attacked. Our barrage was something terrific. I never thought it would be anything like it really was. I went right through to the objective. Our fellows fell like rain. I jumped down into a shell hole, and an explosive bullet from a German Machine Gun hit the sole of my right boot, and embedded itself there. I thought

it had gone into my foot, but was much surprised to find that it had not touched me, only stunned my foot for about three hours. Owing to the flanks not coming up our fellows had to withdraw. I could not walk, so I lay in that shell hole from 5.15am until dark, 9.15pm, about 16 hours. I had four wounded fellows with me. We dared not move because there was a German machine gun each side of us, with heaps of snipers about. The Germans tried to counter attack in the afternoon, and our people dropped a barrage on the ground where we were. A shell burst about a yard from me, and a large piece of earth hit me in the face breaking the skin in several places. That night we went back to the English line, about 800 yards behind and arrived about two o'clock the next morning. I fell in the enemy's wire in the dark and cut my right wrist a little. All day Thursday we kept low in a new line that had been pushed forward. Only one German shell dropped on it, causing three casualties. On Thursday night, we went about 200 yards into No-Man's Land and dug another trench behind two enemy strong points, which were causing a lot of trouble. We stopped out there until we were relieved by another battalion. At 11.30pm we made our way back very quickly, and a train carried us to our billets. When we arrived, we were made a great fuss of and fed well. I never want to have another time like that I had in No-Man's Land. I was covered in mud, dirt and blood. I am lucky to be alive; many of my pals are wounded or killed. It would be easy to write a book about it all. We are still smiling and going to see a concert party tonight."

Frederick was killed, by a German shell, on Sunday 2 September 1917, when 100 men of 2/1st Battalion Ox & Bucks Light Infantry were sent to Wieltje, Belgium as a carrying party. His parents received the following letter from C.Q.M.S. W.F. Taylor:

"I am sorry to inform you that your son, No. 285148 F.C. Lawrence, was killed early this morning. He was one of a carrying party when a shell exploded among them killing your son instantly. Please accept my deepest sympathy from officers, N.C.O.'s and men of C Company, and may God comfort you in your great loss."

Frederick is remembered on the Tyne Cot Memorial and has no known grave.

Private	*William Henry Rodbourne*	*13th Bn Royal Welsh Fusiliers*	
Service No.	235320	Age:	19
Place of birth:	Stratton, Wiltshire	Home Country:	England
Date of death:	02/09/1917	Cause of death:	Killed in action
Memorial:	Great Western Railway Stores Department Memorial, Swindon		
War Cemetery:	Poelcapelle British Cemetery - Grave XLVI. F. 4.		
Next of Kin:	Henry & Mary Ann Rodbourne		
Address:	St Philips Road, Stratton St Margaret, Wiltshire		

William was the eldest son of Henry and Mary Ann Rodbourne and was employed as a warehouse lad in the Stores Department at the Great Western Railway Works in Swindon. It is likely he was either conscripted into the army or enlisted under the Derby Scheme initially joining the Wiltshire Regiment. He was sent to the front and transferred to the 13th Battalion Royal Welsh Fusiliers who on Sunday 2 September 1917 were in the British front line near Alouette Farm, south of Langemarck, Belgium. It is likely William was killed when the 13th Royal Welsh Fusiliers were subjected to German artillery barrages throughout the day. In September 1918 William's parents inserted the following memoriam in a local paper:

One year has passed since that sad day,
When our dear boy was called away;
A son so loving a brother kind,
He is peacefully sleeping in a shell-hole grave.

Left: William Henry Rodbourne

Right: Clement John Strange

After the war William's remains were located west of Pheasant Farm and identified by a disc before being moved to Poelcapelle British Cemetery.

Private Clement John Strange — *2nd Bn Wiltshire Regiment*

Service No.	24146
Place of birth:	Calne, Wiltshire
Date of death:	03/09/1917
Memorial:	Lydiard Millicent, Wiltshire
War Cemetery:	Torreken Farm Cemetery No 1 - Grave D. 11.
Next of Kin:	George & Lottie Matilda Strange
Address:	Greatfield, Wiltshire
Age:	22
Home Country:	England
Cause of death:	Killed in action

Clement was the eldest son of George and Lottie Strange and was employed as a helper in the Loco Department in the Great Western Railway Works at Swindon. It is likely Clement joined the 2nd Battalion Wiltshire Regiment by registering for the Derby Scheme or was conscripted. He was killed in action on Monday 3 September 1914 in the trenches near Wytschaete (now Wijtschate), Belgium. It is likely he was killed by shell fire because the artillery was described as very active. His brother Zenas George Strange was killed in Gallipoli in 1915 while serving with the 5th Battalion Wiltshire Regiment. In 1918, the brother's parents inserted the following memoriam in a local paper:

Not now, but in the coming years,
It may be in that better land,
We'll know the meaning of our fears,
And then perhaps we'll understand.

TUESDAY 4 SEPTEMBER 1917 - TEMPERATURE 21.5°c - OVERCAST - RAINFALL 1.1mm

Private John Percy Brickell — *1st Bn Wiltshire Regiment*

Service No.	9025
Place of birth:	South Wraxall, Wiltshire
Date of death:	04/09/1917
Memorial:	Box - Malmesbury, Wiltshire
Age:	26
Home Country:	England
Cause of death:	Killed in action

War Cemetery: Menin Road South Military Cemetery - Grave II. D. 16.
Next of Kin: Thomas & Susanah Bricknell
Address: Lower High Street, Malmesbury, Wiltshire

Regular soldier John, known as Jack, was the only son of Thomas and Susanah Bricknell and was raised by his uncle, in Box, following the death of his mother during child birth. He arrived in France with the 1st Battalion Wiltshire Regiment. Jack was killed by German 8 inch artillery when the 1st Wiltshires were in reserve at Zillebeke Lake on Tuesday 4 September 1917. In mid September Jack's father received the following letter from Second Lieutenant S.H. Warren of C Company the 1st Wiltshires:

"It is with sincere regret and deepest sympathy that I have to inform you that your son 9025 Pte. J. P. Bricknell was killed in action of the 4 September 1917. He suffered no pain as his death was instantaneous and his body has been buried in a cemetery. He was a willing and good soldier and well liked by all the men of his company. His personal effects will be sent to you as soon as possible., with deepest sympathy in your bereavement."

Jack's father received the following letter from Chaplain T.W. Hart of the 76th Filed Ambulance:

"It is my sad duty to convey to you the sad news of the death of your son, Pte. J. P. Bricknell, 9025, Wilts Regiment, which occurred yesterday. His regiment was back behind the line at the time but a shell fell quite near him. Death was instantaneous so that he suffered no pain. He was buried in the afternoon and a large number of his comrades followed him to the grave. It was my sad duty to officiate at the funeral. It will be some comfort for you to know that he lies buried in a cemetery where his grave will receive every attention. A cross has already been erected at the head of his grave. I feel that this letter will come as a great shock to you, filling your heart with grief and casting deep shadows across your house. May the God of consolation be very near to you, nearer than the sorrow that hides in your heart and nearer than the tears that dim your eyes."

Private Walter Charles Shergold — *1st Bn Wiltshire Regiment*
Service No. 26141
Place of birth: Bemerton, Wiltshire
Date of death: 04/09/1917
Age: 33
Home Country: England
Cause of death: Killed in action
Memorial: Salisbury, Wiltshire
War Cemetery: Menin Road South Military Cemetery - Grave II. D. 14.
Next of Kin: William & Emma Shergold
Address: Homington, Wiltshire

Walter, an asylum attendant, was the youngest son of William and Emma Shergold and it is likely he was either conscripted into the army or enlisted under the Derby Scheme joining the Wiltshire Regiment. He was sent to the front joining the 1st Battalion Wiltshire Regiment who on Tuesday 4 September 1917 were in the reserve line near the dugouts at Zillebeke Lake. During the morning the Germans shelled the position with 8 inch howitzers which caused three casualties. Walter Shergold was one of the men killed in this action.

Private Lewis James Pike — *2/5th Bn Gloucestershire Regiment*
Service No. 242125
Place of birth: Glastonbury, Somerset
Date of death: 04/09/1917
Age: 21
Home Country: England
Cause of death: Died of wounds
Memorial: Devizes Odd Fellows Memorial - Butleigh, Somerset
War Cemetery: Lijssenthoek Military Cemetery - Grave XVIII. F. 14A.
Next of Kin: George & Mary Ann Pike

Address: 42 Butleigh, Glastonbury, Somerset

Twenty one year old Lewis, a masons labourer, was the second son of George and Mary Pike and a member of the Odd Fellows Society. It is likely he was either conscripted into the army or enlisted under the Derby Scheme initially joining the Somerset Light Infantry before being sent to France and being transferred to the 2/5th Battalion Gloucestershire Regiment. He was wounded with shrapnel wounds to the chest, when he was part of a night fatigue party carrying stores to the front north of Ypres, Belgium. He was evacuated to No. 3 Casualty Clearing Station at Lijssenthoek, where he succumbed to his wounds on Tuesday 4 September 1917.

Gunner John James William Crook *150th Bde Royal Field Artillery*

Service No.	109793	Age:	19
Place of birth:	Swindon, Wiltshire	Home Country:	England
Date of death:	04/09/1917	Cause of death:	Killed in action
Memorial:	Swindon Christ Church Memorial, Wiltshire		
War Cemetery:	Vlamertinghe New Military Cemetery - Grave IX. H. 21.		
Next of Kin:	William John & Clara Crook		
Address:	Swindon, Wiltshire		

John was the only son of William John and Clara Crook and it is likely he was either conscripted into the army or enlisted under the Derby Scheme initially joining the Royal Field Artillery. He was sent to the front and sent to the 150th Brigade. He was killed in action on Tuesday 4 September 1917, most likely by German counter battery fire in a gun position east of Vlamertinghe, Belgium.

Private Albert Geoffrey Lawes *8th Bn Royal Inniskilling Fusiliers*

Service No.	41685	Age:	19
Place of birth:	Swindon, Wiltshire	Home Country:	England
Date of death:	04/09/1917	Cause of death:	Died of wounds
Memorial:	Not known		
War Cemetery:	Etaples Military Cemetery - Grave XXV. O. 7A.		
Next of Kin:	Albert H. & Elizabeth Lawes		
Address:	5 Ponting Street, Swindon, Wiltshire		

Albert, known a Geoffrey, was the eldest son of Albert and Elizabeth Lawes and was educated at Sandford Street School. After leaving education, he found employment with C.H. Carpenter, grocers in Manchester Road, Swindon where he was employed for nearly five years. It is likely he was either conscripted into the army or enlisted under the Derby Scheme joining the army on 16 February 1917. He arrived in France on 23 June 1917, four days after his 19th birthday and was sent to 8th Battalion Royal Inniskilling Fusiliers. He was severely wounded in action on 17 August 1917 east of Zonnebeke, Belgium and evacuated to the military hospital at Etaples, France. News of Geoffrey's wound was first received in a letter from the Rev. Robert Howie:

"By the time this reaches you you will doubtless have heard that your son, Pte. A.G. Lawers, has been wounded. He has just been brought into our casualty clearing station. You may be sure he will receive every possible attention, and I hope, by the blessing of God, that he may soon be sent down to the base."

From the same hospital, the Rev. G.M. Ambrose wrote:

"Your son is at present with us, having received serious wounds, which necessitated the amputation of part of his left leg. He seems to be doing well and hopes soon to be on his way to a base hospital, on the journey to England."

Geoffrey wrote or had written letters home to his parents stating:

"I am going on as well as can be expected under the circumstances. I can imagine the shock you received when you received the chaplain's letter sayingthat I was wounded, but cheer up, for I shall soon be home in dear old 'Blighty.'"

In a further letter, he stated:

"I know how sorry you will be to learn that I have lost my left leg, but we out here don't think so much of it as you will at home, because we know of so many others who are worse off. Also we know that when we get better we can have cork legs, so that other people are unable to tell the difference. You would not worry if you saw how cheerful we are."

Geoffrey's condition worsened and he died from his wounds on Tuesday 4 September 1917. Molly Smith from the hospital wrote the following letter to Geoffrey's parents:

"I am writing to you because I knew your son Geoffrey whilst he was in hospital. I am only an occasional visitor at the hospital where he was, but as his bed was next to that of an Australian boy whom I went to see there I got to know Geoffrey, too, and he told me he lived in Swindon. He was always very cheerful and smiling. When the Australian boy left for 'Blighty' I said I would look after him instead. He was splendidly nursed and the sisters were devoted to him and did everything possible to make him happy. I saw him an hour or so before he died, and went again the next day, but he had passed very peacefully away. He was a dear boy, and I thought you would like flowers on his grave I took a lovely bunch today and put them there. He lies in a beautiful little English cemetery close to the sea. I shall take flowers when I go, though the graves are beautifully cared for. I can sympathise deeply with you in your loss and it will comfort you to know that he bore himself so bravely and died so peacefully. The Australian boy was very fond of him and their beds were side by side out of doors as well as in."

Sapper Henry George Panting		*227th Field Company Royal Engineers*	
Service No.	178172	Age:	23
Place of birth:	Chippenham, Wiltshire	Home Country:	England
Date of death:	04/09/1917	Cause of death:	Died of wounds
Memorial:	Calne, Wiltshire		
War Cemetery:	Reninghelst New Military Cemetery - Grave IV. G. 15.		
Next of Kin:	Edith E Panting (wife); Henry George & Rose Panting (parents)		
Address:	25 High Street, Wooton Bassett - 2 Oxford Villas, Pippin Road, Calne		

Henry, known as Harry, was a cabinet maker and the only son of Henry and Rose Panting. In the summer of 1915 he married Edith Ayers in Swindon. It is likely he was either conscripted into the army or enlisted under the Derby Scheme joining the Royal Engineers. He was wounded on Tuesday 4 September 1917, while under taking work on a mule track near Shrewsbury Forest east of Hill 60. He was evacuated to 140th Field Ambulance, at Reninghelst where he succumbed to his wounds later that day.

Wednesday 5 September 1917 - Temperature 23.5°c - Clear- Rainfall 5.1mm

Sapper Robert Thomas Ockwell		*151st Field Coy Royal Engineers*	
Service No.	62893	Age:	37
Place of birth:	South Marston, Wiltshire	Home Country:	England

Date of death: 05/09/1917 Cause of death: Died of wounds
Memorial: Not known
War Cemetery: Bard Cottage Cemetery - Grave IV. F. 19.
Next of Kin: Bertha Emily Ockwell (wife) - George & Sarah Ockwell (parents)
Address: Alresford, Hampshire - 16 Swindon Road Stratton St. Margaret

Robert, known as Thomas and a railway plate layer, was the eldest son of George and Sarah Ockwell and volunteered for service joining the Royal Engineers. He arrived in France on 4 December 1915 and was sent 151st Field Company. At the beginning of 1917 he married Bertha Emily Lush at Alresford, Hampshire soon after returning to the front. Thomas was killed by a bursting German shell on the night of Wednesday 5 September 1917 while repairing a pontoon bridge over the Ypres Canal not far from Bard Cottage. His widow, Bertha received the following letter from his section officer:

"I regret to inform you that your husband, Sapper R.T. Ockwell was killed last night by a shell. He died instantly and without pain, and he was buried this morning by a Church of England Chaplain. All his comrades and myself were fortunately able to attend his funeral. I have been his section officer for about six weeks, and always found him hard working and trustworthy, and he was loved and respected by all the men in the section. We are having a cross made, which we will place over his grave in the Cemetery. I am extremely sorry to lose him, as he has been with the company for a long time, and was looked upon by myself as a valuable and reliable man. He has done his duty, God will repay him."

It is interesting to point out that in the letter it states he died instantly, however official records state he died of wounds, which may indicate that his death was not painless.

THURSDAY 6 SEPTEMBER 1917 - TEMPERATURE 25°c - OVERCAST- RAINFALL 24.6mm

Private Charles James Aylesbury *2/5th Bn Royal Warwickshire Regiment*
Service No. 235035 Age: 26
Place of birth: Corsley, Wiltshire Home Country: England
Date of death: 06/09/1917 Cause of death: Killed in action
Memorial: Frome, Somerset - Abertillery St. Michael's, Monmouthshire
War Cemetery: Tyne Cot Memorial - Panel 23 to 28 and 163A.
Next of Kin: James Jonah & Emily Jane Aylesbury
Address: 5 Friggle Street, Frome, Somerset

Charles, known as Charlie, was the only son of James and Emily Aylesbury and was employed in an iron foundry in South Wales. It is likely he was either conscripted into the army or enlisted under the Derby Scheme initially joining the Monmouthshire Regiment. He was sent to the front and transferred to the 2/5th Battalion Royal Warwickshire Regiment. Charlie was killed during a successful attack on Thursday 6 September 1917 at Hill 35 near the German strong points of the Somme and Gallipoli, west of Zonnebeke. He is remembered on the Tyne Cot Memorial and has no known grave.

Rifleman Edwin James Holton *2/8th Bn London Regiment*
Service No. 372498 Age: 22
Place of birth: Burbage, Wiltshire Home Country: England
Date of death: 06/09/1917 Cause of death: Killed in action
Memorial: Not known
War Cemetery: Track X Cemetery - Grave B. 12.
Next of Kin: Edwin & Elizabeth Holton

Address: South Street, Andover, Hampshire

Post office worker, Edwin, was the third son of Edwin and Elizabeth Holton and it is likely he was either conscripted into the army or enlisted under the Derby Scheme initially joining the 2/8th Bn London Regiment (the Post Office Rifles). He was killed on the night of Thursday 5/6 September 1917, most likely by German Artillery fire, as the 2/8th Londons took into the British front line near Sprigfield south east of Vancouver Corner.

SATURDAY 8 SEPTEMBER 1917 - TEMPERATURE 22°c - FOG- RAINFALL NIL

Private Harold Liney — *2nd Bn Wiltshire Regiment*

Service No. 33000 — Age: 22
Place of birth: Winterslow, Wiltshire — Home Country: England
Date of death: 08/09/1917 — Cause of death: Killed in action
Memorial: Winterslow, Wiltshire,
War Cemetery: Cabin Hill Cemetery - Grave C. 8.
Next of Kin: Philip & Eliza Liney
Address: The Horse Shoe Inn, Winterslow, Wiltshire

Harold, a farm labourer, was the second son of Philip and Eliza Liney and initially enlisted with the Wiltshire Yeomanry. He was sent to the front and transferred to the 2nd Battalion Wiltshire Regiment. It is likely he was killed, by German artillery, while on a night working party on Saturday 8 September 1917, east of Messines, Belgium.

Gunner Harold Percival Morris — *Howitzer Bde Royal Marine Artillery*

Service No. RMA/1052(S) — Age: 26
Place of birth: Shucknall, Herefordshire — Home Country: England
Date of death: 08/09/1917 — Cause of death: Died of wounds
Memorial: Salisbury, Wiltshire
War Cemetery: Dozinghem Military Cemetery - Grave VI. A. 17.
Next of Kin: Percy W & Arabella M Morris
Address: Shucknall Court, Shucknall, Herefordshire

Harold was the youngest son of Percy and Arabella Morris and was employed as a masonry contractor. He volunteered for action on 7 August 1915 joining the Royal Marine Artillery and arrived in France on 1 July 1916. He was wounded, most likely by German counter battery artillery fire north of Ypres, on Saturday 8 September 1917, and taken to a military hospital at Dozinghem, where he succumbed to his wounds later that day.

SUNDAY 9 SEPTEMBER 1917 - TEMPERATURE 21.5°c - FOG- RAINFALL NIL

Private William James Burton — *2/1st Bucks Bn Ox & Bucks Light Infantry*

Service No. 267162 — Age: 28
Place of birth: Salisbury, Wiltshire — Home Country: England
Date of death: 09/09/1917 — Cause of death: Killed in action
Memorial: Salisbury, Wiltshire
War Cemetery: Tyne Cot Memorial - Panel 96 to 98.

William James Burton

Next of Kin: Eliza Caroline Burton (wife) – William & Annie Burton (parents)
Address: 63 Rampart Road, Salisbury, Wiltshire

William, a brewery hand, was the eldest son of William and Annie Burton and at the beginning of 1911 he married Eliza Caroline Whittington at Salisbury. It is likely he was either conscripted into the army or enlisted under the Derby Scheme initially joining the Wiltshire Regiment, but was later transferred to the 2/1st Battalion Oxfordshire & Buckinghamshire Light Infantry. He was killed in action on Sunday 9 September 1917 in the British front line, near Warwick Farm, south of Wieltje, most likely by German artillery. William is remembered on the Tyne Cot Memorial and has no known grave. He left a widow and a young family.

Private Cecil Harold Richardson		*2nd Bn Royal Berkshire Regiment*	
Service No.	36872	Age:	20
Place of birth:	Sutton Veny, Wiltshire	Home Country:	England
Date of death:	09/09/1917	Cause of death:	Died of wounds

Memorial: Broughton Gifford, Wiltshire
War Cemetery: Harlebeke New British Cemetery - Grave XII. D. 11.
Next of Kin: Herbert & Rose Richardson
Address: Broughton Gifford, Wiltshire

Cecil, a farm worker, was the fourth son of Herbert and Rose Richardson and it is likely he was either conscripted into the army or enlisted under the Derby Scheme initially joining the Worcestershire Regiment, before transferring to the 2nd Battalion Royal Berkshire Regiment. It is also likely that Cecil was reported wounded and missing during an attack near Westhoek on 14/15 August 1917. He was captured during a German counter attack and taken to a German medical facility at Izegem, Belgium, where it is believed he succumbed to his wounds on Sunday 9 September 1917. He was buried in Izegem Communal Cemetery German Extension and his remains were relocated to Harlebeke New British Cemetery in May 1923.

Monday 10 September 1917 - Temperature 19°c - Clear- Rainfall Nil

Private Edward Nicholas Rose		*3rd Bn Coldstream Guards*	
Service No.	17579	Age:	19
Place of birth:	Durrington, Wiltshire	Home Country:	England
Date of death:	10/09/1917	Cause of death:	Killed in action
Memorial:	Rollestone, Wiltshire		
War Cemetery:	Tyne Cot Memorial - Panel 9 to 10.		
Next of Kin:	James & Kate Rose		
Address:	Rollestone Cottages, Shrewton, Wiltshire		

Nineteen year old Edward, was the youngest son of James & Kate Rose and it is likely he was either conscripted into the army or enlisted under the Derby Scheme joining the 3rd Battalion Coldstream Guards. He was killed on Monday 10 September 1917, south of Langemarck when the 3rd Coldstreams advanced positions were subjected to German raids. Edward is remembered on the Tyne Cot Memorial and has no known grave.

Private Fred Walter Barrett		*2/4th Bn Ox & Bucks Light Infantry*	
Service No.	203443	Age:	34
Place of birth:	Pewsey, Wiltshire	Home Country:	England
Date of death:	10/09/1917	Cause of death:	Killed in action
Memorial:	Not known		
War Cemetery:	Ypres Reservoir Cemetery - Grave I. C. 12.		
Next of Kin:	Richard & Frances Barrett		
Address:	London		

Fred, a counting house clerk, was the youngest son of Richard and Frances Barrett and initially enlisted with the Royal Bucks Hussars. He was transferred to the 2/4th Battalion Ox & Bucks Light Infantry and sent to the front. On Monday 10 September 1917, the 2/4th Battalion Ox & Bucks attacked Hill 35 northwest of Zonnebeke. At 4pm the attack commenced and the British advanced within 30 yards of the objective, where they were held up by German machine gun fire from Iberian Farm which was situated south of Hill 35 and Aisne House to the north. The 2/4th Battalion Ox & Bucks found it impossible to advance and were forced to withdraw under cover of darkness. Fred was killed during the attack.

TUESDAY 11 SEPTEMBER 1917 - TEMPERATURE 21.5°c - CLEAR- RAINFALL NIL

Private John Durston		*2/4th Bn Ox & Bucks Light Infantry*	
Service No.	25464	Age:	27
Place of birth:	East Pennard, Somerset	Home Country:	England
Date of death:	11/09/1917	Cause of death:	Died of wounds
Memorial:	East Grafton, Wiltshire		
War Cemetery:	Mendinghem Military Cemetery - Grave IV. D. 11.		
Next of Kin:	John & Mary Durston		
Address:	106 Camberwell Road, London, London		

John was the eldest son of John & Mary Durston and was employed as a gardener by Mr MacAndrew of Wexcombe near Marlborough. It is likely he was either conscripted into the army or enlisted under the Derby Scheme initially joining the Worcestershire Regiment, before being transferred to the 2/4th Battalion Ox & Bucks Light Infantry. He was wounded during the attack on Hill 35 on Monday 10 September 1917 and evacuated to a medical facility at Mendinghem, where he succumbed to his wounds the following day.

WEDNESDAY 12 SEPTEMBER 1917 - TEMPERATURE 16.5°c - OVERCAST- RAINFALL NIL

Private Sidney New Massey — *2nd Bn Wiltshire Regiment*

Service No.	6781	Age:	31
Place of birth:	St Lukes, London	Home Country:	England
Date of death:	12/09/1917	Cause of death:	Died of wounds
Memorial:	Salisbury, Wiltshire		
War Cemetery:	Outterstreene Communal Cemetery Extension Bailleul - Grave I. A. 46.		
Next of Kin:	Edward & Annie Massey		
Address:	Rampart Road, Salisbury, Wiltshire		

Regular soldier Sidney was the second son of Edward and Annie Massey and had enlisted with the Wiltshire Militia in 1902. He had served on the island of St. Helena where he guarded Boer prisoners from the South African War and was awarded the King's Medal. He had also served in India and South Africa and returned to England 12 months prior to the outbreak of hostilities. He arrived in France on 22 August 1914 and served as a company stretcher bearer during the retreat from Mons with the 1st Battalion. He completed 14 years with the colours in January 1916 and applied for time expired leave, which he was granted in June 1916 and was home for a month. At some stage, he transferred to the 2nd Battalion Wiltshire Regiment and was wounded in the abdomen on Tuesday 11 September 1917 east of Wytschaete, most likely caused by German artillery as the 2nd Wiltshires were being relieved. He was evacuated to a hospital at Bailleul, where he succumbed to his wounds the following day. His brother Frederick had been killed in March 1915 whilst serving with the 1st Battalion Wiltshire Regiment.

FRIDAY 14 SEPTEMBER 1917 - TEMPERATURE 19°c - OVERCAST- RAINFALL 0.4mm

2nd Lt Arthur Simon Watson-Taylor — *22nd Bn London Regiment*

Service No.	N/a	Age:	33
Place of birth:	Erlestoke	Home Country:	British West Indies
Date of death:	14/09/1917	Cause of death:	Killed in action
Memorial:	Erlestoke, Wiltshire		
War Cemetery:	Menin Road South Military Cemetery - Grave II. C. 7.		
Next of Kin:	Arthur Wellesley Watson-Taylor & Mary Emmeline Watson-Taylor,		
Address:	Haughton Grove, Ramble, Jamaica		

Arthur was the eldest son of Arthur Wellesley and Mary Emmeline Watson-Taylor and was educated at Wellington College before attending Cambridge University where he studied art. He enlisted with the army initially joining the 20th Training Reserve, before being transferred to the 15th Rifle Brigade, being promoted to Corporal. He was given a commission with the 22nd London Regiment on 15 June 1917. Arthur was killed on Friday 14 September 1917 most likely by German artillery while commanding a working party at Y Wood, west of Hooge.

Private Francis John Offer — *1st Bn Wiltshire Regiment*

Service No.	10004	Age:	34
Place of birth:	Devizes, Wiltshire	Home Country:	England
Date of death:	14/09/1917	Cause of death:	Died of wounds
Memorial:	Not known		
War Cemetery:	Pond Farm Cemetery - Grave E. 2.		

Next of Kin: Francis & Sarah Ann Offer
Address: 105A New Park Street, Devizes, Wiltshire

Francis, a printer's labourer, was the eldest son of Francis and Sarah Offer. It is likely he was a reservist being called to the colours at the outbreak of hostilities and sent to France arriving on 22 October 1914 where he joined the 1st Battalion Wiltshire Regiment. Francis was wounded, most likely by German artillery fire, and taken to a field ambulance near Wulvergem, south west of Ypres, Belgium, where he died on Friday 14 September 1914 and was buried in Pond Cemetery.

SATURDAY 15 SEPTEMBER 1917 - TEMPERATURE 19.5°c - OVERCAST- RAINFALL 0.1mm

Gunner Arthur James Bird *128th Bty Bn Royal Field Artillery*
Service No. 172955
Age: 33
Place of birth: Preshute, Wiltshire
Home Country: England
Date of death: 15/09/1917
Cause of death: Killed in action
Memorial: Norton Bavant, Wiltshire
War Cemetery: Dozinghem Military Cemetery - Grave V. C. 8.
Next of Kin: Harriet Mabel Bird (wife) – Frederick & Elizabeth Bird (parents)
Address: 13, Regent Street, Clifton, Gloucestershire

Arthur was the eldest son of Frederick and Elizabeth Woodings and was employed as a footman for Percy Archer Clive MP for south Herefordshire, where he met his future wife Harriet Mabel Woodings. They married in the summer of 1911 at Hereford and it is likely he was either conscripted into the army or enlisted under the Derby Scheme initially joining the Royal Field Artillery. He was wounded while serving with the 128th Battery, most likely by German artillery and evacuated to a medical facility at Dozinghem where he succumbed to his wounds on Saturday 15 September 1917. His employer Percy Archer Clive MP was killed in 1918 while serving with the 1/5th Lancashire Fusiliers.

SUNDAY 16 SEPTEMBER 1917 - TEMPERATURE 23°c - OVERCAST- RAINFALL NIL

Corporal George Frederick Sutton *40th Bde Bn Royal Field Artillery*
Service No. 71029
Age: 22
Place of birth: Swindon, Wiltshire
Home Country: England
Date of death: 16/09/1917
Cause of death: Died of wounds
Memorial: Not known
War Cemetery: Ypres Reservoir Cemetery - Grave I. E. 38.
Next of Kin: Walter & Annie Sutton
Address: 6 Byron Street, Swindon, Wiltshire

Regular soldier George was the third son of Walter and Annie Sutton and had joined the Royal Warwickshire Regiment Special Reserve at the age of 17 years and 3 months. He then transferred to the Royal Field Artillery who he was serving with at the outbreak of hostilities. He arrived in France with the 36th Brigade on 16 August 1914. He was wounded in the arm on 23 October 1914 and sent to a No. 8 General Hospital at Rouen. Following a short convalescence, he was transferred to the 40th Brigade Royal Field Artillery, early in 1915. George was again wounded, on Sunday 16 September 1917, most likely by German artillery and evacuated to the 2/1st Wessex Field Ambulance at Ypres, where he succumbed to his wounds later that day.

Private Oliver Dyer — *2nd Bn Wiltshire Regiment*

Service No.	22264	Age:	32
Place of birth:	Wilcote, Warwickshire	Home Country:	England
Date of death:	16/09/1917	Cause of death:	Died of wounds
Memorial:	Ramsbury, Wiltshire		
War Cemetery:	Bailleul Communal Cemetery Extension Nord - Grave III. E. 188.		
Next of Kin:	Walter & Sarah Jane Dyer		
Address:	Warwickshire		

Gardener Oliver, was the second son of Walter and Sarah Jane Dyer and was a popular member of Ramsbury Cricket Club. It is likely he was either conscripted into the army or enlisted under the Derby Scheme joining the Wiltshire Regiment and was sent to the front being attached to the 2nd Battalion. It is likely he was wounded on Tuesday 11 September 1917 east of Wytschaete, most likely caused by German artillery as the 2nd Wiltshires were being relieved. Oliver was evacuated to a military hospital at Bailleul, where he succumbed to his wounds on Sunday 16 September 1917.

MONDAY 17 SEPTEMBER 1917 - TEMPERATURE 23°c - OVERCAST- RAINFALL NIL

Private Albert Edward Wallis — *153rd Coy Bn Machine Gun Corps*

Service No.	103209	Age:	19
Place of birth:	Brinkworth, Wiltshire	Home Country:	England
Date of death:	17/09/1917	Cause of death:	Killed in action
Memorial:	Not known		
War Cemetery:	Poelcapelle British Cemetery - Grave L. F. 16.		
Next of Kin:	Matthew H & Fanny Wallis		
Address:	72 George Street, Coventry, Warwickshire		

Nineteen year old, Albert, was the youngest son of Matthew and Fanny Wallis and it is likely he was either conscripted into the army or enlisted under the Derby Scheme initially joining the Royal Warwickshire Regiment, before transferring to the Machine Gun Corps. He was sent to the front and attached to the 153rd Company who on Monday 17 September 1917, were targeting German positions at and around Rose House, south west of Poelcapelle, with eight Vickers machine guns. Albert and one other soldier were killed during this action. In November 1920, Albert's remains were located south of Alouette Farm, near Langemarck. He was identified by means of a disc before his remains were moved to Poelcapelle British Cemetery.

TUESDAY 18 SEPTEMBER 1917 - TEMPERATURE 18.5°c - CLEAR- RAINFALL 0.4mm

Gunner Sydney Herbert Goodall — *221st Siege Bty Royal Garrison Artillery*

Service No.	152650	Age:	24
Place of birth:	Winterbourne, Wiltshire	Home Country:	England
Date of death:	18/09/1917	Cause of death:	Killed in action
Memorial:	Chute, Wiltshire		
War Cemetery:	Klein-Vierstraat British Cemetery - Grave III. C. 11		
Next of Kin:	Henry & Elizabeth Ann Goodall		
Address:	St Mary Bourne, Hampshire		

Sydney, known a Herbert and a carter, was the youngest son of Henry and Elizabeth Ann Goodall. It is likely he was either conscripted into the army or enlisted under the Derby Scheme initially joining the Royal Garrison Artillery. He was killed on Tuesday 18 September 1917, most likely by German artillery fire, while serving with 221st Siege Battery, in a gun position south of Ypres.

Private Charles Score		*70th Aux Petrol Coy Army Service Corps*	
Service No.	M2/184202	Age:	29
Place of birth:	Donhead St Andrew, Wiltshire	Home Country:	England
Date of death:	18/09/1917	Cause of death:	Killed in action
Memorial:	Semley Baptist Chapel, Wiltshire – Hove Library, Hove Sussex		
War Cemetery:	Brandhoek New Military Cemetery No 3 - Grave I. F. 9.		
Next of Kin:	Mary Ann Score (wife) - George & Kate Score		
Address:	32 Montgomery Street, Hove, Sussex - Barkers Hill, Semley.		

Charles, a car man was the only son of George and Kate Score and toward the end of 1913 he married Mary Ann Tomblinson at Steyning, Sussex. It is likely he was either conscripted into the army or enlisted under the Derby Scheme initially joining the Army Service Corps. He was sent to the front and served with the 70th Aux. Petrol Company. During the third battle of Ypres he was attached to the 38th Division. He was killed on Tuesday 18 September 1917, most likely by German artillery fire, west of Ypres.

Gunner William John Frank Dunford		*294th Siege Bty Royal Garrison Artillery*	
Service No.	75265	Age:	27
Place of birth:	Brockenhurst, Hampshire	Home Country:	England
Date of death:	18/09/1917	Cause of death:	Killed in action
Memorial:	Not Known		
War Cemetery:	Tyne Cot Memorial - Panel 6 to 7 and 162.		
Next of Kin:	Olive Sarah Dunford (wife) - William & Eunice K. Dunford (parents)		
Address:	46 Portway, Warminster, Wiltshire – Brockenhust, Hampshire		

William, a bricklayer, was the eldest son of William and Eunice Dunford and married Olive Sarah Lockyer on 12 May 1915 at Warminster. He enlisted under the Derby Scheme on 11 December 1915 and was called up on 7 April 1916 joining the Royal Garrison Artillery. After completing his training, he was posted to Singapore on 11 July 1916 and returned to England on 27 May 1917. He was sent to France on 5 September 1917 serving with the 294th Siege Battery from 15 September 1917. He was killed just three days later, on Tuesday 18 September 1917, most likely by German artillery, south of Ypres. William's personal possessions were returned to Olive Durnford and consisted of a disc, letters, photos and a purse. He is remembered on the Tyne Cot Memorial and has no known grave. He left a widow and three children.

Wednesday 19 September 1917 - Temperature 22°c - Clear- Rainfall 5.1mm

Captain Geoffrey Stafford Wallington		*10th Bn Kings Royal Rifle Corps*	
Service No.	N/A	Age:	20
Place of Birth:	Bury, Lancashire	Home Country:	England
Date of Death:	19/09/1917	Cause of death:	Killed in action
Memorial:	Eton School		
War cemetery:	Poelcapelle British Cemetery - Grave Sp. Mem. 7.		
Next of Kin:	Colonel Charles D. & Edith Margaret Wallington		
Address:	41 Portchester Road, Bournemouth, Dorset		

Geoffrey Stafford Wallington

Twenty year old Geoffrey, known as Geoff, was the elder son of Charles and Edith Wallington who had lived at The Priory, Chippenham and was the grandson of Sir John Wallington of Keevil Manor. He was educated at Eton from 1910 to 1915 and was an exceptional athlete. He won the junior high jump in 1912 and in 1914 he won the school Field and Ophidian Wall colours, for the high jump and the hurdles. He played in the Eton XI gaining his colours for 12th man and in 1915 he was placed third for the Victor Ludorum Cup. Geoff was an active member of "pop" being secretary of the Musical Society and was Company Sergeant Major of the Officer Training Corps. He went to Sandhurst in August 1915 and joined the 60th Rifles in December 1915. He was sent to France in July 1916 and appointed Adjutant and promoted to Lieutenant in early 1917. He was mentioned in dispatches on 25 May 1917 and promoted to Captain. On Wednesday 19 September 1917, the 10th Kings Royal Rifle Corps were near Reires Farm just west of Langemarck. At about 5.30pm Geoff was killed together with his Colonel when a shell struck the dug out in which they were sheltering. His commanding officer wrote:

"We all loved Geoff and cannot yet realize that he has left us. One has had from time to time to see other officers go, whom one could hardly bear to lose, but Geoff was quite apart. It was such a privilege to live with his wonderful personality, and the recollection of his cheerfulness, his ability, his own self, will always be a very great possession, a memory that will never, never fade. We cannot bear to think too much of what has happened, and it would be a presumption to tell you what you already know of his qualities as a man and as a leader of men, he was of course, ideal. That he and the Colonel should have been killed side by side is a great tragedy, but it was in battle, and some great comfort to us all."

Geoff's House master from his school wrote:

"We were all so proud of him and he was in life and death a worthy son of Eton."

He is remembered on a special memorial in Poelcapelle British Cemetery.

Gunner Francis Victor Sage — *19th Heavy Bty Royal Garrison Artillery*

Service No.	109153	Age:	20
Place of birth:	Calne, Wiltshire	Home Country:	England
Date of death:	19/09/1917	Cause of death:	Killed in action
Memorial:	Calne, Wiltshire		
War Cemetery:	Canada Farm Cemetery - Grave III. C. 9.		
Next of Kin:	Benjamin & Emily A Sage		
Address:	10 Alma Terrace, Calne, Wiltshire		

Francis, known as Vic and a labourer, was the youngest son of Benjamin and Emily Sage and enlisted on 16 May 1916, at Winchester, aged 18 years. He joined the Royal Garrison Artillery and after completing his training arrived in France on 3 October 1916 and was sent to the 19th Heavy Battery. He was killed on Wednesday 19 September 1917 most likely by German artillery fire north west of Ypres.

Above: A Ration Party near Zillebeke on 21 September 1917

Below: Sanctuary Wood with Mount Sorrel in the background 25 October 1917

8
The Battle of the Menin Road Ridge

Map page 423

THURSDAY 20 SEPTEMBER 1917 - TEMPERATURE 19°c - OVERCAST- RAINFALL NIL

The comparative quiet on the different battle fronts was broken on Thursday morning when the forward movement began at 6am and most of what was aimed at was done in four or five hours, but fighting continued right through Friday, Sir Douglas Haig reported complete success and over 3000 prisoners were taken in Thursdays fighting, but evidently not many guns were captured, as the Germans, taught by bitter experience, now withdraw their guns well to the rear when they know these pushes are impending. It was said by prisoners that the word went down the German trenches on early Thursday morning that the British attack would begin at the very hour that it was timed to begin. The advance was on a width of eight miles, one mile in depth, east of Ypres, north and south of the road to Menin. It was a fight for more of that high ground the Germans are holding on to with desperation, positions that are very important to them. They flung in dense masses of troops in the endeavour to re-capture the ground they have lost, but all their efforts failed. This was a continuation of the 31 July and nothing but the horrible weather of August and the early part of September had prevented the commanders plan from initial success. In the sodden fields of Flanders an operations success is dependent on the weather. The infantry were not to be sent forward without the cover of the guns and fine weather is needed before the guns could be moved. Any delay in the prosecution of the attack once it is launched is disadvantageous and during the delay the enemy can withdraw shattered troops and guns and within three weeks to send his regiments back into the line and to reorganise reserves. This was the case of the 31 July 1917 the main objective of the British troops was completely exposed by that days fighting, and the Germans ever since have piled up defences and accumulated troops to arrest the British advance on the Menin road. A maze of strong places, provided with every defensive and offensive apparatus known to man, was created, and in the rear, there was an unusually large number of divisions held in reserve and obviously retained for counter-attacks. The British commanders not only overcame these defences but held all the ground gained on the 20 September 1917, in the face of powerful and reiterated counter-attacks delivered with the greatest determination by fresh German reserves.

A correspondent at British Headquarters states that the Germans are fighting a purely defensive fight and are in terror of the British artillery. With the help of the Royal Flying Corps the British do roughly 10 times the destruction of the German batteries than the Germans do to the British. The majority of the German's heavy guns have been moved farther back, and only isolated field guns remain in forward positions.

The official message of the British Headquarters states:

"There is nothing to report except the great artillery activity, which continues on both sides of the Ypres sector."

A successful raid near Inverness copse was carried out by men of the York and Lancaster Regiment.

6th Battalion Wiltshire Regiment War Diary

Thursday 20th September 1917 - Opaque Wood north east of Hollebeke, Belgium.

On Thursday 20th September 1917, the 6th Wiltshires formed the right flank in the attack by the 2nd and 5th Armies on the Menin Road the adjoining ridges having the 9th Welsh on left and 2nd Bedfords of the 37th Division on the west bank of Canal. The Battalion was organised in the following way; D Company right assaulting Company, C Company left assaulting Company, B Company right supports, A Company left support. At 5.40am the 6th Wiltshires advanced to the attack under a heavy creeping barrage by British artillery. The left front Company met with little opposition except for continuous German machine gun fire from the direction of Cemetery Embankment. The German machine guns appeared to be located beyond the objective line and to fire through the British barrage. German dugouts in the wood were dealt with resulting in 3 Germans being killed and 19 taken prisoner. D Company on the right met considerable resistance and Captain Williams commanding C Company ordered his right front lewis gun to open a brisk fire on the dugouts in front of D Company. On the left the 9th Welch did not reach their objective until 30 minutes after C Coy of the 6th Wiltshires had begun consolidating. To cover his left flank Captain Williams formed a defensive flank of posts and asked for assistance. These posts from the left rear platoon were subsequently withdrawn when the 9th Welch advanced. The 6th Wiltshires Company reached their objective within 37 minutes of the start of their attack and flares were lit in response to aeroplane calls soon after. The consolidation was covered by Lewis guns and the company snipers who were busily engaged endeavouring to pick off Germans moving down the railway embankment and keeping down enemy sniping on the immediate front - one platoon sniper remained isolated in a forward position from the morning of the 20 September until relieved on the night 21/22 September. The left support company consolidated its section of the intermediate line and several casualties were caused by German sniping. The ground was very wet and water logged in places but firesteps were formed with sandbags. Two platoons were ordered to operate vigorously against German positions in Hessian Wood which was believed to be holding up the 9th Welsh. A battle patrol was sent out from the company when the barrage lifted, although it discovered no enemy on the immediate front of the objective, it came across a German bombing post recently vacated and some consolidated shell holes with iron shelters destroyed by artillery fire. All the 6th Wiltshires officers of D Company were killed on attaining their objectives. On the embankment, the attack was pushed well forward and a post established beyond the actual objective, this post was held until relief on the night 21/22 September although at times heavily shelled. Contact was maintained with the 2nd Bedfords on the right near the canal. To the east of the embankment Captain Langley led the attacks upon the dugouts south of Graves Copse. After he was killed the right section of his party took up positions in shell holes south of the Copse and dug in at dusk. The left of the party which had reached the side of the cemetery found the ground in the immediate front broken and wet and without field of fire and withdrew to the north side of the cemetery to obtain a better field of fire.

B Company had a short way to go and they began digging a line before it was sufficiently light to recognise the landmarks previously reconnoitred with the result that when it became light the position had to be rectified. Throughout the day, they were troubled by German sniping from left front and German machine gun fire from right front. A battle patrol was sent out but came back under considerable German machine gun fire and suffered several casualties. Subsequently two platoons were moved to the embankment which it was considered advisable to hold in greater strength covering the whole of the valley towards Hessian Wood. Carrying parties assembled with loads of wire and stakes behind each of the supporting Companies whom they followed through but German sniping and machine Gun fire made it impossible for them to work in daylight.

Captain Herbert Henry Williams *6th Bn Wiltshire Regiment*

Service No.	N/a	Age:	23
Place of birth:	Swindon, Wiltshire	Home Country:	England
Date of death:	20/09/1917	Cause of death:	Killed in action
Memorial:	Swindon Christ Church, Euclid Street School		
War Cemetery:	Kemmel Chateau Military Cemetery - Grave H. 23.		
Next of Kin:	Thomas Henry & Sarah Ann Williams		
Address:	85 Curtis Street, Swindon, Wiltshire		

Herbert was the only surviving child of Thomas and Sarah Williams and was educated at Sandford Street School before attending the Secondary School, where he attained honours and distinctions. He then carried on his education at St. Paul's College, Cheltenham, from 1912 to 1914 and passed 1st Class. He then became a teacher with Swindon Education Committee and was employed at Ferndale Road School. He volunteered for service on 8 September 1914 with the Royal Army Medical Corps and on 27 December 1914 he was given a commission with the 6th Battalion Wiltshire Regiment. He arrived in France in July 1915 and was promoted to Captain in September 1916. Mr T. Butler the chairman of the Swindon Education Committee stated:

"He is a smart young fellow, and one is pleased to hear that he has made such progress and advancement."

Herbert was wounded on Thursday 20th September 1917 during the attack on German positions near Opaque Wood north east of Hollebeke, Belgium. He succumbed to his wounds soon after on the same day.

Private Reginald John Gurd *6th Bn Wiltshire Regiment*

Service No.	32997	Age:	24
Place of birth:	Wardour, Wiltshire	Home Country:	England
Date of death:	20/09/1917	Cause of death:	Killed in action
Memorial:	Tisbury, Wiltshire		
War Cemetery:	Tyne Cot Memorial - Panel 119 to 120		
Next of Kin:	Henry John & Cecily Ellen Gurd		
Address:	Furzelease, Tisbury Row, Tisbury, Wiltshire		

Reginald a farm labour was the third son of Henry and Cecily Gurd and enlisted with the Royal Wiltshire Yeomanry. He was transferred at some stage to the 6th Battalion Wiltshire Regiment and sent to the front. He was killed on Thursday 20th September 1917 during the attack on German positions near Opaque Wood north east of Hollebeke, Belgium. Reginald is remembered on the Tyne Cot Memorial and has no known grave. His younger brother Ernest Walter was to be killed in March 1918 while also serving with the 6th Battalion Wiltshire Regiment.

Private Herbert Henry Rumming *6th Bn Wiltshire Regiment*

Service No.	18391	Age:	23
Place of birth:	Bremhill, Wiltshire	Home Country:	England
Date of death:	20/09/1917	Cause of death:	Killed in action
Memorial:	Bremhill, Wiltshire		
War Cemetery:	Bedford House Cemetery - Enclosure No.4 Grave XII. G. 25.		
Next of Kin:	Frederick & Sarah Rumming		
Address:	East Tytherton, Wiltshire		

Herbert, a baker's assistant, was the second son of Frederick and Sarah Rumming and volunteered for service with the Wiltshire Regiment and arrived in France on 1 June 1915. He was killed on Thursday

20th September 1917, while serving with the 6th Battalion Wiltshire Regiment during the attack on German positions near Opaque Wood north east of Hollebeke. It is likely Herbert advanced in to an islotated position and his body was moved by the Germans to the rear area behind the German front line. In May1922 his remains were located near Kruiseecke, east of Zandvoorde and identified by means of a disc and clothing, before being moved to Bedford House Cemetery.

Private Sidney Waite		*6th Bn Wiltshire Regiment*	
Service No.	18576	Age:	39
Place of birth:	Bishops Cannings, Wiltshire	Home Country:	England
Date of death:	20/09/1917	Cause of death:	Killed in action
Memorial:	Bishops Cannings, Wiltshire		
War Cemetery:	Bedford House Cemetery - Grave Enclosure No.4 XII. G. 24.		
Next of Kin:	Edwin & Martha Waite		
Address:	Bishops Cannings, Wiltshire		

Labourer Sidney was the youngest son of Edwin and Martha Waite and before the Great War he had been employed by Mr E.G. De Mestre at the training stables at Bishops Cannings. He volunteered for service joining the Wiltshire Regiment and arrived in France in September 1915 being sent to the 6th Service Battalion. Sidney was killed on Thursday 20th September 1917 during the attack on German positions near Opaque Wood north east of Hollebeke, Belgium. Sidney's nephew William Waite had been killed in July 1917 while serving with the Canadians near Loos, France. It is likely Sidney advanced in to an isolated position and his body was moved by the Germans to the rear area behind the German front line. In May 1922 his remains were located near Kruiseecke, east of Zandvoorde and identified by means of a disc and clothing, before being moved to Bedford House Cemetery.

Private Herbert William Tuck		*6th Bn Wiltshire Regiment*	
Service No.	24525	Age:	19
Place of birth:	Collingbourne Kingston, Wilts	Home Country:	England
Date of death:	20/09/1917	Cause of death:	Killed in action
Memorial:	Not known		
War Cemetery:	Tyne Cot Memorial - Panel 119 to 120.		
Next of Kin:	Emanuel & Kate Tuck		
Address:	52 Collingbourne Kingston, Wiltshire		

Herbert, a carter on a farm, was the eldest son of Emanuel and Kate Tuck and it is likely Robert was either conscripted into the army or enlisted under the Derby Scheme joining the 6th Battalion Wiltshire Regiment. He was killed on Thursday 20th September 1917 during the attack on German positions near Opaque Wood north east of Hollebeke, Belgium. Herbert is remembered on the Tyne Cot Memorial and has no known grave.

Private Walter Burton		*6th Bn Wiltshire Regiment*	
Service No.	12213	Age:	22
Place of birth:	Bradford on Avon, Wiltshire	Home Country:	England
Date of death:	20/09/1917	Cause of death:	Killed in action
Memorial:	Bradford on Avon, Wiltshire		
War Cemetery:	Tyne Cot Memorial - Panel 119 to 120.		
Next of Kin:	George & Emily Burton		
Address:	Bradford on Avon, Wiltshire		

Walter, a cloth dyer, was the youngest son of George and Emily Burton and volunteered for service

Wiltshire Regiment, arriving in France on 27 April 1915. It is likely he was either wounded or suffered from illness or disease and following his recovery he was returned to the front being transferred to the 6th Battalion Wiltshire Regiment. He was wounded on Thursday 20th September 1917 during the attack on German positions near Opaque Wood north east of Hollebeke, Belgium. He succumbed to his wounds soon after.

Private Henry Stoneham — *6th Bn Wiltshire Regiment*
Service No. 18117 — Age: 20
Place of birth: Hullavington, Wiltshire — Home Country: England
Date of death: 20/09/1917 — Cause of death: Died of wounds
Memorial: Hullavington
War Cemetery: Bus House Cemetery - Grave H. 20.
Next of Kin: William & Bertha Stoneham
Address: The Street, Hullavington, Wiltshire

Henry was the second son of William and Bertha Stoneham and volunteered for service joining the Wiltshire Regiment, arriving in France on 27 April 1915. It is likely he was either wounded or suffered from illness or disease and following his recovery he was returned to the front being transferred to the 6th Battalion Wiltshire Regiment. He was wounded on Thursday 20th September 1917 during the attack on German positions near Opaque Wood north east of Hollebeke, Belgium. He succumbed to his wounds soon after.

Lance Corporal Charles Henry Ponting — *6th Bn Wiltshire Regiment*
Service No. 20880 — Age: 21
Place of birth: Kington St Micheal, Wiltshire — Home Country: England
Date of death: 20/09/1917 — Cause of death: Died of wounds
Memorial: Leigh Delemere, Wiltshire
War Cemetery: Locre Hospice Cemetery - Grave II. B. 13.
Next of Kin: William George & Florence Eliza Ponting
Address: Sevington, Wiltshire

Charles, a farm labourer, was the eldest son of William and Florence Ponting and it is likely he was conscripted or joined the army under the Derby Scheme joining the 6th Battalion Wiltshire Regiment. He had only just returned from home leave in England when he was wounded on Thursday 20th September 1917, during the attack on German positions near Opaque Wood north east of Hollebeke, Belgium. He was evacuated to a Field Ambulance at Loker, south west of Ypres where he succumbed to his wounds on Thursday 20 September 1917. In September 1918 Charles's parents inserted the following memoriam in a local paper:

Sleep on dear one in an unknown grave
Your life for your country you nobly gave
No loved ones were with you to say goodbye
But safe in God's keeping now you lie

Private Ernest Frayling — *6th Bn Wiltshire Regiment*
Service No. 22832 — Age: 23
Place of birth: Corston, Wiltshire — Home Country: England
Date of death: 20/09/1917 — Cause of death: Killed in action
Memorial: Not known
War Cemetery: Birr Cross Roads Cemetery - Grave I. C. 25.

Next of Kin: Worthy & Annie Frayling
Address: Corston, Wiltshire

Ernest, a farm labourer, was the second son of Worthy and Annie Frayling and it is likely he was conscripted or joined the army under the Derby Scheme joining the 6th Battalion Wiltshire Regiment. He was killed on Thursday 20th September 1917 during the attack on German positions near Opaque Wood north east of Hollebeke. In June 1922 Ernest's remains were located south east of Graves Copse, south of Opaque Wood and were identified by means of a disc, before being moved to Birr Cross Roads Cemetery.

Private Samuel Sutton Romain *6th Bn Wiltshire Regiment*

Service No. 22289
Place of birth: Wilton, Wiltshire
Date of death: 20/09/1917
Age: 29
Home Country: England
Cause of death: Killed in action
Memorial: Wilton, Wiltshire
War Cemetery: Tyne Cot Memorial - Panel 119 to 120.
Next of Kin: Florence Susan Romain (wife) - James & Annie Romain (parents)
Address: 17 North Street, Wilton - 4 Fancy Row, Wilton, Wiltshire

Samuel, a grocer's traveller, was the second son of James and Annie Romain and married Florence Susan Green on 24 May 1915 at Wilton. It is likely he was conscripted or joined the army under the Derby Scheme joining the 6th Battalion Wiltshire Regiment. He was killed on Thursday 20th September 1917 during the attack on German positions near Opaque Wood north east of Hollebeke, Belgium. Samuel is remembered on the Tyne Cot Memorial and has no known grave. He left a widow and young son.

Private Frederick John Long *6th Bn Wiltshire Regiment*

Service No. 20712
Place of birth: Warminster, Wiltshire
Date of death: 20/09/1917
Age: 33
Home Country: England
Cause of death: Died of wounds
Memorial: Not known
War Cemetery: Locre Hospice Cemetery - Grave II. B. 16.
Next of Kin: Mary Elizabeth 'Polly' Long (wife) - Edward Thomas & Eliza Jane Long (parents)
Address: Bath, Somerset - Pound Street, Warminster, Wiltshire

Frederick, a photographer and printer, was the youngest son of Edward and Eliza Long and toward the end of 1912 he married Mary Elizabeth 'Polly' Slade at Bath. On 10 May 1914, the couple had their first and only child Dennis. It is likely Frederick was conscripted or joined the army under the Derby Scheme joining the 8th Battalion Wiltshire Regiment. Soon after he joined, Frederick wrote the following letter to his wife from Bovington Camp:

"My Dearest Wife, Just a few lines in answer to your most welcome letter. Hoping to find you and Babs well. My cold is better, but my throat is still bad. I have a nasty cough at night. There is a possibility of us coming to Sutton Veny of Codford. Our commanding Officer has gone to the War Office to see about it. As there was a mistake us coming here. It is like Hampton Downs for miles round. You do not see many people here. I shall get a pass as soon as I possibly can. I am longing to see you and Babs. I expect he grows now. Baldwins did not get a man very quick. He will not find such a fool as I was for them. Well dear, I do not expect I shall go to France very quick. But I am picked for the first draft from this battalion. But the sergeant stopped it so as far as I know I am as alright as the officer that we are under, thinks a lot of the drums. Well dearest if we should get the back to Bovington Camp to Sutton Veny. You

Left: Frederick John Long

Right: Herbert Stanley Bricker

would be able to come to Warminster and live with mother for a time and we should not be far apart then. There will be a cheer if we go from. Not half. It has been very hot here mow but we have only been out once the week is quiet. We are at practice as there is another Drum and Fyfe Band in the camp. But we do not mean to let them beat us. We have learnt 6 tunes since we have been here and we have to remember it all in our head too, we never carry our music. Well dearest I am longing to see you and babes again it seems a long time since I saw you. Hoping to hear from you soon."

Frederick was sent to France with a draft to serve with the 6th Battalion Wiltshire Regiment. He was killed on Thursday 20th September 1917 during the attack on German positions near Opaque Wood north east of Hollebeke, Belgium. He left a widow and young son.

Sergeant Herbert Stanley Bricker		*D Company 6th Bn Wiltshire Regiment*	
Service No.	18954	Age:	23
Place of birth:	Bradford on Avon, Wiltshire	Home Country:	England
Date of death:	20/09/1917	Cause of death:	Killed in action
Memorial:	Holy Trinity Church, Bradford on Avon, Wiltshire		
War Cemetery:	Tyne Cot Memorial - Panel 119 to 120.		
Next of Kin:	Frank and Sarah Bricker		
Address:	42 Trowbridge Road, Bradford on Avon, Wiltshire		

Herbert was the third son of Frank and Sarah Bricker and was employed as a gardener at the Priory. He volunteered for service joining the 6th Battalion Wiltshire Regiment and arrived in France on 8 September 1915. Herbert was killed on Thursday 20th September 1917 during the attack on German positions near Opaque Wood northeast of Hollebeke, Belgium. His company officer Lieutenant Oxley wrote the following letter to Herbert's parents:

"It is with great regret that I have to inform you that your son was killed in the advance on the 20 September. He was with me ever since I have had No. 13 Platoon, and I have always found him an excellent platoon sergeant, and is a great loss to me. I was not in the attack myself, but I understand death was instantaneous. He has been buried and a cross erected close to his company commander, who was killed at the same time. Any of his personal belongings which have been recovered will be forwarded to you by the usual channels, but if there is anything I can do I shall be only too pleased to do it if you let me know. I should like to express my sympathy with you in your sorrow, and I am sure the platoon would like to express theirs. Your son was liked by all, and we are very sorry to lose him."

Herbert's grave was lost in later fighting and he is today remembered on the Tyne Cot Memorial. His parents inserted the following memoriam in a local paper:

Mother, I must go; she is calling
For men to fight her foes;
I feel that I am needed;
I'll volunteer and go.

His King and Country called him
The call was not in vain;
On Bradford's Roll of Honour
You will find our dear one's name.

Private Sidney Charles Everett		*6th Bn Wiltshire Regiment*	
Service No.	20862	Age:	19
Place of birth:	Sutton Veny, Wiltshire	Home Country:	Wales
Date of death:	20/09/1917	Cause of death:	Killed in action
Memorial:	Sutton Veny, Wiltshire		
War Cemetery:	Tyne Cot Memorial - Panel 119 to 120.		
Next of Kin:	John Thomas & Emma Everett		
Address:	Sutton Veny, Wiltshire		

Nineteen year old Sidney was the third son of John and Emma Everett and it is likely he was conscripted or joined the army under the Derby Scheme joining the 3rd Battalion Wiltshire Regiment. After completing his training, he was sent to the front to serve with the 6th Service Battalion. Sidney was killed on Thursday 20th September 1917 during the attack on German positions near Opaque Wood north east of Hollebeke, Belgium. He is remembered on the Tyne Cot Memorial and has no known grave.

Lance Sergeant Ernest Norris		*6th Bn Wiltshire Regiment*	
Service No.	7182	Age:	30
Place of birth:	Mere, Wiltshire	Home Country:	England
Date of death:	20/09/1917	Cause of death:	Killed in action
Memorial:	Mere, Wiltshire		
War Cemetery:	Tyne Cot Memorial - Grave Panel 119 to 120.		
Next of Kin:	James & Mary Norris		
Address:	North Row, Mere, Wiltshire		

Regular soldier Ernest was the sixth son of James and Mary Norris and arrived in France on 28 August 1914 with the 1st Battalion Wiltshire Regiment. It is likely he was either wounded or suffering from illness or disease and following his recovery he returned to the front, being transferred to the 6th Battalion Wiltshire Regiment. He was killed on Thursday 20th September 1917 during the attack on German positions near Opaque Wood north east of Hollebeke, Belgium. Ernest is remembered on the Tyne Cot Memorial and has no known grave. His brother Sidney had been killed in January 1915 while serving with the 1st Battalion Wiltshire Regiment.

2nd Lieutenant Robert Henry Curtis		*10th Bn Royal West Surrey Regiment*	
Service No.	N/a	Age:	28
Place of birth:	Salisbury, Wiltshire	Home Country:	England

Date of death: 20/09/1917
Cause of death: Killed in action
Memorial: Salisbury, Wiltshire
War Cemetery: Tyne Cot Memorial - Panel 14 to 17 and 162 to 162A
Next of Kin: William & Sarah Anne Curtis
Address: 3 New Street, Salisbury, Wiltshire

Robert was the younger and only surviving son of William and Sarah Anne Curtis and was educated at St Mark's School, Salisbury, and St Mark's Training College, Chelsea. While he was a pupil teacher at Sarum St Mark's, he passed first of all England in the Archbishop's examination in religious knowledge. After leaving education he became a master at Tottenham Council School. It is likely Robert was either conscripted into the army or enlisted under the Derby Scheme initially joining the Honourable Artillery Company, and served with them in France some months before being given a commission with the 10th Battalion Royal West Surrey Regiment on 7 January 1917, where he had acted as signalling officer for his battalion. At 5.40am on Thursday 20 September 1917, following previous days' intense barrage, the 10th Royal West Surrey's followed the 32nd Royal Fusiliers attacking German positions at Tower Hamlets Ridge, east of Hooge, south of the Menin Road. As they advanced in close formation they were met by heavy fire from two German machine gun fire which caused havoc and led to the deaths of many of the 10th Royal West Surrey's officers. The German machine guns were eventually outflanked and captured allowing the 10th Royal West Surrey's to capture their objectives. It is likely Robert was killed by one of these German machine guns. He is remembered on Tyne Cot Memorial and has no known grave.

Private Harry Brewer
28th Bn Australian Infantry AIF
Service No. 5817
Age: 27
Place of birth: Melksham, Wiltshire
Home Country: England
Date of death: 20/09/1917
Cause of death: Killed in action
Memorial: Melksham, Wiltshire
War Cemetery: Ypres Menin Gate - Panel 7 - 17 - 23 - 25 - 27 - 29 - 31.
Next of Kin: George & Eliza Brewer
Address: Semington Road, Melksham, Wiltshire

Harry was the second son of George and Eliza Brewer and had been a postal worker in Melksham. He left England in 1913, emigrating to Australia where he worked as a farm hand. He volunteered for service on 17 March 1916 enlisting with the Australian Infantry. He arrived back in England on 2 December 1916 and then onto France arriving on 22 December 1916. He joined the 28th Battalion on 5 February 1917. At 5.40am on Thursday 20 September 1917 the 28th Battalion were in reserve preparing to attack German positions north of Nonne Boschen. The attack was preceded by an intense British barrage to which the Germans retaliated shelling the Australians position. At 8.10am after a report that the first and second objectives had been taken the 28th Battalion advanced only a few casualties were suffered and by 9.53am the 28th Battalion's objective had been secured. The Australians then dug in north of Polygon Wood and were subjected to German barrage but a German counter attack did not develop. Harry was killed during the advance and his personal property was sent to his father, George, and consisted of tweezers, 6 books, pencil case, razor and brush. He is remembered on the Ypres Menin Gate and has no known grave. His brother Herbert who also served with the 28th Battalion was to die from wounds in June 1918.

Private Alfred Groves
28th Bn Australian Infantry AIF
Service No. 6322
Age: 26
Place of birth: Wandsworth, London
Home Country: Australia
Date of death: 20/09/1917
Cause of death: Killed in action
Memorial: Not known

War Cemetery: Ypres Menin Gate - Panel 7 - 17 - 23 - 25 - 27 - 29 - 31.
Next of Kin: Thomas John & Sarah Elizabeth Groves
Address: The Gables, Lockeridge, Wiltshire

Alfred, a farmer, was the youngest son of Thomas and Sarah Groves and emigrated to Australia before the Great War. He volunteered for service with the Australian Infantry on 23 August 1916. After completing his training, he arrived in England on 3 March 1917. He was found to be suffering from rubella and after a short stay at a hospital in Salisbury he returned to his unit. He arrived in France on 16 June 1917 and was sent to the 28th Battalion being taken on strength on 3 July 1917. He was killed on Thursday 20 September 1917 when the 28th Battalion attacked German positions north of Nonne Boschen and Polygon Wood in the same action as Harry Brewer.

Corporal Albert Victor Lloyd *124th Coy Machine Gun Corps*
Service No. 27677
Age: 21
Place of birth: Trowbridge, Wiltshire
Home Country: England
Date of death: 20/09/1917
Cause of death: Killed in action
Memorial: Frome, Somerset
War Cemetery: Tyne Cot Memorial - Panel 154 to 159 and 163A.
Next of Kin: Josiah & Mary Lloyd
Address: 32 Catherine Street, Frome, Somerset

Albert, known as Bertie and a letter press printer, was the second son of Josiah and Mary Lloyd. It is likely he was conscripted or enlisted under the Derby Scheme initially joining the Somerset Light Infantry, later transferring to the Machine Gun Corps. He served with the 124th Company Machine Gun Corps who on Thursday 20 September 1917 were supporting the 124th Brigade attacking German positions east of Shrewsbury Forrest. Bertie was killed during the attack and is remembered on Tyne Cot Memorial and has no known grave.

Private Albert Clarke White *214th Coy Bn Machine Gun Corps*
Service No. 106347
Age: 20
Place of birth: Corsley, Wiltshire
Home Country: England
Date of death: 20/09/1917
Cause of death: Killed in action
Memorial: Longbridge Deverill, Wiltshire
War Cemetery: Tyne Cot Memorial - Panel 154 to 159 and 163A
Next of Kin: Harry & Emma White
Address: 152 Paradise Lane, Crockerton, Wiltshire

Albert, a farm worker, was the third son of Harry and Emma White and it is likely he was conscripted or enlisted under the Derby Scheme initially joining the Royal Army Ordinance Corps, later transferring to the Machine Gun Corps. He served with the 124th Company Machine Gun Corps who on Thursday 20 September 1917 were supporting the 124th Brigade attacking German positions east of Shrewsbury Forest. Albert was killed during the attack and is remembered on Tyne Cot Memorial and has no known grave.

Sapper Raymond Henry Knott *228th Field Coy Bn Royal Engineers*
Service No. 166451
Age: 35
Place of birth: Devizes, Wiltshire
Home Country: England
Date of death: 20/09/1917
Cause of death: Killed in action
Memorial: Devizes, Wiltshire
War Cemetery: Tyne Cot Memorial - Panel 8 and 162.

Next of Kin: George H & Emma S Knott
Address: 76 New Park Street, Devizes, Wiltshire

Monumental sculptor Raymond was the youngest son of George and Emma Knot. It is likely he was either conscripted into the army or enlisted under the Derby Scheme joining the Royal Engineers, being sent to the front with 228th Field Company. Raymond was killed in action when the 41st Division attacked German positions at Tower Hamlets Ridge on Thursday 20 September 1917, the eve of his 36th Birthday. The 228th Field Company carried forward bridges to cross the Bassevilbeek under heavy German machine gun fire. The engineers then attempted to consolidate the captured positions installing wire entanglements until they were forced to stop because of the continuing German machine gun fire. He is remembered on the Tyne Cot Memorial and has no known grave.

Rifleman Arthur Thomas Foster — *21st Bn Kings Royal Rifle Corps*

Service No.: R/32895 — Age: 32
Place of birth: Wandsworth, Surrey — Home Country: England
Date of death: 20/09/1917 — Cause of death: Killed in action
Memorial: Not known
War Cemetery: Tyne Cot Memorial - Panel 115 to 119 and 162A and 163A
Next of Kin: Margaret Elizabeth Foster (wife) – Thomas & Charlotte Foster (parents)
Address: 290 Cricklade Road, Swindon, Wiltshire

Arthur, a milk carrier was the eldest son of Thomas and Charlotte Foster and married Margaret Elizabeth Smith at All Saints, Clapham Park, Lambeth on 12 Jan 1910. It is likely he was either conscripted into the army or enlisted under the Derby Scheme joining the 21st Battalion Kings Royal Rifle Corps. He was killed on Thursday 20 September 1917 during an attack on German positions east of Shrewsbury Forest, south of the Menin Road. He left a widow and two small children and is today remembered on the Tyne Cot Memorial. He has no known grave.

Private Daniel Skinner — *6th Bn Ox & Bucks Light Infantry*

Service No.: 25972 — Age: 39
Place of birth: Cirencester, Gloucestershire — Home Country: England
Date of death: 20/09/1917 — Cause of death: Killed in action
Memorial: Wroughton, Wiltshire
War Cemetery: Tyne Cot Memorial - Panel 96 to 98.
Next of Kin: Florence Jane Skinner (wife) - Edward & Sarah Skinner (parents)
Address: Wroughton, Wiltshire

Daniel, a journeyman baker, was the eldest son of Edward and Sarah Skinner and in the summer of 1900 he married Florence Jane Richens at Swindon. It is likely he was either conscripted into the army or enlisted under the Derby Scheme joining the 6th Battalion Ox & Bucks Light Infantry. He was reported missing during an attack on Thursday 20 September 1917, on German held Eagle trench east of Langemarck, Belgium. Florence Skinner later received official information stating Daniel was presumed to have been killed on the day he was reported missing. He is remembered on the Tyne Cot Memorial and has no known grave. He left a widow and young family.

Private Albert Henry Cornish — *10th Bn Worcestershire Regiment*

Service No.: 242152 — Age: 21
Place of birth: Corsham, Wiltshire — Home Country: England
Date of death: 20/09/1917 — Cause of death: Killed in action

Left: *Albert Henry Cornish*

Right: Francis Henry Blower

Memorial:	Twyning War Memorial
War Cemetery:	Tyne Cot Memorial - Panel 75 to 77.
Next of Kin:	Edward Ernest Albert & Naomi Ann Cornish
Address:	Tewkesbury, Gloucestershire

Albert, known as Bert, was the eldest son of Edward and Naomi Cornish and was employed as a butcher's assistant. It is likely he was either conscripted into the army or enlisted under the Derby Scheme joining the Worcestershire Regiment. Bert was reported missing on Thursday 20 September 1917 when the 10th Worcesters were on a working party on a duckboard track and drying rooms. In November 1917 Bert's mother received official information stating that Bert was presumed to have been killed on the day he was reported missing. He is remembered on the Tyne Cot Memorial and has no known grave.

Sapper Francis Henry Blower		*227th Field Company Royal Engineers*	
Service No.	19781	Age:	26
Place of birth:	Bradford on Avon, Wilts	Home Country:	England
Date of death:	20/09/1917	Cause of death:	Killed in action
Memorial:	Trowbridge, Wiltshire		
War Cemetery:	Tyne Cot Memorial - Panel 8 and 162		
Next of Kin:	Henry & Anne Blower		
Address:	2 Ansties's Court, Mortimer Street, Trowbridge, Wiltshire		

Regular soldier Francis was the only son of Henry and Annie Blower and lived with his grandmother in Trowbridge. He had served several years in India and in January 1917 he was invalided home and spent 6 months at the depot in Chatham before being sent to France in July 1917. While on active service he sent a letter home explaining whilst at work his officer and two men were killed beside him and two others were severely wounded, but he had escaped unhurt. In early October 1917 Francis's grandmother received the following letter from Lieutenant McRae of the Royal engineers dated 24 September:

"It is with deep regret that I have to advise you that your grandson was killed in action on the morning of the attack on the 20 September. I was his section officer, and he was one of the party to accompany me in a reconnaissance of our new front line. We were heavily shelled and took refuge in some dugouts. Shortly afterwards a shell burst in the entrance of the dug out, and he was badly wounded. We did all

we could for him, but he died almost immediately. As it was impossible to do anything else we buried him on the battlefield. No words of mine can comfort you in your great sorrow, but no man can die better than to die for his country facing the foe. I only had your son a short time with me, but I invariably found him brave, cheerful and willing to do his duty whenever the call came. Please accept from myself and all the officers and men of this Company our heartfelt sympathy."

Francis was killed on Thursday 20 September 1917, at Welbeck Grange near Bulgar Wood south east of Shrewsbury Forest, after coming under heavy German machine gun and shell fire. He is remembered on the Tyne Cot Memorial and has no known grave.

Sergeant Frederick John Jefferies		*58th Div Royal Engineers*	
Service No.	510187	Age:	21
Place of birth:	Westbury, Wiltshire	Home Country:	England
Date of death:	20/09/1917	Cause of death:	Killed in action
Memorial:	Westbury, Wiltshire		
War Cemetery:	Tyne Cot Memorial - Panel 8 and 162		
Next of Kin:	Herbert Lenthell & Frances Jefferies		
Address:	3 Church Terrace Church Street, Westbury, Wiltshire		

Frederick was the second son of Herbert and Frances Jefferies and was employed as a clerk by Snailum Architects of Westbury. He was a prominent member of the Scouting movement and a solo singer at Westbury Parish Church. When he became assistant Scout master he was presented with a walking stick with a silver band with his name engraved thereon. He volunteered for service in September 1914 and was attached to the Royal Engineers signals service. He was sent to the 58th Division at Sutton Veny and arrived in France with them in January 1917. Frederick was killed on Thursday 20 September 1917 just south of Vancouver Corner. Frederick's parents received the following letter from his section commander Lieutenant D. Cecil-Henry:

"I am sorry to be the sender of bad news to you. Your son, Sergeant F. Jefferies, who has been my section sergeant for some time now, was killed in action the day before yesterday. He was in charge of a small party who were laying a telegraph line forward to the fighting troops in the battle we have just fought and won. His party got scattered, and your son very bravely and persistently attempted to get them back together again. While waiting for two men who were bringing up fresh supplies of cable, he was hit by a number of fragments from a large shell, which burst very close to him. He was knocked senseless at once and died without any pain. I know very well what a blow this loss is to you I can only hope that the thought of the bravery of your son and the good work he has done for his country will be some consolation to you in your grief. My loss, of course, cannot compare with yours, his mother, but I cannot tell you how sorry I personally am that he has been killed. He was the best man in my section, popular, hard working, conscientious and cheerful, and I always regarded him as a very good friend. There were three good men in the section whom I valued and esteemed most especially, and of these three he was the foremost. He was, I have reason to know, a good Christian man and a brave soldier. He was buried the same evening by two men of the party who were with him. Another man of the section is making a cross, which we will place over his grave. I will write again when this is done, and let you know exactly where he is buried as I know you will wish to picture the resting place of his mortal body. I wish anything I could do would avail to lessen your grief, I can only pray God will comfort you and give you strength to bear your loss. You can indeed be proud of you son; he lived and died a brave and unselfish soldier."

In October 1917 Frederick's parents received a further letter from his section commander Lieutenant D. Cecil-Henry, describing the spot where Frederick was buried, within a few yards of where he fell:

"We put a cross at the head of his grave, made by sapper brown, a man of the section who new Sergeant

Jefferies well. It was a very fine bit of work, simple and dignified. The cross is of wood painted white, with an oaken tablet, with your son's name, regiment, and the date of his death. As a precaution in case the weather should obliterate the lettering the same lettering was stamped on a brass plate, and the latter screwed at the base of the cross. The cross was carried up to Springfield on the early morning of the 27 September, by Rifleman Clarke, who was in Sergeant Jefferies' party, and myself. We fixed it securely, gave Sergeant Jefferies a last salute, and returned to the station, where we were that day entraining for our present position. Again, I tell you my deep sympathy, and my love for "my little sergeant" of whom, as you say, I am justly proud."

Springfield was a German strong point on Zonnebeke Straat. From Vancouver Corner head toward Zonnebeke, straight across the first cross roads and you will see a farm on the left-hand side. Opposite the farm is an uncultivated field with two entrances. This is the site of the original farm fortified by the Germans and is almost definitely where Frederick was buried and could still rest today. For some reason the grave site and the ornate cross were lost and Frederick is today remembered on the Tyne Cot Memorial.

2nd Lieutenant Trevor Blake Jolly		*3rd Bn. attd. 12th Bn Bn East Surrey Regiment*	
Service No.	N/a	Age:	23
Place of birth:	Sydenham, Kent	Home Country:	England
Date of death:	20/09/1917	Cause of death:	Killed in action
Memorial:	Marlborough College – Sydenham, St. Bartholomew Church, Kent		
War Cemetery:	Tyne Cot Memorial - Panel 79 to 80 and 163A		
Next of Kin:	Catherine Blake Jolly (wife) – Sydney Blake & Maud Jolly (parents)		
Address:	48 Fulham Road, South Kensington, London		

Trevor was the second son of Sydney and Maud Jolly and was educated at Marlborough College. He volunteered for service joining the Officer Training Corps and in March 1915 was given a commission with the 3rd Battalion East Surrey Regiment. He was sent to France and served at the Somme in 1916, until he was invalided home with an attack of fever. At the beginning of 1917 he married Catherine Riley at Chelsea, and in the summer of 1917 returned to the front and was attached to the 12th Battalion East Surrey Regiment. Trevor was reported missing during an attack on Thursday 20 September 1917, on German positions near Bitter Wood, south of Tower Hamlets on the south side of the Menin Road. His widow later received official information stating Trevor was presumed to have been killed on the day he was reported missing. He is remembered on the Tyne Cot Memorial and has no known grave.

2nd Lieutenant John Bently Freeman		*3rd Bn., attd. 11th Bn Royal West Kent Regiment*	
Service No.	N/a	Age:	20
Place of birth:	Soho, London	Home Country:	England
Date of death:	20/09/1917	Cause of death:	Killed in action
Memorial:	Marlborough College, Wiltshire		
War Cemetery:	Tyne Cot Memorial - Panel 106 to 108		
Next of Kin:	Herbert Bently & Ira Gertrude B. Freeman		
Address:	The Vicarage, Burton on Trent, Staffordshire		

John was the only son of Herbert and Ira Freeman and was educated at Waveny House, Burton on Trent, and Marlborough College. He was given a commission with the Special Reserve in August 1916 and attached to the Guards at Chelsea. He arrived in France on 23 October 1916 and served as Bombing Officer with the 11th Battalion Royal West Kent Regiment. John was killed by a German sniper, while leading his men during an attack on Thursday 20 September 1917, on German positions at Tower Hamlets on the south side of the Menin Road. The first two objectives had been taken and he fell during the advance on the "green line," final objective. John with 40 men attempted to make a defensive line on

Left: *Trevor Blake Jolly*

Right: *John Bently Freeman*

the right of their position but were cut down by German rifle and machine gun fire. He was buried near where he fell, his commanding officer wrote:

"I had not intended that he should go into action on 20 September, but at the very last moment, as all the officers of one company had been wounded, and he was up helping me, I had to order him to go with this company. I can see his face now, when I gave him the order. I think he was glad to have the chance to be in it. I saw him once more on the early morning of 20 September, gallantly leading his men in the attack, and I am told he was shot in the head by a sniper. He was a very great favourite with us all, and I was very much interested to watch him developing from a school boy to a fine manly soldier. It may be some small consolation to you and his father in your great sorrow to know that your son always did his duty, and never complained from the day he joined me to the day of his death."

The battalion Adjutant wrote:

"Your son was so popular with us all, that each one of us has hesitated to send you details of his death. We went up the line into tunnels on 19 September, preparatory to making the attack on the following day. Just as the battalion was moving out on the night of the 19 September, one company lost all its officers by shell fire, and your son was detailed to lead this company. When reaching their final objective near Tower Hamlets, he was shot by a sniper through the head. I was very friendly indeed with your son. I have lived in the same mess with him since he was made bombing officer, and although I have seen many officers come and go in the battalion, I can honestly say I never felt the loss of anyone so much as of him. In the headquarters mess we all used to chaff your son, he was so young and boyish, but we all had a very deep affection for him. He was the best type of public school boy. The Colonel will be very upset, as your son was, if I may say so, his favourite in the battalion. The other officer in the company your son was with when he was killed says he was magnificent right through the attack until he was shot, and if he had lived he would have had the Military Cross."

John's grave was lost in further fighting and he is remembered on the Tyne Cot Memorial and has no known grave.

Lance Corporal William John Fussell — *503rd Field Company Royal Engineers*

Service No.	504468	Age:	25
Place of birth:	Bath, Somerset	Home Country:	England
Date of death:	20/09/1917	Cause of death:	Killed in action
Memorial:	Calne, Wiltshire		

Left: The original grave marker of William John Fussell

Right: Bertie Edward Davies

War Cemetery:	Buffs Road Cemetery - Grave E. 22.
Next of Kin:	Olive Edith Fussell (wife) – Samuel & Elizabeth Fussell (parents)
Address:	1 Back Row London Road, Calne, Wiltshire

William, known as Billy, an electrical engineer, was the youngest son of Samuel and Elizabeth Fussell. He married Olive Drew at the beginning of 1916 at Bath, Somerset. It is likely he was conscripted into the army or enlisted under the Derby Scheme joining the Royal Engineers. He was killed in action on Thursday 20 September 1917, most likely by German artillery north west of Zonnebeke, north of the road to Langemarck, when the 4th Section, 503rd Field Company were repairing duckboard tracks near Abre and Genoa pill boxes. Billy's sister Emily wrote and sent the following letter to him on 23 September 1917, not knowing her brother was already dead:

"My dearest darling Billy, today we are all in home and mother tells us she received two letters from you this morning she was so delighted, of course you have mother's letters by now we can't understand what's become of them. Mother is writing to you tomorrow, she would have written today but I am writing and she thought she would wait until tomorrow thinking perhaps she might hear from you again saying you have received this. Whilst I am writing this mother is looking at your views you sent. Oh, they are interesting especially if we knew all about it. Now my darling from the papers it is terrible and dread day after day, what we might hear, but we make the best of it to mother and father. Now my dear have you received my box, hope it arrived to you quite safe and also mother's pears. I do hope you have received mother's letters now. We heard from olive last week and she said how much better they felt of for the change. We were pleased to hear you had some nice new pants. Mind and ask for whatever you want. Oh, my darling I do hope please god it will soon be over. Oh, I pray so hard for you my darling. You do the same. The weather is better here this past week. I do hope now we shall get it fine for the farmers to finish harvesting. Rose is sending pad with her box. Now my darling I haven't any more news hoping this will find you well. Do take care my darling, best love from us all hoping to have you home soon, kisses from all of us, from you ever loving sister Em."

"George sends his love – he will give you a job when the war is over."

Sergeant Allen Edgar Bryant		*503rd Field Coy Royal Engineers*	
Service No.	504565	Age:	27
Place of birth:	Bletchinley, Surrey	Home Country:	England
Date of death:	20/09/1917	Cause of death:	Killed in action

Memorial: St Mary's Swindon, Wiltshire
War Cemetery: Buffs Road Cemetery - Grave E. 21.
Next of Kin: Albert & Mary Ann Bryant
Address: 69 Oxford Buildings, Rodbourne Road, Swindon, Wiltshire

Allen, a railway platelayer, was the third son of Albert and Mary Ann Bryant and volunteered for service on 30 December 1914, originally joining Territorial Wilts Fortress Royal Engineers joining the 2/1st Wessex Division Royal Engineers. He was transferred to the 503rd Field Company and arrived in France with them on 23 January 1917. Allen was killed in action on Thursday 20 September 1917, most likely by German artillery north west of Zonnebeke, north of the road to Langemarck, when the 4th Section, 503rd Field Company repairing duckboard tracks near Abre and Genoa pill boxes, in the same action as William Fussell.

Private Bertie Edward Davies *12th Bn Durham Light Infantry*
Service No. 301180 Age: 23
Place of birth: Bushbury, Staffordshire Home Country: England
Date of death: 20/09/1917 Cause of death: Died of wounds
Memorial: Stores Department Memorial, Great Western Railway Works, Swindon
War Cemetery: Lijssenthoek Military Cemetery - Grave XIX. A. 20A.
Next of Kin: Henry & Alice Davies
Address: Shaw Hall Lane, Coven, Wolverhampton, Staffordshire

Bertie was the youngest son of Henry and Alice Davies and was employed in the Stores Department, Wolverhampton for the Great Western Railway Company. It is likely he was either conscripted into the army or enlisted under the Derby Scheme joining the 12th Battalion Durham Light Infantry. He was wounded during attack on German positions south of the Menin Road, South of Tower Hamlets on Thursday 20 September 1917. Bertie was evacuated to a casualty clearing station at Lijssenthoek, where he succumbed to his wounds later the same day.

Private William Arthur Wheeler *13th Bn Durham Light Infantry*
Service No. 203433 Age: 24
Place of birth: Trowbridge, Wiltshire Home Country: England
Date of death: 20/09/1917 Cause of death: Killed in action
Memorial: Devizes, Potterne, Wiltshire
War Cemetery: Tyne Cot Memorial - Panel 128 to 131 and 162 and 162A
Next of Kin: Emily Elija Dale Wheeler(wife) - Arthur J & Mary A Wheeler (parents)
Address: Glinton The Down, Trowbridge, Wiltshire

William, a house painter, was the oldest son of Arthur and Mary Wheeler and employed by F. Walters of New Park Street, Devizes. He married Emily Elija Dale Sheppard on 20 February 1915 prior to joining the army and after completing his training he was sent to France in 1916. In mid October 1917 Emily Wheeler received the following letter from W.J. Acres, Williams platoon officer:

"It is with the greatest sorrow that I notify you that your husband was killed in action on 20 September 1917. As his platoon officer, I can speak of him as a most willing and cheerful soldier and he is mourned amongst his many comrades. I am very pleased to be able to inform you that he was buried and a cross erected by his comrades, which will be carefully looked after."

William was killed in action during an attack on German positions south of the Menin Road, and south of Tower Hamlets on Thursday 20 September 1917. His grave was not looked after but lost during subsequent fighting. He is remembered on the Tyne Cot Memorial and has no known grave.

Private William Stokes — *8th Bn North Staffordshire Regiment*

Service No.	40258	Age:	19
Place of birth:	Laverstock, Wiltshire	Home Country:	England
Date of death:	20/09/1917	Cause of death:	Killed in action
Memorial:	Bemerton, Wiltshire		
War Cemetery:	Tyne Cot Memorial - Panel 124 to 125 and 162 to 162A		
Next of Kin:	Edward Christopher & Emma Jane Stokes		
Address:	Quidhampton, Wiltshire		

William was the second son of Edward and Emma Stokes and was employed at the sorting office at Fisherton. He was conscripted into the army, being called up in February 1917 and arriving in France in the last week of July 1917 joining the 8th Battalion North Staffordshire Regiment. On Thursday 20 September 1917 Williams' unit attacked German positions at Belgium Wood north of the Ypres canal north east of Hollebeke. He was killed when he was hit by a piece of German shell while advancing in muddy conditions during the attack. He is remembered on the Tyne Cot Memorial and has no known grave.

FRIDAY 21 SEPTEMBER 1917 - TEMPERATURE 16.5°c - 25% CLOUD COVER- RAINFALL NIL

Lance Corporal Fred Cope — *3rd MGC Austrailian Infantry AIF*

Service No.	1327	Age:	29
Place of birth:	Great Bedwyn, Wiltshire	Home Country:	England
Date of death:	21/09/1917	Cause of death:	Killed in action
Memorial:	Great Bedwyn, Wiltshire		
War Cemetery:	Ypres Menin Gate - Panel 31.		
Next of Kin:	Ambrose & Susan Cope		
Address:	Folly Farm, Shalbourne, Berkshire		

Fred was the youngest son of Ambrose and Susan Cope and emigrated to Australia before the Great War, finding employment as a railway car builder. He volunteered for service with the Australian Infantry on 3 November 1914 and after completing his training was sent to Gallipoli arriving on 7 May 1915. While serving with the 11th Battalion he was slightly wounded, on 20 July 1915, with a wound to the upper lip. He was taken to the 1st Casualty Clearing Station and evacuated on the Hospital Ship Clacton, to St. Georges Hospital, Malta. Following his recovery, he returned to Gallipoli on 15 October 1915, where he remained until 7 January 1916 during the evacuation of the peninsular. He was sent to Egypt where he transferred to the 3rd Australian Machine Gun Company and was then sent to France on 24 July 1916. He was wounded for a second time on 26 July 1916 with a gun shot wound to the wrist and evacuated to the 13 General Hospital at Boulogne and following his convalescence, returned to his unit on 11 September 1916. He was slightly wounded for a third time on 7 May 1917 with a wound to the left hand and after his recovery he returned to his unit on 12 June 1917. From the 11 August 1917 to 10 September 1917, he was on a course at the Brigade Instruction School. Fred was killed by a German shell on Friday 21 September 1917. Two Red Cross reports were written and one from Lieutenant Hoge of the 3rd Australian Machine Gun Company states:

"Cope was killed instantaneously by a shell. Two other men were killed by this shell, at Glencourse Wood. On that day, we lost half our officers and half our men in the 60. We had a very hot time. They were buried where they fell."

Infantry man H. Igham stated:

"He was killed one evening by a shell at Glencourse Wood I did not see it happen, but came up in charge of a ration party immediately afterwards, and he had just been buried. The same shell killed L/Cpl. Marsh and Pte. Morgan as well. All three were on the same Vickers gun. I cannot locate the spot of his grave exactly, but they hopped over on the morning of the 20th taking our objective, which was the first German line. That was where they were then, and he fell and was buried there."

However, Lieutenant V Collis of the 3rd Machine Gun Company stated:

"L/Cpl. Cope was killed by a shell at Holebeke on duty and was buried at Holebek Cemetery. His relatives have been written to."

The location of Fred's grave was lost and remains unknown. Today he is remembered on the Ypres Menin Gate.

Private Richard Frank Franks		*3rd Bn South African Infantry*	
Service No.	11670	Age:	48
Place of birth:	Cricklade, Wiltshire	Home Country:	South Africa
Date of death:	21/09/1917	Cause of death:	Killed in action
Memorial:	Not known		
War Cemetery:	Perth Cemetery China Wall - Grave IV. E. 14.		
Next of Kin:	Ida Ovidia Franks (wife) – John & Anne Franks (parents)		
Address:	1 Talana Villa Hope Road, Rosebank, Cape Town - Marlborough		

Chemist Richard was the second son of John and Anne Franks who had lived for many years at Manor Farm, Rowde. He was educated at Devizes Grammar School and on completion of his studies he was articled to Mr Edwards, a chemist at the Brittox, Devizes. He then emigrated to South Africa, married Ida Ovidia Imsland and at the outbreak of hostilities joined the South African army. He was reported missing in action during operations against German positions at Potsdam, west of Zonnebeke, on Friday 21 September 1917. His remains were later located and he is today buried in Perth Cemetery China Wall. In August 1919 Richard's remains were located near Vampir, just north of the old Zonnebeke Road and was identified by means of a disc, before being moved to Perth Cemetery China Wall.

Sergeant Lancelot Ethelbert Barnes		*2nd Bn South African Infantry*	
Service No.	10040	Age:	30
Place of birth:	Swindon, Wiltshire	Home Country:	South Africa
Date of death:	21/09/1917	Cause of death:	Died of wounds
Memorial:	Not known		
War Cemetery:	Brandhoek Military Cemetery No 3 - Grave I. F. 32		
Next of Kin:	Ellen Barnes (wife) – William George & Ellen Barnes (parents)		
Address:	18 Fanns Lane, Durban		

Lancelot was the second son of William George and Ellen Barnes and enlisted with the Wiltshires in 1904. In 1910, while serving in South Africa he decided to leave the army and bought himself out for the sum of £26. He married while in South Africa and found employment as a french polisher. He volunteered for service, joining the South African Infantry, and arrived in France on 28 November 1916. He was wounded in action on 17 April 1917, with a slight wound to the head. Lancelot was again wounded on Friday 21 September 1917 during operations against German positions at Potsdam, west of Zonnebeke. He was taken to a casualty clearing station at Brandhoek where he succumbed to his wounds on the same day.

Gunner Albert Charles Dewey Drewett		*132nd Heavy Bty RGA*	
Service No.	116706	Age:	19
Place of Birth:	Calne, Wiltshire	Home Country:	England
Date of Death:	21/09/1917	Cause of death:	Killed in action
Memorial:	Calne		
War cemetery:	The Huts Cemetery – Grave V. D. 18.		
Next of Kin:	Albert & Emma Drewett		
Address:	15 North Street, Calne, Wiltshire		

Albert was the oldest son of Albert and Emma Drewett and he was educated at Marden School, Calne. On leaving school he was apprenticed as a grocer at the Co-operative Stores, where he served for four years and then moved to the Co-operative stores in Trowbridge where he remained for nearly a year. During his youth, he was a member of the Castle Street chapel and he was described as a steady lad, giving evidence of a high Christian character. For many years, he was a teacher at Castle Street Sunday School, a work which he delighted in up to the time he enlisted. Albert was conscripted into the army and attested on 23 May 1916. He was called up in September 1916 joining the Royal Garrison Artillery. He then spent some time at the Signalling School at Southampton. He left for France in January 1917 and joined the 132nd Heavy Battery. At the start of October 1917, the first news of Albert's death was conveyed in a letter from Major J. Williams writing to Albert's parents, stating:

"It is my sad task to inform you that your son, Gunner A.C.D. Drewett was killed in action on September 21st. He was on duty at the time as an aeroplane look out in a battery position and was killed instantly by a fragment of a bomb dropped by an enemy aeroplane. It will be some comfort to you and your family to know that he died doing his duty and did not suffer any pain. The funeral took place yesterday behind the lines in a little cemetery and I will arrange to have his resting place permanently marked. Your son always did his work cheerfully and well and was respected and loved by all ranks in the battery. His death is a great blow to us all. May God comfort you in your great loss."

The small cemetery referred to was the Huts Cemetery, named after a row of huts that were at Dickebusch (now Dikkebus), Belgium. It contains the graves of over 1000 casualties of the Great War.

Private Charles Fortune		*15th Bn Hampshire Regiment*	
Service No.	33158	Age:	36
Place of birth:	Bromham, Wiltshire	Home Country:	England
Date of death:	21/09/1917	Cause of death:	Died of wounds
Memorial:	Box, Wiltshire		
War Cemetery:	Lijssenthoek Military Cemetery - Grave XXIV. H. 12.		
Next of Kin:	George & Jane Fortune		
Address:	Wharf House, Box, Wiltshire		

Charles, known as Charlie and a stone mason, was the eldest son of George and Jane Fortune and was conscripted into the army, being called up in November 1916. He was sent to France in 1917 and attached to the 15th Battalion Hampshire Regiment. He was wounded on 20 September 1917 during an attack south of Tower Hamlets, south of the Menin Road. Charlie was evacuated to No. 2 Canadian Casualty Clearing Station at Lijssenthoek, where he succumbed to his wounds on Friday 21 September 1917.

Private Percival Edward Rattue		*23rd Bn Middlesex Regiment*	
Service No.	TF/206179	Age:	25
Place of birth:	Salisbury, Wiltshire	Home Country:	England
Date of death:	21/09/1917	Cause of death:	Killed in action

Left: The original grave marker of Albert Charles Dewey Drewett

Right: Percival Edward Rattue

Memorial: Salisbury, Wiltshure
War Cemetery: Tyne Cot Memorial - Panel 113 to 115.
Next of Kin: Olive Henrietta Rattue (wife) – William & Annie Rattue (parents)
Address: 7 Fair View Road Elm Grove, Salisbury, Wiltshire

Percival, an engine cleaner, was the second of William and Annie Rattue and it is likely he was either conscripted into the army or enlisted under the Derby Scheme initially joining the 7th Territorial Battalion Middlesex Regiment. Just before his departure to France he married Olive Henrietta Walton at Salisbury in the spring of 1917. On arrival on the continent he was transferred to the 23rd Battalion Middlesex Regiment. Percival was killed on Friday 21 September 1917 during an attack on Tower Hamlets south of the Menin Road. He is remembered on the Tyne Cot Memorial and has no known grave.

Corporal George Herbert Moody *10th Bn West Riding Regiment*

Service No. 235444 Age: 29
Place of birth: Romsey, Hampshire Home Country: England
Date of death: 21/09/1917 Cause of death: Killed in action
Memorial: Calne, Wiltshire
War Cemetery: Tyne Cot Memorial - Grave Panel 82 to 85 and 162A.
Next of Kin: Clara Moody (wife) - Thomas & Mary Moody (parents)
Address: 25 Curzon Street, Calne - Narrow Lane, Romsey, Hampshire

George was the second son of Thomas and Mary Moody. He married in 1910 and was employed as a scout with the Automobile club in the Calne district. It is likely he was either conscripted into the army or enlisted under the Derby Scheme joining the West Riding Regiment. He was sent to France in the first week of September 1916 and attached to the 10th Service Battalion. George was killed on Friday 21 September 1917 following an attack on German positions at Inverness Copse on the Menin Road. George's widow received news of her husband's death on 30 September 1917. He had only been on the Continent three weeks when he was killed. She was left with four young children. He is remembered on the Tyne Cot Memorial and has no known grave.

Private Albert Edward Scull		*6th Bn Wiltshire Regiment*	
Service No.	22706	Age:	23
Place of birth:	Broadtown, Wiltshire	Home Country:	England
Date of death:	21/09/1917	Cause of death:	Died of wounds
Memorial:	Stratton St. Margaret.		
War Cemetery:	Outterstreene Communal Cemetery Extension Bailleul - Grave I. A. 56.		
Next of Kin:	Charles William & Ellen Scull		
Address:	66 The Street, Lower Stratton, Wiltshire		

Farm labourer, Albert, was the eldest son of Charles and Ellen Scull and it is likely he was either conscripted into the army or enlisted under the Derby Scheme joining the Wiltshire Regiment. He was wounded in action on 20 September 1917 during the attack on German positions near Opaque Wood north east of Hollebeke, Belgium, and evacuated to a medical facility at Bailleul where he succumbed to his wounds on Friday 21 September 1917. In 1918 Albert's family inserted the following memoriam in a local paper:

We loved our boy, but he has gone,
And now for him we yearn;
The only hope that's left us now,
Is his brothers safe return.

Some may think we all forget him.
When they sometimes see us smile;
But they know not of the feeling
That the smile hide all the while.

Lieutenant William Thomas Granger		*6th Bn Wiltshire Regiment*	
Service No.	N/a	Age:	24
Place of birth:	Chippenham, Wiltshire	Home Country:	England
Date of death:	21/09/1917	Cause of death:	Died of wounds
Memorial:	Chippenham, St. Pauls Church		
War Cemetery:	Bus House Cemetery - Grave I. 6.		
Next of Kin:	Thomas & Emily Granger		
Address:	40 Park Lane, Chippenham, Wiltshire		

William, known as Will, was educated at St. Pauls School in Park lane, Chippenham and was a member of the Boy Scout movement. He rose to the position of assistant scout master from which he resigned when he found employment with the Great Western Railway at Swindon. He lived with his Uncle and Aunt in Ferndale Road, Swindon, taking an active role in the Scouting movement in the town. He initially worked as a porter before taking a role as a clerk, and at the outbreak of hostilities he was working in the Loco and Carriage Department. He volunteered for service in September 1916 with the Wiltshire Territorials and was sent to India on garrison duties. He was promoted to lance corporal and later recommended for a commission. He returned to England and in the qualifying examination he received the maximum marks and gained a first-class military education certificate. He was gazetted to the rank of 2nd Lieutenant on 16 November 1916 and was sent to France on 3 January 1917. He commenced service with the 6th Battalion Wiltshire Regiment on 16 January 1917 joining them at Sailly in France. He was wounded in action near Battle Wood not far from Hill 60 and the Menin Road south east of Ypres on Thursday 20 September 1917 and died of his wounds the following day. In early October 1917 Will's parents received the following letter from the Adjutant of the 6th Wiltshires:

"I am sorry to tell you that your son died from wounds received in battle on the 20th. He is a great loss to the regiment as he was both battalion musketry officer, and also a platoon commander. He was very keen in everything he did, and his men were ready to follow him at all times. On the 20th he led his men along a very difficult part of the advance, and it was due greatly to his leadership that we were able to

William Thomas Granger

gain the objective in the front allotted to his company. He was always such a cheery fellow, and one could be certain that whatever job he was given to do would be done well. I truly sympathise with you in your great loss, which is felt by every officer and man in his battalion."

Will's cousin Bert Granger, who was also serving with the Wiltshires, made enquires to the fate of Will and ascertained that Will had volunteered to go forward and when he reached a fortified house he was shot through the kidneys. Will was brought to a dressing station and was just able to recognize the doctor, with who he was very friendly. He died shortly after and Bert was informed:

"I am glad to say he is decently buried in a recognized graveyard, and our pioneers have made a nice cross and painted it to put over the grave."

Sergeant Griffin of the Wiltshires wrote the following:

"I should like to mention that I was serving under Lieutenant Granger as a platoon sergeant last February, and I know that by his death the boys have lost a thorough good friend and leader."

Will's father received the following letter from W. R. Bird the District Commissioner North Wilts B.P. Scouts Association:

"I am very distressed to hear that Will has died of wounds received in the service of his country. I shall never forget what a true and faithful friend and loyal helper he was as my assistant officer in the Second Swindon Troop of Boy Scouts. His life here was a very unselfish and happy one, spent in the service of others. From the beginning of the war he has not spared himself in the service of his country, and we have been proud of his advancement to the rank of lieutenant in the Wiltshire Regiment. Now he has made the greatest sacrifice, and the God in whom he trusted has called him to a higher service after a well spent life here. Officers and scouts of the Second Division troop present last night wish to join with me in tendering our very sincere sympathy with you and Mrs Granger and the rest of your family. I pray that our Heavenly Father may grant you all the comfort and consolidation to bear the loss you have sustained with that faith and courage which we all need at this time."

In the London Gazette on 23 November 1917, two months after his death, Will's promotion to Lieutenant was announced and alongside it was written *"died of wounds"*.

British Official Despatch

After an intense artillery preparation, the violence of which has be testified to for some days by the German official despatch, the British yesterday opened an offensive east of Ypres on a wide front, and the day went well for us. The most intense zone of fighting was astride the Ypres-Menin road, the object being to complete our mastery of the Westhoek ridge system. The attack was made on a front of eight miles, and the British Commander in Chief states that great success attended the British Troops. Positions of considerable importance, strongly fortified places which have been fought for before, were carried and over 2,000 prisoners have been taken.

At 5.45am this morning attacks were launched by the British and French Armies east, northeast and north of Ypres. The allied troops are reported to be making satisfactory progress. Rain fell heavily during the latter part of the night and is still continuing.

SATURDAY 22 SEPTEMBER 1917 - TEMPERATURE 17°c - CLEAR- RAINFALL NIL

Lance Corporal Francis Henry Butcher		*2nd Bn Wiltshire Regiment*	
Service No.	11119	Age:	23
Place of birth:	Bradford on Avon, Wiltshire	Home Country:	England
Date of death:	22/09/1917	Cause of death:	Killed in action
Memorial:	Bradford on Avon, Moulton Bradford on Avon		
War Cemetery:	Torreken Farm Cemetery No 1 - Grave B. 10.		
Next of Kin:	Edward & Christina Butcher		
Address:	56 Trowbridge Road, Bradford on Avon, Wiltshire		

Francis was the second and last surviving son of Edward and Christina Butcher and was employed at Kingston Rubber Mills, at Bradford on Avon. He was one of the first to volunteer for service at the outbreak of hostilities enlisting with the Wiltshire Regiment. He arrived in France on 11 December 1914 joining the 2nd Battalion, and had served in every major engagement of the first years of the war. Francis sent many trophies of the fighting home including a German officer's helmet, a soldier's cap, rosary and crucifix, several shell fuses, German pipes, knives in sheaves, German bank notes and a belt with 17 military badges taken from dead soldiers. Francis was a member of a Lewis gun team and had eagerly been awaiting home leave. He was killed instantaneously, by a German shell, when it scored a direct hit on a concrete bunker between Wytschaete and Messines near Lumm Farm on Saturday 22 September 1917. He was killed with his friend, Thomas Henry Walters, and the Regimental Chaplin wrote the following letter to Francis's parents:

"We buried him just after dawn on Sunday, 23rd, with the service of the Churcu of England. His Colonel and company commander were present at the funeral, and the battalion has placed a cross at the head of the grave with his regiment and name on it. Will you try to think of him as one of a great army who have given their lives for the sake of peace and freedom of the world. It is a sacrifice which our Lord himself made. So, we are sure He shares our sorrow and understands. May He comfort you also."

Francis and Thomas Henry Walters lie side by side in Torreken Farm Cemetery No 1. His parents inserted the following memoriam in a local paper:

For these, O God, we lift our prayer;
And leave them sleeping 'neath Thy care.
Their comrades shall m arch home one day;
But they'll be sleeping far away.

Left: Francis Henry Butcher

Right: Gunner George Goddard

Their wars are o'er; their sun is set;
But England never shall forget.
And though the long long years to be,
Their deeds shall live eternally.

Francis's brother, Edward Frank Butcher, had been killed on 15 September 1916 at the Somme.

Sunday 23 September 1917 - Temperature 18.5°c - 25% Cloud Cover- Rainfall Nil

Gunner George Goddard		*5th Siege Bty Bn Royal Garrison Artillery*	
Service No.	167954	Age:	29
Place of birth:	Atworth, Wiltshire	Home Country:	England
Date of death:	23/09/1917	Cause of death:	Killed in action
Memorial:	Frome, Frome Trinity Church		
War Cemetery:	Bard Cottage Cemetery - Grave III. H. 8.		
Next of Kin:	Rose Maude Goddard (wife) – James & Maria Goddard (parents)		
Address:	Berry Hill, Nunney, Somerset		

George was the youngest a son of James and Maria Goddard and was employed as a carter with Mr Armstrong. In the summer of 1914 he married Rose Maude Neal at Frome and was conscripted into the army in January 1917 being sent to the Royal Garrison Artillery. On Sunday 23 September 1917 George was serving with the 5th Siege Battery on the banks of the Yser Canal north of Ypres, when he was killed by German artillery fire. The captain of the 5th Siege Battery wrote to George's widow stating:

"He had only been with the battery a short time, but he was a good and brave soldier."

Driver Jacob Curtis — *187th Bde Royal Field Artillery*

Service No. 108089 — Age: 45
Place of birth: Cricklade, Wiltshire — Home Country: England
Date of death: 23/09/1917 — Cause of death: Died of wounds
Memorial: Cricklade, Wiltshire
War Cemetery: Lijssenthoek Military Cemetery - Grave XXIV. C. 6.
Next of Kin: Fanny Curtis (wife) – Jonathan & Lucy Jane Curtis (parents)
Address: West Mill Lane, Cricklade

Jacob, a farm labourer, was the youngest son of Jonathan and Lucy Jane Curtis and toward the end of 1909 he married Fanny Woodward at Cricklade. It is likely he lied about his age when he volunteered for service and was sent to the Royal Field Artillery. After completing his training, he was sent to the front to serve with the 187th Brigade. Jacob was serving with them on 22 September 1917, when the 187th Brigade were supporting the 41st Division attacking German positions south of the Menin Road. Jacob was one of nine men wounded and one gun put out of action, when they were targeted by German counter battery fire. He was evacuated to a casualty clearing station at Lijssenthoek where he succumbed to his wounds on Sunday 23 September 1917. He left a widow and young family.

MONDAY 24 SEPTEMBER 1917 - TEMPERATURE 23.5°c - 50% CLOUD COVER- RAINFALL NIL

Private Harry Barber — *1st Bn Middlesex Regiment*

Service No. G/50456 — Age: 38
Place of birth: Horningsham, Wiltshire — Home Country: England
Date of death: 24/09/1917 — Cause of death: Killed in action
Memorial: Not known
War Cemetery: Tyne Cot Cemetery - Grave XLIV. B. 14.
Next of Kin: Jeannie Barber (wife) - Joseph & Hannah Barber (parents)
Address: 36, Shielfield Terrace, Tweedmouth, Northumberland

Harry was the youngest son of Joseph and Hannah Barber and was employed as a senior servant, (described as a usefulman), in the household of Weetman Dickinson Pearson, the 1st Viscount Cowdray of Cowdray Park Midhurst, Sussex. At the beginning of 1907 he married Jeannie Purves, also a sat Saffon Walden, Essex. It is likely he was either conscripted into the army or enlisted under the Derby Scheme joining the Middlesex Regiment. He was sent to the front to serve with the 1st Battalion who on Monday 24 September 1917 were in the British front-line south of Polygon Wood. The front line consisted of shell holes some of which had been connected with small stretches of trench. It was a foggy morning but under the cover of a mist the Germans attacked infiltrating the British positions. The two Middlesex companies who were in the front line lost all their officers and Harry was reported missing. Later official news was received stating Harry was presumed to have been killed, between the 24 and 26 September 1917. In 1920 a grave was located and Harry's remains were identified by means of an identity disc and were relocated to Tyne Cot Cemetery. He left a widow and young family.

58-175

Private Edward Frank Eyres — *215th Coy Machine Gun Corps*

Service No. 64606 — Age: 20
Place of birth: Bemerton, Wiltshire — Home Country: England
Date of death: 24/09/1917 — Cause of death: Died of wounds
Memorial: Salisbury, Salisbury Post Office, Wiltshire

War Cemetery: Dozinghem Military Cemetery - Grave VIII. C. 22.
Next of Kin: Frank & Fanny Eyres
Address: 133 Devizes Road, Salisbury, Wiltshire

Edward was the eldest son of Frank and Fanny Eyres and educated at Bishop Wordsworths School. He was employed as a sorting clerk and telegraphist at Salisbury Post Office and enlisted under the Derby Scheme on 10 December 1915 joining the 8th Battalion London Regiment, The Post Office Rifles. He was transferred to the Machine Gun Corps on 14 October 1916 and arrived in France on 16 March 1917, being sent to the 215th Company. On 15 April 1917, he was awarded 3 days Field Punishment No.2, for being improperly dressed on parade, unshaven with dirty equipment. On Monday 24 September 1917, the 215th Company were at Wurst, Tirpitz and Stroppe farms, all former German strong points, north west of Zonnebeke. Edward was acting as a runner and was wounded. One report states he was hit by a German sniper whilst delivering a message up the line. He was evacuated to No. 47 Casualty Clearing Station at Dozinghem. He was admitted with multiple gun shot wounds, to which he succumbed to one hour later. The officer commanding 215th Company wrote the following to Edward's parents:

"I always had the greatest admiration for his pluck, and enjoyed his social qualities, so when possible, picked him out to act as my runner and companion. He was bringing another officer down to relieve me when a shell burst; the officer was immediately killed, but your son escaped for that time in marvellous fashion. I sent him down to headquarters for 24 hours' rest, when at the end of that time the commanding officer told him to go up the line with an important message. He was the most reliable runner we had, so in the usual hard manner was always sent on most important messages. He was a brave boy, your son and was loved and respected by us all."

Private Alfred Strong — *9th Bn Yorkshire Regiment*
Service No. 235476 — Age: 29
Place of birth: Chisenbury, Wiltshire — Home Country: England
Date of death: 24/09/1917 — Cause of death: Killed in action
Memorial: Poulshot, Rushall
War Cemetery: Tyne Cot Memorial - Panel 52 to 54 and 162A.
Next of Kin: Sarah Jane Strong - Edward & Emily Strong (parents)
Address: Poulshot, Wiltshire

Alfred was the eldest son of Edward and Emily Strong and married Sarah J. Bowden in the summer of 1916. It is likely he was either conscripted into the army or enlisted under the Derby Scheme and was sent to France initially to join the Durham Light Infantry before being transferred to the 9th Battalion Yorkshire Regiment. Alfred was killed in action on Monday 24 September 1917, most likely by German artillery while in the British front-line south of Polygon Wood. Alfred is remembered on the Tyne Cot Memorial and has no known grave. In September 1918, his widow inserted the following memoriam in a local paper:

God takes our loved one from our home
But never from our heart
Gone from me but not forgotten
Never shall his memory fade
Sweetest thoughts shall ever linger
Round the spot where he is laid

Gunner Francis Edgar Giles — *280th Siege Bty Royal Garrison Artillery*
Service No. 116326 — Age: 19
Place of birth: Stanton Fitzwarren, Wiltshire — Home Country: England

Date of death:	24/09/1917	Cause of death:	Killed in action
Memorial:	Stanton Fitzwarren, Wiltshire		
War Cemetery:	Tyne Cot Memorial - Panel 6 to 7 and 162.		
Next of Kin:	John Robert & Martha Giles		
Address:	Stanton Fitzwarren, Wiltshire		

Nineteen year old Francis, known as Frank, a farm labourer was the youngest son of John and Martha Giles and was conscripted into the army and called up on 21 August 1916, joining the Royal Garrison Artillery. After completing his training, he arrived in France on 8 September 1917 and was sent to the 280th Siege Battery serving with them from 17 September 1917. He was killed instantaneously by a German shell on Monday 24 September 1917, just eight days after he arrived at the unit. Frank's parents received the following letters, one from his major and one from his comrade:

"I am very sorry to have to acquaint you with the very sad news that your son was killed in action on the 24th of this month. He had only been with me a few days and I cannot say I knew him well, but everyone tells me what a nice lad he was and what a good soldier he was making. He was killed by a shell instantaneously, so was spared any suffering. You have the sympathy of myself and the whole battery. I feel perhaps the more so, as I look upon any one coming from your part of the country as neighbours, having lived near for several years."

The following letter from his comrade:

"It is on behalf of my chums and myself that I write this letter, and assure you that it was a terrible blow to us all when Frank was knocked out, as he was loved by us all. The blow came home to me very hard, as Frank and myself have been together for nearly a year, and naturally became very attached to one another, and when at Codford we had our photos taken together. In Frank you had a very honourable son, as he was always waiting and ready to help anyone, and his mother was for ever in his thoughts. All my pals beg to enclose their deepest sympathy with you, and if I am spared to come home I will give you a call."

Frank is remembered on the Tyne Cot Memorial and has no known grave. His brother Herbert was to be killed in September 1918.

TUESDAY 25 SEPTEMBER 1917 - TEMPERATURE 24°c - MIST- RAINFALL NIL

Private Francis Luther Edwards		*2nd Bn Worcestershire Regiment*	
Service No.	242560	Age:	23
Place of birth:	Enford, Wiltshire	Home Country:	England
Date of death:	25/09/1917	Cause of death:	Killed in action
Memorial:	Fittleton, Wiltshire		
War Cemetery:	Tyne Cot Memorial - Panel 75 to 77		
Next of Kin:	Frank & Edith Fanny Edwards		
Address:	Enford, Wiltshire		

Francis, known as Luther, a carter on a farm, was the youngest son of Frank and Edith Fanny Edwards. It is likely he was either conscripted into the army or enlisted under the Derby Scheme joining the Worcestershire Regiment. He was sent to the front to serve with the 2nd Battalion who on Tuesday 25 September 1917 were near Inverness Copse, or what was left of it. The area was a mass of shell holes interspersed with marshes. The only landmarks were various German concrete dugouts. and there were numerous derelict tanks. Luther was killed most likely by German artillery while the Worcesters held this part of the British line. He is remembered on Tyne Cot Memorial and has no known grave.

Frederick Dennis Tucker

2nd Lieutenant Frederick Dennis Tucker		*1st Bn Royal West Surrey Regiment*	
Service No.	N/a	Age:	19
Place of birth:	Redhill, Surrey	Home Country:	England
Date of death:	25/09/1917	Cause of death:	Killed in action
Memorial:	Reigate, Surrey, Marlborough College		
War Cemetery:	Tyne Cot Memorial - Panel 14 to 17 and 162 to 162A		
Next of Kin:	James Charlton & Janet Margaret Tucker		
Address:	Redhill, Surrey		

Nineteen year old Frederick was the youngest son of James and Janet Tucker and was educated at Sunningdale School and Marlborough College, where he won the school 100 yards race. He then went to Sandhurst where he was given a commission with the Royal West Surrey Regiment in April 1917. He was sent to the front joining the 1st Battalion. Frederick was killed on Tuesday 25 September 1917 while in the British front line, on the Menin Road near Veldhoek, when practically the whole of the front-line company's of the 1st Battalion were wiped out by German artillery. He is remembered on the Tyne Cot Memorial and has no known grave.

Private Frank Ernest Barton		*1st Bn Royal West Surrey Regiment*	
Service No.	G/21922	Age:	36
Place of birth:	Melksham, Wiltshire	Home Country:	England
Date of death:	25/09/1917	Cause of death:	Killed in action
Memorial:	Melksham, Wiltshire		
War Cemetery:	Tyne Cot Memorial - Panel 14 to 17 and 162 to 162A.		
Next of Kin:	Elsie Lucy Barton (wife) - William J & Amelia Barton (parents)		
Address:	Hanwell, Middlesex -Melksham, Wiltshire		

Frank, a house painter, was the youngest son of William and Amelia Barton and toward the end of 1912 married Elsie Lucy Standfield at Brentford, Middlesex. It is likely he was either conscripted into the army or enlisted under the Derby Scheme joining the Royal West Surrey Regiment, and was sent to the front joining the 1st Battalion. Frank was reported missing on Tuesday 25 September 1917, while in the British front line, on the Menin Road near Veldhoek, when practically the whole of the front-line company's of the 1st Battalion were wiped out by German artillery. Later information was received stating Frank was presumed to have been killed on the day he was reported missing. He is remembered on the Tyne Cot Memorial and has no known grave. Frank left a widow and young son.

9
The Battle of Polygon Wood

Map page 424

WEDNESDAY 26 SEPTEMBER 1917 - TEMPERATURE 20°c - MIST- RAINFALL 0.5mm

Field Marshal Sir Douglas Haig reporting from British Headquarters states:

Our attack on the morning of Wednesday 26 September 1917, was delivered on a total front of nearly six miles from south of Tower Hamlets to east of St. Julien. Our operations were entirely successful. Later in the day the enemy delivered a series of heavy counter attacks along our new front, resulting in hard fighting, which is still continuing at certain points.

South of the Menin Road the attack carried out by English troops successfully completed the capture of the Tower Hamlets spur and gained possession of the German strong field works on its eastern slopes, which formed our objective. A powerful counter attack from the direction of Gheluvelt was repulsed. On the right of our main attack north of the Ypres-Menin road, our troops met with obstinate resistance, and heavy fighting took place in the area across which the enemy counter attacked yesterday. After a severe struggle lasting through the greater part of the day. English and Scottish battalions drove the enemy from his position, and accomplished the task allotted to them of securing the flank of our principle attack. In their advance our troops relieved two companies of Argyll and Sutherland Highlanders, who had held out with great gallantry during the night in a forward position in which they had been isolated by the enemy's attack yesterday morning.

Later in the afternoon the enemy developed another counter attack in great strength in this sector, where fierce fighting is still continuing. Further north Australian troops cleared the remainder of Polygon Wood, and captured the German trench system to the east of it which formed their objective for the day.On their left English, Scottish and welsh battalions penetrating the enemy's defences to the depth of nearly a mile, stormed Zonnebeke and gained the line of their objectives.

During the afternoon, a counter attack directed our new positions east of Polygon Wood was repulsed. On the left of our attack North Midland and London Territorial's, attacking on both sides of the Wieltje-Gravenstafel and St. Julien-Gravenstafel road, also captured their objectives and beat off a counterattack. In this area, our line has been advanced to a depth of half a mile across country defended by a large number of fortified farms and concrete redoubts.

Early in the afternoon the enemy delivered a second counter attack in this area, with larger forces, and succeeded in pressing back our line a short distance on a narrow front. Our troops counter attacking in turn, at once re-captured the greater part of the lost ground. Over 1,000 prisoners have been taken by us in these operations. Very large numbers of German dead have been found on the ground captured by our troops, and the enemy's losses both in our attack and in his subsequent counter attacks have again been heavy.

Private Joseph Henry Balcombe		*1st Bn Royal West Surrey Regiment*	
Service No.	G/37006	Age:	26
Place of birth:	Partridge Green, Surrey	Home Country:	England
Date of death:	26/09/1917	Cause of death:	Killed in action
Memorial:	Not known		
War Cemetery:	Tyne Cot Memorial - Panel 14 to 17 and 162 to 162A		
Next of Kin:	Rebecca Balcombe (wife) – George Walter & Kate Balcombe		
Address:	Pewsey Hill, Milton, Wiltshire – Red Hill, Surrey.		

Joseph, a printer, was the youngest son of George Walter and Kate Balcombe and on Christmas Day 1912 he married Rebecca Miles at St. Johns Church, Red Hill, Surrey. It is likely he was either conscripted into the army or enlisted under the Derby Scheme joining the Royal West Surrey Regiment, and was sent to the front joining the 1st Battalion. He was killed on Wednesday 26 September 1917, while in the British front line, on the Menin Road near Veldhoek, when the 1st Battalion were halted within 50 yards of their objective, then repulsed a German counter attack. He is remembered on the Tyne Cot Memorial and has no known grave. Frank left a widow and a young family.

Private William J. Evans		*11th Bn Royal Sussex Regiment*	
Service No.	TF/290264	Age:	31
Place of birth:	Malmesbury, Wiltshire	Home Country:	England
Date of death:	26/09/1917	Cause of death:	Killed in action
Memorial:	South Heighton, Sussex		
War Cemetery:	Hooge Crater Cemetery - Grave VII. L. 1.		
Next of Kin:	James & Lucy Evans		
Address:	South Heighton, Sussex		

William was the third son of James and Lucy Evans and had been a regular soldier with the 1st Battalion Royal Sussex Regiment before the Great War. It is likely he was time expired but rejoined some time after the outbreak of hostilities, joining the 11th Service Battalion Royal Sussex Regiment. He was killed by German artillery fire on Wednesday 26 September 1917, when the 11th Royal Sussex were supporting an attack on Tower Hamlets, west of Gheluvelt. In April 1919 William's remains were located north of the Menin Road, south of Veldhoek and identified by means of a disc, before being moved to Hooge Crater Cemetery.

Private Albert George Yates		*2/4th Bn Ox & Bucks Light Infantry*	
Service No.	203750	Age:	31
Place of birth:	Stratton St Margaret, Wiltshire	Home Country:	England
Date of death:	26/09/1917	Cause of death:	Died of wounds
Memorial:	Not known		
War Cemetery:	Etaples Military Cemetery - Grave XXVI D 4A		
Next of Kin:	Albert & Mary Ann G. Yates		
Address:	55 Haydon Street, Swindon, Wiltshire		

Albert was the eldest son of Albert and Mary Yates and it is likely he was either conscripted into the army or enlisted under the Derby Scheme initially joining the Hampshire Regiment. He was transferred to the Ox & Bucks Light Infantry and was sent to the front to serve with the 2/4th Battalion. It is likely he was wounded around 10 September 1917, north east of St. Julien and evacuated to a medical facility at Etaples, where he succumbed to his wounds on Wednesday 26 September 1917.

Private William Gibbs — *177th Coy Machine Gun Corps*

Service No.	57865
Age:	Not known
Place of birth:	Swindon, Wiltshire
Home Country:	England
Date of death:	26/09/1917
Cause of death:	Killed in action
Memorial:	Not known
War Cemetery:	Tyne Cot Memorial - Panel 154 to 159 and 163A.
Next of Kin:	George Gibbs
Address:	Not known

William was the son of George Gibbs and it is likely he was either conscripted into the army or enlisted under the Derby Scheme initially joining the Shropshire Light Infantry. He transferred to the Machine Gun Corps and was sent to the front to serve with the 177th Company. He was reported missing on Wednesday 26 September 1917, while supporting an attack by the 177th Infantry Brigade near Dochy Farm, a German strong point, north west of Zonnebeke. Later official information was received stating William was presumed to have been killed on the day he was reported missing. He is remembered on the Tyne Cot Memorial and has no known grave.

Private Frank Victor Chapman — *1st Bn Cambridgeshire Regiment*

Service No.	36599
Age:	21
Place of birth:	Steeple Ashton, Wiltshire
Home Country:	England
Date of death:	26/09/1917
Cause of death:	Killed in action
Memorial:	Steeple Ashton, Wiltshire
War Cemetery:	Tyne Cot Memorial - Panel 148.
Next of Kin:	Frank Victor & Mabel Jane Chapman
Address:	High Street, Steeple Ashton, Wiltshire

House painter, Frank, was the eldest son of Frank and Mabel Chapman and volunteered for service initially joining the Wiltshire Regiment and arriving on the Gallipoli peninsular on 30 June 1915. It is likely he was wounded or suffering from disease and was evacuated; following his recovery he was transferred to the Suffolk Regiment. At some time later he was transferred to the again to the 1st Battalion Cambridgeshire Regiment. He was reported missing on Wednesday 26 September 1917 during an attack on Tower Hamlets, west of Gheluvelt. Later official information was received stating Frank was presumed to have been killed on the day he was reported missing. He is remembered on the Tyne Cot Memorial and has no known grave.

Private Charles Henry Lansley — *1st Bn Middlesex Regiment*

Service No.	TF203000
Age:	30
Place of birth:	Ludgershall, Wiltshire
Home Country:	England
Date of death:	26/09/1917
Cause of death:	Killed in action
Memorial:	Ludgershall, Wiltshire
War Cemetery:	Hooge Crater Cemetery - Grave VIII. C. 8.
Next of Kin:	Elsie Maud Lansley (wife) – Fred & Mary Lansley (parents)
Address:	17 Bell Street, Ludgershall, Wiltshire

Charles was the second son of Fred and Mary Lansley and was employed as a camp porter at Tidworth. He married Elsie Maud Blackman on 7 April 1915 and enlisted under the Derby Scheme on 7 December 1915. He was called up on 29 May 1916 and sent to the Middlesex Regiment. After completing his training, he arrived in France on 30 November 1916 and from 27 December 1916 he was attached to the 4th Entrenching Battalion. He was then posted, on 7 April 1917, to the 1st Battalion Middlesex Regiment, who he was serving with when he was killed in action between 24/ 26 September 1917, just south of Polygon Wood. In April his remains were located near Glencorse Wood and identified by means of a disc, before being moved to Hooge Crater Cemetery. Charles's personal property was returned to his family and consisted of; two discs, letters, and a small note book. He left a widow and a young son. In October 1917, Elsie inserted the following memoriam in a local paper:

Sleep on, dear one, in a foreign grave,
Your life for your country you nobly gave;
No friend stood near you to say good-bye,
But safe in God's keeping now you lie.

Private James Berry		*14th Bn Hampshire Regiment*	
Service No.	381007	Age:	28
Place of birth:	Sherston, Wiltshire	Home Country:	England
Date of death:	26/09/1917	Cause of death:	Killed in action
Memorial:	Sherston, Wiltshire		
War Cemetery:	Tyne Cot Memorial - Panel 88 to 90 and 162.		
Next of Kin:	George & Mary Ann Berry		
Address:	Rose Cottage, Pinkney, Wiltshire		

Farm labourer James was the eldest son of George and Mary Ann Berry and it is likely he was either conscripted into the army or enlisted under the Derby Scheme joining the Hampshire Regiment. He was sent to the 14th Service Battalion and killed while serving with them on Wednesday 26 September 1917, during an attack on Tower Trench at Tower Hamlets, west of Gheluvelt. He is remembered on the Tyne Cot Memorial and has no known grave.

Private Bertie Harold Bennett		*14th Bn Hampshire Regiment*	
Service No.	32568	Age:	33
Place of birth:	Donhead St. Mary, Wiltshire	Home Country:	England
Date of death:	26/09/1917	Cause of death:	Killed in action
Memorial:	Not known		
War Cemetery:	Tyne Cot Memorial - Panel 88 to 90 and 162		
Next of Kin:	Thomas & Annie Bennett		
Address:	Haydown Lodge, Amport, Hampshire.		

Bertie, a game keeper, was the eldest son of Thomas and Annie Bennett and in the spring of 1910 he married Mabel Mary E. Gray at Donhead St. Mary. It is likely he was either conscripted into the army or enlisted under the Derby Scheme joining the Hampshire Regiment. He was sent to the 14th Service Battalion and reported missing while serving with them on Wednesday 26 September 1917, during an attack on Tower Trench at Tower Hamlets, west of Gheluvelt. Later official information was received stating Bertie was presumed to have been killed on the day he was reported missing. He left a widow and a young son, and is remembered on the Tyne Cot Memorial. He has no known grave.

Major Roger Alvin Poore DSO		*2nd Bn Royal Welsh Fusiliers*	
Service No.	N/a	Age:	47
Place of birth:	Bath, Somerset	Home Country:	England
Date of death:	26/09/1917	Cause of death:	Killed in action
Memorial:	Sherborne School		
War Cemetery:	Poelcapelle British Cemetery - Grave LV. F. 11.		
Next of Kin:	Lorna Margery Poore (wife) - Maj. Robert & Juliana Poore (parents)		
Address:	Fernyhurst, Rownhams, Hampshire		

Left: oger Alvin Poore DSO

Right: Sidney Miles Toppin MC

Roger was the third son of Major Robert and Juliana Poore and was educated at Warminster Preparatory School and Sherborne School, before attending Hertford College, Oxford. He was employed as a solicitor and joined the Royal Wiltshire Yeomanry. He served through the South African War with the Yorkshire Light Infantry (mounted infantry) where he was mentioned in despatches and awarded the Distinguished Service Order. On 9 December 1913 Roger married Lorna Margery Dennistoun. He served 24 years in total with the Royal Wiltshire Yeomanry and commanded the 2/1st Regiment, where he was serving at the outbreak of hostilities. He was transferred to the 2nd Battalion Royal Welsh Fusiliers and appointed second in command. On Wednesday 26 September 1917, Roger was commanding the battalion in the front line at Black Watch Corner on the edge of Polygon Wood. While he was talking to assistant adjutant and another officer a German 5.9 shell fell between them killing all three. The colonel of the 2nd Royal Welsh Fusiliers, writing to Lorna Poore stated:

"There is one thing that you will hear with pride and that is that the battalion under your husband's command behaved most gallantly in the action and has covered itself with glory. Your husband had endeared himself to everybody in the battalion, and his loss will be most acutely felt. He had helped and supported me most loyally; indeed, I do not know how I will get on without his wise advice. He was one of the most gallant gentlemen I have ever met."

Roger left a widow and a young son. Inn June 1923 Roger's remains were located in Polygon Wood and identified by the badges on his uniform, the crown of a majors rank and a handkerchief with the initials R.A.P. on it. They were then re-interred in Poelcapelle British Cemetery.

THURSDAY 27 SEPTEMBER 1917 - TEMPERATURE 19.5°c - OVERCAST- RAINFALL NIL

Major Sidney Miles Toppin MC		*151st Heavy Bty Royal Garrison Artillery*	
Service No.	N/a	Age:	39
Place of birth:	Cloumel, Ireland	Home Country:	England
Date of death:	27/09/1917	Cause of death:	Died of wounds
Memorial:	Sandown, Branksome, Dorset		
War Cemetery:	Lijssenthoek Military Cemetery - Grave XXIV. G. 6.		
Next of Kin:	Jessie Viva Toppin (wife) - James Morris & Jane Toppin (parents)		
Address:	Rose Bank, Sandown, Isle of Wight - Blacklands Park, Calne		

Sidney was the younger son of Major-General James and Jane Toppin. He was educated at Clifton College and Gonville and Cains College, Cambridge. While studying for a medical degree he was offered a commission in the Royal Artillery and was gazzetted in May 1900. He was then posted to India and after learning Hindustani, was given charge of a mountain battery on the Afghan frontier at Chitra. After two years he was transferred to Burma. He was then appointed Company Commander and transferred to Egypt and then returned to England in 1914. On 17 August 1914, ten days after war had been declared, he married Jessie Viva Coleman. He was initially sent to Ireland where he formed an artillery battery and then on to France. He was mentioned in dispatches for his services at the Battle of Loos and was awarded the Military Cross. He was wounded near Ypres and taken to the Military Hospital at Lijssenthoek, where he succumbed to his wounds on Thursday 27 September 1917, leaving a widow and infant child. His elder brother Harry Toppin had been killed during the Battle of the Aisne in 1914.

Private Arthur Walter Ford — *99th Field Ambulance Royal Army Medical Corps*

Service No.	66413	Age:	40
Place of birth:	Box, Wiltshire	Home Country:	England
Date of death:	27/09/1917	Cause of death:	Died of wounds
Memorial:	Box, Wiltshire		
War Cemetery:	Bedford House Cemetery - Grave Enclosure No.2 I. A. 25.		
Next of Kin:	William & Sarah Anne Ford		
Address:	Twinhoe Farm, Midford, Wiltshire		

Arthur was the youngest son of William and Sarah Ford and served an apprenticeship as a cabinet maker with Horton Brothers and was afterwards employed by Mallet and Sons for ten years. Eventually he established his own business in Bath near St. Andrews Church. On 14 June 1911, he left Bristol for Canada where he purchased some land. In 1915 he returned to England and volunteered for service on 31 August 1915 with the Royal Army Service Corps. After completing his training he was sent to 99th Field Ambulance on 22 October 1915 and proceeded to France with them arriving on 16 November 1915. Arthur was wounded on Thursday 27 September 1917 while supporting the 33 Division near Polygon Wood. He was evacuated to an advanced dressing station at Ecole de Bienfaisance British Cemetery, located on the Menin Road in Ypres, behind Menin Road South Cemetery where he died the same day. In 1921 Arthur's remains were relocated to Bedford House Cemetery. Arthur's parents inserted the following memoriam in a local paper:

We were not there to see him die,
The one we loved so dear,
But we know he died a hero,
And died without a fear.

He fought for King and country,
He died a hero's death,

When last we saw his smiling face
He looked so strong and brave,
We little thought how soon he'd be
Laid in a soldiers grave.

Private Ernest Ewart Cook — *13th Bn Royal Sussex Regiment*

Service No.	G/17152	Age:	19
Place of birth:	Chiseldon, Wiltshire	Home Country:	England
Date of death:	27/09/1917	Cause of death:	Killed in action

Memorial:	Blunsdon, Wiltshire
War Cemetery:	Tyne Cot Memorial - Panel 86 to 88
Next of Kin:	William & Elizabeth Cook
Address:	Kings Down Lane, Blunsdon, Wiltshire

Nineteen year old Ernest was the youngest son of William and Elizabeth Cook and it is likely he was either conscripted into the army or enlisted under the Derby Scheme joining the Royal Sussex Regiment. After completing his training, he was sent to the front and attached to the 13th Battalion. Ernest was reported missing on Thursday 27 September 1917 and had not been seen since "going over the top," near Tower Hamlets, west of Gheluvelt. Later Ernest's parents received official information stating Ernest was presumed to have been killed on the day he was reported missing. He is remembered on the Tyne Cot Memorial and has no known grave.

Sergeant Walter James Wickham Elsip — *240th Bde TF Bn Royal Field Artillery*

Service No.	825032	Age:	37
Place of birth:	Luckington, Wiltshire	Home Country:	England
Date of death:	27/09/1917	Cause of death:	Killed in action
Memorial:	Luckington, Wiltshire		
War Cemetery:	Vlamertinghe New Military Cemetery - Grave XII. G. 4.		
Next of Kin:	Elaine Carla Elsip (wife) – James & Mary Elsip (parents)		
Address:	10 Bellevue, Clifton, Bristol – Luckington, Wiltshire		

Walter, a commercial traveller selling stationary, was the only son of James and Mary Elsip and was educated at Tetbury School. In the summer of 1910 he married Elaine Carla Peters at Bristol. He volunteered for service joining the 240th Brigade Territorial Force (south Midland) Royal Field Artillery, arriving in France on 30 March 1915. Walter was killed on Thursday 27 September 1917, most likely by German counter battery artillery fire, near Vlamertinghe. He left a widow and a young son.

Thursday 27 September 1917

Field Marshal Sir Douglas Haig reporting from British Headquarters states:

"More detailed accounts of yesterday's battle confirm the completeness of our success. During the evening, local attacks were delivered in the neighbourhood of Tower Hamlets and northeast of Langemarck, and cleared up a number of strong points and completed the capture of our objectives. In these localities, there were many enemy counter attacks. His casualties were unusually great in every case. The advancing lines of German infantry were destroyed by concentrated fire. Our troops consolidated the positions during the night undisturbed. Our losses were light."

FRIDAY 28 SEPTEMBER 1917 - TEMPERATURE 18.5°c - 25% CLOUD COVER- RAINFALL NIL

Private Percy Herbert Keel — *7th Bn Loyal North Lancashire Regiment*

Service No.	33752	Age:	32
Place of birth:	Berwick St James, Wiltshire	Home Country:	England
Date of death:	28/09/1917	Cause of death:	Killed in action

Memorial: Not known
War Cemetery: Bedford House Cemetery - Grave Enclosure No.4 IX. D. 3.
Next of Kin: Ellen Keel (wife) – Robert & Kate Keel (parents)
Address: Boveney Road, Honor Oak Park, London

Percy was the only son of Robert and Kate Keel and originally joined the army on 23 April 1902 enlisting with the 7th Dragoon Guards, serving in South Africa and on home duties. He left the regulars on 22 April 1905 and was transferred to the army reserve, his service expiring on 22 April 1914 on completion of 12 years service. After leaving the army in 1905 Percy found employment as an insurance agent and married Ellen Fiddian on 18 April 1914 at St. John the Evangelist, Walworth. After the outbreak of hostilities Percy re-enlisted joining the Army Cyclists Corps and at some stage he was transferred to the 7th Service Battalion Loyal North Lancashire Regiment. It is likely Percy was killed on Friday 28 September 1917, near Klein Zillebeke, when a German shell entered the dugout that A Company H.Q. were occupying, killing one officer and four other ranks. Percy was buried near where he fell southeast of Groenenburg Farm. His remais were located and identified by means of a disc, before being moved to Bedford House Cemetery in July 1921. He left a widow and young daughter. In 1918 Percy's family inserted the following memoriam in a local paper:

Days of sadness still come o'er us
Secret tears do often flow
Memory keeps our loved one near to us
Though it's now one year ago

I often think and talk of him
And think how he died
To think he could not say good-bye
Before he closed his eyes

Could I but kneel beside his grave
And Shed a Silent Tear
But now he sleeps somewhere in France
The one I love so dear

Gunner Arthur George Mapson — *160th Siege Bty Royal Garrison Artillery*
Service No. 60133
Place of birth: Stratton, Wiltshire
Date of death: 28/09/1917
Age: 19
Home Country: England
Cause of death: Killed in action
Memorial: Not known
War Cemetery: The Huts Cemetery - Grave VIII. A. 18.
Next of Kin: Arthur Henry & Sarah Ann Mapson
Address: 2 Station Road Kingsdown, Swindon, Wiltshire

Arthur, a general labourer, was the youngest son of Arthur and Sarah Ann Mapson and volunteered for service on 23 October 1915 joining the Royal Garrison Artillery. After completing his training, he was sent to France, arriving on 31 March 1916, serving with the 160th Siege Battery. On 20 January 1917 Arthur was evacuated from the front, to No.8 General Hospital, Rouen, suffering from trench foot. He was then sent back to England and following his recovery he returned to the front on 24 July 1917. Arthur was killed, most likely by German artillery on Friday 28 September 1917, south of Ypres. In 1918 his family inserted the following memoriam in a local paper:

Thou art not forgotten, brother dear,

Nor ever wilt thou be;
As long as life and memory last
We shall remember thee.

Gunner Edward Phillips — *101st Siege Bty Bn Royal Garrison Artillery*

Service No.	129635	Age:	31
Place of birth:	Devizes, Wiltshire	Home Country:	England
Date of death:	28/09/1917	Cause of death:	Died of wounds
Memorial:	Keynsham, Somerset		
War Cemetery:	Dozinghem Military Cemetery - Grave VII. E. 1.		
Next of Kin:	Nora Phillips (wife) - John & Susan Phillips (parents)		
Address:	Stoneleigh, 12 Chewton Road, Keynsham, Somerset		

Butcher Edward was the third son of John and Susan Phillips and married Nora Harry at Keynsham in the summer of 1916, most likely prior to being conscripted into the army. After completing his training he was sent to the front joining the 101st Siege Battery Royal Garrison Artillery. He was wounded probably by German artillery fire and taken to a casualty clearing station near Westvleteren, Belgium, where he succumbed to his wounds on Friday 28 September 1917. Edward was buried in Dozinghem Military Cemetery.

Private William Richard John Janes — *1st Bn Northumberland Fusiliers*

Service No.	46934	Age:	22
Place of birth:	Gosport, Hampshire	Home Country:	England
Date of death:	28/09/1917	Cause of death:	Died of wounds
Memorial:	Not known		
War Cemetery:	Tyne Cot Memorial - Panel 19 to 23 and 162.		
Next of Kin:	John & Martha Janes		
Address:	10 Leonard Road, Forton, Gosport, Hampshire		

William, a copper smith, was the eldest son of John and Martha Janes and had lived in Salisbury up to the start of the war. It is likely he was either conscripted into the army or enlisted under the Derby Scheme, initially joining the Hampshire Regiment. At some time later he was transferred to the 1st Battalion Northumberland Fusiliers who on Friday 28 September 1917 were in the British front line at Hill 40, north west of Zonnebeke. William was wounded and succumbed to his wounds soon after. He is remembered on the Tyne Cot Memorial, having no known grave.

Corporal Fred Hudd — *332nd Siege Bty Royal Garrison Artillery*

Service No.	125696	Age:	34
Place of birth:	Hilperton, Wiltshire	Home Country:	England
Date of death:	28/09/1917	Cause of death:	Died of wounds
Memorial:	St. Andrews Church & Chippenham Secondary School		
War Cemetery:	Dozinghem Military Cemetery - Grave VII. E. 4.		
Next of Kin:	Ada Hudd (wife) - Samuel & Emily Hudd (parents)		
Address:	20 Athelstan Road, Clive Vale, Hastings – Chippenham		

Fred, a solicitor's clerk, was the eldest son of Samuel and Emily Hudd of Foghamshire Nursery, Chippenham. In January 1896 at the opening of Chippenham Secondary School Fred was no.1 on the secondary school register and on leaving school was employed as a clerk with Wood and Audrey Solicitors. He was also a teacher at the Wesleyan Sunday School in the Causeway Chippenham. In 1901, he became a clerk with Gaby Stapleton and Smith of Bexhill and in 1906 he married Ada Ward in

Bromley, Kent. It is likely he was either conscripted into the army or enlisted under the Derby Scheme, joining the Royal Garrison Artillery. He was sent to the front to serve with the 332nd Siege Battery. Fred was badly wounded on 14 September 1917 and succumbed to his wounds at the 61st Casualty Clearing Station on Friday 28 September 1917. He left a widow and two small children.

Mr R.H. Gaby, Fred's employer, wrote to Samuel Hudd stating:

"I have always appreciated him and how much I have felt his absence. He was always doing something and always to be relied on. It is poor consolation to say that he was a son that you might well be proud of, but his steady, solid qualities commended him very much to me. A more loyal servant no man could have had."

Private Harry Osmond *2nd Bn Wiltshire Regiment*

Service No.	24534	Age:	19
Place of birth:	Fisherton, Wiltshire	Home Country:	England
Date of death:	28/09/1917	Cause of death:	Died of wounds
Memorial:	Salisbury, Wiltshire		
War Cemetery:	Outterstreene Communal Cemetery Extension Bailleul - Grave I. C. 21.		
Next of Kin:	William & Edith Osmond		
Address:	13 Fisherton Street, Salisbury, Wiltshire		

Nineteen year old Harry was the youngest son of William and Edith Osmond and volunteered for service in March 1915, joining the Wiltshire Regiment. He trained as a signaler and arrived in France in 1916 and was sent to serve with the 2nd Battalion. He was wounded most likely near Messines and evacuated to a military hospital at Bailleul, where he succumbed to his wounds on Friday 28 September 1917.

Corporal Frederick Dobson Beaven *2/6th Bn Sherwood Foresters*

Service No.	241775	Age:	23
Place of birth:	Trowbridge, Wiltshire	Home Country:	England
Date of death:	28/09/1917	Cause of death:	Killed in action
Memorial:	Not known		
War Cemetery:	Tyne Cot Cemetery - Grave LIII. D. 1.		
Next of Kin:	Frederick William & Catherine Beaven		
Address:	Priestcliffe, Taddington, Buxton, Derbyshire		

Frederick, known as Fred, was the eldest son of teachers Frederick and Catherine Beaven. It is likely he was either conscripted into the army or enlisted under the Derby Scheme joining the Sherwood Foresters. He was sent to the front to serve with the 2/6th Battalion who on Friday 28 September 1917, attacked German positions at Downing Trench north west of Zonnebeke. Fred was killed during the attack and his remains were relocated to Tyne Cot Cemetery in 1920.

Major Henry Clissold DSO *474th Field Coy Royal Engineers*

Service No.	N/a	Age:	46
Place of birth:	Horsley, Gloucestershire	Home Country:	England
Date of death:	28/09/1917	Cause of death:	Killed in action
Memorial:	Marlborough College, Wiltshire - Nailsworth, Gloucestershire		
War Cemetery:	Duhallow ADS Cemetery - Grave I. C. 49		
Next of Kin:	William George & Julia Grosvenor Clissold		
Address:	Chestnut Hill, Nailsworth, Gloucestershire		

Left: Henry Clissold DSO

Right: Walter Stanley Jones

Henry, known as Harry, was the eldest son of William and Julia Clissold, his father was the owner of Nailsworth Brewery. He was educated at Wycliffe College, Stonehouse and Clifton College, before attending Trinity College Cambridge, where he took a first-class degree in Natural Sciences. He became an assistant master at Marlborough College in 1893, followed by Clifton College in 1894, he also joined Clifton RFC in 1894-95 and was made Captain in 1900-01. While at Clifton he commanded the Officer Training Corps and at the outbreak of hostilities, he volunteered for service and was given a commission with the Royal Engineers. He was awarded the Distinguished Service Order in 1916 and was twice mentioned in despatches. Harry was killed by a German shell on Friday 28 September 1917, while work was being carried out on shelters behind California Trench, north of Wieltje. He was sheltering in a dug-out when a heavy shell came through the roof and exploded inside. The Commander of the Royal Engineers of the 48 Division, stated:

"I have had the greatest admiration for his splendid character, his gallantry, and his unquenchable spirit. He will live in my memory as the ideal of what a soldier should be."

Saturday 29 September 1917 - Temperature 18.5°c - Clear- Rainfall Nil

Private Walter Stanley Jones		*8th Bn Yorkshire Light Infantry*	
Service No.	37597	Age:	25
Place of birth:	Westbury, Wiltshire	Home Country:	England
Date of death:	29/09/1917	Cause of death:	Killed in action
Memorial:	Southwick, Wiltshire		
War Cemetery:	Tyne Cot Memorial - Panel 108 to 111.		
Next of Kin:	Frank & Jane Jones		
Address:	Nain Road, Southwick, Wiltshire		

Walter was the eldest son of Frank and Jane Jones and was employed in the gardens at Wingfield House. It is likely he was conscripted into the army in September 1916 and after completing his training went to France in August 1917 with the Suffolk Regiment. Shortly after his arrival he was transferred to the King's Own Yorkshire Light Infantry and was sent to Belgium. He was killed in action on Saturday 29 September 1917 in trenches near Hollebeke, east of Ypres Belgium, during a very heavy German bombardment. Walter's platoon Sergeant wrote to Frank and Jane Jones explaining that during the bombardment Walter was struck by a piece of shell just above the heart and he passed away a few minutes afterwards. He was one of six men to be killed by the same shell. The Sergeant wrote:

"I hope it will be of some comfort and help to console you to know that he was a very brave lad, and gave his life fighting for the life of the dear ones at home, never failing to do his duty, no matter how hard or great the risk always ready and willing to do his best. I cannot express my own personal loss in so brave and gallant a lad, for he was dearly loved by one and all in the platoon."

Walter's Commanding Officer also wrote the following to Frank and Jane Jones:

"It is with great sorrow to me to have to inform you of the death of Private W. S. Jones, which happened last night, caused by a shell just one hour before we were relieved from the trenches. All of us felt the loss very much, but of course it will be a greater blow to you, and I hope you may find some consolation in the fact that he fell doing his duty. Trust in the Almighty and you will find some solace to heal the wound this great loss has caused, and out of the darkness may you see some light believing that God's will be done."

Walter is remembered on the Tyne Cot Memorial and has no known grave.

Lance Corporal Frederick Bertram Pinfield		*13th Bn Kings Royal Rifle Corps*	
Service No.	R/38020	Age:	36
Place of birth:	Goytre, Monmouthshire	Home Country:	England
Date of death:	29/09/1917	Cause of death:	Killed in action
Memorial:	Chippenham, St. Pauls Church, Wiltshire		
War Cemetery:	Tyne Cot Memorial - Panel 115 to 119 and 162A and 163A		
Next of Kin:	Rosa Gertrude Pinfield (wife) - Henry G & Emily Pinfield (parents)		
Address:	17 Audley Road, Chippenham - 44 Park Lane, Chippenham		

Frederick, known as Bert, was the eldest son of Henry and Emily Pinfield and was educated at St.Paul's School and then completed his education at the North Wilts Technical College at Swindon. At the age of 16 years he gained employment with Collen Brothers at Chippenham Flour Mills initially as a clerk before being promoted to outdoor representative and was employed with them for twenty years. Bert also had a great love of sport, he was Captain of Chippenham Football Club for several years before becoming a referee. He was a keen cricketer being a skilful batsman and played a good game of tennis. He helped form the Amateur Dramatic Society and was a member of St. Pauls Church choir and regularly took part in the services. In 1912 Bert married Rosa Gertrude Buckland at Doncaster and the couple set up home in Chippenham. At the outbreak of hostilities Bert joined the Wiltshire volunteers (Home Guard) and was in the cyclist section, he was described as a skilful marksman. Bert was called up initially joining the Army Service Corps but was later transferred to the 13th Kings Royal Rifle Corps and was sent to France in February 1917 while also being promoted to Lance Corporal. He took part in the fighting at Arras and was killed on Saturday 29 September 1917, when the 13th Kings Royal Rifle Corps were near Bodmin Copse south of the Menin Road. In early October 1917 Rosa Pinfield received the following letter from a Captain, Bert's company commanding officer:

"I am very sorry to have to inform you of the death of your husband who was a non commissioned officer in the company in which I command. I only wish to say something to soften the shock of the sad news for you, but at such times words from anyone are very little good. I can only hope that in the course of time the fact that he made the supreme sacrifice in the fight for the freedom of the future generations may help you a little. Your husband was killed by a shell this morning at 6.45, during a heavy bombardment; he was only a few yards away from me at the time, in our trenches. I do not think he could have had time to realise he was even hit. You may feel glad, therefore, that he suffered no agony or physical pain. I had recommended your husband for a commission and he was expected very shortly to return to England for his course of training. I can only assure you of the sympathy felt by the whole of his company with you in your loss. Your husband was very popular with all his comrades."

Bert had written the following in a letter prior to his death:

"As you say, it is in the hands of God. I believe when I go over the great divide I am going to a better place, and I don't want any funeral music sung for me."

Bert's favourite hymn had been *"Hark, tis the watchman's cry"* and the words of the hymn seem to echo his message. He left a widow and small child and is today remembered on the Tyne Cot Memorial and has no known grave.

Gunner Frederick Sweeting *275th Siege Bty Royal Garrison Artillery*

Service No.	91617	Age:	36
Place of birth:	High Easter, Essex	Home Country:	England
Date of death:	29/09/1917	Cause of death:	Died of wounds
Memorial:	Tollard Royal, Wiltshire		
War Cemetery:	Tyne Cot Memorial - Panel 6 to 7 and 162.		
Next of Kin:	Florence Maria Sweeting (wife) - William & Sophia Sweeting (parents)		
Address:	Rushmore Park, Tollard Royal, Wiltshire		

Frederick was the fourth son of William and Sophia Sweeting and on 4 February 1905 he married Florence Maria Fairs at Cobham, Surrey. He was employed as a game keeper at Rushmore Park and on 11 December 1915, he enlisted in the army under the Derby Scheme. He was called up on 3 June 1916 joining the Royal Garrison Artillery and arrived in France on 15 March 1917. He was wounded on Saturday 29 September 1917 most likely by German counter battery fire, south of Ypres and succumbed to his wounds soon after. He is remembered on the Tyne Cot Memorial and has no known grave. Frederick left a widow and a young family.

Private Albert Victor Millard *Gun Carrier Sect Tank Corps*

Service No.	95127	Age:	34
Place of birth:	Bradford on Avon, Wiltshire	Home Country:	England
Date of death:	29/09/1917	Cause of death:	Killed in action
Memorial:	Bradford on Avon, Bradford on Avon Christ Church		
War Cemetery:	Birr Cross Roads Cemetery - Grave II. C. 12.		
Next of Kin:	Mary Ann Millard (wife) – Frank & Emma Millard (parents)		
Address:	3 Regent Place, Bradford on Avon, Wiltshire		

Albert was the third son of Frank and Emma Millard and was employed as a labourer at the gas company in Bradford on Avon. He married Mary Ann Walton on 22 December 1906 and it is likely he was either conscripted into the army or enlisted under the Derby Scheme, initially joining the Somerset Light Infantry. He was transferred to the Tank Corps and was attached to the Gun Carrier Section. The Gun Carriers looked like tanks but were specifically designed for transporting 60 pounder guns and ammunition. He was killed on Saturday 29 September 1917 most likely by German counter battery fire, south of the Menin Road, east of Ypres. In June 1919 Albert's grave was located south east of Zouave Wood and his remains moved to to Birr Cross Road Cemetery. He left a widow and a young daughter. His brother Frank had been killed in April 1917 serving with the Wiltshire Regiment.

SUNDAY 30 SEPTEMBER 1917 - TEMPERATURE 19.5°c - CLEAR- RAINFALL NIL

Lance Corporal William John Aldridge *2nd Bn Wiltshire Regiment*

Service No.	18241	Age:	26
Place of birth:	Wootton Rivers, Wiltshire	Home Country:	England
Date of death:	30/09/1917	Cause of death:	Killed in action

Memorial: Not known
War Cemetery: Messines Ridge British Cemetery - Grave Lumm Farm Cem. Mem. 10.
Next of Kin: William & Hannah Aldridge
Address: 2 Wootton Rivers, Wootton Rivers, Wiltshire

Farm Labourer William, was the eldest son of William and Hannah Aldridge and volunteered for service joining the Wiltshire Regiment. He arrived in France on 4 May 1915 and was sent to the 2nd Battalion. William was killed on Sunday 30 September 1916 by German shelling near Lumm Farm north of Messines. His remains were moved to Messines Ridge British Cemetery after the war.

Private Cyril Henry Ellison — *717th Mech. Trans. Coy Army Service Corps*

Service No. M2/265467
Place of birth: Cholderton, Wiltshire
Date of death: 30/09/1917
Age: 20
Home Country: England
Cause of death: Killed in action
Memorial: Not known
War Cemetery: Locre Hospice Cemetery - Grave III. B. 5.
Next of Kin: Henry & Annie K Ellison
Address: Hayling Island, Hampshire

Cyril was the eldest son of Henry and Annie Ellison and it is likely he was either conscripted into the army or enlisted under the Derby Scheme, joining the Army Service Corps. After completing his training, he was sent to the front and attached to 717th Mechanical. Transport Company. He was killed, most likely by German artillery or aircraft, on Sunday 30 September 1916.

Gunner Philip Charles Drury — *86th Bde Ammunition Col Royal Field Artillery*

Service No. 3259
Place of birth: Swindon, Wiltshire
Date of death: 30/09/1917
Age: 22
Home Country: England
Cause of death: Killed in action
Memorial: Great Western Railway Works Swindon
War Cemetery: The Huts Cemetery - Grave VIII. D. 14.
Next of Kin: Tom & Mary Jane Drury
Address: 66 Westcott Place, Swindon, Wiltshire

Philip was the second son of Tom and Mary Jane Drury and was educated at Hook School. He was employed as a labourer in the Masons Yard at the Great Western Railway Works at Swindon, and was described as a quiet lad. It is likely he was either conscripted into the army or enlisted under the Derby Scheme, joining the Royal Field Artillery. After completing his training, he was sent to France to swith the 86th Brigade Ammunition Column. He was killed south of Ypres on Sunday 30 September 1916. His mother received the following letter from Philips Captain:

"I very much regret to inform you that your son, No. 3259 Gunner P Drury, was killed yesterday evening, September 30th. The circumstances under which he met his death are these: As we were experiencing a bombing raid by enemy air planes I issued orders for all men to take cover. About six or eight bombs were dropped close to our camp, and one at 8.15pm dropped right in it, instantaneously killing your son and wounding several others. You have the consolation of knowing that he died a painless death as a piece penetrated his heart. His funeral takes place today and is being attended by every available officer, N.C.O and men, who all join me in expressing our deepest sympathy in your great loss. He was a really good brave fellow and universally liked by everyone. I will let you know the location of his grave later and other particulars, and I should be obliged if you would inform me of any particular inscription you would like inscribed on the cross."

Left: Philip Charles Drury

Right: *Percy Harold Comley*

MONDAY 1 OCTOBER 1917 - TEMPERATURE 20.5°c - CLEAR- RAINFALL NIL

Sapper Percy Harold Comley		*2nd Light Railway Op. Coy Royal Engineers*	
Service No.	218815	Age:	28
Place of birth:	Swindon, Wiltshire	Home Country:	England
Date of death:	01/10/1917	Cause of death:	Died of wounds
Memorial:	Great Western Railway Works Swindon		
War Cemetery:	Lijssenthoek Military Cemetery - Grave XXV. J. 6.		
Next of Kin:	Mary Elizabeth Comley (wife) - Albert & Mary Ann Comley (parents)		
Address:	8 Ashford Road, Swindon, Wiltshire		

Percy was the youngest son of Albert and Mary Ann Comley and was educated at King William Street School, Swindon. He was employed as a clerk in the loco and carriage department at the Great Western Railway Works at Swindon. He enlisted under the Derby Scheme on 24 November 1915 joining the Royal Engineers, and married Mary Elizabeth Hutchings on 26 October 1916 at Christchurch, Swindon. Percy was called up on 6 January 1917 and after just a few weeks training he was sent to France arriving on 4 February 1917 and attached to the 2nd Light Railway Operating Company. He was wounded, on Monday 1 October 1917, while walking with a friend when a bomb was dropped from a German aeroplane and landed about 20 yards away. His friend was unscathed, but Percy was badly injured in the abdomen. He was taken to No.2 Canadian Casualty Clearing station at Lijssenthoek, where he succumbed to his wounds on the same day.

Rifleman Sidney Albert Carpenter		*1st Bn Rifle Brigade*	
Service No.	B/200221	Age:	20
Place of birth:	Mere, Wiltshire	Home Country:	England
Date of death:	01/10/1917	Cause of death:	Killed in action
Memorial:	Not known		
War Cemetery:	Tyne Cot Memorial - Panel 145 to 147		
Next of Kin:	Albert & Martha Ann Carpenter		
Address:	Lower Woodford, Wiltshire		

Sidney a dairy worker was the second son of Albert and Martha Ann Carpenter and it is likely he was

Left: *Walter John Ellison*

Right: *Private Edward Tom Jefferies*

either conscripted into the army or enlisted under the Derby Scheme, initially joining the 3/8th London Regiment. At some time after he was sent to the front and transferred to the 1st Battalion Rifle Brigade. Sidney was killed on Monday 1 October 1917, when the 1st Rifle Brigade were subjected to a heavy German barrage while in the British front line at Trout Line, east north east of Langemarck. He is remembered on the Tyne cot memorial and has no known grave.

Sapper Walter John Ellison		*133rd Army Troops Coy Royal Engineers*	
Service No.	37390	Age:	25
Place of birth:	Ashton Keynes, Wiltshire	Home Country:	England
Date of death:	01/10/1917	Cause of death:	Died of wounds
Memorial:	Great Western Railway Works - Ashton Keynes, Wiltshire		
War Cemetery:	Godewaersvelde British Cemetery - Grave I. L. 2.		
Next of Kin:	Walter John & Julia Ellison		
Address:,	Ashton Keynes, Wiltshire		

Walter was the eldest son of Walter John and Julia Ellison and was employed as a wheel wright at the Great Western Railway Works at Swindon. He volunteered for service joining the Royal Engineers and arrived in France on 29 November 1915. He was wounded most likely by German artillery fire, while working near Ypres and taken to No. 11 Casualty Clearing Station at Godewaersvelde, where he succumbed to his wounds on Monday 1 October 1917.

Private Edward Tom Jefferies		*22nd Coy Machine Gun Corps*	
Service No.	63088	Age:	27
Place of birth:	Bulkington, Wiltshire	Home Country:	England
Date of death:	01/10/1917	Cause of death:	Killed in action
Memorial:	Keevil, Wiltshire		
War Cemetery:	Railway Dugouts Burial Ground - Grave I. P. 13.		
Next of Kin:	Ada Jefferies (wife) - Tom & Annie Jefferies (parents)		
Address:	Martin's Road, Keevil, Wiltshire		

Edward, known as Ted was the youngest son of Tom and Annie Jefferies and at the start of 1915 married Ada Symonds at Droxford, Hampshire. It is likely he was either conscripted into the army or enlisted under the Derby Scheme, initially joining the Wiltshire Regiment. He transferred to the Machine Gun

Corps and was sent to the front to serve with the 22nd Company. Ted and a comrade were killed by a German shell on whilst Monday 1 October 1917, near Glencourse Wood, whilst carrying the machine guns up to the British front line. The officer commanding Ted's section wrote:

"Pte. Jefferies was killed by a shell whilst carrying machine guns to the front line and two comrades were killed at the same time by the same shell."

Ted and the comrade J.H. Mitchell's remains were located in August 1924 and Ted was identified by his shoulder titles and clothing, before being moved to Railway Dugouts Burial Ground. Ted left a widow and a young son. In 1918 Ada Jefferies inserted the following memoriam in a local paper:

Gone is the Face we loved so dear
Silent the voice we loved to hear
Too far way from sight and speech
But not too far for thought to reach

His parents inserted the following memoriam:

Sleep on dear Ted, in a far off land
In a grave, I may never see
But as long as life and memory last
We will Remember thee

TUESDAY 2 OCTOBER 1917 - TEMPERATURE 24.5°c - SHOWERS- RAINFALL 2.7mm

Tuesday 2 October 1917- Eye witness account

"Through the haze which lies over Flanders, though above is still a blue sky, the noise of great gunfire goes on, rising and falling, in gusts, and like the beat of surf to people who live by the sea, it is the constant sound in men's ears, not disturbing their work unless they are close enough to suffer from the power behind the thunder strokes.

The trees are yellowing into crinkled gold, and there is the touch and smell of Autumn in the night air, and in the orchards in France are heavy with fruit. Wonderful weather, the soldiers say.

The artillery battle is endless, and on both sides, is intense and widespread. It was followed yesterday by five German counter attacks, which did not reach the British lines. It a very desperate way the Germans are trying to push the British back from positions that are essential to the strength of his defence, all the German guns are at work.

Our men have hope in their hearts, and fight more grimly and with higher spirit because of it. The success of the last two battles has deepened the hope, and men come back from the line, back to the rest billets, with the old conviction newly revived that at last they have the enemy down and under and very near hopelessness.

In the rest billets are the men who come back. They come marching back along dusty roads from the fire swept zone, first across ground pitted with new made shell holes, with the howl of shells overhead, and then through broken villages on the edge of the battlefields, and then through standing villages where only a gap or two shows where a haphazard shell has gone, and then at last to the clean, sweet country which no high explosives reach, unless a hostile airman comes over with his bombs.

In any old billet in Flanders one hears the tale of battle told by men who were there, and it is worthwhile, as yesterday, when I sat down at table with the officers of an English county battalion in a Flanders farmhouse. The men were camped outside, and as I passed I liked the look of these lads, who had just come out of one of the stiffest fights of the war. They looked amazingly fresh after one night's rest, and they stood in groups telling their yarns in the good old dialect of their county, laughing as though it had all been a joke, though it was more than a joke with death on the prowl.

"Your men look fit," I said to the colonel, and he smiled as though he liked my words, and said: "You couldn't get their tails down, with a crowbar. It was a good show, and that makes all the difference. They have been telling the Australian boys that you have only got to make a face at the Hun and he puts his hands up. They knocked the stuffing out of the enemy."

Lance Corporal Ernest William Groves		*152nd Field Coy Bn Royal Engineers*	
Service No.	61151	Age:	35
Place of birth:	Romsey, Hampshire	Home Country:	England
Date of death:	02/10/1917	Cause of death:	Died of wounds
Memorial:	Not known		
War Cemetery:	Lijssenthoek Military Cemetery - Grave XXV. E. 7.		
Next of Kin:	Mary Ellen Groves (wife) – William & Harriet Groves (parents)		
Address:	4 Marlborough Road, Swindon, Wiltshire		

Ernest, a gamekeeper, was the eldest son of William & Harriet Groves and on 27 October 1906, married Mary Ellen Pinnell at Hungerford. He volunteered for service on 6 February 1915 with the Royal Engineers, arriving in France on 31 May 1915 and was attached to the 69th Field Company as a driver. He was transferred to the Head Quarters of the 38th Division on 9 July 1916 and then on to the 152nd Field Company. He was severely wounded on the night of 1 October 1917 south of Polygon Wood, while building a trench board track. He was evacuated to No. 2 Canadian Casualty Clearing Station at Lijssenthoek suffering from a gun shot wound to the back which penetrated his abdomen. Ernest succumbed to his wounds on Tuesday 2 October 1917. Ernest left a widow and a young family.

WEDNESDAY 3 OCTOBER 1917 - TEMPERATURE 18°c - OVERCAST- RAINFALL 1.2mm

Private Francis Samuel Maidment		*11th Bn Royal Sussex Regiment*	
Service No.	L/9344	Age:	29
Place of birth:	Amesbury, Wiltshire	Home Country:	England
Date of death:	03/10/1917	Cause of death:	Died of wounds
Memorial:	Not known		
War Cemetery:	Etaples Military Cemetery - Grave XXVII. D. 4.		
Next of Kin:	Alice Maud Maidment (wife) – James & Mary Anne Maidment (parents)		
Address:	Coombe Cottages, Littleham, Bideford, Devon		

Regular soldier Francis, was the fourth son of James and Mary Anne Maidment and enlisted with the Royal Sussex Regiment on 1 February 1911. He arrived in France on 12 August 1914 with the 2nd Battalion. It is likely he was wounded or suffered illness or disease and was evacuated to England. At the beginning of 1916 he married Alice Maud Wise at Bideford, Devon. Following his recovery, he returned to the front and was transferred to the 11th Battalion. He was wounded during fighting on the Menin Road in late September 1917. He was evacuated to No. 18 General Hospital at Camiers, where he succumbed to his wounds on Wednesday 3 October 1917.

Private Leonard Harris		*2nd Bn Wiltshire Regiment*	
Service No.	22821	Age:	24
Place of birth:	Haxon, Wiltshire	Home Country:	England
Date of death:	03/10/1917	Cause of death:	Died of wounds
Memorial:	Fittleton, Wiltshire		
War Cemetery:	Outterstreene Communal Cemetery Extention Bailleul - Grave I. C. 62.		
Next of Kin:	Alfred & Louisa Ann Harris		
Address:	Haxon, Netheravon, Wiltshire		

Leonard, a farm labourer, was the youngest son of Alfred and Louisa Ann Harris and it is likely he was either conscripted into the army or joined under the Derby Scheme, joining the Wiltshire Regiment. He was sent to the front to serve with the 2nd Battalion. Leonard was wounded most likely near Messines and evacuated to a military hospital at Bailleul, where he succumbed to his wounds on Wednesday 3 October 1917.

Private William Harold Cripps		*12th Bn Gloucestershire Regiment*	
Service No.	31504	Age:	19
Place of birth:	Devizes, Wiltshire	Home Country:	Wales
Date of death:	03/10/1917	Cause of death:	Died of wounds
Memorial:	Not known		
War Cemetery:	Lijssenthoek Military Cemetery - Grave XXIV. E. 20A.		
Next of Kin:	George & Mary Cripps		
Address:	5 High Street, Chepstow, Monmouthshire		

Nineteen year old William was the second son of George and Mary Cripps and it is likely he was either conscripted into the army or joined under the Derby Scheme, joining the 12th Service Battalion Gloucester Regiment. He was wounded on Wednesday 3 October 1917, most likely by German artillery with injuries to the face and legs, as the 12th Gloucesters were making their way to attack positions south of Polygon Wood. He was evacuated to No.3 Canadian Casualty Clearing Station at Lijssenthoek where he succumbed to his wounds later that day.

Private Christopher Tom Drew		*1st Bn Royal West Kent Regiment*	
Service No.	242152	Age:	29
Place of birth:	Tettenall, Staffordshire	Home Country:	England
Date of death:	03/10/1917	Cause of death:	Killed in action
Memorial:	Not known		
War Cemetery:	Poelcapelle British Cemetery - Grave IX. H. II.		
Next of Kin:	George & Ellen Emma Drew		
Address:	89 Dixon Street, Swindon, Wiltshire		

Christopher, a clerk, was the only son of George and Ellen Emma Drew and enlisted under the Derby Scheme on 8 December 1915, enlisting with Royal West Kent Regiment. He was called up on 6 February 1917 and after completing his training he arrived in France on 12 September 1917 and joined 1st Battalion on 16 September 1917. He was killed on Wednesday 3 October 1917, most likely by German artillery, when the 1st Royal West Kents were making their way to attack German positions between the Menin Road and Polygon Wood. His personal property consisting of photos and letters were returned to his parents. In 1923, Christopher's remains were located south of Herenthage Chateau, south of the Menin Road. Initially he was recorded as an unknown British soldier as his identity disc was unreadable. However, also recovered were his shoulder titles and a broken knife and luckily, he also still had in his possession a postcard which was used for his identification. The disc and the postcard were returned to his parents in 1924. His remains we moved to Poelcapelle British Cemetery.

10
The Battle of Broodseinde

Map page 424

THURSDAY 4 OCTOBER 1917 - TEMPERATURE 15.5°c - OVERCAST- RAINFALL 4.6mm

The British inflicted a great defeat on the Germans, and the victorious troops were thoroughly representative of the Empire. An attack was launched over an eight-mile front between the south of Tower Hamlets to the north of Langemarck, and rapid progress was made, the enemy being driven from villages and woods. The British established themselves well over the crest of the main ridge five miles to the east of Ypres.
Over 3,000 prisoners were collected and a few guns captured, and much war material. The enemy casualties were very heavy and the British light. Berlin stated the British penetrated only one kilometre deep into the German defensive system and that especially bitter fighting took place.

An unofficial statement declared 4 October 1917, would stand out as one of the great days of glory in the annals of the British Army and the victory achieved is the greatest since the Battle of the Marne. A correspondent told how five German divisions gathered for an attack on Zonnebeke came under curtain fire, with the result that the slaughter was described as the worst of the war, stating:

"Never have our men fought more superbly. It was remarked to me last night by one whose opinion on the matter merits the utmost respect that if any troops could carry the different positions which we were attacking, the men who were going over at dawn would do it. And very completely has this prophecy been vindicated. But another factor which has largely contributed to the fulness of our success is that we forestalled the Germans in a big projected attack, having for it's obvious purpose the attempt to recover Zonnebeke Ridge. No fewer than five divisions had been brought into position for this operation, and their attack is said to have been fixed for 7am. Our own attack was launched an hour earlier, and this was the enemy's undoing."

Private Thomas Charles Goodfellow — *1/6th Bn Royal Warwickshire Regiment*

Service No.	30505	Age:	32
Place of birth:	Chilmark, Wiltshire	Home Country:	England
Date of death:	04/10/1917	Cause of death:	Killed in action
Memorial:	Hindon, Chilmark - Wiltshire		
War Cemetery:	Tyne Cot Memorial - Panel 23 to 28 and 163A		
Next of Kin:	Gertrude Nellie Goodfellow (wife) – George & Annie Goodfellow (parents)		
Address:	Hindon, Wiltshire		

Thomas, a road labourer, was the second son of George and Annie Goodfellow and married Gertrude Nellie Lawes on 15 June 1912 at Coombe Bisset. It is likely he was either conscripted into the army or joined under the Derby Scheme, initially joining the Worcester Regiment. He was sent to the front and

Left: Thomas Charles Goodfellow

Right: George Henry Fry

transferred to the 1/6th Battalion Royal Warwickshire Regiment. Thomas was reported missing on Thursday 4 October 1917, during attacks on German positions south of Poelcapelle. All the objectives were taken except Burns House and Vacher Farm. Later official information was received stating Thomas was presumed to have been killed on the day he was reported missing. He is remembered on the Tyne Cot memorial and has no known grave. He left a widow and a young daughter.

Private George Henry Fry		*9th Bn Yorkshire Light Infantry*	
Service No.	44026	Age:	31
Place of birth:	Boughton Gifford, Wiltshire	Home Country:	England
Date of death:	04/10/1917	Cause of death:	Killed in action
Memorial:	Trowbridge, Broughton Gifford, Wiltshire		
War Cemetery:	Hooge Crater Cemetery - Grave XIII. C. 12/15.		
Next of Kin:	Ellen Louisa Fry (wife) - Francis & Mary Fry (parents)		
Address:	58 Dursley Road, Trowbridge, Wiltshire		

George was the second son of Francis and Mary Fry and was employed by the Trowbridge Cooperative Society as a van man. He married Ellen Louisa Stillman at the start of the year in 1910 and at the outbreak of hostilities he joined the Royal Field Artillery. He was later transferred to the King's Own Yorkshire Light Infantry and arrived in France in December 1916. On Thursday 4 October 1917, the 9th Battalion Yorkshire Light Infantry had advanced eastward from Polygon Wood under heavy German Machine gun fire. After a difficult fight at Joist Farm it was captured, but the 9th Yorkshire Light Infantry faced a march lined with German concrete strong points to the right. These were attacked by British bombers (hand grenades) and Juniper Trench was captured. Other German blockhouses were attacked and the 9th Yorkshire Light Infantry secured their objective. The attackers then came under German machine gun fire but this was put out of action by a British tank. At about 12 noon the Germans launched a counter attack but this was beaten off by British artillery. George was killed during the attack and his commanding officer wrote to Ellen Fry speaking in high terms of her husband's abilities as a soldier and added he was reverently buried behind the lines. In June 1919 his grave was located in Polygon Wood and his remains moved to Hooge Crater Cemetery.

Private Fred Barnes		*1st Bn Somerset Light Infantry*	
Service No.	26735	Age:	20
Place of birth:	Upton Scudamore, Wiltshire	Home Country:	England

Date of death:	04/10/1917	Cause of death:	Killed in action
Memorial:	Not known		
War Cemetery:	Tyne Cot Memorial - Panel 41 to 42 and 163A.		
Next of Kin:	William John & Fanny Barnes		
Address:	Long Lane Cottages, Wanstrow, Somerset		

Fred was the second son of William John and Fanny Barnes and it is likely he was either conscripted into the army or joined under the Derby Scheme, joining the Somerset Light Infantry. He was sent to the front joining the 1st Battalion. On Thursday 4 October 1917, the 1st Somersets attacked German positions west of Poelcapelle. At 6am the British barrage fell and the advance began, the attackers were close up to the creeping barrage and got too close causing some casualties. Kangaroo Trench was found to be occupied by the Germans but the trench was taken with little opposition. The first real opposition was encountered on a track leading south from Lemnos House after a short fire fight the 1st Somersets again advanced. The attack was held up for a time by German machine guns in fortified houses, but after killing a number of Germans and capturing a further 16 and two machine guns the British advance came under fire from a German machine gun in Ferdan House and the British barrage halted. The first objective was consolidated. After a short time, the advance continued and with the aid of stokes mortars Ferdan house was captured, along with two German officers and thirty other ranks together with two machine guns and two trench mortars. By this time the Germans defence was getting weaker although the 1st Somersets had some casualties from a machine gun firing from 19 Metre Hill. The Green objective was achieved and in the afternoon the Germans counter attacked on a point held by the Seaforth Highlanders. This left the 1st Somersets in an exposed position and they were forced to fall back, while being continuously shelled by the British artillery. Fred was reported missing during the attack. Later official information was received stating Fred was presumed to have been killed on the day he was reported missing. He is remembered on the Tyne Cot memorial and has no known grave.

Private Arthur Henry Powell		*1st Bn Somerset Light Infantry*	
Service No.	28261	Age:	19
Place of birth:	Swindon, Wiltshire	Home Country:	England
Date of death:	04/10/1917	Cause of death:	Killed in action
Memorial:	Not known		
War Cemetery:	Tyne Cot Memorial - Panel 41 to 42 and 163A.		
Next of Kin:	James & Annie Elizabeth Powell,		
Address:	Stratton St Margaret, Wiltshire		

Nineteen year old Arthur was the youngest son of James and Annie Elizabeth Powell and it is likely he was either conscripted into the army or joined under the Derby Scheme, joining the Somerset Light Infantry. He was sent to the front joining the 1st Battalion. He was killed on Thursday 4 October 1917, when the 1st Somersets attacked German positions west of Poelcapelle. In the same action as Fred Barnes, he is remembered on the Tyne Cot memorial and has no known grave.

Private Douglas Sidney Collier		*1st Bn Somerset Light Infantry*	
Service No.	28159	Age:	19
Place of birth:	Dilton Marsh, Wiltshire	Home Country:	England
Date of death:	04/10/1917	Cause of death:	Killed in action
Memorial:	Dilton Marsh, Wiltshire		
War Cemetery:	Tyne Cot Memorial - Panel 41 to 42 and 163A.		
Next of Kin:	Sidney & Frances Collier		
Address:	Dilton Marsh, Wiltshire		

Douglas was the only son of Sidney and Frances Collier and it is likely he was either conscripted into the army or joined under the Derby Scheme, joining the Somerset Light Infantry. He was sent to the front joining the 1st Battalion. He was reported wounded and missing on Thursday 4 October 1917, when the 1st Somersets attacked German positions west of Poelcappelle in the same action as Fred Barnes. Later official information was received stating Douglas was presumed to have been killed on the day he was reported missing. He is remembered on the Tyne Cot memorial and has no known grave. In 1918 his family inserted the following memoriam in a local paper:

The only comfort that I have is we shall meet again
His smiling face will greet me when the gate I enter in;
I prayed that God would keep a watch and shield him from the fray
But alas! My hopes were blighted when the sad news came that day

We mourn for you dear brother
But not with outward show
For the heart that mourns sincerely
Mourns silently and low

Sweet be the rest dear brother;
'Tis sweet to breathe thy name
In life I loved you dearly;
In death I do the same

Private George Chandler		*1st Bn Devonshire Regiment*	
Service No.	44445	Age:	31
Place of birth:	Chippenham, Wiltshire	Home Country:	England
Date of death:	04/10/1917	Cause of death:	Killed in action
Memorial:	Chippenham, St. Pauls Church		
War Cemetery:	Tyne Cot Memorial - Panel 102.		
Next of Kin:	George & Anna Chandler		
Address:	Ashes Hamlet, Langley Burrell, Wiltshire		

George, a carpenter and joiner, was the eldest son of George and Anna Chandler and it is likely he was either conscripted or enlisted under the Derby Scheme joining the Devonshire Regiment. He was sent to the front to serve with the 1st Battalion. On the evening of 3 October 1917, the 1st Devons advanced to assembly positions just east of Veldhock, Belgium. The tracks were described as very slippery and they were shelled by the Germans continuously. At 6am the assault commenced; the 1st Devons objective was Polderhoek Chateau and they had to pick their way over a land of swamps, mud and German shells. The 1st Devons were met in no mans land by hard fighting as the Germans had at the same time been assembling for attack on the British. As they proceeded across no man's land, (which probably had a stream running through it at some point), it became a bog and continued to hamper the 1st Devons progress; however, it was so soft and deep that it smothered shell bursts. The 1st Devons advance was finally brought to a halt west of Polerhoek Woods where they were forced to consolidate their position and repulse a number of German counter attacks. George was one of over a hundred men of the 1st Devons to be killed on Thursday 4 October 1917. He is remembered on the Tyne Cot Memorial and has no known grave. No one made an application for George's medals and in 1922 the Army Records Office applied to have the medals disposed of and, as with many others, it is likely they were melted down for scrap.

Private Harold Henry Kitley		*1st Bn Devonshire Regiment*	
Service No.	30753	Age:	19
Place of birth:	Havant, Hampshire	Home Country:	England

Date of death:	04/10/1917	Cause of death:	Killed in action
Memorial:	Imber, Wiltshire		
War Cemetery:	Tyne Cot Memorial - Panel 38 to 40.		
Next of Kin:	Henry & Frances Kitley		
Address:	Imber, Wiltshire		

Nineteen year old Harold was the second son of Henry and Frances Kitley and it is likely he was either conscripted into the army or enlisted under the Derby Scheme initially joining the Wiltshire Regiment. He was sent to the front and transferred to the 1st Battalion Devonshire Regiment. He was killed on Thursday 4 October 1917 when the 1st Devons attacked German positions west of Polerhoek Woods in the same action as George Chandler. He is remembered on the Tyne Cot Memorial and has no known grave.

Private Thomas William Wootton *1st Bn Devonshire Regiment*

Service No.	30748	Age:	19
Place of birth:	Ramsbury, Wiltshire	Home Country:	England
Date of death:	04/10/1917	Cause of death:	Died of wounds
Memorial:	Ramsbury, Wiltshire		
War Cemetery:	Godewaersvelde British Cemetery - Grave I. J. 36.		
Next of Kin:	Thomas & Mary Ann Wootton		
Address:	Sanham Green, Hungerford, Berkshire		

William was the eldest son of Thomas and Mary Ann Wootton and it is likely he was either conscripted into the army or enlisted under the Derby Scheme initially joining the Wiltshire Regiment. He was sent to the front and transferred to the 1st Battalion Devonshire Regiment. He was wounded on Thursday 4 October 1917 when the 1st Devons attacked German positions west of Polerhoek Woods in the same action as George Chandler. He was evacuated to a casualty clearing station at Godewaersvelde, France, where he succumbed to his wounds the same day.

Private Henry Pinnock *1st Bn Devonshire Regiment*

Service No.	205150	Age:	27
Place of birth:	Cricklade, Wiltshire	Home Country:	England
Date of death:	04/10/1917	Cause of death:	Killed in action
Memorial:	Cricklade, Wiltshire		
War Cemetery:	Tyne Cot Memorial - Panel 38 to 40.		
Next of Kin:	Deborah Pinnock (wife) – Peter & Sarah Pinnock		
Address:	10 Calcult Street, Cricklade, Wiltshire		

Henry was the eighth son of Peter and Sarah Pinnock and was employed by Mrs Carter's butchers shop. He was a member of the local Court of Foresters and in the spring of 1912 he married Deborah Young at Devizes. It is likely he was either conscripted into the army or enlisted under the Derby Scheme initially joining the Wiltshire Regiment on 1 January 1917. He was sent to the front on 22 March 1917 and transferred to the 1st Battalion Devonshire Regiment. He was reported missing on Thursday 4 October 1917 when the Devons attacked over boggy waterlogged ground near Polderhoek Chateau east of Ypres, in the same action as George Chandler. Later, official information was received stating it was presumed that Henry had been killed on the day he was reported missing. He is remembered on the Tyne Cot Memorial and has no known grave. He left a widow and two small children. His brother James had died in 1915 while serving with the 5th Battalion Wiltshire Regiment at Gallipoli.

Left: Herbert Samuel Young

Right: Edward John Gayer

Private Herbert Samuel Young		*1st Bn Devonshire Regiment*	
Service No.	205152	Age:	33
Place of birth:	Trowbridge, Wiltshire	Home Country:	England
Date of death:	04/10/1917	Cause of death:	Killed in action
Memorial:	Trowbridge, Wiltshire		
War Cemetery:	Tyne Cot Memorial - Panel 38 to 40		
Next of Kin:	Florence Young (wife) – Samuel & Sarah Young (parents)		
Address:	50 Islington, Trowbridge - 36 Islington, Trowbridge		

Herbert was the youngest son of Samuel and Sarah Young and was employed as a grocer at the Down, Trowbridge. In the summer of 1915 he married Florence Bloodworth and took employment with Haden and Son's. It is likely he was either conscripted into the army or enlisted under the Derby Scheme initially joining the Wiltshire Regiment in January 1917. He was sent to the front and transferred to the 1st Battalion Devonshire Regiment. He was reported missing on Thursday 4 October 1917 when the Devons attacked over boggy waterlogged ground near Polderhoek Chateau east of Ypres. Florence received the following letter from an army Chaplain:

"I am afraid your husband was killed in the battle a week ago today; at least his name appears in the provisional list of casualties, although that is always liable to correction. It is more sad, as he joined us so recently. I am a Wesleyan chaplain to the brigade, and made his acquaintance at services held when we were out for a rest. I pray that God our Father may comfort you in your great trouble."

Herbert is remembered on the Tyne Cot Memorial and has no known grave. Florence Young inserted the following memoriam in a local paper:

We did not know the pain he bore
We did not see him die
We only know he passed away
And never said goodbye
From his sorrowing wife and friends

2nd Lieutenant Edward John Gayer		*1st Bn Lincolnshire Regiment*	
Service No.	N/a	Age:	19
Place of birth:	Calcutta, India	Home Country:	Burmah

Date of death: 04/10/1917 Cause of death: Killed in action
Memorial: Marlborough College, Wiltshire
War Cemetery: Tyne Cot Memorial - Panel 35 to 37 and 162 to 162A
Next of Kin: Arthur Henry & Mary Agnes Gayer
Address: Burmah

Edward was the son of Arthur and Mary Gayer and was educated at Marlborough College. On leaving the college he went to Sandhurst in December 1915 and was given a commission with the 3rd Battalion Lincolnshire Regiment in August 1916. He arrived in France on 11 July 1917 and was attached to the 1st Battalion. On Thursday 4 October 1917, the 1st Battalion advanced from Polygon Wood crossing the Polygonbeek and the adjacent marsh. The advance continued capturing Judge Trench. The 1st Lincoln's were subjected to heavy German machine gun fire from Judge Copse to the east but consolidated their position. John was killed while leading his lewis gun team to the second objective. He is remembered on the Tyne Cot Memorial and has no known grave.

Lance Corporal Walter Edgar George Perrett *1st Bn Duke of Cornwalls Light Infantry*
Service No. 27335 Age: 27
Place of birth: Fovant, Wiltshire Home Country: England
Date of death: 04/10/1917 Cause of death: Killed in action
Memorial: Fovant, Wiltshire
War Cemetery: Tyne Cot Memorial - Panel 80 to 82 and 163A.
Next of Kin: Ellen Perrett (wife) - Edwin & Elizabeth Perrett (parents)
Address: Fovant, Wiltshire

Walter, a game keeper, was the youngest son of Edwin and Elizabeth Perrett and on 27 March 1913 he married Ellen Johnson at Swallowcliffe. It is likely he was either conscripted into the army or enlisted under the Derby Scheme joining the Duke of Cornwalls Light Infantry. He was sent to the front to serve with the 1st Battalion. Walter was killed on Thursday 4 October 1917 when the 1st Duke of Cornwalls attacked German positions from the south side of Polygon Wood to Juniper Hill. Walter is remembered on Tyne Cot Memorial and has no known grave. He left a widow and a young son named Walter Edgar George Perrett, and it is likely Walter senior never met him.

Private Headley Walter Golden *9th Bn Kings Own Yorkshire Light Infantry*
Service No. 44029 Age: 21
Place of birth: Bowerchalke, Wiltshire Home Country: England
Date of death: 04/10/1917 Cause of death: Killed in action
Memorial: Bowerchalke, Wiltshire
War Cemetery: Tyne Cot Memorial - Panel 108 to 111.
Next of Kin: Walter Parson & Ellen Maria Golden
Address: Middle Chase Farm, Bowerchalke, Wiltshire

Headley was the second son of Walter and Ellen Golden and was employed on his father's farm. It is likely he was either conscripted into the army or enlisted under the Derby Scheme initially joining the Royal Field Artillery, but transferred to the King's Own Yorkshire Light Infantry. He was sent to the front to serve with the 9th Battalion and was reported missing on Thursday 4 October 1917 when the 9th Battalion Yorkshire Light Infantry advanced eastward from Polygon Wood under heavy German Machine gun fire, in the same action as George Fry. Later his family received official information stating Headley was presumed to have been killed on the day he was reported missing. He is remembered on the Tyne Cot Memorial and has no known grave.

Sergeant Walter Charles Henry Feltham		*1st Bn Hampshire Regiment*	
Service No.	6877	Age:	32
Place of birth:	Chitterne, Wiltshire	Home Country:	England
Date of death:	04/10/1917	Cause of death:	Killed in action
Memorial:	Iping, Sussex,		
War Cemetery:	Tyne Cot Memorial - Panel 88 to 90 and 162		
Next of Kin:	Evelyn Feltham (wife) - Hannah Elizabeth Toomer (mother)		
Address:,	2 London Road Ifield Sussex - Twyford, Hampshire		

Reservist Walter was the eldest son of Hannah Toomer and had enlisted with the Hampshire Regiment prior to the Great War. In the summer of 1910 he married Evelyn Yarndley at Horsham and they lived in Ifield where Walter was employed as a cowman. At the outbreak of hostilities Walter was recalled to the colours and arrived in France, with the 1st Battalion Hampshire Regiment on 23 August 1914. On Thursday 4 October 1917, the 1st Hampshires attacked German positions at Beek Villas and Kangaroo Trench east of Poelcapelle. They advanced behind a creeping barrage but the British barrage was described as ragged and responsible for most of the 1st Hampshires casualties. Walter was killed during the attack. He is remembered on the Tyne Cot Memorial and has no known grave.

Private Robert Musten Everley		*1st Bn Hampshire Regiment*	
Service No.	27781	Age:	26
Place of birth:	Chitterne, Wiltshire	Home Country:	England
Date of death:	04/10/1917	Cause of death:	Killed in action
Memorial:	Breamore, Hampshire		
War Cemetery:	Tyne Cot Memorial - Panel 88 to 90 and 162		
Next of Kin:	Robert & Susan Everley		
Address:	Breamore, Hampshire		

Robert, a cook, was the youngest son of Robert and Susan Everley and volunteered for service with the Wiltshire Regiment on 12 August 1914. However, he was discharged on 5 October 1914, the reason given was he was not likely to become an efficient soldier, most likely because of his eyesight. It is likely he was then either conscripted into the army or enlisted under the Derby Scheme when standards were not so high, joining the Hampshire Regiment. He was sent to the front to serve with the 1st Battalion, who on Thursday 4 October 1917 attacked German positions at Beek Villas and Kangaroo Trench east of Poelcapelle. They advanced behind a creeping barrage but the British barrage was described as ragged and responsible for most of the 1st Hampshires casualties. Robert was reported missing during the attack. Later his parents received official information stating that he was presumed to have been killed on the day he was reported missing. He is remembered on the Tyne Cot Memorial and has no known grave.

Private Arthur George Lightfoot		*1st Bn Hampshire Regiment*	
Service No.	25122	Age:	33
Place of birth:	East Harnham, Wiltshire	Home Country:	England
Date of death:	04/10/1917	Cause of death:	Killed in action
Memorial:	Not known		
War Cemetery:	Tyne Cot Memorial - Panel 88 to 90 and 162.		
Next of Kin:	Eva Kate Lightfoot (wife) - Arthur Edward & Laura Olive Lightfoot		
Address:	39 Bemister Road Winton, Bournemoth, Dorset		

Arthur, a house painter, was the eldest son of Arthur and Laura Lightfoot and in the spring of 1909 married Eva Kate Parker. It is likely he was either conscripted into the army or enlisted under the Derby Scheme joining the Hampshire Regiment. He was sent to the front to serve with the 1st Battalion, who

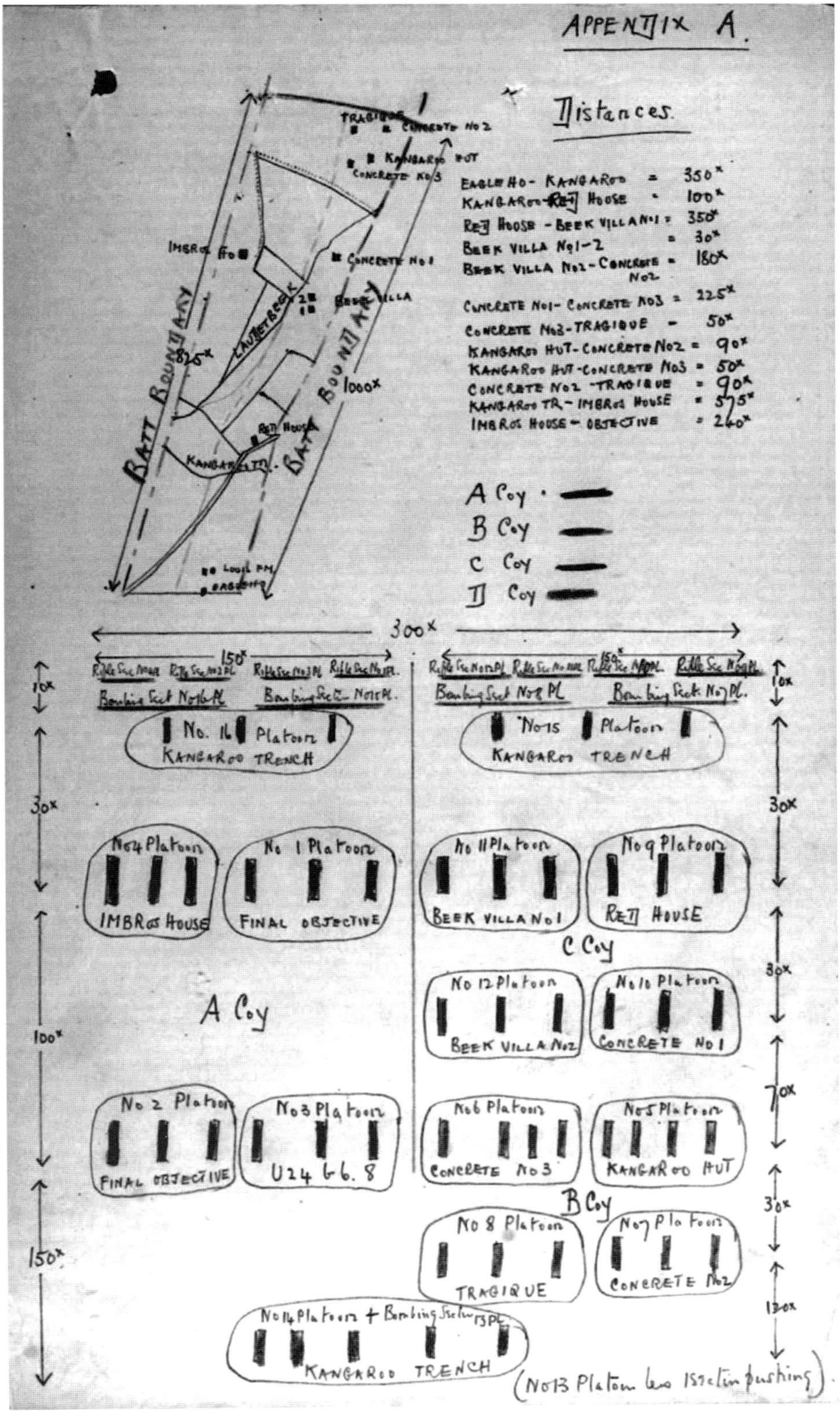

Map of the attack made by the 1st Battalion Hampshire Regiment on 4 October 1917

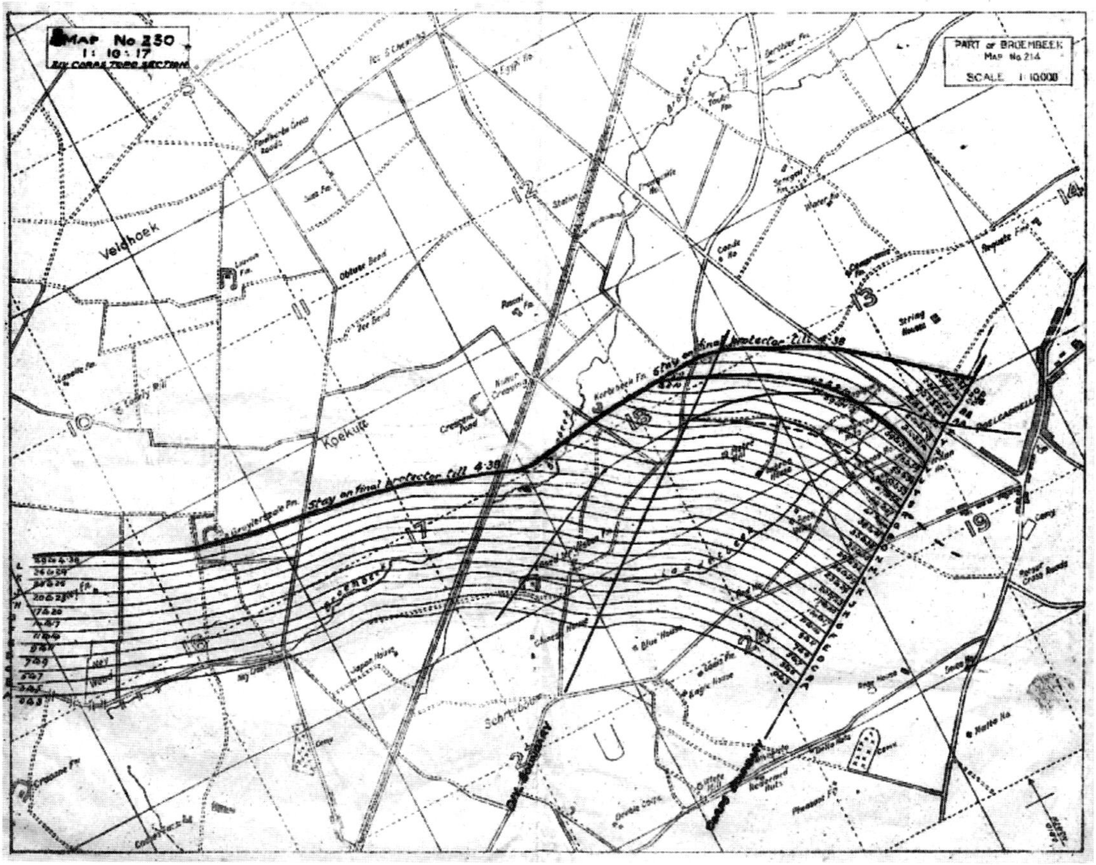

Above: Artillery map of the attack made by the 1st Battalion Hampshire Regiment on 4 October 1917, showing the lines of lift for the creeping barrage.

Below: British 18 pounder near Zillebeke stuck in the Flanders mud.

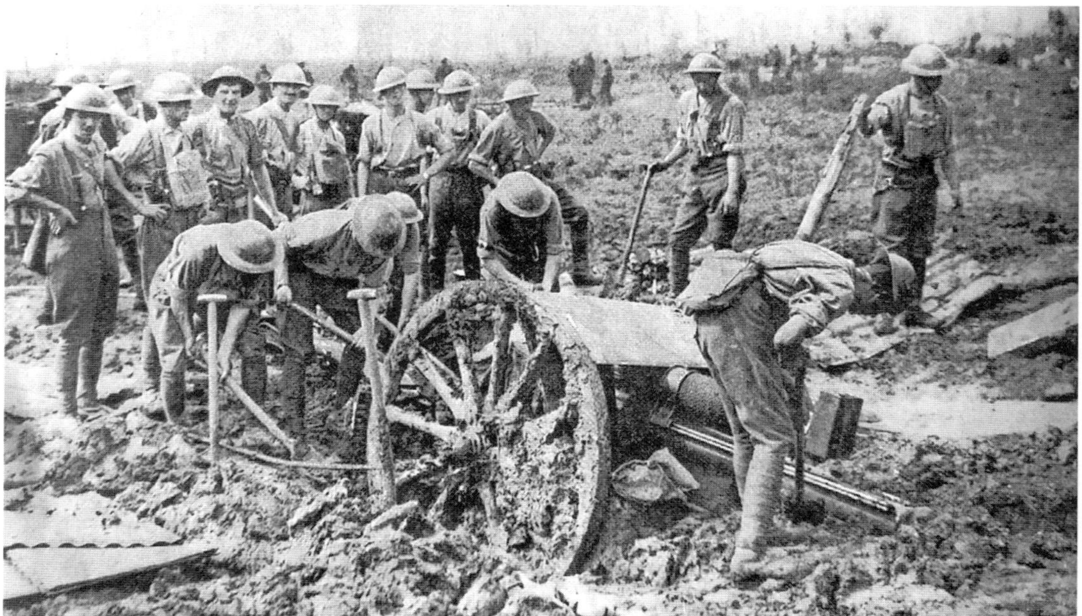

on Thursday 4 October 1917 attacked German positions at Beek Villas and Kangaroo Trench east of Poelcapelle. They advanced behind a creeping barrage but the British barrage was described as ragged and responsible for most of the 1st Hampshires casualties. Arthur was killed during the attack and is remembered on the Tyne Cot Memorial, he has no known grave.

2nd Lieutenant John Oliver Ethell		*23rd Bn Australian Infantry A I F*	
Service No.	N/a	Age:	21
Place of birth:	Kalk Bay, South Africa	Home Country:	Australia
Date of death:	04/10/1917	Cause of death:	Killed in action
Memorial:	Not known		
War Cemetery:	Ypres Menin Gate - Panel 7 - 17 - 23 - 25 - 27 - 29 - 31.		
Next of Kin:	Rev. Alfred William & May Willett Shott Ethell		
Address:	The Rectory, Laidley, Queensland		

School teacher John was the son of Rev. Alfred and May Willett Shott Ethell and the grandson of George David Shott of Swindon. He was a patrol leader with Baden Powell's scouts and had intended to take holy orders at the outbreak of hostilities. He volunteered for service on 8 November 1915 joining the Australian Engineers, arriving in France on 24 May 1916. He was evacuated to England suffering from synovitis of the right knee in May 1916 returning to France in October 1916. He was given a commission with the 23rd Battalion Australian Infantry in April 1917 and wounded at Bullecourt in May 1917 whilst in charge of a bombing (hand grenade) party. He was again evacuated to England suffering from multiple gun shot wounds to the arms and legs. Following his recovery, he returned to on France 23 August 1917. On Thursday 4 October 1917, the 23rd Battalion was part of the 6th Australian Division, which skirted Zonnebeke Lake and helped to capture the village. They chased the fleeing Germans capturing four anti tank field guns and all their objectives were taken including the village of Broodseinde. John was killed during the attack. His Colonel wrote the following to his parents:

"In his death, I have lost one of my most promising officers. He was buried on the battlefield close to Zonnebeke Lake and a small temporary cross marks the position of his grave."

The Padre wrote:

"We all expected him to take a big place in the army as he had all the qualities of a good officer".

The position of John's grave was lost in further fighting and his parents wrote to the Australian Secretary of Defence in 1919. John's sisters came to Europe in 1922 but failed to secure any further information about his last resting place. He is today remembered on the Ypres Menin Gate.

Private Thomas Charles Evershed		*8th Bn Devonshire Regiment*	
Service No.	291149	Age:	39
Place of birth:	Chobham, Surrey	Home Country:	England
Date of death:	04/10/1917	Cause of death:	Killed in action
Memorial:	Whiteparish, Wiltshire		
War Cemetery:	New Irish Farm Cemetery - Grave XXXIII. B. 20		
Next of Kin:	Lavinia Emma Evershed (wife) - George & Ruth Evershed (parents)		
Address:	Whiteparish, Wiltshire - Chobham, Surrey		

Thomas, a grocer's assistant, was the third son of George and Ruth Evershed and on 1 February 1910, he married Lavinia Emma Spare at Whiteparish. It is likely he was either conscripted into the army or enlisted under the Derby Scheme joining the 7th Devonshire Regiment. He was sent to the front and transferred to the 8th Battalion Devonshire Regiment. Thomas was killed during an attack on the German position north east of Polygon Wood. In April 1921 Thomas's remains were located near Veldhoek and identified by means of a disc, before being moved to New Irish Farm Cemetery in 1921.

2nd Lieutenant Harold Henry Reynolds		*1st Bn Bedfordshire Regiment*	
Service No.	N/a	Age:	20
Place of birth:	Chippenham, Wiltshire	Home Country:	England
Date of death:	04/10/1917	Cause of death:	Killed in action
Memorial:	Not known		
War Cemetery:	Hooge Crater Cemetery - Grave XVIII. A. 8.		
Next of Kin:	Frank & Martha Reynolds		
Address:	21 Ladyfield Road, Chippenham, Wiltshire		

Twenty year old Harold was the fifth son of Frank and Martha Reynolds and was educated at Winterslow School. It is likely he volunteered for service with the Wiltshire territorials in India where he was promoted to Lance Sergeant. He was offered a commission and returned to England where he passed the army examinations with merit. He received his commission in March 1917 and was sent to France joining the 1st Battalion Bedfordshire Regiment. He was killed instantaneously by a shell south of Polygon Wood, near Polderhoek Chateau, on Thursday 4 October 1917. He was described by his commanding officer as a young officer of exceptional promise. In August 1919 Harold's grave was located between Stirling Castle and Bodmin Copse and his remains were moved to Hooge Crater Cemetery.

Private Henry James Reeves		*8th Bn Somerset Light Infantry*	
Service No.	27781	Age:	37
Place of birth:	Lyneham, Wiltshire	Home Country:	England
Date of death:	04/10/1917	Cause of death:	Killed in action
Memorial:	Hilmarton, Wiltshire		
War Cemetery:	Tyne Cot Memorial - Panel 41 to 42 and 163A.		
Next of Kin:	Lydia Reeves (wife) - George & Sarah Reeves (parents)		
Address:	Snow Hill, Hilmarton, Wiltshire		

Henry, the village postman, was the second son of George and Sarah Reeves and in the spring of 1903 he married Lydia Thorpe at Hilmarton. He was also a member of the Foresters Friendly Society and one of four brothers serving in the forces. It is likely he was either conscripted into the army or enlisted under the Derby Scheme joining the Somerset Light Infantry and was sent to the front to serve with the 8th Battalion. On Thursday 4 October 1918, the 8th Somersets were south of the Menin Road near the Village of Gheluvelt. They were to attack two German strong points. At this point in the third battle of Ypres the landscape around this area was a mass of shell holes and there was an absence of landmarks. Even the Menin Road had been obliterated. Communication with the front line was only possible during the hours of darkness; during the day, even individual runners were shot at as soon as they left headquarters. The Somersets reached their assembly points without incident. Due to the hurried preparations and the state of the ground the assembly trenches were limited and over crowded for the attack. At 6am the British barrage began but it was at once noticed that the veil of fire appeared very thin. As the Somersets advanced the barrage was already beyond the first objective and there was no chance of getting close to it; the enemy was holding a number of posts north and south of the strong point. As soon as the Somersets reached the ridge line they came under heavy machine gun and rifle fire. With a series of sectional rushes the Somersets reached their objective and attempted to consolidate the position, but again came under heavy fire from four German machine guns positioned to the right.

It had been hoped that these guns would have been put out of action by the British barrage. The Germans now counterattacked; each of their bombers advanced carrying no equipment and each threw two stick bombs simultaneously. Two of the Somersets' companies tried to overcome the German machine guns but were almost annihilated in the process. Another attack was tried by Lieutenant Smith of the Somersets, unfortunately the brave Lieutenant was killed before the attack had gone far and none of the thirty men who made the attack were able to reach the strong point. At the end of the day the Somersets were back in their original positions. The casualties were 30 killed, 77 wounded and 12 missing. The action was part of the Battle of Broodseide. Official dispatches stated;

"The success of this operation marked a definite step in the development of our advance. Our line had now been established along the main ridge line, 9,000 yards starting from Mount Sorrel. From the farthest point reached the well marked Gravenstafel Spur offered a defensible feature which our line could be bent back from the ridge."

Henry was described as always cheerful and obliging. The following memoriam appeared in the local paper:

We think we can see his smiling face
As he bade us his last Goodbye
And left his home for ever
In a foreign land to die
But the bitterest blow is yet to come
When the warriors all return
And we miss among the cheering crowd
The face of our dear son
He little thought when he left us
He never would return
His heart was good, his spirit brave
He is now resting in a soldier's grave

It is likely Henry was killed by one of the German machine guns on the ridge near the Menin Road, he has no known grave and is remembered on the Tyne Cot Memorial. He left a widow and four children.

Private William Henry Howcutt		*8th Bn Somerset Light Infantry*	
Service No.	27766	Age:	24
Place of birth:	Aldershot, Hampshire	Home Country:	England
Date of death:	04/10/1917	Cause of death:	Killed in action
Memorial:	Enford, Wiltshire		
War Cemetery:	Tyne Cot Memorial - Panel 41 to 42 and 163A		
Next of Kin:	John Thomas & Fanny Howcutt		
Address:	Newtown, Enford, Wiltshire		

William was the second son of John Thomas and Fanny Howcutt and it is likely he was either conscripted into the army or enlisted under the Derby Scheme joining the Somerset Light Infantry. He was sent to the front to serve with the 8th Battalion. He was killed on Thursday 4 October 1918, when the 8th Somersets were south of the Menin Road near the Village of Gheluvelt, in the same action as Henry John Reeves. William is remembered on the Tyne Cot Memorial and has no known grave.

Private Robert Willis		*1/8th TF Bn Royal Warwickshire Regiment*	
Service No.	306694	Age:	39
Place of birth:	Urchfont, Wiltshire	Home Country:	England

Date of death:	04/10/1917	Cause of death:	Killed in action
Memorial:	Urchfont, Devizes Odd Fellows		
War Cemetery:	Tyne Cot Memorial - Panel 23 to 28 and 163A.		
Next of Kin:	James & Jane Willis		
Address:	Peppercombe Lane, Urchfont, Wiltshire		

Robert, a labourer and second son of James and Jane Willis, was employed by Drew & Company of Devizes. He had served in South Africa and held the South African Medal. He attested under the Derby Scheme and was called up in March 1916, joining the 1/8th Territorial Battalion Royal Warwickshire Regiment, and after completing his training he was sent to the front. He was posted as missing in action South of Poelcapele, near Burn's House and Vacher Farm, on Thursday 4 October 1917. Later official information was received stating he was presumed to have been killed on the day he was reported missing. He is remembered on the Tyne Cot Memorial and has no known grave. In October 1918, his parents inserted the following memoriam in a local paper:

Just one year has passed away, how we miss his loving face
But he has left us to remember, none on earth can take his place

Private Frank Judd		*1st Bn Royal West Kent Regiment*	
Service No.	242190	Age:	37
Place of birth:	Lyndhurst, Hampshire	Home Country:	England
Date of death:	04/10/1917	Cause of death:	Killed in action
Memorial:	Nomansland, Redlynch, Britford, Wiltshire; Bramshaw, Hampshire		
War Cemetery:	Tyne Cot Memorial - Panel 106 to 108		
Next of Kin:	Mary Jane Judd (wife) - William & Mary Ann Judd (parents)		
Address:	Nomansland, Wiltshire		

Farmer Frank was the third son of William and Mary Ann Judd and in the spring of 1904 he married Mary Jane Russell. It is likely he was either conscripted into the army or enlisted under the Derby Scheme joining the Royal West Kent Regiment and was sent to the front to serve with the 1st Battalion. Frank was reported missing on Thursday 4 October 1917 as the 1st Royal West Kents attacked German positions between Polygon Wood and the Menin Road. As they advanced they came under German machine gun fire from a pill box south of the Menin Road, most likely Leis Farm. The 1st Royal West Kents were halted and forced to adopt a defensive line facing the German held pill box. Later official information was received stating Frank was killed on the day he was reported missing. He is remembered on the Tyne Cot Memorial and has no known grave. He left a widow and three children.

Private James Carey		*6th Bn Wiltshire Regiment*	
Service No.	10283	Age:	41
Place of birth:	Seagry, Wiltshire	Home Country:	England
Date of death:	04/10/1917	Cause of death:	Died of wounds
Memorial:	Not known		
War Cemetery:	Tyne Cot Memorial - Panel 119 to 120.		
Next of Kin:	John & Sarah Carey		
Address:	Seagry, Wiltshire		

James was the second son of John and Sarah Carey and was employed by the Great Western Railway as a coach and wagon repairer. It is likely he was either conscripted into the army or enlisted under the Derby Scheme joining the Wiltshire Regiment and was sent to the front to serve with the 6th Battalion. On Thursday 4 October 1917 the 6th Wiltshires were in trenches near Zillebeke south east of Ypres. The front line consisted of a number of posts loosely connected and the Wiltshires spent the day improving these posts and improving the barbed wire. All through the day the Wiltshires were shelled by German artillery and it is likely James was wounded by a German shell and succumbed to his wounds soon after. He is remembered on the Tyne Cot Memorial and has no known grave.

Private Percy Tom Hedges		*6th Bn Wiltshire Regiment*	
Service No.	25476	Age:	25
Place of birth:	Purton, Wiltshire	Home Country:	England
Date of death:	04/10/1917	Cause of death:	Killed in action
Memorial:	Purton, Wiltshire		
War Cemetery:	Oxford Road Cemetery - Grave II. A. 2.		
Next of Kin:	Thomas Nelson & Sarah Ann Hedges		
Address:	Locks Lane, Purton, Wiltshire		

Percy, a labourer, was the eldest son of Thomas and Sarah Ann Hedges and it is likely he was either conscripted into the army or enlisted under the Derby Scheme joining the Wiltshire Regiment and was sent to the front to serve with the 6th Battalion. He was killed, most likely by German shell fire, on Thursday 4 October 1917 when the 6th Wiltshires were in trenches near Zillebeke south east of Ypres, in the same action as James Carey. He was initially buried in Fusilier Wood Cemetery near Zillebeke and later moved to Oxford Road Cemetery. In 1918 his parents inserted the following memoriam in a local paper:

How short was his stay in this valley below,
How soon were his sufferings past:
He has left this wide world of affliction and woe,
He was nipped like a rose in the bud of a blast,
Peace, perfect, Peace.

Private Ernest David Hanks		*5th Bn Dorsetshire Regiment*	
Service No.	19988	Age:	19
Place of Birth:	Great Somerford, Wiltshire	Home Country:	England
Date of Death:	04/10/1917	Cause of death:	Killed in action
Memorial:	Chippenham & St. Paul's Church Memorial - Grave XLVII. D. 10.		
War cemetery:	Poelcapelle British Cemetery – Grave XLVII. D. 10		
Next of Kin:	Richard & Elizabeth Hanks		
Address:	3 Old Road, Chippenham, Wiltshire		

Nineteen year old Ernest, a farm labourer, was the youngest son of Richard and Elizabeth Hanks. It is likely he was either conscripted into the army or enlisted under the Derby Scheme joining the Dorsetshire Regiment and was sent to the front to serve with the 5th Battalion. On Thursday 4 October 1917, the 5th Dorsets were supporting an attack west of Poelcapelle, near Bulow Farm. In the early hours of the morning as they moved into position they sustained some casualties' due to German shelling. Just after noon of the same day the 5th Dorsets were ordered forward to support attacking units, reaching the new forward positions at 3pm. Then it was realised that with all the force well forward the British were in a pronounced salient which would be hard to defend. The 5th Dorsets were ordered to return to their original position. The 5th Dorsets suffered over 60 casualties and Ernest was reported missing. In August 1920 his remains were located northwest of New Houses, South of Langemark and identified by means of a disc, before being moved to Poelcapelle British Cemetery.

2nd Lieutenant Arthur Fyfe Forge *8th Bn Lincolnshire Regiment*

Service No.	N/a	Age:	25
Place of birth:	Grimsby, Lincolnshire	Home Country:	England
Date of death:	04/10/1917	Cause of death:	Killed in action
Memorial:	Wilton, Wiltshire - Grimsby St. James, Holton le Clay, Lincolnshire		
War Cemetery:	Tyne Cot Memorial - Panel 35 to 37 and 162 to 162A		
Next of Kin:	Arthur & Mary Louisa Fyfe Forge		
Address:	13 Albert Road Cleethorpes, Grimsby, Lincolnshire		

Arthur was the only child of Arthur and Mary Louisa Fyfe Forge and was employed as an insurance clerk. It is likely he was either conscripted into the army or enlisted under the Derby Scheme joining the Lincolnshire Regiment. He was promoted to Corporal and later given a commission and was sent to the front and attached to the 8th Service Battalion. Arthur was killed on Thursday 4 October 1917 during an unsuccessful attack on German positions on Tower Hamlets Spur, south of the Menin Road when the 8th Lincolns sustained heavy casualties. He is remembered on the Tyne Cot Memorial and has no known grave.

Lieutenant Alexander Egan Barrow *B Coy 3/4th Bn Royal West Surrey Regiment*

Service No.	N/a	Age:	29
Place of birth:	North West Provinces, India	Home Country:	England
Date of death:	04/10/1917	Cause of death:	Killed in action
Memorial:	Marlborough College, Wiltshire – Bexhill on Sea, Sussex		
War Cemetery:	Tyne Cot Memorial - Panel 14 to 17 and 162 to 162A		
Next of Kin:	Rev. Kingston Egan & Amy Eliza Barrow		
Address:	Springbank, Uplyme, Devon		

Alexander was the younger son of Kingston and Amy Barrow and was educated at Marlborough College and won a classical scholarship to Trinity College, Oxford and gained a First Class in Classical Moderations. He then took employment with the Home Civil Service, in the National Health Insurance Commission. He was given a commission with the 3/4th Battalion Royal West Surrey Regiment and arrived in France on 31 May 1917. Alexander was killed while leading his men on Thursday 4 October 1917 during an attack on German positions east of Polygon Wood, between Polygon Beek and Jetty Warren. He is remembered on the Tyne Cot Memorial and has no known grave.

Lance Corporal Sydney Thomas Harvey *2nd Pontoon Park Royal Engineers*

Service No.	11514	Age:	34
Place of birth:	Lingwood, Norfolk	Home Country:	England
Date of death:	04/10/1917	Cause of death:	Died of wounds
Memorial:	Durrington, Wiltshire		
War Cemetery:	Lijssenthoek Military Cemetery - Grave XX. H. 13		
Next of Kin:	Lillian Harvey (wife) – Frederick Rudling & Harriet Emma Harvey (parents)		
Address:	1 Spearmint Cottages, Durrington, Wiltshire – Norfolk		

Reservist, Sydney, was the eldest son of Frederick and Harriet Harvey and originally enlisted with the Royal engineers on 30 September 1902. He served at home for seven years until he was transferred to the Army Reserve on 15 May 1909. The following month on 14 June 1909 he married Lillian Sandiland at the registry office at Amesbury. At the outbreak of hostilities Sydney was recalled to the colours and arrived in France on 20 August 1914. He was wounded while returning from the front line on Thursday 4 October 1917, and succumbed to his wounds soon after. In December 1917 Lillian Harvey received the following letter from Sydney's commanding officer.

Left: Sydney Thomas Harvey

Right: Eric Luker

"I very much regret to have to inform you that your husband Cpl Harvey was killed in action on the 4th October, near Ypres. He was returning to camp from the lines and on his way back he noticed some wounded men sitting and lying down on the roadside. As he had an empty pontoon wagon with him, he decided to give some of the wounded a lift in it to the nearest dressing station. Just as he had drawn up alongside these men a Bosche shell fell quite close to him and exploded. He was immediately picked up with the two riders of the wagon team, who were both seriously injured by the fragments of the shell, and was carried to the nearest Ambulance, but he was so badly wounded that nothing could be done for him. He was quite unconscious and passed quietly away. The shock of the explosion was so great that he could not have suffered any pain. We are all very sorry to lose Corporal Harvey, he was an excellent N.C.O. and very popular with all ranks. I am trying to ascertain the correct address of the cemetery where he was buried and shall send it to you. Please accept our sympathy for your great loss."

Sydney left a widow and five children.

FRIDAY 5 OCTOBER 1917 - TEMPERATURE 11°c - 50% CLOUD COVER- RAINFALL 3.1mm

British Official Despatch

During the night, the enemy heavily shelled our new positions east of Ypres, but has made no further counter attack. Our troops have been engaged in organising the captured positions.

Private Eric Luker		*3rd Bn Canterbury Regiment NZEF*	
Service No.	32193	Age:	23
Place of birth:	Kingstone Bazpup, Berkshire	Home Country:	England
Date of death:	05/10/1917	Cause of death:	Killed in action
Memorial:	Wroughton, Wiltshire		
War Cemetery:	Tyne Cot Memorial - N.Z. Apse, Panel 2		
Next of Kin:	Henry & Mary Luker		
Address:	8 Green's Lane, Wroughton, Wiltshire		

Eric, a gardener, was the second son of Henry and Mary Luker and emigrated to New Zealand on 13 November 1913. He joined the New Zealand Rifles on 22 July 1916 and arrived in England on 29

January 1917, being sent to Sling Camp on Salisbury Plain. He left for France on 28 May 1917 and was sent to the 3rd Battalion Canterbury Regiment. Eric was killed on Friday 5 October 1917 the day after New Zealanders attacked German positions north west of Zonnebeke. He was buried 100 yards north west of Otto Farm Pill Box, but his grave was lost in subsequent fighting and he is today remembered on Tyne Cot Memorial. In November 1917 his parents inserted the following memoriam in a local paper:

A son and brother both true and kind,
He was to us all in heart and mind;
A careful one who loved us all well,
While he with us on earth did dwell.

Lance Corporal Randolph Jones		*1st Bn Somerset Light Infantry*	
Service No.	27937	Age:	20
Place of birth:	Pewsey, Wiltshire	Home Country:	England
Date of death:	05/10/1917	Cause of death:	Died of wounds
Memorial:	Pewsey, Wiltshire		
War Cemetery:	Dozinghem Military Cemetery - Grave V. H. 8.		
Next of Kin:	Hugh & Theresa Jones		
Address:	Laurels, High Street, Pewsey, Wiltshire		

Randolph was the youngest son of Hugh and Theresa Jones and volunteered for service with the Wiltshire Yeomanry before the Great War. In September 1916, he was transferred to the Wiltshire Regiment and sent to Salonika. In December 1916, he was invalided back to England suffering from dysentery. Following his recovery he was sent to France in April 1917 and was attached to the 1st Battalion Somerset Light Infantry. He was wounded on Thursday 4 October 1917, when the 1st Somersets attacked German positions west of Poelcapelle, in the same action as Fred Barnes. He was evacuated to a casualty clearing station at Dozinghem, suffering from severe gunshot wounds to the abdomen and succumbed to his wounds on Friday 5 October 1917. His brother Harry Harold Jones had been killed in Palestine in August 1917.

Private Alfred George Diaper		*7th Bn Somerset Light Infantry*	
Service No.	28043	Age:	23
Place of birth:	Little Langford, Wiltshire	Home Country:	England
Date of death:	05/10/1917	Cause of death:	Died of wounds
Memorial:	Little Langford, Wiltshire		
War Cemetery:	Etaples Military Cemetery - Grave XXVII. F. 12A.		
Next of Kin:	George & Sarah Diaper		
Address:	Little Langford, Wiltshire		

Farm worker, Alfred was the youngest son of George and Sarah Diaper and it is likely he was either conscripted into the army or enlisted under the Derby Scheme initially joining the Wiltshire Regiment. He was sent to the front and transferred to the 7th Battalion Somerset Light Infantry. It is likely he was wounded in fighting near Langemarck in late September 1917 and evacuated to a military hospital near Etaples, where he succumbed to his wounds on Friday 5 October 1917.

SATURDAY 6 OCTOBER 1917 - TEMPERATURE 8.5°c - 50% CLOUD COVER- RAINFALL 2.1mm

Private James Hubert Skyrme		*1st Bn Royal Warwickshire Regiment*	
Service No.	25463	Age:	19
Place of birth:	Combe St Nicholas, Somerset	Home Country:	England
Date of death:	06/10/1917	Cause of death:	Killed in action
Memorial:	Blunsdon, Wiltshire		
War Cemetery:	Cement House Cemetery - Grave 3.		
Next of Kin:	James H. R. & Minnie Skyrme		
Address:	School House, Blunsdon, Wiltshire		

James, known as Hubert was the youngest son of James and Minnie Skyrme and was employed as an apprentice wool stapler with Chaffey's of Chard, Somerset. He joined the army on 3 May 1917 and after completing his training at Sutton Veny and Newport on the Isle of Wight, he left for France on 22 August 1917, serving with the 1st Bn Royal Warwickshire Regiment. He was killed on Saturday 6 October 1917 near 19 Metre Hill north west of Poelcapelle, the area had been captured in the British advance on 4 August 1917 and the 1st Warwicks consolidated the area.

2nd Lieutenant Arthur Amyor Steward		*11th Balloon Coy Bn Royal Flying Corps*	
Service No.	N/a	Age:	35
Place of birth:	Salisbury, Wiltshire	Home Country:	England
Date of death:	06/10/1917	Cause of death:	Killed in action
Memorial:	Downton, Boyton & Corton, Wiltshire		
War Cemetery:	Duhallow ADS Cemetery - Grave I. D. 25.		
Next of Kin:	Miriam Agnes Steward (wife) – Edward & Margaret Steward (parents)		
Address:	The Moot, Downton, Wiltshire – Boyton Rectory, Wiltshire.		

Arthur was the younger son of Canon Edward and Margaret Steward and was educated at Wellington and Magdalen College, Oxford. He held a commission in the Norfolk Militia during the South African War, in which he saw active service. He subsequently resigned his commission and was ordained by the Archbishop of York to a curacy in Hull on 9 June 1912. He married Miriam Carver on 18 June 1912, at Laverstock, Wiltshire and at the outbreak of hostilities was on the staff of St. Mary's, Johannesburg. He returned to England, offered his services as a combatant officer, and was given a commission in 1915 in the Royal Field Artillery proceeding to the front in April 1916. He was transferred in mid 1917 to the Royal Flying Corps as an observation officer. Arthur was killed on Saturday 6 October 1917, whilst asleep in his dugout by a German shell. He left a widow and three young daughters.

Private Harry William Stagg		*9th Bn Devonshire Regiment*	
Service No.	291050	Age:	26
Place of birth:	Salisbury, Wiltshire	Home Country:	England
Date of death:	06/10/1917	Cause of death:	Killed in action
Memorial:	Salisbury, Wiltshire		
War Cemetery:	Tyne Cot Memorial - Panel 38 to 40.		
Next of Kin:	Lillian Stagg (wife) - George & Lucy Ann Stagg (parents)		
Address:	St Martin, Salisbury, Wiltshire		

Harry, a butcher was the eldest son of George and Lucy Ann Stagg and on 3 August 1914 he married Lilian Theresa Claudia Vincent. It is likely he was either conscripted into the army or enlisted under the Derby Scheme initially joining the Devonshire Regiment. He was sent to the front to serve with the 9th Battalion who on Saturday 6 October 1917 were in dugouts at Hooge Crater. They were shelled during the morning and at 7.30pm the 9th Battalion were marched to the Butts east of Polygon Wood. They were heavily shelled on the way by German artillery and it is likely Harry was killed by a German shell.

He is remembered on the Tyne Cot Memorial and has no known grave. He left a widow and a young daughter.

Private William Henry Fry Vines		*3/4th Bn Royal West Surrey Regiment*	
Service No.	205792	Age:	31
Place of birth:	Christian Malford, Wiltshire	Home Country:	England
Date of death:	06/10/1917	Cause of death:	Died of wounds
Memorial:	Not Known		
War Cemetery:	Godewaersvelde British Cemetery - Grave I. N. 44.		
Next of Kin:	Mary Campbell Vines (wife) - Joseph Daniel & Jane Vines (parents)		
Address:	3 Hamilton Road, Southville, Bristol - Calstone, Wiltshire		

William, a grocer's assistant, was the youngest son of Joseph Daniel and Jane Vines and on 1 July 1914 he married Mary Campbell Cree at Clifton, St Andrews. It is likely he was either conscripted into the army or enlisted under the Derby Scheme initially joining the Royal West Surrey Regiment and was sent to the front to serve with the 3/4th Battalion. He was wounded on Thursday 4 October 1917 during an attack on German positions east of Polygon Wood, between Polygon Beek and Jetty Warren and was evacuated to a casualty clearing station at Godewaersvelde where he succumbed to his wounds on Saturday 6 October 1917.

Private John Habgood		*3/4th Bn Royal West Surrey Regiment*	
Service No.	T/205460	Age:	19
Place of birth:	Brinkworth, Wiltshire	Home Country:	England
Date of death:	06/10/1917	Cause of death:	Died of wounds
Memorial:	Not known		
War Cemetery:	Etaples Military Cemetery - Grave XXVII. F. 10A.		
Next of Kin:	Edwin James & Eliza Esther Habgood		
Address:	Cox's Farm Dunfield, Marston Meysey, Gloucestershire		

John was the fourth son of Edwin and Eliza Habgood and was employed on his father's farm. It is likely he was either conscripted into the army or enlisted under the Derby Scheme initially joining the Royal West Surrey Regiment and was sent to the front to serve with the 3/4th Battalion. It is likely he was wounded on Thursday 4 October 1917 during an attack on German positions east of Polygon Wood, between Polygon Beek and Jetty Warren and was evacuated to a military hospital at Etaples where he succumbed to his wounds on Saturday 6 October 1917. In 1918 his parents inserted the following memoriam in a local paper:

Do not ask us if we miss him, there is such a vacant place,
Can wee'er forget his footsteps and the dear familiar face;
How we miss that cheery voice and a happy smile of yours,
God's will be done, we'll meet again and then we'll part no more.

2nd Lieutenant Arthur Berkeley Penlington MC		*15th Army Bde Bn Royal Field Artillery*	
Service No.	N/a	Age:	20
Place of birth:	Edmonton, Middlesex	Home Country:	England
Date of death:	06/10/1917	Cause of death:	Killed in action
Memorial:	Seale St Lawrences, Marlborough College, Wiltshire		
War Cemetery:	Tyne Cot Memorial - Panel 4 to 6 and 162		
Next of Kin:	Charles Berkeley & Emilie Penlington		
Address:	10 Arlington Road, Eastbourne, Sussex		

Left: Arthur Berkeley Penlington MC

Right: Jack Rowland Phillips

Arthur was the only son of Charles and Emilie Penlington and was educated at Marlborough College. After leaving Education in 1915 he went to Woolwich and in August 1916 was sent straight to fight at the Somme. He was then in action at Vimy and was then attached to the Australian Corps for the third battle of Ypres. He was killed on Saturday 6 October 1917 near Hooge by a chance German shell. He is remembered on the Tyne Cot Memorial and has no known grave.

SUNDAY 7 OCTOBER 1917 - TEMPERATURE 11.5°c - CLOUD COVER- RAINFALL 10.4mm

Private Jack Rowland Phillips		*162nd Coy Labour Corps*	
Service No.	190257	Age:	41
Place of birth:	Chippenham, Wiltshire	Home Country:	England
Date of death:	07/10/1917	Cause of death:	Died of wounds
Memorial:	Chippenham, St. Andrews Church Chippenham		
War Cemetery:	Lijssenthoek Military Cemetery - Grave XX. I. 7.		
Next of Kin:	Emily Florence E Phillips (wife) - Matthew & Ann Phillips (parents)		
Address:	27 River Street, Chippenham, Wiltshire		

John, known as Jack, was the youngest son of Mathew and Ann Philips and was employed as a milk seller. In the summer of 1904 he married Emily Florence E. Whyman at Chippenham. He joined the army under the Derby scheme enlisting with the Wiltshire Regiment on 24 November 1915 and was mobilised and sent to the 3rd Battalion on 14 June 1916. He was transferred to the Labour Corps on 9 June 1917 and sent to France on 4 July 1917. He was wounded during fighting at the third battle of Ypres, most likely by German shell fire, and evacuated to No. 3 Casualty Clearing Station at Lijssenthoek where he succumbed to his wounds on Sunday 7 October 1917. He left a widow and five children. Soon after Emily Phillips received the news of the death of her husband, the family had another tragedy when her son, George, fell into a chaff cutting machine. George was taken to the Cottage Hospital in Chippenham but his arm was so badly mangled it had to be amputated. Jack's personal property was returned to his family and consisted of writing pad, letters, 2/6' stamps war saving, button brush and stick, tooth brush, nail brush, razor, hair clipper, braces, nibs, 3 pairs of socks, 1 pair gloves, hair brush, shaving brush, kit bay handle and lock, 2 handkerchiefs, 3 keys on ring, comb and 1 pair scissors.

Private Charles Jessie Cox		*2nd Bn Wiltshire Regiment*	
Service No.	18480	Age:	32
Place of birth:	Westbury, Wiltshire	Home Country:	England

Date of death:	07/10/1917	Cause of death:	Died of wounds
Memorial:	Westbury, Wiltshire		
War Cemetery:	Pond Farm Cemetery - Grave A. 6.		
Next of Kin:	Maria Cox (wife) – Thomas & Jane Cox (parents)		
Address:	4 Eden Vale, Penleigh Road, Westbury, Wiltshire		

Charles was the eldest son of Thomas and Jane Cox and at the start of 1912 he married Maria Scott at Westbury. He volunteered for service joining the Wiltshire Regiment and arrived in France on 8 June 1915, being sent to the 2nd Battalion. He was wounded most likely while on a working party near Messines and taken to one of the field ambulances at Pond Farm where he succumbed to his wounds on Sunday 7 October 1917. He left a widow and a young family.

Lieutenant James Cromwell Bush MC *22 Sqdn Royal Flying Corps*

Service No.	N/a	Age:	26
Place of birth:	Salisbury, Wiltshire	Home Country:	England
Date of death:	07/10/1917	Cause of death:	Killed in action
Memorial:	Salisbury, Seend, Wiltshire - St. Edwards School, Oxford		
War Cemetery:	Neuville En Ferrain Communal Cemetery - Grave Under War Memorial.		
Next of Kin:	Rev. Herbert Cromwell Bush & Mabel August Holdsworth Bush		
Address:	Wishford Rectory, Salisbury, Wiltshire		

James was the eldest son of Herbert and Mabel Bush and was educated at Fritham and St. Edwards School, Oxford, where he was in the Rowing IV and the 1st XV rugby team. At the age of 19 he went to Ceylon to become a tea planter, but was invalided home. He went next to India but was again invalided home. At the outbreak of hostilities, he was leaning to be a land agent and in September 1914, he volunteered for service with the Wiltshire Regiment. He was given a temporary commission with the 5th Service Battalion. He was sent to Gallipoli with the 5th Wiltshires and arrived on the peninsular in July 1915 as machine gun officer. On 10 August 1915, the 5th Wiltshires and the Loyal North Lancashires were attacked in the north of the peninsular by a whole Turkish Division. The 5th Wiltshires had been led to a part of the line which was considered safe and at sunrise they came under fire with terrible results. Those who could, retired down a narrow gully, only to find that the Turks had sited machine guns on all sides where the two-remaining senior officer were killed. James found himself in command and with the aid of two sergeants, rallied the men and lined them against the side of the gully, just out of reach of the Turkish machine guns. He then went up and across the gully, finding a fairly practicable though terribly steep way up and got the men across by twos and threes, and led them to a place of safety under the top of the cliffs. Leaving them with the two remaining subalterns with orders not to move till after dark, if he did not return, and then make their way to the beach, he then went across the open ground, under a machine gun and rifle fire a distance of about 300 yards, finally reaching a New Zealand trench. From there he was passed down to Headquarters, and was able to pass word all along the line to look out for the men as they came in after dark. A party was sent out to clear the bottom of the gully, and about 150 to 200 men came in that night. James was evacuated from the peninsular about 10 days later suffering from dysentery. He was mentioned in General Sir Ian Hamilton's despatches and in October 1916 was presented with the Military Cross by the King at Buckingham Palace for conspicuous service during the Gallipoli campaign. Following his recovery from dysentery he was sent to Egypt as Aide de Camp to a Brigadier General. In September 1916, having received a permanent commission with the Dorset Regiment he volunteered for service with the Royal Flying Corps. After completing his flying training at Shoreham, he received his "wings," flying certificate in April 1917 and was sent to France arriving with 22 Squadron on 5 May 1917. Initially he was flying F.E. 2B aircraft but from July 1917 these were replaced by Bristol F 2 Fighters, known as "Brisfits". In July 1917 James wrote the following letter describing his flying experiences to his parents.

James Cromwell Bush MC

"We had the greatest fun of Sunday, six of us on an offensive patrol at 11,000 feet above great masses of white cloud; it was perfectly lovely, but bitterly cold: they look quite flat, just what I should imagine Arctic snow fields to be like. We went along way over but saw no Huns, Archie popping at us through the gaps. Our leader gave us the signal and we came down from 11,000 feet to join just under 2,000 feet in one glorious rush of 110 miles per hour. I had my knee jammed behind the joystick to keep her down. Their Archie was wonderful and came down almost as quickly as we did. We then flew up and down the Hun lines for a quarter of an hour, shooting at them: we could easily see the wretched Hun rushing wildly up and down his trenches with the most awful wind up; they simply loathe it and nothing demoralises troops quicker. Of course, they retaliated not only with their Archie but field guns and machine guns, it was a mad, merry quarter of an hour. I finished up at barely 1,500 feet. I got hit: an awful jolt on the engine which chucked her nose down. Joy riding, one would probably have been frightened; in the excitement, it didn't worry me a bit, but I beetled off to our side to see what was up. Everything seemed all right except for awful vibration, and still having some rounds left I re-joined the fray. I flew home very canny and found great chunks knocked out of my prop, so that I have to have a new one; also holes all over the planes and a large one just outside my seat in the lower plane. But I don't ever remember enjoying a quarter of an hour more. One day later we saw a Hun come over and go for one of our balloons. He was a sportsman, came down under 2,000 feet, firing like mad. They were hauling the balloon down all the time. Finally, the observer had evidently had enough, for he walked over the side with his parachute. It looked horrible, and he looked so awfully small dangling there, but he got down all right and landed quite near us in a pile of firewood, and I couldn't help laughing as the parachute fell on top of him and completely enveloped him! The old Hun got away, and deserved to. The dawn patrols are rather wonderful: quite dark when we start, so that we have to use the little electric lights for the instruments, but at 8,000 feet we got into glorious sunshine."

On the 12 August 1917 James scored the first of his air victories while flying near Lens two Albatros's, which were shared kills with other pilots. He later went on to be credited with a further four kills while flying over Belgium between late August and early October 1917. James was reported missing along with his observer, Lieutenant William Chapman, on Sunday 7 October 1917 while flying near Kruishoek, north of Koortrijt. In November 1917, James's parents received news that a German flyer had dropped a message on a British aerodrome stating that James and his observer had been killed. They had been shot down by Hans von Habler of Jasta 36 and the two British officers were initially buried in the German plot of Neuville en Ferrain Communal Cemetery. His commanding officer wrote:

"He was such a cheerful and efficient officer."

Another officer wrote:

"He was always keen and eager."

Soon after the Armistice the officers exhumed and re-buried in another part of the cemetery and a War Memorial in remembrance to them and the men of the village place on their burial spot.

MONDAY 8 OCTOBER 1917 - TEMPERATURE 12°c - OVERCAST WITH SHOWERS- RAINFALL 10.4mm

Private Jesse Frank Tavenor Billett		*7th Bn Leicestershire Regiment*	
Service No.	25255	Age:	23
Place of birth:	North Wraxall, Wiltshire	Home Country:	England
Date of death:	08/10/1917	Cause of death:	Died of wounds
Memorial:	North Wraxall, Wiltshire		
War Cemetery:	Etaples Military Cemetery - Grave XXX. A. 9A		
Next of Kin:	Jesse & Dora Jane Billett		
Address:	46 Hungerford Road, Lower Weston, Bath, Somerset		

Jesse, a farm labourer, was the eldest son of Jesse and Dora Jane Billett and it is likely he was either conscripted or enlisted under the Derby Scheme joining the Leicestershire Regiment. He was sent to the front to serve with the 7th Service Battalion. Jesse was wounded most likely by German shelling in early October, when the 7th Leicesters were in support at Polygon Wood. He was evacuated to a military hospital near Etaples where he succumbed to his wounds on Monday 8 October 1917.

Private Henry Thomas Sandy Golding		*5th Bn Dorsetshire Regiment*	
Service No.	19968	Age:	28
Place of birth:	Pitton, Wiltshire	Home Country:	England
Date of death:	08/10/1917	Cause of death:	Killed in action
Memorial:	Quarley, Hampshire		
War Cemetery:	Tyne Cot Memorial - Panel 92		
Next of Kin:	James Dennis & Ida Golding		
Address:	The Home Farm, Quarley, Hampshire		

Farmers son Henry was the fourth son of James and Ida Golding and it is likely he was either conscripted into the army or enlisted under the Derby Scheme joining the Dorsetshire Regiment. He was sent to the front to serve with the 5th Battalion. Henry was reported missing on Monday 8 October 1917, when the 5th Dorsets were in the British front line near Poelcapelle. Later his family received official information that Henry was presumed to have been killed on the day he was reported missing. He is remembered on the Tyne Cot Memorial and has no known grave.

Driver Joseph Ewart Thompson		*51st Div. Ammo Col Royal Field Artillery*	
Service No.	645260	Age:	28
Place of birth:	Malmesbury, Wiltshire	Home Country:	England
Date of death:	08/10/1917	Cause of death:	Died of wounds

Memorial: Malmesbury, Wiltshire
War Cemetery: Dozinghem Military Cemetery - Grave VIII. G. 20.
Next of Kin: Mathew & Mary Jane Thompson (uncle & aunt)
Address: Malmesbury, Wiltshire

Joseph was the only son of Joseph Thompson, both his parents died and he was raised by his uncle Mathew Thompson, who became the Mayor of Malmesbury. Joseph served an apprenticeship with Walter Hays coach builders of Malmesbury and in 1912 he emigrated to America where he worked for a coach building company owned and run by German immigrants. His employer would often exasperate him by bringing to his notice German victories in the early part of the war. Joseph returned to England and after a short break at home, volunteered for service with the Royal Field Artillery Territorials in February 1915. He arrived in France on 6 May 1915 and was sent to serve as a driver, with the 51st Highland Division Ammunition Column. While on a home leave he had a strong presentiment that he was not coming back again and he put all his affairs in order. He had taken part in many of the battles on the Western Front and had several narrow escapes. He was wounded on 6 October 1917 and was evacuated to No. 47 Casualty Clearing Station, where he succumbed to his wounds on Monday 8 October 1917. Joseph's Captain wrote the following to his uncle:

"It is with deep regret I have to inform you that your son, Driver Thompson, was this morning whilst on duty wounded in the thigh and abdomen. All possible medical was rendered him, almost immediately placed in hospital and receiving the best possible attention. Driver Thompson has always been one of the most diligent drivers, and he will be a sad loss to my unit. I assure you of my sincere sympathy, and trust that before long you will have your dear son at home."

Sister May Winter of No. 47 Casualty Clearing Station wrote:

"Your son, Driver J. E. Thompson, passed away this morning in my ward. The poor boy told me he was your only son, and my heart always goes out to the mothers who are called upon to make the tremendous sacrifice. He was quite happy, and I don't think he had the least idea he was dying, for when I told him I should write to you and asked for a message, he said, "Tell her I shall be home in a few days, and my wounds are very slight." He was a lovely boy and we are very sad at losing him. I am an Australian sister, and we are very fond of our soldiers and they of us. May God help you to bear this great sorrow. The Church of England minister, Padre Rankin, was with him at the last."

The Padre wrote stating:

"Your son's grave will be properly marked and will be well cared for in the future. My very deep sympathy with you in your sad loss. Your son was a brave, capable and excellent driver, always willing and ready to do his duty, no matter how dangerous it might be, and by the faithful and fearless discharge of duty won the esteem and respect of his colleagues, who deeply regret his loss, and join with me in a hearty expression of sorrow and sympathy to you and your husband. When I saw him Saturday evening he was just recovering from an operation, so I was able to speak to him, and he was greatly concerned about the two other men who were with him when the fatal injuries were received and were also wounded. I may say one of them is dead, but everything possible was done for him. My sincere sympathies are with you, and you can console yourself that your son died at his country's call and was faithful unto death."

Gunner Thomas Roger Fraser — *B Bty 92nd Bde Royal Field Artillery*

Service No.	16199	Age:	22
Place of birth:	Aberdeen, Aberdeenshire	Home Country:	Scotland
Date of death:	08/10/1917	Cause of death:	Killed in action

Memorial: Box, Wiltshire
War Cemetery: Canada Farm Cemetery - Grave III. A. 41.
Next of Kin: Francis & Annie Mason Mitchell Fraser
Address: Wellwood Cottage, Cults, East Peterculter, Aberdeenshire

Thomas was the second son of Francis and Annie Fraser and it is likely he was employed at one of the stone quarries in Box. He volunteered for service joining the 92nd Brigade Royal Field Artillery and arrived in France on 21 July 1915. He was killed on Monday 8 October 1917, most likely by German counter battery artillery fire, north of Ypres.

Above: Poelcapelle had a tank in place for a long time at the Guynemer Monument, and it stayed in the market square until the Second World War when the Germans acquired this British property. - Below: The current Tank Memorial in the square at Poelcapelle.

11
The Battle of Poelcapelle

Map page 425

TUESDAY 9 OCTOBER 1917 - TEMPERATURE 11.5°c - CLEAR- RAINFALL NIL

German General von Arnim persevered with counter attacks against British positions on the ridge east of Ypres. At dawn on Tuesday 9 October 1917, German infantry advanced between Tower Hamlets and Polygon Wood. They failed to get through the British artillery barrage except at points immediately north of the Menin road, and the British Infantry dealt with them adequately. The British line is intact. Throughout the day the artillery fire on both sides was very heavy.

Corporal William Drury		*7th Bde Bn Australian Field Artillery*	
Service No.	18450	Age:	22
Place of birth:	Pontypridd, Glamorgan	Home Country:	England
Date of death:	09/10/1917	Cause of death:	Died of wounds
Memorial:	Not known		
War Cemetery:	Nine Elms British Cemetery - Grave IV. B. 12.		
Next of Kin:	William & Bessie Drury		
Address:	44 Fleet Street, Swindon, Wiltshire		

William was the eldest son of William and Bessie Drury and was educated at Swindon Secondary School. From 1909 to 1911 he was employed as a book room clerk at the school. He then emigrated to New Zealand and in autumn 1915 he enlisted with the New Zealand Army. So enthusiastic was he to go into training that, finding he could not at once get in to a camp in New Zealand, he set out for Australia and volunteered with the Australian Field Artillery on 17 November 1915. He arrived in England on 10 July 1916 and was sent to France on 29 December 1916. William was wounded on 8 October 1917 most likely by German artillery fire, and evacuated to 11th Field Ambulance, where it was found he had gun shot wounds to the right thigh, head, face, hands and legs. He was then sent to No. 44 Casualty Clearing Station, where he succumbed to his wounds on Tuesday 9 October 1917.

Rev. L.T. Pearson, an army chaplain, wrote to William's parents stating:

"I am very sorry to have to tell you that your dear son, Corporal W. Drury, was admitted to this clearing station after being most seriously wounded in action. He was hit in the right thigh, leg and head. Everything possible was done for him, but he passed away on the 9th at 11.30am. It will be of some comfort to you to know he received the utmost care and comfort while he was with us. I have buried his remains in our military cemetery, and a cross will be erected to his memory. These are sad, sad days, but Jesus lives! God bless you in your sorrow."

Private Frederick Albert Brownett Giles		*20th Bn Manchester Regiment*	
Service No.	51677	Age:	31
Place of birth:	Cricklade, Wiltshire	Home Country:	England
Date of death:	09/10/1917	Cause of death:	Killed in action
Memorial:	Cricklade, Wiltshire		
War Cemetery:	Tyne Cot Memorial - Panel 120 to 124 and 162 to 162A and 163A		
Next of Kin:	Anna Helena Giles (wife) - Albert B. & Sarah A. B. Giles (parents)		
Address:	5 Abingdon Court Road, Cricklade, Wiltshire		

Frederick, known as Fred, was the third son of Albert and Sarah Giles and was employed as a fruit and hay dealer. He was a keen athlete and competed in a large number of local meetings and had a fair amount of success as a cyclist. Toward the end of 1910 he married Anna Helena Bush at Cricklade, and it is likely he was either conscripted into the army or enlisted under the Derby Scheme joining the Army. He was called up on 3 September 1916 and sent to the Army Service Corps (Motor Transport) and was later transferred to a training reserve battalion. He was home on a final leave in June 1917 and was sent to France on 9 August 1917 being attached to the 20th Battalion Manchester Regiment. On 7 October 1917, the 20th Manchesters left Hooge Crater where they had dinner to relieve the 9th Devons north west of Beselare. It was raining heavily and they were hampered by deep mud. At 5.20am on Tuesday 9 October 1917, a British barrage to help the advance of the remainder of the 22nd Infantry Brigade fell on the S.O.S. line of the 20th Manchesters and 2 platoons of B Company were rushed forward to fill the gap in the front line. It is likely Fred was killed during this barrage, his platoon officer wrote the following to his family:

"It is with the deepest regret that I have to inform you that your husband, 51677 Pte. F.A. Giles, was killed in action on October 9th. He was killed during a severe enemy bombardment, when assisting to hold ground recently won from the enemy. His loss is felt, not only by myself and the other officers of the company, who all fully realised his sterling qualities, but by every non-commissioned officer and all his comrades, who always regarded him as a 'Pal.' I trust you may find comfort and consolation in your sad loss in the fact that he died nobly for a just cause. Please accept my most sincere sympathy."

Fred is remembered on the Tyne Cot Memorial and has no known grave. He left a widow and two young children.

Private William Edward Corderoy		*1/4th TF Bn York & Lancaster Regiment*	
Service No.	33334	Age:	42
Place of birth:	Brixton, London	Home Country:	England
Date of death:	09/10/1917	Cause of death:	Killed in action
Memorial:	Calne, Wiltshire		
War Cemetery:	Tyne Cot Memorial - Panel 125 to 128.		
Next of Kin:	Charlotte Annabella Corderoy (wife) - Clement & Lucy Corderoy (parents)		
Address:	The Chantry, Calne, Wiltshire - Dulwich London		

William was the eldest son of Clement and Lucy Corderoy and arrived in Calne in 1899 as a works Manager for Harris & Co. At the end of four years he relinquished that position and in the summer of 1904 he married Charlotte Annabella Coleman in London and went to South America, where he remained for a time. He left South America to accept an appointment as a tourist conductor in the East for Cook and Son, Travel Company. He received a commission in the Royal Army Service Corps in August 1915 and was promoted to full Lieutenant in December 1915. In 1916 William was attached to the Guards in London and was in charge of forage supply. On 5 January 1917 Dorothy Lindsell-Stewart, known as Meum, went to William's commanding officer, Major Cleve, and accused William of threatening her. Meum had been a secretary in the office where William worked but had left to take a post at a Canadian Hospital in London. She produced a letter that was allegedly written by William which stated;

"Meum Stewart, You must resign your present post *immediately. You are no longer a fit or proper person either to associate with decent girls or to hold any appointment in any department of His Majesty's Government. If you let me have the M.O.'s (medical officer) acceptance of your resignation before 10am on Saturday 6th inst. I shall place before him proofs that what I say is true, before lunch that day."*

In a statement Meum stated that William had threatened to murder her if she did not go and live with him at his flat. Stating also that on 3 January 1917 he called at her home at 11 o'clock, was very violent and told her that he would fix her because he would not have anything to do with her. On Thursday 4 January, Meum stated that William had handed in a most libellous statement concerning her to an orderly at her place of employment with instructions to; *"pass it all round the office."* She again stated she was in great fear that he would do her some violence as he carried a fully loaded revolver and a large knife about 8 inches long. On 6 January Meum again wrote to Major Cleeve and attached a letter addressed to her husband that had been received by Jacob Epstien, Meum said the letter was from William, though it was not signed, she stated she recognized the hand writing. Meum described the contents of the letter as fabrication but since it was addressed to her husband, she was worried what her husband would do. The letter stated:

"To 2nd Lieutenant Lindsell- Stewart, Sir, the following facts may interest you. Your wife Meum, against the advice of her friends has left Sally, lost her government job and is in all probability, since she admits it, the Mistress of the sculptor Jacob Epstein who lives at 23 Guilford Street, Russell Square. Epstein's Wife is agreeable to the arrangement, presumably to encourage his art. Your wife posses for him in the nude. In case you have not made suitable arrangement for your pension re your next of kin, should you be unlucky, lose no time in doing so. She is in with a very fast crowd at the Café Royal and booked for hell, also worthy of no mans sympathy."

Major Cleeve made a decision to hand all the information to the Provost Marshall and a Captain Trevor took up the case. Captain Trevor went to William's lodgings, William was not in but he managed to gain entrance and conducted a search. Captain Trevor found a loaded automatic pistol and a long-pointed knife. He took possession of these items along with some letters and other things. The following day Captain Trevor returned to William's lodgings and having again gained entrance found William in pyjamas and an old pair of flannel trousers. According to Captain Trevor's statement:

"Corderoy said he thought I (Captain Trevor) was Mr Epstien and having turned sideways to conceal his intentions then suddenly swung round and produced a fully loaded revolver which he pointed at my head".

Captain Trevor disarmed William after a struggle and took him in his own car to Millbank Hospital, where he handed William over to the Provost Marshall and he was placed in a cell. At the time of these events William had been on sick leave from the army and it was assumed by the Provost Marshall William had had a nervous breakdown. Meum, wrote to one of the officers involved in the case stating:

"Dear Billy, Write and tell me what has happened about W.E.C. I am very anxious to know – not so much out of curiosity, as I am placed in a rather awkward position with regard to the letter he sent to my husband. If Tony takes it seriously I am let in for a divorce, which I want very much to avoid. But if as I strongly suspect, W.E.C. has gone a trifle insane, and would be likely to be put under supervision, I can make it alright with my husband since I can write to put the facts before him. Send me a few lines addressed here, Miss D. Stewart, C/o A/D.D.M.S. Canadians, 86 Strand, W.C. I will be awfully obliged

to you, Billy, if you will. I am rather worried, although Major Cleeve has been such a brick over the matter. Yours, Meum"

Meum typed the letter on official note paper from the department where she worked, after she hand wrote;

"you may rely that I would regard anything you might tell me as confidential in haste."

On the 14 February 1917 William was Court Martialled at the Guild hall, Westminster. He was charged with;

"Offering violence to his superior officer being in execution of his office, in that he at No. 7 Crown Office Row, Temple, London, E.C., on the 6 January 1917 pointed a loaded revolver at Captain Keith Trevor, MC., Assistant Provost Martial, London District, who was at the time about to put him under arrest."

William was found guilty and sentenced to be dismissed from His Majesty's Service. However, William was still liable for service under the Military Service Act and the director of Recruiting, Major Sinclair, insisted he was called up at once. On 10 March 1917 William was conscripted into the Royal Army Service Corps as a private soldier and at the end of Mach 1917 he was compulsorily transferred to the infantry joining the 1/4th York & Lancaster Regiment on the continent in July 1917.
William's commanding officer wrote to Charlotte Corderoy on 16 October 1917;

"Dear Mrs Corderoy, - I take this first opportunity of sending my deepest sympathy on the death of your husband. He was killed instantly by a bullet through the heart on the 9th October 1917, during a British attack. Though he had been with us a short time he had endeared himself to all around by his gentle manners and indomitable courage. He had been offered posts that would keep him out of the front line, but he refused as he wanted to get at the enemy, and even the short periods of rest behind the lines seemed irksome to him. He went over the top with his Battalion at 5.20am on the 9th and his conduct throughout was heroic. He was killed by a sniper soon after the capture of the enemy position. I only rejoined the battalion myself on the 1st September after being wounded, but at once I realized your husband was a man of unusual ability. I had many talks with him and we were friends, and knowing him as I did I can more deeply realize your terrible loss. Assuring you of my deepest sympathy, in which the whole platoon and officers of A Company Join me. - I am your sincerely William Ryan O.C."

William was killed west of Passchendaele near Snipe Hall, which lies north of Tyne Cot Cemetery on the old German front line, when the 1/4th York & Lancaster Regiment were consolidating captured ground.

In May 1918 Charlotte Corderoy received William's personal possessions which consisted of photos, disc, metal mirror, notebook, diary and letters, and a pension of 20 shillings and 5 pence per week. William is remembered on the Tyne cot memorial and has no known grave. It is interesting that at Williams Court Martial no mention was made of Meum, or the fact that Captain Trevor gained entry to Williams lodging's, without permission, on two occasions. There was also the question of why did he remove personal letters and other things, and what were the other things? It is now known that Meum was Jacob Epstein's mistress and the mother of his first child. Meum was a model for Epstein who sketched her and made four busts between 1916 and 1918.

Private Herbert John Strong		*21st Bn Australian Infantry AIF*	
Service No.	2389	Age:	33
Place of birth:	Charlton, Wiltshire	Home Country:	Australia
Date of death:	09/10/1917	Cause of death:	Killed in action

Left: Herbert John Strong

Right: James Henry Davis

Memorial:	Not known
War Cemetery:	Ypres Menin Gate - Panel 7 - 17 - 23 - 25 - 27 - 29 - 31
Next of Kin:	John & Mary Ann Strong
Address:	Charlton, Wiltshire

Herbert, a driver, was the eldest son of John and Mary Ann Strong and emigrated to Australia before the Great War. He volunteered for service with the 21st Battalion Australian Infantry on 13 July 1915 and after completing his training was sent to Egypt, arriving on 7 January 1916. He was then sent to France and arrived at Marseilles on 23 March 1916. He was wounded on 16 November 1915 with a gunshot wound to the right thumb and was evacuated initially to the 12th General Hospital at Rouen before being sent to England. After a stay at the 3rd Aux Hospital at Dartford, he was sent to Weymouth in December 1916 and after a short furlough he was sent to Wareham. He returned to France arriving on 13 September 1917 re-joining his unit on 22 September 1917. He was reported missing on Tuesday 9 October 1917 near Daisy and Dairy Woods north east of Broodseide. Shortly after he was officially reported to have been killed in action on the day he was reported missing. He is remembered on the Ypres Menin Gate and has no known grave.

Guardsman James Henry Davis — *2nd Bn Grenadier Guards*

Service No.	29052	Age:	27
Place of birth:	Ansty, Wiltshire	Home Country:	England
Date of death:	09/10/1917	Cause of death:	Killed in action
Memorial:	Cholderton, Wiltshire		
War Cemetery:	Tyne Cot Memorial - Panel 9.		
Next of Kin:	James Henry & Emma Davis		
Address:	Quarley Down Cottages, West Chaldon, Wiltshire		

James, known as Harry and a horseman on a farm was the eldest son of James Henry and Emma Davis. It is likely he was either conscripted into the army or enlisted under the Derby Scheme joining the Grenadier Guards. He was sent to France to serve with the 2nd Battalion. On 5 October 1917, the 2nd Battalion Grenadier Guards relieved the 1st Battalion north west of Langemarck immediately on the left of the Staden Railway. The line held was a series of posts running across the Broenbeek stream. The war diary states:

The line is a very unpleasant one to occupy as the nature of the ground makes movement by day practically impossible and the ground is extremely marshy.

Harry was killed on Tuesday 9 October 1917 most likely by German artillery fire north east of the current position of the Langemarck German Cemetery He is remembered on the Tyne Cot Memorial and has no known grave.

Private Bertram George Henstridge		*2nd Bn Coldstream Guards*	
Service No.	19344	Age:	32
Place of birth:	South Newton, Wiltshire	Home Country:	England
Date of death:	09/10/1917	Cause of death:	Killed in action
Memorial:	South Newton		
War Cemetery:	Tyne Cot Memorial - Panel 9 to 10.		
Next of Kin:	Henry William & Martha Henstridge.		
Address:	South Newton, Wiltshire		

Bertram was the eldest son of Henry and Martha Henstridge and was employed as a gardener and domestic servant at Wilton Park. It is likely he was either conscripted into the army or enlisted under the Derby Scheme initially joining the Army Service Corps before being transferred to the 2nd Battalion Coldstream Guards. On Tuesday 9 October 1917, the 2nd Coldstreams attacked and captured a German post on the far side of the Broenbeek stream, north east of the Langemarck German Cemetery. Many of the British attackers had to wade waist deep through the water. A large number of the German defenders, who were completely surprised by the attack, rushed forward to surrender. The 2nd Coldstreams captured one German office and around 100 other ranks and ten machine guns. Bertram was killed during the attack and is today remembered on the Tyne Cot Memorial, he has no known grave.

Lance Corporal Frank Bryant		*3rd Bn Coldstream Guards*	
Service No.	15618	Age:	23
Place of birth:	Bromham, Wiltshire	Home Country:	England
Date of death:	09/10/1917	Cause of death:	Killed in action
Memorial:	Bromham, Wiltshire		
War Cemetery:	Tyne Cot Memorial - Panel 9 to 10.		
Next of Kin:	George & Alice Bryant		
Address:	The Leaze, Bromham, Wiltshire		

Frank, a farm labourer and eldest son of George and Alice Bryant, volunteered for service soon after the outbreak of hostilities. He was tall and well built and this was probably the main reason why he was sent to the Coldstream Guards arriving in France on 2 November 1915, joining the 3rd Battalion. Frank was killed in action on Tuesday 9 October 1917 when the 3rd Coldstream Guards crossed the Broenbeek stream, north of Langemarke German Cemetery and advanced 800 yards with the Staden Railway on the right from the second objective taking the final objective of the attack Egypt House east of Veldhoek. George and Alice Bryant received a letter form one of Frank's comrades expressing sympathy and stating how sorrowful the company was at the loss of one so brave and popular. This was the second son George and Alice Bryant had lost in the war, Arthur Bryant had been posted missing in action at Salonika, Greece in April 1917. Frank is remembered on the Tyne Cot Memorial and has no known grave.

Sergeant Harry Lucas Hillier Perrett		*3rd Bn Coldstream Guards*	
Service No.	5279	Age:	35
Place of birth:	Rowde, Wiltshire	Home Country:	England
Date of death:	09/10/1917	Cause of death:	Killed in action
Memorial:	Calne, Rowde		
War Cemetery:	Artillery Wood Cemetery - Grave XI. E. 1.		

Harry Lucas Hillier Perrett

Next of Kin: Rhoda Perrett (Wife) – Caroline Perrett (grandparent)
Address: Marsh Lane, Rowde, Wiltshire

Reservist Harry was well known in Rowde and had been a member of the church choir and was remembered for the solos he performed. He had enlisted with the Coldstream Guards prior to the Great War and was a first-class shot having won many prizes in various competitions while serving in the army. At the outbreak of hostilities Harry was called to the colours and arrived in France on 12 August 1914 and in the summer of 1915 while on leave Harry married Rhoda Brewer at Calne. He then served until January 1917 when he was given one months leave on the expiry of his service contract. At the end of his leave Harry re-joined the army and returned to the front joining the 3rd Battalion Coldstream Guards. On Tuesday 9 October 1917, the 3rd Coldstream Guards crossed the Broenbeek stream, north of Langemarke German Cemetery and advanced 800 yards with the Staden Railway on the right from the second objective taking the final objective of the attack Egypt House east of Veldhoek. Towards the end of October unofficial information was received stating that Harry had been killed in action. In early November, official information was received that Harry had been killed on the day the 3rd Coldstreams had advanced. Rhoda Perrett received a letter from a comrade of Harry's in the Coldstreams who was also a native of Rowde. Enclosed were some photos that had been taken from Harry's body by a stretcher bearer. Harry was initially buried close to where he fell north of Langemarck and later his remains were moved to Artillery Wood Cemetery, he left a widow and a little daughter. On 11 November 1917, a memorial service was held for Harry at the Rowde parish church.

Private Isaac Henry Slade — *1st Bn Coldstream Guards*

Service No. 20447 — Age: 28
Place of birth: Devizes, Wiltshire — Home Country: England
Date of death: 09/10/1917 — Cause of death: Killed in action
Memorial: Not known
War Cemetery: Tyne Cot Memorial - Panel 9 to 10
Next of Kin: Lucy Slade (wife) – Isaac and Mary A. Slade (parents)
Address: 130 Wright's Lane, Old Hill, Staffordshire

Isaac was the eldest son of Isaac and Mary Slade and had worked as a servant at Stoke Lacy, Herefordshire. In the spring of 1915 he married Lucy Tennant at Dudley and it is likely he was either conscripted into the army or enlisted under the Derby Scheme joining the Coldstream Guards and after completing his training he was sent to France and attached to the 1st Battalion. Isaac was killed in action

Tuesday 9 October 1917 when the 1st Battalion crossed the Broenbeek stream and advanced almost unopposed north east to Veldhoek crossroads. He is remembered on the Tyne Cot Memorial and has no known grave.

Gunner Henry James Hughes — *35th Bde Bn Royal Field Artillery*

Service No.	119299	Age:	22
Place of birth:	Devizes, Wiltshire	Home Country:	England
Date of death:	09/10/1917	Cause of death:	Killed in action
Memorial:	Swindon, Wiltshire		
War cemetery:	Birr Cross Roads Cemetery - Grave III. D. 6.		
Next of kin:	James & Alice Hughes		
Address:	123 Morrison Street, Swindon, Wiltshire		

Labourer Henry, known as Harry, was the second son of James and Alice Hughes and lived at Nursteed, Devizes with his uncle prior to the Great War. It is likely he was either conscripted into the army or enlisted under the Derby Scheme and after completing his training he was sent to France joining 12th Battery of the 35th Brigade Royal Artillery. He was killed in action on Tuesday 9 October 1917, most likely by German artillery fire, near Zillebeke, and buried near where he fell. In 1918 his sister inserted the following memoriam in a local paper:

Some time, some day, our eyes shall see
The face we hold in memory,
And Christ will link the broken chain
Closer when we meet again.

In January 1919 Henry's grave was located east of the moated grange, south of Hell Fire Corner and his remains were moved to Birr Cross Roads Cemetery.

Private Calverley Richard Brown — *6th Bn Wiltshire Regiment*

Service No.	18818	Age:	19
Place of birth:	Beamish, Durham	Home Country:	England
Date of death:	09/10/1917	Cause of death:	Killed in action
Memorial:	Not known		
War Cemetery:	Duhallow ADS Cemetery - Grave Fusilier Wood Memorial.		
Next of Kin:	Charles Edward & Alice Brown		
Address:	Birtley, Durham		

Calverley, known as Dick, was the youngest son of Charles Edward and Alice Brown and it is likely he came to Corsham for work. It is also likely he was either conscripted into the army or enlisted under the Derby Scheme joining the Wiltshire Regiment. He was sent to the front to serve 6th Battalion and was killed on Tuesday 9 October 1917, when the 6th Wiltshire were being relieved they were shelled by German artillery at the junction of Oaf Trench and the Embankment near Spoild Bank on the canal south of Ypres. He was originally buried in Fusilier Wood Cemetery but his grave was destroyed by the shelling and he is today remembered on a memorial in Duhallow ADS Cemetery. His brother Charles had been killed at the Somme on 1 July 1916.

Private Joseph Percy Herrington — *1/6th Bn Gloucestershire Regiment*

Service No.	36707	Age:	41
Place of birth:	Stourton, Wiltshire	Home Country:	England
Date of death:	09/10/1917	Cause of death:	Killed in action

Memorial: Mere, Wiltshire
War Cemetery: Tyne Cot Memorial - Panel 72 to 75.
Next of Kin: Alfred & Hester Herrington
Address: Church Street, Mere, Wiltshire

Grocer's assistant Joseph was the fourth son of Alfred and Hester Herrington and it is likely he was either conscripted into the army or enlisted under the Derby Scheme joining the Gloucestershire Regiment. After completing his training, he was sent to the front to serve with the 1/6th Battalion. Joseph was killed on Tuesday 9 October 1917 when the 1/6th Gloucesters advanced and came under considerable opposition as they attacked German position near Vacher Farm south east of Poelcapelle. He is remembered on the Tyne Cot Memorial and has no known grave.

Private Walter Herbert Saunders *1/6th Bn Gloucestershire Regiment*
Service No. 285104 Age: 37
Place of birth: Sherston, Wiltshire Home Country: England
Date of death: 09/10/1917 Cause of death: Died
Memorial: Sherston, Wiltshire
War Cemetery: Tyne Cot Memorial - Panel 72 to 75
Next of Kin: Rose Saunders (wife) – Alfred & Margaret Saunders (parents)
Address: Silver Street, Sherston Magna, Wiltshire

Walter, a gardener, was the eldest son of Alfred and Margaret Saunders and in the spring of 1906 he married Rose Amelia Toghill at Chipping Sodbury. It is likely he was either conscripted into the army or enlisted under the Derby Scheme joining the Gloucestershire Regiment. After completing his training, he was sent to the front to serve with the 1/6th Battalion. Walter was reported missing on Tuesday 9 October 1917 when the 1/6th Gloucesters advanced and came under considerable opposition as they attacked German position near Vacher Farm south east of Poelcapelle. Later official information was received stating Walter was presumed to have died on the day he was reported missing. He left a widow and a young family and is remembered on the Tyne Cot Memorial, having no known grave.

Private Donald Horder *B Coy 26th Bn Royal Fusiliers*
Service No. 19659 Age: 21
Place of birth: Salisbury, Wiltshire Home Country: England
Date of death: 09/10/1917 Cause of death: Died of wounds
Memorial: Salisbury, Wiltshire
War Cemetery: Godewaersvelde British Cemetery - Grave I. H. 13.
Next of Kin: Harry Tom & Edith Maria Horder
Address: 16 Queens Road, Salisbury, Wiltshire

Donald was the youngest son of Harry and Edith Horder and was educated at Bishop Wordsworth's School. He volunteered for service in mid 1915 with the 26th Battalion Royal Fusiliers, the Bankers Battalion. He was sent to France and was wounded at the Somme in July 1916 and evacuated to England where he spent four Months at Summerdown Convalescence Camp, Eastbourne. Following his recovery, he was given home leave at Christmas 1916 and in early 1917 was sent to Dover for a signalling course and passed as a first-class signaler. Following this he was sent to the front and was seriously wounded in the right side and ankle on 20 September 1917 in an attack at Tower Hamlets ridge south of the Menin Road. He was evacuated to a casualty clearing station at Godewaersvelde where he succumbed to his wounds on Tuesday 9 October 1917.

Private Sidney Walter Eyers		*2/7th Bn Lancashire Fusiliers*	
Service No.	282537	Age:	20
Place of birth:	Upavon, Wiltshire	Home Country:	England
Date of death:	09/10/1917	Cause of death:	Killed in action
Memorial:	Marlborough, Wiltshire		
War Cemetery:	Tyne Cot Memorial - Panel 54 to 60 and 163A.		
Next of Kin:	Walter Henry & Annie Elizabeth Eyers		
Address:	4 Mount Pleasant, Marlborough, Wiltshire		

Sidney, a farm labourer was the eldest son of Walter and Annie Eyers and it is likely he was either conscripted into the army or enlisted under the Derby Scheme initially joining the Suffolk Regiment. He was sent to the front and transferred to the 2/7th Battalion Lancashire Fusiliers, who on Tuesday 9 October 1917 attacked German positions at Heine House north of Tyne Cot Cemetery. The objective was reached however the 197 Brigade, which the 2/7th Lancashire Fusiliers were a part, lost touch with the brigades on each flank and was compelled to fall back to the rear of the first objective Hillside Farm to the railway crossing. Sidney was reported missing during the attack and later official information was received by his family stating Sidney was presumed to have been killed on the day he was reported missing. He is remembered on the Tyne Cot Memorial and has no known grave.

Private Bertram John Gardner		*2nd Bn Royal Warwickshire Regiment*	
Service No.	306657	Age:	28
Place of birth:	Salisbury, Wiltshire	Home Country:	England
Date of death:	09/10/1917	Cause of death:	Killed in action
Memorial:	Salisbury, Wiltshire		
War Cemetery:	Tyne Cot Memorial - Panel 23 to 28 and 163A.		
Next of Kin:	George Nathaniel & Naomi Ruth Gardner		
Address:	29 Meadow Cottages Friary, Salisbury, Wiltshire		

Bertram, a labourer, was the eldest son of George and Ruth Gardner and it is likely he was either conscripted into the army or enlisted under the Derby Scheme joining the Royal Warwickshire Regiment. He was sent to the front to serve with the 2nd Battalion and reported missing on Tuesday 9 October 1917, when the 2nd Royal Warwicks attacked German positions at Judge Copse north east of Beselare. They passed through Judge Copse but failed to mop up the remaining Germans. Bertrams parents later received official information stating Bertram was presumed to have been killed on the day he was reported missing. He is remembered on the Tyne Cot Memorial and has no known grave.

Driver Robert Thomas Colton		*888th MT Coy Army Service Corps*	
Service No.	M/282154	Age:	38
Place of birth:	Brinkworth, Wiltshire	Home Country:	England
Date of death:	09/10/1917	Cause of death:	Died of wounds
Memorial:	Not known		
War Cemetery:	Brandhoek New Military Cemetery No 3 - Grave I. K. 24.		
Next of Kin:	Emily R Colton (wife) – Thomas & Eliza Colton (parents)		
Address:	92 Lupus Street, Pimlico, London		

Robert, was the eldest son of Thomas and Eliza Colton and was employed as a chauffeur before the Great War. He enlisted under the Derby Scheme on 30 November 1917 and on 18 January 1916, he married Emily Hawkins at St. Peters Church, Pimlico. He was mobilised on 4 January 1917 and sent to the Army Service Corps, Motor Transport Reserve Depot at Grove Park. He arrived in France on 22 February 1917 joining 888th Mechanical Transport Company of the 66th Division supply column. On 25 September 1917 he was attached to the 2/1st, East Lancs, Field Ambulance. Robert was wounded near Ypres on Tuesday 9 October 1917 and taken to a casualty clearing station at Brandhoek, where he succumbed to his wounds later that day.

Lieutenant Edwin Donald Palethorpe		*2nd (South Mid.)*	*Bde R.F.A. attd R.H.A*
Service No.	N/a	Age:	24
Place of birth:	Barnt Green, Worcestershire	Home Country:	England
Date of death:	09/10/1917	Cause of death:	Killed in action
Memorial:	Not Known		
War Cemetery:	Canada Farm Cemetery - Grave III. D. 11		
Next of Kin:	Edwin & Sarah Annie Palethorpe		
Address:	Hermitage, Stratford on Avon, Warwickshire		

Edwin, known as Donald, was the only son of Edwin and Sarah Palethorpe and was educated at the Lickey Hills School and Marlborough College. He was a keen sportsman and particularly fond of boating, swimming, fishing and boating. On leaving education he became a director of Palethorpe and Cond of Fleet Street, Birmingham. He volunteered for service on 27 September 1915 with the Inns of Court Officer Training Corps and on 8 August 1916 was given a commission with the 2nd South Midland Royal Field Artillery. He arrived in France in November 1916, where he was attached to the Warwickshire Battery of the Royal Horse Artillery and involved in the fighting at the Somme and Arras. Donald was instantly killed by a German shell on Tuesday 9 October 1917, near Langemarck whilst on duty as the forward observation officer. His brigade colonel wrote:

"He was one we could ill spare, and I don't think we could have had a more universally popular and also hard working and efficient officer. Alas! That it should always be the best that are taken."

His Major wrote:

"Your son is a very great loss to the battery. I looked upon him as one of the best officers I had, always active and willing and ready for any kind of work."

Edwin Donald Palethorpe

Corporal Arthur George Tilley — *4th Bn Worcestershire Regiment*

Service No.	31483	Age:	20
Place of birth:	Hook, Wiltshire	Home Country:	England
Date of death:	09/10/1917	Cause of death:	Killed in action
Memorial:	Bishopstone, Wiltshire		
War Cemetery:	Tyne Cot Memorial - Panel 75 to 77.		
Next of Kin:	William & Eliza Tilley		
Address:	Bishopstone, Wiltshire		

Arthur was the third son of William and Eliza Tilley and it is likely he was either conscripted into the army or enlisted under the Derby Scheme joining the Worcestershire Regiment. He was sent to the front to serve with the 4th Battalion who on Tuesday 9 October 1917, attacked along the Ypres – Standen Railway line, north east of Langemarck. Arthur was killed, most likely by a German artillery barrage which was particularly heavy along the Broembeek. He is remembered on the Tyne Cot Memorial and has no known grave.

WEDNESDAY 10 OCTOBER 1917 - TEMPERATURE 9°c - 25% CLOUD COVER WITH SHOWERS - RAINFALL 2.5mm

Private James Henry Dangerfield — *15th Bn Royal Warwickshire Regiment*

Service No.	32848	Age:	23
Place of birth:	Marlborough, Wiltshire	Home Country:	England
Date of death:	10/10/1917	Cause of death:	Killed in action
Memorial:	Not known		
War Cemetery:	Tyne Cot Memorial - Panel 23 to 28 and 163A.		
Next of Kin:	Frederick & Lydia Dangerfield		
Address:	Wootten Rivers, Wiltshire		

James, a groom, was the only son of Frederick and Lydia Dangerfield it is likely he was either conscripted into the army or enlisted under the Derby Scheme initially joining the 10th Hussars. He was transferred to the infantry and sent to France where he was to serve with the 15th Service Battalion Royal Warwickshire Regiment. James was reported missing on Wednesday 10 October 1917, near Stirling Castle, most likely by German artillery. An attack on German positions was cancelled and the 15th Warwicks were forced to withdraw during daylight hours. Later official information was received stating James was presumed to have been killed on the day he was reported missing. He is remembered on the Tyne Cot Memorial and has no known grave.

Private Thomas Edwin Dunning — *2nd Bn West Riding Regiment*

Service No.	26081	Age:	23
Place of birth:	Exeter, Devon	Home Country:	England
Date of death:	10/10/1917	Cause of death:	Killed in action
Memorial:	Salisbury, Wiltshire		
War Cemetery:	Cement House Cemetery - Grave XIII. B. 16.		
Next of Kin:	Richard & Emma Dunning		
Address:	21 Elm Grove, Salisbury, Wiltshire		

Thomas, a motor lorry driver, was the youngest son of Richard and Emma Dunning and volunteered for service on 11 February 1915, with the Army Service Corps. He arrived in France on 25 February 1915 and was attached to the 1/3rd North Midlands Field Ambulance as a driver. He was given one week's home leave in June 1916 and in August he was evacuated to No. 3 General Hospital, suffering from trench foot. On returning to duty he was attached to various ammunition parks again as a driver. On 27 September 1917, he was compulsorily transferred to the West Riding Regiment and sent to the 2nd Battalion. On Wednesday 10 October 1917, the 2nd West Riding Regiment were in the support line at Tragique Farm north west of Poelcapelle and continuously shelled by German artillery. Thomas was reported missing on that day and on 27 February 1918 official information was received stating he was presumed to have been killed on the day he was reported missing. On 14 January 1921 Thomas's remains were located and re interred in Cement House Cemetery.

Private Samuel Job Hill		*8th Bn Somerset Light Infantry*	
Service No.	27863	Age:	19
Place of birth:	Westbury, Wiltshire	Home Country:	England
Date of death:	10/10/1917	Cause of death:	Killed in action
Memorial:	Chapmanslade, Wiltshire		
War Cemetery:	Tyne Cot Memorial - Panel 41 to 42 and 163A.		
Next of Kin:	John Thomas & Ellen Hill		
Address:	Goss Roads, Chapmanslade, Wiltshire		

Nineteen year old Samuel, known as Job, was the fourth son of John and Ellen Hill and was employed as a farm labourer. It is likely he was either conscripted into the army or enlisted under the Derby Scheme joining the Somerset Light Infantry and was sent to the front to serve with the 8th Service Battalion. He was killed on Wednesday 10 October 1917 most likely by German artillery in the British front line near Jute Cotts, west of Gheluvelt. He is remembered on the Tyne Cot Memorial and has no known grave. His brother Frederick, was to die from the effects of his service in 1920.

Private Wilfred John King		*1/8th TF Bn Worcestershire Regiment*	
Service No.	242271	Age:	20
Place of birth:	All Cannings, Wiltshire	Home Country:	England
Date of death:	10/10/1917	Cause of death:	Died of wounds
Memorial:	All Cannings, Wiltshire		
War Cemetery:	Duhallow ADS Cemetery - Grave I. D. 48		
Next of Kin:	Frederick & Elizabeth Lawrence King		
Address:	77 The Street, All Cannings, Wiltshire		

Twenty year old Wilfred was the second son of Frederick and Elizabeth King and had been employed as an attendant at the Wiltshire County Asylum at Devizes prior to joining the army. It is likely he was either conscripted into the army or enlisted under the Derby Scheme joining the Worcestershire Regiment where he was to become an excellent shot winning the cross guns for marksmanship. After completing his training, he was sent to France arriving in September 1916 and sent to the 1/8th Territorial Battalion Worcestershire Regiment. Official records state that Wilfred died of wounds on Wednesday 10 October 1917, however a letter from the captain of his company stated that Wilfred was killed instantly on 9 October 1917 when he was hit by a piece of shell while going forward in attack, just south of Vancouver Corner. The letter continued:

"Your son was a man in whom I had the greatest confidence; he was brave, kind hearted, and in every way a good soldier. It is a great personal blow to me to lose such men as your son, and words will not express my sorrow. He was a great favourite in the company, and his death was a great shock to them."

Wilfred was killed while attacking German positions at the Battle of Poelcapelle and is buried at Duhallow ADS Cemetery.

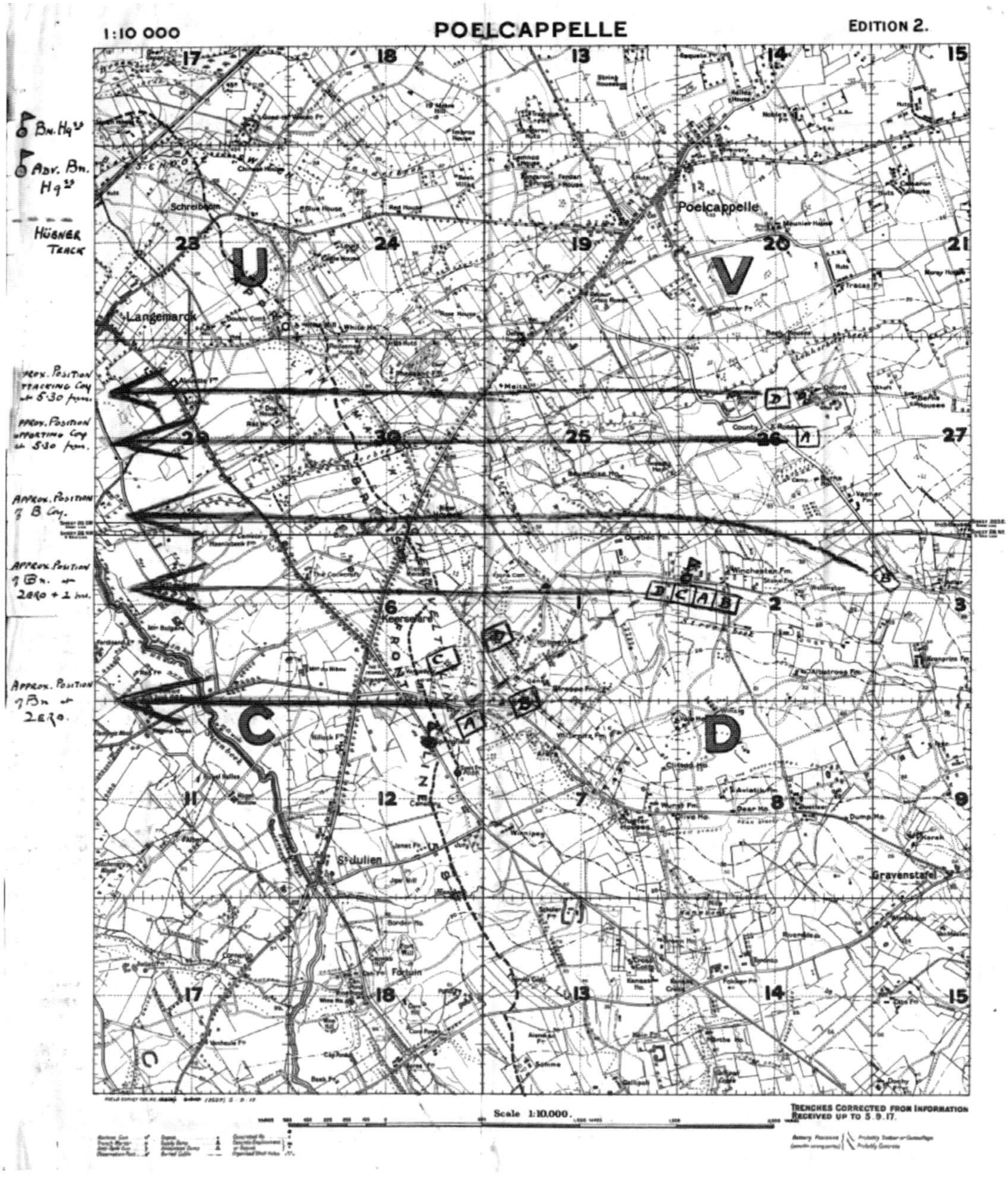

Attack map used by the 1/8th TF Bn Worcestershire Regiment

Private Arthur Thomas Benham		*9th Bn Devonshire Regiment*	
Service No.	291950	Age:	25
Place of birth:	Alresford, Hampshire	Home Country:	England

Date of death:	10/10/1917	Cause of death:	Killed in action
Memorial:	Lacock Church, Lacock Village		
War Cemetery:	Tyne Cot Memorial - Panel 38 to 40.		
Next of Kin:	Mary Tryphena Benham (wife) - Thomas & Mary Benham (parents)		
Address:	Address:High Street Lacock - Spring Garden's Tichborne, Hampshire		

Arthur, a butcher, was the eldest son of Thomas and Mary Benham and married Mary Tryphena Farmer of Lacock at the end of 1914 at Tichborne, Hampshire. It is likely he was either conscripted into the army or enlisted under the Derby Scheme initially joining the Cyclists Corps and was later transferred to the 9th Service Battalion Devonshire Regiment. In October 1917, the 9th Devons were at the Butte.

Private William Charles Reynolds *204th Coy Machine Gun Corps*

Service No.	65879	Age:	31
Place of birth:	Hamptwoth, Wiltshire	Home Country:	England
Date of death:	10/10/1917	Cause of death:	Killed in action
Memorial:	Redlynch, Wiltshire		
War Cemetery:	Tyne Cot Memorial - Panel 154 to 159 and 163A.		
Next of Kin:	Elsie J. Reynolds (wife) – Frank & Fanny Reynolds (parents)		
Address:	1 Natanbury Cottages, Downton, Wiltshire		

William was the eldest son of Frank and Fanny Reynolds and in the summer of 1915 married Elsie J Hatton. It is likely he was either conscripted into the army or enlisted under the Derby Scheme initially joining the Bedfordshire Regiment, before being transferred to the Machine Gun Corps. He was sent to the front to serve with the 204th Company who on Wednesday 10 October 1917 were North of Zonnebeke covering the British attacks. It is likely William was killed by German artillery. He is remembered on the Tyne Cot Memorial and has no known grave. He left a widow and a young son.

Corporal George Edwards MM *6th Bn Wiltshire Regiment*

Service No.	12120	Age:	29
Place of birth:	Damerham, Wiltshire	Home Country:	England
Date of death:	10/10/1917	Cause of death:	Killed in action
Memorial:	Not known		
War Cemetery:	Oxford Road Cemetery - Grave II. C. 10.		
Theatre of War:	Belgium		
Next of Kin:	George & Sarah Ann Edwards		
Address:,	Rockbourne, Hampshire		

George, a farm labourer, was the second son of George and Sarah Ann Edwards and volunteered for service joining the 6th Service Battalion Wiltshire Regiment. He arrived in France on 19 July 1915 and at some stage of his service won the Military Medal for gallantry. He was killed on Wednesday 10 October 1917, most likely by German shelling, east of Spoil Bank on the canal south of Ypres, when the 6th Wiltshires were in a series of posts in the front line.

THURSDAY 11 OCTOBER 1917 - TEMPERATURE 10°c - 50% CLOUD COVER WITH SHOWERS - RAINFALL 4.9mm

Left: *Frederick Edward Croker*

Right: Francis Edgar Payne

Private Frederick Edward Croker — *6th Bn Wiltshire Regiment*

Service No.	203261	Age:	20
Place of birth:	Pewsham, Wiltshire	Home Country:	England
Date of death:	11/10/1917	Cause of death:	Died of wounds
Memorial:	Lacock Church, Lacock Village		
War Cemetery:	Tyne Cot Memorial - Panel 119 to 120		
Next of Kin:	Frederick & Julia Croker		
Address:	Bridge House, Lacock, Wiltshire		

Under age soldier Frederick was the eldest son of Frederick and Julia Croker and volunteered for service with the Wiltshire Yeomanry at the age of 17. He was transferred to the 6th Service Battalion Wiltshire Regiment and arrived in France on 4 December 1915. Frederick had spent 20 months on the continent before receiving his first leave, of ten days, in August 1917. On 10 October 1917 the 6th Wiltshire were east of a position called the Spoil Bank on the canal south east of Ypres. Frederick was wounded by a German shell and died soon after on Thursday 11 October 1917 as the Wiltshires were being relieved and returning to a rest camp. It was the day after his twentieth birthday and he is today remembered on the Tyne Cot Memorial and has no known grave.

Lance Corporal Francis Edgar Payne — *6th Bn Wiltshire Regiment*

Service No.	203134	Age:	23
Place of birth:	Chilmark, Wiltshire	Home Country:	England
Date of death:	11/10/1917	Cause of death:	Killed in action
Memorial:	Melksham, Wiltshire		
War Cemetery:	Tyne Cot Memorial - Grave Panel 119 to 120.		
Next of Kin:	David James & Sarah Jane Payne		
Address:	Bank Street, Melksham, Wiltshire		

Francis was the second son of David and Sarah Payne and was employed at the Avon Rubber Works at Melksham. He volunteered for service with the Royal Wiltshire Yeomanry in 1911 and was transferred to the 6th Service Battalion Wiltshire Regiment and sent to the front in early 1916. At the end of 5-year engagement he came home on leave in July 1917 and rejoined the army and returned to the front on 10 August 1917. Francis was killed by a German shell on Thursday 11 October 1917, east of spoil Bank, on the canal south east of Ypres, as the Wiltshires were being relieved and returning to a rest camp. He is remembered on the Tyne Cot Memorial and has no known grave. He left Miss Giles, his sorrowing fiancée.

Private Reginald Witt		*6th Bn Wiltshire Regiment*	
Service No.	203389	Age:	24
Place of birth:	Salisbury, Wiltshire	Home Country:	England
Date of death:	11/10/1917	Cause of death:	Died of wounds
Memorial:	Salisbury, Wilktshire		
War Cemetery:	Duhallow ADS Cemetery - Fusilier Wood Memorial.		
Next of Kin:	Charles & Julia Witt		
Address:	52 St Ann Street, Salisbury, Wiltshire		

Labourer, Reginald, was the third son of Charles and Julia Witt and he volunteered for service with the Royal Wiltshire Yeomanry in 1911 and was transferred to the 6th Service Battalion Wiltshire Regiment and sent to the front in early 1916. Reginald was wounded by a German shell on Thursday 11 October 1917, near spoil Bank, on the canal south east of Ypres, as the Wiltshires were being relieved and returning to a rest camp. He succumbed to his wounds on the same day and was originally buried in Fusilier Wood Cemetery, but his grave was lost during further fighting. He is today remembered on Fusilier Wood Memorial at Duhallow ADS Cemetery.

Private Albert Edwin Few		*7th Bn Royal West Surrey Regiment*	
Service No.	G/24663	Age:	25
Place of birth:	Poulshot, Wiltshire	Home Country:	England
Date of death:	11/10/1917	Cause of death:	Killed in action
Memorial:	Not known		
War Cemetery:	New Irish Farm Cemetery - Grave XXI. B. 6.		
Next of Kin:	Albert & Harriet Few		
Address:	35 Greenclose Road, Ilfracombe, Devon		

Albert, known as Edwin, was a grocer and provision merchant and the eldest son of Albert and Harriet Few. It is likely he was either conscripted into the army or enlisted under the Derby Scheme initially joining the Royal Fusiliers but was later transferred to the 7th Battalion Royal West Surrey Regiment. Edwin was reported missing on Thursday 11 October 1917 when the 7th Royal West Surrey's attacked German positions south of Poelcapelle. Albert was originally buried where he fell and in 1920 his remains were located on the bank of the Steenbeek Stream, south of Mon. Bulgare, west of Vancouver Crossroads. He was identified by means of an identity disc and his remains were moved to New Irish Farm Cemetery.

Private Albert Charles Vincent		*27th Coy Bn Machine Gun Corps*	
Service No.	108084	Age:	30
Place of birth:	Wilton, Wiltshire	Home Country:	England
Date of death:	11/10/1917	Cause of death:	Killed in action
Memorial:	Wilton, Wiltshire		
War Cemetery:	Tyne Cot Memorial - Panel 154 to 159 and 163A		
Next of Kin:	Daisy Nellie Selina Vincent (wife) – Charles Henry & Elizabeth Vincent (parents)		
Address:	21 Highcliffe Road, Winchester, Hampshire – Wilton, Wiltshire		

Albert, a clerk, was the youngest son of Charles and Elizabeth Vincent and married Daisy Nellie Selina Collins on 9 June 1913 at Bemerton, Wiltshire. It is likely he was either conscripted into the army or enlisted under the Derby Scheme initially joining the Royal Warwickshire Regiment. He was transferred to the Machine Gun Corps and sent to the front to serve with the 27th Company. Albert was killed on Thursday 11 October 1917, most likely by German artillery, near Winchester House north of Gravenstafel. He is remembered on the Tyne Cot Memorial and has no known grave.

Left: John Wheeler

Right: Albert Milton

Private John Wheeler		*8th Bn Somerset Light Infantry*	
Service No.	17771	Age:	19
Place of birth:	Witham Friary, Somerset	Home Country:	England
Date of death:	11/10/1917	Cause of death:	Died of wounds
Memorial:	Witham Friary, Somerset		
War Cemetery:	Outterstreene Communal Cemetery Extention Bailleul - Grave I. D. 33.		
Next of Kin:	Henry W & Annie Wheeler		
Address:	Witham Friary, Somerset		

Under age soldier John, known as Jack, was the third son of Henry and Annie wheeler and was employed as a farm labourer. He lived in Trowbridge prior to joining the army and volunteered for service at seventeen years of age with the Somerset Light Infantry and after completing his training he arrived in France on 4 October 1915. He was wounded most likely by German artillery in the British front line near Jute Cotts, west of Gheluvelt and succumbed to his wounds on Thursday 11 October 1917 at a casualty clearing station at Outterstreene. His elder brother Henry was to die from the effects of the conflict in Fovant Military Hospital in 1919.

Bombardier Albert Milton		*64th Bde Bn Royal Field Artillery*	
Service No.	151944	Age:	31
Place of birth:	Ecclesfield, Yorkshire	Home Country:	England
Date of death:	11/10/1917	Cause of death:	Killed in action
Memorial:	Not known		
War Cemetery:	Tyne Cot Memorial - Panel 4 to 6 and 162.		
Next of Kin:	Agnes Milton (wife) – John & Emily Milton (parents		
Address:	6 Stansfield Street, Roker, Sunderland, Durham		

Albert was the sixth son of John and Emily Milton and was a professional footballer playing for South Kirby Bansley in 1907, then Sunderland Football Club from 1908 to 1913. At the beginning of 1912 he married Agnes Gibson at St. Marks, Lincoln and in that season 1912 to 1913 he struggled with injury but prevailed helping Sunderland to win the title. In 1914 to 1915 he played left back, for Swindon Town Football Club making 27 league and 2 FA appearances. It is likely he was either conscripted into the army or enlisted under the Derby Scheme joining the Royal Field Artillery. Before he left for the front to serve with the 64th Bde he told a friend he did not expect to come back. Albert was killed near Ypres on Thursday 11 October 1917. He is remembered on the Tyne Cot Memorial and has no known grave. He left a widow and a young daughter.

2nd Lieutenant George Frederick Austin		*6th Bn Royal Berkshire Regiment*	
Service No.	N/a	Age:	31
Place of birth:	Eaton Hastings, Berkshire	Home Country:	England
Date of death:	11/10/1917	Cause of death:	Killed in action
Memorial:	Not known		
War Cemetery:	Bard Cottage Cemetery - Grave V. A. 41.		
Next of Kin:	George & Mary Austin		
Address:	Wroughton Porchester Road, Newbury, Berkshire		

George, known as Dick, was the only son of George and Mary Austin and the grandson of Mathew Austin of Broad Hinton. At the outbreak of hostilities, he was sent to France as a signaller with the Royal Engineers. He travelled to France on the same ship as Field Marshall French arriving on 9 August 1914. He took part in the retreat from Mons and served continuously in France until July 1916 when he was evacuated to hospital in England, with an injury to his eyes. He returned to France in November 1916 with a draft and in January 1917 he was sent back to England to take a commission. He joined the officer's cadet battalion at Crookham near Aldershot and passed his examination and was given a commission with the Royal Berkshires on 30 May 1917. He returned to France on 14 July 1917 being sent to the 6th Battalion. Dick was killed on Thursday 11 October 1917, most likely by a German shell, leading a platoon to a forming up position near Cane Trench, north of Wieltje. A fellow officer wrote:

"He had only recently taken over the duties of signalling officer, and showed very great promise in his work. He was greatly respected and beloved by all his fellow officers and men, and is now greatly missed by all."

Garter Point 25 October 1917

12
The First Battle of Passchendaele

Map page 425

FRIDAY 12 OCTOBER 1917 - TEMPERATURE 13°c - RAIN- RAINFALL 7.9mm

Trooper William Walter Baxter		*Household Battallion*	
Service No.	2427	Age:	19
Place of birth:	Ogbourne, Wiltshire	Home Country:	England
Date of death:	12/10/1917	Cause of death:	Killed in action
Memorial:	Not known		
War Cemetery:	Cement House Cemetery - Grave IX. B. 29.		
Next of Kin:	Henry Thomas & Jane Elizabeth Baxter		
Address:	Pusey, Berkshire		

Nineteen year old William, a farm labourer, was the youngest son of Henry and Jane Baxter and it is likely he was either conscripted into the army or enlisted under the Derby Scheme joining the Household Battalion. On Friday 12 October 1917, the Household Battalion attacked German positions north of Poelcapelle. William was killed during the attack and his body was buried where he fell. In 1918 William's parents inserted the following memoriam in a local paper:

Days pf sadness still come o'er us,
Tears in silence often flow
Memory keeps him ever near us,
Though he died a year ago.

In August 1919, William's remains were located west of Mousse Farm, just south of the Bixchoote - Langemarck Road and identified by means of an identity disc, before being moved to Cement House Cemetery.

Private William James Humphries		*63rd Coy Machine Gun Corps*	
Service No.	102771	Age:	19
Place of birth:	Reading, Berkshire	Home Country:	England
Date of death:	12/10/1917	Cause of death:	Killed in action
Memorial:	Marlborough, Wiltshire		
War Cemetery:	Larch Wood Railway Cutting Cemetery - Grave V. A. 18.		
Next of Kin:	Walter & Amy Louisa Humphries		
Address:	Fosbury, Wiltshire		

Nineteen year old William was the eldest son of Walter and Amy Louisa Humphries and it is likely he was either conscripted into the army or enlisted under the Derby Scheme joining the Machine Gun

Corps. He was sent to France to serve with the 63rd Company who were attached to the Royal Naval Division. William was killed south east of Ypres on Friday 12 October 1917. The war diary states it was difficult to keep the Vickers guns clean because of the rain and mud.

Private William Frank Grant		*6th Bn Royal Berkshire Regiment*	
Service No.	23652	Age:	27
Place of birth:	Chitterne, Wiltshire	Home Country:	England
Date of death:	12/10/1917	Cause of death:	Died of wounds
Memorial:	Shrewton, Wiltshire		
War Cemetery:	Tyne Cot Memorial - Panel 105 to 106 and 162.		
Next of Kin:	Joseph & Elizabeth Jane Grant		
Address:	Shrewton, Wiltshire		

William, a farm labourer, was the eldest son of Joseph and Elizabeth Grant and it is likely he was either conscripted into the army or enlisted under the Derby Scheme initially joining the Somerset Light Infantry. He was sent to the front and transferred to the 6th Battalion Royal Berkshire Regiment. He was reported wounded and missing on Friday 12 October 1917, most likely near Beek Houses south of Poelcapelle. Later his family received official information stating he was presumed to have died of wounds on the same day he was reported missing. He is remembered on the Tyne Cot Memorial and has no known grave.

Sergeant Edward Charles Drew		*6th Bn Royal Berkshire Regiment*	
Service No.	16081	Age:	23
Place of birth:	Kintbury, Berkshire	Home Country:	England
Date of death:	12/10/1917	Cause of death:	Killed in action
Memorial:	Little Bedwyn, Wiltshire		
War Cemetery:	Poelcapelle British Cemetery - Grave XXXVII. D. 4		
Next of Kin:	Edwin & Annie Drew		
Address:	Little Bedwyn, Wiltshire		

Edward known as Charles and a horseman on a farm was the eldest son of Edwin Drew. He volunteered for service joining the 6th Service Battalion Royal Berkshire Regiment, arriving in France on 25 July 1915. He was killed on Friday 12 October 1917, most likely near Beek Houses south of Poelcapelle. Edward was originally buried east of Poelcapelle and after the war his remains located east of Poelcapelle Brewery, south of the Westroosebeke Road. His remains were identified by means of an identity disc and then moved to Poelcapelle British Cemetery.

Private James Barnes		*6th Bn Royal Berkshire Regiment*	
Service No.	202184	Age:	29
Place of birth:	Highworth, Wiltshire	Home Country:	England
Date of death:	12/10/1917	Cause of death:	Killed in action
Memorial:	Shellingford, Berkshire		
War Cemetery:	Tyne Cot Memorial - Panel 105 to 106 and 162		
Next of Kin:	George & Emily Barnes		
Address:	Shellingford, Berkshire		

James, a horseman on a farm was the fourth son of George and Emily Barnes and it is likely he was either conscripted into the army or enlisted under the Derby Scheme joining the Royal Berkshire Regiment. He was sent to the front to serve with the 6th Battalion and was reported missing on Friday 12 October 1917, most likely near Beek Houses south of Poelcapelle. Later his family received official

Left: 2nd Lieutenant Charles Hatt Todd

Right: Charles Robert Windeyer

information stating he was presumed to have been killed on the same day he was reported missing. He is remembered on the Tyne Cot Memorial and has no known grave.

2nd Lieutenant Charles Hatt Todd		*6th Bn Royal Berkshire Regiment*	
Service No.	N/a	Age:	33
Place of birth:	Englefield, Berkshire	Home Country:	England
Date of death:	12/10/1917	Cause of death:	Killed in action
Memorial:	Wanborough, Wiltshire		
War Cemetery:	Tyne Cot Memorial - Panel 105 to 106 and 162		
Next of Kin:	Elsie Anne Todd (wife) – Richard & Mary Hall Todd (parents)		
Address:	Lotmead, Wanborough, Wiltshire – Bettsworth Reading		

Charles was youngest son of Richard and Mary Todd and was employed as a clerk with Lloyds Bank at Swindon before being transferred to Folkestone. It is likely he was either conscripted into the army or enlisted under the Derby Scheme initially joining the 26th Battalion Royal Fusiliers, the Bankers Battalion. Before he was called up he married Elsie Anne Wiseman at the beginning of 1916 at Swindon. He was given a commission with the Royal Berkshire Regiment on 26 June 1917 and was sent to the front to serve with the 6th Service Battalion, joining them on 20 August 1917. Charles was killed on Friday 12 October 1917, while leading his men, most likely near Beek Houses south of Poelcapelle. Captain N. B. Hudson wrote the following to Charles's widow:

"It is my painful duty to have to write to tell you of the death in action of your husband Second Lieutenant Todd, who was in my company. He was doing perfectly magnificently, running about under heavy fire, looking after his men, leading them and encouraging them. I know the blow to you will be unspeakable, but it may be of some comfort to know that he was killed at once and suffered no pain, and also that he died doing his job magnificently. His men loved him, and are always telling of his brave behaviour. It will be hard to fill the gap that his loss has made. It is doubtful whether his body will be able to be brought back, as it is in a very exposed place, but his men have collected some personal belongings of his and they will be sent as soon as possible. Please accept the deepest sympathy of myself and all."

Charles is remembered on the Tyne Cot Memorial and has no known grave.

2nd Lieutenant Charles Robert Windeyer		*49th Bn Australian Infantry A I F*	
Service No.	N/a	Age:	21
Place of birth:	Sydney, New South Wales	Home Country:	Australia

Date of death: 12/10/1917 Cause of death: killed in action
Memorial: Not Known
War Cemetery: Ypres Menin Gate - Panel 7 - 17 - 23 - 25 - 27 - 29 - 31.
Next of Kin: Richard & Mabel Fuller Windeyer
Address: The Peel, Elizabeth Bay Road, Sydney, New South Wales

School teacher, Charles, known as Charlie, was the eldest son of Richard and Mabel Windeyer and was the brother of Mrs Simpson of Thornbury, Westlecott Road, Swindon. He volunteered for service with the 6th Australian Light Horse on 18 September 1914 at the age of 18 and 9/12 years. He arrived on the Gallipoli peninsular on 13 July 1915 and was evacuated suffering from dysentery on 31 July 1915. He was evacuated to Egypt where his condition was found to be worse and he was sent back to Australia suffering from colitis. Following his recovery, he was sent back to Egypt arriving in June 1916, where he was transferred to the 49th Battalion Australian Infantry arriving on 20 November 1916. In April 1917, he was sent to England to undertake an officers course and on completion was given a commission on 8 August 1917. He returned to the 49th Battalion on 23 August 1917. Charlie was reported missing on Friday 12 October 1917 not far from Tyne Cot Cemetery. His mother came to London to make enquiries about her missing son writing the following to the Red Cross:

"I heard through a corporal in my boy Charlie's Battalion that they went into the line on the 9th October and that Charlie was ordered with his platoon to outflank a German point. This they did on the evening of the 9th and held the position well on the 10th and 11th, and on the morning of the 12th a shell hit Charlie on the head killing him instantly and wounding his runner. He was buried behind his position and a small wooden cross put up and the position of the grave is known by the Military Authorities."

Corporal M. Nolan made the following statement:

"I buried him myself in the front line before Passchendaele Village at night time. There was no chance to mark his grave. Private J. Hawke of the same Platoon, 5 of B Company, helped me. Lieutenant W. was my platoon officer. We were sitting down talking to each other when a piece of shell caught him in the head and killed him outright."

B Company were in the front line on the southeast side of Broodseinde crossroads and this is the likely position where Charlie was buried. The location of his grave was lost in subsequent fighting and he is today remembered on the Ypres Menin Gate Memorial.

Sergeant Arthur James *49th Bn Australian Infantry AIF*
Service No. 1637A Age: 24
Place of birth: Australia Home Country: Australia
Date of death: 12/10/1917 Cause of death: Killed in action
Memorial: Not known
War Cemetery: Ypres Menin Gate - Panel 7 - 17 - 23 - 25 - 27 - 29 - 31.
Next of Kin: Fred James
Address: Jootho, South Gripperland, Victoria

Arthur, a bushman, was the son of Fred James and was the nephew of Mrs J. James of Corsham, Wiltshire. He volunteered for service on 10 February 1915 with the Australian Infantry arriving on the Gallipoli peninsular on 6 May 1915, being attached to the 9th Battalion. He was evacuated from the peninsular suffering from sickness on 27 August 1915 and sent to 25th Casualty Clearing Station on Murdos. Following his recovery, he returned to Gallipoli on 28 September 1915 and served there until the evacuation of the peninsular. He was then sent to Egypt and in February 1916 he was transferred to the 49th Battalion and arrived in France on 12 June 1916. He was wounded in September 1916 and evacuated to England suffering from gun shot wounds to the hand and shoulder. Following his recovery, he remained in England and was transferred to the 69th Battalion at Weymouth then Hurdcott Camp. He returned to France on 21 August 1917 and was transferred back to the 49th Battalion rejoining them in early September 1917. Arthur was reported missing on Friday 12 October 1917 there were two differing reports of his death. The first was from Corporal Quigley who stated:

"Sergeant Arthur James was killed in a dug-out with Corporal Siddell and Private Austin. Sergeant Waltisbuhl was unhurt, all were from D Company, 49th Battalion. The dug-out was near and to the right of (going toward Broodseinde) a big gasometer between Zonnebeke and Broodseinde. They were buried where they fell and a cross erected but nothing was on it when I saw it. I saw them lying dead and saw them buried by pioneers."

Private Bradbury of the 49th Battalion states:

"I saw him killed by a shell whilst in a shell hole in front of Passchendaele ridge. He was buried close by, by a party from the company."

Sergeant Waltisbuhl wrote in March 1918 stating:

"Re Sergeant Arthur James, whom you have posted as killed on 12.10.17. I beg to inform you that this report is perfectly correct. You may tell your enquirers that he was killed in the same dug-out as myself and spoke to me a second before his death. My other two mates both were killed by the same shell at 4.15am. All were killed instantaneously so none of them suffered any pain at all. The other two were Corporal Siddell and Private W. Hayes. All three were buried in the field and their positions were marked with rifles stuck butt up into the ground. Sergeant James was a fair faced man of about 24 or 25 years of age, with reddish brown hair."

Arthur's personal property was returned to his brother and consisted of a wallet, post card, photos and 10 coins. He is today remembered on the Ypres Menin Gate and has no known grave.

Private Allan Frederick Shepherd		*55th Field Amb Royal Army Medical Corps*	
Service No.	38295	Age:	24
Place of birth:	Bermondsey, Middlesex	Home Country:	England
Date of death:	12/10/1917	Cause of death:	Killed in action
Memorial:	Savernake, Wiltshire		
War Cemetery:	Cement House Cemetery - Grave IX. D. 20.		
Next of Kin:	Daniel John & Elizabeth Ann Shepherd		
Address:	5, Bedwyn Common, Wiltshire		

Allan was the only son of Daniel and Elizabeth Shepherd and volunteered for service joining the Royal Army Medical Corps. He was attached to the 55th Field Ambulance and arrived in France on 27 July 1915. In October 1917 Allan was given a short leave returning to the front on 4 October 1917. He was killed on Friday 12 October 1917, by a German shell just west of the centre of Poelcapelle. His officer wrote the following to his mother:

"He was killed instantaneously by a shell when engaged in bringing in the wounded and in the most dangerous and difficult circumstances."

After the war, his remains were located just south of Poecapelle Church and identified by means of an identity disc, before being moved to Cement House Cemetery.

Private Leslie Penn — *7th Bn Royal West Kent Regiment*

Service No.	266157	Age:	28
Place of birth:	Ampfield, Hampshire	Home Country:	England
Date of death:	12/10/1917	Cause of death:	Killed in action
Memorial:	Kilmington, Wiltshire		
War Cemetery:	Tyne Cot Memorial - Panel 106 to 108.		
Next of Kin:	Walter & Cecilia Decima Penn		
Address:	School House, Kilmington, Wiltshire		

Leslie, a pianist, was the eldest son of Walter and Cecilia Penn and volunteered for service with the Kent Cyclist Battalion on 7 August 1915 and was sent to the 2/1st Battalion. He served in England for 1915 and 1916 and it would appear he had no desire to serve overseas. It would also appear he had bad teeth because he was marked in category D condition because of them. He refused dental treatment from the army and this led to the army changing his fitness category to A and on 20 January 1917, he was told to report sick and the medical officer upgraded him to A on the grounds of the refusal of dental treatment had made him ineligible for a lower grading. He was transferred to the Royal West Kent Regiment and arrived in France on 27 July 1917, joining the 7th Battalion on 24 August 1917. On Friday 12 October 1917, the 7th Royal West Kents attacked German positions at Meunier House south of Poelcapelle. They lost the attack as the creeping barrage and the German machine gun fire was too strong. They were forced to to establish a series of posts just beyond the original line. The war diary states:

"The heavy loss which occurred among the officers and N.C.O.'s were due to the efforts to gain ground by fire and movement after the barrage had thus been lost. The mud and water were so bad that to move rapidly from shell hole to shell hole was out of the question. Rifles also got covered with mud and even after they had been cleaned it was difficult to keep them in action for more than a few rounds without cleaning the breach again, since the men's hands were plastered with mud and each time a fresh clip was put in some mud inevitably went in with it."

Leslie was reported missing on Friday 12 October 1917, in August 1918 his parents received official information that Leslie was presumed to have been killed on the day he was reported missing. He is remembered on the Tyne Cot Memorial and has no known grave.

Private Frederick Charles Smith — *7th Bn Royal West Kent Regiment*

Service No.	241254	Age:	24
Place of birth:	Calne, Wiltshire	Home Country:	England
Date of death:	12/10/1917	Cause of death:	Killed in action
Memorial:	Calne, Wiltshire		
War Cemetery:	Cement House Cemetery - Grave IX. B. 23.		
Next of Kin:	James & Annie Smith		
Address:	35 London Road, Calne, Wiltshire		

Frederick, known as Fred was the second son of James & Annie Smith and it is likely he was either conscripted into the army or enlisted under the Derby Scheme initially joining the Somerset Light Infantry. He was sent the front and transferred to the Royal West Kent Regiment. He was reported missing on Friday 12 October 1917 when the 7th Royal West Kents attacked German positions at Meunier House south of Poelcapelle. They lost the attack as the creeping barrage and the German machine gun fire was too strong. They were forced to to establish a series of posts just beyond the original line, in the same action as Leslie Penn. Fred was buried near where he fell and in August 1919 his remains were located near the centre of Poelcapelle and identified by means of his regimental badge and identity disc. His parents were informed that his body had been found and his remains were moved to Cement House Cemetery.

Bombardier Ernest Prevett Godden *40th Bde Royal Field Artillery*

Service No.	68976	Age:	20
Place of birth:	Trowbridge, Wiltshire	Home Country:	England
Date of death:	12/10/1917	Cause of death:	Killed in action
Memorial:	Not known		
War Cemetery:	Tyne Cot Memorial - Panel 4 to 6 and 162.		
Next of Kin:	Lilian Jane Vyle		
Address:	106 Crewe Street, Derby, Derbyshire		

Under age regular soldier Ernest was the youngest son of Lilian Jane Vyle and enlisted with the Royal Field Artillery before the Great War. He arrived in France on 19 August 1914 at 17 years of age with the 40th Brigade. Prior to joining the army, he was a butcher's errand boy. He was killed in action during near Ypres on Friday 12 October 1917. He is remembered on the Tyne Cot Memorial and has no known grave.

Private Wilfred Edwin Moore *7th Bn Lincolnshire Regiment*

Service No.	43343	Age:	30
Place of birth:	Steeple Langford, Wiltshire	Home Country:	England
Date of death:	12/10/1917	Cause of death:	Killed in action
Memorial:	Steeple Langford, Wiltshire		
War Cemetery:	Tyne Cot Memorial - Panel 35 to 37 and 162 to 162A		
Next of Kin:	Charles & Jane Moore		
Address:	Charterhouse Hinton, Somerset		

Wilfred, a miller's carter, was the eldest son of Charles and Jane Moore and it is likely he was either conscripted into the army or enlisted under the Derby Scheme initially joining the Army Service Corps, before being transferred to the North Staffordshire Regiment. He was sent to the front and transferred again to the 7th Battalion Lincolnshire Regiment. Wilfred was killed on Friday 12 October 1917 while taking part in an attack on German positions near the railway north of Poelcapelle. His grave was lost in subsequent fighting and he is today remembered on the Tyne Cot Memorial.

Private Frederick James Austin *1st Bn Royal Warwickshire Regiment*

Service No.	25409	Age:	36
Place of birth:	Bradford on Avon, Wiltshire	Home Country:	England
Date of death:	12/10/1917	Cause of death:	Killed in action
Memorial:	Bradford on Avon Wesleyan Chapel – Ilminster, Somerset		
War Cemetery:	Cement House Cemetery - Grave X. E. 8.		
Next of Kin:	Gladys Emily Austin (wife) - Thomas & Mary Jane Austin (parents)		
Address:	West Street Ilminster - 20 Trowbridge Road, Bradford on Avon, Wiltshire		

Frederick, a hairdresser, was the only son of Thomas and Mary Jane Austin and in the spring of 1906 he married Gladys Emily Taylor at Chard. It is likely he was either conscripted into the army or enlisted under the Derby Scheme joining the Royal Warwickshire Regiment and was sent to the front to serve with the 1st Battalion. On Friday 12 October 1917, the 1st Royal Warwicks attacked German positions of Landing Farm, Water House and Besage Farm, north of Poelcapelle. The attackers were forced to halt 50 yards to the west of Memling because of enfilade German machine gun fire from Requete Farm and the swampy condition of the ground. Frederick was reported missing during the attack. After the war Frederick's remains were found on the battlefield, just south of the Watervliet Beek stream, north of Poelcaplle and he was identified by means of an identity disc. His remains were moved to Cement House Cemetery. He left a widow and young daughter.

Iain Rose Paterson

2nd Lieutenant Iain Rose Paterson		*3rd Bn attd 5th Bn Cameron Highlanders*	
Service No.	N/a	Age:	19
Place of birth:	Cardiff, Glamorgan	Home Country:	Wales
Date of death:	12/10/1917	Cause of death:	Killed in action
Memorial:	Marlborough College, Wiltshire		
War Cemetery:	Tyne Cot Memorial - Panel 136 to 138		
Next of Kin:	Donald Rose & Constance Mary Paterson		
Address:	15 St Andrews Crescent, Cardiff, Glamorganshire		

Iain was the eldest son of Donald and Constance Paterson and was educated at Marlborough College, where he was a member of the rugby XV. On leaving Marlborough he went to Kings College, Cambridge, but left almost immediately, joining the Honourable Artillery Company, before he was given a commission with the 3rd Battalion Cameron Highlanders. He was sent to the front and attached to the 5th Battalion who on Friday 12 October 1917 were in support for an attack by the 26th Brigade south of Poelcapelle. As the attack advanced it was noticed the attacking battalions were receiving enfilade German machine gun fire (from the flank or side) from the German pill box in a small copse. The Cameron Highlanders made a number of unsuccessful attempts to silence the machine gun and on the final assault as the attackers advanced the German defenders put out a white flag. The attacking party got closer and the Germans threw out a few bombs (hand grenades) but did no harm. The Germans then came out of the pill box led by an officer who shot the first of the British attackers, the German officer in turn was shot by one of the British attackers. The whole German garrison of 25 men, with the exception of 4 men who were taken prisoner, were killed. The pill box was searched and it was found the Germans had run out of ammunition. During the indiscriminate killing of the prisoners an officer of the Kings Own Scottish Borderers unfortunately was killed. Iain was killed during the action on Friday 12 October 1917. He is remembered on the Tyne Cot Memorial and has no known grave.

Saturday 13 October 1917 - Temperature 11°c - 50% Cloud Cover - Rainfall 10.7mm

Richard Guy Titley MC

Captain Richard Guy Titley MC		*1/6th Bn Gloucestershire Regiment*	
Service No.	N/a	Age:	24
Place of birth:	Clifton, Gloucestershire	Home Country:	England
Date of death:	13/10/1917	Cause of death:	Died of wounds
Memorial:	Marlborough College, Wiltshire		
War Cemetery:	Dozinghem Military Cemetery - Grave XII. F. 17		
Next of Kin:	William Alfred & Isabel Titley		
Address:	Wynton Lodge, Durdham Down, Bristol, Gloucestershire		

Richard was the eldest son of William Alfred and Isabel Titley and was educated at Marlborough College. At the outbreak of hostilities, he joined the Bristol University Officer Training Corps and was later given a commission with the 1/6th Battalion Gloucestershire Regiment arriving in France on 7 March 1916. In September 1916 at the Somme, Richard was awarded the Military Cross the citation states:

For conspicuous gallantry during operations. He captured and consolidated an enemy barricade, and when on the next night the enemy attacked and killed or wounded all the garrison, he with one wounded sergeant held on to the barricade until reinforcements arrived.

On 9 October 1917 1/6th Gloucesters attacked German positions south east of Poelcappelle and C Company, advanced through Vacher Farm. The war diary states:

It is thought that they reached a point about 200 yards north east of Burns House - Vacher Road. Estimated losses of C Company in the attack - 2 Officers and 55 other ranks.

Richard was missing for 3 days, he was wounded and was found lying on the battlefield by members of the 9th Division. He was evacuated to a casualty clearing station at Dozinghem where he succumbed to his wounds on Saturday 13 October 1917.

Private Ernest Tanswell		*1/6th Bn Royal Warwickshire Regiment*	
Service No.	30509	Age:	36
Place of birth:	Rockbourne, Hampshire	Home Country:	England
Date of death:	13/10/1917	Cause of death:	Died of wounds
Memorial:	East Knoyle, Wiltshire		
War Cemetery:	Boulogne Eastern Cemetery - Grave VIII. I. 52.		

Next of Kin:	Sarah Jane Tanswell (wife) – John & Emily Tanswell (parents)
Address:	17 Upton Road, East Knoyle, Wiltshire

Ernest was the eldest son of John and Emily Tanswell and in the summer of 1902 he married Sarah Jane Small. It is likely he was either conscripted into the army or enlisted under the Derby Scheme initially joining the Somerset Light Infantry. He was transferred to the Royal Warwickshire Regiment and was sent to the front to serve with the 1/6th Battalion. It is likely he was wounded on Thursday 4 October 1917, during attacks on German positions south of Poelcapelle. He was evacuated to a military hospital near Boulogne, where he succumbed to his wounds on Saturday 13 October 1917. He left a widow and two small children.

Corporal Wilfred Henry Scott MM		*V Bty 9th TM Bde Royal Garrison Artillery*	
Service No.	35416	Age:	22
Place of birth:	Fisherton, Wiltshire	Home Country:	England
Date of death:	13/10/1917	Cause of death:	Killed in action
Memorial:	Salisbury, Wiltshire		
War Cemetery:	Tyne Cot Memorial - Panel 6 to 7 and 162.		
Next of Kin:	Henry John & Eva May Scott		
Address:	18 Harcourt Terrace, Salisbury, Wiltshire		

Wilfred was the third son of Henry and Eva Scott and enlisted with the Royal Garrison artillery on 15 June 1911, stating he was 18 years of age. He was 15 years of age and had lied but served six months in England before being sent to serve in Bermuda. He returned to England on 19 April 1915 where he served until he was sent to France arriving on 27 February 1916. Wilfred was awarded the Militay Medal, for bravery in the field, most likely in August 1917 and was killed near Passchendaele Ridge on Saturday 13 October 1917. Wilfred's personal property was returned to his parents and consisted of some photos and in August 1918 his parents received their sons Military Medal. He is remembered on the Tyne Cot Memorial and has no known grave.

Private John Stratton		*6th Bn Kings Own Yorkshire Light Infantry*	
Service No.	44114	Age:	35
Place of birth:	Pewsey, Wiltshire	Home Country:	England
Date of death:	13/10/1917	Cause of death:	Killed in action
Memorial:	Marden, Wiltshire		
War Cemetery:	Tyne Cot Memorial - Panel 108 to 111		
Next of Kin:	Ethel Emily Ann Stratton (wife) – Joseph & Sarah Stratton (parents)		
Address:	Marden, Wiltshire		

John, a gardener and domestic servant, was the eldest son of Joseph and Sarah Stratton and at the beginning of 1904 he married Ethel Emily Ann Pratt at Pewsey. It is likely he was either conscripted into the army or enlisted under the Derby Scheme initially joining the Royal Field Artillery. He was transferred to the Kings Own Yorkshire Light Infantry and sent to the front to serve with the 6th Battalion. On 11 October 1917, the 6th Yorkshire Light Infantry to over the British front like south east of Polygon Wood, between the Polygon Beek stream and the Reutel Beek stream. The line was described as shell holes and badly damaged trenches. The two streams had become a practically impassable marsh of water logged shell holes for a width of 30 yards which formed very safe flanks. In front of their position had also become a marsh at the junction of the two streams. John was killed on Saturday 13 October 1917, most likely in the evening when the 6th Yorkshire Light Infantry, were heavily shelled by German artillery. He is remembered on the Tyne Cot Memorial and has no known grave. He left a widow and young family.

Denys John Bressey

Rifleman George Vernon Lafford		*7th Bn Rifle Brigade*	
Service No.	Z/102	Age:	22
Place of birth:	Swindon, Wiltshire	Home Country:	England
Date of death:	13/10/1917	Cause of death:	Died of wounds
Memorial:	Parkstone St Johns, Heatherlands, Dorset		
War Cemetery:	Godewaersvelde British Cemetery - Grave I. P. 46.		
Next of Kin:	John William & Mary Lafford		
Address:	317 Ashley Road, Parkstone, Dorset		

George was the second son of John and Mary Lafford and volunteered for service joining the 7th Battalion Rifle Brigade, arriving in France on 17 February 1915. On 10 October the 7th Rifle Brigade, went in to the British front-line south of Polygon Wood, between the Reutel Beek stream and the Menin road. It is likely George was wounded by German shelling while in the front line and evacuated to No. 37 Casualty Clearing Station, where he succumbed to his wounds on Saturday 13 October 1917.

SUNDAY 14 OCTOBER 1917 - TEMPERATURE 11°c -OVERCAST WITH SHOWERS - RAINFALL NIL

2nd Lieutenant Denys John Bressey		*12th Bty Bn Royal Field Artillery*	
Service No.	N/a	Age:	19
Place of birth:	Ceylon	Home Country:	England
Date of death:	14/10/1917	Cause of death:	killed in action
Memorial:	Marlborough College, Wiltshire		
War Cemetery:	The Huts Cemetery - Grave XIII. A. 14		
Next of Kin:	Herbert & Amy Bressey		
Address:	Durlstone, Hayes Lane, Bromley, Kent		

Denys was the only son of Herbert and Amy Bressey and was educated at Marlborough College. Before the outbreak of hostilities, he had intended to join the army and went to Woolwich in July 1915. He was given a commission with the Royal Field Artillery on 10 May 1916 and arrived in France on 26 August

1916. He was attached to the 7th Division ammunition column and later appointed Aide de Camp to Brigadier General Stanley Clarke, Royal Artillery. He was then sent to base to train young soldiers and was posted to the 12th Battery Royal Field Artillery in the autumn of 1917. He was just over nineteen years of age when he was killed by a direct hit from a German shell.

MONDAY 15 OCTOBER 1917 - TEMPERATURE 11°c - FOG THEN OVERCAST - RAINFALL NIL

Private Wilfred John Godfrey Judd		*12th Bn Durham Light Infantry*	
Service No.	54149	Age:	30
Place of birth:	Winterslow, Wiltshire	Home Country:	England
Date of death:	15/10/1917	Cause of death:	Killed in action
Memorial:	Winterslow, Wiltshire		
War Cemetery:	Tyne Cot Memorial - Panel 128 to 131 and 162 and 162A.		
Next of Kin:	Allen & Lydia Sarah Judd		
Address:	Grenville Hill, Winterslow, Wiltshire		

Wilfred, a cowman, was the only son of Allen and Lydia Judd and enlisted under the Derby Scheme on 10 December 1915. He was called up on 19 September 1916 and transferred to the Training Reserve on 25 November 1916. He was sent to France on 8 January 1917 and transferred to the 12th Battalion Durham Light Infantry, joining them on 10 February 1917. On 13 October 1917, the 12th Durhams relieved the 10th Northumberland Fusiliers in the right sub sector, east of Polygon Wood. They were constantly shelled by German artillery throughout their tour and Wilfred was killed on Monday 15 October 1917. He is remembered on the Tyne Cot Memorial and has no known grave.

TUESDAY 16 OCTOBER 1917 - TEMPERATURE 12°c - CLEAR - RAINFALL 0.1mm

For the fourth time within 19 days the British Army again attacked on Tuesday 16 October 1917, at the Ypres front, this time in co-operation with the French on their left. The French and British allies were both successful, the day's objectives being promptly reached.

The new thrust of the allies was aimed mainly at the German positions in the low ground northeast of Ypres, between Houthulst Forest and Passchendaele Ridge. The objectives were strictly limited scope. On the British side, it was essential to eliminate several awkward salient's left as a result of the attack on 4 October 1917. The objective of the French troops, under the command of General Anthoine, was to obtain possession of points which would dominate the strong position established by the Germans in Houthulst Forest, the biggest forest in this part of Belgium. On the allied left French troops advanced in conjunction with English, Welsh and Irish Battalions and the Guards. Their work was completed rapidly and brilliantly. The villages of St. Jean, Mangelaere, Koekuit and Veldhoek were stormed, as well as numerous fortified farms, ground being won to a depth averaging a mile and a quarter. The allied troops on this wing reached the outskirts of the Houthulst Forest.

In the left centre British troops completed the capture of the village of Poelcappelle, two miles southeast of Houthulst, and from here they won their way along the road to Westroosebeek. The advance in this

region is described by Sir Douglas Haig as considerable; it included the capture of many fortified farms and concrete redoubts.
A third line Territorial Division comprising the Manchester, East Lancashires and Lancashire Fusiliers, placed a fine feat to its credit in the right centre, thrusting a mile eastward in the direction of Passchendaele under most trying and difficult circumstances. The mud of the battlefield was studded everywhere with German bodies, the victims of the last battle. The British found them still unburied in the country they took, lying everywhere in swamps, packed closely together in craters where they had been killed by a single shell, piled around the exits of redoubts, all telling by their attitude the same story of headlong flight agony and terror. Never before have British troops encountered so many enemy dead as during the fighting of the past week.

There was heavy fighting along the front of the new British positions in the evening, the Germans counter attacked heavily against the British left wing in the neighbourhood of the Ypres-Standen railway, between Houthulst Forest and Poelcapelle. The attacks were all repulsed, but south of the railway the British troops were forced back a short distance along a front of about a mile and a quarter. Other counter attacks northeast of Broodseinde failed completely.

Private Frederick George Jones		*6th Bn Duke of Cornwalls Light Infantry*	
Service No.	29342	Age:	18
Place of birth:	Wallingford, Berkshire	Home Country:	England
Date of death:	16/10/1917	Cause of death:	Killed in action
Memorial:	Not known		
War Cemetery:	Hooge Crater Cemetery - Grave XV. G. 15.		
Next of Kin:	George & Eliza Jane Jones		
Address:	41 Cheltenham Street, Swindon, Wiltshire		

Frederick, an under-age soldier, was the only son of George and Eliza Jones and volunteered for service joining the Duke of Cornwalls Light Infantry. He was sent to France to serve with the 6th Battalion, who on Tuesday 16 October 1917 were in support in Sanctuary Wood in dugouts and shelters. Frederick was killed when the 6th Duke of Cornwalls were shelled by German artillery with gas and high explosive shells. He was buried near where he fell in old British Cemetery at Sanctuary Wood and moved to Hooge Crater Cemetery in July 1919. In 1918 his parents inserted the following memoriam in a local paper:

"Greater love hath no man than this – that a man lay down for his friends."

Act. Bombardier Arthur George Short		*93rd Cornwall Siege Bty TF R.G.A.*	
Service No.	322157	Age:	22
Place of birth:	Chippenham, Wiltshire	Home Country:	England
Date of death:	16/10/1917	Cause of death:	Killed in action
Memorial:	Chippenham, St. Andrews Church Chippenham		
War Cemetery:	Klein-Vierstraat British Cemetery - Grave III. D. 19.		
Next of Kin:	Azor & Eliza Short		
Address:	11 Emery Lane, Chippenham, Wiltshire		

Twenty two year old Arthur was the eldest son of Azor and Eliza Short, Azor Short was a postman in Chippenham. Arthur took employment with the post office firstly as a telegraph messenger boy, then an assistant postman and then being promoted to postman and transferring to Truro in Cornwall. Soon after the outbreak of hostilities Arthur volunteered for service with the 93rd Siege Battery, Royal Garrison Artillery, part of the Cornish Territorial force, and was sent to France in May 1916. He was killed most likely by German counter battery fire near Kemmel, south east of Ypres, Belgium, on Tuesday 16 October 1917. His younger brother Maurice William Short was to be killed in France in May 1918.

George Frederick Dean

2nd Lieutenant George Frederick Dean		*162nd Bty Royal Field Artillery*	
Service No.	N/a	Age:	28
Place of birth:	Swindon, Wiltshire	Home Country:	England
Date of death:	16/10/1917	Cause of death:	Killed in action
Memorial:	Chief Accountants Office Memorial Great Western Railway Works		
War Cemetery:	Tyne Cot Memorial - Panel 4 to 6 and 162		
Next of Kin:	Robert & Sarah Dean		
Address:	11 Gloucester Terrace, Swindon, Wiltshire		

George, known as Fred, was the second son of Robert and Sarah Dean and was educated at Sandford Street Schools before attending the Technical School for three years. He was a prominent sportsman and well-known for playing football and cricket. On leaving education he found employment as a staff clerk in the Chief Accountants Office at the Great Western Railway works in Swindon. He volunteered for service joining the Army Service Corps and arrived in France on 30 April 1915. He returned to England in 1917 and was given a commission with the Royal Field Artillery on 2 June 1917 and after a period at Larkhill returned to the front at the beginning of October 1917. On 13 October 1917, the 162nd Battery left the Bedford House where they had been engaged in supporting an attack by the 5th Division at Polderhoek Chateau and moved to La Clytte for a period of rest. Fred was killed on Tuesday 16 October 1917, when a German shell struck the dug-out in which he and two men were sleeping. Second Lieutenant McNab wrote the following to Fred's parents:

"Receiving this letter, you will have heard from the War Office the very sad news of your son Fred's death. I feel I must write and tell you of the keen sorrow I feel for you all in this very sad affliction that has come so suddenly upon you. Fred and I had been together almost daily for about eight months, so naturally got to known each other very well. To some extent, therefore, I can share your sorrow, for I feel that I have lost a real true friend. From what I learn a German shell struck the dug-out in which your son and two men were sleeping. Fred was killed instantly, and the other two men were seriously wounded. The deceased was buried near the Gun position, and his grave will be suitably marked with a cross"

The location of Fred's grave was lost in subsequent fighting and he is remembered on the Tyne Cot Memorial.

The grave of Robert William Renyard in uttes New British Cemetery Polygon Wood

Lance Corporal Robert William Renyard		*7th Bn Rifle Brigade*	
Service No.	S/2070	Age:	29
Place of birth:	Witham Friary, Somerset	Home Country:	England
Date of death:	16/10/1917	Cause of death:	Killed in action
Memorial:	Not known		
War Cemetery:	Buttes New British Cemetery Polygon Wood - Grave I. D. 10		
Next of Kin:	William & Mary Amelia Renyard		
Address:	14 Longhedge, Corsley, Wiltshire		

Robert, a gamekeeper, was the eldest son of William and Mary Renyard and volunteered for service with the 7th Battalion Rifle Brigade, arriving in France on 21 July 1915. He was a sniper and wounded, being shot through the shoulder, in the advance at Guillemont, at the Somme on 3 September 1916. He was evacuated to a military hospital and following his recovery returned to his unit. Robert was killed by a German shell on Tuesday 16 October 1917, while in the British front-line south of Polygon Wood,

between the Reutel Beek stream and the Menin Road. Official records state he was killed on 16th but in the following letter to Robert's mother, Lieutenant J.S. Hall states he was killed on 15th October:

"With the greatest regret, I write to inform you that your son Lance Corporal R. Renyard, was killed in action on the 15th October. He was in the front-line trenches when a small shell landed on the pararpet and killed him instantaneously and at the same time wounded another man severely. I know this must be a terrible blow to you, and that nothing that I can say can mitigate it, but it will, I am sure, be some consolation to you to know that your son was killed at once, and did not suffer as many have to. We buried him just behind the trenches, and a record of the spot has been kept. No doubt some mark will be put there in time, but it is impossible to do so now because it is in the front line. All ranks, I know, will join me in offering you oour warmest sympathy, as your son was liked and respected by all who knew him, and was one of our best lance corporals."

Robert was buried near Polderhoek and his grave location was found in February 1920 and he was identified by means of an identity disc. His remains were relocated to Buttes New British Cemetery Polygon Wood. His brother Walter had died of wounds while serving with Wiltshire Regiment in March 1915.

WEDNESDAY 17 OCTOBER 1917 - TEMPERATURE 13.5°C - CLEAR - RAINFALL 7.1mm

There was some small fighting on Wednesday 17 October 1917 near the Ypres-Standen railway, but generally the British troops were able so spend the day in organising their new positions between the Houthulst Forest and the Passchendaele Ridge. The number of German prisoners taken in the battle is 2,038, of which the French share is 400.

On the British left the French have extended their hold on the valley of the Corverbeek.

In a strong gale and thick clouds British airmen kept touch with the infantry throughout the battle, marked for artillery, and harassed the enemy with machine gun fire. In fighting four German machines were destroyed, and two sent down out of control. Two British aeroplanes were lost.

"The Germans newest theory of defence pillbox fortifications has proved to be a complete failure. They were not proof against British guns and even when they were not directly struck the concussion caused by the British shell fire had a most disabling effect on their garrisons."

Corporal William John Barlow		*1st Bn Devonshire Regiment*	
Service No.	49008	Age:	38
Place of birth:	Devizes, Wiltshire	Home Country:	England
Date of death:	17/10/1917	Cause of death:	Died of wounds
Memorial:	Devizes, Wiltshire		
War Cemetery:	Godewaersvelde British Cemetery - Grave I. O. 25.		
Next of Kin:	Minnie E Barlow		
Address:	4 Castle Lane, Market Place, Devizes, Wiltshire		

Oil retailer William was the eldest son of John and Selina Barlow and married Minnie Elizabeth Goosey in the spring of 1899. It is likely he was either conscripted into the army or enlisted under the Derby Scheme and after completing his training he was sent to France joining the 1st Battalion Devonshire Regiment. William was wounded most likely south of Polygon Wood and evacuated to No. 41 Casualty Clearing Station at Godewaersvelde, France, where he succumbed to his wounds on Wednesday 17 October 1917. He was buried in Godewaersvelde British Cemetery and left a widow and young family.

Lt. Col. Alan Bryant D.S.O.		*1st Bn Glos Reg. attd. Cdg 9th Bn Northumberland Fusiliers*	
Service No.	N/a	Age:	48
Place of birth:	Chippenham, Wiltshire	Home Country:	England
Date of death:	17/10/1917	Cause of death:	killed in action
Memorial:	St. George Church, Dunster		
War Cemetery:	Talana Farm Cemetery - Grave III. K. 1.		
Next of Kin:	Millicent Bryant (wife) - George Rourke & Hannah Bryant		
Address:	3 Nelson Terrace, Westward Ho, Devon		

Alan was the eldest son of George and Hannah Bryant and was educated at Marlborough College. In 1890, he was given a commission with the Gloucestershire Regiment, serving in Ireland, Malta, Egypt and India. In October 1899, on the outbreak of the South African War, he was sent to Natal, and fought at Rietfontein, and at Ladysmith, where he was captured. Later he fought in Transvaal and Orange River State, receiving the Queen's Medal with 3 clasps. He was promoted to Captain in 1900, sent to Staff

Right: Alan Bryant D.S.O.

Left: Sidney Philip Matthews

College in 1901 and from 1903 to 1905 was an instructor at Sandhurst. From there he was promoted becoming a Brigade Major at Plymouth 1905 to 1907 and from 1908 to 1912 he served with the Coast Defence Dover. In 1912, he was sent to Canada as a Major and General Service Officer. He returned to England at the outbreak of hostilities and was promoted to Lieutenant Colonel in 1916, arriving in France 12 October 1916. He was awarded the Distinguished Service Order in 1916 and mentioned twice in dispatches. In 1917 Alan was given command of the 9th Battalion Northumberland Fusiliers. He was killed on Wednesday 17 October 1917 at Stray Farm east of Pilckem. At about 9am the Germans shelled Stray Farm and a shell struck Battalion Headquarters killing Alan and all inside instantaneously. He left a widow and a young family.

Private Sidney Philip Matthews		*12th Bn Royal Sussex Regiment*	
Service No.	G/16934	Age:	19
Place of birth:	Paddington, Middlesex	Home Country:	England
Date of death:	17/10/1917	Cause of death:	Died of wounds
Memorial:	Chief Accountants Office Memorial, Great Western Railway Works Swindon		
War Cemetery:	Voormezeele Enclosure No1 and No2 - Grave I. L. 16.		
Next of Kin:	Philip Griffin & Emma C. Matthews		
Address:	Kensal Green, London		

Sidney, a clerk was the eldest son of Philip Griffin and Emma C. Matthews and it is likely he was either conscripted into the army or enlisted under the Derby Scheme joining the Royal Sussex Regiment. He was sent to the front to serve with the 12th Battalion and it is likely he was wounded near Tower Hamlets, east of Hooge on the Menin Road. He was evacuated to a casualty clearing station near Voormezeele, where he succumbed to his wounds on Wednesday 17 October 1917.

THURSDAY 18 OCTOBER 1917 - TEMPERATURE 13.5°c - CLEAR - RAINFALL NIL

Private Ernest Sidney Phillips		*109th Coy Bn Labour Corps*	
Service No.	65168	Age:	30
Place of birth:	Salisbury, Wiltshire	Home Country:	England
Date of death:	18/10/1917	Cause of death:	Killed in action

Memorial: Salisbury - St Martin's Church Memorial - Wiltshire
War Cemetery: Artillery Wood Cemetery - Grave I. D. 7.
Next of Kin: Arthur & Bessie Phillips
Address: 18 St Anne Street, Salisbury, Wiltshire

Ernest was the third son of Arthur and Bessie Phillips and it is likely he was either conscripted into the army or enlisted under the Derby Scheme initially joining the Gloucester Regiment. He was later transferred to 109th Company Labour Corps and sent to the front. Ernest was killed, most likely by German artillery fire near Pilckem on Thursday 18 October 1917.

Gunner Henry James Whiting *B Bty 78th Bde Bn Royal Field Artillery*

Service No. 128518
Place of birth: Great Cheverell, Wiltshire
Date of death: 18/10/1917
Age: 27
Home Country: England
Cause of death: Killed in action
Memorial: Great Cheverell, Wiltshire
War Cemetery: Cement House Cemetery - Grave V. B. 24.
Next of Kin: Hugh & Mary Jane Whiting
Address: Laurel House, Great Cheverell, Wiltshire

Carter, John, was the second son of Hugh and Mary Whiting and it is likely he was either conscripted into the army or enlisted under the Derby Scheme joining the Royal Field Artillery. After completing his training, he was sent to the front joining B Battery, 78th Brigade. He was killed on Thursday 18 October 1917 most likely by German artillery fire south east of Poelcapelle, Belgium, not far from Goudberg, and was buried where he fell. His remains were relocated to Cement House Cemetery in August 1919.

Private William Weeks *attd. X Corps Ammo. Park Army Service Corps*

Service No. M1/07673
Place of birth: Colerne, Wiltshire
Date of death: 18/10/1917
Age: 29
Home Country: England
Cause of death: Died of wounds
Memorial: Colerne, Wiltshire
War Cemetery: Lijssenthoek Military Cemetery - Grave XXIV. A. 16
Next of Kin: Edwin & Grace Selina Weeks
Address: Thickwood, Colerne, Wiltshire

William, a groom, was the second son of Edwin and Grace Weeks and volunteered for service joining the Army Service Corps. He arrived in France on 10 September 1915 and was attached to X Corps Ammunition Park. William was wounded by German artillery fire, near his lorry, at about 5.30pm on Wednesday 17 October 1917. He was evacuated to No. 10 Casualty Clearing Station at Lijessenthoek, where he succumbed to his wounds the following morning. William's mother received the following letters, the first from Captain Basil Pearson:

"I am writing to tell you of the Great loss which the Company has had in the death from wounds received under shell fire of your son, William Weeks. He was hit when near his lorry at about 5.30 yesterday evening, and passed away about 6 o'clock this morning in hospital. Since being with this company I have heard nothing but praise of your son's work, and recently, when he had left the Company, special application was made for his return. The funeral took place at two o'clock this afternoon and was attended by all his friends who could be spared from their work. Please accept my deepest sympathy."

The second letter was from Chaplain H. Clarke from No. 10 Casualty Clearing Station.

William Weeks

"Your son W. Weeks, was brought to this hospital late last evening with bomb wounds in legs and arm. He was very severely injured and died in spite of every care and all skilful attention. I had a nice talk with him and prayed with him, and I think he was comforted a good deal. He told me about his home and was pleased to find I knew the West Country and his old Rector Rev. Maxwell-Smith. He asked me to send you all his love and to tell you not to worry; he would write as soon as he could, poor lad. He was very brave and patient. I enclose a little card which I gave him, which he kissed and which I promised to send you as a little souvenir. The unit has put a most lovely carved oak cross up in memory of your boy, quite the nicest thing in the cemetery. May I assure you of my real sympathy, and thank God for his bright, brave, useful life, and for his example and service."

William's brother George had been killed on 9 April 1917 at the Somme, while serving with the Australian Infantry.

FRIDAY 19 OCTOBER 1917 - TEMPERATURE 9°c - CLOUD COVER - RAINFALL 2.9mm

Fitter Harry Crumplin		*76th Bde Bn Royal Field Artillery*	
Service No.	94532	Age:	19
Place of birth:	Breamore, Hampshire	Home Country:	England
Date of death:	19/10/1917	Cause of death:	Killed in action
Memorial:	Harnham, Wiltshire		
War Cemetery:	Solferino Farm Cemetery - Grave I. C. 2.		
Next of Kin:	George & Lucy Caroline Crumplin		
Address:	Hatts Cottage, Semley, Wiltshire		

Harry was the third son of George and Lucy Crumplin and volunteered for service at seventeen years of age joining the Royal Field Artillery. He arrived in France with the 76th Brigade on 22 June 1915 and was employed as a fitter. He was killed on Friday 19 October 1917, most likely by German artillery, north west of Ypres.

Sapper Walter Harold Townsend — *233rd Field Coy Royal Engineers*

Service No.	166786	Age:	20
Place of birth:	Stratton, Wiltshire	Home Country:	England
Date of death:	19/10/1917	Cause of death:	Killed in action
Memorial:	Not known		
War Cemetery:	Coxyde Military Cemetery - Grave IV. H. 1.		
Next of Kin:	John & Clara Townsend		
Address:	King Street, Swindon, Wiltshire		

Walter, a wheelwright, was the youngest son of John and Clara Townsend and it is likely he was either conscripted into the army or enlisted under the Derby Scheme joining the Royal Engineers. He was sent to the front joining the 233rd Field Coy, who in October 1917 were working in the Nieuport Bains area, improving dugouts and trenches. Walter was killed on Friday 19 October 1917, most likely by German Artillery fire and was buried in Coxyde Military Cemetery.

SUNDAY 21 OCTOBER 1917 - TEMPERATURE 12°c - HEAVY RAIN - RAINFALL 1.3mm

Pioneer Frank Bailey — *343rd Road Construction Coy Bn Royal Engineers*

Service No.	274174	Age:	36
Place of birth:	Potterne, Wiltshire	Home Country:	England
Date of death:	21/10/1917	Cause of death:	Died
Memorial:	Potterne, Wiltshire		
War Cemetery:	Nine Elms British Cemetery - Grave V. C. 21.		
Next of Kin:	Thomas & Matilda Bailey		
Address:	The Butts, Potterne, Wiltshire		

Bricklayer's labourer Frank was the second son of Thomas and Matilda Bailey and was employed by Mr Miller, a builder of Potterne. It is likely he was either conscripted into the army or enlisted under the Derby Scheme and after completing his training he was initially sent to the Durham Light Infantry before being transferred to the Royal Engineers. He was sent to France and attached to the Australian Royal Engineers and on 18 October 1917 Frank fell ill and was evacuated to a casualty clearing station where he died the following day, Sunday 21 October 1917, after suffering a cerebral haemorrhage. The Corporal of Frank's platoon wrote the following to Matilda Bailey:

"He was always of a quiet and retiring nature, and commanded the respect of all the men in the platoon. I trust it may be of some consolation to you to know, and I do say it with all reverence and sincerity, that no one has served his country more loyally than your son, he being always ready and anxious to do his duty."

The Chaplain of the regiment also wrote to Mrs Medlicott of Sandfield:

"The physician in charge tells me that it was not due to any accident or injury, but simply to the bursting of an artery owing to some natural weakness. He did not recover consciousness. We laid his body to rest in Nine Elms Cemetery. Please convey my deepest sympathy to Private Bailey's parents. It may help them to think of their son as having emigrated from a land of sorrow and strife to a life of progress and enlightenment where men evermore rejoice in God's holy comfort and no brave, loving soul can be in anyway a loser by passing on to the brighter and fuller life."

Private James Emanuel Curtis — *2nd Bn Wiltshire Regiment*

Service No.	203055	Age:	31
Place of birth:	Fisherton Delamere, Wiltshire	Home Country:	England
Date of death:	21/10/1917	Cause of death:	Killed in action
Memorial:	Not known		
War Cemetery:	Derry House Cemetery No 2 - Grave II. F. 5.		
Next of Kin:	Edith Ellen Curtis (wife) – Henry James & Susanah Curtis		
Address:	4 Exeter Terrace, Exeter Street, Salisbury, Wiltshire		

James, a farm waggoner, was the eldest son of Henry and Susanah Curtis and at the start of 1911 he married Edith Ellen Andrews at Salisbury. It is likely he was either conscripted into the army or enlisted under the Derby Scheme initially joining the Somerset Light Infantry. He was transferred to the Wiltshire Regiment and sent to the front joining the 2nd Battalion. He was killed on Sunday 21 October 1917, by German artillery near Derry House east of Wytschaete. He left a widow and a young family.

Sapper Lewis George Elling — *21st Light Railway Operating Coy Royal Engineers*

Service No.	256313	Age:	25
Place of birth:	Warminster, Wiltshire	Home Country:	England
Date of death:	21/10/1917	Cause of death:	Killed in action
Memorial:	Not known		
War Cemetery:	Reninghelst New Military Cemetery - Grave IV. C. 24.		
Next of Kin:	Louisa Elling (wife) – William & Alice Elling (parent)		
Address:	20 Hilperton Road, Trowbridge - Codford St. Mary		

Lewis, a carpenter and joiner, was the eldest son of William and Alice Elling and originally joined the army on 9 March 1909, leaving on 1 January 1913. While serving in the army he married Louisa Seviour in spring 1911 at Frome. It is likely he rejoined the army at the beginning of hostilities, and was called to the colours and sent to the continent in March 1917 with the 21st Light Railway Operating Company. He was killed in action most likely by German shell fire south west of Ypres, Belgium, on Sunday 21 October 1917.

Gunner Harold Frederick O'Brien — *D Bty 82nd Bde Bn Royal Field Artillery*

Service No.	94084	Age:	19
Place of birth:	Swindon, Wiltshire	Home Country:	England
Date of death:	21/10/1917	Cause of death:	Killed in action
Memorial:	Euclid Street School, Swindon, Great Western Railway		
War Cemetery:	Minty Farm Cemetery - Grave I. B. 1.		
Next of Kin:	Frederick & Eliza Mary O'Brien		
Address:	60 Elmina Road, Swindon, Wiltshire		

Harold, known as Frederick, was the only son of Frederick and Eliza O'Brien and was educated at Euclid Street School, Swindon. After leaving education he became an apprentice brass fitter at the Great Western Railway Works in Swindon. He was under age when he volunteered for service in 1915 joining the Royal Filed Artillery and arrived in France with the 82nd Brigade on 26 July 1915. Frederick was killed on Sunday 21 October 1917 west of Poelcapelle, most likely by German counter battery artillery fire. He was buried at Minty Farm Cemetery.

Sergeant Charles William Baker — *155th Siege Bty Royal Garrison Artillery*

Service No.	86023	Age:	39
Place of birth:	Hastings, Sussex	Home Country:	England

Left: The grave marker of Lewis George Elling in Reninghelst New Military Cemetery

Right: Harold Frederick O'Brien

Date of death:	21/10/1917	Cause of death:	Died of wounds
Memorial:	Not known		
War Cemetery:	Etaples Military Cemetery - Grave XXX. F. 7A		
Next of Kin:	Nellie Maria Baker (wife) - Moses & Elizabeth B. Baker (parents)		
Address:	Lower Pavenhill, Purton, Wiltshire – 113 South Street, Walworth, London		

Charles was the eldest son of Moses and Elizabeth Baker and originally enlisted with the Royal Engineers on 5 May 1899. He served in the South African War, arriving on 8 May 1900. He was awarded the Kings and Queens South Africa Medals with clasps for Cape Colony, Orange Free State, and Transvaal. He returned to England in 1902 and served with the regular army until March 1905, when he was transferred to the reserve. His service expired and he was discharged from the reserves on 4 May 1911. Charles took employment as the Manager of a Public House and on 24 January 1913 he married Nellie Maria Driscoll at the registery office at St. Pancras. It is likely Charles was called up and re-enlisted with the Royal Garrison Artillery on 20 May 1916. He arrived in France on 29 August 1916 and seved with 155th Siege Battery. Charles was wounded most likely by German artillery fire on 6 October 1917 and evacuated to No.1 Canadian Casualty Clearing Station at Etaples, where he succumbed to his wounds on Sunday 21 October 1917. He left a widow and a young family.

MONDAY 22 OCTOBER 1917 - TEMPERATURE 13.5°c - OVERCAST - RAINFALL 3.2mm

Private Wilfred Gordon Anson		*14th Bn Gloucestershire Regiment*	
Service No.	265915	Age:	27
Place of birth:	Littleover, Derbyshire	Home Country:	England
Date of death:	22/10/1917	Cause of death:	Killed in action
Memorial:	Not known		
War Cemetery:	Tyne Cot Memorial - Panel 72 to 75.		
Next of Kin:	Rev Harcourt Suft & Edith Anson		
Address:	The Close, Salisbury, Wiltshire		

Wilfred was the eldest son of Rev. Harcourt and Edith Anson and was educated at Eastfield House

Ditching and the Technical College, Brighton. After leaving education he was employed as an engineer by the Bristol Aeroplane Works. Wilfred volunteered for service on 3 October 1914, joining the 14th Service Battalion Gloucestershire Regiment. He arrived in France on 31 March 1915 and during his service was wounded and evacuated to England. Captain Coates wrote to Wilfred's parents in a letter dated 22 April 1915:

"Your boy has already proved himself a real good lad, plucky and a splendid worker."

He returned to the front in September 1917 and on Monday 22 October 1917 the 14th Gloucesters attacked German positions south of Houthulst Forest. At 5.35am they advanced from the British line east of Veldhoek and met strong opposition, but by 6.15am they had taken their frist objective including Panama House. They continued their advance and by 7.45am had consolidated their final objective. At 4.39pm the Germans counter attacked and the 14th Gloucesters dropped their right flank back to continue the line. Wilfred was killed during the attack. Colonel Walker-Nott D.S.O. wrote the following letter to his parents:

"Your son was in my company when we came out two years ago, and so I know him pretty well. He was an extremely plucky boy, and his spirit was always willing, though his flesh was weak. I used to admire him very much for the grit which he showed by sticking it out even on the worst march, and also for his absence of fear under fire."

Wilfred is remembered on the Tyne Cot Memorial and has no known grave.

Private Fred Newman		*14th Bn Gloucestershire Regiment*	
Service No.	241938	Age:	29
Place of birth:	Downton, Wiltshire	Home Country:	England
Date of death:	22/10/1917	Cause of death:	Killed in action
Memorial:	Downton, Wiltshire - Lyme Regis, Dorset		
War Cemetery:	Tyne Cot Memorial - Panel 72 to 75		
Next of Kin:	Edith Mary Anne Newman (wife) – George & Ellen Newman (parents)		
Address:	48 Church Street, Lyme Regis, Dorset		

Fred, a carpenter, was the eldest son of George and Ellen Newman and on 13 April 1914 he married Edith Mary Anne Gibbs at Lyme Regis. It is likely he was either conscripted into the army or enlisted under the Derby Scheme joining the Gloucestershire Regiment and was sent to the front to serve with the 14th Service Battalion. He was wounded in December 1916 and following his recovery returned to the front in September 1917. Fred was killed on Monday 22 October 1917 when the 14th Gloucesters attacked German positions south of Houthulst Forest, in the same action as Wilfred Anson. He is remembered on the Tyne Cot Memorial and has no known grave. His brother William was awarded the Military Medal and the Distinguished Service Medal during the Great War.

Private William Charles Edwards		*18th Bn Lancashire Fusiliers*	
Service No.	45468	Age:	19
Place of birth:	Alvediston, Wiltshire	Home Country:	England
Date of death:	22/10/1917	Cause of death:	Killed in action
Memorial:	Not known		
War Cemetery:	Tyne Cot Memorial - Panel 54 to 60 and 163A.		
Next of Kin:	Charles & Sarah Edwards		
Address:	Reeve's Farm, Bratton, Wiltshire		

Nineteen year old William was the eldest son of Charles and Sarah Edwards and originally joined the

Royal Wiltshire Yeomanary. He was sent to the front and transferred to the 18th Battalion Lancashire Fusiliers, who on Monday 22 October 1917 were attacking German positions near Veldhoek south of Houthulst Forest. They advanced at 5.35am and found the British creeping barrage was too slow causing some casualties to the 18th Lancashire Fusiliers. One company wandered too far to the left and entered Houthulst Forest but were forced back to the edge. William was reported missing during the attack. Later his parents received official information stating that William was presumed to have been killed on the day he was reported missing. He is remembered on the Tyne Cot Memorial and has no known grave.

Gunner Frederick George Sainsbury *B Bty 75th Bde Royal Field Artillery*

Service No.	19576	Age:	22
Place of birth:	Figheldean, Wiltshire	Home Country:	England
Date of death:	22/10/1917	Cause of death:	Killed in action
Memorial:	Figeldean, Wiltshire		
War Cemetery:	Canada Farm Cemetery - Grave III. E. 22		
Next of Kin:	George & Sarah Sainsbury		
Address:	305, Figheldean, Wiltshire		

Frederick was the eldest son of George and Sarah Sainsbury and before the Great War worked at the officer's mess at Netheravon. He volunteered for service joining B Battery, 75th Brigade Royal Field Artillery and arrived in France on 2 September 1915. He was killed on Monday 22 October 1917, most likely by German counter battery fire north of Ypres and is buried at Canada Farm Cemetery.

Corporal Charles King Woodford MM *54th Field Coy Royal Engineers*

Service No.	22348	Age:	25
Place of birth:	Pewsey, Wiltshire	Home Country:	England
Date of death:	22/10/1917	Cause of death:	Killed in action
Memorial:	Enford, Wiltshire		
War Cemetery:	Railway Dugouts Burial Ground - Grave VII. S. 2.		
Next of Kin:	Tom & Lydia Woodford		
Address:	Long Street, Enford, Wiltshire		

Charles, a bricklayer, was the eldest son of Tom and Lydia Woodford and volunteered for service with the Royal Engineers. He arrived in France on 20 November 1914, serving with the 54th Field Company and was awarded the Military Medal. He was killed on Monday 22 October 1917, most likely by German artillery fire, near Tower Hamlets south of the Menin Road. He was buried in Railway Dugouts Burial Ground.

Private Fred Charles Martin *9th Bn Kings Own Yorkshire Light Infantry*

Service No.	44069	Age:	25
Place of birth:	Potterne, Wiltshire	Home Country:	England
Date of death:	22/10/1917	Cause of death:	Killed in action
Memorial:	Devizes, Wiltshire		
War Cemetery:	Tyne Cot Memorial - Grave Panel 108 to 111.		
Next of Kin:	Edwin and Caroline Martin		
Address:	1 Hare and Hounds Court, Devizes, Wiltshire		

Fred, a farm labourer, was the fourth son of Edwin and Caroline Martin and it is likely he was either conscripted into the army or enlisted under the Derby Scheme and after completing his training he was initially sent to the Royal Garrison Artillery. With a need for more infantrymen Fred was transferred to the 9th Service Battalion Kings Own Yorkshire Light Infantry. Fred was killed in action on Monday 22 October 1917, when the 9th Kings Own Yorkshire Light Infantry were heavily shelled by German artillery, while in the British front line near Reutel east of Polygon Wood. He is remembered on the Tyne Cot Memorial and has no known grave.

Gunner Charles Edward Westall		*103rd Bde Bn Royal Field Artillery*	
Service No.	198546	Age:	31
Place of birth:	Aldbourne, Wiltshire	Home Country:	England
Date of death:	22/10/1917	Cause of death:	Killed in action
Memorial:	Trowbridge, Aldbourne, Wiltshire		
War Cemetery:	La Clytte Military Cemetery - Grave III. E. 28.		
Next of Kin:	Rosina Westall (wife) - Jacob & Hannah Westall (parents)		
Address:	11 York Buildings, Timbrell Street, Trowbridge - Aldbourne, Wiltshire		

Charles, a labourer, was the second son of Jacob and Hannah Westall and originally volunteered for service with the Wiltshire Regiment on 21 August 1914, but was discharged on 22 September 1914 being declared unfit for service. He was then conscripted into the Royal Engineers in 1916 and married Rosina Taylor in January 1917 being transferred to the Royal Field Artillery before being sent to France in May 1917, serving with the 103rd Brigade. Charles was killed, by German artillery fire, near Bedford House on Monday 22 October 1917. In mid November 1917 Rosina received the following letter from an army chaplain Rev. A.W. Chute:

"He was serving with the guns. The position was a dangerous spot as it was always liable to hostile shelling. On this occasion, your husband was resting in a dugout with several of his companions when a shell burst on the very spot, and breaking through into the place where they were, he and three others were killed. I think it will be of some relief to know that his death was probably quite instantaneous, so that he would have been saved any suffering. I can only say how sorry I am to have to write you this sad news. Your husband had been such a short time with us and it seems hard that he should have been taken like this, but you will feel satisfaction, perhaps, in some small degree in knowing that he fell while doing his duty, and while serving the cause he knew to be right, and if it was to be, he could not have died more nobley. We held his funeral, which I conducted myself in a cemetery some seven miles behind the firing line. It is a quiet little spot and a cross will be placed to mark the grave. I think it will help you to bear this blow if you remember after all, though he is parted from you for a time he is not really dead, but has only passed on into a new and fuller life the other side of the grave."

TUESDAY 23 OCTOBER 1917 - TEMPERATURE 10°c - SHOWERS - RAINFALL 4mm

Sergeant Oliver Charles Gerrard MM		*2nd Bn Rifle Brigade*	
Service No.	2561	Age:	29
Place of birth:	Corsham, Wiltshire	Home Country:	England
Date of death:	23/10/1917	Cause of death:	Killed in action
Memorial:	Corsham, Wiitshire		
War Cemetery:	Prowse Point Military Cemetery - Grave III. D. 9.		
Next of Kin:	Joseph & Mary Gerrard		
Address:	Westrip, Corsham, Wiltshire		

Regular soldier, Oliver was the third son of Joseph and Mary Gerrard and enlisted with the army on 30

Left: Charles Edward Westall

Right: Oliver Charles Gerrard MM

December 1907 joining the Rifle Brigade. He was sent to India where he was at the outbreak of hostilities and arrived back in England on 18 November 1915. He was sent to France on 20 December 1914 and was wounded with a gunshot wound to the leg on 23 April 1915. He was evacuated to England on 27 April 1915 and following his recovery he returned to France arriving on 6 October 1915. He was awarded the Military Medal for gallantry and devotion to duty, between 15 and 17 August 1917 north of Nonne Boschen Wood. Oliver was killed on Tuesday 23 October 1917, when the 2nd Rifle Brigade were continuously shelled by German trench mortars, at Le Basse-Ville, south of Warneton. His parents received the following letter:

"It is with the greatest regret I have to write to tell you of the death of your son Sergeant Gerrard. He was my platoon sergeant and we were great friends as we have known each other for some time. He was well liked by everyone in the Company, and his death is a sad blow to us. He was killed by the explosion of a bomb and his death was instantaneous, as he was killed by concussion. He was a brave boy and recently won the Military Medal, which I hope you will receive as a memento of his brave deeds during fighting near Ypres on the 16 August. Please accept the deepest sympathy of all ranks in the Company in your great loss. Myself I cannot tell you how grieved I am to lose him as he was an excellent soldier and died doing his duty."

In February 1918 Oliver's parents received their son's Military Medal, they also received his personal processions consisting of a wallet and photos, note book, dominoes in a case, a disc and letters.

Private Harold Pearcey		*6th Bn Somerset Light Infantry*	
Service No.	28861	Age:	19
Place of birth:	Salisbury, Wiltshire	Home Country:	England
Date of death:	23/10/1917	Cause of death:	Killed in action
Memorial:	Salisbury, Wiltshire		
War Cemetery:	Hooge Crater Cemetery - Grave XI. F. 8.		
Next of Kin:	Emma Philpott (grandparent)		
Address:	3 Curtiss Court Endess Street, Salisbury, Wiltshire		

Nineteen year old Harold, known as Harry, was the grandson of Emma Philpott and grew up in Salisbury Workhouse. It is likely he was conscripted into the army initially joining the Wiltshire Regiment. He was sent to the front and transferred to the 6th Battalion Somerset Light Infantry. Harry was killed on Tuesday 23 October 1917, most likely by German artillery, in the British frontline north of Polderhoek, just east of Cameron House and buried near where he fell. In May 1919 Harry's remains were found, identified by his name and number on the rifle cover he had used when he was in the Wiltshire Regiment, and moved to Hooge Crater Cemetery.

Private Leonard Victor Roots — *12th Bn Middlesex Regiment*

Service No.	G/5652	Age:	30
Place of birth:	Hackney, London	Home Country:	England
Date of death:	23/10/1917	Cause of death:	Killed in action
Memorial:	Not known		
War Cemetery:	Tyne Cot Memorial - Panel 113 to 115.		
Next of Kin:	Mabel E. Roots (wife) - Herbert & Hannah Roots (parents)		
Address:	New Southgate, London		

Leonard was the third son of Herbert and Hannah Roots and lived in Swindon before the outbreak of hostilities. He volunteered for service joining the 12th Battalion Middlesex Regiment and married Mabel E. Parnell at Strood, Kent, in the Summer of 1915. Soon after his marriage he was sent to France, arriving on 23 September 1915. Leonard was killed on Tuesday 23 October 1917, most likely by German artillery fire, near Pheasant Farm, south west of Poelcapelle. He is remembered on the Tyne Cot Memorial and has no known grave.

Private Victor Arthur Bull — *12th Bn Middlesex Regiment*

Service No.	TF235005	Age:	22
Place of birth:	Walcot, Somerset	Home Country:	England
Date of death:	23/10/1917	Cause of death:	Killed in action
Memorial:	Calne, Wiltshire		
War Cemetery:	Tyne Cot Memorial - Panel 113 to 115.		
Next of Kin:	Arthur William & Alice Bull		
Address:	1 Bennetts Cottages, Walcot, Somerset		

Victor was the fifth son of Arthur and Alice Bull and volunteered for service with the 7th Battalion Somerset Light Infantry arriving in France on 24 July 1915. It is likely he was wounded or suffered from illness or disease and was evacuated to England. Following his recovery, he was transferred to the 12th Battalion Middlesex Regiment and returned to the front. He was killed in action on Tuesday 23 October 1917, most likely by German artillery fire, near Pheasant Farm, south west of Poelcapelle. He is remembered on the Tyne Cot Memorial and has no known grave.

WEDNESDAY 24 OCTOBER 1917 - TEMPERATURE 9°c - 25% CLOUD COVER - RAINFALL 7.7mm

Gunner Frederick William Scott — *228th Siege Bty Royal Garrison Artillery*

Service No.	66554	Age:	30
Place of birth:	Westbury, Wiltshire	Home Country:	England
Date of death:	24/10/1917	Cause of death:	Died of wounds

Frederick William Scott

Memorial:	Bratton, Westbury Congregational Church
War Cemetery:	Menin Road South Military Cemetery - Grave III. I. 23.
Next of Kin:	Lilian Annie Scott (wife) – Alfred & Rebecca Scott (parents
Address:	Park View Terrace, Dilton Marsh, Wiltshire

Frederick was the third son of Alfred and Rebecca Scott and was employed as a lamp man in the traffic department of the Great Western Railway Company at Swindon. His father, Alfred, was a veteran of the Crimean War. Frederick married Lilian Annie Pearce on 31 May 1909 at Westbury and it is likely he was either conscripted into the army or enlisted under the Derby Scheme joining the Royal Garrison Artillery and sent to the front in mid 1917, to serve with the 228th Siege Battery. Frederick was killed on Wednesday 24 October 1917, by hostile German artillery fire east of Ypres near the Menin Road. Frederick's widow received the following letter from an officer of the battery:

"Gunner Scott was working with other members of the gun team in a new position when hostile shelling commenced and he and three comrades were killed by the same shell. He had not been with battery very long, but had made himself liked by his companions. Both officers and men deeply regret his death."

Frederick brother in law Harry Pearce had been killed on H.M.S. Invincible in 1916 at Jutland. Frederick left a widow and a little boy.

Rifleman Frank Deadman		*16th Bn Kings Royal Rifle Corps*	
Service No.	C/1548	Age:	24
Place of birth:	Thornton Heath, Surrey	Home Country:	England
Date of death:	25/10/1917	Cause of death:	Died of wounds
Memorial:	Malmesbury, Wiltshire		
War Cemetery:	Wimereux Communal Cemetery - Grave VI. E. 26.		
Next of Kin:	George & Ada S Deadman		
Address:	Cowbridge, Malmesbury, Wiltshire		

Frank was the second son of George and Ada Deadman and was employed as a gardener by Sir Philip Rose of Penn, Buckinhamshire. He had been a prominent member of the Boy Scout Movement and volunteered for service in September 1915 joining the 16th Battalion Kings Royal Rifle Corps, being sent to France early in 1916. He was wounded in fighting at the Somme near Trones Wood, with a shrapnel wound to the side. He was evacuated to England and sent to Brighton Hospital and then on to shrapnel wound to the side. He was evacuated to England and sent to Brighton Hospital and then on to Lewes, the shrapnel was never removed. Following his recovery, he returned to France and in January 1917 he was evacuated again to England suffering from trench foot. He was sent to Malmesbury Red Cross Hospital, which was a great surprise for his parents who new nothing of his arrival. In mid 1917, he returned to the front and in October 1917 was wounded again, most likely by German artillery east of Messines. This time he was suffering from a compound fracture to the right forearm and a wound in the back. He was evacuated to the 2nd Australian General Hospital at Wimereux, France, where complications set in and he succumbed to his wounds on Thursday 25 October 1917. Matron E. Gray at the hospital wrote the following letter to Frank's mother:

"It is with much regret that I am writing to let you know the sad news of your son's death. During the last few days we have been very anxious about him, a haemorrhage (internal) causing us much anxiety. I saw him this morning and had a good talk with him. He was so very bright and cheerful, and always had a bright smile for us. This evening he became worse, and though everything was done for him that could be done he quietly passed away at 7.30pm. He will be buried in the little cemetery where so many of our brave men and boys have been laid. The Chaplain was with him when he passed away, and I am sure he will write to you. With so many thoughts and much sympathy."

The Chaplain, Rev. W. K. Douglas, the vicar of Port Esperance, Tasmania wrote:

"Just a line of my sincere sympathy with you all over your splendid boy's death. He passed away as easily and gently tonight as possible. We were all so fond of him, and he put up such a plucky fight, but God wanted him, and though he did not want to go, he was quite ready. I was with him about ten minutes before he died; we expected then that he would live for some hours. All day he had been very weak, but almost to the last we were hoping he would pull through. His thoughts and prayers have been all along with you at home, with his aunt at Portsmouth, and with his little girl. He was so very fond of you all and so anxious to get home. Now he waits for you in Paradise. We all pray for you and for him."

Private Walter John Rixon		*23rd Field Amb. Royal Army Medical Corps*	
Service No.	90700	Age:	26
Place of birth:	Swindon, Wiltshire	Home Country:	England
Date of death:	25/10/1917	Cause of death:	Died of wounds
Memorial:	No 15 Shop Memorial Swindon Railway Museum		
War Cemetery:	Lijssenthoek Military Cemetery - Grave XXII. A. 15A.		
Next of Kin:	Daisy May Rixon (wife) - William & Elizabeth Rixon (parents)		
Address:	139 Rodbourne Road, Swindon, Wiltshire		

Walter, known John, was the fourth son of William and Elizabeth Rixon and was employed as a boiler riveter in No. 15 Shop, Great Western Railway Works at Swindon. Toward the end of 1912 he married Daisy May Lock at Swindon. It is likely he was either conscripted into the army or enlisted under the Derby Scheme joining the Royal Army Medical Corps and was sent to the front to serve with the 23rd Field Ambulance. Walter was wounded, most likely near Hooge Crater by German artillery shelling and was evacuated to No. 10 Casualty Clearing Station at Lijssenthoek where he succumbed to his wounds on Thursday 25 October 1917. He left a widow and young daughter.

2nd Lieutenant Arthur Edward Holt		*233rd Siege Bty Royal Garrison Artillery*	
Service No.	N/a	Age:	19
Place of birth:	Burnham on Sea, Somerset	Home Country:	England
Date of death:	25/10/1917	Cause of death:	Died of wounds
Memorial:	Burnham on Sea, Somerset – Marlborough College		
War Cemetery:	Menin Road South Military Cemetery - Grave III. J. 30		

Left: *Walter John Rixon*

Right: Arthur Edward Holt

Next of Kin: Thomas & Margaret Jane Holt
Address: The Hall, Burnham on Sea, Somerset

Nineteen year old Arthur was the eldest son of Thomas and Margaret Holt and was educated at Connaught House School and Marlborough College. He left education in December 1916 to train for a commission with the Royal Garrison Artillery. He was given a commission in March 1917 and was sent to France in September 1917 to serve with the 233rd Siege Battery. Arthur was wounded on Thursday 25 October 1917; he was hit by a German shell splinter while in charge of an ammunition party near Hooge. He succumbed to his wounds a few hours later.

Sapper George Polden Ledgley — *54th Field Coy Royal Engineers*

Service No.	139542	Age:	29
Place of birth:	Windsor, Berkshire	Home Country:	England
Date of death:	25/10/1917	Cause of death:	Killed in action

Memorial: Not known
War Cemetery: Tyne Cot Memorial - Panel 8 and 162.
Next of Kin: Mary Anne Ledgley (wife) – James George & Harriet Ledgley
Address: Lethbridge Hersham Road, Walton on Thames, Surrey - 40 Albany Road Windsor

George a carpenter was the eldest son of James and Harriet Ledgley and lived at Pavenhill, Purton. It is likely he was either conscripted into the army or enlisted under the Derby Scheme joining the Royal Engineers. He married Mary Anne Shailer on 20 August 1917 at St Mary, Walton on Thames and soon after the wedding was sent to the front to serve with the 54th Field Company. He was killed on Thursday 25 October 1917, most likely by German artillery fire, near Scottish Wood, west of Voormezeele. He is remembered on the Tyne Cot Memorial and has no known grave.

12
The Second Battle of Passchendaele

Map page 425

FRIDAY 26 OCTOBER 1917 - TEMPERATURE 9°c - OVERCAST- RAINFALL 7.8mm

Private Ernest George Barter — *44th Bn New Brunswick Regiment*

Service No. 865034
Age: 32
Place of birth: Shrewton, Wiltshire
Home Country: Canada
Date of death: 26/10/1917
Cause of death: Killed in action
Memorial: Shrewton, Wiltshire
War Cemetery: Ypres Menin Gate - Panel 26 - 28
Next of Kin: John & Charlotte Barter
Address: High Street, Shrewton, Wiltshire

Ernest was the youngest son of John and Charlotte Barter and was a member of the Shrewton Rifle Club where he was described as a consistent shot. He emigrated to Canada prior to the Great War, where he was employed as a bar tender. He enlisted with the Canadian Infantry on 10 February 1916 and after completing his training in Canada arrived in England on 29 April 1917. He arrived in France on 16 June 1917 and was sent to serve with the 44th Battalion, joining them on 21 June 1916. He was killed on Friday 26 October 1917, most likely from German artillery fire when the 44th Battalion were in support of an attack toward Passchendaele from Abraham Heights west of Tyne Cot. He is remembered on the Ypres Menin Gate and has no known grave.

Corporal William Charles Beaven — *4th Canadian Mounted Rifles Central Ontario Rgt.*

Service No. 172007
Age: 24
Place of birth: Salisbury, Wiltshire
Home Country: Canada
Date of death: 26/10/1917
Cause of death: Killed in action
Memorial: Salisbury, Wiltshire
War Cemetery: Tyne Cot Cemetery - Grave XXX. E. 15.
Next of Kin: Michael & Alice Beaven
Address: The Close, Salisbury, Wiltshire

William, a civil sailor, was the third son of Michael and Alice Beaven and emigrated to Canada before the Great War. He volunteered for service with the militia and on 16 July 1915 he enlisted with the 83rd Overseas Battalion of the Canadian Army. On 7 July 1915, he arrived in England and was transferred to the 12th Battalion and on 28 July 1916 was again transferred to the 4th Canadian Mounted Rifles. He arrived in France on 29 July 1916 but was wounded in December 1916 when he was buried by a shell and was evacuated to the Royal Victoria Hospital, Netley, England, suffering from a fractured pelvis. He returned to the front and the 4th Canadian Mounted Rifles on 23 September 1917. William was killed on Friday 26 October 1917, during an attack on German positions just south east of Wolf Copse, west of Passchendaele. The 4th Canadian Mounted Rifles had a hard fight from shell hole to shell hole and sustained many casualties. They were later forced to fall back 300 yards to link up with the attacking division on their left. William was buried where he fell and after the war his remains were identified by the means of a disc and relocated to Tyne Cot Cemetery.

Private Victor Maurice Haines — *1st RM Bn RN Div Royal Marine Light Infantry*

Service No.	CH/1859(S)	Age:	19
Place of birth:	South Newton, Wiltshire	Home Country:	England
Date of death:	26/10/1917	Cause of death:	Killed in action
Memorial:	Norton Bavant, Wiltshire		
War Cemetery:	Tyne Cot Memorial - Panel 1 and 162A.		
Next of Kin:	Tom & Mary Haines		
Address:	North Farm, Norton Bavant, Wiltshire		

Victor, a carter, was the youngest son of Tom and Mary Haines and enlisted with the Royal Marines on 16 November 1916. Joining the Brigade on 26 January 1917 and after completing his training he was sent to France on 29 April 1916. He was initially sent to the Base Depot in Calais, before being sent to the 1st Royal Marine Battalion on 20 May 1917. At 5.40am on Friday 26 October 1917, 16 officers and 597 other ranks of the 1st Royal Marines attacked German positions south east of Poelcaplle, near the Lekkerboterbeek stream. They advanced with very great difficulty, rain had fallen heavily during the night and shell holes were full of water, the mud made the ground almost impassable. However, all the objects were taken including Berks Houses, Banff House and Bray Farm. The position was consolidated but the 1st Royal Marines sustained a considerable amount of casualties from German snipers on the left where the British brigade was unable to advance. Toward nightfall the garrison in Banff Farm was forced to withdraw. Victor was reported missing during the advance on Friday 26 October 1917. Later official information was received by his parents stating he was presumed to have been killed on the day he was reported missing. He is today remembered on the Tyne Cot Memorial and has no known grave.

Private Audley Clark — *1st RM Bn RN Div Bn Royal Marine Light Infantry*

Service No.	PO/2218(S)	Age:	23
Place of birth:	Burbage, Wiltshire	Home Country:	England
Date of death:	26/10/1917	Cause of death:	Killed in action
Memorial:	Brokenborough, Wiltshire		
War Cemetery:	Tyne Cot Memorial - Panel 1 and 162A.		
Next of Kin:	Francis & Natalia Moore Clark		
Address:	30 Brokenborough, Wiltshire		

Audley was the second son of Francis and Natalia Clark and was employed as a carter at Mr Sellwood's Brook Farm. He and his brother Bernard were members of the Malmesbury Volunteers and he took a keen interest in drill. He attested under the Derby Scheme on 11 December 1915 and was mobilised on 26 May 1917, being sent to the Royal Marines at Deal Depot. After completing his training with Victory Royal Marine Brigade, he was sent to France on 25 September 1917 to serve with the 1st Royal Marine Battalion. He was killed on Friday 26 October 1917 when the 1st Royal Marines attacked German positions southeast of Poelcapplle, near the Lekkerboterbeek stream, in the same action as Victor Haines. Walter was described as a smart intelligent young man and took his place in the marines cheerfully. He is remembered on the Tyne Cot Memorial and has no known grave.

Private Walter Lewis Hames		*1st RM Bn RN Div Bn Royal Marine Light Infantry*	
Service No.	PO/18652	Age:	19
Place of birth:	Pewsey, Wiltshire	Home Country:	England
Date of death:	26/10/1917	Cause of death:	Killed in action
Memorial:	Marden, Wiltshire		
War Cemetery:	Tyne Cot Memorial - Panel 1 and 162A.		
Next of Kin:	Mary J. Hames		
Address:	Marden, Wiltshire		

Walter, was the only son of Mary Hames and had been employed as a farm labourer by Mr Hibberd of Connock. He lied about his age and was only sixteen years of age when he enlisted with the Royal Marines on 28 May 1915. He was sent to Murdos where he arrived on 24 February 1916 and then on to France arriving 12 May 1916 and joined the 1st Royal Marine Battalion. He was killed on Friday 26 October 1917 when the 1st Royal Marines attacked German positions south east of Poelcaplle, near the Lekkerboterbeek stream, in the same action as Victor Haines. Walter is remembered on the Tyne Cot Memorial and has no known grave.

Private Robert Henry Pearce		*1st R.M. Bn. R.N. Div. Royal Marine Light Infantry*	
Service No.	PLY/2031(S)	Age:	32
Place of birth:	Rowde, Wiltshire	Home Country:	England
Date of death:	26/10/1917	Cause of death:	Killed in action
Memorial:	Melksham, Steeple Ashton, Wiltshire		
War Cemetery:	Tyne Cot Memorial - Panel 1 and 162A.		
Next of kin:	Helen M. Pearce (wife) - Henry & Elizabeth Pearce (parents)		
Address:	Broughton Road, Melksham, Wiltshire		

Robert, known as Bob and a rubber worker, was the eldest son of Henry and Elizabeth Pearce and married Helen M. Pearce toward the end of 1915 most likely just before he attested for military service under the Derby Scheme on 11 December 1916. He was mobilised on 9 April 1917 and sent to the Royal Marine Light Infantry and after completing his training was sent to the front in June 1917. Roberts' sister who lived at Weston-Super-Mare had not seen her brother for four years and she did not know her brother was in the forces until she met a resident of Melksham. She dispatched a parcel to her brother at the front but Robert was killed two days later on Friday 26 October 1917, when the 1st Royal Marines attacked German positions southeast of Poelcapplle, near the Lekkerboterbeek stream, in the same action as Victor Haines. Bob never received the parcel. He is remembered on the Tyne Cot Memorial and has no known grave. Robert's sister inserted the following memoriam in a local paper:

Peaceful be thy rest, dear Bob
It is sweet to breathe thy name
In life I loved you dearly
In death I'll do the same
No One knows the silent heartache
Only those can tell
Why have lost their best and dearest
Without saying farewell

Private George Webster		*1st RM Bn RN Div Bn Royal Marine Light Infantry*	
Service No.	PO/2216(S)	Age:	19
Place of birth:	Rowington, Warwickshire	Home Country:	England
Date of death:	26/10/1917	Cause of death:	Killed in action
Memorial:	Great Bedwyn, Wiltshire		

Left to right: Walter Hames - Robert Henry Pearce - George Webster

War Cemetery:	Tyne Cot Memorial - Panel 1 and 162A
Next of Kin:	Joseph & Emily Webster
Address:	183 Brook Street, Great Bedwyn, Wiltshire

George was the eldest son of Joseph and Emily Webster and was employed as a porter at the Traffic Department at Codford for the Great Western Railway Company. It is likely he was either conscripted into the army or enlisted under the Derby Scheme joining the Royal Marines. He arrived in France on 24 September 1917 joining the 1st Royal Marine Battalion on 4 October 1917. George was reported missing on Friday 26 October 1917 when the 1st Royal Marines attacked German positions southeast of Poelcapelle, near the Lekkerboterbeek stream, in the same action as Victor Haines. Later information was received by his parents stating George was presumed to have been killed on the day he was reported missing. He is remembered on the Tyne Cot Memorial and has no known grave.

Private Arthur Frederick Stone		*2nd R M Bn R N Div Royal Marine Light Infantry*	
Service No.	PO/2217(S)	Age:	19
Place of birth:	Salisbury, Wiltshire	Home Country:	England
Date of death:	26/10/1917	Cause of death:	Killed in action
Memorial:	Bemerton, Wiltshire		
War Cemetery:	Tyne Cot Memorial - Panel 1 and 162A		
Next of Kin:	Albert & Selina Stone		
Address:	St Andrews Road, Bemerton, Wiltshire		

Arthur was the fifth son of Albert and Selina Stone It is likely he was either conscripted into the army or enlisted under the Derby Scheme joining the Royal Marines. He arrived in France on 24 September 1917 joining the 2nd Royal Marine Battalion. Arthur was reported missing on Friday 26 October 1917 when the 2nd Royal Marines were in support of the attack on German positions south east of Poelcapplle, near the Lekkerboterbeek stream. As the attack proceeded the 2nd Royal Marines became intermingled with the 1st Royal Marines. Later information was received by his parents stating Arthur was presumed to have been killed on the day he was reported missing. He is remembered on the Tyne Cot Memorial and has no known grave.

Eltham Bryan Brown

Private Eltham Bryan Brown		*2nd R M Bn R N Div Royal Marine Light Infantry*	
Service No.	PLY/1413(S)	Age:	24
Place of birth:	Christchurch, Dorset	Home Country:	England
Date of death:	26/10/1917	Cause of death:	Died of wounds
Memorial:	Wootton Bassett, Wiltshire		
War Cemetery:	Tyne Cot Memorial - Panel 1 and 162A.		
Next of Kin:	Ethel Brown (wife) - Frederick John & Florence Brown		
Address:	11 New Street, Oakham, Rutland - Cross Keys Wootton Bassett		

Eltham, known as Brian, was the second son of Frederick and Florence Brown and he was employed as a motor driver for the Post Office. He married Ethel Marriott toward the end of 1914 at Oakham, Rutland. He enlisted with the Royal Marines on 16 February 1916 and was sent to the recruit depot at Deal. He arrived in France on 22 November 1916 and joined the 2nd Royal Marine Battalion the following month. He suffered from pyrexia from 27 December 1916 to 23 February 1917 and infalmation of the connecting tendons in his legs from 11 May 1917 to 28 June 1917. Brian was reported wounded and missing on Friday 26 October 1917 when the 2nd Royal Marines were in support of the attack on German positions south east of Poelcapelle, near the Lekkerboterbeek stream. As the attack proceeded the 2nd Royal Marines became intermingled with the 1st Royal Marines, the 2nd Royal Marines suffered 308 casualties. In June 1918 Brian's wife received information stating Brian was presumed to have been killed on the day he was reported missing. He is remembered on the Tyne Cot Memorial and has no known grave.

Private Maurice Heath		*2nd R M Bn R N Div Royal Marine Light Infantry*	
Service No.	PO/17776	Age:	20
Place of birth:	West Tytherton, Wiltshire	Home Country:	England
Date of death:	26/10/1917	Cause of death:	Killed in action
Memorial:	St. Andrews Church Chippenham		
War Cemetery:	Tyne Cot Memorial - Panel 1 and 162A.		
Next of Kin:	Sidney & Kate Heath		
Address:	West Tytherton, Wiltshire		

Maurice, a farm labourer ,was the fifth son of Sidney and Kate Heath and at the age of seventeen years, seven months and twenty-eight days Maurice volunteered for service with his brother Fred on 9 September 1914 at Bristol ith the Royal Marines. He arrived in France on 19 May 1917 and was attached to the 2nd Royal Marine Battalion. Maurice was reported missing on Friday 26 October 1917 when the 2nd Royal Marines were in support of the attack on German positions south east of Poelcapelle, near the Lekkerboterbeek stream. As the attack proceeded the 2nd Royal Marines became intermingled with the 1st Royal Marines, the 2nd Royal Marines suffered 308 casualties. Later information was received by his parents stating Maurice was presumed to have been killed on the day he was reported missing. He is remembered on the Tyne Cot Memorial and has no known grave. His brother Fred was to die in November 1918 when H.M.S. Britania was torpedoed by a German submarine.

Able Seaman Ernest Hoare		*Hood Royal Naval Div. R.N.V.R.*	
Service No.	R/735	Age:	27
Place of birth:	Bideford, Devon	Home Country:	England
Date of death:	26/10/1917	Cause of death:	Killed in action
Memorial:	Marlborough, Wiltshire		
War Cemetery:	Tyne Cot Memorial - Panel 2 to 3 and 162 to 162A.		
Next of Kin:	Rosina Hoare (wife) - Edward & Martha Hoare (parents)		
Address:	3 Mount Pleasant, Marlborough, Wiltshire		

Ernest, a boot maker, was the eldest son of Edward and Martha Hoare and in the spring of 1912 he married Rosina Buse at Bideford, Devon. He attested under the Derby Scheme 10 December 1915 and was mobilised on 14 February 1917, being sent to The Royal Naval Volunteer Reserve. After completing his training, he was sent to France on 6 May 1917, joining Hood Battalion Royal Naval Division on 30 June 1917. On Friday 26 October 1917, Hood Battalion were in support of an attack by Anson and Howe Battalions on German positions near Varlet Farm, south east of Poelcapelle. Hood Battalion were subjected to German bombardment throughout the day and at 7pm Hood Battalion was ordered forward to take over the positions of Anson and Howe Battalions. This included the most forward position at Varlet Farm. Ernest was killed at some point during Friday 26 October 1917, it is likely his death was caused by shelling by German artillery. He is remembered on the Tyne Cot Memorial and has no known grave.

Private Herbert William North		*8th Bn Devonshire Regiment*	
Service No.	290852	Age:	34
Place of birth:	Pewsey, Wiltshire	Home Country:	England
Date of death:	26/10/1917	Cause of death:	Killed in action
Memorial:	Manningford Bruce, Wiltshire		
War Cemetery:	Hooge Crater Cemetery - Grave VIII. B. 14.		
Next of Kin:	James & Mary North		
Address:,	Manningford Bruce, Wiltshire		

Herbert, a farm labourer, was the youngest son of James and Mary North and it is likely he was either conscripted into the army or enlisted under the Derby Scheme joining the Devonshire Regiment. He was sent to the front to serve with the 8th Service Battalion, who at 5.40am on Friday 26 October 1917 attacked German positions at Gheluvelt from north of the Menin Road. The plan was to capture the Zandvoorde spur to secure the hold on Tower Hamlets Ridge. The 8th Devons were in the second wave and the attack was carried out with a creeping British barrage. As they advanced they suffered from heavy enfilade (from the side) and frontal German machine gun and rifle fire. The majority of the second wave who had lost all their officers made an attempt on German pill boxes south of the Menin Road. A right attacking platoon of the 8th Devons got into Gheluvelt, but nothing more was heard of them. At 10am the Germans made a determined counter attack from the railway cutting north of Gheluvelt. By the end of the day the 8th Devons had almost been forced back to their start point. Herbert was reported missing during the attack on Friday 26 October 1917 and later his parents received official information

Charles Eric Jupe

stating Herbert was presumed to have been killed on the day he was reported missing. Some time later Herbert's remains were found near Stirling Castle, the report stated he was identified by his pay book, which stated it was in an unsanitary condition. His remains were moved to Hooge Crater Cemetery.

Captain Charles Eric Jupe *8th Bn Devonshire Regiment*

Service No.	N/a	Age:	27
Place of birth:	Longbridge Deverill, Wiltshire	Home Country:	England
Date of death:	26/10/1917	Cause of death:	Killed in action
Memorial:	Bristol Grammar School. - Singapore Cenotaph & Cricket Club - Winscombe		
War Cemetery:	Tyne Cot Memorial - Panel 38 to 40.		
Next of Kin:	Charles William & Mary Jane Jupe		
Address:	Lorraine, Winscombe, Somerset		

Charles was the eldest son of Charles and Mary Jupe and was educated at Wooford House School, Birchington, Kent and Bristol Grammar School. He left England for Singapore in 1910 where Paterson Symonds Commercial Company employed him, one of the largest trading companies in Singapore. He was a keen cricketer and a member of Singapore Cricket Club. He joined the Volunteer Artillery and at the outbreak of hostilities served the forts keeping a lookout for the renowned German surface raider the Emden. By the end of 1914 he had returned to England with some friends who volunteered for service with the 10th Battalion Royal Fusilers, arriving in France on 31 July 1915. On 1 August 1916, he was given a commission with the 8th Service Battalion Devonshire Regiment and was promoted to Captain in October 1917. He was killed while commanding A Company, who were a reserve company on Friday 26 October 1917. He was leading his company against a German stong point that was holding up the advance at Gheluvelt from north of the Menin Road, in the same action as Herbert North. One of his fellow officers wrote to Charles's parents stating:

'We shall always cherish the memory of your son as a good friend and a splendid officer.'"

He is remembered on the Tyne Cot Memorial and has no known grave.

Private Bertie Roland Day *8th Bn Devonshire Regiment*

Service No.	33828	Age:	32
Place of birth:	Swindon, Wiltshire	Home Country:	England

Date of death: 26/10/1917 Cause of death: Killed in action
Memorial: Okehampton, Devon
War Cemetery: Tyne Cot Memorial - Panel 38 to 40
Next of Kin: Minnie Day (wife) - William & Susanah Day (parents)
Address: Okehampton, Devon

Bertie was the fourth son of William and Susanah Day and at the beginning of 1913 married Minnie Fuse at Okehampton. It is likely he was either conscripted into the army or enlisted under the Derby Scheme initially joining the Dorset Regiment before being transferred to the 8th Service Battalion Devonshire Regiment. Bertie was reported missing on Friday 26 October 1917 when the 8th Devons attacked German positions at Gheluvelt from north of the Menin Road, in the same action as Herbert North. Later official information was received stating Bertie was presumed to have been killed on the day he was reported missing. He is remembered on the Tyne Cot Memorial and has no known grave. He left a widow and young daughter

Private Reginald Godfrey Harris *9th Bn Devonshire Regiment*
Service No. 204924 Age: 21
Place of birth: Fordingbridge, Hampshire Home Country: England
Date of death: 26/10/1917 Cause of death: Killed in action
Memorial: Salisbury, Wiltshire
War Cemetery: Hooge Crater Cemetery - Grave VIA. E. 17.
Next of Kin: William & Kate Harris
Address: 125 Gigant Street, Salisbury, Wiltshire

Reginald, an outfitters assistant, was the youngest son of William and Kate Harris and it is likely he was either conscripted into the army or enlisted under the Derby Scheme initially joining the Wiltshire Regiment before being transferred to the 9th Service Battalion Devonshire Regiment. At 5.50am on Friday 26 October 1917 when the 9th Devons attacked German positions at Gheluvelt from north of the Menin Road. As they advanced they were continuously harassed by German machine gun fire from pill boxes. The mud and water was so bad that the majority of the 9th Devons rifles and lewis guns had got clogged with mud and were no use without being cleaned. At 8am a small party of the 9th Devons who had entered Gheluvelt were seen to be falling back as the Germans began to re-occupy the positions they had left earlier. The enemy advanced in small parties covered by machine gun fire and were working around the 9th Devons flanks and few of the 9th Devons rifles would work. At 10am the Germans made a determined counter attack from the railway cutting north of Gheluvelt. By the end of the day the 8th Devons had almost been forced back to their start point. The 9th Devons casualties were 143 killed or missing and 151 wounded and there was only one officer who was not hit. Reginald was reported missing on Friday 26 October 1917 during the attack at Gheluvelt, later his parents received official information stating he was presumed to have been killed on the day he was reported missing. After the war, Reginald's remains were found north of the Menin Road opposite Gheluvelt Wood. He was identified by means of his identity disk and his remais moved to Hooge Crater Cemetery.

Private Arthur Slade *9th Bn Devonshire Regiment*
Service No. 31360 Age: 29
Place of birth: Lea, Wiltshire Home Country: England
Date of death: 26/10/1917 Cause of death: Killed in action
Memorial: Lea, Wiltshire
War Cemetery: Tyne Cot Memorial - Panel 38 to 40.
Next of Kin: John E. & Ellen Slade
Address: Lea, Wiltshire

Arthur was the youngest son of John and Ellen Slade and it is likely he was either conscripted into the army or enlisted under the Derby Scheme initially joining the Wiltshire Regiment before being transferred to the 9th Service Battalion Devonshire Regiment. He was reported missing on Friday 26 October 1917 when the 9th Devons attacked German positions at Gheluvelt from north of the Menin Road, in the same action as Reginald Harris. In August 1918 Arthur's mother received official information stating her son was presumed to have been killed on the day he was reported missing. He is remembered on the Tyne Cot Memorial and has no known grave.

Private William Arthur Elliott Witchell		*9th Service Bn Devonshire Regiment*	
Service No.	31264	Age:	33
Place of birth:	Berwick St James, Wiltshire	Home Country:	England
Date of death:	26/10/1917	Cause of death:	Killed in action
Memorial:	Parkstone St Johns Heatherlands, Dorset		
War Cemetery:	Tyne Cot Memorial - Panel 38 to 40.		
Next of Kin:	Eliza Mary Witchell (wife) – John & Leah Witchell (parents)		
Address:	Dessa Cottage, Pine Road, Upper Parkestone, Dorset		

William, a carter, was the third son of John and Leah Witchell and on 1 April 1907 he married Eliza Mary Tuffin. It is likely he was either conscripted into the army or enlisted under the Derby Scheme joining the 9th Service Battalion Devonshire Regiment. He was reported missing on Friday 26 October 1917 when the 9th Devons attacked German positions at Gheluvelt from north of the Menin Road, in the same action as Reginald Harris. Later official information was received stating William was presumed to have been killed on the day he was reported missing. He is remembered on the Tyne Cot Memorial and has no known grave. He left a widow and young family.

Private Herbert Mead		*9th Bn Devonshire Regiment*	
Service No.	31065	Age:	39
Place of birth:	Steeple Langford, Wiltshire	Home Country:	England
Date of death:	26/10/1917	Cause of death:	Killed in action
Memorial:	Steeple Langford, Wiltshire		
War Cemetery:	Tyne Cot Memorial - Panel 38 to 40.		
Next of Kin:	Alice Martha Mead (wife) – Charles & Mary Mead (parents)		
Address:	Steeple Langford, Wiltshire		

Herbert was the second son of Charles and Mary Mead and on 18 September 1909 he married Alice Martha Moore. It is likely he was either conscripted into the army or enlisted under the Derby Scheme initially joining the Dorset Regiment before being transferred to the 9th Service Battalion Devonshire Regiment. He was reported missing on Friday 26 October 1917 when the 9th Devons attacked German positions at Gheluvelt from north of the Menin Road, in the same action as Reginald Harris. Later official information was received stating Herbert was presumed to have been killed on the day he was reported missing. He is remembered on the Tyne Cot Memorial and has no known grave. He left a widow and young family.

Private Elliot Woolford Cove		*9th Bn Devonshire Regiment*	
Service No.	290873	Age:	20
Place of birth:	Queington, Gloucestershire	Home Country:	England
Date of death:	26/10/1917	Cause of death:	Killed in action
Memorial:	Not known		
War Cemetery:	Tyne Cot Memorial - Panel 38 to 40.		
Next of Kin:	Dinah Reeve Cove (mother)		
Address:	Park Farm, Garsdon, Wiltshire		

Elliott was the only son of Dinah Reeve Cove and it is likely he was either conscripted into the army or enlisted under the Derby Scheme joining the 9th Service Battalion Devonshire Regiment. He was reported missing on Friday 26 October 1917 when the 9th Devons attacked German positions at Gheluvelt from north of the Menin Road, in the same action as Reginald Harris. Later official information was received stating Elliott was presumed to have been killed on the day he was reported missing. He is remembered on the Tyne Cot Memorial and has no known grave.

Private Christopher George Hinder		*9th Bn Devonshire Regiment*	
Service No.	290939	Age:	22
Place of birth:	Wroughton, Wiltshire	Home Country:	England
Date of death:	26/10/1917	Cause of death:	Killed in action
Memorial:	Not known		
War Cemetery:	Tyne Cot Memorial - Panel 38 to 40		
Next of Kin:	Henry George & Rhoda Louisa Hinder		
Address:	Rodbourne Cheney, Swindon, Wiltshire		

Christopher, a slot collector's labourer, was the third son of Henry and Rhoda Hinder and it is likely he was either conscripted into the army or enlisted under the Derby Scheme joining the 9th Service Battalion Devonshire Regiment. He was reported missing on Friday 26 October 1917 when the 9th Devons attacked German positions at Gheluvelt from north of the Menin Road, in the same action as Reginald Harris. Later official information was received stating Christopher was presumed to have been killed on the day he was reported missing. He is remembered on the Tyne Cot Memorial and has no known grave.

Private George Henry Fennell		*9th Bn Devonshire Regiment*	
Service No.	31371	Age:	26
Place of birth:	Chippenham, Wiltshire	Home Country:	England
Date of death:	26/10/1917	Cause of death:	Killed in action
Memorial:	Chippenham, St. Pauls Church		
War Cemetery:	Tyne Cot Memorial - Panel 38 to 40.		
Next of Kin:	Thomas & Mary Fennell		
Address:	17 Lowden, Chippenham, Wiltshire		

George, a butcher, was the eldest son of Thomas and Mary Fennell and it is likely he was either conscripted into the army or enlisted under the Derby Scheme joining the 9th Service Battalion Devonshire Regiment. He was reported missing on Friday 26 October 1917 when the 9th Devons attacked German positions at Gheluvelt from north of the Menin Road, in the same action as Reginald Harris. Later official information was received stating George was presumed to have been killed on the day he was reported missing. He is remembered on the Tyne Cot Memorial and has no known grave.

Private James Stone		*9th Bn Devonshire Regiment*	
Service No.	204926	Age:	26
Place of birth:	Winterslow, Wiltshire	Home Country:	England
Date of death:	26/10/1917	Cause of death:	Killed in action
Memorial:	Winterslow, Wiltshire		
War Cemetery:	Tyne Cot Memorial - Panel 38 to 40		
Next of Kin:	Silas & Elizabeth Matilda Stone		
Address:	The Causeway, Winterslow, Wiltshire		

James, a horseman on a farm, was the youngest son of Silas and Elizabeth Stone and it is likely he was either conscripted into the army or enlisted under the Derby Scheme joining the 9th Service Battalion Devonshire Regiment. He was reported missing on Friday 26 October 1917 when the 9th Devons attacked German positions at Gheluvelt from north of the Menin Road, in the same action as Reginald Harris. Later official information was received stating James was presumed to have been killed on the day he was reported missing. He is remembered on the Tyne Cot Memorial and has no known grave. His brother Harry had been killed in Mesoptamia in April 1917 while serving with the Wiltshire Regiment.

Private Aaron George Webb		*9th Bn Devonshire Regiment*	
Service No.	204927	Age:	29
Place of birth:	Colerne, Wiltshire	Home Country:	England
Date of death:	26/10/1917	Cause of death:	Killed in action
Memorial:	Colerne, Wiltshire		
War Cemetery:	Tyne Cot Memorial - Panel 38 to 40.		
Next of Kin:	Aaron & Hettie Webb		
Address:	Euridge Manor, Colerne, Wiltshire		

Arron, known as George, was the only son of Aaron and Hettie Webb and was employed on his father's farm. He volunteered for service with the Royal Wiltshire Yeomanry in September 1914, but was later transferred to the Infantry. Initially to the Wiltshire Regiment and then to the 9th Service Battalion Devonshire Regiment. He was reported missing on Friday 26 October 1917 when the 9th Devons attacked German positions at Gheluvelt from north of the Menin Road, in the same action as Reginald Harris. Later official information was received stating George was presumed to have been killed on the day he was reported missing. He is remembered on the Tyne Cot Memorial and has no known grave.

Private Maurice Silver Pond		*9th Bn Devonshire Regiment*	
Service No.	31358	Age:	36
Place of birth:	Chippenham, Wiltshire	Home Country:	England
Date of death:	26/10/1917	Cause of death:	Killed in action
Memorial:	Chippenham, St. Pauls Church		
War Cemetery:	Tyne Cot Memorial - Panel 38 to 40.		
Next of Kin:	George William & Mary Ann Pond		
Address:	1 High Street, Chippenham, Wiltshire		

Maurice was the youngest son of George and Mary Pond and was employed by his father as a grocer's assistant at their store at 1 High Street, Chippenham and it is likely he was either conscripted into the army or enlisted under the Derby Scheme joining the 9th Service Battalion Devonshire Regiment. He was reported missing on Friday 26 October 1917 when the 9th Devons attacked German positions at Gheluvelt from north of the Menin Road, in the same action as Reginald Harris. Later official information was received stating Maurice was presumed to have been killed on the day he was reported missing. He is remembered on the Tyne Cot Memorial and has no known grave.

Private Frank Loader		*9th Bn Devonshire Regiment*	
Service No.	290965	Age:	26
Place of birth:	Bishopstone, Wiltshire	Home Country:	England
Date of death:	26/10/1917	Cause of death:	Killed in action
Memorial:	Broad Chalke, Wiltshire		
War Cemetery:	Tyne Cot Memorial - Panel 38 to 40.		
Next of Kin:	Elsie Jane Loader (wife) – John & Eliza Loader (parents)		
Address:	Cliffside, Broad Chalke, Wiltshire		

Frank a farm labourer was the second son of John and Eliza Loader and on 24 April 1911 he married Elsie Jane Goodfellow at Broad Chalke. It is likely he was either conscripted into the army or enlisted under the Derby Scheme joining the 9th Service Battalion Devonshire Regiment. He was reported missing on Friday 26 October 1917 when the 9th Devons attacked German positions at Gheluvelt from north of the Menin Road, in the same action as Reginald Harris. Later official information was received stating Frank was presumed to have been killed on the day he was reported missing. He is remembered on the Tyne Cot Memorial and has no known grave. He left a widow and a young son.

Private Harold Stanley Gale		*2nd Bn Royal West Surrey Regiment*	
Service No.	G/5397	Age:	28
Place of birth:	Salisbury, Wiltshire	Home Country:	England
Date of death:	26/10/1917	Cause of death:	Killed in action
Memorial:	Salisbury - Harnham, Wiltshire		
War Cemetery:	Tyne Cot Memorial – Panel 14 to 17 and 162 to 162A.		
Next of Kin:	Leonora Gale (wife) – James & Matilda Julia Gale (parents)		
Address:	5 The Drove West Harnham, Salisbury, Wiltshire		

Harold, an iron monger's assistant was the third son of James and Matilda Gale and at the beginning of 1908 he married Leonora Earney. He volunteered for service joining the Royal West Surrey Regiment and after completing his training he arrived in France on 15 June 1915, being sent to the 2nd Battalion. Harold was killed on Friday 26 October 1917 when the 2nd Royal West Surreys attempted to capture the German fortified position at Lewis House north west of Gheluvelt, but were driven back to their start line. Harold is remembered on the Tyne Cot Memorial and has no known grave. He left a widow and two young children.

Private Frederick Burgess		*14th Bn Royal Warwickshire Regiment*	
Service No.	28046	Age:	36
Place of birth:	Warminster, Wiltshire	Home Country:	England
Date of death:	26/10/1917	Cause of death:	Killed in action
Memorial:	Warminster, Wiltshire		
War Cemetery:	Tyne Cot Memorial - Panel 23 to 28 and 163A.		
Next of Kin:	Samuel & Ellen Burgess		
Address:	27 Marsh Street, Warminster, Wiltshire		

Frederick was the youngest son of Samuel and Ellen Burgess and it is likely he was either conscripted into the army or enlisted under the Derby Scheme joining the Royal Warwickshire Regiment. After completing his training, he was sent to the front to serve with the 14th Battalion. On Friday 26 October 1917, the 14th Warwicks attacked German position between the Reutelbeek stream and Polderhoek Chateau. Initially the attacks went well and reports coming back said the attacking British troops had passed the Chateau and it was now surrounded. Though there had been stiff opposition from the German held Chateau and surrounding German held pill boxes and after some heavy hand to hand fighting the Chateau and the pill box on the right had been taken. A message for more Lewis guns and rifles was then received, owing to the indescribable mud conditions the 14th Warwicks Lewis guns and rifles were practically all out of action. As soon as the Germans knew the Chateau had been captured they put down a very heavy barrage causing many British casualties. At about 11am it was decided by a senior officer to retire to the 14th Warwicks start positions, because the Germans were massing for a counter attack on the right and the front and too many Lewis guns and rifles were out of action. The Germans then re-occupied the Chateau and front-line positions. Frederick was killed during the attack on Friday 26 October 1917 and is remembered on the Tyne Cot Memorial. He has no known grave.

Sergeant William George Russell		*14th Bn Royal Warwickshire Regiment*	
Service No.	993	Age:	25
Place of birth:	Chippenham, Wiltshire	Home Country:	England
Date of death:	26/10/1917	Cause of death:	Killed in action
Memorial:	Bloxham, Oxfordshire		
War Cemetery:	Tyne Cot Memorial - Panel 23 to 28 and 163A.		
Next of Kin:	James William & Annie Russell		
Address:	Near Little Green, Bloxham, Oxfordshire		

William, a grocer's assistant, was the only son of James and Annie Russell and lived at Kenilworth prior to the Great War. He volunteered for service joining the 14th Service Battalion Royal Warwickshire Regiment and arrived in France on 21 November 1915. He was killed on Friday 26 October 1917 when the 14th Warwicks attacked German position between the Reutelbeek stream and Polderhoek Chateau, in the same action as Frederick Burgess. William is remembered on the Tyne Cot Memorial and has no known grave.

Private Sidney Geogre Albert Tancock		*1st Bn Royal West Kent Regiment*	
Service No.	206637	Age:	23
Place of birth:	Bath, Somerset	Home Country:	England
Date of death:	26/10/1917	Cause of death:	Killed in action
Memorial:	Warminster, Horningsham, Wiltshire		
War Cemetery:	Hooge Crater Cemetery - Grave VII. E. 11.		
Next of Kin:	George Henry & Florence Tancock		
Address:	Horningsham, Wiltshire		

Sidney, known as George anda farm labourer, was the eldest son of George and Florence Tancock. He volunteered for service joining the North Somerset Yeomanry. It is likely he was transferred to the infantry and sent to the 1st Battalion Royal West Kent Regiment, who on Friday 26 October 1917 were attacking German positions between Polderhoek Chateau and the Scherriabeek stream. As they advanced down the Scherriabeek valley they found it to be an impassable morass. They attempted to push on under fire from Gheluvelt, sustaining very heavy casualties. George was killed during the attack. George's remains were originally buried south east of Tower Hamlets in a small cemetery and after the war his remains were relocated to Hooge Crater Cemetery.

Private Horace Henry Barber		*1st Bn Royal West Kent Regiment*	
Service No.	G/23252	Age:	28
Place of birth:	Battersea, London	Home Country:	England
Date of death:	26/10/1917	Cause of death:	Killed in action
Memorial:	Not known		
War Cemetery:	Hooge Crater Cemetery - Grave VIA. D. 10.		
Next of Kin:	Helen Barber (wife) – Charles J. & Ellen Barber (parents)		
Address:	19 Kingshill Road, Swindon, Wiltshire		

Horace, a print compositor was the third son of Charles and Ellen Barber and at the start of 1915 he married Helen M. Penney at Wandsworth. It is likely he was either conscripted into the army or enlisted under the Derby Scheme joining the Royal West Kent Regiment and after completing his training he was sent to the front, to serve with the 1st Battalion. Horace was reported missing on Friday 26 October 1917 when the 1st Royal West Kents attacked German positions between Polderhoek Chateau and the Scherriabeek stream, in the same action as George Tancock. Later official information was received by Horace's widow stating he was presumed to have been killed on the day he was reported missing. In May 1919 Horace's remains were located near the Scherriabeek stream and identified by means of a disc, before being relocated to Hooge Crater Cemetery.

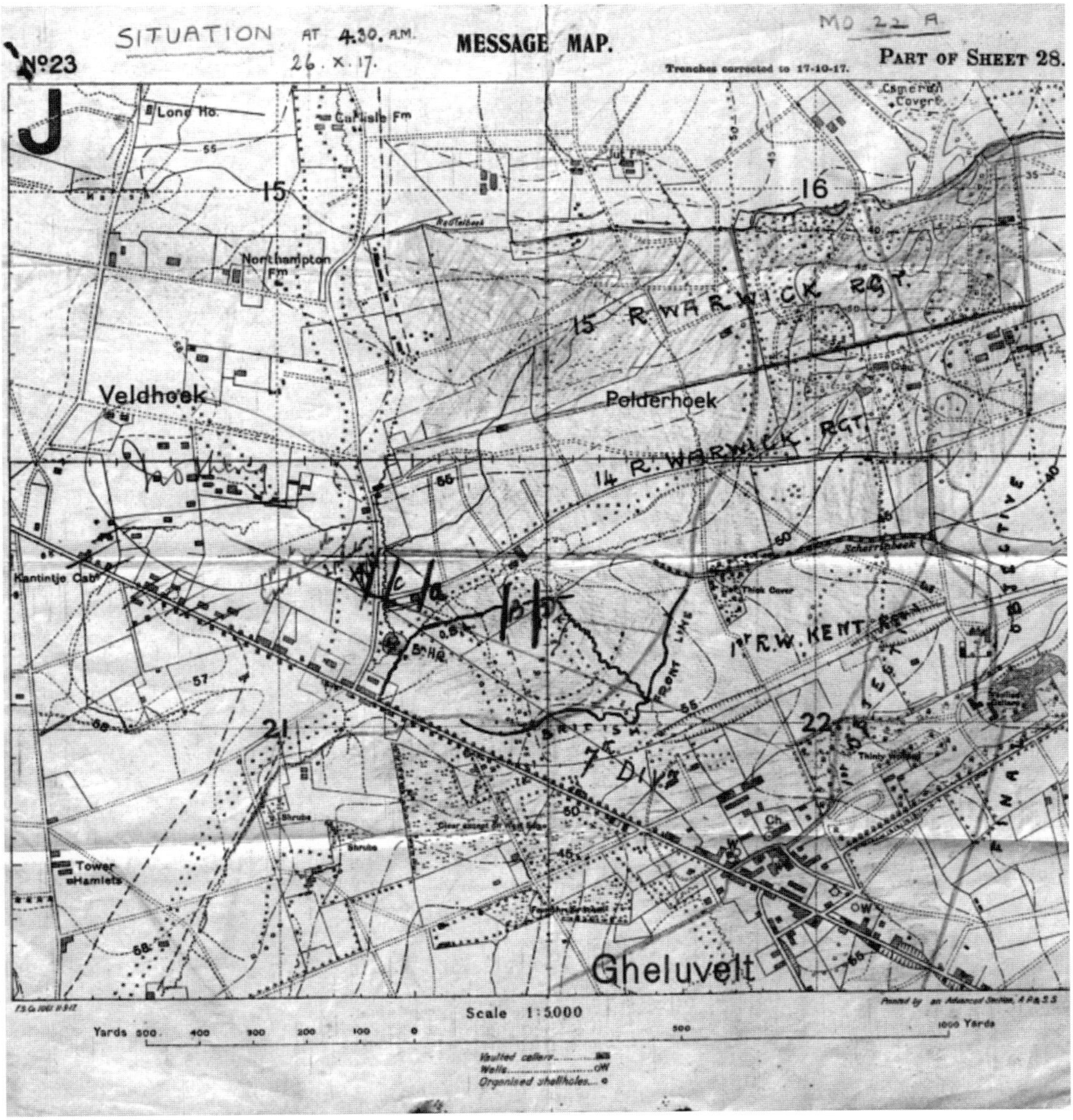

Above: Map showing the positions of the Warwicks and Royal West Kents north of Gheluvelt.

2nd Lieutenant Edward Gamman		*306th Siege Bty Royal Garrison Artillery*	
Service No.	N/a	Age:	26
Place of birth:	Kingham, Buckinghamshire	Home Country:	England
Date of death:	26/10/1917	Cause of death:	Killed in action
Memorial:	Andover, Hampshire – Marlborough College		
War Cemetery:	Tyne Cot Memorial - Panel 6 to 7 and 162		
Next of Kin:	Henry & Isabella Gamman		
Address:	Bishops Way, Andover, Hampshire		

Edward was the eldest son of Henry and Isabella Gamman and was educated at Marlborough College. After completing his education, he went to the School of Mines before proceeding to northern Nigeria. At the outbreak of hostilities, he joined the Nigerian Land Force and later returned to England, joining

Edward Gamman

the Royal Garrison Artillery as a cadet. He was given a commission 19 July 1916 and arrived in France on 2 April 1917. He was killed on Friday 26 October 1917, while acting as the forward observation officer west of Passendaele. Edward is remembered on the Tyne Cot Memorial and has no known grave. His younger brother Gilbert had been killed on 10 August 1915 while serving with the 5th Battalion Wiltshire Regiment at Gallipoli.

Lance Corporal Arthur Leonard D Watts — *2/5th Bn Royal Lancaster Regiment*

Service No.	15013	Age:	27
Place of birth:	Westbury, Wiltshire	Home Country:	England
Date of death:	26/10/1917	Cause of death:	Killed in action
Memorial:	Not known		
War Cemetery:	Tyne Cot Memorial – Panel 18 to 19.		
Next of Kin:	Oliver & Mary Anne Watts		
Address:	Elliotts Green, Frome, Somerset		

Arthur was the second son of Oliver and Mary Anne Watts and it is likely he was either conscripted into the army or enlisted under the Derby Scheme joining the Royal Lancaster Regiment. After completing his training he was sent to the front to serve with the 2/5th Battalion. He was killed on Friday 26 October 1917 when the 2/5th Royal Lancasters attacked German positions near Rubens and Memling Farms north east of Poelcapelle. As they advanced they found that the ground was impassable and the attack came to a stop about 300 yards from the start point. Two posts were established near Rubens and Memling Farms. Arthur is remembered on the Tyne Cot Memorial and has no known grave.

Private Reginald William Toogood — *2/2nd Bn London Regiment Royal Fusiliers*

Service No.	67090	Age:	25
Place of birth:	Devizes, Wiltshire	Home Country:	England
Date of death:	26/10/1917	Cause of death:	Killed in action
Memorial:	Monkton Farleigh, Wiltshire		
War Cemetery:	Tyne Cot Memorial - Panel 28 to 30 and 162 to 162A and 163A.		
Next of Kin:	William Adams & Susannah Toogood		
Address:,	Farleigh Wick, Wiltshire		

Farm worker Reginald was the eldest son of William and Susannah Toogood and it is likely he was either conscripted into the army or enlisted under the Derby Scheme initially being sent to the Army Service Corps. After completing his training, he was transferred to the 2/2nd London Regiment. He was reported missing on Friday 26 October 1917 during attacks on German positions of Cameron House and Moray House east of Poelcapelle. Later official information was received stating Reginald was presumed to have been killed on the day he was reported missing. He is remembered on the Tyne Cot Memorial and has no known grave.

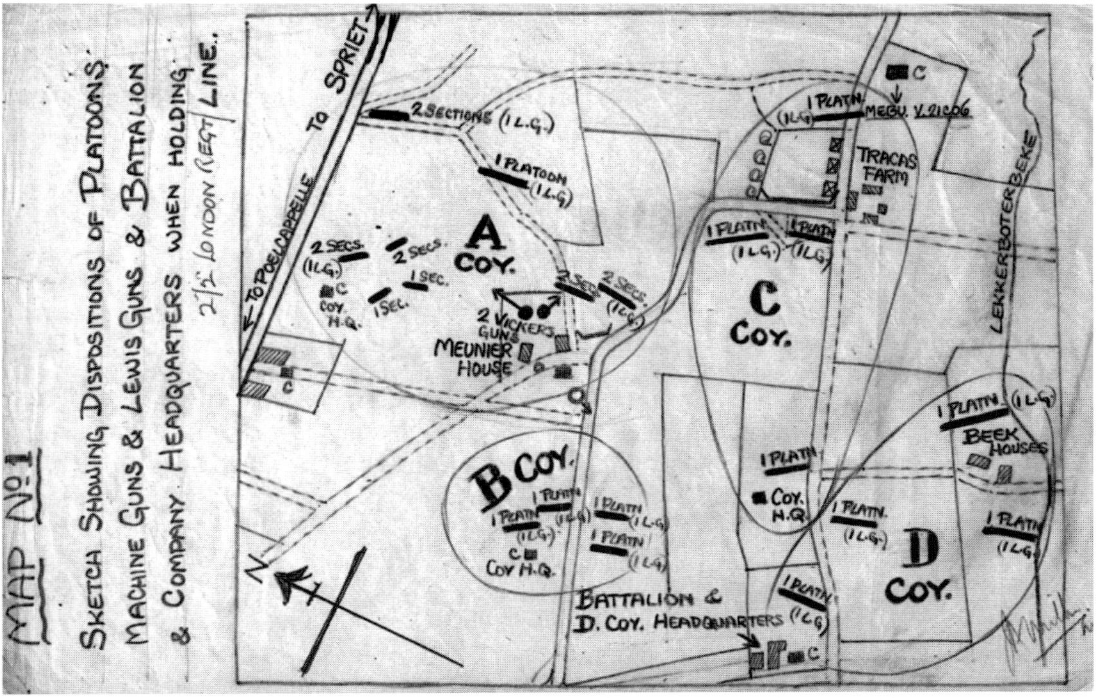

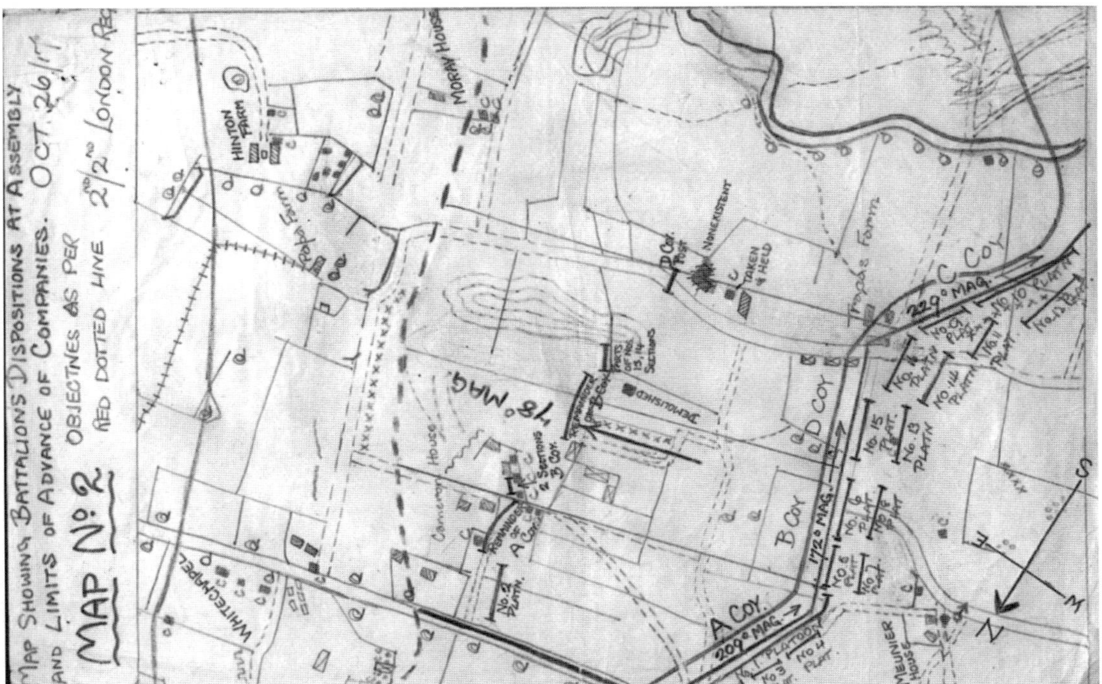

Maps showing the dispositions of the 2/2nd Bn London Regiment Royal Fusiliers on Friday 26 October 1917

Saturday 27 October 1917 - Temperature 9.5°c - 50% Cloud Cover - Rainfall Nil

Private William Henry Head		*21st Bn Manchester Regiment*	
Service No.	52651	Age:	34
Place of birth:	Swindon, Wiltshire	Home Country:	England
Date of death:	27/10/1917	Cause of death:	Killed in action
Memorial:	Swindon Christ Church, Wiltshire		
War Cemetery:	Tyne Cot Memorial - Panel 120 to 124 and 162 to 162A and 163A.		
Next of Kin:	William & Sarah Anne Head		
Address:	68 Newport Street, Swindon, Wiltshire		

William, a confectioner, was the only son of William and Sarah Anne Head and it is likely he was either conscripted into the army or enlisted under the Derby Scheme joining the Manchester Regiment. After completing his training, he was sent to the front, joining the 21st Battalion. On Friday 26 October 1917, the 21st Manchesters attacked German positions near Lewis House south of the Menin Road, west of Gheluvelt As they advanced over very muddy ground they were forced to retire to their start line under heavy German machine gun fire. William was reported missing on Friday 26 October 1917, it was thought he may have been wounded during the attack. William's mother received the following letter from 2nd Lieutenant J. McMahon of the 21st Manchesters:

"I regret to inform you that since October 26th your son, 52651 Pte. Head, has up to the present been missing, and that we have no means of knowing what happened to him. We have been unable to find out from his chums anything definite about him, and are sorry that we should have to send you such vague news. If, however, any information should come through about him, you can depend on our forwarding it to you. We are sorry to have lost your son, and sympathise with you in you great trouble. He has made many friends among our men, and we shall miss such a good and cheerful soldier. Again saying how sorry we are that we cannot give you any definite news of his fate, and hoping you will accept this expression on behalf of the officers and men of your son's old company."

Later William's mother received a further letter from the chaplain:

"I write to let you know that I buried your son Pte. W. H. Head, on November 9th. I found his body while going round the line on that night. He was killed some time before, but I do not know the date. Death must have been instantaneous, and I think the cause was shell fire. He had to be buried where he fell, as it was not possible to get his body brought back to a cemetery. Only his pay book and a purse were found on him and these will be sent to the base, and the purse, at any rate, to you. May god be with you in your loss and sorrow."

The location of William's grave was later lost and he is today remembered on the Tyne Cot Memorial.

Private Reginald Alfred Freegard		*2nd Bn Devonshire Regiment*	
Service No.	30939	Age:	19
Place of birth:	Sutton Benger, Wiltshire	Home Country:	England
Date of death:	27/10/1917	Cause of death:	Killed in action
Memorial:	Bremhill, Foxham, East Tytherton Morovian Church, Wiltshire		
War Cemetery:	Lancashire Cottage Cemetery - Grave III. A. 3.		
Next of Kin:	William & Sophia Freegard		

Address: Foxham, Wiltshire

Reginald, a rural postman, was the eldest son of William and Sophia Freegard and was well known in the Foxham area. It is likely he was conscripted into the army in late 1916 and sent to Exmouth, Devon for training. After completing his training, he was sent to the front in July 1917. He was killed in action on Saturday 27 October 1917 in the front line, east of Ploegsteert Wood. The Chaplain, who buried Reginald beside two of his comrades who were killed at the same time by the same shell, wrote the following to Reginald's mother;

"The men were in a Lewis gun position and the shell burst in the middle of them, killing all three on the spot. One consolation is he did not suffer for an instant. Another consolation is that he died doing his duty, and doing it well, and has gone to join the noble army of men who have given their lives for the good of humanity."

The Corporal of the platoon wrote to Reginald's sister;

"Your brother was killed by the concussion of the shell as he had only a slight wound on his leg. He had been in my section of bombers all the time until last week, he was taken from me and put in the machine gun section, so as one of my old boys I knew him well. I always considered him one of the best in my section and for digging a bit of trench he was the master piece. You should be quite proud of Reg; he was a brave lad. He and four others were with me in a tight corner, but came through safe, so I knew his worth. He was quiet, reliable, and fond of you and home, also his girl."

Miss Hillier, Reginald's fiancée, received two letters, one from the Company Sergeant Major and the other from a private, one of Reginald's pals. The former stated that;

"Reginald was well liked by the company and was admired by all the officers and N.C.O's. for his great coolness under fire. He would have done well if he had pulled through this terrible war."

His comrade also wrote to Miss Hillier;

"Bare your loss bravely and remember that he died fighting for you and he will be sadly missed by us all in the company, but much more so you and his dear mother."

In October 1918, the following memoriam was inserted in the local paper;

In loving memory of Reg
A few more struggles here
A few more partings o'er
A few more tolls a few more tears
And we shall weep no more

Sergeant Albert Edward Woolford — *C Bty 83rd Bde Royal Field Artillery*

Service No.	21871	Age:	35
Place of birth:	Swindon, Wiltshire	Home Country:	England
Date of death:	27/10/1917	Cause of death:	Killed in action
Memorial:	Not known		
War Cemetery:	Duhallow ADS Cemetery - Grave III. A. 19.		
Next of Kin:	George & Alice Woolford		
Address:	25 Albion Street, Swindon, Wiltshire		

Regular soldier Albert was the second son of George and Alice Woolford and enlisted with the Royal

Field Artillery before the Great War. He arrived in France on 27 September 1914 with C Battery of the 83rd Brigade. Albert was killed on Saturday 27 October 1917, most likely by German counter battery artillery fire, near St. Julian and buried in Duhallow ADS Cemetery. His brother Sidney had been killed while serving the the 1st Wiltshires at Messines in June 1917.

Pioneer Arthur John Jenner		*5th Army HQ Signal Coy Royal Engineers*	
Service No.	148096	Age:	23
Place of birth:	Swindon, Wiltshire	Home Country:	England
Date of death:	27/10/1917	Cause of death:	Killed in action
Memorial:	Wroughton, Euclid Street, Stores Department G.W.R. Swindon Works		
War Cemetery:	Bard Cottage Cemetery - Grave V. B. 7.		
Next of Kin:	William Henry & Susan Jenner		
Address:	18 High Street, Wroughton, Wiltshire		

Arthur was the youngest son of William and Susan Jenner and was employed in the stores department of the Great Western Railway Works in Swindon. It is likely he was either conscripted into the army or enlisted under the Derby Scheme joining the Royal Engineers. He was killed on Saturday 27 October 1917, most likely by German artillery fire, north of Ypres and buried at Bard Cottage Cemetery.

Corporal William Edwin Collett MM		*82nd Bde Royal Field Artillery*	
Service No.	48324	Age:	21
Place of birth:	Battersea, London	Home Country:	England
Date of death:	27/10/1917	Cause of death:	Killed in action
Memorial:	Lacock Church, Lacock Village		
War Cemetery:	Tyne Cot Memorial - Panel 4 to 6 and 162.		
Next of Kin:	Maria Collett (mother)		
Address:	Nethcote Hill, Lacock, Wiltshire		

Twenty one year old William was the eldest son of Maria Collett and volunteered for service joining the Royal Field Artillery in October 1914. He arrived in France on 25 July 1915 serving continuously on the continent and being awarded the Military Medal in August 1917 for conspicuous work in the field. He was killed on Saturday 27 October 1917 most likely by German artillery fire, near Fusilier Farm north east of Ypres. In November 1917 Maria Collett received the following letter from and officer of her son's battery:

"I am writing on behalf of the officers and men of the battery to offer you the deepest sympathy in the loss of your son in action. Corporal W. Collett was one of the most valuable N.C.O.'s in the battery, especially in signalling, at which he had log training, but lately he was in charge of a gun detachment. We all miss him very much. He was wounded in the arm on the 27 October, and was on his way down to the dressing station when another shell burst near him and a piece struck him in the head, killing him instantly. He was buried on the battlefield, and his grave marked by a cross. I feel for you very deeply and trust that God will give you strength to bear your great sorrow."

William's grave was lost in subsequent fighting and he is today remembered on the Tyne Cot Memorial.

Private Cecil Herbert Cox		*15th Bn Royal Warwickshire Regiment*	
Service No.	370	Age:	22
Place of birth:	Salisbury, Wiltshire	Home Country:	England
Date of death:	27/10/1917	Cause of death:	Died of wounds
Memorial:	Not known		
War Cemetery:	Lijssenthoek Military Cemetery - Grave XXII. C. 20A.		

Next of Kin: Herbert Porch & Emily Cox
Address: Nortonbury, Easemore Road, Redditch, Worcester

Cecil was the eldest son of Herbert and Emily Cox and was employed in a leather warehouse. It is likely he was either conscripted into the army or enlisted under the Derby Scheme joining the Royal Warwickshire Regiment and after completing his training was sent to the front to serve with the 15th Battalion. He was wounded during an attack on German positions north of Gheluvelt, on 26 October 1917 and evacuated to a casualty clearing station at Lijssenthoek, where he succumbed to his wounds on Saturday 27 October 1917.

Sunday 28 October 1917 - Temperature 5°c - 50% Cloud Cover - Rainfall 1.3mm

Gunner Albert Cave — *129th Heavy Bty Royal Garrison Artillery*

Service No. 159288 — Age: 35
Place of birth: Esclusham Below, Denbigh — Home Country: England
Date of death: 28/10/1917 — Cause of death: Died of wounds
Memorial: Not known
War Cemetery: Dozinghem Military Cemetery - Grave IX. B. 11.
Next of Kin: Minnie Gertrude Cave (wife) – Thomas and Elizabeth Cave (parents)
Address: 1 Southside, Street Andrew's Road, Bemerton, Wiltshire

Albert, a paper maker, was the third son of Thomas and Elizabeth Cave and on 15 November 1913 married Minnie Gertrude Ford at Bemerton. It is likely he was either conscripted into the army or enlisted under the Derby Scheme joining the Royal Garrison Artillery. After completing his training, he was sent to the front to serve with the 129th Heavy Battery. He was seriously wounded near Ypres and taken to No. 47 Casualty Clearing Station north of Poperinge, where he succumbed to his wounds on Sunday 28 October 1917. He left a widow and a young daughter.

2nd Corporal Charles Lewis — *12th Field Coy Bn Canadian Engineers*

Service No. 504770 — Age: 39
Place of birth: South Marston, Wiltshire — Home Country: Canada
Date of death: 28/10/1917 — Cause of death: Died of wounds
Memorial: Not known
War Cemetery: Ypres Reservoir Cemetery - Grave I. I. 35.
Next of Kin: William & Charlotte Lewis
Address: South Marston, Wiltshire

Charles, was the second son of William and Charlotte Lewis, was well known in Swindon and originally enlisted with the British army on 22 August 1899, joining the 3rd Dragoon Guards. He served in the South African War and was awarded the Queen's Medal with 4 Clasps; Cape Coloney, Orange Free State, South Africa 1901 and South Africa 1902. After serving for eight years he left the Dragoons in 1907 on the termination of his engagement and was placed on the army reserve. He emigrated to Canada with his brother and other members of his family where he was employed as a driver and miner by the Western Fuel Company of Nanaimo Vancouver Island. He volunteered for service with the Canadian army on 6 March 1916 and was sent to No. 13 Field Company Canadian Engineers. He arrived in England on 29 May 1916 and transferred to No. 12 Field Company and was sent to France on 12 August 1916. On Sunday 28 October 1917, Charles was in charge of a pack train proceeding from Potijze towards Zonnebeke, with ammunition for the forward area, when he was severely wounded by shrapnel from a

Henry Fred Hardiman

German shell. His comrades administered first aid and he was taken to No. 11 Canadian Field Ambulance where he succumbed to his wounds. His brother John had been killed while serving with the Royal Engineers in July 1917

Able Seaman Henry Fred Hardiman *Nelson Bn Royal Naval Div RNVR*

Service No.	R/1489	Age:	19
Place of birth:	Fovant, Wiltshire	Home Country:	England
Date of death:	28/10/1917	Cause of death:	Killed in action
Memorial:	Fovant, Wiltshire, Commemorated on his parent's grave.		
War Cemetery:	Tyne Cot Memorial - Panel 2 to 3 and 162 to 162A		
Next of Kin:	Frank & Charlotte Hardiman		
Address:	East Farm, Fovant, Wiltshire		

Henry, known as Fred, was the eldest son of Frank and Charlotte Hardiman and was conscripted in to the army and put on to the reserve on 5 June 1916. He was mobilised on 29 May 1917 and after completing his training he was sent to France on 6 August 1917. He was sent to the front to serve with Nelson Battalion on 4 October 1917. Fred was killed on Sunday 28 October 1917, most likely by German artillery on the east side of the Ypres Canal not far from Essex Farm. He is remembered on the Tyne Cot Memorial and has no known grave.

MONDAY 29 OCTOBER 1917 - TEMPERATURE 8.5°c - 50% CLOUD COVER - RAINFALL NIL

Private Victor James *2nd Bn Wiltshire Regiment*

Service No.	24529	Age:	20
Place of birth:	Newton Abbot, Devon	Home Country:	England
Date of death:	29/10/1917	Cause of death:	Died of wounds
Memorial:	Newton Abbott - London City & Midland Bank Memorial, Canary Wharf.		
War Cemetery:	Trois Arbres Cemetery Steenwerck - Grave II. B. 1.		
Next of Kin:	Henry David & Flora Almeda Asenath James		
Address:	40 Abbotsbury Road, Newton Abbot, Devon		

Victor was the second son of Henry and Flora James and was employed by the London City & Midland Bank Ltd at Salisbury, where he was much esteemed. It is likely he was either conscripted into the army or enlisted under the Derby Scheme joining the Wiltshire Regiment and was mobilized in May 1916. After completing his training, he was sent to France in December 1916 to serve with the 2nd Battalion. On 29 October 1917, the 2nd Wiltshires had been in the British support line near Wall Farm east of Oostaverne and were on their way to rest billets at Parrain Farm west of Wytschaete when they were bombed by German aircraft. Victor was wounded and was evacuated to the 2nd Australian Casualty Clearing Station at Trois Arbres Cemetery at Steenwerck. His parents received the following letter from the casualty clearing station:

"He was brought into a clearing-station hospital on the 29th, suffering from internal injuries received in action and, although everything possible was done for him, there was no hope for him from the first and he passed away the same day. He was buried at Trois Arbres Cemetery and a cross was erected over the grave."

The official intimation was accompanied by a message of sympathy from the King and Queen.

Private Arthur Stewart Butcher		*2nd Bn Wiltshire Regiment*	
Service No.	11032	Age:	21
Place of birth:	Stratton St Margaret, Wiltshire	Home Country:	England
Date of death:	29/10/1917	Cause of death:	Died of wounds
Memorial:	Not known		
War Cemetery:	Bailleul Communal Cemetery Extension Nord - Grave III. E. 86.		
Next of Kin:	John & Annie Butcher		
Address:	10 Dixon Street, Swindon, Wiltshire		

Arthur was the youngest son of John and Annie Butcher and had been an apprentice at the Great Western Railway Works at Swindon. He volunteered for service on 7 September 1914 with the Wiltshire Regiment and after completing his training he was sent to France arriving on 17 February 1915. On 29 October 1917, the 2nd Wiltshires had been in the British support line near Wall Farm east of Oostaverne and were on their way to rest billets at Parrain Farm west of Wytschaete when they were bombed by German aircraft. Arthur was wounded and was evacuated to a casualty clearing station at Bailleul, where he succumbed to his wound later that day.

TUESDAY 30 OCTOBER 1917 - TEMPERATURE 6.5°c - CLEAR SHOWERS - RAINFALL 2.3mm

Private Francis Thomas Rose		*4th Bn Bedfordshire Regiment*	
Service No.	21274	Age:	35
Place of birth:	Cirencester, Gloucestershire	Home Country:	England
Date of death:	30/10/1917	Cause of death:	Killed in action
Memorial:	Sutton Benger, Wiltshire		
War Cemetery:	Tyne Cot Memorial - Panel 48 to 50 and 162A.		
Next of Kin:	Florence Mary Rose (wife) – Isaac & Emma Rose (parents)		
Address:	Sutton Benger, Wiltshire - 53 Castle Street, Cirencester		

Thomas, known as Frank and a gardener, was the eldest son of Isaac and Emma Rose and married

In Loving Memory

OF

MY DEAR SON,

Company Sergeant Major

ISRAEL FISHER,

Killed in action, October 30th, 1917,

AGED 43 YEARS.

Above: Memorial card for Israel John Fisher - Right: Coleridge Marchment

Florence Mary Weakley at the beginning of 1912 at Sutton Benger. The couple moved to Holt and it is likely Frank was conscripted into the army or enlisted under the Derby Scheme initially joining the Royal Horse Artillery, before being transferred to the 4th Battalion Bedfordshire Regiment. At 5.50am on Tuesday 30 October 1917 the 4th Bedfords attacked south east of Poelcapelle. As they advanced they were held up and eventually checked by the boggy ground that surrounded the Paddebeek stream to the west of Passchendaele. An advance of between 150 and 200 yards was made and over ninety men of the 4th Bedfords were killed. Frank was reported missing during the attack and later official information was received stating he was presumed to have been killed on Tuesday 30 October 1917. He is remembered on the Tyne Cot Memorial and has no known grave. He left a widow and two small children.

Private Coleridge Marchment — *4th Bn Yorkshire Regiment*

Service No. 203478
Place of birth: Salisbury, Wiltshire
Date of death: 30/10/1917
Memorial: Not known
War Cemetery: Tyne Cot Memorial - Panel 52 to 54 and 162A
Next of Kin: Teresa M Marchment
Address: Llanelly, Carmarthenshire

Age: 30
Home Country: Wales
Cause of death: Killed in action

Coleridge was born in Salisbury in 1887 and in the spring of 1913 he married Teresa M. McCoy at Llanelli. It is likely he was either conscripted into the army or enlisted under the Derby Scheme joining the Yorkshire Regiment. After completing his training, he was sent to the front joining the 4th Battalion. Coleridge was killed on Tuesday 30 October 1917, most likely by German artillery, while in the British support line near Colombo House north of Langemarck. He is remembered on the Tyne Cot Memorial and has no known grave. He left a widow and a young daughter.

Private Israel John Fisher — *38th Bn Eastern Ontario Regiment*

Service No. 246095
Place of birth: Greatfield, Wiltshire
Date of death: 30/10/1917
Memorial: Not known
War Cemetery: Passchendaele New British Cemetery - Grave III. D. 15.

Age: 43
Home Country: Canada
Cause of death: Killed in action

Next of Kin: Alice Fisher (wife) – William & Mary Fisher (parents)
Address: 201 Hopewell Avenue, Ottawa, Ontario – Greatfield, Wiltshire

Israel, known as John, was the second son of William and Mary Fisher and originally joined the British army, enlisting with the Wiltshire Regiment on 4 December 1893. After two years serving in England he served a further seven years in India before serving in South Africa in 1902. He then returned to England where he served until leaving the Wiltshires on 3 December 1909. Shortly after leaving the army he emigrated to Canada, and lived in Ottawa. He married, then joined the local militia and was promoted to Company Sergeant Major of the 43rd D.C.O.R. He found employment in the inspection room of the Militia Department. He enlisted with the Canadian Army on 1 April 1916 and in June 1916 came to England spending a short leave with his parents. John was killed at 4pm on Tuesday 30 October 1917, he was instantly killed by concussion from a bursting shell, whilst occupying the enemy front line trench in front and just south of Passchendaele. His remains were located in February 1920, identified by means of a disc, then moved to Passchendaele New British Cemetery.

Private William McArthur Vokins *78th Bn Canadian Infantry*

Service No.	625160	Age:	29
Place of birth:	Ramsbury, Wiltshire	Home Country:	England
Date of death:	30/10/1917	Cause of death:	Killed in action
Memorial:	Ramsbury, Wiltshire		
War Cemetery:	Ypres Menin Gate – Panel 24 - 26 - 28 - 30.		
Next of Kin:	William & Mary E. Vokins		
Address:	Oxford Street, Ramsbury, Wiltshire		

William, a farmer, was the second and twin son of William & Mary Vokins and emigrated to Canada in 1910. He volunteered with the militia in 1913 joining the 22nd Saskatchewan Light Horse and on 13 March 1916 he enlisted with the Canadian Expeditionary force. After completing his training he was sent to England and then onto France, to serve with the 78th Battalion Canadian Infantry. William was killed on Tuesday 30 October 1917, near the east side road to Broodseinde, just south of Passchendaele. William's mother received the following letter from one of his comrades:

"It is likely you will have heard the unwelcome news of your dear son's death before this reaches you, but as one of his pals I feel I must write a few lines of sympathy in your great loss. 'Bill,' as we affectionately called him, died gallantly doing his bit in a recent push which put the Hun on the run. It is some small comfort to know that he suffered no pain, but passed away quickly. Although yours is a greater loss, we all mourn his departure from among us, for his ever cheery nature was always an inspiration to keep up our spirits, and his good manly character was such that the best of men might be proud to follow his example. He and I were in the same platoon, in the ----st, and although that unit was broken up we both eventually came to the --th Scout Section, where he has always been, since joining it, one of its most popular members and friend to all. It was the morning of October 30th that 'Bill' crossed the Great Divide to a better land, where we must have patience to meet him at the last Great Day. I again ask you to accept my sympathy and offer of any slight service I might be able to render you."

William is remembered on the Ypres Menin Gate and has no known grave.

Private John Reginald Tunnicliffe Paradise *1st/28th Bn London Regiment*

Service No.	756371	Age:	23
Place of birth:	Kingston, Surrey	Home Country:	England
Date of death:	30/10/1917	Cause of death:	Killed in action
Memorial:	Marlborough College - St John the Evangelist, Kingston		

Left: John Reginald Tunnicliffe Paradise

Right: John Piggott Wheeler MC

War Cemetery:	Tyne Cot Memorial - Panel 153
Next of Kin:	Dr Thomas Decimus & Mary Lomax Paradise
Address:	Athol House, Kingston on Thames, Surrey

John, known as Jack, was the only child of Dr Thomas and Mary Paradise and was educated at Marlborough College, before attending Pembroke College Oxford. He was given a commission with the 11th Battalion Royal Warwickshire Regiment. However, Jack was not with the 11th Warwicks when they crossed to France in July 1915 and he relinquished his commission on 11 November 1915. It is likely he was conscripted into the army on 2 March 1916 and was placed on the army reserve. He was called up for service on 14 March 1917 and on the front of his attestation paper was the underlined word, Unitarian. The term Unitarian means religious beliefs that have a respect for all life, Jack may have been a conscientious objector on the grounds of religion. He was sent to France on 13 September 1917 to serve with the 28th Battalion London Regiment, the Artists Rifles. Jack was reported missing on Tuesday 30 October 1917, when the Artists Rifles attacked German positions west of Passchendaele at Source Trench. At 5.50am the Germans dropped a counter barrage 100 yards behind the British barrage and caught the British attackers struggling in the mud. Later official information was received stating Jack was presumed to have been killed on the day he was reported missing. He is remembered on the Tyne Cot Memorial and has no known grave.

Major John Piggott Wheeler MC | *82nd Bde Royal Field Artillery*

Service No.	N/a	Age:	25
Place of birth:	Reading, Berkshire	Home Country:	England
Date of death:	30/10/1917	Cause of death:	Killed in action
Memorial:	Marlborough College, Wiltshire		
War Cemetery:	Vlamertinghe New Military Cemetery - Grave IX. E. 23		
Next of Kin:	Samuel & Elizabeth Wheeler		
Address:	30 Craven Road, Reading, Berkshire		

John was the youngest son of Samuel and Elizabeth Wheeler and was educated at Marlborough College. On leaving education he was given an apprenticeship with Vickers Company and joined the 4th Home Counties Brigade, Royal Field Artillery, Territorial Force at Erith. After serving as a gunner he was given a territorial force commission in April 1911 and was promoted to Lieutenant in February 1912. At the outbreak of hostilities John was given a regular commission with 82nd Brigade Royal Field Artillery and arrived in France in July 1915, being promoted to Captain. He was awarded the Military

Cross in April 1917 and the citation reads:

"For conspicuous gallantry and devotion to duty. He, with great coolness and disregard of danger, reorganised his drivers and teams, and succeeded in getting his guns into action under the most trying conditions."

In June 1917, he was promoted to Major and on Tuesday 30 October 1917 the 82nd Brigade were near Fusilier Farm, north of St. Jean. They were supporting an attack by the 58th Division and were targeted by German counter battery fire, with high explosive and gas shells. The 82nd Brigade suffered heavily and lost all their officers and a good number of other ranks. John was killed during the barrage and was buried in Vlamertinghe New Military Cemetery.

Wednesday 31 October 1917 - Temperature 12°c - Clear - Rainfall Nil

Private Albert Edgar Dew		*9th Bn Leicestershire Regiment*	
Service No.	39559	Age:	27
Place of birth:	Westbury, Wiltshire	Home Country:	England
Date of death:	31/10/1917	Cause of death:	Killed in action
Memorial:	Westbury, Wiltshire		
War Cemetery:	Hooge Crater Cemetery - Grave I. J. 10.		
Next of Kin:	Annie Dew (wife) – Simon & Jane Dew (parents)		
Address:	147 Harrington Street, Derby- Leigh Road, Westbury		

Albert, a gardener, was the fifth son of Simon and Jane Dew and it is likely he was conscripted into the army and placed on the reserve on 21 June 1916. On April 14 1917 he married Annie Horby at St. Thomas's Church. He was called up on 11 June 1917 joining the Sherwood Foresters and after completing his training arrived in France on 6 October 1917, being transferred to the 9th Battalion Leicestershire Regiment on 15 October 1917. On Wednesday 31 October 1917, the 9th Leicesters were in the British line in front of Polygon Wood and were ordered at 6.30pm back to reserve at Zillebeke Railway Dugouts. The relief was very slow owing to a heavy German gas shell barrage between Polygon Wood and Chateau Wood. Albert was reported missing on Wednesday 31 October 1917 and in March 1918, Albert's widow received official information stating he was presumed to have been killed on the day he was reported missing. After the war Alberts grave with a cross erected on it with his name number and date of death 5 November 1917, was located near the British line near Railway Wood, north of Hooge. It contained a full body with shoulder titles and a silver watch made in Nottingham., his remains were moved to Hooge Crater Cemetery. In May 1919 Albert's widow received his personal possessions consisting of disc, safety razor and blades, touch card, 1 franc, 50 centimes note, defaced. No mention was made of the silver watch. He left a widow and young daughter.

Airman 2nd Class George Chapman Bradbury		*6th Sqdn Royal Flying Corps*	
Service No.	51746	Age:	36
Place of birth:	Shepton Mallett, Somerset	Home Country:	England
Date of death:	31/10/1917	Cause of death:	Killed in action
Memorial:	Frome, Somerset		
War Cemetery:	Lijssenthoek Military Cemetery - Grave XXI. DD. 16A.		
Next of Kin:	Margaret E. Bradbury (wife) – Frederick G. & Elizabeth M. Bradbury (parents)		
Address:	22 Hockmore Street Cowley, Oxford – Marshlands, Warminster		

George was the eldest son of Frederick and Elizabeth Bradbury and was educated at the Wells Blue School. After leaving education he was employed as a photographer for Bells & Sons in Frome. In spring

Left: *George Chapman Bradbury*

Right: *Ernest Henry King's* memorial scroll

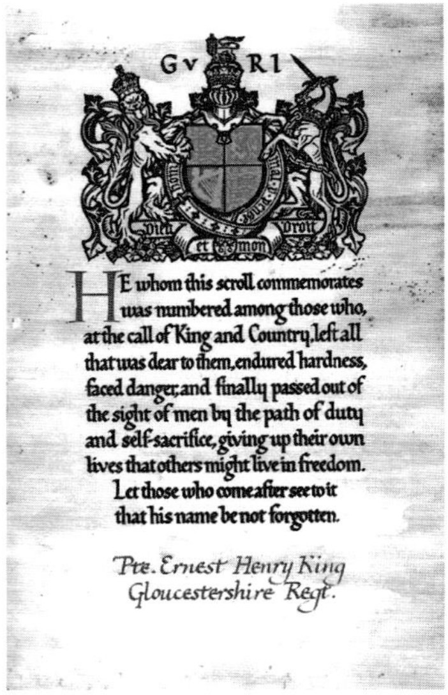
GV RI

HE whom this scroll commemorates was numbered among those who, at the call of King and Country, left all that was dear to them, endured hardness, faced danger, and finally passed out of the sight of men by the path of duty and self-sacrifice, giving up their own lives that others might live in freedom. Let those who come after see to it that his name be not forgotten.

Pte. Ernest Henry King
Gloucestershire Regt.

1916, he married Margret E. Middleton at Witney, Oxfordshire. It is likely he was either conscripted into the army or enlisted under the Derby Scheme initially joining the Somerset Light Infantry in August 1916. He was transferred to the Hampshire Regiment and then applied for a transfer to the Royal Flying Corps He was sent to France in January 1917, to serve with 6th Squadron, where his professional skill was in demand and used in aerial photography of the German lines. On 30/31 October 1917, there was a full moon during the night. George was nine miles behind the front line, at Abele Aerodrome, in a photo studio when it was bombed by German aircraft. According to his diaries the aerodrome had been receiving special attention from the "Hun" airman. George was one of the four men killed during the raid, the intelligence officer of the squadron wrote the following to George's widow:

"Your husband was killed early this morning by an act of the enemy. No words of mine can fully express my feelings in regard to the loss of your husband, who was, without a doubt, the most gentlemanly, trustworthy, sincere and efficient photographer in my section. I shall miss him greatly, not only for his work, but for the good qualities which he possessed. Please accept my heartfelt sympathy for you and your family in the loss of your dear husband, who died as an English gentleman, and who has been called to a higher service."

THURSDAY 1 NOVEMBER 1917 - TEMPERATURE 10.5°c - OVERCAST - RAINFALL 0.2mm

Private Ernest Henry King		*14th Bn Gloucestershire Regiment*	
Service No.	20694	Age:	21
Place of birth:	Donhead, Wiltshire	Home Country:	England
Date of death:	01/11/1917	Cause of death:	Killed in action
Memorial:	Not known		
War Cemetery:	Canada Farm Cemetery - Grave III. F. 14		
Next of Kin:	Fred John & Emma Jane King		
Address:	Donhead St Andrew, Wiltshire		

Ernest, a farm labourer, was the eldest son of Fred and Emma King and it is likely he was either conscripted into the army or enlisted under the Derby Scheme joining the Gloucestershire Regiment. After completing his training he was sent to France to serve with the 14th Battalion. On Thursday 1 November 1917, the 14th Gloucesters were in the British front line near the Houthulst Forrest and during the night they were relieved by the 17th Royal Scots. It is likely Ernest was killed by German artillery fire as the 14th Gloucesters made their way to Dykes camp east of Elerdinghe.

Able Seaman Cecil Victor Simmonds		*Drake Bn RN Div RNVR*	
Service No.	R/990	Age:	20
Place of birth:	Salisbury, Wiltshire	Home Country:	England
Date of death:	01/11/1917	Cause of death:	Died
Memorial:	Salisbury, Wiltshire		
War Cemetery:	Mendinghem Military Cemetery - Grave VI. F. 39.		
Next of Kin:	William Carey & Louisa Jane Simmonds		
Address:	93 Rampart Road, Salisbury, Wiltshire		

Cecil, a print compositor ,was the youngest son of William and Louisa Simmonds and it is likely he was conscripted into the forces enlisting with the Royal Naval Volunteer Reserve on 26 March 1917. After completing his training, he was sent to France on 9 July 1917 and joined Drake Battalion of the Royal Naval Division on 30 August 1917. Cecil was wounded on 24 October 1917 when Drake Battalion supplied 550 men to work with the 7th Canadian Railway Troops on Railway work south west of Elverdinge. Two other ranks were killed, two died of wounds and 3 were wounded. Cecil was evacuated to the 64th Casualty Clearing Station north west of Poperinge where it was found he had a bomb wound and his 4th finger was fractured and he had a penetrating wound to the head. Cecil succumbed to his wounds at 10am on Thursday 1 November 1917 and was buried in Mendinghem Military Cemetery.

Private Francis Harry Farmer		*9th Bn Devonshire Regiment*	
Service No.	31367	Age:	19
Place of birth:	Cahore Point, Ireland	Home Country:	England
Date of death:	01/11/1917	Cause of death:	Died of wounds
Memorial:	Not known		
War Cemetery:	Wimereux Communal Cemetery - Grave VI. F. 15.		
Next of Kin:	Joseph Richard & Sarah Jane Farmer		
Address:	18 Regent Place, Swindon, Wiltshire		

Nineteen year old Francis, was the son of Joseph and Sarah Farmer and it is likely he was either conscripted into the army or enlisted under the Derby Scheme initially joining the Wiltshire Regiment. He was later transferred to the 9th Battalion Devonshire Regiment. It is likely he was wounded in the British front line at Gheluvelt and evacuated to a military hospital at Wimereux where he succumbed to his wounds on Thursday 1 November 1917.

Lance Sergeant William Smith DCM MM		*99th Field Amb Bn Royal Army Medical Corps*	
Service No.	66599	Age:	45
Place of birth:	Manchester, Lancashire	Home Country:	England
Date of death:	01/11/1917	Cause of death:	Killed in action
Memorial:	West Lavington, Wiltshire		
War Cemetery:	Kandahar Farm Cemetery - Grave I. D. 13.		
Next of kin:	Ada Emma Smith (wife) - William Boyle Smith (parent)		
Address:	Bush Bottom Farm, West Lavington - Lancashire		

William, a poultry manager, was the son of William Boyle Smith and on 3 February 1895, he married Ada Emma Briscoe at St. Cyprian, Edge Hill, Lancashire. He volunteered for service joining the Royal

The original grave marker of George Arthur Keith Buskin, now in the cloisters at Salisbury Cathedral.

Army Medical Corps and arrived in France on 16 November 1915 being sent to 99th Field Ambulance. He was awarded the Military Medal and the Distinguished Service Medal while serving, and the citation for the D.C.M. states:

For conspicuous gallantry and devotion to duty. He worked continuously for forty eight hours directing stretcher bearers and accompanying them through heavy shell fire over difficult ground and carried in a wounded man under heavy shell fire. His coolness and energy inspired all ranks

William was killed in action near Wulvergem, on Thursday 1 November 1917. He was one of the members of a party that was visiting the front line and on their return, were heavily shelled by German artillery. He was buried in Kandahar Farm Cemetery which at the time was the base for 99th Field Ambulance. His son, John Wilfred Smith, had been killed at the Somme on 1 July 1916.

Saturday 3 November 1917 - Temperature 11°c - Overcast - Rainfall Nil

Gunner George Arthur Keith Buskin — *1st Bde Bn Australian Field Artillery*

Service No.	318	Age:	23
Place of birth:	Gorakpur, India	Home Country:	Australia
Date of death:	03/11/1917	Cause of death:	Killed in action
Memorial:	Memorial Cross Salisbury Cathedral Cloisters		
War Cemetery:	The Huts Cemetery - Grave XIV.B.4		
Next of Kin:	Alexander & Laura May Buskin		
Address:	Canterbury, Kent		

George was the younger son of Alexander and Laura May Buskin and was educated at Fort Street Sydney, before taking work as a clerk with the Sydney Morning Herald. He volunteered for service joining the 3rd Battery Royal Filed Artillery on 24 August 1914 and after completing his training was sent to Egypt and then landed at Gallipoli on 25 April 1915. He was evacuated from Gallipoli suffering from neurasthenia, a condition caused by chronic fatigue, in mid July 1915 and returned to the peninsular on 1 August 1915. He was evacuated again on 30 December 1915 suffering from bronchitis and re-joined his unit in Egypt. He left Egypt at the start of August 1916, being sent to England and after a year at Larkhill arrived in France on 17 August 1917. George was killed on Saturday 3 November 1917, most likely near Halfway House south east of Hellfire Corner, not far from the Menin Road, most likely by

German artillery fire. The 1st Australian Field Artillery were registering the guns to support an attack the following day. George was buried at The Huts Cemetery, near Dickebusch. In the late 1920's the original cross grave markers were replaced by headstones and the wooden crosses were offered to the next of kin. George's cross was sent to his mother, whose brother, a clergyman may have had connections with Salisbury Cathedral, where George Buskin's Cross is displayed in the cloisters today. His older brother Alexander Buskin had been killed at Gallipoli in September 1915.

Sunday 4 November 1917 - Temperature 8.5°c - Overcast - Rainfall Nil

Private Percy Alfred Clinch		*1st Bn Devonshire Regiment*	
Service No.	27630	Age:	20
Place of birth:	Westbury, Wiltshire	Home Country:	England
Date of death:	04/11/1917	Cause of death:	Died of wounds
Memorial:	Westbury, Wiltshire		
War Cemetery:	Lijssenthoek Military Cemetery - Grave XXI. HH. 19.		
Next of Kin:	Oliver & Mary Ann Clinch		
Address:	Penleigh, Dilton, Westbury, Wiltshire		

Percy was the third son of Oliver and Mary Ann Clinch and was employed as a labourer in a tanner's yard. It is likely he was either conscripted into the army or enlisted under the Derby Scheme joining the Devonshire Regiment. After completing his training, he was sent to France joining the 1st Battalion. It is likely Percy was wounded in the British front line near Polderhoek Chateau at the end of October and evacuated to a casualty clearing station at Lijssenthoek, where he succumbed to his wounds on Sunday 4 November 1917.

Gunner Albert Burton		*76th Siege Bty Royal Garrison Artillery*	
Service No.	62934	Age:	27
Place of birth:	Monkton Farleigh, Wiltshire	Home Country:	England
Date of death:	04/11/1917	Cause of death:	Killed in action
Memorial:	Monkton Farleigh, Wiltshire		
War Cemetery:	Vlamertinghe Military Cemetery - Grave XII. E. 12.		
Next of Kin:	Thomas & Emily Burton		
Address:	Farleigh Wick, Monkton Farleigh, Wiltshire		

Albert was the second son of Thomas and Emily Burton and was a policeman with the Bristol City Police Force. He volunteered for service on 6 November 1915 with the Royal Garrison Artillery. After completing his training, he was sent to France 1 April 1916, joining the 76th Siege Battery. He was given ten days leave to go to England on 1 August 1917 and after this leave returned to his unit. Albert was killed on Sunday 4 November 1917 north of Ypres. His mother received the following letter from Lieutenant R. G. Wallis:

"We had been in action ourselves in the afternoon, but later the Germans started shelling our position. Our men took cover in their dug-outs, but buy an evil chance, a direct hit was obtained on the one in which your son was sheltering with his mates, and we had seven brave fellows killed by that one shell. Your boy's death is a great loss to us, a far greater one to you, but you will be proud to know he died bravely for the home folk."

Left: Albert Burton

Right: The laid down grave marker of Armar Edward Acton at Wimereux Communal Cemetery

A letter was received from Lieutenant G. Chapman, Chaplain to the Forces:

"We trust that the knowledge that your son died in the path of honour and duty may soften the force of the heavy blow. He is buried with others of his comrades who were killed by the same shell, and we laid him to rest in the sure and certain hope of Resurrection to eternal life, which we trust will bring you consolation in this hour of sorrow. The country must ever hold in the highest esteem the memory of our brave dead heroes and their noble deeds, men who have laid down their lives for the security of English homes."

Albert's mother wrote to Lieutenant Wallis asking for the particulars of her son's death and received the following:

"I am glad to be able to assure you that your dear boy suffered no pain; he was killed instantly. His dug-out was next to the cook-house and help was immediately available, but your son had passed away, and we could do nothing. The shell penetrated the dug-out before bursting. Your son died to save the womenfolk of England from the beastly Germans, and his own country from their domination."

Chaplain 4th Class Armar Edward Acton		*Army Chaplains Department*	
Service No.	N/a	Age:	28
Place of birth:	Galway, Ireland	Home Country:	Ireland
Date of death:	04/11/1917	Cause of death:	Died of wounds
Memorial:	Aravon School Memorial, Trinity College, Dublin		
War Cemetery:	Wimereux Communal Cemetery - Grave IV. L. 2.		
Next of Kin:	Lt. Col. James Lowery Cole & Maud Julia Lowery Acton		
Address:	Dunmore, Glenageary, Dublin		

Armar was the eldest son of Lt. Col. James and Maud Acton and was a nephew of the Mrs Millman of Devizes. He was educated at Aravon School before attending Trinity College Dublin. He volunteered for service with the Army Chaplains Department and arrived in France on 9 June 1916. He was attached to the 2nd Battalion Border Regiment, who on 26 October attacked German positions near Gheluvelt. Armar was visiting the troops in the front line and was wounded in the knee with shrapnel. He was evacuated to a military hospital at Wimereux where it was found the shrapnel had broken his knee but his wound was not thought to be serious. An infection set in and his leg had to be amputated but his condition worsened and he succumbed to his wounds on Sunday 4 November 1917.

William Herbert Fry

Driver William Herbert Fry — *84th Bde. Ammo Col Royal Field Artillery*

Service No. 94083
Age: 20
Place of birth: Swindon, Wiltshire
Home Country: England
Date of death: 04/11/1917
Cause of death: Died of wounds
Memorial: L2 Shop, Locomotive Department, Great Western Railway Works, Swindon
War Cemetery: Wimereux Communal Cemetery - Grave VI. G. 5A.
Next of Kin: William & Annie Maria Fry
Address: Exmouth Street, Swindon, Wiltshire

William, known as Herbert, was the only son of William and Annie Fry and was under age when he volunteered for service with the Royal Field Artillery. He arrived in France on 28 July 1915 and to serve as a driver, with the 84th Brigade Ammunition Column. Herbert was wounded, most likely by German artillery fire, near Ypres in October 1917. He was evacuated to a military hospital near Wimereux, where he succumbed to his wounds on Sunday 4 November 1917.

Gunner William James Dobson — *238th Siege Bty Royal Garrison Artillery*

Service No. 86947
Age: 21
Place of birth: Froxfield, Wiltshire
Home Country: England
Date of death: 04/11/1917
Cause of death: Killed in action
Memorial: Froxfield, Wiltshire
War Cemetery: Potijze Chateau Grounds Cemetery - Grave I. C. 32
Next of Kin: Job & Louisa Ann Dobson
Address: 42 The Hill, Froxfield, Wiltshire

William, a butcher's assistant, was the second son of Job and Louisa Dobson and it is likely he was either conscripted into the army or enlisted under the Derby Scheme joining the Royal Garrison Artillery. After completing his training, he was sent to serve with the 238th Siege Battery. William was killed on Sunday 4 November 1917, most likely by German artillery fire, north east Ypres.

Corporal Sidney Ernest Matthews — *121st Bty 27th Bde Royal Field Artillery*

Service No. 19980
Age:
Place of birth: Salisbury, Wiltshire
Home Country: England
Date of death: 04/11/1917
Cause of death: Killed in action
Memorial: Salisbury, Wiltshire

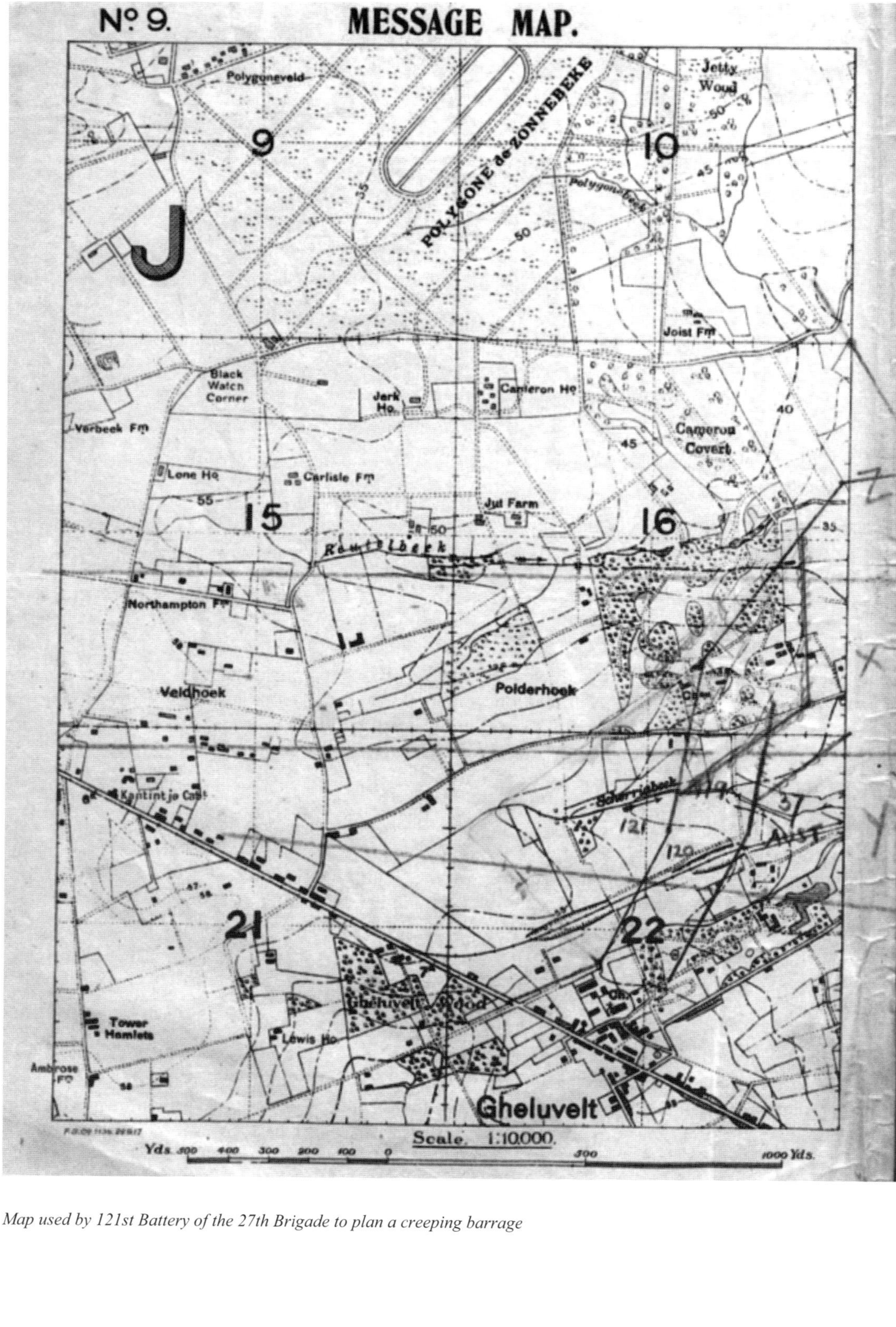

Map used by 121st Battery of the 27th Brigade to plan a creeping barrage

Joseph Brown

War Cemetery:	La Clytte Military Cemetery - Grave III. F. 22.
Next of Kin:	Frank William & Sarah Matthews
Address:	Britford, Wiltshire

Sidney, a mental nurse, was the eldest son of Frank and Sarah Matthews and volunteered for service joining the Royal Field Artillery. After completing his training, he was sent to France arriving on 9 September 1915 to serve with the 121st Battery of the 27th Brigade. Sidney was killed on Sunday 4 November 1917, near Halfway House south east of Hellfire Corner, not far from the Menin Road, most likely by German artillery fire. He was buried at La Clytte Military Cemetery.

MONDAY 5 NOVEMBER 1917 - TEMPERATURE 9.5°c - OVERCAST FOGGY - RAINFALL NIL

Gunner Joseph Brown — *Y Bn Royal Field Artillery*

Service No.	155397	Age:	39
Place of birth:	Englefiel Green, Sussex	Home Country:	England
Date of death:	05/11/1917	Cause of death:	Killed in action
Memorial:	13 Shop Memorial, Great Western Railway Works, Swindon		
War Cemetery:	Bedford House Cemetery - Grave Enclosure No.2 III. C. 2.		
Next of Kin:	Caroline Edith Brown (wife) – David J. & Elizabeth Brown (parents)		
Address:	20 Newport Street, Swindon, Wiltshire		

Joseph was the eldest son of David and Elizabeth Brown and originally enlisted with the army on 18 December 1894, joining the Hussars. He served at home for 5 years and from November 1899 to November 1902 he served in the South African War being awarded the Queens Medal with clasps for the Relief of Kimberly, Transvaal, Paarderberg and Driefontein. After this he returned to England and served one more year in the army, being transferred to the reserve in 1903. In the spring of 1905 he married Caroline Edith Lancaster at Tendering, Essex and in 1906, he was discharged from the army reserves. At the outbreak of hostilities, he was employed as a frame builder assistant, in 13 Shop, at the Great Western Railway Works at Swindon. It is likely he was either conscripted into the army or enlisted under the Derby Scheme joining the Royal Field Artillery and after completing his training he was sent to the front to serve with the 5th Trench Mortar Battery. Joseph was killed on Monday 5 November 1917, most likely by German artillery fire, east of Ypres. He left a widow and a young family.

Tuesday 6 November 1917 - Temperature 9.5°c - Overcast Foggy - Rainfall Nil

Private William John Lugg		*1st Bn East Surrey Regiment*	
Service No.	26201	Age:	24
Place of birth:	Swindon, Wiltshire	Home Country:	England
Date of death:	06/11/1917	Cause of death:	Killed in action
Memorial:	No. 3 Shop Memorial Great Western Railway Works Swindon		
War Cemetery:	Hooge Crater Cemetery - Grave VIII. A. 9.		
Next of Kin:	Annie Violet Lugg (wife) - John Thomas & Eveline E. Lugg (parent)		
Address:	2 Moreton Street, Swindon, Wiltshire		

William was the only child of John and Eveline Lugg and was educated at Clarence Street Schools. After leaving education he was employed as a grocer's assistant to Mr H. James in Fleet Street for 5 years before taking employment as a machine man in No. 3 Shop at the Great Western Railway Works at Swindon. On 6 September 1916, he married Annie Violet Coole at St. Mark's, Swindon. It is likely that soon after he was either conscripted into the army or enlisted under the Derby Scheme and was called up, initially joining the Essex Regiment. He was sent to the front in 1917 and transferred to the 1st Battalion East Surrey Regiment. One month after leave in England William was killed on Tuesday 6 November 1917, by a German artillery shell, north east of Gheluvelt Wood. William's father received the following information from a Captain of the 1st East Surrey's:

"Your son was in the Lewis gun section of my platoon and went into the line on November 5th. The next morning, soon after daylight, we were heavily shelled, and a piece of shell struck your son in the head. He was killed outright, and buried in the spot that night by Pte. Lake, of the same Lewis gun section."

In March 1919, William's remains were located north east of Gheluvelt Wood, just south of the Menin Road and were removed to Hooge Crater Cemetery. He left a widow and a young daughter.

Lt. Wynond Nicholas Richard Pole-Carew		*1st Bn Duke of Cornwalls Light Infantry*	
Service No.	N/a	Age:	21
Place of birth:	Hatton, Ceylon	Home Country:	England
Date of death:	06/11/1917	Cause of death:	Killed in action
Memorial:	Antony, Wye College		
War Cemetery:	Tyne Cot Memorial - Grave Panel 80 to 82 and 163A		
Next of Kin:	Charles Edward & Ellen Henrietta Pole-Carew		
Address:	Parkhill, Totnes, Devon		

Wynond was the youngest son of Charles and Ellen Pole-Carew and educated at Marlborough and Wye Agricultural College. He was a keen sportsman and had an interest in big game hunting. At the outbreak of hostilities, he was given a commission with the 2/4th Territorial Wiltshire Regiment and was sent to India where he was Aids de Camps to Lord Willington the Governor of Bombay in 1915 to 1916. In 1916, he was sent to Sandhurst passing out first and winning the Kings Medal and Anson Memorial Sword. He was given a commission with the 1st Battalion Duke of Cornwalls Light Infantry in October 1916 and arrived in France on 23 March 1917. Wynond was killed early in the morning on Tuesday 6 November 1917 at Polderhoek while commanding D Company during an attack at the Chateau. His commanding officer wrote to his parents stating:

Left: Right: William John Lugg

Right: Wynond Nicholas Richard Pole-Carew

"He was killed in an attack on a strong hostile position on 6 November. He was commanding D Company, and led them to the assault in the early morning. He had a reputation for gallantry in previous actions and had been recommended for the Military Cross after operations on 4 October 1917 for gallantry and distinguished service in the field."

He is remembered on the Tyne Cot Memorial and has no known grave.

Private Charles James Cockerell — *1st Bn Duke of Cornwalls Light Infantry*

Service No.	29458	Age:	24
Place of birth:	Trowbridge, Wiltshire	Home Country:	England
Date of death:	06/11/1917	Cause of death:	Killed in action
Memorial:	Bridgwater, Somerset		
War Cemetery:	Tyne Cot Memorial - Panel 80 to 82 and 163A.		
Next of Kin:	George Charles & Sarah Ann Cockerell		
Address:	7 West Quay, Bridgwater, Somerset		

Charles, a cabinet maker, was the eldest son of George and Sarah Ann Cockerell and a member of the 2/1st Somerset Yeomanry. He was transferred to the Duke of Cornwalls Light Infantry and then sent to the front joining the 1st Battalion. He was killed in action on Tuesday 6 November 1917 during an unsuccessful attack through the sticky Belgium mud at Polderhoek Chateau. He is remembered on the Tyne Cot Memorial and has no known grave.

Private Percival John Hacker — *1st Bn Devonshire Regiment*

Service No.	205147	Age:	23
Place of birth:	Hilmarton, Wiltshire	Home Country:	England
Date of death:	06/11/1917	Cause of death:	Killed in action
Memorial:	Nettleton, Wiltshire		
War Cemetery:	Hooge Crater Cemetery - Grave IXA. A. 12.		
Next of Kin:	Eli & Elizabeth Hacker		
Address:	Keeper's Cottage, West Kington, Wiltshire		

Percy was a cowman and carter employed at Fosse Farm. He was conscripted in late 1916 and originally joined the Dorset Regiment before being transferred to the Wiltshire Regiment and then on to the 1st

Battalion Devonshire Regiment. He was killed in action on Tuesday 6 November when the 1st Devons captured a German position called the Mound near Polderhoek Chateau, Passchendaele, Belgium; the same day the Canadians captured the Passchendaele village. Thirty-one men of the 1st Battalion Devonshire Regiment were killed on the same day. Percy was buried near where he fell, just east of Polderhoek Chateau. His remains were discovered in May 1919 and he was identified by means of a disc and a letter. His remains were subsequently removed and buried in Hooge Crater Cemetery. Percy's brother Ernest had been killed at the Somme in October 1916

Private Arthur Edwin Clifford — *1st RM Bn RN Div Royal Marine Light Infantry*

Service No.	PLY/1918(S)	Age:	19
Place of birth:	Bristol, Gloucestershire	Home Country:	England
Date of death:	06/11/1917	Cause of death:	Killed in action
Memorial:	Melksham, Wiltshire		
War Cemetery:	Tyne Cot Memorial - Panel 1 and 162A		
Next of Kin:	Arthur & Emily Jane Clifford		
Address:	7 Self Cottages Beanacre Road, Melksham, Wiltshire		

Arthur, a driller, was the second son Arthur and Emily Clifford and enlisted on 3 June 1916. He was placed on the army reserve and called up on 23 February 1917. After completing his basic training, he was sent to the Recruiting Depot at Deal on 20 April 1917. He was sent to France on 29 May 1917 and joined 1st Royal Marine Battalion on 23 June 1917. On Tuesday 6 November 1917, Y company of the 1st Royal Marines was sent for duty with 2nd Royal Marines in the British front line southeast of Poelcapelle. Arthur was killed, most likely by German artillery fire and is remembered on the Ypres Menin Gate. He has no known grave.

Private Tom Zebedee — *2nd RM Bn RN Div Royal Marine Light Infantry*

Service No.	CH/2006(S)	Age:	37
Place of birth:	Salisbury, Wiltshire	Home Country:	England
Date of death:	06/11/1917	Cause of death:	Killed in action
Memorial:	Salisbury, Wiltshire		
War Cemetery:	Tyne Cot Memorial - Panel 1 and 162A.		
Next of kin:	Sophie Zebedee (wife); late William & Mary Kate Zebedee (parents)		
Address:	22 Harnham Road Salisbury, Wiltshire St Edmunds, Salisbury, Wiltshire		

Tom, a butcher was the only son William and Mary Zebedee and in the summer of 1915 he married Sophie Gourdin at Salisbury. It is likely he was either conscripted into the army or enlisted under the Derby Scheme and was put on the Army reserve. He was called up on 28 December 1917 and was sent to the Recruiting Depot at Deal on 23 February 1917. He was sent to France on 3 April 1917 and joined the 11th Entrenching Battalion on 21 April 1917. He was transferred to the 2nd Royal Marine Battalion on 2 May 1917 and accidentally sprained his ankle on 19 May 1917. After his recovery, he re-joined the 2nd Royal Marines on 23 July 1917. Tom was killed on Tuesday 6 November 1917, most likely by German artillery fire, in the British front line southeast of Poelcapelle. He is remembered on the Ypres Menin Gate and has no known Grave. He left a widow and a young son called Tom.

Gunner Harry Thomas Read — *108th Bde Royal Field Artillery*

Service No.	212563	Age:	30
Place of birth:	Bishopstone, Wiltshire	Home Country:	England
Date of death:	06/11/1917	Cause of death:	Killed in action
Memorial:	Bishopstone, Broad Chalke, Wiltshire		
War Cemetery:	Ruisseau Farm Cemetery - Grave B. 11.		
Next of Kin:	Henry & Sarah Read		

Address:	Bishopstone, Wiltshire

Harry, a Farm labourer, was the only child of Henry and Sarah Read and it is likely he was either conscripted into the army or enlisted under the Derby Scheme joining the Royal Field Artillery. After Completing his training, he was sent to the front to serve with the 108th Brigade. He was killed on Tuesday 6 November 1917, most likely by German artillery fire, near Langemarck and was buried in Ruisseau Farm Cemetery.

Private Edwin Frank Cook		*1/8th Bn Durham Light Infantry*	
Service No.	40542	Age:	25
Place of birth:	Swindon, Wiltshire	Home Country:	England
Date of death:	06/11/1917	Cause of death:	Killed in action
Memorial:	Wroughton, St Mary's Swindon, Wiltshire		
War Cemetery:	Tyne Cot Memorial - Panel 128 to 131 and 162 and 162A		
Next of Kin:	Henry & Mary Elizabeth Cook		
Address:	7 Moredon Road Rodbourne Cheney, Swindon, Wiltshire		

Edwin was the third son of Henry and Mary Cook and was employed as a shunter driver for the Great Western Railway Company. It is likely he was either conscripted into the army or enlisted under the Derby Scheme joining the Durham Light infantry. After completing his training, he was sent to the front to serve with the 1/8th Battalion. Edwin was killed on Tuesday 6 November 1917. Most likely caused by German artillery shelling West of Westroosebeke. He is remembered on the Tyne Cot Memorial and has no known grave.

WEDNESDAY 7 NOVEMBER 1917 - TEMPERATURE 9°c - OVERCAST - RAINFALL 1.4mm

Private Fred James Haddrell		*15th Bn Central Ontario Regiment*	
Service No.	35429	Age:	24
Place of birth:	North Newton, Wiltshire	Home Country:	England
Date of death:	07/11/1917	Cause of death:	Died of wounds
Memorial:	Not known		
War Cemetery:	Lijssenthoek Military Cemetery - Grave XXII. G. 10A.		
Next of Kin:	William Frederick & Eliza Haddrell		
Address:	Exeter Lodge Parker Road Winton, Bournemouth, Dorset		

Driver Fred was the eldest son of William and Eliza Haddrell and had been employed by Northgate Brewery at Devizes before emigrating to Canada. He volunteered for service on 22 September 1914 and after returning to England on 20 April 1915 he was sent to France in January 1916. He was wounded in action east of Ypres on 6 November 1917; he had got through the action and was helping to bring in the wounded. Official information states:

"Whilst one of a stretcher bearing party on duty collecting the wounded after an attack on Passchendaele Ridge on November 6th, 1917, the enemy subjected the ground over which they were working to a heavy bombardment and he was wounded in the back and lungs by fragments of a shell. He was taken to the nearest field ambulance and evacuated to No. 3 Casualty Clearing Station where he died the following day."

He was evacuated to a military hospital at Lijssenthoek, Belgium where he succumbed to his wounds, on Wednesday 7 November 1917, and was buried in Lijssenthoek Military Cemetery. His parents received the following letter from a company officer:

"It is with the deepest regret that I have to convey my most sincere sympathy to you on the death of your boy Freddie. Before transferring to the 15th Company Infantry Battalion, Freddie was my section corporal, and I never had a more efficient and hard working N.C.O. since I came out here in February 1915. He was not only liked but loved and worshiped by every N.C.O. and man in the company, and I can assure you that all the boys of this company feel the loss very, very keenly, and desire that I should convey to you both their deepest sympathy. I have located Freddie's grave, and it is situated in a very nice spot. I am having a cross made to place over the boy as a lasting remembrance of us all, and will endeavour to have a photo of the same sent to you."

Private Percy Robert Cook — *5th Coy Bn Canadian Machine Gun Corps*

Service No.	721105	Age:	24
Place of birth:	Salisbury, Wiltshire	Home Country:	England
Date of death:	07/11/1917	Cause of death:	Died of wounds
Memorial:	Broughton Gifford, Wiltshire		
War Cemetery:	Potijze Chateau Grounds Cemetery - Grave I. C. 36		
Next of Kin:	Norah Cook (wife) Charles William & Winifred Cook (parents)		
Address:	114 Selkirk Avenue Winnipeg, Manitoba, Broughton Gifford, Wiltshire		

Percy, a farmer, was the fourth son of Charles and Winifred Cook and emigrated to Canada in 1911. He volunteered for service on 2 December 1916 joining the 108th Overseas Battalion, Canadian Army. He married Norah Mary Annette on 2 September 1916 at Winnipeg, Manitoba and left Canada, soon after on 18 September 1916 arriving at Liverpool on 25 September 1916. He was transferred to the 14th Reserve Battalion and on 15 March 1917, was sent to the Canadian Machine Gun Depot at Crowborough. After completing his Vickers machine gun training he was sent to France arriving on 11 July 1917 and attached to the 5th Machine Gun Company on 24 August 1917. He was wounded on 6 November 1916, by shrapnel from German artillery fire. The 2nd Canadian Division attacked Passchendaele village and swept through with little opposition. The machine guns of the 5th Company accompanied the advance and were set up almost in the centre of the village. Percy was evacuated to No. 6 Canadian Field Ambulance at Potijze Chateau, where he succumbed to his wounds on Wednesday 7 November 1917. He left a widow and a young son.

Able Seaman William John Collins — *Howe Bn RN Div Royal Naval Volunteer Reserve*

Service No.	R/1188	Age:	34
Place of birth:	Liverpool, Lancashire	Home Country:	England
Date of death:	07/11/1917	Cause of death:	Killed in action
Memorial:	Winterslow, Wiltshire		
War Cemetery:	Tyne Cot Memorial - Panel 2 to 3 and 162 to 162A		
Next of Kin:	Uriah & Annie Collins		
Address:	Forest View, Tytherley Road, Winterslow, Wiltshire		

William, known as John and a baker and shop keeper, was the only son of Uriah and Annie Collins and enlisted under the Derby Scheme on 9 December 1915. He was placed on the Army reserve and called up on 20 April 1917 and sent to the Royal Naval Division. He arrived in France on 6 August 1917, to serve with Howe Battalion joining them on 27 September 1917. On 5 November 1917 two companies, B & C, were attached to Anson Battalion in the British front line near Vapour Farm west of Goudberg Copse not far from the Westroosbeke and Passchendaele Road. On the 6 November 1917, the First Canadian division on the right of Anson's position attacked Passchendaele and Anson Battalion were caught in the artillery barrage. Fifty casualties were caused by German artillery and 8 to 10 caused by fire from the British and Canadian guns supporting the attack. John was reported missing on Wednesday 7 November 1917. Later official information was received stating John was presumed to have been killed on the day he was reported missing. He is remembered on the Tyne Cot Memorial and has no known grave.

Private Alfred Chew — *2nd Bn Welsh Regiment*

Service No.	46453	Age:	36
Place of birth:	Swindon, Wiltshire	Home Country:	Wales
Date of death:	07/11/1917	Cause of death:	Killed in action
Memorial:	Not known		
War Cemetery:	Tyne Cot Memorial - Panel 93 to 94.		
Next of Kin:	Annie Louise Chew (wife) – Alfred & Susan Chew (parents)		
Address:	3 Duffryn Back Terrace, Church Village, Pontypridd, Glamorganshire		

Alfred, a house painter, was the eldest son of Alfred and Susan Chew and toward the end of 1902 he married Mina Alicia Jarvis at Swindon. In 1911, he is living in South Wales with his wife and three children. In 1914, he has another child with Annie Louise Chew his new wife. It is likely he was either conscripted into the army or enlisted under the Derby Scheme joining the Welsh Regiment. After completing his training he was sent to the front to serve with the 2nd Battalion. On Wednesday 7 November 1917, the 2nd Welsh were relieving the troops in the British front line at Passchendaele and met their guide at Wieltje. On the way to the front they were shelled by German artillery and Alfred was killed. He is remembered on the Tyne Cot Memorial and has no known grave. His medals and war gratuity were never claimed.

THURSDAY 8 NOVEMBER 1917 - TEMPERATURE 9°c - 25% CLOUD COVER - RAINFALL 2.6mm

Sapper Harold James Matthews — *5th Field Coy Royal Engineers*

Service No.	23669	Age:	29
Place of birth:	Swindon, Wiltshire	Home Country:	England
Date of death:	08/11/1917	Cause of death:	Killed in action
Memorial:	Not known		
War Cemetery:	Tyne Cot Cemetery - Grave XIII. D. 20.		
Next of Kin:	Frederick & Mary Matthews		
Address:	Manchester, Lancashire		

Regular soldier Harold, was the youngest son of Frederick and Mary Matthews and enlisted with the army before the Great War. He initially joined the Wiltshire Regiment but transferred to 5th Field Company Royal Engineers and arrived in France on 15 August 1914. Harold was killed on Thursday 8 November 1917, by German artillery fire, when the 5th Field Company were repairing the road from St. Julian to Winnipeg. He is remembered on the Tyne Cot Memorial and has no known grave.

SATURDAY 10 NOVEMBER 1917 - TEMPERATURE 7.5°c - RAIN - RAINFALL 13.4mm

Private Alfred Reginald Yeates — *5th Bn Saskatchewan Regiment*

Service No.	268060	Age:	25
Place of birth:	Highworth, Wiltshire	Home Country:	England
Date of death:	10/11/1917	Cause of death:	Killed in action

Memorial:	Not known
War Cemetery:	Ypres Menin Gate - Panel 18 - 26 - 28.
Next of Kin:	George & Martha Yeates
Address:	The Bungalow Dippenhall, Farnham, Surrey

Alfred, known as Reginald and a framer, was the second son of George and Martha Yeates and emigrated to Canada in 1910. He volunteered for service with the Canadian Army on 8 November 1916 and was sent to England and then on to France joining the 5th Saskatchewan Battalion. On Saturday 10 November 1917, the 5th Saskatchewans were in support, at Venture, Vocation and Virtue Farms, when the 1st Canadian Division made an attack on German positions between Westoosebeke and Passchendaele. B Company was sent forward and dug in 80 yards from the British front line at Vindictive crossroads. During this time, the 5th Saskatchewans were subjected to hostile enemy artillery shelling and it is likely that German artillery was responsible for Reginald's death. He is remembered on the Ypres Menin Gate and has no known grave.

Private Harold Lyttleton George Tayler		*8th Bn Manitoba Regiment*	
Service No.	830322	Age:	22
Place of birth:	Wootton Bassett, Wiltshire	Home Country:	Canada
Date of death:	10/11/1917	Cause of death:	Killed in action
Memorial:	Wootton Bassett, Wiltshire		
War Cemetery:	Ypres Menin Gate - Panel 24 - 26 - 28 - 30.		
Next of Kin:	Evelyn May Tayler (wife) – James & Alice Tayler (parents)		
Address:	178 High Street, Wootton Bassett, Wiltshire		

Harold was the youngest son of James and Alice Tayler and in the summer of 1912 he married Evelyn May Tuck at Wootton Bassett. In November 1912, the couple emigrated to Canada where Harold was a farmer. On 26 July 1916, he volunteered for service with the Winnipeg Rifles and was sent to England arriving in September 1916, before being sent on to France in April 1917. On Saturday 10 November 1917, the 8th Manitoba Battalion attacked German positions north of Passchendaele. The 1st South Wales Borders who were attacking on the left lost direction and ran into the British barrage in front of the 8th Manitoba Battalion and then began to retire causing much confusion on the battlefield. The 8th Manitoba Battalion was forced to put out a left defensive flank. On 27 November 1917 Harold's wife received an intimation from the Canadian Records Office to the effect that Pte. Tayler was "missing, believed killed," since 10 November 1917. In January 1918, Harold's wife received the following letter from his Commanding Officer:

"I am sorry that I cannot add anything to the official intimation referred to in your letter of the 1 January 1918. Your husband was in my platoon, and from the information I have obtained he and others were in a shell hole, when a shell fell and blew them out. One of them was killed, but the others escaped, but your husband could not be found after that. As you will understand, it is difficult to assume anything definite in the regard to it. He might have been killed or he might have been wounded and made prisoner. I always found Tayler a splendid soldier, trustworthy and brave. He was well liked by all his comrades, and I always saw much to admire in him; in fact, had him in line for promotion. I regret that I cannot give you anything more definite, but you will understand that in battles of the nature of that of November 10th, or even any, one has to mostly rely on his men for information as to missing casualties, and unfortunately the information obtainable is usually meagre. I can assure you that you have my heartfelt sympathy, and if it eventually transpires that your husband has made the supreme sacrifice I know that the Great Ruler, Who is ever with us in the hour of tribulation, will tender you that great condolence and spiritual comfort which is His alone to bestow."

Later Harold's widow received official information that her husband was presumed to have died on or since 10 November 1917. He is remembered on the Ypres Menin Gate and has no known grave.

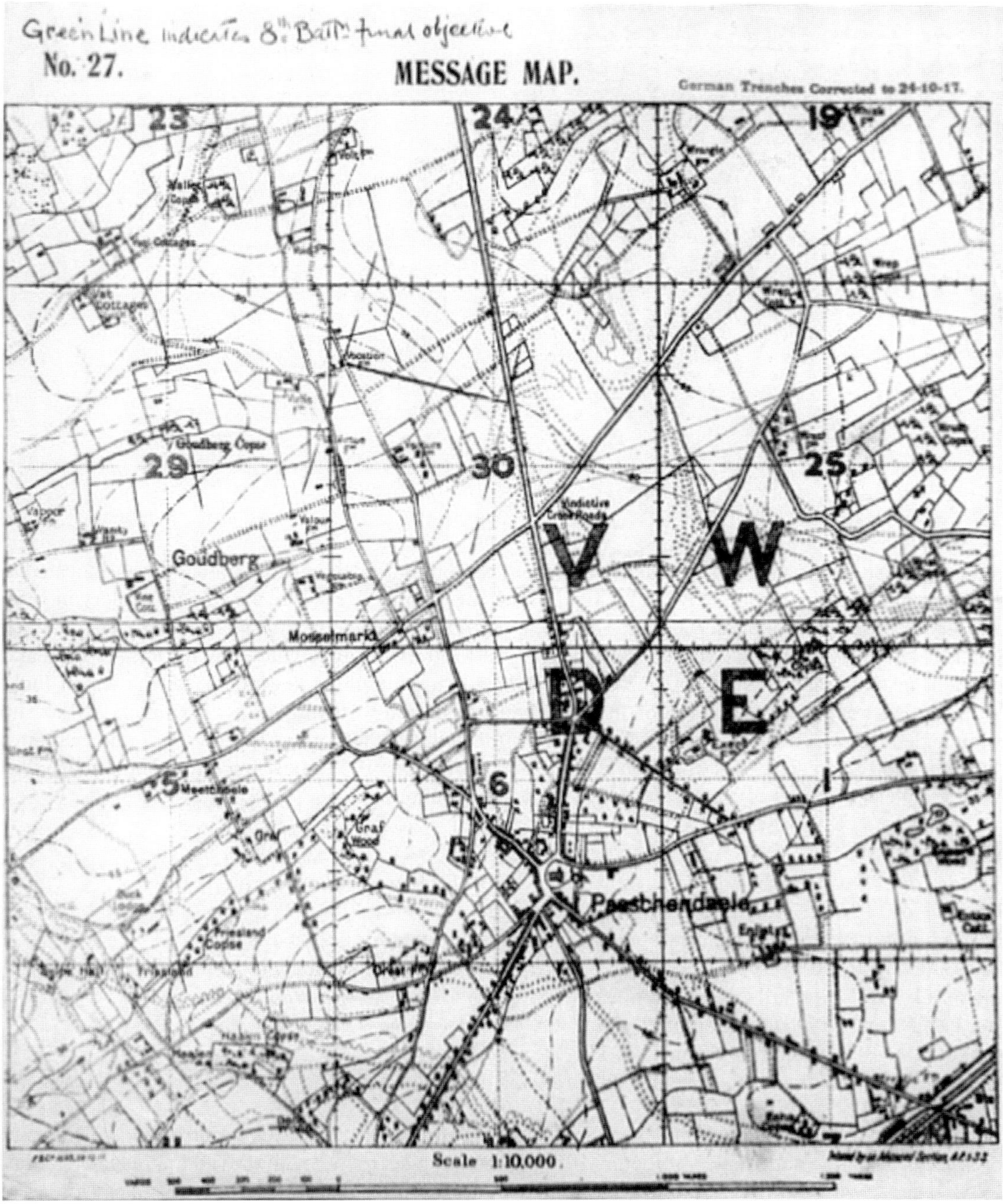

Map of Passchendaele and the objectives of the 8th Manitoba Battalion.

Maj.Frederic Ekershall Nixon-Eckersall MID		*157th Siege Bty Royal Garrison Artillery*	
Service No.	N/a	Age:	48
Place of birth:	Aghmacart, Ireland	Home Country:	England
Date of death:	10/11/1917	Cause of death:	Killed in action
Memorial:	Marlborough College, Wiltshire - St. Brendan's Church, Birr, Ireland		
War Cemetery:	Ypres Reservoir Cemetery - Grave I. A. 40		
Next of Kin:	Florence Nixon- Eckersall (wife) - Eckersall N. & Constantia Nixon-Eckersall		
Address:	Gainsborough, College Road, Cheltenham, Gloucestershire		

Frederic Ekershall Nixon-Eckersall

Frederic, was the eldest son of Rev. Eckersall Nixon & Constantia Nixon-Eckersall and was educated at Marlborough College, where he was a member of the Rifle Corps. He joined the Royal Artillery in 1888 and served in India, Malta and Gibraltar and was promoted to Captain. In 1904, he married Florence Eleanor Scobel at Newent and retired from the army in 1910. He re-joined the army in October 1914 and was sent to France on 6 October 1915 and served with an ammunition column with the Royal Field Artillery. He was promoted to Major in 1916, and transferred to the 157th Siege Battery, which he commanded. He was mentioned in despatches after the battle of the Somme in May 1917 and again in December 1917. Frederic was killed on Saturday 10 November 1917, most likely by German artillery counter battery fire, east of Ypres. He left a widow and young Family.

Private John Alexander Harrod		*1st Bn Bn South Wales Borderers*	
Service No.	18871	Age:	24
Place of birth:	Wolverton, Buckibghamshire	Home Country:	England
Date of death:	10/11/1917	Cause of death:	Killed in action
Memorial:	Fonthill Gifford, Wiltshire		
War Cemetery:	Tyne Cot Memorial - Panel 65 to 66		
Next of Kin:	William & Annie Harrod		
Address:	Wood Lane, Fonthill Gifford, Wiltshire		

John, known as Alexander and a gardener, was the only son of William and Annie Harrod and volunteered for service with the South Wales Borderers. After completing his training, he arrived in France on 2 May 1915, to serve with the 1st Battalion. On Saturday 10 November 1917, the 1st South Wales Borderers attacked German positions north west of Passchendaele and were forced to move to the right during the attack because of a ragged British creeping barrage which forced them ahead of the Canadians on their right and into their barrage. This caused a gap to open to the left of the 1st South Wales Borderers and prevented Virile Farm and Goudberg Copse being taken. The Germans counter attacked into the gap that had been formed. The 1st South Wales Borderers were forced to retire. Alex was killed during the attack on Saturday 10 November 1917. He is remembered on the Tyne Cot Memorial and has no known grave.

Private Sidney Hall		*1st Bn South Wales Borderers*	
Service No.	13643	Age:	36
Place of birth:	Swindon, Wiltshire	Home Country:	Wales

Date of death:	10/11/1917	Cause of death:	Killed in action
Memorial:	Cwmynyscoy, Monmouthshire		
War Cemetery:	Tyne Cot Memorial - Panel 65 to 66.		
Next of Kin:	Elizabeth Hall (wife)		
Address:	135 Star Row, Cwmynyscoy, Monmouthshire		

Sidney was a labourer in a brick works and married Elizabeth Hick at the beginning of 1911 at Cwmynyscoy, Monmouthshire. It is likely he was either conscripted into the army or enlisted under the Derby Scheme joining the South Wales Borderers. After completing his training, he was sent to France, to serve with the 1st Battalion. Sidney was reported missing on Saturday 10 November 1917, when the 1st South Wales Borderers attacked German positions north west of Passchendaele in the same action as Alexander Harrod. Later official information was received stating Sidney was presumed to have been killed on the day he was reported missing. He is remembered on the Tyne Cot Memorial and has no known grave.

German Bunker Scott Post in Polygon Wood captured by the 56th Australian Battalion on 26 September 1917.

14
November 1917

Official End of Passchendaele – The Third Battle of Ypres

Sunday 11 November 1917 - WEATHER FINE

Sergeant Edgar Robert Smith		*2nd Bn Welsh Regiment*	
Service No.	9183	Age:	28
Place of birth:	Salisbury, Wiltshire	Home Country:	England
Date of death:	11/11/1917	Cause of death:	Died of wounds
Memorial:	Frome, Somerset		
War Cemetery:	Lijssenthoek Military Cemetery - Grave XXII. HH. 29		
Next of Kin:	William Hogarth & Annie Smith		
Address:	Floral Cottage, 64 Marston Road, Frome, Somerset		

Regular soldier Edgar was the fourth son of William and Annie Smith and enlisted on 7 December 1906. He served seven years with the colours at South Africa and Khartoum and was discharged on 19 February 1914. He re-joined the 2nd Welsh Regiment at the outbreak of hostilities and arrived in France on 13 August 1914. On 10 November 1917, the 2nd Welsh were in support east of Passchendaele. Edgar was with his platoon, who he had been with for fifteen months. On the morning of 10th of November 1917, while he was taking rations to another company in the front line, a shell exploded and wounded a lance corporal. Edgar went to his aid, and was wounded by another shell. He was evacuated to a casualty clearing station at Lijssenthoek where he succumbed to his wounds on Sunday 11 November 1917. The Captain commanding his company wrote the following to Edgar's mother:

"He died of wounds in a casualty clearing station soon after he was badly wounded by a shell. He met a soldier's death. He was leading his platoon carrying water and rations to a forward post. Sergeant Smith was most conscientious and did his duty with the utmost vigour. He was a very gallant soldier and during the summer while acting as Q. M. S. and C. M. S. I got to know him very well and looked on him as a personal friend."

Captain Cyril Knox Barrow Mogg		*7th Bn British Columbia Regiment*	
Service No.	N/a	Age:	30
Place of birth:	Clifton, Gloucestershire	Home Country:	England
Date of death:	11/11/1917	Cause of death:	Killed in action
Memorial:	Bishops Cannings, Wiltshire		

Left: Edgar Robert Smith

Right: Cyril Knox Barrow Mogg

War Cemetery: Ypres Menin Gate - Panel 18 - 28 - 30.
Next of Kin: Rev Cannon Henry H & Emma L Mogg
Address: Bishops Cannings Vicarage, Bishops Cannings, Wiltshire

Cyril was the third son of Rev. Henry Mogg, the vicar of Bishops Cannings, and Emma Mogg and was one of three sons to volunteer. He was educated at Wilkinson's then King's College Taunton and after completing his education he emigrated to British Columbia, Canada, where his father had lived in the 1870's. He was employed as a banker by the Canadian Bank of Commerce and was serving at the Seattle branch at the outbreak of hostilities. He volunteered for service in December 1914 initially joining the Canadian Royal Garrison Artillery but on finding that the regiment was not due to go to the front he transferred to the Canadian Infantry. Cyril obtained a commission with the 48th Battalion and was then transferred to the 7th Battalion and came to England in March 1916 and was sent to France in June 1916. He was given charge of the trench mortar section and took part in the taking of Vimy Ridge and the Battle of the Somme. While serving at the Somme he spent five days and two nights sleeping in four feet of water and as a result he was brought to the verge of contracting rheumatic fever and invalided to England. On his recovery Cyril returned to the front and was offered a choice of either returning to the trench mortar battery or taking charge of an infantry company with the 7th Battalion. He took the command of the company and led his men in the assault on Passchendaele, Belgium, on 10 November 1917. Cyril got safely through the attack and survived a heavy German counter attack but the next day Sunday 11 November 1917 he was killed by a shell near Vindictive Cross roads north of Passchendaele. A Major of the 7th Battalion wrote the following letter to Cyril's parents:

"He must have had a very strenuous day. He was to be relieved, and when within about two hours of the relief he was sitting in a shell hole with three more officers a shell came and killed them all. There is no doubt that death was instantaneous, and that he never knew what struck him."

Cyril's brother Aubrey had been killed in August 1916 at St. Eloi, Belgium and both brothers are remembered on the Ypres Menin Gate and have no known grave.

Private Thomas George Hunt		*18th Bn Western Ontario Regiment*	
Service No.	775920	Age:	31
Place of birth:	South Rakaia, New Zealand	Home Country:	Canada
Date of death:	11/11/1917	Cause of death:	Killed in action

Memorial:	Toronto Railway Memorial, Toronto Old City Hall, Canada
War Cemetery:	Passchendaele New British Cemetery - Grave VI. C. 9.
Next of Kin:	Ellen Hunt (wife) - William & Lucy Hunt (parents)
Address:	13 North Street, Swindon, Wiltshire – 46 North Street, Swindon

Thomas was the second son of William and Lucy Hunt and grew up in Wootton Bassett. He was employed as a locomotive fireman and on 24 August 1907 he married Ellen Sellmand at Wootton Bassett. In 1911 the couple emigrated to Canada where Thomas found employment as a motor man for the Toronto Street Railway Company. Thomas Volunteered for service with the Canadian Army joining the 126th Overseas Battalion on 3 March 1916. After completing his training, he arrived in England on 24 August 1916 and on 28 November 1916 was sent to France, to serve with the 18th Battalion Western Ontario Regiment. On 9 November 1917, the 18th Battalion were holding the front line just to the east of Passchendaele Village and the war diary states:

"During the whole of this tour, the officers and men held this part of the line under the most severe conditions possible. Great difficulty was experienced in the evacuating of casualties from the line to Regimental aid post's and dressing stations. Front line trenches were subjected to frequent barrages and the rear country was also heavily shelled and bombed. The supports on this front were reached by a series of tracks, being trench mat walks, and rations had to be carried by mules up these tracks, each track being subjected to continual shell fire, the transport and ration parties were fortunate in escaping the loss of 3 men killed and 1 mule which fell off the duckboard track and owing to the depth of the mud, had to be shot."

Thomas was killed by a German shell on Sunday 11 November 1917 in the front line at Passchendaele. His widow received the following letter from his Lieutenant:

"It is with extreme regret that I have to report to you of the death of 775920 Pte. T. G. Hunt, who was killed in action on November 11th, 1917. He was hit by a shell and killed instantly, so suffered no pain. Our battalion has left the vicinity. Particulars of his place of burial, I expect, will be sent to you later by the authorities. As his platoon commander, kindly accept my sincere condolence in your sad bereavement, as I feel the loss of a good, dependable man who always did his share and was like by all his comrades. He died manfully and fearlessly doing his duty under intense shell fire. Therefore, I cannot but say that I feel his loss keenly."

In January 1920 Thomas's grave was located near the centre of Passchendaele village and was identified by means of an identity disc. His remains were relocated to Passchendaele New British Cemetery.

MONDAY 12 NOVEMBER 1917 - WEATHER FINE

Lance Coporal Frank Channing		*Royal Wiltshire Yeomanry*	
Service No.	320467	Age:	33
Place of birth:	Britford, Wiltshire	Home Country:	England
Date of death:	12/11/1917	Cause of death:	Killed in action
Memorial:	Not known		
War Cemetery:	Tyne Cot Memorial - Panel 3.		
Next of Kin:	Emanuel & Annie Channing		
Address:,	Dog Dean, Wiltshire		

Frank, a gardener and groom, was the only son of Emanuel and Annie Channing and volunteered for service with the Royal Wiltshire Yeomanry in September 1914. It is likely he was sent to France in 1916 and transferred to the Corps of Hussars. Frank was killed on Monday 12 November 1917, most likely caused by German artillery fire. He had recently been attached to Brigade Headquarters at the time of his death. He is remembered on the Tyne Cot Memorial and has no known grave.

Gunner Charles Large *31st Bde Bn Royal Field Artillery*

Service No.	238354	Age:	39
Place of birth:	Upton Tetbury, Glos.	Home Country:	England
Date of death:	12/11/1917	Cause of death:	Died of wounds
Memorial:	Not known		
War Cemetery:	Wimereux Communal Cemetery - Grave VI. G. 21A		
Next of Kin:	Elsie Elizabeth Large (wife) - Thomas & Hannah Large (parents)		
Address:	18 St Marys Street, Chippenham - Northfields, Tetbury		

Charles, a groom and gardener, was the youngest son of Thomas and Hannah Large and married Elsie Elizabeth Harris at the end of 1900. It is likely he was either conscripted into the army or enlisted under the Derby Scheme. Likely as a result of his work with horses Charles was sent to the Royal Field Artillery and after completing his training was sent France to serve with the 31st Brigade. He was wounded in fighting, most likely by German counter battery fire east of Ypres and evacuated to No. 8 Stationary Hospital at Wimereux, where he succumbed to his wounds on Monday 12 November 1917. He left a widow and two children.

Private Eric Hunt Harding *8th Bn Manitoba Regiment*

Service No.	441162	Age:	24
Place of birth:	Holt, Wiltshire	Home Country:	Canada
Date of death:	12/11/1917	Cause of death:	Died of wounds
Memorial:	Holt, Wiltshire		
War Cemetery:	Lijssenthoek Military Cemetery - Grave XXII. HH. 17.		
Next of Kin:	Harry & Anne Harding		
Address:	Hamcroft, Holt, Wiltshire		

Eric, a farmer, was the eldest son of Harry and Anne Harding and emigrated to Canada before the Great War. He volunteered for service with the Canadian Amy on 10 April 1915 and after completing his training he was sent to England arriving on 13 September 1915. He was then sent to France arriving on 1 December 1915 to serve with the 8th Manitoba Battalion. Eric was wounded during fighting just north of Passchendaele and evacuated to No. 2 Casualty Clearing Station at Lijssenthoek, where he succumbed to his wounds on Monday 12 November 1917.

WEDNESDAY 14 NOVEMBER 1917 - WEATHER FINE

Major Cyril Bartlett MC MID *13th Bn Royal Sussex Regiment*

Service No.	N/a	Age:	25
Place of birth:	Shrawley, Worcestershire	Home Country:	England
Date of death:	14/11/1917	Cause of death:	Died of wounds
Memorial:	Not known		
War Cemetery:	Outterstreene Communal Cemetery Extension Bailleul - Grave II. B. 56.		
Next of Kin:	Charles & Emma Thirza Bartlett		
Address:	White House, Great Witley, Worcestershire		

Cyril was the eldest son of Charles and Emma Thirza Bartlett and was educated at King Charles I Grammar School, Kidderminster, followed by Dean Close School, Cheltenham. After leaving education he found employment in the Witley Court estate office and after this he acted as Secretary for the Earl of Dudley at Aldershot before becoming Secretary and Accountant to the Countess of Dudley. Cyril lived in Malmesbury before the Great War and volunteered for service, being given a commission with 13th Battalion Royal Sussex Regiment on 22 September 1915. He served in Ireland during the Rebellion in April 1916 and was sent to France in July 1916. He was promoted to Lieutenant in August 1916 and at the start of the Third Battle of Ypres was recommended for the Military Cross and mentioned in despatches by field Marshall Haig, the citation states:

"For most conspicuous bravery and good leading in the Battle of Ypres on 31st July and August 1st and 2nd. Lieutenant Bartlett was Adjutant of this Battalion. Throughout the three days of the battle he displayed courage, coolness, cheerfulness and devotion to duty, and gallantly assisted dressing a large number of wounded under a heavy barrage. His fine courage throughout was an inspiring example to the whole battalion."

In August 1917 Cyril was promoted to Captain and Major in October 1917 and was awarded the Military Cross by the King at Buckingham Palace on 19 October 1917. He was wounded in early November, most likely by German artillery shelling, near Tower Hamlets. He was evacuated to No. 1 Australian Casualty Clearing Stating at Outterstreene, where he succumbed to his wounds on Wednesday 14 November.

Cyril's father received the following letter from his commanding officer:

"During my whole service in France I have never had a better officer or a better friend. I know I speak for my brother officers and all the men when I say that his loss is more deeply felt than I thought possible,"

A former Commanding Officer wrote:

"He was one of the most conscientious and hardworking officers and also one of the bravest that ever set foot in France, and he will be sadly missed in the Battalion."

Private Charles Henry Alexander		*1st Bn Loyal North Lancashire Regiment*	
Service No.	34511	Age:	39
Place of birth:	Box, Wiltshire	Home Country:	England
Date of death:	14/11/1917	Cause of death:	Killed in action
Memorial:	Box, Wiltshire		
War Cemetery:	Tyne Cot Memorial - Panel 102 to 104.		
Next of Kin:	Mabel Alexander (wife) – Henry & Harriet Alexander (parents)		
Address:	West View, Freshford, Somerset – Box, Wiltshire		

Charles, a banker mason, was the youngest son of Henry and Harriet Alexander and toward the end of 1904 he married Mabel Brown. It is likely he was either conscripted into the army or enlisted under the Derby Scheme initially joining the Royal Engineers. After completing his training, he was transferred to the infantry and sent to France to serve with the 1st Battalion Loyal North Lancashire Regiment. On the night of 13/14 November 1917, the 1st Loyal North Lancashire's had been in Passchendaele and were sent to the front line north of the village. Unfortunately they failed in the position until after day break and were subjected to a persistent German barrage which inflicted heavy losses. Charles was reported missing on Wednesday 14 November 1917, during the German barrage. Later Charles's widow received official information stating Charles was presumed to have been killed on the day he was reported missing. He is remembered on the Tyne Cot Memorial and has no known grave. He left a widow and young family.

Left: William Henry Collins

Right: Hugh Lennox Fleming Boyd

Sapper William Henry Collins — *262nd Coy Bn Royal Engineers*

Service No.	171623	Age:	31
Place of birth:	Collingbourne, Wiltshire	Home Country:	England
Date of death:	14/11/1917	Cause of death:	Killed in action
Memorial:	Marlborough, Wiltshire		
War Cemetery:	Brandhoek New Military Cemetery No 3 - Grave II. N. 13.		
Next of Kin:	Francis Ellen Collins (wife) - Frederick & Sarah Collins (parents)		
Address:	Marten, Grafton, Wiltshire		

William was the eldest son of Frederick and Sarah Collins and was employed as a packer in the Engineering Department, at Marlborough, for the Great Western Railway Company. On 17 February 1912, he married Francis Ellen Hobbs at East Kennett. It is likely he was either conscripted into the army or enlisted under the Derby Scheme joining the Royal Engineers. He was sent to the front to serve with the 262nd Company Railway Construction Troops, who were used to repair and construct railways in the rear areas. He was killed, most likely by German artillery fire, near Brandhoek on Wednesday 14 November 1917. He left a widow and two young children.

SATURDAY 18 NOVEMBER 1917 - WEATHER FINE AND DRY - GOOD VISIBILITY

Captain Hugh Lennox Fleming Boyd — *1st Bn Black Watch*

Service No.	N/a	Age:	27
Place of birth:	Kensington, London	Home Country:	England
Date of death:	18/11/1917	Cause of death:	Killed in action
Memorial:	Marlborough College, Wiltshire - Shalford – Guildford Holy Trinity		
War Cemetery:	Poelcapelle British Cemetery - Grave XII. C. 1		
Next of Kin:	Hugh Fenwick & Elizabeth Boyd		
Address:	Noddings, Wormley, Surrey		

Hugh was the only son of Hugh and Elizabeth Boyd and was educated at Marlborough College before attending New College Oxford. He was about to be called to the bar at the outbreak of hostilities and was given a commission with the 7th Territorial Force, London Regiment. He Later was given a commission with the regular army joining the 1st Battalion the Black Watch and arrived in France on

20 March 1916. He was severely wounded in May 1916 and after recovering from his wounds returned to the front in August 1917 and was promoted to the rank of Captain. Hugh was killed on Saturday 18 November 1917 by a German sniper near Vocation Farm, which formed a salient in the British front line, north west of Passchendaele. He was initially buried near where he fell and in November 1919 he his remains were moved to Poelcapelle British Cemetery.

Private Thomas Henry Boyles — *152nd Coy Labour Corps*

Service No. 90670 — Age: 27
Place of birth: Ogbourne St. George, Wiltss — Home Country: England
Date of death: 18/11/1917 — Cause of death: Died of wounds
Memorial: Ogbourne St. George, Wiltshire
War Cemetery: Solferino Farm Cemetery - Grave II. B. 5.
Next of Kin: Eleanor May Boyles (wife) – Henry & Julia Ann Boyles
Address: 92 Broad street, Swindon - Ogbourne St. George, Wiltshire

Thomas was the eldest son of Henry and Julia Boyles and enlisted under the Derby Scheme on 11 December 1915 initially joining the Wiltshire Regiment. He was mobilized on 8 February 1916 and was transferred to the 12th Labour Battalion Devonshire Regiment. On 27 May 1916 he married Eleanor May Gutridge at Swindon Registry office and after a short leave he was sent to France, arriving on 15 June 1916. In 1917 the 12th Labour Battalion under an Army Council Order, changed their name to the 152nd Company Labour Corps. On 19 October 1917 Thomas was granted home leave, returning to the front on 30 October 1917. He was wounded on Saturday 18 November 1917, most likely by German artillery. He was taken to the 52nd Field Ambulance, north west of Ypres with gun shot wounds to the groin and right leg and succumbed to his wounds soon after. Thomas left a widow and young daughter.

Wednesday 21 November 1917

Gunner Frederick John Bunce — *86th Bde Bn Royal Field Artillery*

Service No. 62525 — Age: 31
Place of birth: Purton, Wiltshire — Home Country: England
Date of death: 21/11/1917 — Cause of death: Killed in action
Memorial: Not known
War Cemetery: The Huts Cemetery - Grave XIV. D. 11.
Next of Kin: William James & Ellen Elizabeth Bunce
Address: Swindon, Wiltshire

Frederick was the eldest son of William and Ellen Bunce and was employed as a labourer with the Great Western Railway Company. He volunteered for service with the Royal Field Artillery arriving in France with the 86th Brigade on 18 July 1915. He was killed on Wednesday 21 November 1917, most likely by German artillery fire, near Dickebusch.

Thursday 22 November 1917 - Weather Fine in the Morning to Dull and Wet

Private Harry Barrett — *53rd Field Ambulance Royal Army Medical Corps*

Service No. 30302 — Age: 24
Place of birth: Lechlade, Glocestershire — Home Country: England
Date of death: 22/11/1917 — Cause of death: Died of wounds

Frederick George Phelps

Memorial: Lechlade, Gloucestershire
War Cemetery: Wimereux Communal Cemetery - Grave VI. H. 20A.
Next of Kin: Nellie Selina Barrett (wife) - John Frank & Ann Barrett (parent)
Address: Longdoles, Lechlade, Gloucestershire

Harry, an agricultural Labourer, was the fourth son of John and Ann Barrett and volunteered for service on the 17 August 1914, joining the Royal Army Medical Corps. On 13 July 1915, he married Nellie Selina Cole at Longbridge Deverill. Straight after the wedding he left for France arriving on 14 July 1915 to serve with 53rd Field Ambulance. At about 10pm on 18 November 1917 53rd Field Ambulance were at Advanced Dressing Station at Cement House, southwest of Langemarck. A German mustard gas shell burst in the doorway blowing in the gas curtain causing many casualties. Harry was gassed and evacuated to 53rd General Hospital at Boulogne where he died on Thursday 22 November 1917. The cause of death was stated as broncho pneumonia and heart failure caused by the mustard gas. His personal property was returned to his wife and consisted of disc, letters, photos, 2 wallets, pocket knife, note case, soldiers companion, cap badge, gold shell ring, leather purse, card, cotton badge and a stamp. His widow inserted the following memoriam in a local paper:

A bitter grief, a shock severe,
To part with one I loved so dear;
My loss is great, I'll not complain,
But hope in heaven to meet again.

His brother James had been killed in 1915.

Gunner Frederick George Phelps — *123rd Bde Royal Field Artillery*
Service No. 102288 — Age: 23
Place of birth: Box, Wiltshire — Home Country: England
Date of death: 22/10/1917 — Cause of death: Died of wounds
Memorial: Box, Wiltshire
War Cemetery: Outterstreene Communal Cemetery Extension Bailleul - Grave II. B. 50.
Next of Kin: Violet Louise Phelps (wife) - Henry & Jane Phelps (parents)
Address: Market Place, Box, Wiltshire

Frederick, known as Fred and a carter, was the fourth son of Henry and Jane Phelps and married Violet

Louise Sinclair on 10 April 1915 at Box. He volunteered for service in August 1915 joining the Royal Field Artillery and was sent to France arriving on 16 December 1915 to serve with the 123rd Brigade. In early November Fred was recommended for the Military Medal for rescuing, tending and dressing the wounds of the wounded under heavy shell fire. Soon after Fred became a casualty when the gun positions at Locre were continually shelled with mustard gas. Two thirds of 123rd Brigade Royal Field Artillery became casualties after repeated small doses of the gas. Fred was evacuated to No. 1 Australian Casualty Clearing Station at Outterstreene where he succumbed to the effects of the gas on Thursday 22 November 1917. The bombardier of his section wrote:

"It is a great blow to us all, he was such a good and brave fellow and loved by us all. It was hard he did not live to receive his well earned decoration. The deed for which Fred earned his Military Medal was worthy of a V.C. He rescued and dressed the wounds of men under heavy shell fire, and showed utter contempt of danger to himself."

His brother Reginald had been killed at the Somme in 1916.

SUNDAY 25 NOVEMBER 1917 - WEATHER FAIR WITH HIGH WINDS

Driver Henry Edward Johnson		*104th Bde Royal Field Artillery*	
Service No.	109862	Age:	22
Place of birth:	Swindon, Wiltshire	Home Country:	England
Date of death:	25/11/1917	Cause of death:	Killed in action
Memorial:	No 15 Shop Memorial Great Western Railway Works, Swindon		
War Cemetery:	The Huts Cemetery - Grave XIV. D. 13.		
Next of Kin:	Walter Johnson		
Address:	20 Regent Street, Swindon, Wiltshire		

Henry was the youngest son of Walter Johnson and was employed as a machinist in No. 15 shop at the Great Western Railway Works, Swindon. It is likely he was either conscripted into the army or enlisted under the Derby Scheme joining the Royal Filed Artillery. After completing his training, he was sent to the front to serve with 104th Brigade. He was killed on Sunday 25 November 1917, most likely by German artillery fire, near Dickebusch.

Private Walter Samuel Clark		*2nd Bn Devonshire Regiment*	
Service No.	291753	Age:	23
Place of birth:	Melksham, Wiltshire	Home Country:	England
Date of death:	25/11/1917	Cause of death:	Killed in action
Memorial:	Not known		
War Cemetery:	Tyne Cot Memorial - Panel 38 to 40		
Next of Kin:	Mabel Clark (wife) – Samuel & Annie Clark.		
Address:	18 Scotland Road, Melksham, Wiltshire		

Walter was the second son of Samuel and Annie Clark and was employed by Hurn Brothers, Timber Merchants. At the start of 1917 he married Mabel M. Langdon at Melksham. It is likely he was either conscripted into the army or enlisted under the Derby Scheme joining the Devonshire Regiment in January 1917. After Completing his training, he was sent to the front in July 1917, to serve with the 2nd Battalion. On Sunday 25 November 1917, the 2nd Devons were in the British front-line north of Passchendaele at Metcheele and made an advance to push the front forward about 150 yards during the hours of darkness. Walter was killed during the advance and is remembered on the Tyne Cot Memorial

Left: Henry Edward Johnson

Right: Walter Samuel Clark

and has no known grave. He left a widow and young child. In 1918 his family inserted the following memoriam in a local paper:

Fondly we loved him he is still dear to us
But in grief we must bend to God's holy will
Our sorrow is great our loss hard to bear
But angels will guard our dear loved one with care

Private George Smart		*2nd Bn Devonshire Regiment*	
Service No.	291108	Age:	28
Place of birth:	Sherston, Wiltshire	Home Country:	England
Date of death:	25/11/1917	Cause of death:	Killed in action
Memorial:	Sherston, Wiltshire		
War Cemetery:	Tyne Cot Memorial - Panel 38 to 40.		
Next of Kin:	Henry & Rubena Smart		
Address:	Long Newnton, Tetbury, Gloucestershire		

George, a gardener was the only son of Henry and Rubena Smart and it is likely he was either conscripted into the army or enlisted under the Derby Scheme joining the Devonshire Regiment. After completing his training, he was sent to the front, to serve with the 2nd Battalion. On Sunday 25 November 1917, the 2nd Devons were in the British front-line north of Passchendaele at Metcheele and made an advance to push the front forward about 150 yards during the hours of darkness. George was reported missing during the advance. Later official information was received stating George was presumed to have been killed on the day he was reported missing. He is remembered on the Tyne Cot Memorial and has no known grave.

Lance Sergeant Stanley Wilberforce Davis		*11th Bn Border Regiment*	
Service No.	35017	Age:	28
Place of birth:	Bradford on Avon, Wiltshire	Home Country:	England
Date of death:	25/11/1917	Cause of death:	Killed in action
Memorial:	Not known		
War Cemetery:	Tyne Cot Cemetery - Grave XXI. G. 23.		
Next of Kin:	James Bull & Sarah Jane Davis		

Address: 134 Cowesley Street, Moss Side, Manchester, Lancashire

Stanley was the youngest son of James and Sarah Davis and was educated at Princess Road School, Manchester, where he was never absent or late and every year received a framed certificate. At the last concert before leaving he was presented with a Gold Medal for regular attendance. On leaving education he was employed by J. F. & H. Roberts, woollen merchants, where initially he was employed as a clerk, before becoming a salesman. He was connected with Great Western Street Primitive Methodist Sunday School, the church choir, and also the football and tennis clubs and was a life abstainer and non-smoker, being a member of the Good Templar Order. Stanley enlisted under the Derby Scheme on 7 December 1915 and was placed on the Army Reserve. He was mobilized on 22 February 1916 and initially posted to the King's Liverpool Regiment and was rapidly promoted to Sergeant. He was then transferred to the Middlesex Regiment, then back to the Liverpool Regiment. He was sent to France on 29 June 1917 and transferred again, to the 11th Border Regiment. Stanley was killed on Sunday 25 November 1917, by a German shell, near Mosselmarkt north west of Passchendaele, when C and A Company's of the 11th Borders were moving into the British front line. A friend of Stanley's, James McCann, wrote the following to his parents:

"Even though this is my first letter to you, I feel I cannot commence it in any other way, for your son Stan and I were close chums in the old 16th King's, and slept together when we were at Crawley and Tunbridge Wells with the Middlesex. I was handed a letter yesterday which came from a sergeant who has been with Stan in France and who had lost Stan's home address. In the letter, he asks me to do him a favour, not a pleasant one inasmuch as it is to convey sad news to you, but which at the same time may bring some small ray of comfort. I hardly know how to break it to you, for I know how I felt when I heard it. It is one of the terrible trials of the war, poor Stan has given his life for his country. The sergeant tells me that a large shell burst near him, and that Stan was killed instantly. Another of our corporals was severely wounded by the same shell, has since died of wounds. I know it must be a great trial for you to bear up, for Stan was a good living lad, and we had both hoped to renew our friendship when this awful war was at an end. I feel his loss very much and ask you to accept my deepest sympathy with you in your sad bereavement. He was killed on November 25th, last Sunday week. Those who knew him here are very grieved to hear the sad news, for he was a very popular N.C.O. and esteemed by those who came under his influence. If you have not already heard from the War Office I trust I have done my duty in such a manner as not to give you too great a shock. If you have already heard, then please forgive me for reaping up what must have been a terrible shock to you. He was my army chum, and as I have said I hoped to renew that friendship in the peace, but God's will is not ours, and often particularly when death takes from us one we love, we feel that we have been harshly treated. Is there not some comfort to be found in the thought that Stan is now in that home to which we hope to gain. He is there, and we have to struggle on. He led a good life, set a fine example and won his reward."

His company commander wrote:

"He joined my company in July last, and was with us from then until his death in action. At all times he served most faithfully, and was liked by all in the company, officers, N.C.O.'s and men. As one of my senior non-commissioned officers, I had ample opportunity of observing his many good qualities, and these, combined with his capabilities, enabled me to trust him with many important things. I had recommended him to the Commanding Office for a commission, and had he been spared I should have had the pleasure of addressing him as a brother officer."

Stanley was buried near where he fell at Furst Farm, west of Meetcheele and in 1920 his remains were identified by means of a disc and removed to Tyne Cot Cemetery.

MONDAY 26 NOVEMBER 1917

Gunner Cyril Richard Manners		*47th Bde Royal Field Artillery*	
Service No.	184989	Age:	26
Place of birth:	Chippenham, Wiltshire	Home Country:	England
Date of death:	26/11/1917	Cause of death:	Killed in action
Memorial:	Corsham, Wiltshire		
War Cemetery:	Tyne Cot Cemetery - Grave XX. E. 7.		
Next of Kin:	Charles and Martha Manners		
Address:	Corshamside, Corsham, Wiltshire		

Cyril, known as Richard, was employed as a footman at Belton House, Grantham, Lincolnshire. He was the youngest son of Charles and Martha Manners who had previously run the Hare and Hounds Public House, at Corsham. It is likely he was either conscripted into the army or enlisted under the Derby Scheme joining the Royal Field Artillery and was called up in August 1916. After completing his training, he was sent to the front, in May 1917, to serve with the 47th Brigade, who on Monday 26 November 1917 were near Abraham Heights west of Passchendaele. Richard was killed by a German shell. His commanding officer Major R.W. Ling wrote the following to Richard's mother:

"I regret to have to inform you that your son, Gunner R. Manners, was killed instantaneously by a shell with three comrades. We buried him with his comrades where they fell, and are erecting crosses to their memory over their graves. I regret to say that all his personal belongings were destroyed by the shell, as he was lying down in a shelter with his things beside him, and we could find nothing. Since your son came out here last May he has been servant to one of my officers, and I cannot speak too highly of him. Always cheerful and doing his work splendidly, I feel his loss very deeply, and so can sympathise with you on your great grief. I am sure it will be a great consolation for you to know he died heroically for his country and had no suffering at the last. All ranks of the battery under my command join with me in expressing their deepest sympathy to you for the loss of your son, who was very popular us all and immensely liked."

In late 1919 Richard and his comrade's graves were located near Abram Heights. They still had the crosses over them that had be placed there in 1917. All are now buried in Tyne Cot Cemetery.

2nd Lieutenant Ernest Archibald Skinner		*24th Coy Machine Gun Corps*	
Service No.	N/a	Age:	24
Place of birth:	Wallingford, Berkshire	Home Country:	England
Date of death:	26/11/1917	Cause of death:	Died of wounds
Memorial:	Winterbournes, Wiltshire		
War Cemetery:	Nine Elms British Cemetery - Grave IX. A. 12.		
Next of Kin:	William & Lydia Jessie Skinner		
Address:	11 Park Street, Islington, London		

Ernest, a civil servant, was the only child of William and Lydia Skinner and was the grandson of Mrs Smith of the Beeches, Winterbourne Gunner. He volunteered for service with the 11th Battalion London Regiment and arrived in Egypt on 10 August 1915, before being sent to Gallipoli. After the evacuation of the peninsular, the 11th Battalion returned to Egypt. It is likely Ernest volunteered to serve with the Machine Gun Corps and at some stage was recommended for a commission and returned to England. Ernest was given a commission on 25 April 1917 and sent to the front joining the 24th Company. He was wounded, most likely east of Ypres and evacuated to a casualty clearing station south west of Poperinge, where he succumbed to his wounds on Monday 26 November 1917.

TUESDAY 27 NOVEMBER 1917 - WEATHER HEAVY RAIN ALL MORNING CLEARING LATER

Left: Charles Edward Osgood

Right:James Norman Ellis

Corporal Charles Edward Osgood — *228th Coy Machine Gun Corps*

Service No.	18068
Age:	21
Place of birth:	Brookley, Hampshire
Home Country:	England
Date of death:	27/11/1917
Cause of death:	Died of wounds
Memorial:	Durnford, Wiltshire
War Cemetery:	Lijssenthoek Military Cemetery - Grave XXVI. A. 10.
Next of Kin:	Herbert & Sarah Ann Osgood
Address:	Upper Woodford, Wiltshire

Charles, a farm labourer, was the third son of Herbert and Sarah Osgood and volunteered for service initially joining the Wiltshire Regiment. He arrived in France on 30 June 1915 and soon after volunteered again and transferred to the Machine Gun Corps joining the 228th Company. He was wounded most likely by German artillery fire at Ridge Wood north of Vierstraat on 26 November 1917. He was evacuated to No.3 Canadian Casualty Clearing Station suffering from gunshot wounds to the head and a compound fracture to the scull. Charles succumbed to his wounds on Tuesday 27 November 1917.

WEDNESDAY 30 NOVEMBER 1917 - WEATHER DULL - WET AT INTERVALS

Private Edric Alfred Baker — *Royal Lancaster Regiment - Army Service Corps*

Service No.	S2/SR/03975
Age:	28
Place of birth:	Marlborough, Wiltshire
Home Country:	England
Date of death:	30/11/1917
Cause of death:	Killed in action
Memorial:	Marlborough, Wiltshire
War Cemetery:	Tyne Cot Memorial - Grave Panel 160.
Next of Kin:	Frank John & Sarah Ann Baker
Address:	18 Caterham Road, Lewisham, London

Edric, a cook, was the only child of Frank and Sarah Ann Baker and volunteered for service with the Army Service Corps. He arrived in France on 19 July 1915 and was attached to the 4th Field Bakery. In 1917, he was recommended for a commission and attached to the Royal Lancaster Regiment. He was killed on Friday 30 November 1917, near Ypres. Edric is remembered on the Tyne Cot Memorial and has no known grave.

15
December 1917

SATURDAY 1 DECEMBER 1917 - WEATHER FINE

2nd Lieutenant James Norman Ellis — *2nd Bn Kings Own Yorkshire Light Infantry*

Service No. N/a
Age: 19
Place of birth: Dewsbury, Yorkshire
Home Country: England
Date of death: 01/12/1917
Cause of death: Killed in action
Memorial: Mirfiled, Yorkshire – Marlborough College, Wiltshire
War Cemetery: Tyne Cot Cemetery - Grave IX. E. 24
Next of Kin: George & Elizabeth Ellis
Address: Easthorpe, Mirfield, Yorkshire

James was the third son of George and Elizabeth Ellis and was educated at Marlborough College. He volunteered for service initially joining the Ox & Bucks Light Infantry. He was given a commission with the 3rd Battalion Yorkshire Light Infantry and sent to the front and attached to 2nd Battalion Yorkshire Light Infantry. At 1.55am on Saturday 1 December 1917 the 2nd Yorkshire Light Infantry took part in an attack on German positions northeast of Passchendaele in the direction of Westroosbeke with the object of driving the Germans from Passchendaele Ridge. James was commanding 13 Platoon of D Company and was killed leading his men against two German pill boxes on the left of the attack as they reached the Passchendaele – Westroosbeke Road. The British attackers failed to find the entrances and worked round the pill boxes digging in 80 yards beyond them. Over the next two days the Germans counter attacked driving the British back almost to the original start line. James body was recovered and buried alongside his company commander Captain H.R. Ford MC just south of Mosselmarkt, northeast of Passchendaele. After the war, his grave site was identified by means of a regimental cross and his remains were moved to Tyne Cot Cemetery. His brothers George and Clifford were both killed during the war.

Private Thomas Probets — *2nd Bn Wiltshire Regiment*

Service No. 8100
Age: 26
Place of birth: Swindon, Wiltshire
Home Country: England
Date of death: 01/12/1917
Cause of death: Killed in action
Memorial: Not known
War Cemetery: Zantvoorde British Cemetery - Grave II. A. 12.
Next of Kin: George & Ellen Probets
Address: 3 Byron Street, Swindon, Wiltshire

Regular soldier Thomas, known as Tom, was the fifth son of George and Ellen Probets and enlisted

Thomas Probets

with the Wiltshire Regiment before the Great War. He served with the 2nd Battalion and landed at Zeebrugge on 7 October 1914. On Saturday 1 December 1917, the 2nd Wiltshires were in the British reserve line near Gheluvelt. Tom was a member of a ration party that were shelled bringing food to the 2nd Wiltshires. At about 7.30pm the ration party was shelled by German artillery near Shrewsbury forest just east of Cokes Cottage. Tom was initially reported missing and several horses were killed and 4 men wounded. Tom's body was later located and buried near where he fell. In November 1919 Tom's grave site was identified by means of a regimental cross and his remains were moved to Zantvoorde British Cemetery. Six of Tom's brothers served in the army during the Great War.

SUNDAY 2 DECEMBER 1917 - WEATHER FINE

Rifleman Walter John Cook Brittain *16th Bn Kings Royal Rifle Corps*

Service No.	C/1591	Age:	20
Place of birth:	Foxham, Wiltshire	Home Country:	England
Date of death:	02/12/1917	Cause of death:	Killed in action
Memorial:	Bremhill, Wiltshire		
War Cemetery:	Passchendaele New Cemetery - Grave XII. B. 6.		
Next of Kin:	William & Emma Brittain		
Address:	Lower Lodge, Pewsham, Wiltshire		

Twenty-year-old Walter, a farm labourer, was the youngest son of William and Emma Brittain and it is likely he was either conscripted into the army or enlisted under the Derby Scheme joining the Kings Royal Rifle Corps. After Completing his training he was sent to France to serve with the 16th Battalion. He was wounded in the leg and foot at the Somme in August 1916 and after spending some time in the 3rd Western General Hospital at Cardiff once recovered he returned to the front. Walter was killed on Sunday 2 December 1917, when the 16th Kings Royal Rifle Corps were subjected to a German Artillery barrage on Passchendaele village. Walter was buried near where he fell, just south of Passchendaele church. In March 1920, Walter's remains were located and identified by means of a disc and his remains were relocated to Passchendaele New Cemetery.

2nd Lieutenant Victor John Horton MID *161st Bde Bn Royal Field Artillery*

Service No.	N/a	Age:	20
Place of birth:	Swindon, Wiltshire	Home Country:	England

Date of death:	02/12/1917	Cause of death:	Killed in action
Memorial:	Dauntseys School Memorial, Wiltshire		
War Cemetery:	Duhallow ADS Cemetery - Grave II. D. 16.		
Next of kin:	Noah & Arabella Horton		
Address:	Day House Coate, Swindon, Wiltshire		

Victor, known as Jack, was the younger son of Noah and Arabella Horton and was educated at Swindon High School and Dauntseys Agricultural College. He was a good horse rider, a thorough sportsman and had a kindly disposition. He volunteered for service at 17 years of age, in August 1914 with the Royal Field Artillery and was in training at Newbridge Barracks, Ireland until August 1915. He was then sent to Cairo, Egypt and arrived at Gallipoli in September 1915 and was invalided home with dysentery in October 1915 and evacuated to England. Following his recovery, he was sent to the barracks at Colchester in December 1915 and in February 1916 arrived in France and at the Somme volunteered for service with a Trench Mortar Battery. He was promoted to sergeant, and received a parchment for gallantry and devotion to duty in the field. He was then mentioned in dispatches and offered a commission. He returned to England and was sent to the cadet school at Brighton until August 1917. From there he went to Salisbury Plain for a gunnery course and was then given home leave, while waiting for his rank to be substantiated. In October 1917, he was sent to Kessingland, Suffolk, where he took charge of a section until the inspection of a general. He was then given a few days' leave and left England for France on 21 November 1917. On Sunday 2 December 1917, near Passchendaele, Victor was at an advanced observation post with another officer and seven men, when a shell German exploded and killed all of them. Victor's mother received a letter from a fellow officer who stated:

"We have lost an officer of experience, such loss as we can ill afford."

He was buried in Duhallow ADS Cemetery, Belgium. ADS refers to an Advance Dressing Station which was based at Duhallow and established the cemetery.

Private Albert Victor Ashley		*2nd Bn Royal Berkshire Regiment*	
Service No.	38488	Age:	19
Place of birth:	Devizes, Wiltshire	Home Country:	England
Date of death:	02/12/1917	Cause of death:	Killed in action
Memorial:	Devizes, Devizes Odd Fellows		
War Cemetery:	Poelcapelle British Cemetery - Grave IV. E. 30.		
Next of Kin:	William & Sarah A Ashley		
Address:	36 Sheep Street, Devizes, Wiltshire		

Nineteen-year-old Albert, known as Vic, was the third son of William and Sarah A Ashley and was an old Scout. In 1913 he had been a member of the gymnastic squad that represented the Devizes troop at the International Scouts Rally at Birmingham. Vic was also a member of the Odd Fellows Society and had been employed by George Dallaway, a harness maker, in the High Street, Devizes where he had worked for nearly ten years. Vic joined the army in February 1917 and after three weeks training contracted spotted fever and was in hospital for nine weeks. After a further six weeks sick leave he completed his training and in September 1917 was sent to France joining the 2nd Battalion Royal Berkshire Regiment. In November 1917 Vic wrote to his father stating:

"Don't worry about me, I am happy enough, although it takes some doing out here."

Official records state he was killed by German artillery fire on Sunday 2 December 1917. However the following letter from Vic's company officer states he was killed the previous day on 1 December 1917 near Passchendaele:

"It is with much regret that I have to inform you of the sad news of the death of your son, No. 38488 Private A. Ashley. He was killed on December 1st by shell fire, and buried where he fell so nobly doing his duty, and the only consolation I can offer you is that he was killed instantly and did not suffer any pain."

Vic was buried where he fell on the right of the road at the northern edge of the village of Passchendeale. In January 1920, his grave was located and he was identified by means of a disc. His remains were relocated to Poelcapelle British Cemetery.

MONDAY 3 DECEMBER 1917 - WEATHER FINE

Corporal Hubert James Cook		*14th Bde Bn Royal Field Artillery*	
Service No.	94712	Age:	25
Place of birth:	Swindon, Wiltshire	Home Country:	England
Date of death:	03/12/1917	Cause of death:	Killed in action
Memorial:	Not known		
War Cemetery:	The Huts Cemetery - Grave XV. A. 3.		
Next of Kin:	Mildred Cook (wife) – James & Elizabeth Cook (parents)		
Address:	19 Tennyson Street, Swindon, Wiltshire		

Hubert was the eldest son of James and Elizabeth Cook and served his apprenticeship as a boiler maker in the Great Western Railway Works at Swindon. He was very popular and an enthusiastic footballer and the centre forward for Swindon United, where he was known as "Captain Cook". On leaving the Railway Works he moved to work in Hull and it was there he volunteered in September 1914, joining the Royal Field Artillery. In the spring of 1915 he married Mildred Adey at Swindon and soon after was sent to the front, arriving in France on 13 May 1915 to serve with the 88th Battery of the 14th Brigade. In March 1917 Hubert's wife became ill and he was given home leave and after her death he returned to the front. He was killed on Monday 3 December 1917, by a German shell near Dickebusch. His mother received the following letters, the first from Major Megee states:

"Corporal cook was firing his gun when shell burst in the gun-pit, and killed him instantaneously. He was always an excellent worker and was liked by all. He is a great loss to the battery. It must be some little consolation for you to know that he would not have suffered any pain. I beg you to accept my deepest sympathy in your bereavement."

Lieutenant G.F. Sadler wrote stating:

"I was your son's section commander and was in the same dug-out for some days in the position where he was killed. It was a very hot place, but nevertheless your son was always cheery and worked hard, as he always did. He met his death when at his post as No. 1 of the gun, and from all accounts I hear he behaved splendidly in spite of the heavy shelling. He was a brave man, I know from experience. Only a few days before his death he went to the assistance of a stretcher party who had been wounded by a shell, and helped to carry them into safety. He is a great loss to the battery and to me personally, as I knew him so well. You can console yourself with the fact that your son died at his post doing his duty, and what finer death can a man die?"

Lance Corporal Oliver James Turner		*2nd Bn Wiltshire Regiment*	
Service No.	26957	Age:	18
Place of birth:	Wanborough, Wiltshire	Home Country:	England

Date of death: 03/12/1917 Cause of death: Killed in action
Memorial: Not known
War Cemetery: Hooge Crater Cemetery - Grave XVII. J. 11.
Next of Kin: John & Kezia Turner
Address: Farringdon, Berkshire

Eighteen-year-old Oliver, was the second son of John and Kezia Turner and grew up in the Farringdon Work House. It is likely he volunteered for service initially joining the Royal Berkshire Regiment before being transferred to the Dorsetshire Regiment and finally the 2nd Battalion Wiltshire Regiment. On Monday 3 December 1917, the 2nd Wiltshires were in the British support line east of Gheluvelt. The Wiltshire's war diary states:

"Our artillery very active at 5am. The 2nd New Zealand Infantry Brigade attacked Polderhooek Chateau, zero 12 noon. Enemy retaliated on our support and back areas B coy suffered 7 casualties."

One of those killed was Oliver and he was buried near where he fell in a grave with seven comrades with a single cross bearing their names, regiment and date of death inscribed on it. In August 1919, the grave was located west of Tower Hamlets. Oliver was identified by means of a disc and he and his comrades remains were removed to Hooge Crater Cemetery.

Private William Reuben Morris *2nd Bn Wiltshire Regiment*
Service No. 22922 Age: 25
Place of birth: Idmiston, Wiltshire Home Country: England
Date of death: 03/12/1917 Cause of death: Killed in action
Memorial: Salisbury, Winterbournes, Wiltshire
War Cemetery: Hooge Crater Cemetery - Grave XVII. J. 12.
Next of Kin: James & Fanny Morris
Address:, Winterbourne Earls, Wiltshire

William, known as Willie and a farm labourer, was the second son of James and Fanny Morris and it is likely he was either conscripted into the army or enlisted under the Derby Scheme joining the Wiltshire Regiment. After Completing his training, he was sent to the front to serve with the 2nd Battalion. He was killed on Monday 3 December 1917, by a German shell, in the British support line east of Gheluvelt, at the same time as Oliver Turner. He was buried near where he fell in a grave with seven comrades and a single cross bearing their names, regiment and date of death inscribed on it. In August 1919, the grave was located west of Tower Hamlets. Willie was identified by means of a disc and he and his comrades remains were removed to Hooge Crater Cemetery.

Private Albert Wareham *2nd Bn Wiltshire Regiment*
Service No. 10958 Age: 31
Place of birth: Hinton, Wiltshire Home Country: England
Date of death: 03/12/1917 Cause of death: Killed in action
Memorial: Bulkington, Keevil, Wiltshire
War Cemetery: Hooge Crater Cemetery - Grave XVII. J. 16.
Next of Kin: James & Elizabeth Wareham
Address: Oxenleaze Farm, Keevil, Wiltshire

Farm labourer Albert was the youngest son of James and Elizabeth Wareham and volunteered for service with the Wiltshire Regiment arriving in France on 26 January 1916 to serve with the 2nd Battalion. He was killed on Monday 3 December 1917, by a German shell, in the British support line east of Gheluvelt, at the same time as Oliver Turner. He was buried near where he fell in a grave with seven comrades and

Left: Herbert Abrams

Right: Wilfred Frederick Stanley Groves

a single cross bearing their names, regiment and date of death inscribed on it. In August 1919, the grave was located west of Tower Hamlets. Albert was identified by means of a disc and he and his comrades remains were removed to Hooge Crater Cemetery.

Sergeant Herbert Abrams — *2nd Bn Wiltshire Regiment*

Service No.	19041	Age:	19
Place of birth:	Trowbridge, Wiltshire	Home Country:	England
Date of death:	03/12/1917	Cause of death:	Killed in Action
Memorial:	Trowbridge, Wiltshire		
War Cemetery:	Hooge Crater Cemetery - Grave XVII. J. 10.		
Next of Kin:	Joseph & Lavinia Abrams		
Address:	10 St. Thomas Passage, Trowbridge		

Under age soldier Herbert, known as Bert, was the third son of Joseph and Lavinia Abrams and had voluntarily enlisted with the Wiltshire Regiment in 1915 at sixteen years of age. He had joined the Trowbridge Church Lads Brigade in 1910 and was an apprentice of the Cooperative Society at the Mortimer Street Branch. He was also an active member of St. Thomas' Church Sunday School. He was sent to France in 1916 to serve with the 2nd Battalion and was twice wounded being sent home to recover. At the age of nineteen he had attained the rank of Sergeant. Bert was killed in action on Monday 3 December 1917 by a German shell, in the British support line east of Gheluvelt, at the same time as Oliver Turner. Joseph and Lavinia Abrams received letters from Captain A. J. Smart and 2nd Lieutenant F. J. E. Spencer extracts from which are below:

"He was a splendid example of a man and you have every reason to be proud of him. He was hit by a piece of shell and killed instantaneously."

"I cannot praise him too highly for his work in the platoon of which I am in command. His name, I can assure you will not be forgotten by his comrades and myself. He was a very keen sportsman and helped me many times to organise games, and concerts and sports, for the welfare of the platoon."

He was buried near where he fell in a grave with seven comrades and a single cross bearing their names, regiment and date of death inscribed on it. In August 1919, the grave was located west of Tower Hamlets. Bert was identified and he and his comrades remains were removed to Hooge Crater Cemetery. In 1918 his family inserted the following memoriam in a local paper:

Fondly we loved him, he is still dear to us,
But in grief we must bent to Gods holy will;
Our sorrow is great and our loss hard to bear
But angels will guard our dear loved one with care.

TUESDAY 4 DECEMBER 1917 - WEATHER COLD AND FROSTY

Private Wilfred Frederick Stanley Groves		*2nd Bn Wiltshire Regiment*	
Service No.	24213	Age:	19
Place of birth:	Trowbridge, Wiltshire	Home Country:	England
Date of death:	04/12/1917	Cause of death:	Killed in action
Memorial:	Trowbridge, Trowbridge UFC	War Cemetery:	Tyne Cot Memorial - Panel 119 to 120.
Next of Kin:	Emma Groves (grandmother)		
Address:	6 Newtown, Trowbridge, Wiltshire		

Nineteen-year-old Wilfred was raised by his Grandmother and volunteered for service on 10 May 1915 with the Wiltshire Regiment. After completing his training he was sent to the front to serve with the 2nd Battalion and was wounded at Messines in 1917. He was killed in action on Tuesday 4 December 1917, by a German shell, in the British support line east of Gheluvelt. The War Diary states:

Enemy artillery still active. During the afternoon "A" coy in right front position sustained 10 casualties, 5 killed and 5 wounded from hostile trench mortar fire.

His Grandmother received the following letter from 2nd Lieutenant Gerald M. Jeans:

"It is with the greatest sorrow that I write to inform you that your grandson was killed at 10am on the 4 December by a bursting shell in the front line. It may be some little consolation and comfort to know that he died a painless death. He was under my command and I found him to be a splendid fellow and absolutely trustworthy and always willing to undertake any work, both dangerous and otherwise. Three nights before his death I was sent out on patrol for a certain purpose. I took my servant with me and asked for one volunteer from my platoon to accompany me. Your grandson immediately stepped forward and volunteered to go with me. I was more than grateful. With his assistance we accomplished the work we had to in 'No Man's Land' within an hour, and then returned to our lines. He made the greatest sacrifice of all. You may rest assured he has done his duty most nobly and fearlessly for his country and battalion, and it grieves me to lose him from my platoon. He was not alone when the great call came, and another splendid fellow was killed, while others were wounded by the same shell. May I again offer my deepest sympathy in your loss."

Wilfred is remembered on the Tyne Cot Memorial and has no known grave. His grandmother inserted the following memoriam in December 1918:

One year has passed since that day,
When one we loved was called away.
His loving ways and smiling face;
No one can fill his vacant place.
Sweet be your dreams dear Wilfred;
'Tis sweet to breathe your name.
In life we loved you dearly,
In death, we do the same.

Private George Henry Saunders		*2nd Bn Wiltshire Regiment*	
Service No.	33220	Age:	28
Place of birth:	Bemerton, Wiltshire	Home Country:	England
Date of death:	04/12/1917	Cause of death:	Killed in action
Memorial:	Salisbury, Laverstock, Wiltshire		
War Cemetery:	Tyne Cot Memorial - Panel 119 to 120.		
Next of Kin:	William Henry Saunders		
Address:	Salisbury, Wiltshire		

George was the son of William Henry Saunders and it is likely he was either conscripted into the army or enlisted under the Derby Scheme joining the Wiltshire Regiment. After completing his training, he was sent to the front to serve with the 2nd Battalion. He was killed in action on Tuesday 4 December 1917, by a German shell, in the British support line east of Gheluvelt, at the same time as Wilfred Groves. George is remembered on the Tyne Cot Memorial and has no known grave.

Private Henry John Baker		*A Coy 2nd Bn Wiltshire Regiment*	
Service No.	13608	Age:	29
Place of birth:	Biddestone, Wiltshire	Home Country:	England
Date of death:	04/12/1917	Cause of death:	Killed in action
Memorial:	Biddestone, Wiltshire		
War Cemetery:	Tyne Cot Memorial - Panel 119 to 120		
Next of Kin:	George & Hannah Baker		
Address:	Butts, Biddestone, Wiltshire		

Henry, known as John, a carter on a farm was the second son of George and Hannah Baker and volunteered for service with the Wiltshire Regiment arriving in France on 1 April 1915 to serve with the 2nd Battalion. He was killed in action on Tuesday 4 December 1917, by a German shell, in the British support line east of Gheluvelt, at the same time as Wilfred Groves. John is remembered on the Tyne Cot Memorial and has no known grave.

Private Frank Edward Dyer		*2nd Bn Wiltshire Regiment*	
Service No.	21940	Age:	39
Place of birth:	Avening, Gloucestershire	Home Country:	England
Date of death:	04/12/1917	Cause of death:	Killed in action
Memorial:	Not known		
War Cemetery:	Tyne Cot Memorial - Panel 119 to 120.		
Next of Kin:	John & Sarah Annie Dyer		
Address:	90 Beatrice Street, Swindon, Wiltshire		

Frank was the second son of John and Sarah Dyer and it is likely he was either conscripted into the army or enlisted under the Derby Scheme joining the Wiltshire Regiment. After completing his training, he was sent to the front to serve with the 2nd Battalion. He was killed in action on Tuesday 4 December 1917, by a German shell, in the British support line east of Gheluvelt, at the same time as Wilfred Groves. Frank's mother received the following letter from his company officer stating:

"I found him a splendid fellow, absolutely reliable and always willing to do any work for me. Your son has made the greatest sacrifice of all and you may rest assured he has done his duty most nobly and fearlessly for his country, and it greaves me greatly to lose him from my platoon."

Frank is remembered on the Tyne Cot Memorial and has no known grave.

John Wyndham Maxwell DSOMC

Private Ernest William North *2nd Bn Wiltshire Regiment*

Service No.	203075	Age:	32
Place of birth:	Aldbourne, Wiltshire	Home Country:	England
Date of death:	04/12/1917	Cause of death:	Died of wounds
Memorial:	Ramsbury, Wiltshire		
War Cemetery:	Bailleul Communal Cemetery Extension Nord - Grave III. E. 43.		
Next of Kin:	James & Annie North		
Address:	Back Lane, Ramsbury, Wiltshire		

Ernest, a groom domestic was the only son of James and Annie North and it is likely he was either conscripted into the army or enlisted under the Derby Scheme initially joining the Somerset Light Infantry, before being transferred to the Wiltshire Regiment. He was a keen football player and played for the Regimental Team in the Inter Regimental Championship. After completing his training, he was sent to the front to serve with the 2nd Battalion. He was wounded by a German shell on 2 December 1917, in the British support line east of Gheluvelt, and evacuated to a military hospital near Bailleul. Though everything possible was done for him he succumbed to his wounds on Tuesday 4 December 1917.

Lt. Colonel John Wyndham Maxwell DSOMC *8th Bn King's Royal Rifle Corps*

Service No.	N/a	Age:	36
Place of birth:	Richmond, Surrey	Home Country:	England
Date of death:	04/12/1917	Cause of death:	Died of wounds
Memorial:	Marlborough College, Wiltshire		
War Cemetery:	Ypres Reservoir Cemetery - Grave I. A. 31.		
Next of Kin:	John & Alice Maxwell		
Address:	29 Brock Street, Bath, Somerset		

John was the son of John and Alice Maxwell and was educated at Marlborough College before attending Keeble College, Oxford where he graduated in 1902. He left England for Ceylon in 1907 where he was employed by the Eastern Produce & Estates Company, and was a member of the Ceylon Planters Rifles. He returned to England in 1914 and at the outbreak of hostilities he volunteered for service with the Somerset Light Infantry on 5 August 1914. He left the Somerset Light Infantry on 4 September 1914 and was given a commission with the 7th Battalion Rifle Brigade. He was promoted to Captain in 1915 and attached to the Royal Berkshire Regiment in 1916 and was awarded the Military Cross. He returned to the 7th Rifle Brigade and was promoted to Major and in 1917 was promoted to Lieutenant Colonel and attached to the 8th Battalion King's Royal Rifle Corps. At about 9pm on 3 December 1917 John went with Second Lieutenant R. H. Woods to reconnoitre the front-line northwest Passchendaele. He was discovered by Brigadier General Skinner 200 yards beyond Metchele, both had been badly wounded by the same German shell. They were taken too Waterloo Bunker where Second Lieutenant Woods died on arrival. John succumbed to his wounds the following day.

FRIDAY 7 DECEMBER 1917

Private Richard Salisbury		*884th Coy MT Army Service Corps*	
Service No.	M2/226823	Age:	23
Place of birth:	Sedgehill, Wiltshire	Home Country:	England
Date of death:	07/12/1917	Cause of death:	Died of wounds
Memorial:	Salisbury, Laverstock, Wiltshire		
War Cemetery:	Dozinghem Military Cemetery - Grave XIV.F.3		
Next of Kin:	Lily J Salisbury (wife) – Henry & Lizzie Salisbury (parents)		
Address:	52 St Ann Street, Salisbury- Burrough Hill Lodge, Laverstock		

Richard, a chauffeur, was the third son of Henry and Lizzie Salisbury and toward the end of 1916 he married Lily J. Witt at Salisbury. It is likely he was either conscripted into the army or enlisted under the Derby Scheme joining the Army Service Corps. After completing his training, he was sent to the front to serve with the 884th Mechanical Transport Company. He was attached to XIX Corps Heavy Artillery and was wounded near Ypres. He was evacuated to No. 4 Casualty Clearing Station north of Poperinge where he succumbed to his wounds on Friday 7 December 1917. He left a widow and a young daughter.

SUNDAY 9 DECEMBER 1917

Gunner Albert Ernest Butt		*33rd Trench Mortar Bty Bn Royal Field Artillery*	
Service No.	86507	Age:	26
Place of birth:	Bradford on Avon, Wiltshire	Home Country:	England
Date of death:	09/12/1917	Cause of death:	Killed in action
Memorial:	Bradford on Avon, Moulton Bradford on Avon		
War Cemetery:	Potijze Chateau Grounds Cemetery - Grave I. D. 34.		
Next of Kin:	Edwin & Adelaide Ann Butt		
Address:	117 Trowbridge Road, Bradford on Avon, Wiltshire		

Albert was the second son of Edwin and Adelaide Butt and was employed by Spencer Moulton and Co. Mills at Bradford on Avon. He volunteered for service soon after the outbreak of hostilities answering Lord Kitcheners appeal for more men. He joined the Royal Field Artillery and after completing his training was sent to the front to serve with the 33rd Trench Mortar Battery. Albert was killed on Sunday 9 December 1917, by a German shell behind the lines, north east of Ypres. His father received the following letter from Lieutenant Howell of his battery:

"I am deeply grieved to have to tell you that your son was killed yesterday. He was asleep in a tent with several other men a good way from the line, and a long-range gun put over a burst of shrapnel which killed him and one other and wounded seven others. What will be a small comfort to you is that he must have been killed quite instantaneously while asleep, and can have felt nothing. Your son was one of our

Albert Ernest Butt

best men and will be very much missed in the Battery. It is no use my trying to say any more, except that I sympathise deeply with your sorrow."

TUESDAY 11 DECEMBER 1917

Private George Henry Cole — *16th Bn Lancashire Fusiliers*

Service No.	47153	Age:	37
Place of birth:	Christian Malford, Wiltshire	Home Country:	England
Date of death:	11/12/1917	Cause of death:	Killed in action
Memorial:	Christian Malford, Wiltshire		
War Cemetery:	Tyne Cot Memorial - Panel 54 to 60 and 163A.		
Next of Kin:	John & Lucy Cole		
Address:	Christian Malford, Wiltshire		

George was the third son of John and Lucy Cole and had been employed as a butler with the Schilizzi family at 3 Prince's Gate, London, for 14 years at the outbreak of hostilities. It is likely he joined under the Derby scheme enlisting with the Army Service Corps and arriving in France in January 1916 where he was employed in the Expeditionary Force canteen. In October 1917, he was transferred to the 16th Battalion Lancashire Fusiliers and after completing eight weeks training he was sent to the front. On Tuesday 11 December 1917, the 16th Lancashires were near Kronpriz Farm west of Passchendale and gas shells were fired at the farm and blew back into the trenches. It is likely he was killed during his first tour in the front line as his sister had received a field post card dated 11 December which was the day he was killed. In January 1918 George's mother received the following letter from his commanding officer:

"I am very sorry to have to inform you of the death of Private G. H. Cole, which occurred on December 11th, 1917. He suffered no pain as death was instantaneous. He had not been with the battalion long, but during the time he was in the Company he became very popular with his fellow men, and was a good soldier and a real man. It will be a great loss to you but please rest assured he died nobly doing his duty. Please accept all our heartfelt sympathy and convey the same to his people."

George is remembered on the Tyne Cot Memorial and has no known grave.

WEDNESDAY 12 DECEMBER 1917

Sapper Joseph George Phelps — *255th Tunnelling Coy Royal Engineers*

Service No.	147932	Age:	36
Place of birth:	Bradford on Avon, Wiltshire	Home Country:	England
Date of death:	12/12/1917	Cause of death:	Died
Memorial:	Monkton Farleigh, Wiltshire		
War Cemetery:	Duhallow ADS Cemetery - Grave III. D. 12.		
Next of Kin:	Caroline E Phelps (wife) – Joseph & Alice Phelps (parents)		
Address:	3 Church Street Aberbargoed, Wales - Town Barton, Norton St Philip, Somerset		

Joseph, known as George and a coal miner was the fourth son of Joseph and Alice Phelps and on 24 February 1900 he married Caroline Elizabeth Gait. He volunteered for service with the Welsh Regiment but was transferred to the Royal Engineers and was sent to France on 3 December 1915. He was sent to 255th Tunnelling Company who in late 1917 were engaged constructing dugouts north of Langemarck and Poelcappelle. It is likely George was wounded by German artillery fire and taken to an advanced dressing station north of Ypres where he succumbed to his wounds on Wednesday 12 December 1917. He left a widow and young family.

SATURDAY 22 DECEMBER 1917 COLD AND FROSTY

Gunner Alfred Reginald Hunt — *1/1st Heavy Battery Bn Royal Garrison Artillery*

Service No.	174398	Age:	24
Place of birth:	Wootton Bassett, Wiltshire	Home Country:	England
Date of death:	22/12/1917	Cause of death:	Died of wounds
Memorial:	Wootton Bassett, Wiltshire		
War Cemetery:	Mendinghem Military Cemetery - Grave VI. BB. 30.		
Next of Kin:	Alfred & Mary Hunt		
Address:	1 Victory Row, Wootton Bassett, Wiltshire		

Alfred, known as Reginald, was the eldest son of Alfred and Mary Hunt and volunteered for service with the Royal Field Artillery in September 1914. After completing his training, he was sent to France on 12 May 1915, where he was twice wounded and twice evacuated to hospital in England. He was transferred to the Royal Garrison Artillery and returned to the front to serve with the 1/1st Heavy Battery. Reginald was wounded on 2 December 1917 and taken to No. 64 Casualty Clearing Station near Proven, where he succumbed to his wounds on Saturday 22 December 1917. His brother Joseph Clarence Hunt had been killed at the Somme in July 1916.

Private Percy Harold Nash — *2nd Bn London Regiment*

Service No.	248015	Age:	25
Place of birth:	Figheldean, Wiltshire	Home Country:	England
Date of death:	22/12/1917	Cause of death:	Killed in action
Memorial:	Figheldean, Wiltshire		
War Cemetery:	Tyne Cot Memorial - Panel 148 to 150.		
Next of Kin:	Frederick & Elizabeth Sarah Nash		
Address:	Mill House, Figheldean, Wiltshire		

Rupert Ernest Titcombe

Percy, a farm labourer, was the fourth son of Frederick and Elizabeth Sarah Nash and originally enlisted with the Army Service Corps. It is probable that he was transferred to the Army Training Reserve in 1917 and then sent to the front and transferred to the 2/1st Battalion London Regiment. Saturday 22 December 1917 the 2/1st Londons were ordered to move up to defensive positions south of Poelcapelle, as it was feared there would be a German attack. Percy was killed most likely by German artillery fire. He is remembered on the Tyne Cot Memorial and has no known grave.

SUNDAY 23 DECEMBER 1917

Lance Bombardier Rupert Ernest Titcombe — *14th Siege Bty Royal Garrison Artillery*

Service No.	43694	Age:	23
Place of birth:	Swindon, Wiltshire	Home Country:	England
Date of death:	23/12/1917	Cause of death:	Killed in action
Memorial:	R Shop Memorial Great Western Railway Works, Swindon		
War Cemetery:	Duhallow ADS Cemetery - Grave III. D. 25.		
Next of Kin:	Robert & Rebecca Titcombe		
Address:	Haydon Wick, Swindon, Wiltshire		

Rupert, known as Ernest, was the youngest son of Robert and Rebecca Titcombe and was employed as a machinist in R Shop of the Loco and Carriage Department at the Great Western Railway Works in Swindon. He volunteered for service on 1 September 1914, joining the Royal Garrison Artillery and after completing his training he was sent to the 14th Siege Battery. He was sent to Egypt arriving on 3 April 1915 and was then sent to Gallipoli. After the evacuation of the Gallipoli peninsular in January 1916 he returned to Egypt before being sent to France and arrived on 15 April 1916. Ernest was killed on Sunday 23 December 1917, most likely by a German shell northeast of Ypres. His parents received the following letter from Major T.E. Cameron stating:

"His death was instantaneous, so that he had not much pain. He has been buried today by our clergyman in the local British Cemetery. I am very sorry to lose so good and useful soldier, and I feel greatly with you in your sad loss. Please accept my sympathy."

Ernest's personal property was returned to his parents and consisted of disc, photos, match cover, purse, pair of scissors, wrist watch, strap and guard, pen holder, 2 handkerchiefs, watch key and cards.

SATURDAY 24 DECEMBER 1917

Corporal Percival Frank Witt *156th Siege Bty Royal Garrison Artillery*
Service No. 78744 Age: 23
Place of birth: Wilton, Wiltshire Home Country: England
Date of death: 24/12/1917 Cause of death: Died of woundsMemorial: St. Mary the Virgin Church, Horsell.
War Cemetery: Mendinghem Military Cemetery - Grave VI. BB. 38.
Next of Kin: James & Frances Witt
Address: Moss Rose Villa, South Road, Horsell, Surrey

Frank, a cowman, was the only son of James and Frances Witt and was called up for service on 27 April 1916 and was sent to the Royal Garrison Artillery Depot. After completing his training, he arrived in France on 9 September 1916 and posted to 156th Siege Battery. He was promoted to corporal in February 1917 and given a week's home leave in October 1917. Frank was gassed on Christmas Eve 1917, when the 156th Battery were shelled by German artillery with mustard gas. He was evacuated to No. 4 Casualty Clearing Station near Proven where he died from the effects of Mustard gas later that day. His personal property was returned to his parents and consisted of 2 discs, letter, photos, 2 note books, 2 religious books, tobacco pouch, false teeth, watch and protector, match box holder, cards, 2 purses and 2 coins.

TUESDAY 25 DECEMBER 1917

Corporal Frederick William Bletso *156th Siege Bty Bn Royal Garrison Artillery*
Service No. 284524 Age: 33
Place of birth: Longbridge Deverill, Wiltshire Home Country: England
Date of death: 25/12/1917 Cause of death: Died of wounds
Memorial: Not known
War Cemetery: Mendinghem Military Cemetery - Grave VI. BB. 37
Next of Kin: Emma Mary Bletso (wife) – John & Fanny Bletso (parents)
Address: Poyntington, Sherborne, Dorset - Brixton, Deverill, Wiltshire

Old soldier Frederick was the youngest son of John and Fanny Bletso and originally joined the Royal Garrison Artillery on 11 November 1901. He was sent to Egypt in April 1902 and served there until returning to England in March 1905. In November 1908 he left the army and was transferred to the reserve. He found employment as a gardener and on 26 April 1913 he married Emma Mary Cooper at Westbury. His term with the Army Reserve expired in November 1913 and it is likely he was either conscripted into the army or re-enlisted under the Derby Scheme. He was sent to serve with the 156th Battery Royal Garrison Artillery and it is likely he was gassed on Christmas Eve 1917, when the 156th Battery were shelled by German artillery with mustard gas. He was evacuated to No. 46 Casualty Clearing Station near Proven where he died from the effects of mustard gas the following day. He left a widow and a young son.

Private Walter Frank Phillips — *2nd Bn Wiltshire Regiment*

Service No.: 27147
Age: 26
Place of birth: Pewsey, Wiltshire
Home Country: England
Date of death: 25/12/1917
Cause of death: Died of wounds
Memorial: Pewsey, Wiltshire
War Cemetery: Bailleul Communal Cemetery Extension Nord - Grave III. E. 28.
Next of Kin: Thomas & Ellen Phillips
Address: West End, Pewsey, Wiltshire

Walter, known as Frank, a bricklayer, was the youngest son of Thomas and Ellen Phillips and it is likely he was either conscripted into the army or enlisted under the Derby Scheme initially joining the Somerset Light Infantry. He was transferred to the Worcester Regiment and then to the 2nd Battalion Wiltshire Regiment. He was wounded most likely while serving in trenches east of Gheluvelt and evacuated to a military hospital at Bailleul, where he succumbed to his wounds on Christmas Day 1917.

WEDNESDAY 26 DECEMBER 1917

Private Richard Charles Silley — *17th Bn Manchester Regiment*

Service No.: 51132
Age: 35
Place of birth: Donyatt, Somerset
Home Country: England
Date of death: 26/12/1917
Cause of death: Killed in action
Memorial: Chippenham, St. Andrews Church Chippenham
War Cemetery: Poelcapelle British Cemetery - Grave VIA. A. 1.
Next of Kin: Charles & Flora Anne Silley
Address: Chiselborough, Stoke under Ham, Somerset

Richard, a grocer's assistant, was the second son of Charles and Flora Silley. It is likely he was either conscripted into the army or enlisted under the Derby Scheme initially joining the Army Service Corps. He was sent to the front and transferred to the 17th Battalion Manchester Regiment. He was killed on Boxing day 1917, most likely by German artillery fire, in trenches west of Gheluvelt and south of Polderhoek, astride the Menin Road. In January 1934 Richard's remains were located on the south side of the Menin Road in Bass Wood and were identified by means of a damaged disc and shoulder titles. His remains were relocated and moved to Poelcapelle British Cemetery.

THURSDAY 27 DECEMBER 1917

Lance Sergeant John Henry Liddon — *2nd Bn Wiltshire Regiment*

Service No.: 22499
Age: 21
Place of birth: Stratton St Margaret, Wiltshire
Home Country: England
Date of death: 27/12/1917
Cause of death: Killed in action
Memorial: Not known
War Cemetery: Hooge Crater Cemetery - Grave XVI. J. 11.
Next of Kin: Edwin Charles & Elizabeth Liddon
Address: 99 Bright Street, Swindon, Wiltshire

John, was the youngest son of Edwin and Elizabeth Liddon and was employed by Wilson's Bacon

Factory at Swindon. It is likely he was either conscripted into the army or enlisted under the Derby Scheme initially joining the Wiltshire Regiment. After completing his training he was sent to the front to serve with the 2nd Battalion. John was killed on Thursday 27 December 1917 while working near the British front line west of Gheluvelt. His company officer wrote the following letter to Henry's mother:

"It is with great sorrow that I have to inform you of the death of your son, Sergeant J. H. Liddon, who was killed last night while working up the front line. This news will come as a great shock to you, more so than it did to me, and you have my deepest sympathy in your bereavement. Your son was a very valuable and reliable platoon sergeant, and I was much attached to him, and I will find him hard to replace. He was always most willing, fearles and cheerful even under the most adverse conditions, and was beloved by his men. I was not with him at the time of his death, but I find that he was shot through the heart with a machine gun bullet, death being instantaneous. It is some slight consolation to know that he did not suffer, and is now resting in peace. Out here we are inclined to look upon death as a happy release from a troublesome life, but it leaves sorrow to those that are left behind. I am sending your son's watch and pocket book, which I hope will reach you safely."

John was originally buried in Bass Wood No.2 Cemetery and in 1919 his remains were moved to Hooge Crater Cemetery. His brother Walter was killed in Belgium in 1914 while serving with the 2nd Battalion Wiltshire Regiment.

SATURDAY 29 DECEMBER 1917

Private Edward Wiltshire		*2nd Bn Royal Berkshire Regiment*	
Service No.	38361	Age:	19
Place of birth:	Bishops Cannings, Wiltshire	Home Country:	England
Date of death:	29/12/1917	Cause of death:	Died of wounds
Memorial:	Devizes, Wiltshire		
War Cemetery:	Lijssenthoek Military Cemetery - Grave XXVII. CC. 14.		
Next of Kin:	William and Fanny Wiltshire		
Address:	3 North Close Terrace, Gosport Street, Lymington, Hampshire		

Nineteen-year-old Edward was the youngest son of William and Fanny Wiltshire and it is likely he enlisted in 1917 and after completing his training he was sent to the front joining the 2nd Battalion Royal Berkshire Regiment. Edward was wounded while in the British front line near Passchendaele and evacuated to a casualty clearing station at Lijssenthoek west of Ypres, Belgium, where he died on Saturday 29 December 1917 and was buried in the nearby cemetery.

Maps

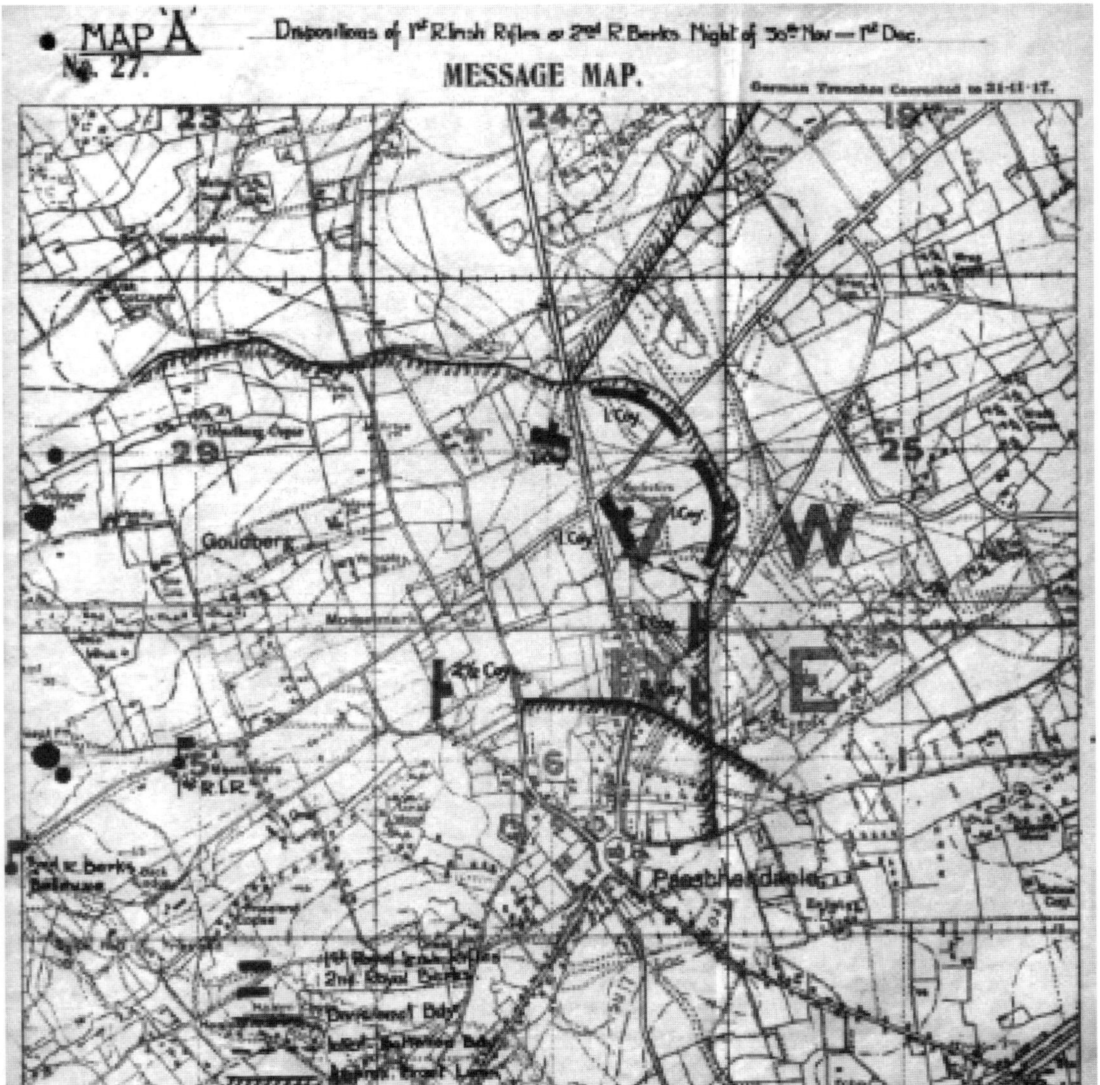

Dispositions of the 1st Royal Irish Rifles & 2nd Royal Berkshires the night of 30 November – 1 December 1917.

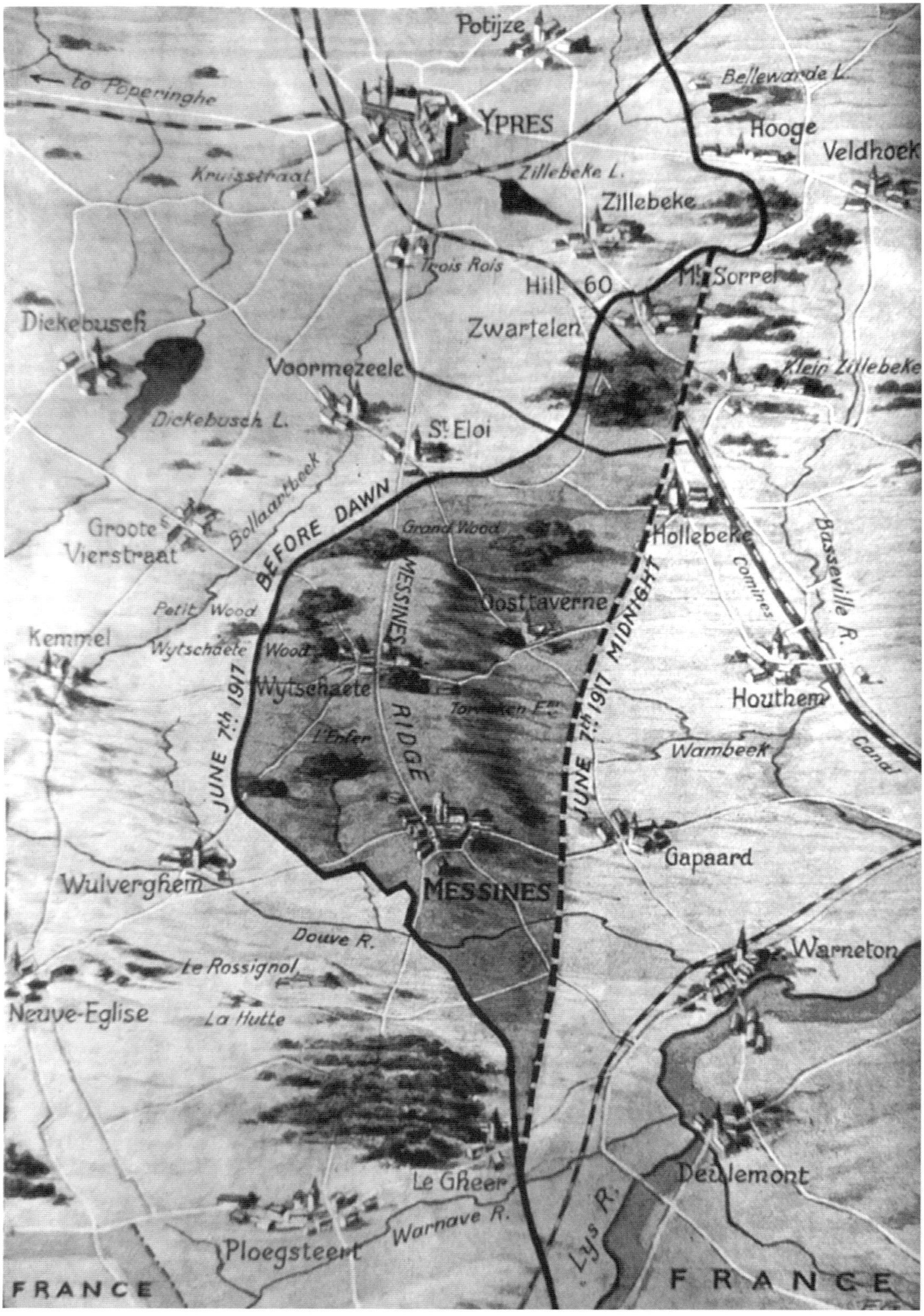

Map showing the area captured by the allies during the Messines attack.

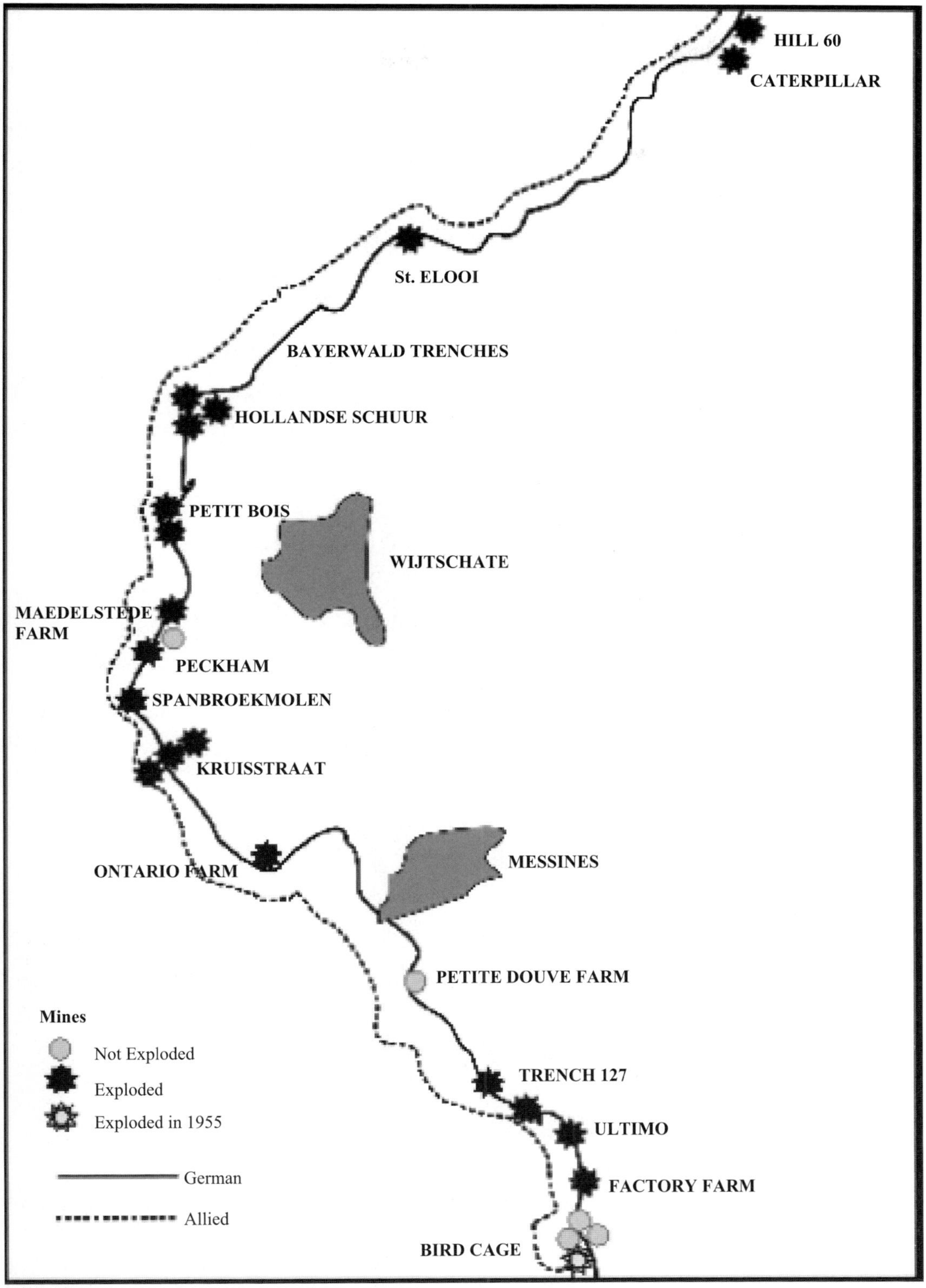

Location of the mines, nineteen of which exploded at Zero hour on Thursday 7 June 1917.

Messines Ridge - extent of advance between Zero hour on 7 June 1917 and 11 June 1917.

The area where the Third Battle of Ypres, known as Passchendaele, was fought.

The front line on the Allies offensive of Tuesday 31 July 1917.

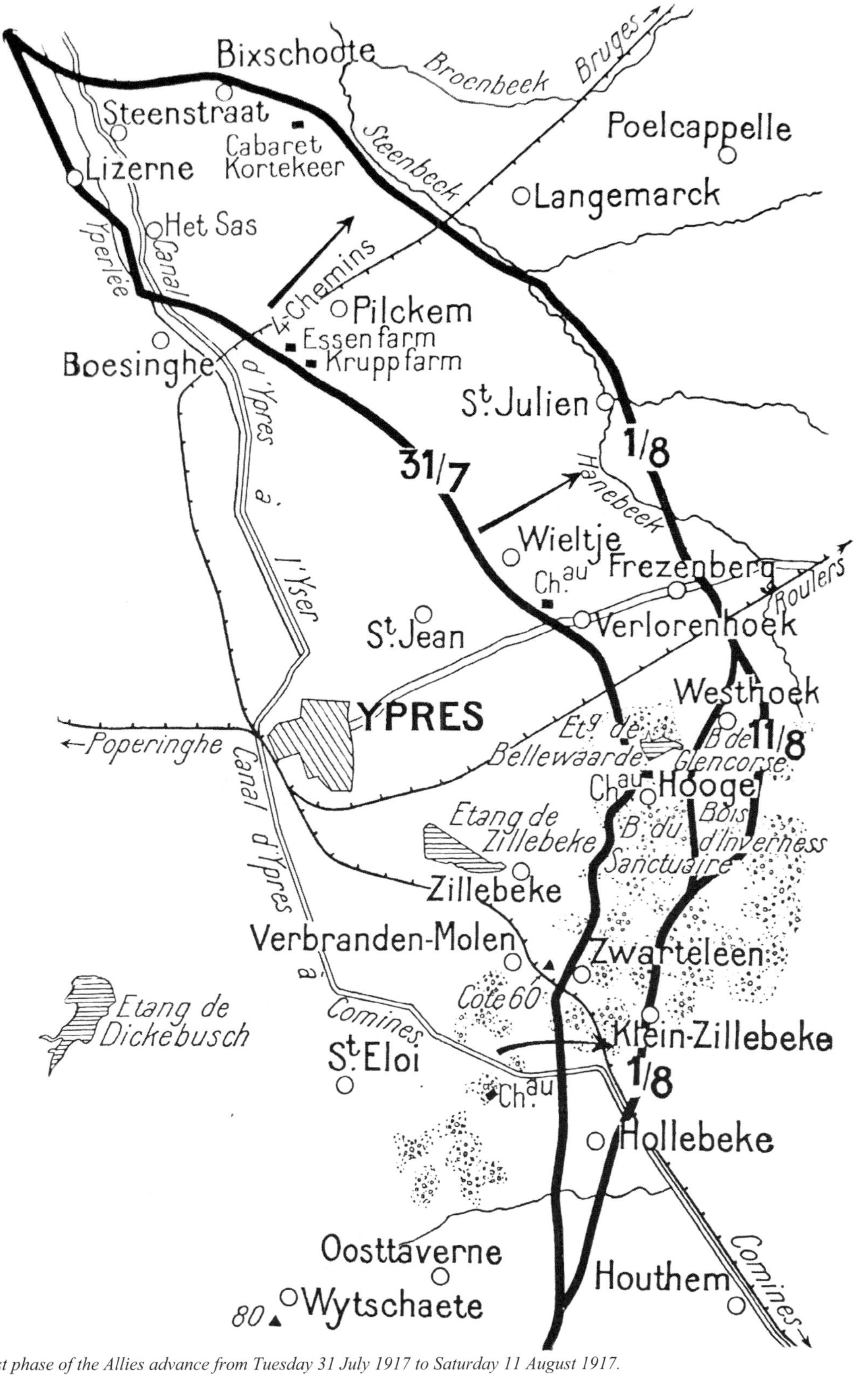

First phase of the Allies advance from Tuesday 31 July 1917 to Saturday 11 August 1917.

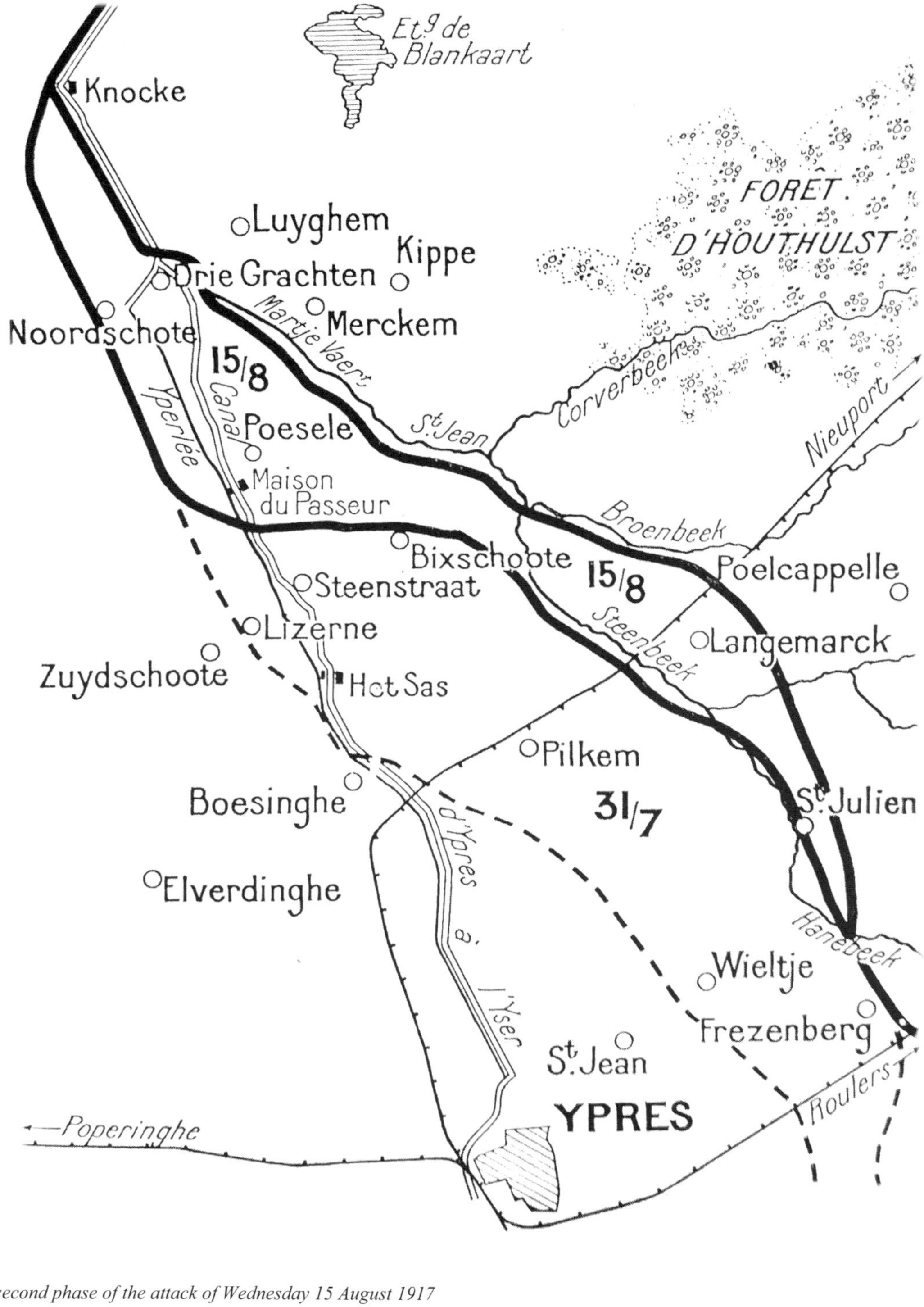

The second phase of the attack of Wednesday 15 August 1917

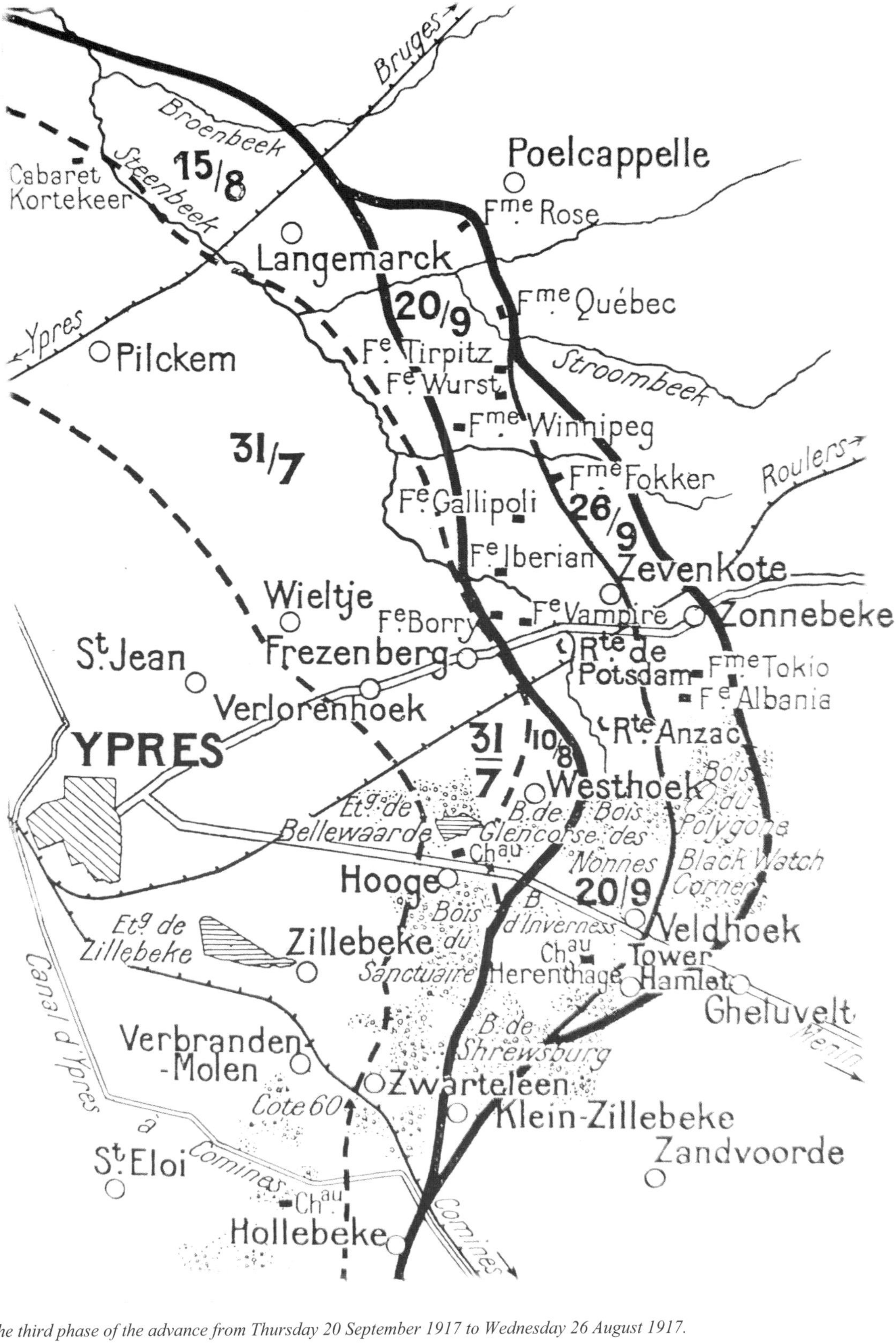

The third phase of the advance from Thursday 20 September 1917 to Wednesday 26 August 1917.

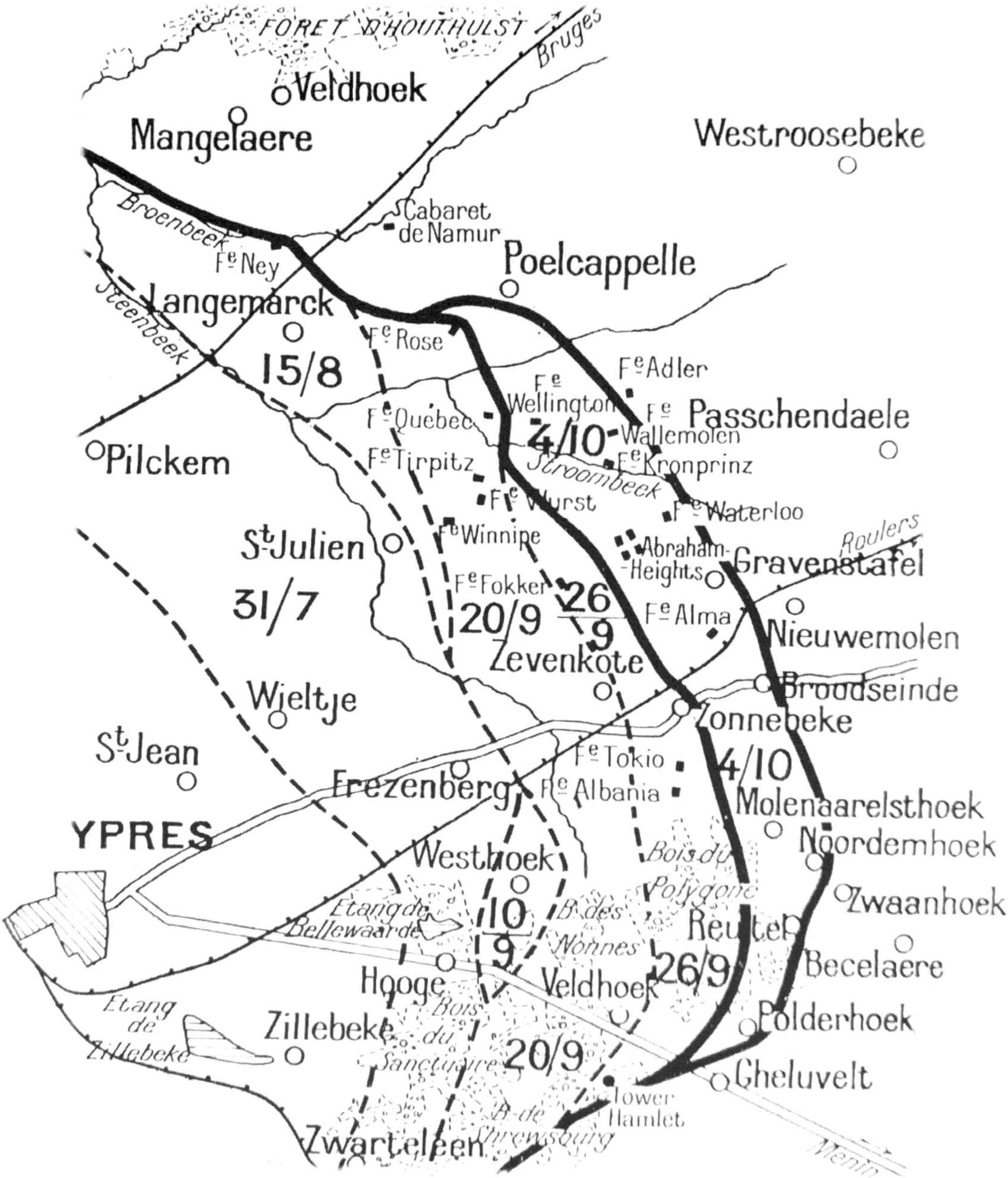

Fourth phase of the advance Thursday 4 October 1917

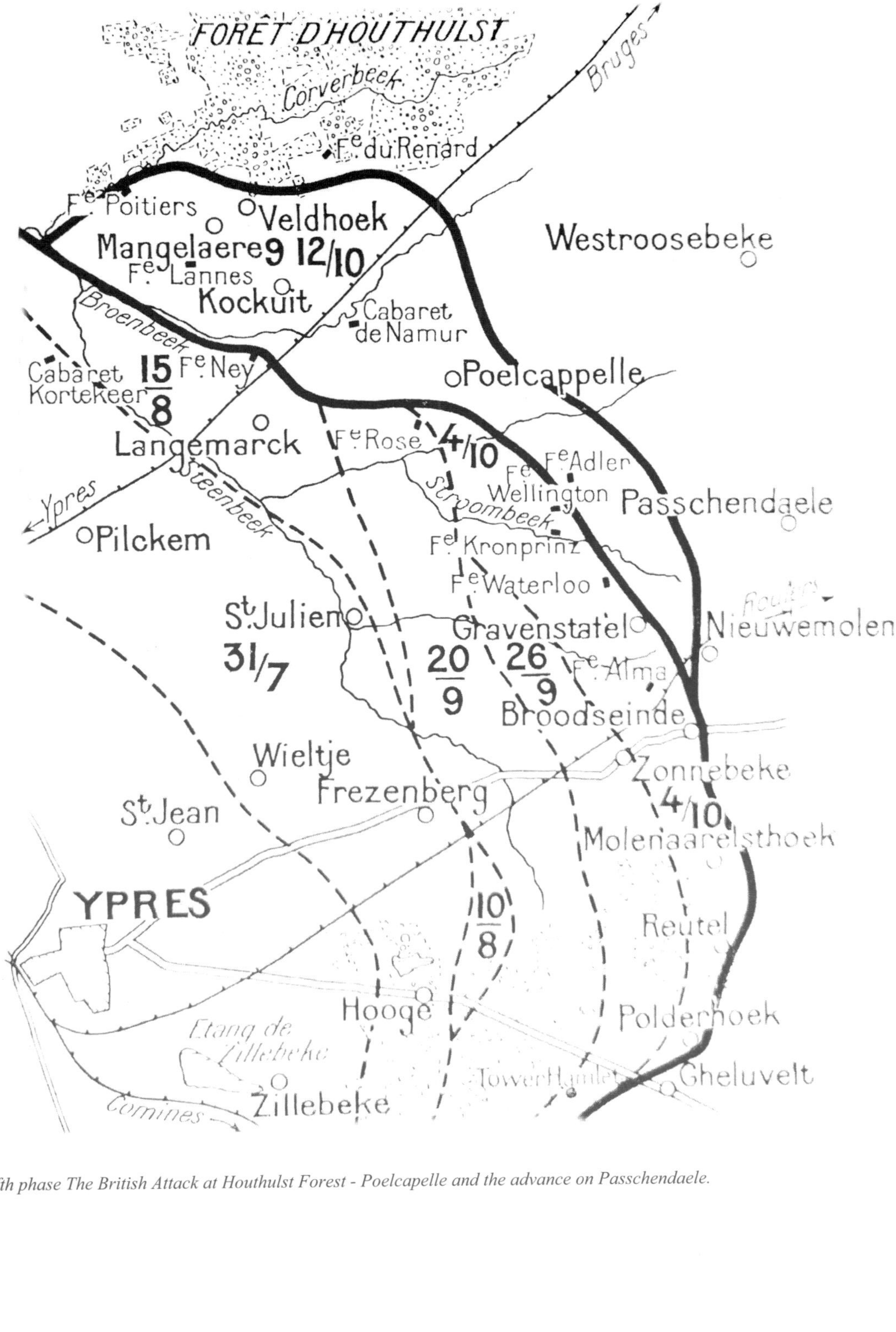

Fifth phase The British Attack at Houthulst Forest - Poelcapelle and the advance on Passchendaele.

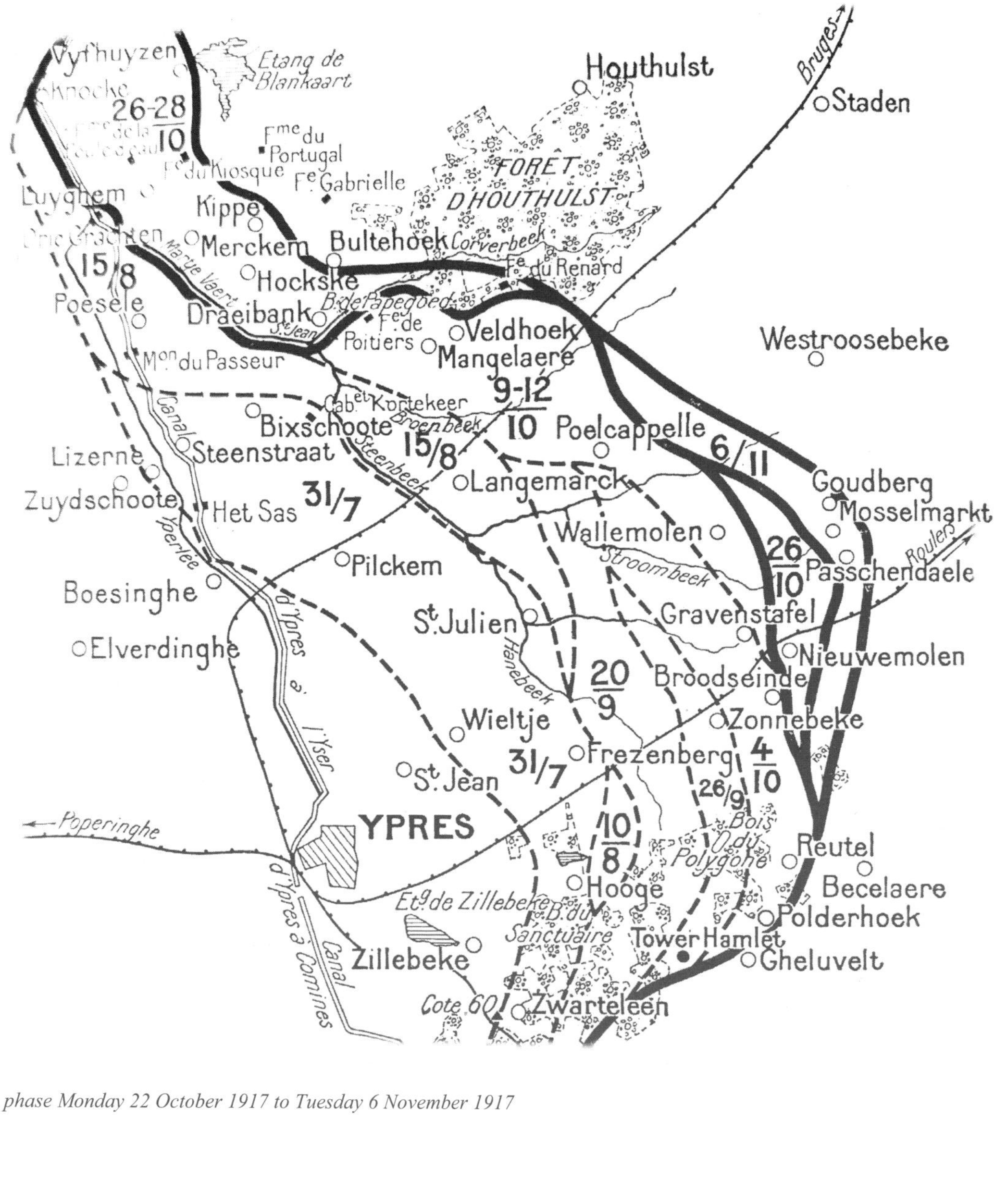

Sixth phase Monday 22 October 1917 to Tuesday 6 November 1917

Images & Diagrams

Above: Poelcapelle British Cemetery commemorates 7478 casualties. - Below: 8th Divisions plan of a strong post that could offer all round defence and could be built from shell holes.

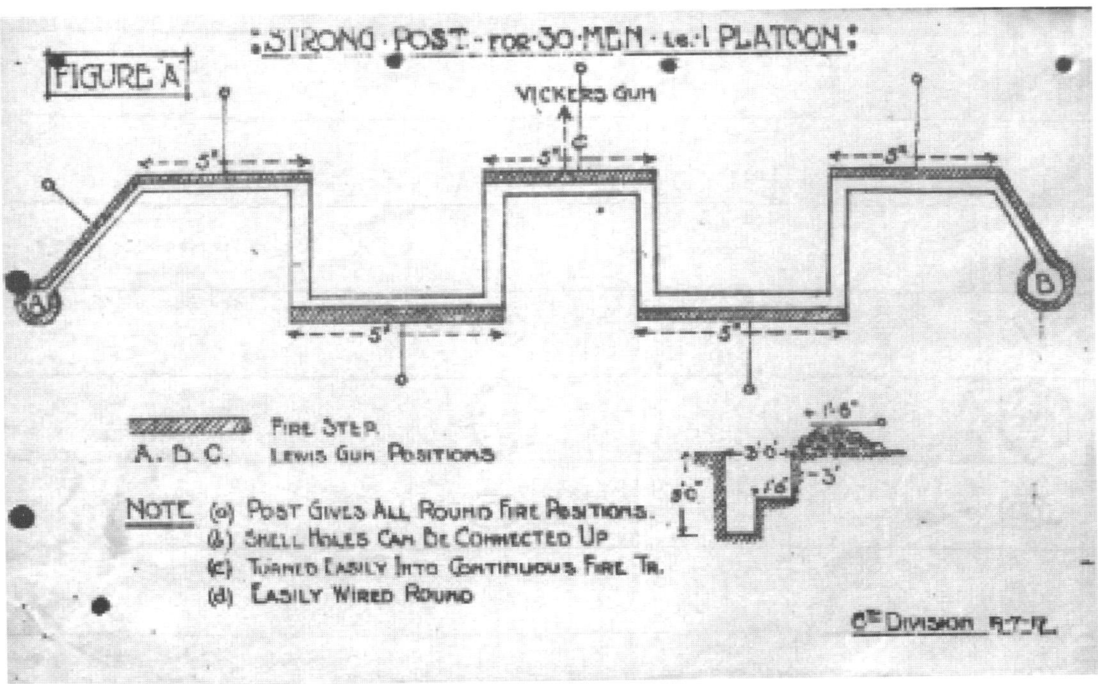

Top: The memorial to the Australian 5th Division at Polygon Wood sits on the pre- Great War Belgian Army rifle butte. Tunnel entrances can still be made out in the butte. The memorial was erected before the New British Cemetery was completed.

Bottom: The view of the memorial to the Australian 5th Division at Polygon Wood today.

Top: The Buttes New British Cemetery entrance from Polygon Wood.

Below: The Buttes New British Cemetery.

Above Left: The Miners Memorial Wytschaete.

Above Right: Memorial to the 1st Australian Tunnellin Company at Hill 60.

Left: Memorial to members of the 177th Tunnelling Company at Railway wood.

Top left: New Zealand Bunkers Polygon Wood built along the edge of the original horse racing track after December 1917.

Top right: Screw pickets from the Great War still in use by Belgian Farmers after 100 years.

Bottom: The Spanbroekmolen crater now the Pool of Peace.

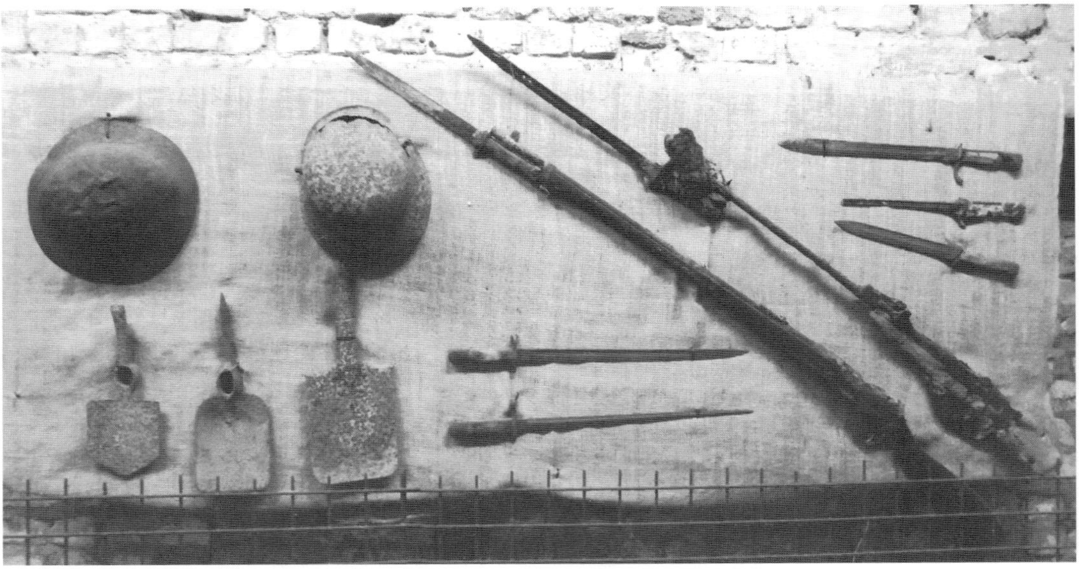

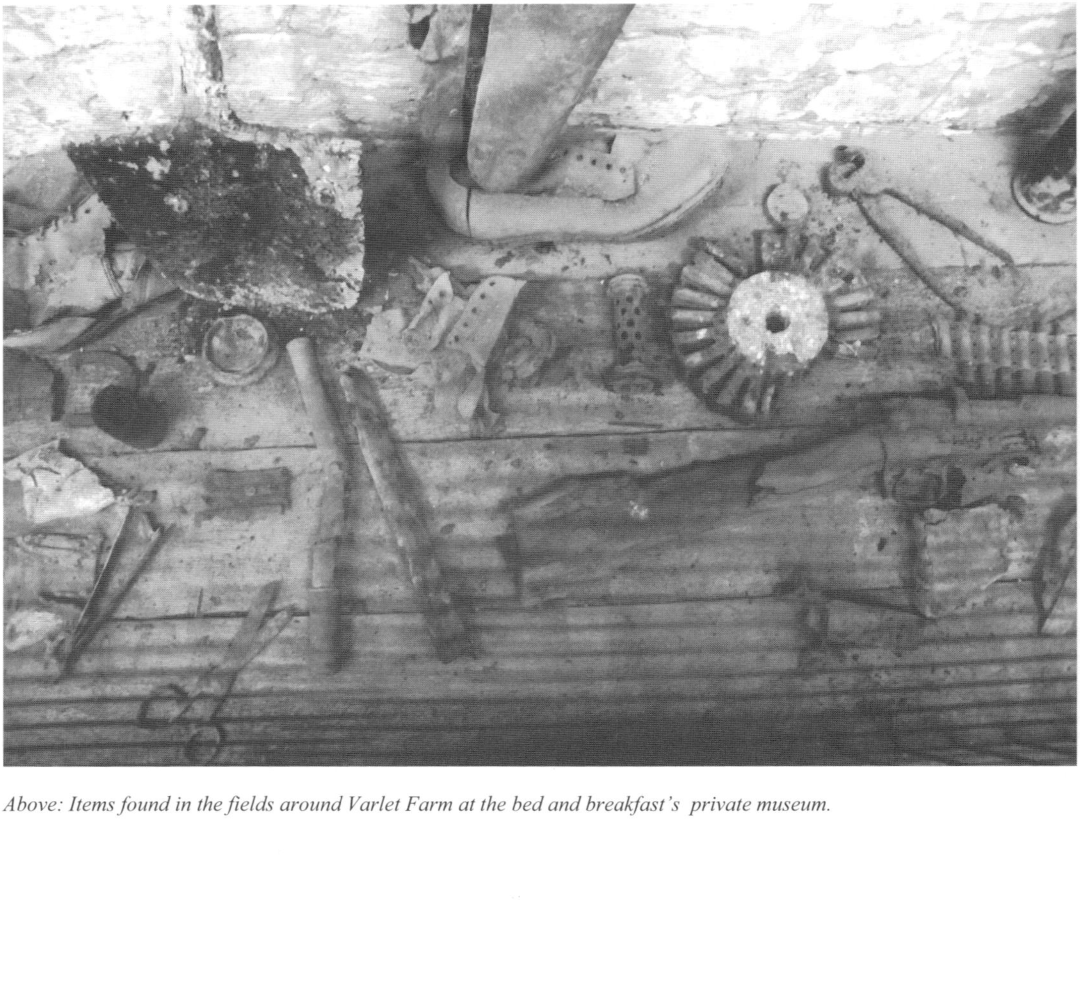

Above: Items found in the fields around Varlet Farm at the bed and breakfast's private museum.

Top left: Memorial to the 16th Irish Division at Wytschaete Military Cemetery.
Top right and above: Wytschaete Military Cemetery.

Above: Hooge Crater Museum.

Below: Part of the "Iron Harvest" at Hooge Crater Museum.

Top: Excavated British Trench at Hooge Crater Museum. - Bottom left: German bunker display at Hooge Crater Museum. - Bottom right: Reconstructed trenches at Hooge Crater Museum.

Top: German bunker at Messines. - Below British bunker built on top of a German bunker at Hill 60.

TO THE MEMORY
OF SEVERAL SOLDIERS
OF THE GREAT WAR
BURIED IN THIS GRAVE

Cemetery & Memorial Index

Hospital Farm was the name given to a farm building used as a dressing station. The cemetery is located 6.5 km west of Ieper town centre, on the Hospitaalstraat, a road leading from the N308 connecting Ieper to Poperinge. It was used particularly in 1915 and in 1917 by regiments and batteries engaged in the fighting around Ypres. The cemetery contains 115 Commonwealth burials of the First World War and one Belgian war grave.

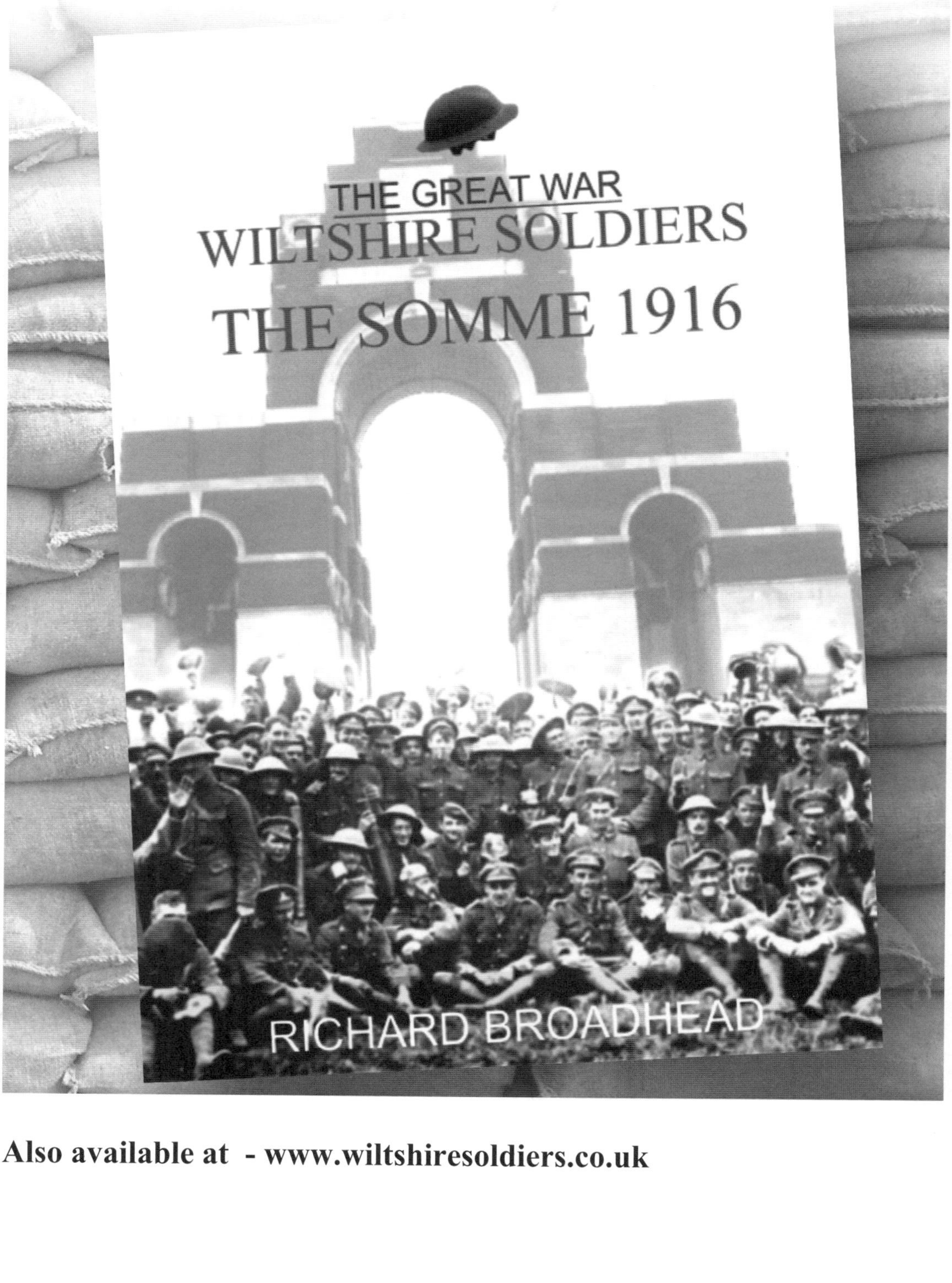
THE GREAT WAR
WILTSHIRE SOLDIERS
THE SOMME 1916
RICHARD BROADHEAD